Issues for Debate in
American Public Policy

Issues for Debate in American Public Policy

Fourth Edition

Selections from *The CQ Researcher*

CQ PRESS

A Division of Congressional Quarterly Inc.
Washington, D.C.

CQ Press
1255 22nd Street, N.W., Suite 400
Washington, D.C. 20037

(202) 729-1900; toll-free, 1-866-4CQ-PRESS (1-866-427-7737)

www.cqpress.com

∞ The paper used in this publication exceeds the requirements of the American National Standard for Information Sciences—Permanence of Paper for Printed Library Materials, ANSI Z39.48-1992.

Printed and bound in the United States of America

07 06 05 04 03   5 4 3 2 1

A CQ Press College Division Publication

Director	Brenda Carter
Acquisitions editor	Charisse Kiino
Marketing manager	Rita Matyi
Managing editor	Christopher Karlsten
Production editor	Joan Gossett
Cover designer	Dennis Anderson
Composition	Olu Davis
Print buyer	Margot Ziperman
Sales manager	James Headley

Library of Congress Cataloging-in-Publication Data

In process

ISBN: 1-56802-853-9

Contents

THE ECONOMY

FOREIGN POLICY

Annotated Table of Contents

The 16 *CQ Researcher* articles reprinted in this book have been reproduced essentially as they appeared when first published. In a few cases in which important new developments have occurred since an article came out, these developments are mentioned in the following overviews, which highlight the principle issues examined.

EDUCATION

Home Schooling Debate

The number of U.S. children educated at home has nearly tripled in the last 10 years, as mainstream parents have embraced a movement once considered the domain of aging hippies and religious fundamentalists. Advocates say home schooling is the best way to ensure a high-quality education and want it exempted from federal and state accountability requirements. But critics warn that removing children from the public schools threatens an essential pillar of democracy while depriving students of vital contact with children and adults from other backgrounds. And school officials complain that when home schooling doesn't work, parents "dump" their children back in the public schools, which are then blamed for the home-schoolers' poor performance.

Charter Schools

A decade after the birth of the charter school movement, reform activists and mainstream educators disagree over whether these experimental public schools are a promising innovation or a damaging distraction. The nation's nearly 2,700 charter schools operate in 39 states, enjoying freedom from many traditional regulations. But they must deliver concrete results in a specified period or risk being shut down. Charters vary as much in their instructional approaches as they do in their genesis, facilities, quality and political constituencies. Yet the evidence remains inconclusive as to whether they are boosting student achievement. The evolving movement remains divided between critics, who see it as the first step in dismembering America's public education system, and those who see it as the system's last best hope.

HEALTH CARE

Covering the Uninsured

The United States is the only industrialized nation that fails to assure universal access to basic health care. Nearly 39 million people — mostly adults and children in wage-earning families — lack health insurance. Nor does holding on to a job guarantee coverage. Seven of every 10 Americans depend on their employers for their insurance, but in today's tight economy employers are chipping away at benefits, compelling employees to pay more of the cost and even eliminating coverage entirely. Four health-care proposals are being considered in Congress, but all would provide only limited benefits. Critics of universal coverage say the nation can't afford to insure everyone. But health-care advocates say the nation's piecemeal approach to insurance doesn't keep Americans healthy — and costs more in the long run.

Medical Malpractice

Doctors in some parts of the country are facing double-digit increases in their malpractice-insurance premiums and blaming the problem on runaway jury verdicts in malpractice suits. Many states already have limited damage awards in malpractice cases. President Bush is now asking Congress to set a $250,000 cap on non-economic or so-called pain-and-suffering damages. But trial lawyers and consumer groups say malpractice suits are not out of control. They claim that insurance companies are raising premiums because of poor underwriting decisions and low investment returns. They also warn that limiting lawsuits hurts victims of egregious medical mistakes and reduces incentives to protect patient safety. But doctors contend that high liability expenses drive up health-care costs, thus reducing access to treatment.

SOCIAL POLICY

Affirmative Action

The U.S. Supreme Court has given supporters of affirmative action a major victory by ruling that universities can consider race as one factor in trying to achieve a racially diverse student body. At the same time, though, the Court barred admissions systems that give a minority candidate a fixed numerical bonus without individually reviewing the applicant's file. The rulings came in two closely watched companion cases brought by unsuccessful white applicants to the University of Michigan's law school and its undergraduate college. In upholding the law school's admissions system, Justice Sandra Day O'Connor said that diversity was a compelling government interest for colleges and universities. But she also said that affirmative action should "no longer be necessary" twenty-five years from now.

Retirement Security

The collapse of Enron Corp. was a wake-up call for Americans who depend on stocks to support them in retirement. It also highlighted the fact that Americans save far less than people in other industrialized countries. Moreover, there has been a dramatic shift in how corporate America helps workers pay for retirement. Employers have been replacing traditional pension plans with voluntary pensions that require workers to contribute their own money and actually make the investment decisions. Meanwhile, the imminent retirement of millions of Baby Boomers threatens Social Security's future. To make matters worse, seniors are living longer, and health-care costs are skyrocketing. But in an election year, Congress may be unwilling to reform Social Security, toughen laws protecting private pension plans or increase Medicare benefits to cover seniors' prescription drugs.

Living-Wage Movement

Since Baltimore became the first U.S. city to adopt a so-called living-wage ordinance in 1994, nearly 100 cities and counties have mandated wage floors above the $5.15-an-hour federal minimum. Relatively few workers take home bigger paychecks — perhaps 100,000 of the nation's 134 million workers. Moreover, living-wage ordinances are banned in one state, and others may follow suit. While the living-wage trend is still gaining momentum, economists disagree whether the pay increases are overshadowed by reductions in the number of jobs.

ENVIRONMENT

SUV Debate

Sport-utility vehicles have become icons of American consumption in the past decade, changing the look of the nation's highways. But few consumer products have attracted such adulation and scorn. Fans of the trucklike passenger vehicles love their spacious interiors, rugged appearance and high-off-the-ground seating. Critics see them as gas-guzzling, turnover-prone behemoths that spew pollutants and endanger the occupants of smaller cars. Like minivans, SUVs are categorized by the government as light trucks, which are held to less stringent fuel-efficiency and safety standards than cars. The Bush administration has ordered automakers to increase light-truck mileage efficiency by a total of 1.5 mpg — to 22.2 mpg — during the 2005–2007 model years. But environmentalists say that's not enough.

Reforming the Army Corps of Engineers

The U.S. Army Corps of Engineers has played an unprecedented role in reshaping the nation's landscape — dredging channels for shipping, building hydroelectric dams to provide rural electricity and erecting levees to guard against lowland flooding. But now an unlikely coalition of environmentalists and fiscal conservatives says the agency uses faulty economic assumptions to press for costly, pork-barrel projects that damage the environment while providing little benefit to society. Environmentalists also say Corps projects in support of developers or large-scale farmers have been especially harmful to the nation's wetlands. The Bush administration is taking aim at the agency budget, but many in Congress insist on continuing to fund big projects back home. Meanwhile, a bipartisan group of lawmakers insists on overhauling Corps procedures before approving any new projects.

CIVIL LIBERTIES, CIVIL RIGHTS AND JUSTICE

Civil Liberties in Wartime

Following the Sept. 11 terrorist attacks on the World Trade Center and Pentagon, the Bush administration and Congress acted forcefully to deter future incidents. A new law was passed giving the government more authority to conduct surveillance and track Internet communications.

The administration also detained more than 600 possible suspects and announced it might use military tribunals to try alleged foreign terrorists. But civil libertarians say the tough, new procedures abridge fundamental constitutional rights like due process and the attorney-client privilege. Some media-watchers, meanwhile, contend that journalists are not aggressively reporting about the crackdown on terrorism out of fear of seeming unpatriotic during wartime.

Cyber-Crimes

Cyber-crime has reached epidemic proportions. More than 90 percent of the corporations and government agencies responding to a recent survey reported computer-security breaches in 2001. Disgruntled employees and hackers commit many cyber-crimes, and others are committed by con artists using the Web to perpetrate auction fraud, identity theft and other scams. Credit-card users are only liable for the first $50 of fraudulent charges, but financial institutions get hit hard. Identity thefts cost them $2.4 billion in losses and expenses in 2000. Some policymakers, wary of Internet-facilitated terrorist attacks, call for tough, new laws to prevent computer crimes. Others fear that such initiatives will trample on civil liberties. Still others want legislation to make Microsoft and other computer-software companies liable for damages caused by their software-security failures.

Abortion Debates

The battle lines on the abortion issue remain clearly drawn 30 years after the Supreme Court's controversial *Roe v. Wade* decision established a constitutional right to the procedure during most of a pregnancy. Anti-abortion groups continue to urge Congress and state legislatures to regulate abortion practices, while abortion-rights supporters say the measures undercut women's reproductive freedom. At the urging of President Bush, Congress is moving to ban a late-stage procedure that opponents call "partial-birth" abortion, although the Supreme Court struck down a similar state law three years ago. The legislative fights continue unabated in the states, where more than 300 anti-abortion laws have been enacted since 1995. Meanwhile, both sides are girding for a possible fight over a Supreme Court nomination from Bush if one or more vacancies occur.

BUSINESS AND THE ECONOMY

Stimulating the Economy

President Bush is proposing a $674 billion plan to boost the economy centered around eliminating the taxes investors pay on corporate dividends. Bush's plan also would speed up tax cuts for high-income Americans due to take effect in 2004 and 2006. Democrats are offering rival stimulus plans that cost less — around $100 billion — and provide more relief for average taxpayers. The Democrats also propose helping fiscally strapped states and extending unemployment benefits. Meanwhile, some experts say the economy is already turning around and that new tax cuts would only worsen long-term fiscal problems, now that budget deficits have returned.

Accountants Under Fire

The accounting profession emerged as one of the biggest victims of the sudden collapse of the once high-flying Enron Corp. The Houston energy-trading company filed for bankruptcy in December 2001 after accounting missteps forced it to restate earnings for several years. Enron executives put part of the blame on Arthur Andersen, the big firm that audited Enron's books. Congress responded by approving legislation in July 2002 to establish a new, five-member accounting industry oversight board. To strengthen auditors' independence, the law also generally bars accounting firms from providing non-audit services to publicly traded companies that they audit. Meanwhile, the Andersen firm collapsed after it was convicted of obstruction of justice in June 2002 for shredding documents related to its Enron audits.

FOREIGN POLICY

North Korean Crisis

While a U.S.-led coalition fought to topple Saddam Hussein's regime in Iraq, a dangerous foreign-policy crisis was brewing on the Korean Peninsula. In 2002, Kim Jong Il resumed North Korea's program to develop nuclear weapons, in violation of the Nuclear Non-Proliferation Treaty and a 1994 agreement with the United States to freeze the program in exchange for food and energy assistance. The Bush administration rejects North Korea's call for bilateral negotiations to resolve the crisis as caving in to "nuclear blackmail" and insists on including other regional powers. Administration critics say that ignoring North Korea — which may have enough material to build at least one nuclear weapon and could soon produce many more — is a recipe for war.

New Defense Priorities

After the Cold War, the Pentagon began downsizing its forces and developing high-tech, mobile weapons designed to deal with "rogue" states like Iraq — less powerful than the Soviet juggernaut but still able to attack the United States and its allies. But the Sept. 11 terrorist attacks forced Pentagon planners back to the drawing board to develop new strategies and weapons. Defense Secretary Donald H. Rumsfeld wants to further transform the military to enable it to counter emerging threats from unconventional forces like the Al Qaeda Islamic terrorist organization. Meanwhile, President Bush put his new preemptive-strike strategy into practice by deposing Iraqi President Saddam Hussein, despite the opposition of most U.S. allies.

Preface

Instructors continually search for material that will spark intelligent and lively debate in the classroom, and questions about current and controversial public policy issues certainly get students thinking and talking. Are tax cuts needed to stimulate the economy? Should colleges use race-based admissions policies to remedy discrimination against minorities? Should the United States adopt a preemptive strike doctrine? As the world becomes more and more complex, we rely on government to handle a greater range of difficult public problems. To add color and insight to a theoretical understanding of how public policy works, provocative, real-world examples are needed to give students a deeper appreciation for the various ways that government responds to different issues. This up-to-date collection of articles from *The CQ Researcher*, the fourth edition of *Issues for Debate in American Public Policy*, illustrates just how broadly contentious policy issues impact citizens and affect government.

The compilation of sixteen recent articles from *The CQ Researcher*, a weekly policy backgrounder, offers in-depth looks at complicated issues on the public agenda. *The CQ Researcher* brings often complex issues down to earth, not by simplifying difficult concepts but by explaining them in plain English. Offering thorough, objective and forward-looking reporting on a specific topic, each article chronicles and analyzes past legislative and judicial action as well as current and possible future political maneuvering, whether at the local, state or federal level. *Issues for Debate* is designed to encourage discussion of these complex topics, to help readers think critically and actively about these vital issues and to facilitate further research.

The collection is organized into seven subject areas that span a range of important public policy concerns. The pieces were chosen to expose students to a wide range of subjects, from civil rights to foreign policy. We are gratified to know that *Issues for Debate* is appealing to several audiences: Teachers are using it as a supplement in both introductory public policy and American government courses, and interested citizens, journalists and business and government leaders are turning to it to familiarize themselves with key issues, actors and policy positions.

The CQ Researcher

The CQ Researcher was founded in 1923 as *Editorial Research Reports* and was sold primarily to newspapers as a research tool. The magazine was given its current name and a re-design in 1991. While *The CQ Researcher* is still used by hundreds of newspapers, some of which reprint all or part of each issue, high school, college and public libraries are now the main subscribers. Thus, students, not journalists, are now the primary audience for *The CQ Researcher*.

The *Researcher's* staff writers — all highly experienced journalists — sometimes compare the experience of writing a *Researcher* report to drafting a college term paper. Indeed, there are many similarities: Each article is as long as many term papers — about 11,000 words — and is written by one person without any significant outside help. One of the key differences is that the writers interview top experts and government officials for each report. In fact, the *Researcher* won the American Bar Association's coveted Silver Gavel award for magazines in 2002 for a series of nine reports on civil liberties and other legal issues.

Like students, staff writers begin the creative process by choosing a topic. Working with the *Researcher's* editors, the writer identifies a subject that has public policy implications and for which there is significant controversy. After a topic is set, the writer embarks on a week or two of intense research. Articles are clipped, books ordered, and information gathered from a variety of sources, including interest groups, universities and the government. Once the writers are well informed about the subject, they begin interviewing academics, officials, lobbyists and people working in the field. Each piece usually requires a minimum of ten to fifteen interviews, while some issues with especially complicated subjects call for more. After much reading and interviewing, the writers develop detailed outlines. Only then does the writing begin.

Chapter Format

Each issue of the *Researcher*, and therefore each selection in this book, is structured in the same way, beginning with an introductory overview of the topic. This first section briefly touches on the areas that will be explored in greater detail in the rest of the chapter.

Following the introduction is a section that chronicles important and current debates in the field. The section is structured around a number of questions, known as "Issue Questions," such as "Can America afford health insurance for all?" or "Are charter schools harming the traditional public school system?" This section is the core of each chapter: The questions raised are often highly controversial and usually the object of much argument among those who work in and think about the field. Hence, the answers provided by the writer are never conclusive but detail the range of opinion within the field.

Following these questions and answers is the "Background" section, which provides a history of the issue being examined. This look back includes important legislative and executive actions and court decisions from the past that inform readers on how current policy evolved.

The "Current Situation" examines important contemporary policy issues, legislation under consideration and legal action being taken. Finally, each selection ends with an "Outlook" section, which gives a sense of what might happen in the next five to ten years, such as new regulations, court rulings and possible initiatives from the White House or Capitol Hill.

Each selection contains other regular features that augment the main text: two or three sidebars that examine issues related to the topic; a pro-con debate by two outside experts; a chronology of key dates and events; and an annotated bibliography, detailing major sources used by the writer.

Acknowledgments

We wish to thank many people for helping to make this collection a reality. Tom Colin, managing editor of *The CQ Researcher*, gave us his enthusiastic support and cooperation as we developed this fourth edition. He and his talented staff of editors and writers have amassed a first-class library of *Researcher* articles, and we are lucky to have access to that rich cache. We also thankfully acknowledge the advice and feedback from current readers and are gratified by their success with the book.

Some readers of this collection may be learning about *The CQ Researcher* for the first time. We expect that many readers will want regular access to this excellent weekly research tool. Anyone interested in subscription information or a no-obligation free trial of the *Researcher* can contact CQ Press at www.cqpress.com or 1-866-4CQ-PRESS (1-866-427-7737, toll-free).

We hope that you will be pleased by the fourth edition of *Issues for Debate in American Public Policy*. We welcome your feedback and suggestions for future editions. Please direct comments to Charisse Kiino, CQ Press, 1255 22nd Street, N.W., Suite 400, Washington, D.C. 20037; or send e-mail to *ckiino@cqpress.com*.

—*The Editors of CQ Press*

Contributors

Charles S. Clark, a senior editor at the Association of Governing Boards of Universities and Colleges, has written on education for *Teacher* magazine, *Phi Delta Kappan, Educational Leadership* and the National Center on Education and the Economy. He is a former *CQ Researcher* staff writer, *Washington Post* editorial writer and *National Journal* managing editor. He graduated with a B.A. in history from McGill University.

Thomas J. Colin, managing editor, has been a magazine and newspaper journalist for more than 25 years. Before joining Congressional Quarterly in 1991, he was a reporter and editor at the *Miami Herald* and *National Geographic* and editor in chief of *Historic Preservation* magazine. He has degrees from the College of William and Mary (English) and the University of Missouri (journalism).

Mary H. Cooper specializes in environmental, energy and defense issues. Before joining *The CQ Researcher* as a staff writer in 1983, she was a reporter and Washington correspondent for the Rome daily newspaper *l'Unità*. She is the author of *The Business of Drugs* (CQ Press, 1990). She also is a contract translator-interpreter for the U.S. State Department. Cooper graduated from Hollins College with a degree in English.

Rachel S. Cox is a freelance writer and contributing writer to *The CQ Researcher*. She also writes for *The Washington Post* and is a former associate editor of *Preservation* magazine. She holds an A.B. in English from Harvard University.

Keith Epstein, Washington correspondent for *The Tampa Tribune* and Media General News Service, has written on a variety of health and technology topics for publications such as *The Washington Post, The Philadelphia Inquirer*, Post-Newsweek's *Techway* magazine and the Discovery Channel's health Web site.

Brian Hansen specializes in environmental issues. He previously reported for the *Colorado Daily* in Boulder and Environment News Service. His awards include the Scripps Howard Foundation award for public service reporting and the Education Writers Association award for investigative reporting. He holds a B.A. in political science and an M.A. in education from the University of Colorado.

David Hosansky is a freelance writer in Denver who specializes in environmental issues. He previously was a senior writer at *CQ Weekly* and the *Florida Times-Union* in Jacksonville, where he was twice nominated for a Pulitzer Prize. His recent *Researcher* reports include "Food Safety" and "Reforming the Army Corps of Engineers."

Kenneth Jost, associate editor, has covered legal affairs as a reporter, columnist and editor since 1970. He is a graduate of Harvard College and Georgetown University Law Center, where he is an adjunct professor. He is the editor of *The Supreme Court A to Z, third edition* (CQ Press, 2003) and a contributor to various legal publications. He was a member of *The CQ Researcher* team that won the 2002 American Bar Association Silver Gavel award for magazines. Jost also served as chief legislative assistant to then-Rep. Al Gore from 1977 to 1980.

Patrick Marshall is the reviews editor at *Federal Computer Week* and a technology columnist for the *Seattle Times*; he is based in Bainbridge Island, Wash. His recent *CQ Researcher* reports include "Three-Strikes Laws" and "Gambling in America." He holds a bachelor's degree in anthropology from the University of California at Santa Cruz and a master's in foreign affairs from the Fletcher School of Law and Diplomacy.

David Masci specializes in social policy, religion and foreign affairs. Before joining *The CQ Researcher* as a staff writer in 1996, he was a reporter at CQ's *Daily Monitor* and *CQ Weekly*. He holds a B.A. in medieval history from Syracuse University and a law degree from George Washington University.

Jane Tanner is a freelancer in Charlotte, N.C., who writes for *The New York Times* and other publications. She earned her B.A. (social policy) and M.A. (journalism) degrees from Northwestern University. Her recent *CQ Researcher* reports include "Future Job Market" and "Unemployment Benefits."

Issues for Debate in
American Public Policy

1 Home Schooling Debate

RACHEL S. COX

When Jane and George Liddle's first child turned 4, they began to think about her formal schooling. Living in the affluent San Francisco Bay Area community of Los Gatos, near Silicon Valley, they had access to some of California's best public schools.

But every Sunday when they attended services at the Saratoga Federated Church, they couldn't help but notice how happy — and successful — the home-schooled children of fellow church members seemed to be.

"At first, I said to myself, 'I will never do this,'" recalls Jane, who was a stockbroker until Caroline was born. "But we saw so many professional, well-educated people who made the choice [to home school] for educational reasons, as well as personal, philosophical ones."

Today, Caroline, nearly 6, starts her day by spending an hour or two working with her mother on language arts and math skills. After family devotions, they move to a classroom set up in a separate building on the rural property to study history and social studies. Two days a week, Caroline and her younger brother, William, 3, visit a home-school co-op to study and play with nearly 60 other children in class-like groupings overseen by their 12 moms.

Jane Liddle concedes that home schooling works for her family for practical as well as philosophical reasons: The extra cost — mainly for books and other educational materials — is minimal. And with the local el-

From *The CQ Researcher,* January 17, 2003.

School begins with the Pledge of Allegiance at the Shapiro home in Tempe, Ariz. Denise Shapiro and her husband Aaron, a chiropractor, decided to home school to raise "very smart" children but also "biblically, morally responsible adults." At least 850,000 U.S. children are home schooled, nearly triple the number a decade ago. Public-school officials worry home schooling undercuts public education and limits students' exposure to children and adults with diverse backgrounds.

ementary school some distance away, she appreciates not having to spend two hours each day in her car or making Caroline ride the bus. Home schooling also improves her quality of life. "I spend such incredible time with my children," she says, "and at night when my husband is home, we really are a family. We avoid a lot of the distractions of popular culture and the pressures to arrange lots of after-school activities. We're not just chasing our tails all the time."

She also believes that, at least for now, home schooling offers the best possible educational experience. "I've learned that you can really shoot the moon with your child. I'm right there with her in the learning process. I know what keeps her challenged and what sabotages her. You can customize. You figure out what works for your child."

The Liddles' approach has grown increasingly popular over the last two decades, as a movement once considered the domain of aging hippies and religious fundamentalists increasingly has been embraced by the mainstream. But school districts complain that when parents give up on home schooling, they "dump" their children back on the public schools, which are then held accountable for the home-schoolers' performance, even if the student is lagging behind his in-school peers. Moreover, critics warn that removing children from the public schools may threaten an essential pillar of democracy, while depriving children of vital contact with other children and adults from diverse backgrounds.

Brian D. Ray, director of the National Home Education Research Institute in Salem, Ore., and a leader in the field, concedes that even as recently as five years ago home-schoolers were considered "kind of weirdo." People thought home-schoolers were all "granola eaters or Bible thumpers," he says. "But now, almost anyone you run into on the street will consider it. It's more common to find support groups, resources are more available and there's less peer pressure against it."

In 1999, the U.S. Education Department estimates, about 850,000 of the nation's 50 million children, ages 5 through 17, were being schooled at home — or 1.7 percent. [1] Ray puts the number at between 1.6 million and 2 million — roughly 2 percent of the school-age population — but his figures are generally considered high.

One thing is certain: The movement has experienced robust growth. Only 30 years ago, few children were being home schooled. [2] By 1991, the Department of Education estimated that

Rise of Home-Schooled Students

The number of U.S. children home schooled nearly tripled during the 1990s, according to estimates by the U.S. Department of Education. Home-schooling advocates, however, say 2 million children now are home schooled.

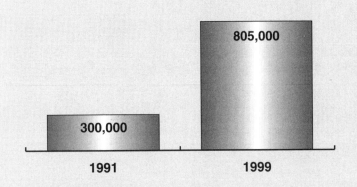

805,000

300,000

1991   1999

Sources: U.S. Department of Education, National Center for Education Statistics, "Parent Survey of the National Household Education Surveys Program, 1999," July 2001; "Issues Related to Estimating the Home-Schooled Population in the United States with National Household Data Survey," September 2000. The next Department of Education report on home schooling is scheduled for release in early 2004.

up to 300,000 school-age children were being educated at home. [3] Thus, according to the department's own conservative estimates, the number of home-schooled children has nearly tripled in just 10 years. [4]

Most home-schooled children come from urban, two-parent families, the study found, with one wage earner and two or more children. The parents are often well educated — a quarter have at least a bachelor's degree — and 36 percent have household incomes above $50,000 per year. White families outnumber minorities by three to one.

Parents say they home-school for five main reasons: to give their children a better education, for religious reasons, to avoid a poor school environment, for family reasons and to instill "character/morality." [5] (*See chart, p. 5.*)

"The core reasons for home schooling are very deep and stable," says Ray, who has studied the movement

since the mid-1980s. "They want their children to learn to read, write and do arithmetic, along with some science and history. They want to individualize the curriculum for each child, meet special interests or needs, provide a safe learning environment and guided social interactions for their kids, nurture strong family ties and transmit certain values and beliefs to their children." [6]

In the 1980s, he notes, the proportion of families choosing home schooling for religious reasons skyrocketed, after tax-code changes forced many religious schools to close.

Critics long have asserted that schooling children at home impedes socialization because home-schooled kids don't learn to get along with their peers in group settings, nor are they exposed to children and adults from different backgrounds. But advocates scoff at the notion.

"I have nothing kind to say about the sort of socialization that occurs in schools," says Holly Albers, an economist in Washington, D.C., who home-schooled her two sons for several years when they were youngsters. "The children are thrown into single-age, often very large groups with no meaningful interactions with adults."

To expose their children to a wide variety of contacts, Albers and other parents organize social and educational activities with other home-schoolers and adults, who often serve as tutors in subject areas that other parents are weak in. As a result, she says, home-schoolers tend to have three advantages: closer family and sibling relationships, more friendships with different ages and genders and more friendships with adults. "There's much more positive socialization for children at home," she says.

In fact, studies appear to refute the argument that home-schoolers are poorly socialized. As early as 1986, John Wesley Taylor, a doctoral candidate at Andrews University, in Berrien Springs, Mich., found that half of the home-schooled children surveyed scored 47 percent higher than the average conventionally schooled child on a well-validated self-concept scale. "This answers the often-heard skepticism suggesting that home-schoolers are inferior in socialization," he concluded. [7]

Home-schoolers win academic kudos as well. In 2000, for instance, home-schooled children took home the top three trophies in the prestigious Scripps Howard National Spelling Bee, just a week after other home-schoolers won four of the top 10 spots at the National Geographic Society's geography bee. [8] And Buchanan, Mich., home-schooler Jeff Joyce recently scored a perfect 1600 on the College Board's Scholastic Assessment Test (SAT) — a feat accomplished by less than 0.5 percent of the students who take the test each year. [9]

In fact, when University of Maryland researcher Lawrence M. Rudner assessed the performance of more than 20,000 K-12 home-schooled students on standardized tests in 1999, their median scores were typically in the 70th to 80th percentile. "The achievement-test scores of this group of home school students are exceptionally high," Rudner concluded. [10]

But Rudner's study, which was funded and widely disseminated by home-schooling advocates, was criticized for failing to acknowledge the narrowness of its sample. The data were gathered exclusively from parents who used the testing services of Bob Jones University, the fundamentalist Christian institution in Greenville, S.C., notorious for its history of racial discrimination. "This data simply cannot be used to reliably compare home-schoolers' achievement levels with those of the general population or to describe the demographics of home-schoolers," scholars Kariane Mari Welner and Kevin G. Welner noted. [11]

Few educators doubt the potential of a customized education when a single adult is working with one child. "There's no doubt that the one-on-one work that parents can do if they're smart or well trained is amazing," says June Million, a spokeswoman for the National Association of Elementary School Principals (NAESP). But home-schooling advocates don't always tell the whole story, she suggests. "The part I never see are the ones who have returned to school after home schooling, and they're behind. It's not always a success."

NAESP President Paul Young agrees. "If families want to work hard at home schooling and do it for the right reasons, they do very well. Others aren't well informed, don't follow through and get frustrated," he says.

When home schooling fails, the problem usually lands in the lap of the public schools, says Young, who is principal at West Elementary

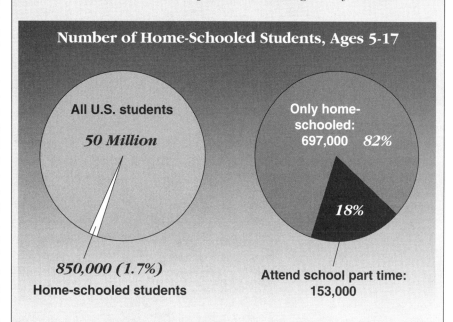

Few Students Are Home-Schooled

About 850,000* of the nation's 50 million school-age children were home-schooled in 1999, according to the U.S. Department of Education. More than three-quarters were taught only at home.

Number of Home-Schooled Students, Ages 5-17

All U.S. students

50 Million

850,000 (1.7%)
Home-schooled students

Only home-schooled:
697,000   *82%*

18%

**Attend school part time:
153,000**

*Home-schooling advocates say the current number may be as high as 2 million.

Note: Students are considered to be home schooled if their parents say they are home schooled, they attend public or private school for less than 25 hours a week and they were not home-schooled due to a temporary illness.

Source: U.S. Department of Education, National Center for Education Statistics, "Parent Survey of the National Household Education Surveys Program," 1999.

School in Lancaster, Ohio. "When the parents realize they can't do it, the kids come back to public school, and then we're held responsible. In some cases these kids have been just running in the street, and the parents are not held accountable for what their children were supposed to be learning."

In addition to its concerns about the lack of adequate socialization, the NAESP worries that home schooling can deny children the full range of curriculum experiences and materials and expose students to unqualified instructors. In addition, the group says home schooling can create an extra burden for administrators re-

sponsible for enforcing compulsory-attendance laws; prevent effective assessment of statewide academic standards; violate health and safety regulations and prevent the accurate diagnosis of learning disabilities or other conditions requiring special attention.

"The public schools' greatest concern is to make sure kids are actually learning," says Julie Underwood, general counsel of the National School Boards Association (NSBA). "There are very strong religious-right organizations that support very conservative [home-schooling] curricula."

Even dedicated home-schoolers acknowledge that home schooling is not

Home Schooling Means Business

Supplying instructional materials for home-schooling families has turned into a $700 million cottage industry, according to Jean C. Halle, chief executive officer of Calvert School Education Services. [1]

For decades the Baltimore-based company, founded in 1906, was the only major institution offering "correspondence courses" for the children of military families, missionaries and other itinerants. In the 1960s, however, they were joined by Christian publishers, whose market share soon exploded, as did the number of religiously motivated home-schooling families.

Today, three major religiously oriented suppliers sell Bible-themed textbooks in all disciplines: Bob Jones University Press, Alpha Omega Publications, of Chandler, Ariz., and Pensacola, Fla.-based A Beka Books. "We have over 100,000 home-schooled pupils using our books, A Beka Sales Manager Eric Fears told *Education Week*.

In addition to books and online curricula, many companies offer testing, record-keeping and teacher consultations as well as class rings, diplomas and caps and gowns.

The growth of the Internet opened national and even global markets to local providers. Core Curriculum, a Florida company offering both Christian and secular curricula, started as a family business in 1989. By 2002 it had reached $1.4 million in revenues, according to Operations Vice President Alexis Thompson, mostly over the Internet.

The rise of publicly funded cyber schools — which allow students to work at home supported by certified teachers — has opened a new market for online curricula providers

William J. Bennett, the outspoken former Secretary of Education under President Ronald Reagan, has joined the ranks of online curriculum providers. The proponent of classical education and author of the best-selling *Book of Virtues* heads K12 Inc., which sells its K-5 curricula to publicly funded cyber schools in nearly a dozen states.

Suppliers of educational materials for home schoolers typically offer both secular and religiously oriented products, including Bible-themed textbooks.

Alpha Omega Publications

Although he questioned cyber learning in his 1999 book *The Educated Child*, saying there is "no good evidence that most uses of computers significantly improve learning," two years later he had changed his views: "There's tremendous promise for technology." [2]

Bennett's company is a subsidiary of Knowledge Universe, Inc — the $1.75 billion educational-products firm established by disgraced junk bond financier Michael Milken. [3]

Until recently, Bennett was a popular speaker at home-schooling conventions because of his endorsement of values-centered, family-based education. But his decision to sell K12 curricula to publicly funded cyber schools has made him a little less welcome. Many home-schoolers say that with public money come regulations, and regulation for cyber-school parents — some of whom are also home schoolers — could lead to regulation for all home-schoolers.

"We home-schoolers need to let other home-schoolers and the general public know that Bennett's commitment to using public money in this way runs counter to what most home-schoolers want and would undermine the very nature of home schooling as we know it," home schooling columnists and advocates Larry and Susan Kaseman wrote in a recent issue of *Home Education Magazine*. [4]

K12's requests to exhibit as a curriculum vendor at home-schooling conferences have been rejected by home-schooling organizations in at least three states, according to the Kasemans. The Christian Home Education Association of California canceled Bennett as its keynote speaker last year "because of the linkage between K12 and publicly funded programs."

[1] Mark Walsh, "Home School Enrollment Surge Fuels 'Cottage' Industry," *Education Week*, June 5, 2002.

[2] "All Things Considered," National Public Radio, Feb. 28, 2001.

[3] Stephen P. Pizzo, "Master of the Knowledge Universe," *Forbes ASAP*, Sept. 10, 2001.

[4] Larry and Susan Kaseman, "How William Bennett's Public E-Schools Affect Homeschooling," *Home Education Magazine*, November-December 2002; online at www.home-ed-magaine.com/HEM/196/ndtch.html.

right for everyone. "It does require a full-time, at-home parent," Albers says, "and it is *relentless* for that parent."

As educators, parents and policymakers struggle with the peculiar mix of personal and public decision-making that home schooling entails, these three questions frequently are being debated:

Should the government regulate home schooling?

"Dog Bites System," read *The Rocky Mountain News* headline, when a Colorado man successfully certified his miniature schnauzer, Missy, as progressing nicely in the third grade while being schooled at home. [12]

Under Colorado's home-schooling law, parents must file a notice of intent with a local school district, then the student must be tested or evaluated to show progress every other year, starting in the third grade. Dog owners Nick and Cheryl Campbell "evaluated" Missy using an evaluation form they found on the Internet, but no one from the school district ever tried to speak to Missy.

"I did it to make a point" about the laxness of the state's oversight of home-schoolers, said Campbell, who was distressed because a 10-year-old neighbor being home schooled had not yet learned to read.

Thanks to adroit lobbying by home-schooling networks, which have access to Republican lawmakers through their links with politically savvy religious conservatives, home schooling is legal in every state, but requirements for eligibility and evaluation vary widely. Thus, policymakers and educators are debating whether local school districts should regulate home schooling more stringently.

"With home schooling now firmly entrenched on the American education scene," New Jersey attorney David Rubin writes, "the legal battleground has shifted in recent years to defining the rights and responsibilities of school districts and home-schooling families." [13]

Many public educators believe that stricter regulation — including testing — is needed to ensure that home-schooled children are being adequately educated. [14] "Kentucky is very lax on its home-school rules," says Martha Lewis, principal of Benton Elementary in rural Marshall County, Ky. "Most of the students that I have seen being home-schooled are ones whose parents get disgruntled with the public school about something. They are weak students who have poor attendance. When they come back, they are even further behind."

Requiring home-schooled students to be tested would help teachers and administrators when home-schoolers return to school, or when they take some courses in public schools, the NSBA's Underwood says. "In some states, there are no regulations, so public school [teachers and officials] are quite frustrated," she says. So when kids enter or return to school, "They don't know if they're really ready. They don't have any information."

Public educators were particularly concerned when President Bush's recently

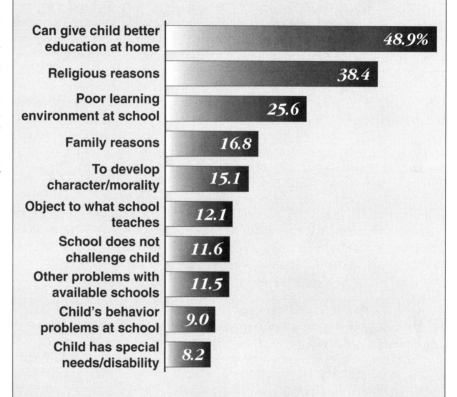

Parents' Reasons for Home Schooling

Nearly half of all parents home-school because they think they can do a better job than the local public schools. High percentages of parents also were motivated by religious reasons and poor school environments.

Parents' Main Reasons for Home Schooling

Reason	%
Can give child better education at home	48.9%
Religious reasons	38.4
Poor learning environment at school	25.6
Family reasons	16.8
To develop character/morality	15.1
Object to what school teaches	12.1
School does not challenge child	11.6
Other problems with available schools	11.5
Child's behavior problems at school	9.0
Child has special needs/disability	8.2

Note: Percentages do not add to 100 because respondents could give more than one reason.

Source: U.S. Department of Education, National Center for Education Statistics, Parent Survey of the National Household Education Surveys Program, "Homeschooling in the United States: 1999," July 2001; new data are now being collected for the next comprehensive report on home schooling, due in early 2004.

enacted No Child Left Behind Act exempted home-schooled students from the new testing requirements it imposed on public-school students. The new law imposes serious financial consequences on schools where students test poorly. Thus, administrators want to make sure that all students are keeping up — including returning home-schoolers.

"When children return to school, that school is held responsible for their performance," says Young of the principals' association. "We need more specific testing requirements so there's some accountability."

"You could have multiple forms of testing," Underwood notes. "It wouldn't have to be standardized testing."

However, to home-schooling advocates like Robert Ziegler, spokesman for the Home School Legal Defense Association, (HSLDA) any regulation is too much. Choosing how to educate one's children is a constitutionally protected parental right, he says. "There should be no regulation of how parents educate their children," he says.

To others, like home-schooling researcher Ray, it is unreasonable to regulate a practice that receives no public financing. "Home-schoolers don't use a single tax dollar," Ray says. "What about children in private schools? Private schools have no regulation. Why do this to us, and not do it to private schools?"

Ray says he doesn't know of "any research suggesting that if you test them, they will do better."

"If the issue is quality in education," Ziegler says, "the argument could be made that heavy government involvement is not a guarantor of success."

Ziegler says stories of children who leave school and are not being educated are irrelevant to debates about regulating home schooling. "It's important to distinguish between home-schoolers and dropouts," he says. "The horror stories are not typical."

Home-schooling parents also point out that children schooled at home can progress at their own pace, so students who might be stigmatized as learning disabled in the public school system often blossom when allowed to pursue their own interests at home on their own schedule. Imposing a state-mandated testing or evaluation regimen would negate these benefits, they say.

Home-schooling advocates often attribute professional educators' efforts to regulate home schooling to their vested interests in keeping the numbers of schoolchildren, teachers and administrators high. "Big-government types have had a monopoly on education," Ziegler says. For teachers' unions like the American Federation of Teachers (AFT), he says, "It's a dollars-and-cents issue. Fewer jobs, fewer teachers in the union."

But Alex Wohl, AFT's director of public affairs, counters: "The number of home-schooled students is so small that it would never interfere with our membership, even if it were a focus, which it's not."

Should the public-school system support home schooling?

In 1999, when 13-year-old Megan Angstadt wanted to play basketball on her local middle-school's team in Williamsport, Penn., her parents obtained a one-year exception to the school-district policy excluding home-schoolers from extracurricular activities. To assure her participation the following year, they enrolled her in Western Pennsylvania Cyber Charter School, a distance-learning public school. They hoped to take advantage of a state law allowing charter school students to participate in extracurricular activities elsewhere if their charter school does not offer them. [15]

But the school district refused to let Megan rejoin the team. Her parents sued, contending her rights had been violated. But the district court questioned whether Megan's interest

in participating in extracurricular activities rose to the level of a constitutionally protected right.

In a change from earlier generations, home-schooling parents like the Angstadts increasingly are augmenting their children's social and educational experiences by seeking access to public-school programs. [16]

And extracurricular activities are not the only public-school resources home-schoolers want to use. According to the 1999 Education Department study, about 18 percent of home schoolers attend public school part time, 11 percent use public-school books or materials and about 6 percent participate in extracurricular activities. [17]

States usually allow local school boards to decide whether or not to honor home-schoolers' requests to take selected courses and join extracurricular activities.

"We do not permit this type of smorgasbord participation in our state," says Robert Heath, principal of W.C. Sullivan Middle School in Rock Hill, S.C. "I believe this to be appropriate, as our students must earn the right to participate in extracurricular activities through grades, behavior and so forth."

New Jersey attorney Rubin says many school districts deny such requests for a variety of reasons, including administrative inconvenience, lack of state aid and equity vis-à-vis other private-school students who would be denied the same opportunities. [18]

Legal challenges to school-district policies prohibiting home-schoolers' participation have generally been defeated. As in Megan's case, courts in Oklahoma, New York, Montana and West Virginia have held that school-district policies or state interscholastic athletic association rules that exclude home-schoolers do not violate the equal-protection rights of home-school or private-school students. [19]

However, a Massachusetts Superior Court ruled in 1995 that home-schooled high-school students may participate in interschool athletics on the grounds that distinguishing between in-school and home-schooled students "was not rationally related to a legitimate state purpose." [20]

When stymied in the courts, home-schooling advocates have turned to the legislative arena. As of spring 2002, 14 states had laws or policies granting home-schoolers access to public-school activities, and several states have legislation pending. [21]

In Oregon, Washington, California, Texas and other states, some public-school districts have gone so far as to design tax-funded school-at-home programs. Local school districts receive all or part of the usual per-pupil funding, while students work off-campus and connect with the schools via computer or at learning centers with computer labs, libraries or science labs. Working closely with parents, teachers at the learning centers may offer curriculum guidance, teach some classes and provide testing and evaluation services.

"Many public educators and the families who send their children full time to public schools . . . look askance at these programs," says Patricia D. Lines, a senior fellow at Seattle's Discovery Institute and longtime observer of home-schooling. "'It's not fair,' complained a public-school parent, 'for them to want the best of what the public school has

Minorities make up only about a quarter of the nation's home-schooled students, compared with 36 percent of the children in public and private schools. Critics say home-schooled students don't have a chance to mix with students and adults from other backgrounds. Advocates respond that music, sports and other outside-the-home activities provide ample opportunities for mixing.

Alpha Omega Publications

to offer without enduring their less-popular aspects.'" [22]

In addition, many home-schoolers are wary of governmental involvement in parent-directed education, viewing it as a Trojan horse by which the state and its employees can gain control over their children's education. "Home-schoolers who get tax dollars for educational expenses will be held accountable by the state, and regulations on them will increase," *Home Education Magazine* warned recently. [23]

"When regulations are increased for some home-schoolers, the increased regulations are very likely to be applied to

all home-schoolers, regardless of whether they are accepting tax money (or enrolling in a public e-school)," wrote home-school advocates Larry and Susan Kaseman.

Moreover, many home-schoolers also fear that accepting public-school services will force them to give up the religious orientation of their home program. [24]

But Lines believes the Trojan-horse analogy may, in fact, work the other way around, with home-schoolers subtly reforming the way public schools do business.

"When public schools open their doors to home-schooling families, they must operate in a very different way," she says in a recent study of school-family partnerships. "Rather than losing control over home schooling, it seems more likely that home-schoolers' ideas will influence public practices and curriculum."

Working with home-school families, she says, can force the public schools to adopt "a radically new service orientation toward families." Because home-schooling parents are unlikely to send their children to a conventional school, public educators will attract home-schoolers "only if they are sensitive to their needs, preferences and goals." [25]

Does home schooling threaten the fundamental American concept of universal public education?

One of the primary goals of American public education is to teach citizens how to knowledgably participate in a democratic society. "The public doesn't realize that is one of the crucial goals of our democracy," says the NSBA's Underwood.

Without a well-educated citizenry, democracy cannot work and might not survive, she says. "Public education makes democracy work well. If people don't recognize that and support it, we're always at risk of losing it."

Home-schooling advocates argue that public-school students have no corner on citizenship, however. "Children do not have to be in the same type of school for them to be productive, kind, free-thinking citizens," says Ray, of the National Home Education Research Institute.

Indeed, home-schooling families tend to be more civically active than the norm, some experts say. A 1999 study based on Education Department data found that home-schoolers were active participants in the political process. "We have reason to believe that the organizations and practices involved in private and home schooling, in themselves, tend to foster public participation in civic affairs," the authors concluded. [26]

Ziegler, of the Home School Legal Defense Association (HSLDA), scoffs at the idea that home-schooling, a tiny fraction of the nation's students, undercuts public education's citizenship goals. "To the degree that having children home-schooled undermines the schools' effectiveness, the government needs to revisit how it structures its public schools."

Others ask how the public-school system can claim to be promoting citizenship and democracy if it is failing to adequately educate all students. The public-school system has "failed us," says California home-school parent Jane Liddle.

Underwood acknowledges that the public schools aren't perfect. "They're run by local elected officials," she says. "Sometimes wacky things happen."

Some supporters of the home-schooling movement, however, believe the public-education system is more focused on producing good workers for U.S. industry than on producing good citizens. Former New York City schoolteacher John Taylor Gatto represents an extreme view of the corporate-influenced goals of state-supported schooling. His massive new book, *Underground History of American Education*, details his vision of the "deliberate transformation of American schooling, corporation-driven, which took place between 1890 and 1920, to . . . subordinate family and individual goals to the needs of 'scientific,' corporate and political managers." [27]

Others see the public schools as an authoritarian "enemy" determined to undermine family values. Much of the home-school movement's literature refers to "government-controlled" or "state-run" schools and reveals grave doubts that any government-controlled agency can operate beneficently, even if the government is a democracy.

Ray himself, in a recent home-schooling guidebook, cast the public schools and their supporters as enemies. "An increasing number of parents are recognizing the battle that is being waged for their children's hearts and minds — a battle that is played out in their education," he wrote. [28]

Educators worry that the home-schooling trend also could jeopardize the role of public education as "the great equalizer in a democracy," in the words of Michael Roberts, a spokesman for the National Parent-Teachers Association. In school, children learn to get along with others from all minorities and all economic backgrounds, he points out, and after graduation they enter the working world equipped with the same basic education. Thus, a public education is designed to, theoretically, give each child a "level playing field" when it comes to economic opportunity and their ability to

achieve success. "If we move away from that, that's detrimental."

Because home-schooling is not an option for poor families in which both parents must work, it tends to attract students from wealthier families, which usually are the most vocal in demanding that public schools perform better.

Home schooling "undermines public education's singular potential to serve as a democratic institution promoting the common good," writes Christopher Lubienski, an assistant professor of education at Iowa State University. He notes that powerful, well-organized groups are encouraging parents, especially Christian parents, to remove their children from public schools — a movement he says includes organizations with mailing lists of millions of families and a radio show with 5 million listeners (James Dobson's "Focus on the Family"). "In view of the influential groups promoting moral mandates for home schooling," Lubienski continues, home schooling should be viewed as "organized exit from public schools." [29]

He sees the growth of the home-schooling movement as the result of active and affluent parents pursuing "the best possible advantages for their own children even if it means hurting other children's chances."

By withdrawing wealthier children from the public schools, "Home schooling is a social threat to public education," Lubienski said. "It is taking some of the most affluent and articulate parents out of the system. These are the parents who know how to get things done with administrators." [30] Indeed, he writes, "Home schooling is not only a reaction to, but a cause of, declining public schools."

"Even self-described liberal, middle-class mothers who profess a loyalty to the idea of equality of educational opportunity are willing to negate such ideals in practice if, by doing so, they can increase educational advantages for their own children," Lubienski writes.

Chronology

19th Century

The notion of the "common school" takes hold. Despite resistance, secular schools that are free and open to all become the norm.

1837

Massachusetts legislators create the first state board of education, centralizing control of common schools at the state level. The first secretary, Horace Mann, awakens public to need for educational reform, establishes first teachers' colleges.

1852

Massachusetts passes first compulsory-education law, requiring children 8-14 to attend school at least 12 weeks a year — unless they were too poor. By 1900, all the northern states follow suit.

1900s-1930s

Progressive Movement replaces rote learning with learning by doing and concern for developmental psychology.

1896-1904

Educator and philosopher John Dewey runs University of Chicago's Laboratory Schools to demonstrate his view of the classroom as a miniature society in which children learn to act democratically.

1918

Mississippi becomes last state to adopt compulsory education.

1920s

Supreme Court rulings define the boundaries of state power over education, validating parents' right to have some choice.

1940s-1950s

Conservative critics assert progressive education and bureaucratic control have weakened education, usurped parental authority.

1953

Launching of *Sputnik* by the Soviet Union focuses Cold War fears on teaching of science and math.

1960s-1970s

Unrest sparked by the Civil Rights Movement and Vietnam War inspires skepticism toward schools and other institutions.

1964

Educator John Holt explains his theories of child-directed learning in *How Children Learn*.

1977

Holt launches *Growing Without Schooling* magazine for the rising number of parents choosing to "unschool" their children.

1979

Educational researcher Raymond S. Moore argues in *School Can Wait* that children suffer from early schooling, laying the foundation for later advocacy of home schooling.

1980s

Home-schooling movement organizes. Increasing numbers of Christian families join the movement; state and local networks form to fight court battles, lobby for favorable legislation and share educational resources.

1983

"A Nation at Risk," a scathing Department of Education critique of public education, appears to confirm home-schoolers misgivings. Washington state attorney Michael Farris launches Home School Legal Defense Association.

1990s-Present

Movement gains credibility and diversity.

1992

Novelist David Guterson (*Snow Falling on Cedars*) helps create program of courses and activities for home-schoolers.

1999

Home School Legal Defense Association breaks ground in Purcellville, Va., for Christian-oriented Patrick Henry College for home-schooled students.

2000

Home-schoolers win top three places in Scripps Howard National Spelling Bee.

2001

Department of Education places number of home-schooled children at an estimated 850,000.

May 2002

Patrick Henry College graduates its first class of 14.

July 2002

California Department of Education sparks a furor when it warns that "home schooling cannot legally be used as a substitute for public-school education."

Most Home-Schooling Families Are White

Minorities make up only 25 percent of home-schooled children, compared to 36 percent of students in traditional schools. A quarter of home-schoolers' parents have at least a bachelor's degree.

Characteristic	Home-Schoolers Percent	Not Educated At Home Percent
Race/ethnicity		
White, non-Hispanic	75.3	64.5
Black, non-Hispanic	9.9	16.1
Hispanic	9.1	14.1
Other	5.8	5.2
Number of children in the household		
1 child	14.1	16.4
2 children	24.4	39.9
3 or more children	61.6	43.7
Number of parents in the household		
2 parents	80.4	65.5
1 parent	16.7	31.0
Non-parental guardians	2.9	3.5
Parents in the labor force		
2 parents, 1 in labor force	52.2	18.6
2 parents, both in labor force	27.9	45.9
1 parent in labor force	11.6	28.0
No parent in labor force	8.3	7.5
Household income		
$25,000 or less	30.9	33.5
25,001-50,000	32.7	30.3
50,001-75,000	19.1	17.1
75,001 or more	17.4	19.2
Parents' highest education level		
High-school diploma or less	18.9	36.8
Voc/tech degree/some college	33.7	30.2
Bachelor's degree	25.1	16.3
Graduate/professional school	22.3	16.7

Source: National Center for Education Statistics, Parent Survey of the National Household Education Surveys Program, "Homeschooling in the United States: 1999."

While home schooling involves less than 2 percent of the public-school population now, Underwood says, it is "one of a series of threats to public education," along with efforts to privatize schools and to provide vouchers and tax credits for private-school tuition. [31] "The underlying threat is a lack of public support for the importance of an educational system that serves all children."

But others point to recent polls indicating that support for the public schools is on the rise. In 2001, the annual *Phi Delta Kappan*/Gallup poll registered the highest level of public satisfaction with local schools in the poll's 33-year history, with 51 percent grading them A or B — an 11-point increase over the 1990 rating. [32]

"Schools have clearly gotten better — there is no doubt about it," said poll director Lowell C. Rose. "The 1990s have been a decade of improvement in public schools, and the upward trend reflects the steady increase in regard people have for the public schools."

Moreover, the poll also showed a major rise in public acceptance of home schooling: 41 percent of respondents called it "a good thing," up from only 15 percent in 1985; similarly, 54 percent called it "a bad thing," down from 73 percent in 1985.

"We're starting to win the battle," Ziegler says. "This may be one reason that the establishment is fighting back." ∎

BACKGROUND

"Common Schools"

Although home schooling is widely regarded as a new phenomenon, that attitude "is simply a reflection of the bias of our times," writes Linda

Dobson, a home-schooling parent and a prominent writer on the subject. Until the middle of the 19th century, when America began transforming from an agrarian to industrial society, Dobson writes, education occurred largely at home. [33]

Nonetheless, there were many education alternatives in the young United States. In Colonial New England villages, primary schools enjoyed public support, while in the agricultural South, where households were more isolated and self-sufficient, education was almost exclusively a family responsibility. In the middle states, some public schools coexisted with church-sponsored or philanthropically established schools. West of the Allegheny Mountains, the tradition of state-mandated education began with the Ordinance of 1787, which reserved a plot of land in every prospective township for schools.

But the notion of universal education in publicly supported institutions is relatively new. In 1827, the Massachusetts legislature ordered towns of more than 500 families to furnish public instruction in American history, algebra, geometry and bookkeeping, in addition to reading, writing and arithmetic. In 1837, following a campaign to document and publicize the state's dire educational conditions, Horace Mann became the first secretary of the Massachusetts Board of Education and launched the "common school," overseen by the state and paid for by taxpayers. The same year, Michigan established a state-supported and -administered system of education.

The controversies that surrounded common schools — whether the state can rightfully levy school taxes and "usurp" parental rights by assuming authority over children's education — continue to this day. Nevertheless, Connecticut and Rhode Island quickly followed in Massachusetts' footsteps. In addition, as the practice spread, the

Home-Schooling Highlights

- *About 850,000 students nationwide — 1.7 percent of U.S. students, ages 5 to 17 — were being home-schooled in 1999, the most recent year for which government data are available. One out of five were enrolled part time in a public or private school.*

- *About 75 percent of home-schoolers are white, compared to 65 percent of children who are not schooled at home.*

- *The parents who home school had household incomes in 1999 similar to those of parents who didn't home school, but parents who home school were more highly educated.*

- *Parents' most common reasons for home schooling were to give their child a better education, religious convictions and because of a poor learning environment at school.*

Source: U.S. Department of Education, National Center for Education Statistics, Parent Survey of the National Household Education Surveys Program, "Homeschooling in the United States: 1999," July 2001.

range of educational opportunities expanded to include high school and college.

Rise of Reformers

The early 20th century brought educational reforms inspired by the Enlightenment views of French philosopher Jean Jacques Rousseau, who viewed education not as the imparting of knowledge but as the drawing out of what resides in the child naturally. Foremost among the reformers was American philosopher-educator John Dewey, who saw the classroom as a miniature society in which the values and methods of democracy were to be nurtured and practiced.

From the soil of this "progressive" tradition sprang modern reformers who first put forward the notion that education should be "child-centered." In 1959, A.S. Neil, founder of the controversial Summerhill school in England, published *Summerhill: A*

Radical Approach to Childrearing, which called for freedom, not coercion, in schools and enjoined teachers always to be on the side of the child. In addition, revolutionary thinker Ivan Illich, in his 1971 book, *DeSchooling Society*, analyzed the corrupting effects of institutionalized education, whereby the pursuit of grades and diplomas comes to replace actual learning.

"We like to say that we send children to school to teach them how to think," Reformer John Holt wrote in the preface to his classic, *How Children Learn*. "What we do, all too often, is to teach them to think badly, to give up a natural and powerful way of thinking in favor of a method that does not work well for them and that we rarely use ourselves." [34]

In 1977, Holt founded the magazine *Growing Without Schooling*, which became a Bible of sorts for families who chose to help their children learn free from the strictures of the classroom — an approach that came to be known as "unschooling."

Meanwhile, in books such as *Better Late than Early: A New Approach to Your Child's Education* and *School Can Wait*, educators like Raymond and Dorothy Moore argued that pushing children into a school setting too early could have dire educational and emotional consequences. The Moores saw the home as a better learning environment than the school. To support their cause, they left academia and created the Hewitt-Moore Research Foundation in Washougal, Wash., to support home-schooling families.

Criticism of the public schools also came from other ideological directions. Reacting to the rise of the counterculture, some home-school advocates, and others, protested the spread of "cultural relativism," which espoused that right and wrong are not absolute, but are relative to the cultural identity of an individual, and "humanistic" teaching that suggested man, not God, should be society's central concern.

In 1983, in response to plummeting standardized test scores, economic strains and disciplinary troubles in the schools, the National Commission on Excellence in Education released "A Nation at Risk," an alarming assessment of U.S. public education that seemed to confirm the misgivings of critics on both the right and the left.

Meanwhile, the ranks of home-schoolers kept growing. In the 1980s, according to Dobson, changes in tax regulations forced smaller Christian schools to close down by the hundreds. Faced with a choice between "government" schools and home schooling, thousands of parents chose to educate their children at home.

"In the mid-1980s, the number of Christian schools exploded," says Ray of the National Home Education Research Institute. "By the time the '90s rolled around, Christian schools were the majority."

States' Rights

In 1852, Massachusetts became the first state to make education compulsory for all children. Mississippi was the last state to do so, in 1918. Ever since, defining the limits on the power of the states to require and regulate education has been a subject for the courts.

"The right of the states to require education under the Constitution is well accepted, but the extent to which that right may be exercised is not unlimited," says education attorney Rubin. The U.S. Supreme Court defined the boundaries of state power in several cases dating back to the 1920s, he points out. "While not dealing specifically with the right of home instruction, these cases form the constitutional backdrop against which home-instruction cases are viewed."

In 1923 in *Meyer v. Nebraska*, the high court struck down a state law prohibiting the teaching of a modern language other than English to students who had not completed the eighth grade. Ruling that the law violated the defendant's right to teach, the student's right to learn and the parents' rights to choose what their children would be taught, the court said such rights are protected by the due-process clause of the 14th Amendment. At the same time, however, the court recognized the "power of the State to compel attendance at some school and to make reasonable regulations for all schools."

Two years later, in *Pierce v. Society of Sisters*, the Supreme Court ruled that an Oregon statute compelling attendance at public school without providing for a private-school alternative "unreasonably interferes with the liberty of parents and guardians to direct the education of children under their control."

States' rights in controlling education came up again in *Farrington v. Tokushige* in 1927. Here the Supreme Court applied the due-process clause of the Fifth Amendment to strike down stringent laws regulating Hawaii's private schools. "The *Farrington* court acknowledged there was a right to regulate private schools, but that right could not be so extensive as to effectively eliminate the alternatives offered by private schools," Rubin commented. [35]

In 1972, the Supreme Court again squarely confronted the issue of state vs. parental power in *Wisconsin v. Yoder*, affirming a Wisconsin Supreme Court's ruling that reversed the conviction of Amish parents for violating the state's compulsory-attendance law. The court held that the conviction had violated the parents' First Amendment right to the free exercise of religion. But the court emphasized that to trigger constitutional protection, the parental interest must be religious rather than philosophical or personal, and it reaffirmed a strong state interest in compulsory education.

In the 1980s, home-schooling advocates turned their attention to the legislative arena. While only two states had home-schooling statutes or regulations in 1980, 37 states had adopted such laws by 2001. [36] States without such statutes still allow home schooling when families designate themselves as private schools or religious schools, according to the Home School Legal Defense Association. ◼

CURRENT SITUATION

Nationwide Movement

By the 1990s — when the pioneering families who launched the movement began their second generation of home schooling — the world of home schooling had changed dramatically.

Colleges Praise Home-Schooled Applicants

Twenty years ago, when Harvard University admitted Grant Colfax, a home-schooled high-achiever from California, the achievement earned him an appearance on Johnny Carson's legendary "Tonight Show."

Today, an estimated 30,000 home-schooled students enter college each year, many at top schools after being actively recruited. Stanford University admitted four out of 15 home-schooled applicants in 1999 — a 27 percent acceptance rate; or more than double the rate of the entire applicant pool. [1]

"Home schoolers are the epitome of Brown students," Dean Joyce Reed wrote recently in the Brown University alumni magazine. "They are self-directed, they take risks and they don't back off." [2]

Colleges and universities generally require home-schooled students to provide a description of their academic work, results from standardized tests — usually the SAT or ACE — and personal recommendations. About a third of the colleges require graduates of "non-accredited" schools to provide GED, or high-school equivalency, test scores, according to the National Center for Home Education, the lobbying arm of the Home School Legal Defense Association." [3]

Some colleges require home-schooled students to take more achievement tests — such as the subject-oriented SAT II tests — than they require of regular high-school seniors. Not long ago, Georgia generated a national flap when it began requiring home-schooled applicants to the state university to take eight SAT IIs.

The more-stringent requirements were set aside after researchers found that home-schooled students "ran every organization at the University of Georgia," says Sean Callaway, director of college placement and internships in the Center for Urban Education at Pace University, in New York City. Callaway oversees e-mail contacts between home-schoolers and admissions officials set up by the National Association for College Admissions Counseling. [4]

But financial-aid issues can pose problems for home-schooled applicants to state universities, Callaway says. Recent changes in federal rules have created conflict between state and federal regulations. "It's different in every state," Callaway says. "Washington state is very friendly [to home-schoolers]; New York state is very unfriendly."

How do home-schoolers fare at college? Systematic research into the question "really needs to be done," Callaway says. But, like other research on home schooling, it's complicated by the difficulty of finding a controlled sample. Anecdotal evidence suggests that home-schooled students do well, however.

"Students from a home-schooled background are almost always in the top half of our applicant pool," says Ken Huus, associate dean of admissions at Indiana's Earlham College, which averages three new home-schooled students per year. "They represent themselves extremely well in personal interviews, tend to be very well read and tend to excel in our learning environment."

"To stereotype [home-schoolers] as being high achievers is a pretty accurate description," Susan Christian, director of admissions at Rider University in New Jersey, told *The New Jersey Times*. "Of the group I've seen over the years, I can't recall too many that weren't exceptional." [5]

Maryalice Newborn, the mother of five home-schooled children, says the experience made the transition to college especially easy. "For my children, going from home-schooling high school to college was just a continuation, and not a paradigm shift, like it is for so many institutionalized high-school students. They are already well acquainted with searching for their own answers and finding their own experts."

Patrick Henry College

Heather Herrick graduates last June from the 14-member inaugural class of Patrick Henry College, and receives a handshake from school President Michael Farris. The Christian-oriented school in Purcellville, Va., serves home-schooled students and currently has 193 students enrolled. Farris is the founder of the Home School Legal Defense Association.

[1] Cafi Cohen, *Homeschoolers' College Admissions Handbook* (2000), p. 6.
[2] Web site for Homeschool.com, www.homeschool.com/articles/Colleges Want You/default.asp.
[3] Cohen, *op. cit.*, p. 11.
[4] To join, send an e-mail to listserv@list.pace.edu and ask to be placed on the HSC-L list.
[5] Robert Stern, "Home Schooled, College-Bound," *The New Jersey Times*, April 8, 2002, p. A1.

Earl Stevens, a Portland, Maine, parent who home-educated his son, remembers how in the 1980s he and a friend, Eileen Yoder, decided to publish a newsletter and create the Home Education Support Network of Southern Maine. It became a model for loosely organized networks of families throughout the country. "I published the newsletter to connect people," he recalls.

He remembers it as a fun and wonderfully harmonious time. For about a dozen years, the network's 200 families and 400-500 kids gathered for activities ranging from baseball to theater productions. "There was always something happening," he recalls. "We were a totally non-directed group. There was never a meeting, never a hierarchy, never a conflict." And dealing with the state of Maine, he said, was a simple matter. "You just had to translate [what your child had accomplished] into a form they could understand."

Today, home-schooling organizations — some formal and some informal — exist in every state. They not only organize softball and basketball games and talent shows but also act as powerful lobbying networks. In addition, the loosely organized groups of families who practice "unschooling" have been joined by more hierarchical, religiously motivated organizations whose families generally prefer a more school-like, top-down approach to teaching and learning.

Members of the Music City Monarchs, a home-schooled baseball team in Mt. Juliet, Tenn., get ready for practice. Advocates of home schooling say sports, music lessons and other outside activities provide home-schooled students with diverse contacts with other students. About 18 percent of home-schoolers take classes or extracurricular activities at public schools.

AP Photo/The Tennessean, Michael Clancy

In 1983 Michael Farris, an attorney in Olympia, Wash., and former executive director of the state's conservative Moral Majority chapter, launched the Home School Legal Defense Association to assist home-schoolers. His nine children grew to maturity schooled primarily by his wife, Vicki, who told reporters that her "first and highest goal for our kids is to love our Lord." [37]

The HSLDA grew in size and influence. By 1993, with headquarters in Purcellville, Va., outside Washington, D.C., the group claimed more than 37,000 dues-paying members, some 90 percent of whom described themselves as evangelical or fundamentalist Christians. [38] That year, Farris ran unsuccessfully for lieutenant governor of Virginia, a move that cemented his ties with the Republican Party.

In 1994, the HSLDA and its home-schooling network demonstrated their political clout by defeating an amendment to the federal Elementary and Secondary Education Act that might have required home-schooling parents in some states and districts to be certified as teachers.

In 1999 the group broke ground for Patrick Henry College in Purcellville. The first students enrolled the next year. The school offers both conventional classroom instruction and an apprenticeship program in government affairs, effectively bringing volunteer workers to the HSLDA.

Today, with a staff numbering close to 60, HSLDA boasts more than 76,000 members, according to spokesman Ziegler.

Other Christian proponents of home schooling have developed veritable home-based industries around their home-schooling experiences and beliefs. For example, Christian Life Workshops, run by Gregg Harris and his family, of Gresham, Ore., centers on organizing seminars to spread the word about Christian home schooling. They also publish and sell home-schooling aids and a magazine. [39]

While conservative Protestant home-schoolers may be more entrepreneurial and media savvy than most, they are only one face of the home-schooling population, notes Mitchell L. Stevens, an associate professor of sociology at Hamilton College in Clinton, N.Y., who studied the home-schooling world for 10 years. "Other home-schoolers have built a decidedly ecumenical home education," he writes. "They have done so according to the rules and with the resources of 'alternative' America: that fragile organizational network left after the ebb of liberal causes of the 1960s and 1970s. This is the world of

At Issue:

Does home schooling promote the public good?

BRIAN D. RAY, PH.D.
PRESIDENT, NATIONAL HOME EDUCATION RESEARCH INSTITUTE

WRITTEN FOR THE CQ RESEARCHER, JANUARY, 2003

*r*esearch, experience and a philosophy of freedom show that home schooling promotes the public good because increasing the number of well-educated, socially stable and civically active individuals advances the public good.

Americans agree that several things benefit society. First, freedom of choice applies to directing the upbringing and education of one's own progeny, as the Supreme Court has affirmed. Second, having authentic educational choices is itself a democratic institution that protects citizens from government controlling knowledge and thought. Choice makes society richer and more diverse. Socially well-adjusted and educated citizens who are industrious and civically involved benefit society. Finally, particular values and principles, such as those listed above, as well as respectfulness and tolerance of others' beliefs and those embodied in the Constitution and Declaration of Independence, advance the common good. Research shows that home schooling promotes these things.

Research also shows home-schooled students score 15 to 30 percentile points above their peers in public schools on academic achievement tests, are above average in their social and psychological well-being and are involved in sports and community activities. Home-educated adults perform well in college and leadership activities and tend to be independent and critical thinkers who are gainfully employed. Home-school parents are more civically active than average.

Studies also show home schooling is accessible to a wide array of people. A rising tide of African-American and Hispanic families is flowing into home-based education and away from the public-good school experiment they discern can never make good on its promises. Many can afford the average $500 per student per year while saving taxpayers the burden of over $7,000 per public-school student.

Home-schooled young adults, regardless of their political, religious, economic or ethnic backgrounds, affirm values and behaviors that promote the common good. I have taught in public and private schools and in the home-school world and been a professor of education at the undergraduate and graduate levels. While 87 percent of Americans attend public schools, illiteracy, drug abuse, and incarceration rates climb and the battles over funding, power and defining "the common good" that riddle these schools continue. Meanwhile, an ever-increasing number of parents will successfully home school one child at a time, for his or her personal good and the furtherance of the public good.

CHRISTOPHER LUBIENSKI
ASSISTANT PROFESSOR, HISTORICAL, PHILOSOPHICAL AND COMPARATIVE STUDIES
COLLEGE OF EDUCATION, IOWA STATE UNIVERSITY

WRITTEN FOR THE CQ RESEARCHER, JANUARY, 2003

*t*he accelerated movement toward home schooling reflects a serious threat to the collective good — a threat encouraged by organized efforts to withdraw from common endeavors such as public education. Home schooling necessarily encourages individuals to focus on their own child, and diminishes concern for the education of other people's children. By emphasizing only personal benefits, the incentives inherent in home schooling essentially privatize the purpose of education. Home schooling fragments the public good into individual concerns that deny the public's interest in the education of all children.

Some argue that such individualization is not only appropriate but preferable in terms of the educational responsiveness home schooling can offer each child. In the aggregate, such a system better approximates the public good than does any bureaucracy, according to this logic.

Of course, home schooling is not an option available to all. While that is no reason to oppose home schooling, it raises questions about the factors that distinguish which child is home schooled and which are not. Home-schooling parents are by definition active and involved, having the means and initiative to guide their children's learning.

While home schooling may have beneficial effects on their own children's academic achievement, their withdrawal from the community's educational endeavors is a double loss for everyone else. Schools depend on such parents to demand accountability and results; if the channels for citizen participation in such institutions are not effectively exercised, atrophy occurs — making concerns about bureaucratic pre-eminence a self-fulfilling prophecy. Moreover, children from articulate and involved families would likely enhance the peer effect in the classroom, where children learn not just from a teacher, but from each other. Thus, while home schooling might produce a handful of academically elite individuals, it may also undermine the capacity to effectively educate the rest.

Home schooling advances from a thin conception of the public good premised on negative notions of liberty: freedom from others, rather than freedom — indeed, responsibility — to be involved with other members of the community. Such an orientation negates the public's legitimate interest in how children are educated. Families necessarily act to reproduce their values, while individual autonomy depends on free and informed choice within a broader social context. Such conditions are reflected more in a school attended by people from other families and backgrounds, than in a single family.

alternative schools, progressive not-for-profits, food co-ops and the occasional surviving commune that carry on the egalitarian ethos of the student movements and the counterculture. [40]

"Both groups have managed to create lively, talkative, durable causes," Stevens observes, "but one version of home education is larger and wealthier and more handily directs the national conversation on home schooling." That group, Stevens says, is the Christian-based wing of the movement.

Into the Mainstream?

M any mainstream Americans now view home schooling as a reasonable and realistic option, and increasing numbers of families are home schooling longer, according to Ray, of the National Home Education Research Institute. "In the early years, the numbers were highly disproportionate, with the great majority in grades K-4, or K-6," Ray says. "Now there's a clear trend of home schooling growing in the upper grade levels."

In August 2001, a *Time* cover story on home schooling's arrival in the mainstream, with a picture of a smiling, stereotypically American-looking family, asked: "Is Home Schooling Good for America?" In a wide-ranging, mostly anecdotal account of the phenomenon, the article stressed the diversity of the movement, with a constituency much like the rest of America and including representa-

Moderator Alex Trebek looks on as the winner of the National Geographic Bee, Calvin McCarter, right, displays his winning answer. The home-schooled 10-year-old from Jenison, Mich., won a $25,000 scholarship.

tives of all political and ethnic backgrounds. It even included a slightly tongue-in-cheek guide to becoming a home-schooler, with a short paragraph describing "How do I design a curriculum?" [41]

Web sites and Web-based businesses have proliferated offering curriculum guidance representing a broad range of educational approaches. (*See story, p. 4.*) Curriculum fairs for home-schoolers are commonplace and well attended. Bookstores have separate sections for home schooling. Amazon.com lists the titles of more than 1,500 home-schooling books. And in pop culture's ultimate acknowledgement of home schooling's rise to mainstream status, IDG Books added *Home Schooling for Dummies* to its popular how-to series.

But not all observers agree that the choice to home school has become so simple. "It's not mainstream yet," says Sean Callaway, director of college placement and internships in the Center for Urban Education at Pace University in New York City. "A lot of home-school families are in a very, very vulnerable position even when they're doing very

well." Callaway, who home-schooled his children off and on for about eight years, has lectured widely on the subject. "You run the risk of having a social-service worker knock on your door. Anyone can accuse you of educational child abuse. It does tend to make people defensive."

Callaway believes that the most useful way to view home-schooled students is as an anarchic school system in which 20 percent of the private-school kids in America are enrolled.

"It's just another way to educate kids, and it works in some situations and not in others," he says. "You have high-end kids and low-end kids. There are both high schools and home schools where the choices are inappropriate, high schools and home schools with a very, very narrow vision." ■

OUTLOOK

"Saber Rattling"

W ith the Republican Party in control of both Congress and the White House, the concerns of home-schoolers will likely find a sympathetic ear on Capitol Hill. "The trend has been to increasingly recognize parents' rights and authority," says Ray of the National Home Education Research Institute.

At the same time, he says, state legislatures are increasingly calling for more testing and more regulation. "Out of the blue, it's been happening

Mark Thiessen/National Geographic Society

more and more," Ray says. "I don't know why."

Among the recent trouble spots, from home-schoolers' perspective, are California, where the state superintendent decided that individual families could no longer qualify as private schools, the arrangement under which they had been allowed to home-school for years.

In Pennsylvania and Illinois, local school superintendents have been "rather aggressive" in trying to ascertain whether home-schooling families are operating according to state regulations, says Ziegler of the Home School Legal Defense Association, adding that the government "saber rattling" has included the issuance of pretrial notifications to some families.

In early 2002, Connecticut state Rep. Cameron Staples, D-New Haven, co-chairman of the legislature's Education Committee, introduced legislation to strengthen state Department of Education home-schooling guidelines by requiring parents to give local school districts copies of their teaching plans, including subjects, materials and a schedule of at least 900 hours of instruction per year. They also were required to obtain an independent assessment of their child's performance. But after a public outcry from home-schooling supporters, he agreed to kill the bill.

And in North Dakota, the House Education Committee is considering a bill — introduced on Dec. 30, 2002, at the request of the superintendent of public instruction — that would require home-schooled students to meet the same math, reading and science requirements as public-school students. [42]

"Some states have pretty strict regulations, others much more freedom," Ziegler says. "We're always working" for more freedom.

Limited Growth?

Advocates predict the home-schooling population will continue growing. "It will continue to grow in absolute numbers and percentage of population," says Ray of the National Home School Research Institute. But, he adds, the movement is also self-limiting. "How many families could or would live on one income? How many are willing to spend that much time with their children? How many believe they can afford to pay property taxes plus the additional expense of home schooling?"

As the movement continues to grow, public-school supporters worry that increasing accountability and assessment in the public schools — without a corresponding increase in accountability of home-schoolers — will create a pronounced educational dichotomy.

"There will be an increasing gap between regulation of public schools and of home schools," says Underwood of the National School Boards Association.

The now-dormant school-voucher issue, meanwhile, could play a role in home schooling. "Probably a minority of home-schooling families strongly want vouchers," Ray says, although vouchers potentially could provide funds for families to underwrite home-schooling costs. But the HSLDA and other home-schooling organizations are wary of accepting state funds. "State-level leaders tend to warn, 'If you take money, there will be strings attached,' " Ray explains.

But Underwood sees commonalities, and thinks the voucher issue will be back on the federal table this year. "The underlying similarity is greater parental control," she says. "In states where home-schooling parents are treated as private schools, it throws up concerns about [parents] keeping children home and keeping the [voucher] money."

For their part, public-school supporters see the trend toward home schooling as part of the broad drive toward privatization of traditionally governmental functions that began after Ronald Reagan's election to the presidency in 1980.

"Like private school, home schooling is a good option for some," says Ohio elementary-school principal Young. But, he adds, "If it just drives privatization, it would be a drastic mistake for our country." ∎

Notes

[1] Stacey Bielick, Kathryn Chandler and Stephen P. Broughman, "Homeschooling in the United States: 1999," U.S. Department of Education, National Center for Education Statistics, July 2001.

[2] J. Gary Knowles, Stacey E. Marlow and James A. Muchmore, "From Pedagogy to Ideology: Origins and Phases of Home Education in the United States, 1970-1990," *American Journal of Education*, Feb. 1992, p. 196.

[3] Nola Kortner Aiex, "Home Schooling and Socialization of Children," *ERIC Digest*, ERIC Clearinghouse on Reading, English and Communication, 1994, www.ed.gov/databases/ERIC_Digests/ed372460.html.

[4] For background, see Charles S. Clark, "Home Schooling," *The CQ Researcher*, Sept. 9, 1994, pp. 769-792.

[5] Greg Toppo, "850,000 Kids are being taught at home, study finds," *USA Today*, Aug. 6, 2001, p. 5D.

[6] For background, see Joan Hennessey, "Teaching Math and Science," *The CQ Researcher*, Sept. 6, 2002, pp. 697-720.

[7] Quoted in Aiex, *op. cit.*, which offers a summary of such findings.

[8] Noreen S. Ahmed-Ullah, "Home-schoolers find vindication in contests," *The Chicago Tribune*, June 21, 2001.

[9] See "Home Schooled Michigan Teen Receives Perfect SAT Score," *The Associated Press*, June 1, 2001.

[10] Lawrence M. Rudner, "Scholastic Achievement and Demographic Characteristics of

Home School Students in 1998," *Education Policy Analysis Archives*, March 23, 1999.

[11] Kariane Mari Welner and Kevin G. Welner, "Contextualizing Homeschooling Data: A Response to Rudner," *Education Policy Analysis Archives*, April 11, 1999.

[12] Nancy Mitchell, "Dog Bites System When She Receives Progress Certificate," *The Rocky Mountain News*, April 30, 2002, p. 4A.

[13] David Rubin, "Home Schooling, Religion and Public Schools: Striking a Constitutional Balance," National School Boards Association, August 2001.

[14] For background on testing, see Kenneth Jost, "Testing in Schools," *The CQ Researcher*, April 20, 2001, pp. 321-344.

[15] For background, see Charles S. Clark, "Charter Schools," *The CQ Researcher*, Dec. 20, 2002, pp. 1033-1056.

[16] *Ibid.*

[17] Toppo, *op. cit.*

[18] Rubin, *op. cit.*

[19] Thomas W. Burns, "Home Schoolers: Eligibility to Participate in Public School Extracurricular Activities," *Inquiry and Analysis*, May/June 2002, p. 6.

[20] *Ibid.*

[21] *Ibid.*, p. 7.

[22] Patricia D. Lines, "When Home Schoolers go to School: A Partnership Between Families and Schools," *Peabody Journal of Education*, January-February 2000, p. 134. Lines has served as a senior research analyst for the U.S. Department of Education and director of the Law and Education Center at the Education Commission of the States.

[23] http://www.home-ed-magazine.com/HEM/196/ndtch.html downloaded (11/12/02).

[24] See Lines, *op. cit.*, p. 133.

[25] *Ibid.*, p. 159.

[26] Christian Smith and David Sikkink, "Is Private Schooling Privatizing?" *First Things 92* (April 1999), www.firstthings.com/ftissues/ft9904/smith.html.

[27] Online at www.JohnTaylorGatto.com.

[28] Brian D. Ray, *2002-2003 Worldwide Guide to Homeschooling* (2002), p. 1.

[29] Christopher Lubienski, "Whither the Common Good? A Critique of Home Schooling," *Peabody Journal of Education*, April 2000, p. 207.

[30] Quoted in John Cloud, "Home Sweet School," *Time*, Aug. 27, 2001, p. 46.

[31] For background on vouchers, see Kenneth Jost, "School Vouchers Showdown," *The CQ Researcher*, Feb. 15, 2002, pp. 124-144

[32] Catherine Gewertz, "Public Support for Local Schools Reaches All-Time High, Poll Finds," *Education Week*, Sept. 5, 2001.

[33] Linda Dobson, "A Brief History of American Homeschooling," *Homeschoolers' Success Stories*, http:www.geocities.com/homeschoolers_success_stories/part1.html 11/6/2002.

[34] John Holt, *How Children Learn* (1964, revised 1982), p. xi.

[35] Rubin, *op. cit.*

[36] *Ibid.*

[37] Mitchell L. Stevens, *Kingdom of Children: Culture and Controversy in the Homeschooling Movement* (2001), p. 3.

[38] *Ibid.*, p. 123.

[39] *Ibid.*, p. 115.

[40] *Ibid.*, p. 7.

[41] Cloud and Morse, *op. cit.*, p. 46.

[42] Robert A. Frahm, "Home School Bill Killed," *The Hartford Courant*, March 15, 2002, p. B1.

FOR MORE INFORMATION

Home Education Magazine, P.O. Box 1083, Tonasket, WA 98855; (800) 236-3278 or (509) 486-1351; www.home-ed-magazine.com. Library Journal's Magazines for Libraries describes the magazine as "informative and commonsense."

Home School Legal Defense Association, P.O. Box 3000, Purcellville, VA 20134; (540) 338-5600; www.hslda.org. HSLDA provides information on state laws and legislative activity that affect home schooling and legal assistance to home-schooling families. Its lobbying arm, the National Center for Home Education, works to protect parents' right to home school.

National Association of Elementary School Principals, 1615 Duke St., Alexandria, VA 22314; (703) 684-3345; www.naesp.com. The NAESP's mission is to "lead in the advocacy and support for elementary and middle level principals and other education leaders in their commitment to all children."

National Home Education Research Institute, P.O. Box 13939, 925 Cottage St. N.E., Salem, OR 97309; (503) 364-2827; www.nheri.org. NHERI publishes the peer-reviewed journal Home School Researcher, undertakes research and provides information and consultation nationally and internationally.

National School Boards Association, 1680 Duke St., Alexandria, VA 22314-3493; (703) 838-6722; www.nsba.org. The foundation's mission is "to foster excellence and equity in public education through innovation in school board leadership and community engagement." It expresses concern that home schooling may expose children to substandard educations and undercut public education.

Practical Homeschooling magazine, P.O. Box 1190, Fenton, MO 63026; (800) 346-6322; www.home-school.com. The Christian-oriented publication offers practical tips on home schooling as well as a daily Bible-reading plan.

The Teaching Home: A Christian Magazine for Home Educators, P.O. Box 20219, Portland, OR 97294; (503) 253-9633; www.teachinghome.com. Publishers Pat and Sue Welch say: "Our purpose has always been to provide information, inspiration and support to Christian home-school families and Christian home-school state and national organizations . . . to the honor and glory of the Lord God."

Bibliography

Selected Sources

Books

Guterson, David, *Family Matters: Why Homeschooling Makes Sense*, Harcourt Brace, 1992.
The public-school teacher who went on to author the bestseller *Snow Falling on Cedars* explains his belief that home schooling is better.

Holt, John, *How Children Learn*, Perseus, 1964, revised 1983.
Holt's clear explication of his theory of children as natural learners played a key role in the growth of home schooling.

Ray, Brian D., *2002-2003 Worldwide Guide to Home-schooling*, Broadman & Holman Publishers, 2002.
One of home schooling's most prolific advocates details the benefits he sees in allowing parents to tailor daily school-work to their children's interests and abilities.

Stevens, Mitchell L., *Kingdom of Children: Culture and Controversy in the Homeschooling Movement*, Princeton University Press, 2001.
After 10 years of research, a sociology professor analyzes growth and change within the home-schooling movement.

Van Galen, J., and M.A. Pitman, eds., *Home Schooling: Political, Historical and Pedagogical Perspectives*, Ablex Publishing, 1991.
This collection of academic articles usefully covers home schooling from a variety of angles.

Articles

Peabody Journal of Education, Vol. 75, January/February 2000.
Several scholarly articles on home schooling offer explanatory theories and historical analyses, describe specific educational programs and assess educational methods.

Archer, Jeff, "Unexplored Territory," *Education Week*, Dec. 8, 1999.
Archer surveys scholarly research on home schooling, providing useful insights into the pitfalls of studying a highly politicized subject.

Cloud, John, *et al.*, "Home Sweet School," *Time*, Aug. 27, 2001, p. 46.
This cover story points out that today's home-schooling parents are a diverse group of parents who are getting results — and putting pressure on public schools.

Knowles, J. Gary, *et al.*, "From Pedagogy to Ideology:

Origins and Phases of Home Education in the United States, 1970-1990," *American Journal of Education*, February 1992, p. 196.
University of Michigan researchers analyze the history of the home-schooling movement.

Lyman, Isabel, "Homeschooling: Back to the Future," *Cato Policy Analysis No. 294*, Jan. 7, 1998.
A home-schooling parent and educator offers a short, useful summary of the case for home schooling.

Ray, Brian D., "Customization Through Homeschooling," *Educational Leadership*, Vol. 59, No. 7, April 2002.
A home-schooling scholar details the benefits of parents tailoring schoolwork to their children's interests and abilities.

Reports and Studies

Bielick, Stacey, *et al.*, "Homeschooling in the United States: 1999," U.S. Department of Education, National Center for Educational Statistics, July 2001.
This is the most detailed study to date of the U.S. home-schooling population.

Bauman, Kurt J., "Home Schooling in the United States: Trends and Characteristics," *Education Policy Analysis Archives*, Vol. 10, No. 26, May 16, 2002.
A Census Bureau demographer argues that home schooling may have significant impacts on the educational system.

Rubin, David, and Perry Zirkel, "Home Schooling in Religion and Public Schools: Striking a Constitutional Balance," *NSBA Council of School Attorneys*, August 2001, available at www.nsba.org/pubs/index.cfm.
This National School Boards Association report analyzes the case law and constitutional issues involved in defining the legal context for home schooling.

Rudner, Lawrence M., "Scholastic Achievement and De-mographic Characteristics of Home School Students in 1998," *Education Policy Analysis Archives*, Vol. 7, No. 8, March 23, 1999, available at http://epaa.asu.edu/epaa/v7n8.
This study found the test scores of more than 20,000 home-schoolers to be exceptionally high. Demographic data also are analyzed.

Welner, Kariane Mari and Kevin G., "Contextualizing Homeschooling Data: A Response to Rudner," *Education Policy Analysis Archives*, Vol. 7, No. 13, April 11, 1999, Available at http://epaa.asu.edu/epaa/v7n13.html.
The Welners warn that Rudner's data are skewed because they came solely from Bob Jones University.

2 Charter Schools

CHARLES S. CLARK

Forget your preconceived notions of dilapidated inner-city public schools. At the Capital City Public Charter School, occupying rented quarters above a CVS drugstore on once-infamous 14th Street in Washington, D.C., the brick building is new, the school well-lighted and clean.

Every morning at 8, when the 180 pre-K through seventh-grade students step off the elevator, abuzz with enthusiasm, they are greeted by Principal Karen Dresden, the city's charter school Principal of the Year last year. Dresden's charges represent 17 Zip codes around the city and diverse racial groups. Four hundred children are on the school's waiting list.

As a charter school, Capital City is a nonprofit, publicly funded experimental school governed by a board, mostly parent volunteers, including many of the school's founders. It is one of 2,696 charter schools established nationwide since the first one opened its doors 10 years ago in St. Paul, Minn. Charter schools are given freedom from most regulations in return for a promise to meet performance goals or lose their charters, usually granted for five-year intervals.

One of Capital City's founders is Anne Herr, a State Department analyst who heads the Board of Trustees. She says starting the school was a "leap of faith" motivated only in part by some parents' dissatisfaction with the traditional public schools their children attended. "The overall motivation was the excitement of starting something new," Herr recalls, though she admits that they might never have started "if we had known all the issues we were going to encounter."

From *The CQ Researcher*, December 20, 2002.

Nearly 680,000 pre-K-12 students attend charter schools in 39 states and the District — slightly more than 1 percent of the 47 million students in traditional public schools. Educators disagree over whether charters — launched 10 years ago in Minnesota — are a promising innovation or a damaging and costly distraction.

AP Photo/Darron Cummings

Capital City built its instructional regime around two increasingly popular programs: Outward Bound's field-trip-heavy Expeditionary Learning, and a pupil-management approach called the Responsive Classroom, which emphasizes developing social skills and a positive attitude towards selves, school and others.

"It's a real opportunity for teachers to exercise leadership and build the school," Dresden says, adding that their pay and benefits are comparable or better than those in traditional D.C. public schools, even though, she admits, "they do work a little harder." All the teachers boast strong elementary-education experience, but were not required to jump through all the "hoops and paperwork" of getting locally certified, she says.

Tuition is free at Capital City, which receives public funds based on the normal student-weighted formula — a per-pupil amount, enhanced for special-education students and those with limited English.

Unlike regular public schools, however, charters must find alternative facilities. Financing the lease on the current building — and purchasing a larger

one to move into next year — required negotiating loans and revenue bonds from area banks, personally backed by a board member. "Our board has the ideal membership for a startup," Dresden says. "They have backgrounds in banking, facilities, grant-writing, law and architecture. You might think it would be good for board members to know education, but we need their expertise in lots of areas that I'm not as strong in."

Across the country, nearly 680,000 pre-K-12 students attend charter schools in 39 states and the District of Columbia — slightly more than 1 percent of the 47 million students attending traditional public schools. Depending on each state's enabling law, charter schools can be authorized by local school districts, state governments or special chartering boards. Their sponsors include universities, social-service agencies, YMCAs, Boys and Girls Clubs and, increasingly, private, for-profit corporations. Instructional themes range from agriculture to the Montessori method to online learning.

Surveys show that families who choose charter schools want small, effective schools that are responsive to special needs, offer a structured environment and operate flexibly. [1] Yet the charter school movement is bipartisan and philosophically broad. Educational liberals value charters for the freedom to experiment, while conservatives stress the freedom for families to move out of failing schools.

Some enthusiasts see charter schools as opportunities to create laboratories of innovation whose potential has yet to be tapped. "This is a revolution in public education, like democracy was a revolution in how people are governed,"

Most States Permit Charter Schools

Since the early 1990s, 39 states and the District of Columbia have passed laws allowing the creation of charter schools, according to the Center for Education Reform, a pro-charter school group that rates state charter laws according to their strengths. Three states — New Hampshire, Tennessee and Iowa — have enabling laws but no charter schools.

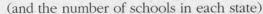

States with Laws Authorizing Charter Schools
(and the number of schools in each state)

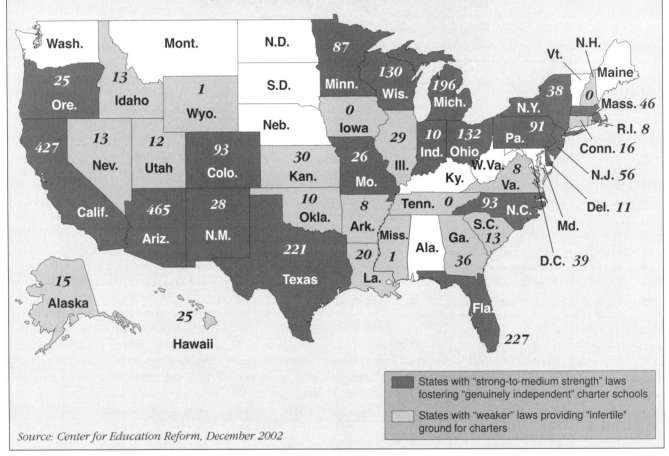

States with "strong-to-medium strength" laws fostering "genuinely independent" charter schools

States with "weaker" laws providing "infertile" ground for charters

Source: Center for Education Reform, December 2002

says Joe Nathan, director of the Center for School Change at the University of Minnesota. "We're seeing far more sophistication in how charters are set up."

Ron Wolk, founder of *Education Week*, predicts that as charter schools become more popular, they will attract private-school students back into the public system.

Others see them as an alternative to the public-school status quo. "The current system rewards good teaching by promoting teachers out of the classroom, which promotes mediocrity," says M.S. "Mike" Kayes, project director of the Phoenix-based National Charter School Clearinghouse, a Department of Education-funded group that supplies information on charter schools. "Public education's failures are systemic and institutionalized, so it's not enough to find a new manager. You have to throw off the yoke of how teachers are hired and rewarded."

But critics point out that a dispro-

portionate number of charter schools are set up in ailing urban districts, making many low-income families with at-risk children the guinea pigs for sketchily funded experimentation. Joan Devlin, associate director of educational issues at the American Federation of Teachers (AFT), says even with some successes, charter schools are "a distraction" from reforming mainstream public schools.

"Charter schools can be good tools if they're carefully done," Devlin says, noting they must be accountable and that their pupils must be required to perform well on the same achievement tests traditional schools are required to give. "And they must be open to all."

Unionized teachers claim that charter schools are a thinly veiled effort to eliminate teachers' unions. Most charter schools do not offer prevailing wages and hours, points out Deanna Duby, a senior policy analyst at the National Education Association (NEA). "They're trying to get rid of union contracts," she says. "They're saying, 'Give us some money and leave us alone, and we'll take care of things.'

"The majority of our 2.7 million members would just as soon have charter schools go away," Duby says. "They're a sign that we're not doing our job, but many feel that the competition is not fair because if you took away all the regulations [mainstream teachers] work under, we could be creative like charters, too."

In fact, Devlin argues, the tendency of many charters to employ teachers "at will" — without tenure or long-term contracts — is why teacher turnover at the schools is so high: about 60-80 percent. "I'm not saying bureaucracy isn't burdensome, but it is not generally what impedes change and progress," she adds. "It's no longer true that unions prevent school principals from hiring who they want or firing incompetent teachers. You just have to show 'just cause' rather than being capricious."

Many administrators and teachers'-union members worry that charter schools are difficult to govern, organize and regulate, like the Los Angeles charter school that reportedly bought its director a sports car. [2] And authorities revoked the license of Gateway Academy — a chain of California charter schools — after it was discovered that some of its 14 schools were teaching Islam, charging parents tuition and hiring convicted felons. [3] The irregulari-

Charter Schools Do Not "Skim"

Contrary to what critics say, charter schools serve a diverse population, according to an Education Department survey. More than half of charter students are minorities. Charter and traditional public schools serve about the same percentage of poor and non-English speakers, but charters serve slightly fewer students with disabilities.

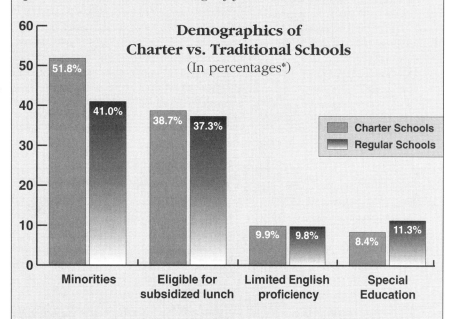

Demographics of Charter vs. Traditional Schools
(In percentages*)

Charter Schools
Regular Schools

Minorities: 51.8% / 41.0%
Eligible for subsidized lunch: 38.7% / 37.3%
Limited English proficiency: 9.9% / 9.8%
Special Education: 8.4% / 11.3%

* Data for charter schools from 1998-1999; for regular public schools, 1997-1998.

Source: RPP International study, "The State of Charter Schools 2000: Fourth-Year Report," U.S. Department of Education, January 2000, pp. 30-38.

ties at Gateway were discovered when a reporter found students praying with their Muslim teachers at a school in Sunnyvale. [4]

Moreover, some studies of student achievement have shown that charter-school test-score gains have been minimal. "If the schools are not effective, they should be curtailed or abandoned," say two Western Michigan University professors. [5]

So far, the Capital City Public Charter School is passing with flying colors. Each year, auditors from the D.C. Public Charter School Board evaluate the school based on students' performance on the Stanford 9 and other standardized tests, as well as non-academic measures like attendance and fulfillment of the school's management

plan. During its first year, Capital City reported the highest reading scores of the district's 33 charter schools.

Far less fortunate were the students, staff and parents of three other charter schools closed by the D.C. Board of Education last June. The World Public Charter School was cited for problems ranging from failing to provide individualized education plans for special-education students and not verifying students' residency to failing to conduct employee background and health checks or supply textbooks.

Nonetheless, charter schools nationwide are on the upswing. President Bush's landmark No Child Left Behind Act proposes new funding and organizational help for charter schools.

Freedom and Headaches: An Educator's Plunge

Taking the plunge into charter schools brings veteran educators freedom — and new headaches. "There was a shocking realization when I went from being in the instructional arena to the business arena in one fell swoop," says Linda Proctor Downing, a former magnet high-school director who started four unique charter schools in Phoenix. "Though I had been an educator for 20 years, I really hadn't understood how hard people in the district bureaucracy have to work to keep instructional programs running day to day."

Downing is now in her sixth year running the nonprofit operation — Arizona Agribusiness and Equine Center (AAEC) — where nearly 300 high school students ride horses and do ranching chores while studying anatomy, physiology, genetics and mathematics.

The Arizona Department of Education funds the schools, housed on community college campuses, but fundraising is always a necessity. Downing is currently in the throes of planning new fundraising to expand the equestrian programs at the two newest centers, started six months ago. "It was an eye-opener that the business aspect meant being on call 24 hours a day, seven days week," she says.

The flexibility Downing has in running the school is reflected in her approach to paying teachers. "We have no salary scale, and we pay what the market demands, with no two similar salaries," she explains. "We hire the best person we can find from an industry, often people whom the school system wouldn't hire because they lack secondary certification."

"We recently stole a biochemist from the local neurological institute," Downing adds. "In my previous school, I had no say in hiring, firing or discipline. Now I can collaborate with staff members and set up an interview team." She can offer job candidates smaller class loads than traditional schools.

The downside to the operation's small size and flexibility is that outside auditors "are a lot harder on us than they are on traditional schools," Downing says. "We're so small that they can spend more time looking at us." The auditors have been impressed both with her students' scores on standardized tests and with the high number of college-level credits they earn

from the community colleges — the average student graduates with a 3.43 grade point average and 46 college credits. "Some students have actually received their community college degrees before they get their diploma from us," Downing says.

The program's intimate size also means "we know every kid and parent in the school," Downing says. Parents and children sign an agreement promising to strive for good grades and good attendance; the school promises zero tolerance for misbehavior. "Parents have immediate access to me by phone."

Managerial flexibility stands as a key attraction for entrepreneurial educators. As a Massachusetts charter principal told a researcher for the Thomas B. Fordham Foundation, "When we get a résumé, we call the number, and we can hire the person on the spot if we like them." Another principal explained that his school "expected more of teachers and paid them less, a guarantee that those who took the job really were imbued with the mission of the school." [1]

Some principals boasted of being able to fire a lunch caterer for late deliveries or take students on a field trip with just two days' notice. Others exulted at being freed from the budget syndrome common in traditional schools, in which funds not specifically earmarked are spent haphazardly at the end of the year merely to avoid "losing" them — having them withheld the following year.

Teachers also like the opportunities charter schools offer for in-depth lessons. Dave Philhower, a fourth-grade teacher at the Capital City Public Charter School in Washington, D.C., has taken his students to the National Zoo more than 30 times to study animals and help write children's-level exhibit labels. At his previous teaching job in the suburbs, "I would never have had the release time or an administration so supportive," he says.

The risks of experimentation, however, are high for charter schools, because they have such high profiles, and the financing is often dicey. "In the charter arena, we don't get a second chance," Downing says. " If you don't get it right the first time, you're likely to end up in the newspaper."

AAEC students Aaron Fontes and Tiana Orberson display their biotech project, "Screening Desert Plants as Potential Antibiotics," at the Future Farmers of America annual competition in Louisville, Ky.

Arizona Agriculture and Equine Center/Robert Sinnott

---

[1] Quoted in Bill Triant, "Autonomy and Innovation: How Do Massachusetts Charter School Principals Use Their Freedom?" Thomas B. Fordham Foundation, December 2001.

"The Clinton administration supported charters as a policy option, but our approach is more entrepreneurial advocacy," says Undersecretary of Education Eugene W. Hickok. "Charter schools are not just an important part of public education, they are an essential part."

As the charter school movement enters its second decade, here are some of the key issues being debated:

Are charter schools harming the traditional public school system?

In suburban Long Island, N.Y., a group of parents have formed the Coalition to Oppose Charter Schools in Glen Cove. "We want to keep our community desirable," said spokeswoman Gloria Wagner. "The connotation of a charter school is, 'The [traditional public] schools are lousy and are not meeting the needs of our children.' [If charter schools are allowed here], our property values will go down, our taxes will increase to keep the standards up." [6]

In Worcester, Mass., Mark Brophy, president of the local teachers' union, blasted charter schools as "a conspiracy to implode public education" by siphoning away funds needed by traditional schools. [7]

In Indianapolis, officials this fall complained that when four new charter schools opened, the school district lost $1.5 million, mostly because the charters attracted many private-school students. [8] And a recent survey of 49 school districts with charter schools, commissioned by the U.S. Education Department, found that at least half of the districts reported negative budgetary impact. [9]

The financial impact on mainstream schools varies by state, says Paul Houston, executive director of the American Association of School Administrators, in Arlington, Va. "It depends on how closely tethered the charters are to district funds," he says. "In some states, the laws burden districts with oversight and monitoring responsibilities without providing new funds. And superintendents gripe that when charters go belly up, the districts have to sweep up the pieces of a problem they had no role in creating."

A school district's overhead costs are largely fixed, regardless of the number of students, until it reaches "a certain breaking point," Houston adds. So if charter schools reduce the number of children in the mainstream district from, say, 3,000 to 2,800, the district loses the funds for those 200 children who left — but without reducing its overhead. "[Thus], you indirectly impact the kids left in the system, because you still have to maintain buildings and provide services."

But Ted Kolderie, a former journalist and Minnesota citizen activist who helped launch the charter movement, dismisses the siphoned-funds complaint. "You have an established industry that sees change occurring, has trouble changing and tries to stop it," he says. "The complaints are self-interested, though they're not couched that way."

Under the charter school concept, "The money moves, and we finance kids," Kolderie says. "That requires districts to think. All of these assertions come when they think inside the box."

Undersecretary Hickok acknowledges "more than a scintilla of truth" to the problem of rigid overhead costs. "Having said that, I remind my friends in school systems that the issue is not funding or managing their systems, but educating children," he says. "Yes, you've got management challenges, but if families feel their children are not getting an education," it is not the district's job to thwart them.

Critics also complain that the charter movement risks re-segregation and the "Balkanization" of public education, tearing the fabric of communities in ways that have had negative consequences in other countries. For example, after New Zealand abolished its national education department in 1989, the subsequent formation of autonomous schools chosen by parents produced overcrowded, homogenized, re-segregated schools that pick their students rather than vice versa, according to Edward B. Fiske, an education consultant, and Helen F. Ladd, a professor of public policy studies and economics at Duke University. [10]

Charter school proponents say that while the Balkanization charge is logical on the surface, it doesn't hold up to scrutiny. "Neighborhood schools based on housing patterns made sense years ago, but we're now in a crisis in the urban schools," says Jeanne Allen, president of the pro-charter school Center for Education Reform, "and if traditional schools are not serving students, then we must be willing to let them leave."

In fact, neighborhood schools have been losing appeal in some areas, including wealthy suburbs where students attend a variety of alternatives to the local public schools, ranging from religious institutions to college-prep private schools.

Chester E. Finn Jr., charter supporter and president of the Thomas B. Fordham Foundation, says public-school choice offers a "dizzying proliferation of hybrid forms — virtual schooling, home schooling in the morning with charter schooling in the afternoon, public schools outsourced to private firms." Balkanization "implies that having a public school system is our foremost object of concern, but my concern is whether the public is being educated. That can be done in a wide variety of ways."

Indeed, charter proponents say fears that charter schools contribute to re-segregation were not borne out in a recent Education Department survey. It showed that charter schools had 52 percent minorities, compared with 40 percent in traditional public schools, that both sectors had about 39 percent of students in the federal lunch program, and both had about 10 percent with limited English proficiency. The traditional public schools, however, had slightly more special-education students

Many Charter Schools Offer Extended Days

More than 40 percent of all charter schools go beyond the traditional school day or year, according to the Center for Education Reform, a pro-charter school group. Both extended days and years are offered at 21 percent of the schools.

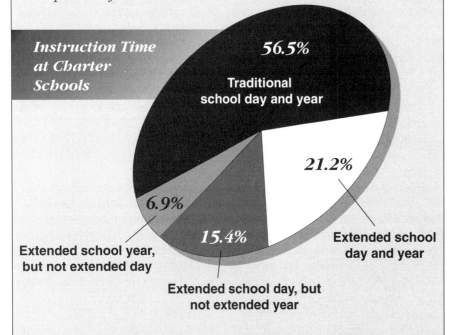

Instruction Time at Charter Schools

56.5% Traditional school day and year

21.2% Extended school day and year

15.4% Extended school day, but not extended year

6.9% Extended school year, but not extended day

Source: Center for Education Reform, October 2002, based on 481 responses from 2,357 charter schools surveyed in September 2001

(about 11 percent vs. about 8 percent in charter schools). [11]

Many strong public-education advocates do not think charter schools threaten the public schools. "Charters exist because many people want to get out of the bureaucratic environment they're mired in, not because they want to avoid the principles and values of public education," says Wendy Puriefoy, president of the Public Education Network (PEN), an association of community organizations known as local education funds (LEFs), dedicated to improving public schools.

Do charter schools foster innovation and achievement?

After 10 years of the charter school movement, evaluators must still rely largely on anecdotal evidence of in-novations and shifting reports of rising or falling test scores — the same complexities and lack of consensus that frustrate discussions of traditional schools.

Skeptics argue that for all the lofty rhetoric about charters being laboratories of innovation that would inspire mainstream schools, mixed results have forced advocates to lower their sights. "The claim was that the schools would be innovative and educators would roll it out on a larger scale," says the NEA's Duby. "We don't hear that now. Instead, you hear, 'Charters provide choice.' That's fine if the schools are innovative and offer something kids can't get in mainstream schools. But if it's just another choice, we're not supportive."

Proponents like Undersecretary Hickok point out that charters were the first to bring in dress codes and instructional programs that weave art and music into the teaching of reading and math. Charters pioneered longer school days and school years and have spotlighted "niche curriculums," such as Core Knowledge and Open Court/Direct Instruction, recently adopted in the Sacramento, Calif., public schools, says the Center for Education Reform's Allen. "The point is not to take one innovation — because the whole charter approach is innovation — but to start with the premise of what can be done differently."

Education scholar Paul Teske found that charter schools deliver innovations more than twice as fast as traditional schools. Among their many innovations: before-and-after-school programs, extra tutoring, high-technology in classes, teacher development, teacher participation in policymaking, pre-K programs, parental contracts and gifted-and-talented programs. [12]

In the Education Department's recent 49-district survey, half of the school leaders with charter schools in their districts reported becoming more customer-oriented, increasing their marketing efforts, tracking students who leave and improving communication with parents. Most districts implemented new programs, or even created new schools with programs like those of the charters. [13]

One superintendent reported that after a second charter school opened in his district, he lost $1 million in state aid. "It's spreading an already-thin budget even thinner," he told researchers, adding that if another charter school opened in his district, he might have to close a school.

The superintendent said he felt competition from the charter schools, even though only 1.3 percent of the district's students had switched to them. He also acknowledged, however, "We're better because of charters. I hate to say it, but we're more aware of the importance of what parents say and have become more customer-service oriented. We're willing to fix anything that parents leave for, like scheduling or busing. The charter schools stole our students; we will steal them back."

As a result of competition from the charter schools, the superintendent implemented several new educational programs, remodeled school buildings, included parents in the hiring process for new principals, encouraged team teaching and directed elementary schools to divide themselves into smaller units, or "families," to increase the sense of community. In addition, he announced that he expected district students to outperform charter school students on future achievement tests and created a new accountability system for district personnel to reinforce that objective.

"There are specialized charter high schools, such as schools for the arts, particularly in urban areas where they're working at reforms," PEN's Puriefoy says. "Urban schools in the standards-based-reform era are like emergency rooms are to medicine. They don't work under antiseptic conditions, and they have people coming in off the streets, but you have the same basic issues of medicine. Urban schools are the real laboratories of learning for public education as a whole."

"In most transitions, the early years are shaky," activist Kolderie says. People complained because "the early automobile was slower than the train, or because the first telephone had a range of only two miles. We never before had a system of autonomous schools. And even when charter schools are using proven learning models, they're still new, in that the organizations created are single-unit operations."

As for student achievement in charter schools, conclusions are complicated because there are no uniform tests or year-to-year data. In the late 1990s, the Phoenix-based Goldwater

Institute, a free-market think tank, studied reading scores at Arizona charter and mainstream schools. "Students enrolled in charter schools for two and three consecutive years have an advantage over students staying in [traditional schools] for the same periods of time," the institute said. [14]

But more recent studies are less glowing. In a review released in September by the Brookings Institution's Brown Center on Education Policy, charter school students in four of the 10 states studied scored significantly below those from similar public schools. The study relied on 1999-2001 data from students in grades 4, 8 and 10 in 376 charter schools. Contrary to expectations, students in the urban charter schools scored higher than those in suburban or rural charter schools, and those from larger schools did better than those from small schools. [15]

Similar findings are reflected in an AFT report released in July. It found negative test-score growth in charter schools in six states — North Carolina, Texas, Michigan, Louisiana, Ohio and Pennsylvania — and mixed results elsewhere. Positive results were found only in New Jersey and Connecticut.

The AFT evaluators also concluded that charter teachers feel less empowered to make changes in their workplaces than those in traditional buildings and hold mixed feelings about administrators and governance structures. They said charters encourage innovation but are less effective at changing instruction; that charters help isolate students by race and class; are not accountable financially and neglect special-needs students. [16]

The proliferation of charter schools in Michigan prompted studies by Western Michigan University's Center for Evaluation. "Some districts may be encouraged to improve, but others are launched on a terminal cycle of decline," wrote researchers Michael Mintrom and David N. Plank. "When assessing students' standardized-test

scores, no evidence suggests that charter schools are doing better than their traditional counterparts in the same districts." [17]

The North Carolina Center for Public Policy Research and scholars writing for the National School Boards Association both gave thumbs-down reviews of charters. [18]

Not surprisingly, charter advocates question the methodology of some of these studies, calling them biased. "Charter schools are all different," says the Center for Education Reform's Allen. "You have to look at how often the state tests, when the schools opened and whom they serve.

"If you look at individual students' scores, not masked by averages, performance is better at 80 percent of the schools," Allen continues. "With oversight boards and audit groups dropping by more frequently than with traditional schools, charter schools are the most scrutinized movement since desegregation. Yet you find a very optimistic picture, succeeding against all odds."

She points out that more than 50 years of longitudinal trends show that Philadelphia's public schools are failing. "We know more about traditional schools," she notes. "Charters know they are under the gun, but tests are expensive. Many of the schools are serving non-traditional, special-ed, at-risk kids, so they struggle to demonstrate progress. But most are, in fact, doing well by any other measures."

For instance, Allen says, charter school mobility rates are stable (charter kids tend to stay put), high-school graduation rates are at 95-99 percent and 63 percent have waiting lists.

Surveys show rates of student, teacher and parental satisfaction in charter schools triple those of traditional public schools. Finn and his colleagues say parents rate charter schools better on class size, individual attention, school size, teaching quality, parent involvement, curriculum, extra help, enforcing standards, accessibility, discipline, basic skills and safety. Traditional schools rated the same or better only on facilities. [19]

"We have a whole menagerie of charter schools," the Fordham Foundation's Finn says. "Many are fabulous, but there are too many bad and mediocre ones. Some get better, others don't."

The University of Minnesota's Nathan, who notes Minnesota has many prized and influential charter schools, says, "The generic thing called 'charter school' is like the word 'business.' Some are effective, some are not. Some shouldn't have been approved.

"But the key is whether the ineffective ones are closed," he continues. "A lot more charter schools have closed than district schools. More close for business reasons than academic ones, and the ones that do poorly in business also do poorly academically."

Kayes of the National Charter School Clearinghouse argues that the low socioeconomic status of many charter-school students makes it imperative that charters be examined with "more-sophisticated value-added" assessments. "If you're getting high-school kids who come in reading at the sixth-grade level, and if, at the end of one year, they're at the seventh- or eighth-grade level, that's phenomenal," he says.

Parents who choose charter schools for their children tend to be more involved with their kids' educations, Kayes says, and charters tend to be two-thirds to three-fourths smaller than traditional schools. "But improving student performance is absolutely what's needed. If these schools only do as well as their traditional counterparts, then why bother?"

Should private companies be allowed to run charter schools?

In Florida, three-fourths of all new charter school seats are being created by private corporations. Companies like Chancellor-Beacon Academies, based in Coconut Grove, work with developers to build new facilities with small classes. By contracting with counties to receive $2,000 less per student than a traditional school district, they pay teachers less than traditional schools, but they offer them stock options, and, in theory, save taxpayers money. [20]

According to the Center for Education Reform, 19 such companies or their nonprofit subsidiaries — called "educational management organizations" (EMOs) — are operating some 350 schools around the nation, many of them charters. They include nationwide companies like Edison Schools and National Heritage Academies. In Ohio, White Hat Ventures LLC, founded by a millionaire industrialist and private-voucher advocate, runs a sixth of the state's 91 charter schools. In New York state, companies run half the charter schools, and in Michigan, two-thirds. [21]

To some public-school purists, such public-private partnerships represent a disturbing trend. "It's based on deception," says the NEA's Duby. "The law says a public school can't be for-profit, so they set up a nonprofit foundation. The big corporate guys believe there is money to be made, so some are diving in to take over the charter movement. It will be interesting to see how many mom-and-pop charters will survive and to what degree the movement will become for-profit."

Critics also scoff at the notion that a "cookie-cutter" design from a large corporation can meet the individual needs of kids and families in diverse neighborhoods. "Education is hard," Duby says. "Learning occurs through day-to-day interaction. Corporations can't come in and say, 'We've got magic.' Which kids? Which environment? On what day? Too often they make decisions based on a test score here, a number there. But it's more complex than you think."

Paul Hill, a University of Washington professor and longtime researcher on public schools, warns that schools may not develop a strong sense of "internal accountability" if they do not control such crucial items as their own budget and curriculum. Authorizers who have a positive opinion of an EMO "may be less likely to look critically at each school affiliated with that EMO during both the application and oversight processes." [22]

The companies deny any deception. "We're not in the business of dummy organizations," says Vickie Frazier-Williams, vice president of community and board relations for Chancellor-Beacon Academies. "Every state law is different. Some allow a for-profit to own, run and operate a public school; others require a nonprofit. It's difficult to keep up with changes. But friendly school boards look to us, research us and invite us in."

As for actually earning a profit, Frazier-Williams points out that her company receives a fixed 10-12 percent of a district's payments, so proceeds from any efficiencies are channeled back into the schools. "The profit comes from growing in many different places," she says. "Charters are the toughest model because the parents vote with their feet. We have to please them."

She also dismisses the common charge that companies try to create cookie-cutter, or "McCharter" schools. "Maybe that happens in the early days, but every child, school and community is different, and each principal sets a different tone," Frazier-Williams says. Chancellor-Beacon partners with land developers to build new schools in overcrowded districts. The school boards consist of parents who all live in the same development, as opposed to traditional school boards, which usually are elected from all parts of a school district.

Marc Egan, director of the Voucher Strategy Center at the Alexandria, Va.-based National School Boards Association, says a local school board — which normally is elected — should be the agency that grants charters. A

Chronology

1970s *Lawmakers and educators experiment with public-school choice programs.*

1971
St. Paul and Minneapolis, Minn., offer the first public choice program in alternative "open" and "free" schools, followed by similar schools in Scarsdale, N.Y., Philadelphia, Pa., and Arlington, Va.

1980s *Nation decides U.S. schools need reform.*

1983
National Commission on Excellence in Education publishes dire warnings about declining quality of U.S. education in "A Nation at Risk" report.

1988
National labor, education and civic leaders hatch idea for charter schools — a concept scribbled on a napkin at Minneapolis foundation conference.

1990s *Charter school movement expands to 36 states and the District of Columbia.*

1991
Minnesota enacts first charter school law.

1992
First charter school opens in St. Paul, Minn. California enacts second charter law.

1993
Charter school laws are enacted in Colorado, Georgia, Michigan, New Mexico and Wisconsin.

1994
Federal government backs charter schools in reauthorization of the 1965 Elementary and Secondary Education Act (ESEA). . . . Arizona enacts one of the nation's most far-reaching charter school laws.

1995
Abandoning earlier opposition, National Education Association (NEA) launches five-year effort that results in four NEA charter schools.

1996
Congress passes District of Columbia School Reform Act granting chartering authority to the D.C. Board of Education and D.C. Public Charter School Board.

1998
ESEA amended with Charter School Expansion Act, which increases federal funding and support.

2000s *Charter school movement continues to expand.*

2000
In presidential campaign, both Republican George W. Bush and Democrat Al Gore promise huge expansion of charter schools; Bush talks of $3 billion in loan guarantees, Gore vows to triple number of schools by 2010.

August 2000
Harvard University's John F. Kennedy School of Government and Ford Foundation award $100,000 to Minnesota for its charter school law, to be used for nationwide advocacy.

Oct. 26, 2000
National Council of La Raza, a nationwide advocacy group for Hispanics, announces it has raised $6.7 million to develop a network of Latino-oriented charter schools.

Nov. 14, 2000
Bill and Melinda Gates Foundation gives nonprofit Aspire Public Schools $3 million to create network of small charter schools, part of larger efforts to create smaller schools.

Jan. 8, 2002
President Bush signs No Child Left Behind Act, requesting $300 million in funding for charter schools and guaranteeing that charters can continue to report their yearly progress to their sponsors, rather than the local school board.

April 29-May 3, 2002
President Bush proclaims National Charter Schools Week. "Charter schools embody the principles of President Bush's No Child Left Behind plan — marrying strict accountability for results, greater options for parents and families, and more freedom and flexibility than traditional public schools," Education Secretary Rod Paige says.

June 19-22, 2002
Education Department convenes fourth national charter school conference in Milwaukee.

June 27, 2002
U.S. Supreme Court rules in favor of Ohio's school voucher program, which allows public-school kids to attend parochial schools in Cleveland, using public education funds for their tuition; some charter school advocates are pleased.

Nov. 5, 2002
GOP election gains boost advocates for voucher programs in Texas, South Carolina and Colorado, in addition to those in effect in Florida, Ohio and Wisconsin.

Are Charter Schools Failing Special Education?

When Patricia Chittams removed her learning-disabled son from the World Public Charter School, in Washington, D.C., she said he wasn't receiving the extra help he needed.

"They provided no special-education services, no matter how much we wrote and begged," said Chittams. "They did nothing." [1]

Ultimately, the city school board closed World Public and another local charter school, charging — among other problems — that they had failed to provide adequate special-education services.

Some parents and educators fear that the nation's 2,700 charter schools, because of their experimental, regulation-exempted structure, may be neglecting children with disabilities. [2] "Its hard to say that the charter school movement has been beneficial to special-education students," says National School Boards Association (NSBA) spokesman Marc Egan.

Others argue that the charter school model allows schools to better serve children with disabilities. "If you're a charter school that serves the deaf or the blind, then you get an economy of specialization, and you can really concentrate on serving those kids' needs," says Herbert J. Walberg, a scholar at the Hoover Institution and charter school board member.

Government assessments of the prevalence of special-education programs at charter schools have produced seemingly contradictory results. A Department of Education study completed in 1999 found that special-education students made up 8.3 percent of the charter school student population, compared to 11.2 percent at regular public schools. However, the same report also cited findings indicating that charter schools enroll special-education students at a slightly higher rate than their regular counterparts. [3] In conclusion, the Education Department

researchers say in most areas data on charter schools and special education "are scant." [4]

And since charter schools are authorized by 39 different state laws, it's difficult to broadly assess their impact. "The federal government is not collecting data on charter schools and special education because the states are responsible for monitoring [them]," says Eileen Ahearn, program director at the National Association of State Directors of Special Education.

While charter schools do not have to comply with many federal and state regulations, they are not exempt from federal laws prohibiting discrimination against the disabled or handicapped. "The laws say [public] schools must provide special-education services to students with disabilities," says Lynda Van Kuren, spokeswoman for the Council for Exceptional Children. "Therefore, it is incumbent on charter schools to provide those services."

A 1975 federal law — now called the Individuals with Disabilities Education Act (IDEA) — says no student can be denied admission or participation in any school program receiving federal financial assistance. [5] Federal funds make up about 7 percent of overall public school monies. "Charter schools are public schools, they're receiving tax dollars and they cannot deny admission to any student," says Egan of the NSBA. [6]

Yet some charter school programs have logged a disproportionate number of special-education-related complaints. For instance, Arizona — which with 465 charter schools has more than any other state — recently revealed that its charter schools accumulate special-education complaints at a rate six times higher than traditional public schools. [7]

"Recently there seems to be an increasing number of hearings requested [under IDEA] regarding charter schools," Ahearn says. Charter schools must accept every student that applies or hold a lottery if there are more applicants than the school can accommodate. [8]

publicly accountable board must decide whether a school meets the public's needs — not a university or a nonprofit that may be a dummy front, he says.

"What is their motivation? To please some financiers 2,000 miles away?" Egan asks. "You can't eliminate public accountability from how the taxpayer education dollar is being spent."

Undersecretary Hickok disagrees. "School boards, as originally structured, are democratic. But what could be more democratic than parents voting with their feet?"

Finn points out that, technically, under most state constitutions, state governments are charged with educating children — not just local school boards.

"Schools we have now are gypping so many kids and have no prospect of turning around," Finn says. "It's unjust to say we must keep these kids trapped in schools that are not doing what they say they are."

Finn also calls the fear of profit-taking a "red herring." Regular schools contract with private companies to provide lunch and bus services, computers, textbooks, building maintenance and tutoring, he points out. "So a non-

trivial part of the budget flows into the coffers of for-profits," he says. "Does that make [those companies] a front? People who don't like choice or charters are trying to get people agitated into thinking EMOs are evil."

Allen also defends the companies. "Anyone who wants to make a quick buck doesn't go into education," she says. "And there is a philanthropic edge to even the most for-profit companies, though there are exceptions. The key is what the company is doing for kids. You can't fire the Miami-Dade County teachers' union, but you can fire Edison."

However, Ahearn is not aware of any federal lawsuits challenging charter schools' treatment of special-ed students. She attributes the lack of complaints to the availability of official avenues of complaint under IDEA.

Advocates for the disabled say some charter schools are "weeding out" the harder-to-educate special-education students. They might be avoiding special-ed students because they score more poorly on standardized tests, and educators are under increasing pressure to show improvement on test scores. [9] Egan admits that he has no hard statistics on how widespread the practice is. "We have some concerns that charter schools may only be admitting children with less-severe disabilities, because they are less costly to educate and provide for," he says.

Charter advocates argue that federally mandating special-education services at charter schools only makes them less effective. "The whole idea of charter schools is to get away from bureaucratic regulation from the federal and state governments," Walberg says. "Special education — because of these bureaucratic and burdensome categories like IDEA — causes a real burden for charter schools. The federal regulations should be loosened."

Because most charter schools are smaller than their traditional public-school counterparts, they may lack the facilities and staff to meet every child's special needs. "You have this huge inefficiency of these federal and state programs. It's a way that the forces of the status quo can prevent charter schools from thriving," Walberg adds.

For some, charter schools offer a middle ground between federally mandated inclusion and non-traditional public schooling. At the CHIME charter school in Los Angeles, Principal Julie Fabrocini and her colleagues integrate children with special needs into mainstream classrooms, a process required by IDEA.

"Being a charter school affords us more opportunities to more thoroughly integrate kids with disabilities, because we start from the ground up and bring in staff and faculty who are of like mind," she says. "We want schools to [reflect] an accurate representation of the community, and we want to stop an institutionalized perspective for people with disabilities."

In the end, until more legitimate research is done, the jury is still out on whether the disabled are being adequately served by charter schools. "The data collection is still being done to see what exactly the charter school movement has given to special education," adds Egan.

Walberg agrees: "It's nearly impossible to answer the question of how well charter schools are serving special-education students because charters are very heterogeneous. What we have right now are arguments rather than evidence."

— Benton Ives-Halperin

[1] Justin Blum, "Revoked Charter Schools Still Open; Facilities Appealing D.C. Board's Order," *The Washington Post*, May 6, 2002, p. B1.

[2] Center for Education Reform, www.edreform.com/pubs/chglance.htm.

[3] See Thomas A. Fiore and Lessley M. Harwell, "Integration of Other Research Findings with Charter Schools and Students With Disabilities: A National Study," U.S. Department of Education, 2000.

[4] *Ibid*.

[5] From the "Twenty-Third Annual Report to Congress on the Implementation of the Individuals with Disabilities Education Act," Office of Special Education Programs, Department of Education, May 14, 2002.

[6] For background, see Kathy Koch, "Special Education," *The CQ Researcher*, Nov. 10, 2000, pp. 905-928.

[7] Pat Kosan, "Charter Schools Exceed in Special Ed Complaints," *The Arizona Republic*, Dec. 10, 2002.

[8] Eileen Ahearn, "Public Charter Schools and Students With Disabilities," Educational Resources Information Center, June 2001.

[9] Maria L. La Ganga, "Charter School's Scores Up, So Why Is Board Unhappy?" *Los Angeles Times*, March 18, 2001, p. A1.

Houston, of the school administrators' group, says he is "more open" to giving EMOs a shot than are many of his colleagues. "Some do a better job than critics say, but they're not the ultimate solution. They're not a cash cow, and some of them may exclude high-cost, special-education kids."

In October, the General Accounting Office, the investigative arm of Congress, released a report saying there is no evidence to prove or disprove EMOs' claims of raising student achievement, because none of the data provided had scientific rigor. Rep. Chaka Fattah, D-Pa., who re-

quested the study, warned Congress to "be leery" of private education companies. ∎

BACKGROUND

Born on a Napkin

The roots of the charter school movement date to the early 1970s, when the "hippie" movement

was trickling down to the high-school level. Reformers in St. Paul, Scarsdale, N.Y., Philadelphia and Arlington, Va., began setting up experimental "free schools" within public schools.

Later, as the national pendulum swung toward a "back to basics" educational approach, the Reagan administration in 1983 released its landmark "A Nation at Risk" report, warning of a rising tide of "mediocrity" in America's public schools. Though educators of all leanings took the harsh report seriously, many felt it was an effort to pave the way for a "school choice" movement that might include taxpayer-supported private-school vouchers.

By the late '80s, California had considered legislation that would have required school districts to offer alternative programs if at least 20 parents expressed an interest. Minnesota, at the behest of then-Gov. Rudy Perpich, enacted two laws that permitted public-school transfers across district lines. And Philadelphia began experimenting with "chartering" new educational structures within districts. Meanwhile, overseas, the British Parliament enacted the 1988 Education Reform Act, which allowed schools to opt out of their local district to join a national network. [23]

But many say the official birth of American charter schools occurred at a 1988 Minneapolis Foundation education conference, where the charter-school concept was scribbled on a napkin by a group of five education and civic leaders: then-AFT President Albert Shanker; Sy Fiegel, a veteran of the East Harlem school-choice plan; Barbara Zohn, president of the Minnesota Parent Teacher Student Association; Elaine Salinas, the Twin Cities education program officer for the Urban Coalition; Kolderie, of the Citizens League in Minneapolis; Ember Reichgott, a Democratic state senator from Minneapolis; and the University of Minnesota's Nathan. [24]

The advocates, Nathan says, shared a worldview as ambitious as that of early women's-suffrage activist Susan B. Anthony. Shanker dubbed the schools as "charter" institutions, borrowing the name from a book by New England educator Ray Budde, who drew on the idea of Renaissance kings giving charters to explorers to find new worlds. [25] Former Education Secretary Lamar Alexander, then-chairman of the National Governors' Association, first proposed allowing charter schools to trade exemptions from regulations for improved results.

Making Do With Less

Charter schools spend about $2,500 less per pupil annually than the average traditional public school. About 4 percent of the average charter school budget must be provided by private donors.

Average cost per pupil

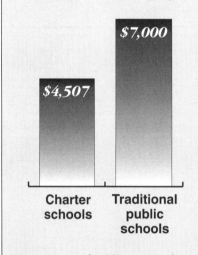

Source: Center for Education Reform, October 2002, based on 481 responses from 2,357 charter schools surveyed in September 2001

States Climb Aboard

Minnesota passed the nation's first charter school law in 1991. Initially, it was opposed by Gov. Arne Carlson and the Minnesota teachers' unions, whose members called the idea "insulting." The NEA told Congress it was "unalterably opposed" to charters; later it would launch its own charter schools.

The Minnesota program began modestly by authorizing eight charter schools, but a year later only one — the City Academy in St. Paul — had opened its doors.

In 1992, California became the second state to authorize charter schools. Republican Gov. Pete Wilson signed charter-school legislation after a competing voucher initiative was defeated at the ballot box. Five more states followed suit in 1993, and in 1994 Arizona enacted one of the country's most activist, free-market-oriented charter-school laws. Arizona's campaign was led by then-state legislator Lisa Graham Keegan, who later became the state's superintendent of education. The same year, Congress authorized experiments with charter schools when it reauthorized the Elementary and Secondary Education Act. [26]

The charter school movement has now spread to 39 states and the District of Columbia, stressing all or parts of four basic theories, according to University of Washington researcher Hill. Some states, like Georgia, pursued innovation/experimentation strategies. Others — California and Colorado — pursued a more traditional, standards-based reform approach. Michigan and Massachusetts adopted a "new supply of schools" strategy, emphasizing broadening the array of operators. The state with the most charter schools, Arizona, used a "competition/market strategy," which gives parents the widest choices possible. [27]

Charter bills were more likely to pass in Republican-controlled states, according to researcher Bryan C. Hassel. [28] In Georgia and Colorado, the governors wanted to keep school boards in charge of charter schools, while governors in Massachusetts and Michigan saw them as a way to bypass the school boards and teachers' unions.

In some states, strange political bedfellows pushed the legislation through. The charter school bill in New York, for example, was stalled due to opposition from teachers' unions and the state education commissioner. To get the law enacted during a

December 1998 lame-duck session, Republican Gov. George Pataki formed an alliance with black leaders from the Urban League, the Rev. Floyd Flake (a former Democratic congressman), Edison Schools and some business leaders.

Most charter schools are in urban areas, "where it's easier to make the argument that you need to do this," says the AFT's Devlin. There is less pressure for such schools in wealthy suburbs, she says, where the public schools are performing relatively well. Some charter laws included specific provisions designed to prevent racial resegregation.

However, charter schools are popular in the suburbs in Colorado, New Jersey and Connecticut, "where proponents have overcome fear of 'unwanted competition' among mainstream educators," one researcher says. [29]

The resulting mosaic of charter schools and related laws is notable for its variations. Minnesota's charter schools, for example, have 43 different sponsoring organizations. In California, 75 percent of charter schools require contracts for parental involvement. And in Indianapolis, the mayor has most of the authority to authorize new charters.

Union opposition, for the most part, has evolved from efforts to block legislation to proposals for charter reforms, such as requirements that the schools hire certified teachers, allow collective bargaining, obtain school board approval, ban contracts with for-profit companies and impose uniform student testing. [30]

But Wolk, of *Education Week*, says unions seeking to reform charters must not remain enamored with "a bureaucracy that can't tolerate deviation or inconsistency." "The Boston teachers' contract alone is six-inches deep with rules that have accreted over the years," he says. "It's OK to have regulations to ban racial and ethnic discrimination, but most of the regulations are just more paperwork."

Creative Resources

The biggest challenge facing budding charter schools has been the shortage of facilities. In Massachusetts, five of the 14 schools set to open in 1994 still had no buildings lined up, five months before the school year was to start. One charter school temporarily used a motel; recess was held in the parking lot. [31]

Charter schools have found homes in office buildings, warehouses, old parochial schools, strip malls and storefronts, says Jon Schroeder, director of the St. Paul-based National Charter Friends Network. Even so, he points out, they must abide by local building codes, since health and safety regulations cannot be waived. Some states provide "transition impact aid" to help charter founders locate appropriate facilities, while other states offer unused public school buildings. The federal government now supplies some funds for charter facilities.

A variety of organizations have sprung up around the country dedicated to helping charter schools secure buildings and other necessities. "We sponsor job fairs for recruiting teachers and help bring in experts on internal systems," says Shirley Monastra, executive director of the District of Columbia Public Charter School Resource Center. The group also meets informally with representatives of other resource centers in several states. Plus, California State University has launched a Charter School Development Center, while the Walton Family Foundation circulates accountability methods in several states.

Outsourcing is a common practice. According to the Education Department, 54 percent of charter schools obtain legal services from a non-district provider, 59 percent do so for insurance, 46 percent for payroll and 42 percent for social services. [32]

Funding levels for charter schools differ by state, and some argue that they are underfunded. In Washington, D.C., the per-pupil funding rate is 100 percent, which means that charter schools receive 100 percent of what traditional schools receive. But New Jersey charter schools only receive 90 percent of that, Monastra says.

A recent survey by the Center for Education Reform found that the average per-pupil cost in charter schools is $4,507 — significantly less than the $7,000 average in traditional public schools.

However, a study of charter school funding conducted by the AFT found that in some cities, like Boston, charters were actually receiving $1,800-$2,000 more than mainstream schools, Devlin says. [33] She notes that there are more elementary-level charter schools than high schools because high schools have many higher fixed expenses, such as biology labs.

But the University of Minnesota's Nathan insists the AFT is wrong. "There is substantially less money in virtually every charter school," he says. And, many states and cities provide a financial cushion to shield districts from the impact of per-pupil funds lost to charter schools.

"The unions want to keep the competition starving," the Thomas B. Fordham Foundation's Finn says. "The public systems are abysmally awful at handling contraction. If they lose 25 kids, they should get rid of a teacher or close a classroom or building instead of insisting that costs are rising."

Some union locals have challenged the constitutionality of charter schools in court, but such lawsuits have been rejected in California, Colorado, Michigan, Minnesota and New Jersey, according to Schroeder of the National Charter Friends Network. A suit by the Ohio Federation of Teachers challenging the diversion of public funds to charter schools is still pending. In California, the affluent Sequoia Union District sued the state to avoid paying $1 million for facilities required by a state-sponsored local charter school because the district never approved the school. A judge ruled in late August that Sequoia must provide the facilities. [34]

"Charter schools are facing challenges and need capital," says Puriefoy of the Public Education Network. "It's as if General Motors announced a new line of cars but would not provide new capital."

Funding charter schools, says the NEA's Duby, should not mean that teachers give up their pension plans. "Yes, the schools are freed from the bureaucracy of the central office, but many are also freed of [the requirement that they provide] support services, such as buses, food and special education. They find themselves spread thin, and many may be more in need of union support."

Seeking Accreditation

Being free and experimental, most charter schools have forgone the traditional accreditation process, designed to assure officials and the public that a given school meets basic standards in its instructional program and physical plant. Some charters, to reassure parents that their children's charter-school credits will be transferable, apply for accreditation with one of the Education Department's six approved regional accrediting bodies. In the early years, the absence of standardized testing was a major obstacle to accreditation, but the Center for Education Reform reports that 98 percent of charter schools now require at least one standardized test.

Many charter school operators feel they need their own accreditation methods, if only to weed out failing schools to avoid tarring the entire movement. Kayes, of the National Charter School Clearinghouse, says some schools are accredited by the Arizona-based Association for Performance-Based Accreditation, while others are working with the Washington-D.C.-based American Academy for Liberal Education. But some regional bodies exclude charters without certified teachers, which Kayes calls "unreasonable."

This fall, California offered a new accreditation program using team visits, conducted jointly over two years by the California Network of Educational Charters and the Western Association of Schools and Colleges. The program was implemented as Democratic Gov. Gray Davis was imposing new regulations on charter schools after revelations about abuses at some schools, and central district officials complained they lacked the resources to properly monitor charter schools. [35]

Similar complaints last winter about the burden of quality control prompted the Pennsylvania School Boards Association and 100 school districts in the Keystone State to sue a group of "virtual" charter schools that had enrolled some 5,100 K-12 students in an online learning program. The suit claimed the schools drain funds from the public schools and were not sufficiently accountable. [36]

However, some observers fear that the accreditation trend — as well as new demands of the No Child Left Behind Act and the academic-standards movement — could force conformity and standardization on charter schools, says Minnesota activist Kolderie. "Some of the most interesting charter schools have no courses and no employees; they break convention," he says.

Others are concerned about the tendency of some charter schools to engage in religious or quasi-religious instruction. In San Bernardino County, Calif., a charter school was recently disciplined for teaching Christianity. [37] And a charter school in Yuba River, Calif., which features the philosophical Waldorf teaching method, was hit with a lawsuit in 2001 accusing it of practicing religion. [38]

The religion question is a difficult one, says the Fordham Foundation's Finn. "We want to teach character — meaning values, ethics and morals — but not religion," he says. "Some educational programs look to some like religion — they light candles and have rites and rituals. But it's not God or theologically based prayers.

"There's plenty of goofy stuff at charters, even at the progressive schools that practice constructivist nonsense that might work well for some but works badly for others, particularly the disadvantaged." ∎

CURRENT SITUATION

Federal Support

The Bush administration has requested an all-time high of $300 million for charter schools for fiscal 2003.

In June, Education Secretary Rod Paige presided over a charter school conference in Milwaukee that drew record attendance and energized the movement with plans to form new, national, charter school alliances, according to Undersecretary Hickok.

Charter advocates, for the most part, are pleased by the boost charter schools received in the No Child Left Behind Act. The law's requirement that all students demonstrate "adequate yearly progress" in proficiencies toward state standards in core subjects may actually be easier for charter schools, says an analysis by the Center for Education Reform, because they have experience with contracts. But unlike the traditional public schools, notes Schroeder of the National Charter Friends Network, new accountability requirements will be overseen by the schools' authorizers and sponsors, rather than by the school districts. "Time will tell how that will work, and to what

At Issue:

Do charter schools help public education?

JEANNE ALLEN
PRESIDENT, CENTER FOR EDUCATION REFORM

WRITTEN FOR THE CQ RESEARCHER, DECEMBER 2002

Since their inception, charter schools have been committing to opening their doors to children who would not normally have a chance. Success for charters means success for all of education. Researchers who have studied the effect of charters on public education found:

- In California, charter schools are more effective than traditional public schools at improving academic achievement for low-income and at-risk students; in Chicago, charter schools performed better on 80 percent of student performance measures; in Arizona, a statewide study of 60,000 youngsters found charter pupils outperforming traditional public school students.
- Higher proportions of disadvantaged and special-needs students attend charter schools — the antithesis of "skimming the cream" from the public schools, as critics allege. Charters enrolled a larger percentage of students of color than all public schools in the charter states. In 1998-99, the most recent year for which data are available, charter schools were more likely than all public schools to serve black students (24 percent vs. 17 percent) and Hispanic students (21 percent vs. 18 percent).
- Academic accountability: Performance is intensively reviewed by authorizers and parents who must annually renew their commitment to a school.
- Parent and teacher satisfaction surpasses that of parents and teachers in traditional public schools.

Critics contend charter schools do no better than traditional ones, citing some "bad apple" stories or low-grade research. Seven percent of all charters that ever opened have been shut down for failing to meet their goals. Yet 11 percent of all public schools are failing, and there are no provisions for closure.

Charter schools are improving education by sparking improvements in the traditional system — leading schools and districts to alter behavior or improve offerings.

Charters offer at-risk programs and state-of-the-art education. They provide arts and music education, Core Knowledge, Montessori, Back to Basics or other thematic instruction; double the reading instruction; raise the expectations; set innovative discipline policies and ensure parental buy-in. Teachers get wide latitude, and more time is spent teaching.

They educate but do not over-label special-needs children. With 80 percent of the funds normally allotted for education, they are still expected to perform, and perform better — and they do. Some people ask why this can't be done in the regular public school system. The answer is quite simple: Educational change doesn't happen without pressure.

JOAN DEVLIN
ASSOCIATE DIRECTOR, EDUCATIONAL ISSUES DEPARTMENT, AMERICAN FEDERATION OF TEACHERS (AFT)

WRITTEN FOR THE CQ RESEARCHER, DECEMBER 2002

in 1988, when former AFT President Albert Shanker first embraced the idea of charter schools, he envisioned them as laboratories of innovation that would offer new curricula and teaching strategies, eliminate burdensome red tape and improve student achievement.

But today, good charter schools are few and far between. A recent AFT report found that most charters have not lived up to their promise to raise student achievement and promote innovation. Of current charter schools, more than half:

- Fail to raise student achievement compared to traditional public schools in the same area;
- Fall far short of meeting expectations to bring innovation into the classroom and the public school system at large;
- Tend to sort children by socioeconomic status; and,
- Spend more money on administration and less on instruction than other public schools.

Charter schools' staunchest defenders may try to dismiss the AFT report as an aberration, but recent independent research — in states like California, North Carolina and Texas — confirms AFT's findings that charter schools are not leading to innovation or higher student achievement, and, in fact, too often are failing to keep pace with the public schools.

States bear some of the blame for the failure of charter schools. Few states provide adequate oversight, leading to mismanagement and fraud. In Ohio, the Coalition for Public Education has filed a suit charging that Ohio's charter-school program violates the state constitution. And California newspapers assert that state's charter schools have used taxpayer dollars to hire convicted felons, buy a sports car for a school official and commit other offenses. More than half of the nation's charter schools are in Arizona, California, Florida, Michigan, Ohio and Texas, yet these states have open-ended charter school laws that allow such abuses to continue unchecked.

Ardent charter school supporters focus on the few positives, while ignoring or distorting the main body of research and will certainly continue to push for more charters and less oversight. That would be a mistake. To date, the charter experiment is a disappointment at best. Charter schools serve only as a distraction from effective reforms that are raising achievement in communities around the country: smaller class sizes, better early childhood education and greater emphasis on putting well-qualified teachers into every classroom. Policymakers owe it to the public to examine the existing research before they give charter schools a blank check for expansion.

extent the existing accountability plans for charters will be incorporated into the overall state plans."

Kayes of the National Charter School Clearinghouse notes that when the time comes for failed schools to be identified under the No Child Left Behind Act, one option would be to turn them into neighborhood charter schools.

Vouchers Link

The November elections, in which Republicans routed Democrats in many parts of the country, were seen as a boon to the school-choice movement in general. Among the winners, 52 percent favor school choice and only 35 percent oppose it, says the Center for Education Reform. Moreover, Republican gains in Congress and in the Florida, Ohio and Wisconsin legislatures were seen as a plus for the related school-voucher movement. [39]

Vouchers are considered more radical than charters, in that many voucher proposals permit public funds to be used for education at private schools, including parochial institutions. Republicans are more inclined toward vouchers than Democrats, even though support for charter schools is evident in both parties. "The parties differ in motivation," the AFT's Devlin says. "Some advocates on the right view charter schools as the camel's nose under the tent for vouchers. Liberal Democrats see them as the moat protecting public schools from vouchers."

Undersecretary Hickok argues that critics create a "false dichotomy" between vouchers and charter schools. "The American public needs to have choice in the broadest sense, and we hope vouchers are part of it," he says.

With vouchers, public funds can be used for tuition at religious schools, as the Supreme Court ruled in a "straightforward decision" last June,

Hickock adds, as long as the purpose of the program is secular education. "This administration has its faith-based initiative in play here. So if a school has a secular instructional purpose, that doesn't mean religious people can't be providers."

Allen of the Center for Education Reform sees a variety of education reforms moving on parallel tracks, all responding to different deficiencies of public education. "The voucher is the more direct, immediate service," she says. "Most in education reform say the system for too long was impervious to change and has failed to educate most kids to the levels we need it to. So there's a significant need for choice, but there's no one-size-fits-all approach."

But the Public Education Network's Puriefoy argues that the goal of charters is to give parents and communities "a point of entry" into improving the public education system.

Education Week's Wolk doesn't agree that charters are "a stalking horse for vouchers." Instead, he feels they are "the best defense against vouchers."

Like the early civil rights movement, there is plenty of vigorous disagreement within the school-choice movement, the University of Minnesota's Nathan says. [Former Supreme Court Justice] "Thurgood Marshall didn't agree all the time with Martin Luther King Jr.," he says. "In any major movement, there are major disagreements.

"I don't think vouchers are a good idea," he continues. Just as there are limits on freedom of speech, so there must be limits on school choice. Schools must be open to all kinds of kids, and voucher advocates want to be sectarian and pick and choose kids."

Steps Forward and Back

Charter schools in the nation's largest school district got a boost this Oc-

tober when newly installed New York City public schools Chancellor Joel Klein announced plans to create additional charter schools. He vowed create a "more welcome environment" for the experimental schools, of which there are currently only 18. The students who go to charter schools only receive two-thirds of the amount traditional school students receive. [40]

In November in Los Angeles, the second-largest system, a newly reconfigured group of school reform activists and academics announced plans to set up 100 charter schools. Members of the Los Angeles Alliance for Student Achievement want to form a "shadow" public school system, run by a nonprofit corporation, to create a more college-bound school culture. [41]

But in Boston, the Massachusetts Department of Education canceled plans to open six additional charter schools next fall, saying that 11 charter schools in the city is enough, given current budget constraints. Ohio, Texas and California also have introduced new curbs on charters. [42] ∎

OUTLOOK

Just a Fad?

No one said the road to a nation of charter schools would be smooth. In Douglas County, Colo., the oldest charter school went through five principals in eight years. [43] Nearly 7 percent of new charter schools fail, according to a recent Center for Education Reform survey — fewer than the 11 percent of public schools the center claims are failing.

"Yes, the closings are wasteful," Kayes of the Charter School Clearinghouse acknowledges, "but what plan do the mainstream schools have for improving?"

Researcher Hassel says the implementation problems and "political compromises" that some charter advocates have been forced to accept "have severely hampered the ability of charter school programs to live up to their promise." [44] For example, 14 states rewrote their charter laws between 1997 and 1998.

The Fordham Foundation's Finn predicts more charter schools will be established in the coming decade, and more data will be available for evaluating them. But the foundation is shifting its focus from the quantity of charter schools to the quality.

Undersecretary Hickok is concerned about losing the movement's "entrepreneurial spirit" to the institutionalization of charter schools. "It could get co-opted" by bureaucracy, he says.

But he is confident the Education Department will help charter schools reach out to disengaged parents and communities. "We can create interest on the part of parents a generation or two removed, for whom there is the possibility of a different kind of community," he says.

Charter schools have a "mixed track record" that in many ways is a distraction for public education, says Houston of the school administrators' association. "They are neither a huge threat nor a landmark innovation," he says. "But if the laws are structured right, administrators should be able to use them for reforms, to leverage and embrace an array of options for improvement."

The movement is "here to stay, at least in the short term, so we will participate," says the NEA's Duby.

"The vista looks promising in terms of the viability of charter school policy innovation," writes Sandra Vergari, an assistant professor of educational administration and policy studies at the State University of New York at Albany. "Symbolically, politically and substantively, the reform appears to hold more long-term significance than the typical fad in educational policy and administration." [45]

But she also asks whether charters might meet individual interests, while not necessarily meeting collective interests. Indeed, as Kayes points out, there is a proposal in Arizona to create a same-sex charter school for grades 4-8. "We wouldn't say it would be best for all communities or parents, but it would be an alternative," he says. [46]

Puriefoy of the Public Education Network believes charter schools will help create a more varied public education system that uniformly imposes higher expectations, helps students meet standards and gives them choices. There should be "fair and multiple assessments" for both students and adults, she adds, but they will be administered differently in different areas of the country.

"We're headed toward significant progress" she says, "but when charter schools reach a certain scale, they too will encounter what feels like bureaucratic roadblocks."

Movement co-founder Kolderie stresses the long-term view. Nearly 20 years after the warnings in "A Nation at Risk," he says, "No one thinks reform has been done, and there's not a lot of reasons to believe it will be done, even with the big hammer of accountability" in the No Child Left Behind Act.

"We're still in the process of creating the schools we need now," Kolderie says. "To rely exclusively on changing the schools we've long had will not work, and it is an unacceptable risk to take with other people's children."

The AFT's Devlin is more wary. "Charters vary in quality, have little impact on the body of knowledge of what children should learn and will have little impact on how 21st-century schools should be organized," she says. "But they're not necessarily a bad idea, and we don't see them going away. Their founders are discovering what we've always known — that running a good school is really hard work." ■

Notes

[1] Survey by RPP International, U.S. Department of Education, cited in Paul T. Hill and Robin J. Lake, *Charter Schools and Accountability in Public Education* (2002), p. 37.

[2] Joe Mathews, "Charter Schools Embracing Standards to Improve Image," *Los Angeles Times*, Oct. 14, 2002.

[3] "Charter Schools Take Root," *The San Francisco Chronicle*, Oct. 6, 2002.

[4] Jessica Brice, "Assembly sends charter school reform bill to governor," The Associated Press, Aug. 30, 2002.

[5] Gary Miron and Christopher Nelson, "What's Public About Charter Schools?" *Education Week*, May 15, 2002.

[6] Kate Zernike, "Suburbs Face Test as Charter Schools Continue to Spread," *The New York Times*, Dec. 18, 2000.

[7] Paul E. Peterson and David E. Campbell (eds.), *Charters, Vouchers & Public Education* (2001), p. 203.

[8] Caroline Hendrie, "Accredited Status Taking on Cache in Charter Schools," *Education Week*, Oct. 23, 2002.

[9] RPP International, "Challenge and Opportunity: The Impact of Charter Schools on School Districts," U.S. Department of Education, June 2001, pp. 41-42.

[10] Peterson, *op. cit.*, p. 77.

[11] RPP International study, January 2000, "The State of Charter Schools 2000: Fourth-Year Report," U.S. Department of Education.

[12] Peterson, *op. cit.*, p. 205.

[13] RPP International, "Challenge and Opportunity," *op. cit.*, pp. 41-42.

[14] See Lewis Solmon, Kern Paark and David Garcia, "Does Charter School Attendance Improve Test Scores?" Goldwater Institute, March 2001, p. 23.

[15] See www.brookings.edu, Sept. 3, 2002.

[16] "Do Charter Schools Measure Up? The Charter School Experiment After 10 Years," American Federation of Teachers, July 2002; http://www.aft.org/edissues/downloads/charterreport02.pdf

[17] Peterson, *op. cit.*, p. 52.

[18] Thomas L. Good, *et. al.*, "Charting a New Course: Fact and Fiction about Charter Schools," National School Boards Association, October 2000.

[19] Chester E. Finn, Jr., Bruno V. Manno and Gregg Vanourek, *Charters Schools in Action: Renewing Public Education* (2000), p. 272.

[20] See Kent Fischer, "Public School Inc.," *The St. Petersburg Times*, Sept. 15, 2002.

[21] Sandra Vergari (ed.), *The Charter School Landscape* (2002), p. 266.

[22] Hill and Lake, *op. cit.*, p. 75.

[23] Bryan C. Hassel, *The Charter School Challenge* (1999), p. 4.

[24] Vergari, *op. cit.*, p. 18.

[25] Ray Budde, *Education by Charter: Restructuring School Districts* (1988).

[26] For background, see Charles S. Clark, "Attack on Public Schools," *The CQ Researcher*, Aug. 2, 1996, pp. 649-672, and Kenneth Jost, "Private Management of Public Schools," *The CQ Researcher*, March 25, 1994, pp. 265-288.

[27] Hill, *op. cit.*, p.17.

[28] Hassel, *op. cit.*, p. 27.

[29] See Jain Pushpam, "The Approval Barrier to Suburban Charter Schools," Thomas B. Fordham Foundation, September 2002.

[30] See "AFT On the Issues," www.aft.org/issues/charterschools.

[31] Hassel, *op. cit.*, p. 113.

[32] Peterson, *op. cit.*, p. 42.

[33] See American Federation of Teachers, "Venturesome Capital: State Charter School Finance Systems," December 2000, online at www.aft.org/charterfinance/venturesome/chapter4.pdf

[34] Bruno V. Manno, "Yellow Flag," *Education Next*, winter 2003, p. 16.

[35] Mathews, *op. cit.*

[36] Michael A. Fletcher, "Rocky Start in 'Cyber' Classrooms," *The Washington Post*, Feb. 26, 2002.

[37] Mathews, *op. cit.*

[38] "The Spirit of Waldorf Education," *Education Week*, June 20, 2001.

[39] See Kenneth Jost, "School Vouchers Showdown," *The CQ Researcher*, Feb. 15, 2002, pp. 121-144, and Kathy Koch, "School Vouchers," *The CQ Researcher*, April 8, 1999, pp. 281-304, and "GOP's Election Gains Give School Vouchers a Second Wind," *The Wall Street Journal*, Nov. 11, 2002, p. B1.

[40] Abby Goodnough, "Chancellor Speaks Up for Charter Schools," *The New York Times*, Oct. 17, 2002.

[41] Caroline Hendrie, " 'Shadow' Idea in the Works," *Education Week*, Nov. 27, 2002.

[42] Megan Tench, "State Rolls Back Number of Boston Charter Schools," *The Boston Globe*, Nov. 11, 2002.

[43] "Charter School Field Plagued by Burnout," *Education Week*, Dec. 6, 2000.

[44] Hassel, *op. cit.*, p. 14.

[45] Vergari, *op. cit.*, p. 273.

[46] For background, see Kenneth Jost, "Single-Sex Education," *The CQ Researcher*, July 12, 2002, pp. 569-592.

FOR MORE INFORMATION

American Association of School Administrators, 1801 N. Moore St., Arlington, VA 22209-1813; (703) 528-0700; www.aasa.org. An association of chief school executives, administrators and teachers of school administration, which promotes excellence in educational administration and organization.

American Federation of Teachers, 555 New Jersey Ave., N.W., Washington, DC 20001; (202) 879-4400; www.aft.org. With more than one million members, AFT is the nation's second-largest teachers' union.

Center for Education Reform, 1001 Connecticut Ave., N.W., Suite 204, Washington, DC 20036; (202) 822-9000; (800) 521-2118; www.edreform.com. An independent advocacy organization founded in 1993 to support those seeking fundamental reforms to public schools.

National Charter School Alliance, 1295 Bandana Blvd., Suite 165, St. Paul, MN 55108; (651) 644-6115; www.charterfriends.org. Formerly the National Charter Friends Network and established in 1996 by the Center for Policy Studies, in cooperation with Hamline University, the alliance promotes quality charter schools.

National Charter School Clearinghouse, 3900 East Camelback Road, Suite 312, Phoenix, AZ 85018; (602) 954-1414; www.ncsc.info. Funded by a U.S. Education Department grant, the center runs an interactive Web site, publishes a monthly newsletter and disseminates policy information to advance the charter school movement.

National Education Association, 1201 16th St., N.W., Washington, DC 20036; (202) 833-4000; www.nea.org. The union of more than 2.7 million educators from preschool to university graduate programs promotes the interest of the teaching profession and monitors legislation and regulations at state and national levels.

National School Boards Association, 1680 Duke St., Alexandria, VA 22314; (703) 838-6722; www.nsba.org. Federation of state school board associations concerned with funding of public education, local governance and quality of education programs.

Thomas B. Fordham Foundation, 1627 K St., N.W., Suite 600, Washington, DC 20006; (202) 223-5452; www.edexcellence.net. A grant-making and research organization that supports education-reform issues at the national level, with a particular focus on projects in Dayton, Ohio.

Bibliography

Selected Sources

Books

Finn, Chester E., Jr., Bruno V. Manno and Gregg Vanourek, *Charter Schools in Action: Renewing Public Education*, Princeton University Press, 2000.

A think tank president, former assistant Education secretary and a charter school specialist at an Internet education firm summarize arguments for and against charter schools and express hopes the movement will save public education.

Hassel, Bryan C., *The Charter School Challenge: Avoiding the Pitfalls, Fulfilling the Promise*, Brookings Institution Press, 1999.

An education consultant examines the politics, policy debates and operational challenges facing the charter school movement, with a focus on developments in Colorado, Georgia, Massachusetts and Michigan.

Hill, Paul T., and Robin J. Lake, *Charter Schools and Accountability in Public Education*, Brookings Institution Press, 2002.

A research professor of public affairs and a public-policy center director at the University of Washington show how charter schools differ from public schools. They explore the unique and controversial accountability systems that give charters their freedom but put them at risk of funding cutoffs.

Nathan, Joe, *Charter Schools: Creating Hope and Opportunity for American Education*, Jossey-Bass, 1999.

This compendium by one of the charter movement's founders offers a history of the charter school movement and numerous interviews with successful charter school operators. He proposes a new charter school role for teachers' unions.

Peterson, Paul E., and David E. Campbell, eds., *Charters, Vouchers & Public Education*, Brookings Institution Press, 2001.

Two leaders at Harvard University's Program on Education Policy and Governance assembled 15 scholarly essays on charter schools, vouchers, school choice and civic education, with evidence for the prospective success of each. They include lessons learned from New Zealand and a discussion of related U.S. constitutional issues.

Schorr, Jonathan, *Hard Lessons: The Promise of an Inner-City Charter School*, Ballantine Books, 2002.

A journalist and former teacher provides an eyewitness account of the early frustrations of a fledgling charter school in economically struggling Oakland, Calif.

Vergari, Sandra, ed., *The Charter School Landscape*, University of Pittsburgh Press, 2002.

Fourteen essays by scholars examine a history of the move-ment and highlight differences among approaches in several states and Canada.

Reports and Studies

American Federation of Teachers, "Do Charter Schools Measure Up? The Charter School Experiment After 10 Years," July 2002; www.aft.org/edissues/downloads/charterreport02.pdf

This study by one of the nation's largest teachers' unions found the vast majority of charter schools have failed to fulfill their promise to bring greater achievement and innovation into the classroom. The report concluded that policy-makers should not expand charter school activities until their effectiveness or viability is proven.

Center for Education Reform, "Public-Private Partnerships: A Consumer's Guide," 2002.

A school-choice advocacy group compiled profiles of 19 educational-management companies, for-profit and nonprofit, now working in 350 schools.

U.S. Dept. of Education, "The State of Charter Schools 2000: Fourth-Year Report," January 2000.

This fourth-year report of the Education Department's National Study of Charter Schools describes charter schools operating in the 1998-99 school year and addresses broad policy issues concerning the charter school movement and its potential effect on America's system of public education.

Good, Thomas L., et. al., "Charting a New Course: Fact and Fiction about Charter Schools," National School Boards Association, October 2000.

In this skeptical examination, three scholars observe that charter districts "appear to be a strange hybrid of tradition grafted onto conservative values and parental hostility toward public education."

Lockwood, Anne Turnbaugh, "Charter Districts: Much Fuss, Little Gain," American Association of School Administrators, November 2001.

An issues analyst at the association examines charter schools in three states, some of which are managed by private companies.

Pushpam, Jain, "The Approval Barrier to Suburban Charter Schools," Thomas B. Fordham Foundation, September 2002.

A University of Maine scholar examines suburban school districts in Colorado, Connecticut and New Jersey, all of which have high proportions of charter schools, to deduce why charters are relatively rare in suburbia.

3 Covering the Uninsured

KEITH EPSTEIN

It did not seem like a big thing. On the swing set at his rural North Carolina preschool three years ago, 5-year-old Dalton Dawes and a classmate bumped into each other. Then began his parents' worst nightmare.

Dalton is a hemophiliac, and he began to bleed internally. Dalton had been receiving twice-weekly injections of a blood-clotting agent almost since birth. Now he would need them more often.

The drug would do more than simply allow him to live a normal child's life, playing soccer and roaming the nearby woods. It would keep him from bleeding to death. Yet the family's health insurer would not provide coverage. Nor could his parents, despite their good jobs, afford the $2,000 weekly expense — for years to come.

So Leonard Poe, a lawyer, and Heather Dawes, a paralegal, impoverished themselves. They sold off land and built a home from logs. They dispensed with the dishwasher and TV. By reducing their earnings to less than $23,000 a year, they qualified for Medicaid, the government health-insurance program for the poor.

After Dalton's seventh birthday, his parents had to cut their income even further — to $15,492 — in order to remain eligible for Medicaid. Instead, they tried to enroll him in the Children's Health Insurance Initiative (CHIP).

Congress passed CHIP in 1997 to tackle a worrisome statistic: the roughly 10 million American children whose families lacked health insurance. The largest single expansion of public health coverage in three decades, CHIP took

From *The CQ Researcher,* June 14, 2002.

Expensive medication makes a normal life possible for Dalton Dawes, a hemophiliac in rural North Carolina, but the cost forced his parents to impoverish themselves to qualify for Medicaid coverage.

Family Photo

direct aim at families too well off for Medicaid but too poor to afford private insurance.

Unfortunately, North Carolina's CHIP program had run out of money by March 2001. And there were more than 23,000 other children besides Dalton waiting to join the program.

To keep up Dalton's medication, his parents relied on drug-company charity and considered moving to a state with a CHIP program that was taking new clients.

By last September, when the North Carolina legislature restarted the program, Dalton had only three weeks' worth of the life-preserving injections left. [1]

"It's incredibly depressing," Heather Dawes says. "The worst thing is, I wasn't just fighting my own battle. There are millions of people in this county who are cut off from good medical care. They don't deserve this. It's awful."

The United States spends $1.3 trillion on health care each year, more than any other industrialized nation, but it is the only developed country that does not assure universal access to basic health care. Unlike the British or Canadians, for instance, all Americans are not entitled to affordable medicine or treatment — or to keeping their existing coverage if their financial circumstances change. Partly as a result, the United States ranks 37th in the World Health Organization's ranking of the world's healthiest countries. [2]

Nearly one in seven Americans — 38.7 million people — lacks insurance, more than the combined populations of Texas, Florida and Connecticut. [3] Eight in 10 of the uninsured are members of working families — too well off for Medicaid and other public programs but too poor to pay private health insurance premiums.

The lack of universal coverage, some critics say, stems from the government's historically piecemeal approach to health insurance — a complicated patchwork of private and government-subsidized coverage more like a sieve than a shield. And while there has been some progress in recent years — establishing the CHIP program and allowing workers to change or lose a job without losing insurance — many people still fall through the cracks in coverage. [4] For example, only 6 percent of the children eligible for CHIP benefits are enrolled in the program. [5]

The absence of universal health coverage has been called "one of the great, unsolved problems facing the United States at the onset of the 21st century." [6]

Most Uninsured Adults Are Young

Nearly a quarter of the adults ages 18-20 — and almost a third of those in their early 20s — did not have health insurance in 2000.

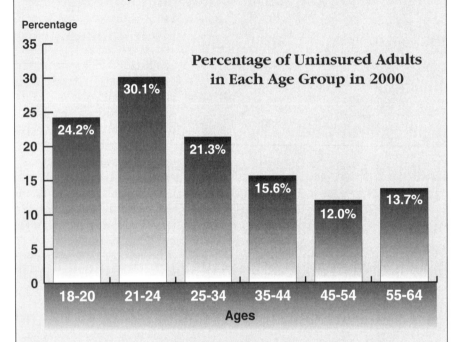

Percentage of Uninsured Adults in Each Age Group in 2000

Percentage

- 18-20: 24.2%
- 21-24: 30.1%
- 25-34: 21.3%
- 35-44: 15.6%
- 45-54: 12.0%
- 55-64: 13.7%

Ages

Note: Percentages add to more than 100 because each age group is measured separately.

Source: Employee Benefit Research Institute, Feb. 5, 2002

The problem affects Americans regardless of their age, education or place of residence. More than half the uninsured are full-time workers or their dependents. Nearly 20 million are white, 11 million are Hispanic and 7 million are black, according to the Census Bureau. [7] Only Americans over 65 are theoretically assured of health security, through Medicare. But Medicare doesn't cover the cost of most drugs, and critics say rising drug prices mean seniors are not really protected if they can see doctors but can't afford the drugs they prescribe.

And the ranks of the uninsured have been rising for most of the last 15 years — even during recent periods of record-breaking economic prosperity. [8] Seven of every 10 American workers depend on their employers for health insurance, but as health-care costs have sky-rocketed in recent years, companies have begun asking employees to pay a greater share of the cost, or eliminating coverage entirely. [9]

In Florida, a Chamber of Commerce survey found that only 77 percent of businesses offered health insurance to employees in late 2001, down sharply from 91 percent in 1999. [10] Nationwide, another survey found that 44 percent of U.S. employers were "very" or "somewhat" likely to increase workers' out-of-pocket premiums during 2002. [11]

Others have solved the problem by downsizing their staffs and outsourcing work to contractors, who by definition do not qualify for medical benefits. During last year's recession and layoffs, 2.2 million Americans lost their insurance, and a third of them probably lost their health coverage at the same time. [12]

"We face a crisis, and we need to act," said Yank D. Coble Jr., president of the American Medical Association (AMA). "The good health of our patients — and our security as a nation — depends on it." [13]

Even before the recession, real income and purchasing power were lagging behind the double-digit rates of inflation for drugs, health services and insurance, which are expected to rise 13 to 16 percent this year. "If we have more years of double-digit increases, people will be priced out of the market," said Paul B. Ginsburg, president of the Center for Studying Health System Change.

And the situation is likely to get worse. According to the Centers for Medicare and Medicaid Services, health spending will reach $2.8 trillion by 2011 — a staggering 17 percent of the gross domestic product. [14]

Cash-strapped state governments — which pay for the bulk of Medicaid — can't keep up with spiraling health costs. "Our challenge is to find a way to not cut services when we have less money than we had the year before," said Gov. Paul E. Patton, D-Ky., vice chairman of the National Governors' Association (NGA). [15]

State governments, collectively billions of dollars in the red, have begun trimming Medicaid benefits, sparking protests from Hawaii to Arkansas. [16] Dozens of states are trying to force drug manufacturers to provide discounts for the poor. [17] In Mississippi, the Medicaid program ran out of money in March. At least 14 states are considering increasing the eligibility requirements for Medicaid and CHIP, thus reducing the number of people who qualify for those safety-net services.

The health implications of inadequate insurance are stark. The Institute of Medicine estimates that 18,000 Americans die prematurely each year as a result of not having health insurance — usually because they discover too late that they have a treatable disease. [18]

Others never receive timely treatment for diabetes, mental illness and other conditions and eventually must be hospitalized, a far more costly solution than early care in a doctor's office. [19]

"The hard truth is that Americans without health-care coverage live sicker and die younger," Coble said. "It's bad fiscal policy. It's bad public policy. And it's bad medicine." [20]

"Charitable physicians and the safety net of community clinics and public hospitals do not substitute for real health coverage," said Adam Searing, project director of the North Carolina Health Access Coalition. "Need a concrete example? Look no farther than Dalton Dawes." [21]

The issue brought together two Washington lobbying groups usually on opposite sides of the health-policy debate: the U.S. Chamber of Commerce and the AFL-CIO. In February, they helped create the Covering the Uninsured coalition — along with business groups, consumer and family advocates and health-care providers — dedicated to solving the problem. [22]

Nearly a third of voters want the health-care system "radically changed," according to Republican pollster Bill McInturff. [23] President Bush has proposed new tax credits to help the uninsured pay for health coverage, a change he said would "reform health care in America." [24] And both political parties have suggested prescription-drug subsidies for the elderly. [25]

Across the country this year, people are peppering campaigners for Congress with questions about health care. A Colorado candidate for the U.S. Senate expected a coal company executive to quiz him on energy issues — only to have him complain about the company's $10 million annual bill for retired workers' prescription drugs. [26]

The problem is hardly new. In 1912, presidential candidate Theodore Roosevelt pledged to make employees, employers and "the people at large" pay

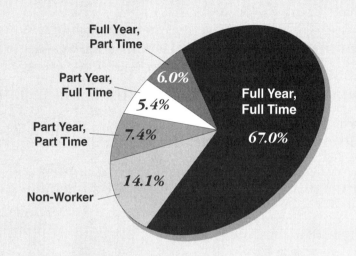

Most Uninsured Children Have Working Parents

More than two-thirds of the 8.4 million children under 18 who don't have health insurance have parents or guardians who work full time.

Work Status of Heads of Household, 2000
(Who have children without insurance)

Full Year, Part Time — 6.0%
Part Year, Full Time — 5.4%
Part Year, Part Time — 7.4%
Non-Worker — 14.1%
Full Year, Full Time — 67.0%

Note: Percentages do not add up to 100 due to rounding.

Source: Employee Benefit Research Institute, Jan. 15, 2002

for insurance against the "hazards of sickness, accident, invalidism, involuntary unemployment and old age." His proposal — often repeated by other politicians over the years — was most recently squelched in 1994, when President Bill Clinton's call for universal coverage foundered spectacularly.

The failure of Clinton's health-care reform "still hangs like a dark cloud over contemporary health-care debates," writes Harvard political scientist Jacob Hacker. [27] And this year Washington again shows every sign of deferring the issue. "We're not going to deal with it in an election year, that's for sure," said a key health-policy player, Sen. John B. Breaux, D-La. [28] People of both parties are "scared of being labeled Clintonites," explained Robert Reischauer, who ran the Congressional Budget Office in 1993. [29]

Thus, while employers, hospitals, doctors and governors clamor for

help, health-care proposals now pending in Congress would offer only limited benefits. Lawmakers believe — despite the opinion surveys — that Americans prefer their health-care progress in small doses and do not think a large federal bureaucracy can solve the problem.

Yet, if the situation isn't remedied, the coming convergence over the next decade of escalating costs, budget shortfalls and vastly increased needs could overwhelm the health-care system and increase the ranks of the uninsured to as many as 61 million. "We are heading for a social and health-care debacle of gigantic proportions," warned Harold G. Koenig, a professor of medicine at Duke University. [30]

As Congress, the White House and local leaders grapple with the nation's uninsured, these are some of the questions being debated:

Can America afford health insurance for all?

On the surface, the nation shows every sign of not being able to afford caring for the uninsured and disenfranchised. Community and public health centers, hospital clinics, inpatient facilities and emergency rooms all are showing stresses from government cutbacks. As spending spirals to new levels, states, Congress, employers and insurers all are in the mood to cut and constrain — not add to financial obligations.

The Balanced Budget Act of 1997, for instance, reduced payments to federally licensed community health centers, cut Medicare reimbursement rates to hospitals and prevented hospitals from challenging the adequacy of Medicaid payments. Since then, states have cut back on Medicaid payments, and some large health plans have pulled out of the Medicaid market altogether. Communities are seeking creative solutions, but few at any level of government or industry are saying they can afford more. [31] (*See sidebar, p. 46.*)

But Don Young, president of the Health Insurance Association of America, believes they can. "It's more of a willingness to pay — and that willingness will have to come from a number of places," he says. The task could be accomplished with expansions in Medicaid, CHIP, tax credits and tax incentives. "If the American public wants to do it, it is certainly affordable."

Ron Pollack, executive director of the national consumer organization Families USA, agrees. "Covering the uninsured has never truly been a question of cost," he says. "We're the richest nation in the history of the planet. The question is whether we have the political will for it."

But Kenneth S. Abramowitz, a managing director of the influential Carlyle Group investment firm and a longtime health-industry analyst, says Americans already pay for universal coverage — through higher health-care costs for everyone else.

Minorities Make Up Most of the Uninsured

Nearly half of America's 39 million uninsured people are black or Hispanic, and 45 percent are white.

Percentages of the Uninsured, by Race
(Excluding those over 65)

Source: Employee Benefit Research Institute, Feb. 5, 2002

"When you or I buy insurance — or the company we work for does — we're paying for the uninsured," says Abramowitz. Most insurance premiums are inflated by about 12.5 percent, he says, to compensate for nonpayment or underpayment by others — a system called "cost shifting."

The uninsured are "freeloaders," he says bluntly. "When someone shoplifts a sweater, the rest of us have to pay for the sweater because it costs us more. The [uninsured] are shoplifters."

Young admits that hospital revenues run at about 114 percent of costs — so the excess can subsidize the uninsured. Also, Medicare and Medicaid compensate hospitals that serve predominantly poor populations at a higher rate than other hospitals. "Those hidden costs are there," Young says. "The uninsured are being covered — they're

getting services, paid for by the government through tax dollars and subsidies from private insurers."

Abramowitz estimates that half the cost of any hypothetical government program to cover the uninsured is already being spent on the uninsured. It would cost less, he says, to compel every citizen to buy health insurance, with the poor receiving government vouchers for part of the cost and the poorest receiving certificates covering the entire amount. Others would receive tax credits, and employers would receive tax deductions.

"It would be cheaper — and everybody would be covered," he says, estimating a total cost of between $11 billion and $86 billion a year. [32]

Under the current system, the uninsured end up using emergency rooms for most of their care because they tend to wait until their condition is critical before seeking care at hospitals, which must treat them. Research for the National Health Policy Forum shows that about three-fourths of all emergency room (ER) visits in which patients are not admitted should have been treated elsewhere.

Because ER care is one of the costliest forms of treatment, the current system helps drive up health-care costs, critics say. The lack of universal coverage prevents the poor from getting treatment more cheaply — in a primary physician's office when their ailments are in their infancy — thus fueling the increase in health-care costs.

When the uninsured cannot afford emergency care, hospitals, businesses, insurers and taxpayers pick up the tab. Hospitals alone absorb an estimated $19 billion per year in uncompensated care for the uninsured. [33]

Such uncovered care amounts to "an unlegislated tax," says Peter Schonfeld, senior vice president for policy of the Michigan Health and Hospital Association. Because legislators don't want to raise taxes, he says, "They shift the cost elsewhere, hiding it from the public."

And the hidden "tax" is going up. The number of emergency room visits increased 15 percent nationally between 1990 and 1999, according to the American Hospital Association, largely due to a surge in uninsured visits. In California, 82 percent of the more than 9.2 million patients who are treated in emergency rooms each year cost the hospitals money — up to $48 in uncompensated care per visit. [34]

Because of the overuse of emergency rooms and state and federal cutbacks in hospital reimbursements for Medicaid and Medicare patients, hospitals nationwide have begun diverting patients to other facilities. A survey by the Democratic staff of the House Government Reform Committee found that overcrowded ERs are causing "substantial problems accessing emergency services" in 22 states — especially in cities with large numbers of uninsured residents. Some hospitals simply close their doors to those unable to pay and for whom the hospital could collect no compensation elsewhere. [35]

More than 90 percent of large hospitals with 300 beds or more report emergency rooms at — or "over" — capacity. Hospitals over capacity place patients in other areas, such as hallways. [36]

"Unless the problem is solved in the near future," cautioned the *Annals of Emergency Medicine*, "the general public may no longer be able to rely on emergency departments for quality and timely emergency care, placing the people of this country at risk." [37]

Her mom gets cancer. They find the tumor early. Her mom is OK.

or

Her mom gets cancer. She's diagnosed too late. Her mom is gone.

When you're uninsured, life turns out differently.

39 million Americans have no health insurance. Women with breast cancer are 49% more likely to die if they're uninsured.

LET'S GET AMERICA COVERED
CoveringTheUninsured.org

U.S. Chamber of Commerce • AFL-CIO • Service Employees International Union • The Business Roundtable • American Medical Association • American Nurses Association Health Insurance Association of America • Families USA • American Hospital Association Federation of American Hospitals • Catholic Health Association of the United States • AARP The Robert Wood Johnson Foundation

Covering the Uninsured Coalition

An unprecedented alliance of normally adversarial business and consumer groups known as the Covering the Uninsured coalition has launched a nationwide publicity campaign to raise awareness about the 39 million Americans who lack health insurance.

Should Medicare cover prescription drugs for the poorest seniors?

If Congress does anything on health care this year, it most likely will involve a distinct population already receiving huge publicly financed benefits — seniors and disabled persons enrolled in Medicare. Currently, Medicare covers only a few drugs, such as certain cancer medications. Some seniors purchase supplemental coverage — such as Medigap or Medicare + Choice, and some states provide additional coverage for services or prescriptions.

President Bush, members of both parties in Congress and a wide range of interest groups want the government to subsidize the skyrocketing cost of pharmaceuticals for Medicare recipients. Their interest in the issue

is not only a sign of the problem — but also of politics: The more than 10 million seniors and persons with disabilities who lack prescription-drug coverage could be critical to the outcome of midterm congressional elections this year, which could alter the balance of power in Washington.

Seniors and the disabled — among the nation's most dependent users of medications — often must pay full price for drugs, while those with private group insurance plans often pay less because of their company's purchasing power. For instance, a cholesterol-lowering medication can cost a senior more than $300 for three months, compared with only about $50 for someone with private insurance.

The big question for lawmakers is not whether to add prescription benefits to Medicare but how many seniors to give it to — in other words, how to pay for it. Facing a budget deficit, even the smallest new benefit would hit taxpayers hard.

The president wants to spend $190 billion over the next 10 years to provide free prescriptions to any Medicare recipient with an annual income under $11,610, or couples earning up to $17,415. The proposal is especially controversial because Medicare has never had salary caps before. Opponents say providing benefits only to the lowest-income seniors undermines Medicare's original covenant with the elderly — to provide coverage to every person over 65, regardless of income. Otherwise, they argue, Medicare becomes a welfare program.

Nevertheless, House Republicans propose covering only the poorest

Tampa's Do-It-Yourself Health Care

Faced with overburdened emergency rooms and sharp drops in state and federal funding for the poor, some local governments are providing health care for their uninsured residents — in some cases with surprising success.

Florida's vast Hillsborough County — a community the size of Rhode Island — raised its sales taxes to buy medical coverage for 29,000 uninsured low-income residents in the Tampa area. The scheme has dramatically lowered hospital admission rates and reduced complications from treatable ailments, such as diabetes and asthma. It also saves the county $50 million a year in property taxes that finance local public hospitals.

The county's benefits "package" — including preventive care, pharmaceuticals, referrals to specialists, hospital services, home health care and vision and dental coverage — rivals the most expensive plans of private health insurers. And yet it costs taxpayers virtually nothing.

Meanwhile, the emergency rooms at Tampa General Hospital are no longer overrun. And the county's costs for covering the uninsured are down from $600 a year per uninsured patient to $262, and average hospital stays are down to only five days — about half what they used to be. Complications from asthma, which accounted for nine in 10 visits to emergency rooms, now amount to fewer than one in 100 visits. Diabetes also is being detected earlier.

"We give better health to more people for less money," says Toni Beddingfield, community relations director for Hillsborough County's Department of Health and Human Services. "We've saved property-tax dollars — and we've saved lives."

Local officials from around the country began taking note of the Hillsborough HealthCare program even before the federal Health Resources and Services Administration two years ago endorsed it as a "model that works."

Similar experiments are under way in other urban areas that have large numbers of uninsured citizens, including Miami, El Paso, Texas, Augusta, Ga., and Kansas City, Mo.

Communities are trying other approaches as well. In Jackson, Miss., and Washington state, public health programs for the poor are financed with money from the $246 billion settlements in the huge 1998 class action lawsuit against tobacco companies. [1] In Portland, Maine, and Detroit, hospitals pool their money to provide primary care — keeping people healthier and out of hospitals.

But Hillsborough is trying to make do with money from the sales tax alone. Since 1999, the Robert Wood Johnson Foundation has been encouraging other communities to follow suit, as have the Ford Foundation and the National Association of Counties.

Tampa's program grew out of the increasing burden of providing care for an estimated 117,000 uninsured residents — nearly 14 percent of the county's population. With health-care costs escalating 17 percent annually, community leaders worried that property taxes would not be able to support the care of the poor forever.

In 1991, the state legislature agreed to a half-cent increase in the sales tax to start the new program. Despite a drop in funding to a quarter-cent after the program reported a surplus in 1997, it still manages to serve the same number of patients, who can earn no more than the federal poverty level — $8,500 for an individual, $14,500 for a family — in order to qualify.

Chief among the beneficiaries are men and women who don't qualify for federal and state medical safety nets like Medicaid and Medicare — mainly mothers of children, young working men and middle-aged women.

All receive care through a network of five hospitals and 1,700 physicians. Generally, doctors are reimbursed at 75 percent of Medicaid rates. The doctors and hospitals bill the county directly.

County officials say the biggest fear when the program started — that it would attract people with HIV, sapping the system of resources — never materialized.

Beddingfield acknowledges that because of politics and other factors most communities may find it difficult to start a local health-care program by raising sales taxes. And yet, she argues, they should try.

"What's the alternative? Raising property taxes? Letting all these people fall between the cracks? Filling emergency rooms and ending up having to spend far more money than you could save?" Emergency room care is far more expensive than primary or preventive care in a doctor's office.

Back in his days as a state legislator, U.S. Rep. Jim Davis, D-Fla., enthusiastically backed Tampa's program. Now, he says proudly, "It's really working. It's made the difference we all expected to see."

---

[1] For background, see Kenneth Jost, "Closing In on Tobacco," *The CQ Researcher*, Nov. 12, 1999, pp. 977-1000; and Kenneth Jost, "High-Impact Litigation," *The CQ Researcher*, Feb. 11, 2000, pp. 89-112.

---

seniors: The plan calls for the government covering part of the first $5,000 a year in drug expenses, and everything above $5,000. Seniors would pay $37 in monthly premiums. The plan would cost the government $350 billion and benefit only half the nation's Medicare recipients. Couples with incomes over $18,000, or individuals earning above $13,000, would not be covered.

Republicans argue that in belt-tightening times — and when so much money is being diverted to fight terrorism — benefits should go to those who need them most. They point out that Medicare beneficiaries who can afford it already pay for supplemental coverage, some of which covers prescriptions. Providing free drugs for all seniors could "bankrupt the program," hurting all Medicare beneficiaries, according to a GOP "Talking Points" memo prepared for House members. Instead, it suggested, any solution should focus on the 35 percent of Medicare recipients "who truly need a prescription-drug benefit."

In the Senate, Democrats propose spending up to $500 billion, arguing that Bush's plan only covers 3 million seniors — a third of those needing help. "The best way to help low-income seniors is to help all seniors," says Rep. John D. Dingell, D-Mich. The president's proposals are "temporary solutions" that "ignore the larger task at hand" — creating a universal Medicare drug benefit.

AARP, the influential seniors' lobby, estimates it would cost around $750 million to cover prescription-drug benefits to every American over 65. Without it, the group says, millions of elderly Americans will continue the dangerous practices they now use to stretch their medicine budgets: skipping doses, splitting pills and sharing medications with friends.

Some seniors go without pills entirely. In a 1995 survey, Medicare beneficiaries lacking drug coverage were less likely than those with drug coverage to fill prescriptions for antihypertensive medications needed to lower the risk of heart attack, heart failure, stroke and kidney failure. [38]

The average Medicare beneficiary with drug coverage fills 22 prescriptions per year, while those without it fill just 14. The ramifications are clear: Those in poor health take far fewer medications than their healthy counterparts. [39]

Price discrimination is not unique to the drug industry. Business travelers, for example, pay much higher airline fares than leisure travelers. In the pharmaceutical world, health maintenance organizations (HMOs) and benefits plan administrators negotiate price breaks.

HMOs and other "third-party" buyers account for more than 90 per-

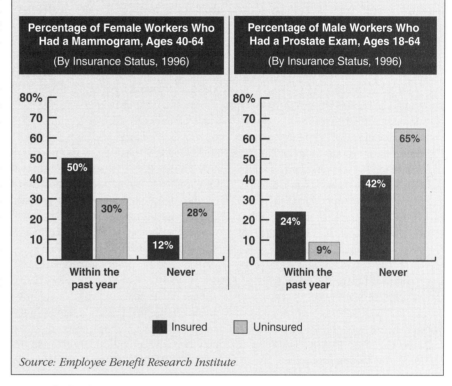

Uninsured Get Fewer Diagnostic Tests

Far more American workers get diagnostic exams when they have health insurance than those without insurance. Among women, half of those with insurance in 1996 got a mammogram that year, compared to only a third of the uninsured. Among men, 65 percent of the uninsured workers in 1996 had never had a prostate exam, compared to 42 percent of those with insurance.

Percentage of Female Workers Who Had a Mammogram, Ages 40-64
(By Insurance Status, 1996)

Percentage of Male Workers Who Had a Prostate Exam, Ages 18-64
(By Insurance Status, 1996)

■ Insured ■ Uninsured

Source: Employee Benefit Research Institute

cent of all pharmaceutical sales. By purchasing large volumes of drugs, they can negotiate steep discounts, sometimes shaving 25 percent or more off the price of a drug. In addition, state prescription-drug assistance plans, programs sponsored by pharmaceutical companies and organizations like AARP offer discounts and other benefits to distinct populations. But uninsured consumers enjoy no such clout.

Meanwhile, average prescription-drug prices have doubled in the past decade. [40] Drug companies have resisted lowering prices, arguing that research, development and testing represent a huge investment, not to mention a high risk.

Clinical trials are more complex and costs have increased, noted an August 2001 Ernst & Young analysis for the Pharmaceutical Research and Manufacturers of America. One successful pill can represent 10-15 years and $802 million of research and development, as the medicine moves from the laboratory bench to the pharmacy shelf, says the analysis. Only three of 10 marketed drugs produce revenues that match or exceed average development costs.

However, rising drug prices could drive up the cost of an eventual Medicare drug benefit, making it impossible to calculate the long-term price tag for a new Medicare benefit. And once in place, such a benefit — despite its high cost or federal budget shortfalls — would be difficult to withdraw. Programs with such a large and influential constituency are not easily eliminated.

Thus, some policymakers have suggested imposing price controls on prescription drugs. The pharmaceutical industry opposes price controls, arguing they would have a chilling effect on the quest for cures and would impede free-market forces.

Adding a prescription-drug benefit to Medicare is widely viewed as in keeping with Medicare's original intent of lessening the burden of health care for all seniors. Nevertheless, both supporters and opponents of Medicare benefits for prescription drugs lament that the nation's biggest health problem — uninsured Americans — remains unaddressed.

"It's really a shame the focus is so much on drugs for seniors," says Chip Kahn, president of the Federation of American Hospitals, "when most of the uninsured are low-income working families. They're the ones who are totally exposed."

Should small businesses be allowed to band together to buy health insurance for their employees?

Ninety-nine percent of the nation's big companies (those with more than 200 employees) offer tax-subsidized health benefits, which cost the average worker about $2,426 a year. Because large employers enjoy greater economies of scale and can pool their risk, their employees pay considerably less than if they purchased health insurance individually.

But small-business owners like John Nicholson, who operates a flower shop in Arlington, Va., have no such purchasing clout. Nicholson could not afford coverage for his 10 employees, and most insurers offered no policies appropriate for a small work force. Eventually, he signed up with a local HMO, paying $3,300 per worker. [41]

Soaring health-care costs hit small businesses harder than larger companies, and their premium rates are rising faster. But it's not just a problem for employers. Since a large percentage of all employees work for small businesses, the lack of affordable health insurance among small businesses dramatically impacts the nation's overall health-care costs. [42] In fact, a third of uninsured Americans work for employers that do not offer any health coverage, and 82 percent of the uninsured are members of families in which at least one person works part or full time. [43]

And the situation is getting worse: Small businesses' cost of insuring employees is expected to jump as much as 20 percent this year — on top of a 10-12 percent increase over the last three years. In some parts of the country, the situation is even more severe. Annual premium increases for small-business owners in Florida were expected to go up 20-30 percent this year, according to the National Federation of Independent Businesses of Florida. [44]

After at least four years of aggressive lobbying for a change, small businesses and their employees may finally be close to having an alternative. Proposed patients'-rights legislation allows small employers to band together across state lines to buy health insurance, giving them greater power to bargain for prices and coverage. The legislation passed the House last August and is awaiting Senate action.

The proposed law would permit trade and professional organizations like the National Restaurant Association or the U.S. Chamber of Commerce to sponsor and negotiate not-for-profit health-care plans known as association health plans. In theory, efficiencies and savings would be passed along to employers and employees through lower premiums.

The measure faces formidable opposition in the Senate, which agreed to a patients'-rights bill — giving patients more of a voice in their treatment by HMOs — but excluded any

provision for association health plans. Similar bills passed the House four times in recent years, only to languish in the Senate, where they couldn't garner sufficient support because of pressure from the insurance industry.

This year, with intensifying pressure to tackle health costs, the tide finally may turn in the Senate. Association health plans are attractive to many, including President Bush, because — at least in theory — they promise to add working Americans to the ranks of the privately insured without spending a dime of public money.

"Before adding millions in new federal spending and more mandates, shouldn't we look for free-market solutions that empower individuals?" Dan Danner, senior vice president of the National Federation of Small Business, asked the House in a letter a year ago. [45]

The Blue Cross and Blue Shield Association, the dominant small-business health insurer in at least half the states, opposes the measure. Danner told the House the group opposes it because "they're against anything that forces them to compete for business."

But Mary Nell Lehnhard, a Blue Cross senior vice president, called the current proposal for association plans "a shell game rather than a serious proposal for the uninsured."

Because the House stipulated that the new plans should not be regulated by the states, they would provide only temporary savings and trigger a collapse of the state-regulated market, Lehnhard said, leading to a return to higher premiums and undoing years of reforms.

Pollack of Families USA said that without being subject to state rules, association plans could exclude mental health services or home health care and might engage in discriminatory underwriting. For example, he said, benefit packages could be designed to attract healthy people, while discouraging sick people from joining. As a result, Pollack says that while he supports businesses banding together

Chronology

1850s-1870s
Early health insurance covers workers and private citizens.

1847
Massachusetts Health Insurance Co. of Boston issues "sickness insurance."

1853
French immigrants in San Francisco found the La Société Française de Bienfaisance Mutuelle — The French Mutual Benevolent Society — the first prepaid medical-insurance program in California and probably the U.S.

1870
Railroad and lumber companies deduct from workers' wages to provide health care.

1900s-1920s
Politicians begin calling for national health insurance.

1912
Presidential candidate Theodore Roosevelt makes his sweeping national health insurance plan a principal plank in the Progressive Party platform.

1915
The first of 16 states consider and reject compulsory insurance.

1929
The forerunner of Blue Cross is born.

1930s-1950s
Passage of Social Security fails to spur support for national health insurance.

1935
President Franklin D. Roosevelt signs the Social Security Act, prompting supporters to urge the second step: a national health insurance system.

1945
President Harry S. Truman seeks to include universal health insurance in Social Security.

1956
Disability-insurance program is added to Social Security.

1960s-1980s
Medicare and Medicaid are created to cover health care for the poor and elderly.

1965
President Lyndon B. Johnson signs bill creating Medicare and Medicaid.

1972
President Richard M. Nixon proposes comprehensive, "high-quality" health care for every American.

1973
The Health Maintenance Organization Act establishes requirements for federally designated HMOs.

1985
The Consolidated Omnibus Budget Reconciliation Act (COBRA) is passed, requiring employers to provide 18 months of continued coverage to terminated employees.

1990s-2000s
Universal coverage is back on the agenda.

1990
President George Bush proposes expanding health insurance through tax breaks.

1991
Democratic Senate candidate Harris Wofford unexpectedly trounces a two-time Pennsylvania governor by declaring that working Americans have "a right to a doctor."

1992
Presidential candidate Bill Clinton rides the public's health-care anxieties to the Democratic nomination. He vows to "take on the health-care profiteers and make health care affordable for every family."

1993-1994
Clinton puts first lady Hillary Rodham Clinton in charge of pushing his Health Security Act. The health-care industry opposes the idea; the plan is resoundingly defeated.

1996
The Health Insurance Portability and Accountability Act prohibits insurers from enforcing pre-existing condition clauses, making it easier for employees to carry insurance between jobs.

1997
The Balanced Budget Act creates the Children's Health Insurance Program, providing federal matching funds to states to expand coverage to families with children whose incomes were below twice the poverty line.

1995
Enrollment in managed-care plans reaches nearly 58 million, from 26 million in 1986.

2001
The House passes a "patients' bill of rights" giving patients more of a voice in managed-care programs.

to buy insurance, "the measure approved by the House could make the problems existing today even worse."

The NGA supports the idea, but not the bill. State oversight is necessary, the governors say, "to protect consumers and small businesses from fraud and abuse and underinsurance." [46]

But Kahn of the hospital federation counters, "Nothing that expands health coverage to more people will be ideal," he says. "We're not talking about Cadillacs here; we're talking about Chevys, at best. But at least we're talking about Chevys for people who now have no car at all."

Just how many people would be newly insured? The Congressional Budget Office (CBO) foresees the innovation worsening conditions for four in five workers. It says 20 million employees would face increases in premiums, while insurance would be less expensive for 4.6 million. Meanwhile, only 330,000 of the uninsured would gain coverage, the CBO said.

But a public-policy research firm, CONSAD, estimates that the measure would extend benefits to 4.5 million workers at affordable rates. According to former Rep. Jim Talent, R-Mo., small businesses could save 10-20 percent in health-care costs.

The key, Talent said, lies in breaking the grip of the Blue Cross monopolies — and conventional wisdom. "Nobody questions that big businesses can offer comprehensive plans," Talent said. "But for some reason, they seem to distrust small businesses." ■

BACKGROUND

Recurring Quest

The quest for guaranteed health care is an old one. Reformers have sought major changes five times during the last century, and at astonishingly regular intervals. From the sweeping pronouncements of Theodore Roosevelt at the dawn of the Progressive Era to President Clinton's foundering attempts led by first lady Hillary in the mid-1990s, the story mostly repeats: Proposals to expand coverage are often considered but rarely enacted, and then only on a piecemeal basis.

Every 15 years or so, movements arouse great enthusiasm, only to fail spectacularly. [47] In the end, peripheral improvements have benefited specific populations — the elderly, the disabled, low-income children and certain low-income adults. But universal coverage, though enticing to both politicians and the body politic, is as elusive as the Holy Grail.

Theodore Roosevelt's "Bull Moose" Progressive Party made national health insurance, modeled on workmen's compensation, a main plank in its party platform in 1912. One of the most sweeping health-reform attempts ever advanced by a presidential candidate, it called for employers, employees and society at large to pay for safeguarding Americans "through insurance" from "the hazards of sickness, accident, invalidism, involuntary unemployment and old age." [48]

Like every major plan to follow, it went nowhere. And yet certain ideas were set in motion. By 1917, model health-insurance bills began popping up in state legislatures, and in 1929 the forerunner of Blue Cross emerged, establishing the pattern: Major proposal, major defeat, small steps forward.

After Social Security was created in 1935, supporters began urging a second step — a national health-insurance system.

In 1945, President Harry S. Truman sought to include universal health insurance with Social Security, noting that "in a nation as rich as ours, it is a shocking fact that tens of millions lack adequate medical care." [49]

In a stirring speech four years later, he again declared his commitment: "We need — and we must have without further delay — a system of prepaid medical insurance which will enable every American to afford good medical care." [50]

Yet Truman faced formidable foes. The AMA branded his plan "socialized medicine." Enemies kept asking his physician, Wallace H. Graham, "are you a socialist, doctor?" [51] By the end of his time in the White House, Truman had given up his vision of universal coverage.

During World War II, health insurance had become a common employee benefit, primarily as a way to attract workers in a tight labor market. During the four decades after the war, the number of Americans with some form of health insurance increased dramatically. In the 1960s, unions made health benefits a key demand in collective-bargaining negotiations. Many experts believed that because so many workers now could visit the doctor without ever seeing a bill, health insurance actually drove up demand for medical services.

Perhaps because of the growing popularity of health insurance, Truman's idea of insuring Social Security beneficiaries persisted. In 1965, President Lyndon B. Johnson signed legislation launching Medicare in a ceremony held, as a tribute, in Truman's hometown of Independence, Mo. It was the cornerstone of Johnson's so-called Great Society program to end poverty.

Johnson also signed Medicaid into law, providing health benefits for low-income pregnant women and children, disabled Americans and low-income elderly needing long-term care. "No longer will older Americans be denied the healing miracle of modern medicine," Johnson said. "No longer will illness crush and destroy the savings they

Universal Health Insurance Not a Cure-All

Minorities and the poor — the largest group of uninsured Americans — suffer disproportionately from health problems. But would guaranteed coverage make everything better?

The short answer: No.

According to a little-noticed finding in a recent Institute of Medicine report: "Health insurance by itself will not eliminate ethnic and socioeconomic disparities in health." [1] The conclusion is based on a University of California at San Francisco analysis of research spanning 16 years.

"While health insurance may alleviate financial barriers to care and improve the choice of providers," the analysis said, "it does not address other individual and societal determinants of poor health experienced by ethnic minorities and the disadvantaged." [2]

In short, the authors cautioned, the United States "should not be content to focus only on insurance [to correct] social disparities in health." Scandinavia, Japan and the United Kingdom, for example, have failed to erase socioeconomic differences despite their well-established systems of universal health coverage. [3]

Less affluent persons might use a free health system more often, but that hardly guarantees the health outcomes enjoyed by the better off. For instance, a study of death rates among English civil servants — all covered by health insurance — determined that unskilled laborers and clerical staff had the greatest risk of dying within 10 years, while professionals and top administrators could be expected to live longer. [4]

In the United States, many assume that disadvantaged minorities would substantially benefit from equal access to medical practitioners, prevention and treatment. After all, racial and ethnic minorities with incomes below the federal poverty level represent a substantial proportion of the uninsured. Hispanics are three times more likely than whites to lack health insurance, and African-Americans twice as likely. [5] Indeed, some researchers suggest that racial and ethnic differences in health are due mostly to differences in socioeconomic status. [6]

Yet the University of California team showed that better care frequently failed to improve the health of minorities, the poor or the lesser educated. A study of 5,986 men, women and children with one of 17 chronic illnesses, all receiving free care or sharing in the cost, found that the poor were less likely to receive "appropriate" care than their better-off counterparts. [7]

Other studies suggest that the rates of receiving hospitalization and preventive care from health professionals depend not solely on whether people have insurance but also on race and ethnicity. Insurance also could narrow but not close the substantial gaps between the races in mortality — whites live an average six years longer than non-whites. Even when adjusting for differences in income, one-third of the difference in the mortality rate remains. [8]

Several factors tend to offset the potentially positive impact of free insurance on a person's health, including low literacy skills, which make it harder to either understand a doctor's instructions or choose between treatments. A person's health beliefs, lifestyle practices and environmental influences can also affect his health. [9] People who are less educated may be less capable of communicating with a doctor, understand possible risks, appreciate the significance of symptoms, schedule an appointment or manage their conditions. [10]

The prejudices of medical professionals, cross-cultural communication failures and overt discrimination also may play a role, experts say. Other studies suggest an association between poor health and crowded neighborhoods, exposure to stressful life events and the inability to take time off from work to see a doctor.

Said Harold Freeman, president of the Ralph Lauren Cancer Center at New York City's North General Hospital and for three decades a surgeon in Harlem: "Giving everyone an insurance card won't solve health disparities." [11]

---

[1] Committee on the Consequences of Uninsurance, Institute of Medicine, "Care Without Coverage: Too Little, Too Late," May 2002. Copies also available at www.nap.edu.

[2] Jennifer S. Haas and Nancy E. Adler, "The Causes of Vulnerability: Disentangling the Effects of Race, Socioeconomic Status and Insurance Coverage on Health," Institute of Medicine, October 2001.

[3] A.E. Kunst and J.P. Machenbach, "The Size of Mortality Differences Associated with Educational Level in Nine Industrialized Countries," *American Journal of Public Health*, June 1994, pp. 932-937.

[4] M.G. Marmot, M.J. Shipley and G. Rose, "Inequalities in Death: Specific Explanations of a General Pattern?" *Lancet*, May 1984, pp. 1003-1006.

[5] Institute of Medicine, "Coverage Matters: Insurance and Health Care," 2001. See also J. Rhodes and M. Chu, "Health Insurance Status of the Civilian Non-Institutionalized Population: 1999," Agency for Healthcare Research and Policy, 2000.

[6] Paul D. Sorlie *et al.*, "Mortality in the Uninsured Compared with that in Persons with Public and Private Health Insurance," *Archives of Internal Medicine*, November 1994, pp. 2409-2416.

[7] The study, known as the "Rand Health Insurance Experiment," is by R.H. Brook *et al.*, "Quality of Ambulatory Care: Epidemiology and Comparison by Insurance Status and Income," *Medical Care*, May 1990, pp. 392-433.

[8] Jan E. Mutchler and Jeffrey A. Burr, "Racial Differences in Health and Health Care Service Utilization in Later Life: The Effect of Socioeconomic Status," *Journal of Health and Social Behavior*, December 1991, pp. 342-356.

[9] Haas and Adler, *op. cit.*, p. 26.

[10] S.K. Behera and Marilyn Winkleby, "Low Awareness of Cardiovascular Disease Risk Among Low-Income African-American Women," *American Journal of Health Promotion*, May/June 2000, pp. 301-305.

[11] Quoted in Gabriele Amersbach, "Through the Lens of Race: Unequal Health Care in America," *Harvard Public Health Review*, winter 2002.

---

have so carefully put away over a lifetime." [52]

President Richard M. Nixon briefly revived the idea of universal health insurance when he proposed making comprehensive, high-quality health care "within the reach of every American." In his 1974 State of the Union address, he suggested expanding Medicaid and Medicare to provide health insurance "to millions of Americans who cannot now obtain it or afford it." [53] His proposal got serious attention in Congress — only to be doomed by the Watergate scandal that engulfed his presidency.

Meanwhile, skyrocketing hospital costs had caught the government's attention. Nixon and another Republican president embraced HMOs as a way to control costs. In 1973, Nixon signed the Health Maintenance Organization Act, requiring businesses with more than 25 employees to offer at least one HMO as an alternative to conventional insurance. Then, in 1982, President Ronald Reagan gave Medicare patients the option of signing up for an HMO. Managed-care organizations composed of loose networks of doctors began to proliferate, and by 1995, nearly three-quarters of covered workers were insured by an HMO. [54]

Clinton Debacle

Suddenly, in 1991, health care resurfaced as a potent political force. Harris Wofford, an upstart Democratic Senate candidate from Pennsylvania, declared: "If a criminal has a right to a lawyer, working Americans have a right to a doctor." His message had such appeal that he resoundingly defeated a popular two-time governor.

On the advice of Wofford's adviser, James Carville, then-Gov. Clinton appropriated Wofford's thunder, riding the health-care theme to the Democratic nomination in 1992. In his acceptance speech, Clinton vowed to "take on the health-care profiteers and make health care affordable for every family."

In 1993, Clinton unveiled his "Health Security Act," a plan largely crafted under the direction of Mrs. Clinton. Employers would pay 80 percent of the premiums to insure all workers, while the government subsidized coverage for everyone else. Clinton said he wanted

"to reform the costliest and most wasteful system on the face of the Earth." [55]

Yet the president's own party fractured badly. Some Democrats proposed a "single-payer" government system, similar to Canada's, which would pay private health-care providers. Others sought a scaled-down version of managed competition, which would have failed to guarantee coverage to many Americans. Republicans, meanwhile, preferred compelling every American to buy insurance, using government dollars only to help the poor.

Congressional Republicans accused Clinton of trying to establish yet another inefficient, expensive and uncaring big-government bureaucracy. Hillary Clinton, too, attracted criticism, in part for her secretive management style. A single, compelling television ad, part of a $17 million campaign by the Health Insurance Association of America, also helped torpedo the plan. Its simple message — in which a fictitious couple, Harry and Louise, tried to make sense of the 1,342 pages of details — preyed on public anxieties. Would people still be able to choose their own doctors? Could employers afford to cover workers? Would health-care decisions be left up to government bureaucrats?

Yet some of Clinton's ideas have been adopted by managed-care plans, helping them achieve some efficiencies and savings. [56] Enrollment exploded between 1986 and 1995, from nearly 26 million to 58 million, according to the American Association of Health Plans — yet people grew disenchanted with having to change doctors, being refused services and losing access to specialists.

Managed care's unpopularity led to the "patients' bill of rights" legislation passed by the House last August, which would allow patients to sue their HMOs, but on a limited basis.

Deep-rooted ambivalence underlies America's stance on health care. It is viewed as a social good, but also a

market commodity. Americans seem to consider it a basic need to which everyone is entitled, but also something to be earned that should be subject to free-market forces. One commentator has described the conflict in health care as the "struggle for the soul of health insurance." [57] ∎

CURRENT SITUATION

Drugs for the Elderly

Even before the distractions of national security, an economic slowdown and the deficits in federal and state budgets, few expected much to happen on the health-care front this year.

The Clinton administration's blistering defeat fragmented and polarized Washington over the subject of health-care reform. With Congress so closely divided, only isolated, dike-plugging initiatives can survive, and action is more likely through the private insurance sector. Meanwhile, the numbers of uninsured undoubtedly will continue rising along with costs.

A longstanding barrier to change is the sheer clout of several players with a lot to win or lose. As commentator Robert G. Evans, a University of British Columbia economics professor, has pointed out, the U.S. health-care system is "inequitable, inefficient, unpopular and spectacularly expensive — but enormously profitable for some Americans." [58]

The health-care industry, its profits severely diminished from the boom years of the 1990s, zealously guards its turf against any threat to the status quo. Health professionals so far have contributed nearly $58 million to the 2000 and 2002 presidential and congressional political campaigns, and the pharmaceutical industry has donated another $37 million. [59]

Another barrier to change is cost. Late last year, for example, while debating legislation to stimulate the economy, Congress avoided any discussion of extending coverage to all Americans, focusing instead on the less expensive option of providing coverage to those who lose their health insurance after losing their jobs.

But even that debate exposed an underlying fault line almost certain to keep Washington in gridlock. Democrats sought subsidies to help the newly unemployed keep their insurance or to cover them in the Medicaid program. Republicans favored giving the newly uninsured tax credits to help them buy insurance. The same philosophical debate underlies current sparring.

This year, at least one major healthcare issue — the cost of prescription drugs for the elderly — appears to be emerging at the top of the political agenda. With both the House and Senate narrowly divided, the balance of power in Washington could rest in the hands of older Americans, who typically play a disproportionate role at the polls in midterm elections.

Winning seven more seats would give the Democrats control of the House; just one seat in the Senate would give Republicans control there. And though the issue certainly isn't new, the volume at which it is being debated is a new wrinkle. Equally intense is the determination of skirmishing party leaders to pass a measure this year — or blame the opposition for the failure to accomplish anything.

"No senior should be forced to choose between putting food on the table or paying the rent or buying the medicines they need," declared House Speaker J. Dennis Hastert, R-Ill., in May as he unveiled the Republicans' $350 billion proposal to add a prescription drug benefit to Medicare.

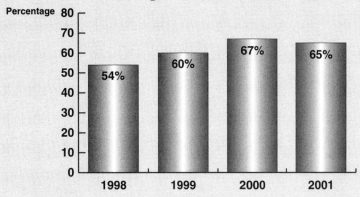

Fewer Small Employers Offer Coverage

The percentage of small businesses offering health insurance declined after 2000, leaving 35 percent of the workers without employer-sponsored health insurance. Nearly all employers with 200 or more workers offer health benefits.

Percentage of Employers Offering Health Benefits, 1998-2001
(Among Firms with 3-199 Workers)

Source: Kaiser/Health Research and Educational Trust Survey of Employer-Sponsored Health Benefits, Jan. 23, 2002

The same day, Senate Democrats unveiled their proposal, with a price tag of $400 billion to $500 billion. Other House Democrats and Senate moderates are working on alternatives, and President Bush has his own 10-year, $190 billion version.

A group supported by the drug industry, the United Seniors Association, launched a $3 million advertising campaign supporting House Republicans. The Democrats, meanwhile, released a video attacking a promise Bush made during the 2000 campaign to "help all people with prescription drugs." Notes the ad: "By his own estimate, Bush leaves out more than two-thirds of seniors in need of prescription-drug coverage."

A Republican campaign memo hinted at the reason for all the fuss: "Republicans passing a prescription-drug benefit would go a long way to leaving Democrats with very little on the table to try to use against us" in the midterm elections. [60]

Despite such traditional divisions, some compromise appears in the wind, given the coalescence of the once-adversarial special interests into the Covering the Uninsured coalition. The group, which includes older Americans, doctors, insurance carriers and hospitals as well as consumer and labor groups, is waging a huge media campaign urging an immediate solution to the problem of the uninsured.

Tax Credits

President Bush proposes to help the uninsured buy private health policies by offering tax credits — $1,000 for adults and $2,000 for families — costing a total of $89 billion. But only individuals with incomes below $30,000 or families with incomes below $60,000 would be eligible. "Too many workers get no coverage at all with their jobs," the president said. Americans should receive "the help they need when they need it." [61]

Economists at the University of Pennsylvania and Yale University say Bush's plan could reduce the number of uninsured by about 8 million. The administration estimates that it would help 6 million uninsured people buy health insurance each year, but the amount of the tax credit and its reach are widely viewed as inadequate. [62]

"It's like throwing a 10-foot rope to someone at the bottom of a 40-foot hole," says Pollack of Families USA. For instance, a healthy, non-smoking 55-year-old woman living at the federal poverty level — less than $8,860 in income — would still have to spend $4,000 to buy health insurance, he points out.

Moreover, some opponents worry that the president's proposal could unravel the current employer-based system, which, in effect, indirectly uses premiums of the relatively healthy to cross-subsidize those needing more care.

However, even the most generous expansion of prescription-drug benefits for the elderly or tax credits for select populations would not tackle the larger problems of rising costs and America's uninsured. Nor will they make up for ground being lost every day, as governments drastically scale back the existing social net.

Shrinking Safety Net

With dwindling discretionary reserves in the federal budget, money for Medicaid and CHIP has vanished, and many private doctors are refusing to accept new Medicare patients, because Medicare HMOs are paying them less. Some Medicare patients who can't afford drugs are turning to the Veterans Affairs hospital system, where rising numbers of patients and pharmaceutical costs — which have nearly doubled since 1996 — are overwhelming an already strained system.

Recession-crippled state budgets, which partially finance and administer Medicaid and CHIP, are running deficits and anticipate fewer revenues. States are tapping rainy-day funds, laying off employees and making across-the-board cuts. The recession, the economic fallout from Sept. 11 and the explosion in Medicaid spending have caused a $40 billion to $50 billion shortfall — the largest ever — in more than 40 states. Thus, legislatures are trimming services and making cuts in the safety net just when the uninsured need it most.

In Illinois, for example, a "welfare-to-work" initiative during the late 1990s added 100,000 women to Medicaid — yet by the end of 2001 Republican Gov. George Ryan felt compelled to eliminate it. The action netted $17 million in savings and sent many of the women — who work in low-paying jobs that lack benefits — back to the ranks of the uninsured.

"Governors are dealing with unprecedented fiscal pressure," said Raymond C. Scheppach, executive director of the National Governors' Association. "The growth rate is simply unsustainable." With Medicaid at a "breaking point," states need more than money from Washington. "Absent serious structural changes to the program down the road, states will be unable to meet the needs of recipients." [63]

Even in better economic times, the safety net misses many. Millions of low-income people who are eligible are not enrolled in government programs. Welfare reform, otherwise known as the Professional Responsibility and Work Opportunity Reconciliation Act of 1996, successfully moved people from cash assistance into jobs — but often into jobs without health coverage. Among women who have been off welfare for more than a year, only half have either Medicaid or private coverage. The other half seek care from strained safety-net institutions like faith-based charities. [64] ∎

OUTLOOK

Major Crisis?

Many commentators believe the nation faces a health-care crisis of phenomenal proportions. They cite the coming convergence of several major trends — rising costs, increasing unemployment, cash-strapped governments and a wave of aging Baby Boomers demanding care.

Joel Miller, policy director for the National Coalition on Health Care, calls it a potential "perfect storm" of economic factors. "We are witnessing an unprecedented set of forces that have converged, which will form what we believe will be the mother of all economic storms as it relates to health care." [65]

Spiraling costs likely will be the biggest culprit. Over the next decade, health-care spending is expected to continue rising faster than the nation's gross domestic product. [66] Premiums are expected to rise at least 50 percent over the next five years. If the sluggish economy persists, employers will cover fewer workers or demand that workers pay an even greater share of their premiums. [67] More than half of all employers plan to require workers to pay more for insurance, according to a survey by Watson Wyatt Worldwide. [68]

Others may cut salaries or jobs. "If health-care premiums continue to explode at their current [rate], employers [will] agonize over which to pay — premiums or salaries," said James Klein, president of the American Benefits Council. At current rates, by 2007 health benefits for an entry-level worker will cost a company half the employee's salary, he points out. "This is a terrible predicament for both the worker and the employer — and we see no help from Congress in solving this problem."

At Issue:

Would tax credits for health insurance help the uninsured?

TOM DONNELLY JR.
BOARD MEMBER, COALITION FOR AFFORDABLE HEALTH CARE COVERAGE

WRITTEN FOR THE CQ RESEARCHER, JUNE 2002

*r*efundable tax credits can make a significant dent in the number of those without health insurance — if we can avoid the temptation to cripple the effectiveness of the marketplace with excessive regulations.

Data suggest that tax credits are a promising solution to the majority of 40 million uninsured Americans. The requirement for such effectiveness is based on allowing it to be used both for employer-based group coverage and in the individual market. If these simple conditions are met, even a credit of modest size will create a significant benefit.

Although there are many segments of the uninsured population, the Census Bureau data report that 87 percent of the uninsured population is under age 45. Every credible study suggests that less than 5 percent of the uninsured population — perhaps closer to 1 percent — is chronically "uninsurable" due to a health condition.

Though smaller, these exceptional populations are no less significant, and policymakers should invest substantially in ideas such as high-risk pools to provide a safety net for such individuals. Doing so will stabilize the health insurance market for all other participants. But opposing tax credits only because they don't reach every exceptional population paralyzes progress on the overall issue. Are the 25 million predominantly healthy "working uninsured" who could benefit from the proposal not worthy of assistance?

The tax-credit proposal of $1,000 for individuals and $3,000 for families provides important financial assistance to individuals to purchase coverage. In addition to other studies with similar conclusions, a recent survey by *eHealthInsurance* of 20,000 individual policies reported an average premium of $1,900 is available for individuals in states representing 93 percent of the U.S. population. This affordability, however, is crippled in states where regulations have stymied the marketplace and driven up the cost of premiums. The policies reported on by *eHealthInsurance* indicate 87 percent would be considered "comprehensive" and that more than two-thirds of those have a deductible of $1,000 or less.

If the goal is to reduce the unacceptable number of 40 million uninsured Americans, let's start with what will work for many while never ignoring those that are most needy. It is simply irresponsible to wait to do anything until we can "do everything for everyone" — that day simply won't come.

RON POLLACK
EXECUTIVE DIRECTOR, FAMILIES USA

WRITTEN FOR THE CQ RESEARCHER, JUNE 2002

*n*early 40 million Americans — the equivalent of 23 states and the District of Columbia — have no health insurance today. Although President Bush agrees that the growing problem of the uninsured merits federal action, his solution is ineffective and potentially dangerous. The administration proposes to offer tax credits — up to $1,000 for individuals with incomes below $15,000, and up to $3,000 for families with incomes below $25,000 — to help people purchase health coverage on their own. This will not make health coverage affordable for uninsured, low-wage, working families. The Bush administration's tax-credit proposal is like throwing a 10-foot rope to a person in a 40-foot hole. It simply fails to make health coverage affordable.

Families USA recently conducted a 50-state survey to assess the affordability of health coverage for healthy, non-smoking 55- and 25-year-old women. For 55-year-olds, the average annual premium of a standard health policy (comparable to the most popular health plan available for federal employees) was $4,934 — unaffordable for people with less than $15,000 in income, even with a $1,000 tax credit. In 47 out of 50 states, there is no insurance policy — not even a bare-bones policy — for a 55-year-old woman at a $1,000 premium.

Even for healthy, non-smoking 25-year-old women, the tax credit falls short. The average cost of a standard policy for such a young woman is $2,459; in 19 states, there are no $1,000 policies available. In the states that do have $1,000 bare-bones policies, the coverage is like Swiss cheese, with more holes than cheese. Those plans usually fail to cover doctors' visits, prescription drugs and maternity care.

By looking at the options available to only healthy, non-smoking women, the data reflect the best-case scenarios in the individual market. People with even the slightest health problems, such as allergies, face the risk of higher premiums, coverage exclusions and possible rejection by insurance companies. Individual tax credits leave people at the mercy of health insurance companies that have the ability to deny them coverage.

The tax-credit proposal makes little sense as a way to expand health coverage to the uninsured, and the individual market is not the answer for most uninsured people. Instead, we should build on existing programs that work well — such as Medicaid and the employer-provided health system — to expand health coverage for low-wage, working families.

As a result, according to risk analysts, by 2009, the number of uninsured Americans could increase to at least 48 million — and perhaps as many as 61 million — if the recession continues and health-cost inflation is unabated. [69]

Medicaid spending, meanwhile, is expected to increase 25 percent over the next two years. "The states are dying on Medicaid," said Greg Scandlen, a senior fellow at the National Center for Health Policy Analysis, a Dallas think tank. "Revenues are down. Expenses are up." [70] Making matters worse, Medicare could be overwhelmed starting in 2011 by the need to provide benefits to retiring Baby Boomers. Medicare's ranks will swell from nearly 40 million to 77 million by 2030. Up to half of them will be over age 84. [71]

Baby Boomers are expected to live longer than their parents' generation, straining the system's ability to provide care for the so-called "old old," generally the sickest and costliest group. Even as President Bush argued to add a prescription-drug benefit this year, the administration acknowledged that Medicare is "not financially secure" for the retirement of the Baby Boomers. [72]

"Most people don't realize the effect that a rapidly increasing elderly population and skyrocketing health-care costs will have on the aging of Americans between now and 2050," said Duke's Koenig. Indeed, Sun Belt states are already getting a taste of things to come. "We are already experiencing the coming health-care crisis," said Florida Secretary of Health Robert Brooks. [73]

The situation could get so bad, predicts Edward Schneider, a professor of gerontology at the University of Southern California School of Medicine, that future hospitals could be reserved only for those in intensive care, with nursing homes handling acute care. Neither government nor the private sector will be able to accommodate ever-larger numbers of poor and frail older Americans, according to Schneider's bleak scenario. People on long waiting lists will flock to organizations affiliated with charities and churches. Rural residents will forgo medical attention altogether. [74]

The crisis of uninsurance eventually may be "so pervasive that it is bound to re-emerge as a major national issue," *The New England Journal of Medicine* predicted. [75]

Election Politics

As in 1992, anxieties of the middle class may prove decisive. Rising unemployment and the growing awareness that anyone could lose their health insurance "could move us toward the tipping point," said Gail Shearer, director of health-policy analysis for Consumers Union. "Congress is going to have to pay more attention." [76]

The reshuffling of traditional alignments that spawned the Covering the Uninsured coalition may get Congress' attention. Significant progress is "more likely than ever" on such issues as expanding Medicaid and CHIP eligibility and adding financial incentives within the tax system for private coverage, says the Health Insurance Association's Young.

Even if the changes were made, however, Young expects competing needs and budget shortfalls over the next 10 years to prevent the number of uninsured Americans from declining by much. Kahn of the Federation of American Hospitals is even less optimistic. "If trends continue, you could lose ground every year," with a few million more joining the ranks of the uninsured, he says.

Election-year campaigns by mainstream groups may have an impact. On the campaign trail, voters are pressing politicians for promises, and business groups are demanding action. Citizens and businesses alike "are really starting to get fed up with the costs," said Laura Pemberton, a lobbyist for the National Federation of Independent Business.

Kate Sullivan, director of health-care policy at the U.S. Chamber of Commerce, says covering the uninsured will be a major issue in the midterm congressional elections this fall. "We will make it an issue," she says.

But many doubt Congress will devise long-term solutions. For now, says health economist Stephen Zuckerman of the Urban Institute, "everyone is trying to put a Band-Aid on different parts of the system."

"As long as hospitals can overcharge you and me to pay for the uninsured, and as long as politicians can get away with ignoring their responsibility, nothing will happen," says the Carlyle Group's Abramowitz. "Democracies work best in crises, and it will take the perception of a crisis for politicians to act."

But Arthur Kellerman says the crisis is already here — at least as far as the nation's already-crowded emergency rooms are concerned.

"I'm dumbfounded that no one in Washington — not the president and no one in Congress — seems to be concerned about it, particularly since Sept. 11," says Kellerman, chairman of the Department of Medicine at the Emory School of Medicine and co-chair of the Institute of Medicine's Committee on the Uninsured. "How are we going to deal with 200, 2,000, 209,000 casualties?

"Yet nobody's listening," he continues. "In Washington it's all about prescription drugs for seniors — rather than the immediate threat to the health and safety of every man, woman and child in this country, regardless of health insurance and their status." ∎

Notes

[1] Dawes' plight is described in Trish Wilson, "Kids' Insurance Needs CPR," *News and Observer*, March 9, 2001, and Karen Tumulty, "Health Care Has a Relapse," *Time*, March 11, 2002, p. 42.

[2] World Health Organization, "World Health Report," 2000.

[3] "Health Insurance Coverage 2000," U.S. Census Bureau, Sept. 28, 2001.

[4] Terminated workers can continue the same health coverage for 18 months under COBRA, the Consolidated Omnibus Budget Reconciliation Act of 1995, which became law in 1996.

[5] See Elizabeth Simpson, "State Reaches Out to Uninsured," *Virginian-Pilot/Ledger Star*, March 7, 2002.

[6] Karen Davis, "Universal Coverage in the United States: Lessons from Experience of the 20th Century," *Journal of Urban Health: Bulletin of the New York Academy of Medicine 78* (March 2001), p. 46-58.

[7] Census Bureau, *op. cit.*

[8] John Holahan and Johnny Kim, "Why Does the Number of Uninsured Americans Continue to Grow?" *Health Affairs*, July/August 2000, pp. 188-196.

[9] Census Bureau, *op. cit.*

[10] Florida Chamber of Commerce Federation, Jan. 24, 2002.

[11] "Employer Health Benefits: 2001 Annual Survey," Kaiser Family Foundation and Health Research and Educational Trust, September 2001.

[12] Jeanne Lambrew, "How the Slowing Economy Threatens Employer-Based Health Insurance," Commonwealth Fund, November 2001. Paul Fronstin, "Sources of Health Insurance and Characteristics of the Uninsured: Analysis of the March 2000 Current Population Survey," *Issue Brief No. 228*, Employee Benefit Research Institute, 2000.

[13] Press conference, Coalition to Cover the Uninsured, Washington, D.C., Feb. 12, 2002.

[14] Mary Agnes Carey, "Analysts See a Seismic Shift in Health Policy Debate," *CQ Weekly*, March 23, 2002.

[15] *Ibid.*

[16] In their biennial reports, the National Governors' Association and National Association of State Budget Officers blamed the recession, fallout from the Sept. 11 terrorist attacks and Medicaid cost increases for creating a record $40 billion to $50 billion budget shortfall in more than 40 states in fiscal 2002.

Meanwhile, 28 states had combined deficits of $7.1 billion in their Medicaid budgets.

[17] A federal judge in March 2002 allowed Maine to force pharmaceutical makers to provide discounts of up to 25 percent for those with incomes 300 percent of the poverty level. Under Maine's law, the state would leverage its buying clout — $210 million in Medicaid drug purchases — to negotiate discounted prices for the 325,000 residents who lack health insurance and are not covered by Medicaid. If the drug makers refuse, the state could impose price caps in 2003. The industry is appealing the decision in *Pharmaceutical Research and Manufacturers of America v. Commissioner, Maine Department of Human Services*. The 1st U.S. Circuit Court of Appeals in Boston is considering the earlier ruling by U.S. District Judge D. Brock Hornby.

[18] "Care Without Coverage: Too Little Too Late," Institute of Medicine, National Academy of Sciences, May 2002.

[19] Paul W. Newacheck, "Health Insurance Access to Primary Care for Children," *The New England Journal of Medicine*, May 15, 2000, pp. 513-519.

[20] Quoted in Vicki Kemper, "Unlikely Coalition Declares Health Care Crisis," *Los Angeles Times*, Feb. 13, 2002, p. A30.

[21] North Carolina Health Access Coalition newsletter, *op. cit.*

[22] The coalition also includes the American Medical Association, Service Employees International Union, Business Roundtable, American Nurses Association, Health Insurance Association of America, Families USA, American Hospital Association, Federation of American Hospitals, Catholic Health Association, AARP and the Robert Wood Johnson Foundation.

[23] From a September 2001 survey for the Institute for Legal Reform and the U.S. Chamber of Commerce.

[24] Speech at the Medical College of Wisconsin in Milwaukee, Feb. 25, 2002.

[25] For background, see Adriel Bettelheim, "Drugmakers Under Siege," *The CQ Researcher*, Sept. 3, 1999, pp. 753-776, and Julie Rovner, "Prescription Drug Prices," *The CQ Researcher*, July 17, 1992, pp. 597-620.

[26] Tumulty, *op. cit.*

[27] Jacob Hacker, "Health Care Reform: A Century of Defeat," *Harvard Health Policy Review*, fall 2000.

[28] Carey, *op. cit.*

[29] Quoted in David Wessel, "After a Few Years of Relaxation, Health-Care Costs Rise Again," *The Wall Street Journal*, May 9, 2002.

[30] Quoted in Bob Condor, "Look Beyond Politics Before Writing Off the Faith-Based Initiative," *Chicago Tribune*, March 18, 2001, p. C3.

[31] For background, see Adriel Bettelheim, "Hospitals' Financial Woes," *The CQ Researcher*, Aug. 13, 1999, pp. 689-704.

[32] The amount depends largely on the breadth of benefits that would be offered, he says.

[33] Cited in testimony by Mary R. Grealy, president, Healthcare Leadership Council, House Energy and Commerce Subcommittee on Health, Feb. 28, 2002. HLC members include CEOs of pharmaceutical companies and major hospitals and clinics.

[34] California Medical Association figures, as of November 2001, cited by Norman Label, president, Emergency Physicians Medical Group, writing in the Sacramento, Calif., *Business Journal*, Feb. 1, 2002.

[35] "Emergency Crews Worry as Hospitals Say 'No Vacancy,' " *The New York Times*, Dec. 17, 2000. See also "Trouble in the ER," *National Journal*, May 19, 2001.

[36] "Emergency Department Overload: A Growing Crisis," The Lewin Group for the American Hospital Association, April 2002.

[37] Robert W. Derlet and John R. Richards, "Overcrowding in the nation's emergency departments: Complex causes and disturbing effects," *Annals of Emergency Medicine*, January 2000, pp. 63-68.

[38] Jan Blustein, "Drug Coverage and Drug Purchases by Medicare Beneficiaries with Hypertension," *Health Affairs*, March/April 2000, pp. 219-230.

[39] J.A. Poisal and L. Murray, "Growing Differences Between Medicare Beneficiaries With and Without Drug Coverage," *Health Affairs*, March/April 2001, pp. 74-85.

[40] *AARP Bulletin*, March 2002.

[41] See J. Gabel *et al*, "Class and Benefits at the Workplace," *Health Affairs*, May/June 1999, pp. 144-150.

[42] Small Business Administration, www.sba.gov/advo/stats/sbfaq.txt

[43] Catherine Hoffman and Mary Pohl, *Health Insurance Coverage in America: 1999 Data Update*, Kaiser Commission on Medicaid and the Uninsured, 2000.

[44] National Federation of Independent Business (nationwide data); for Florida, "Florida's Small Businesses Struggle with Rapidly Rising Health Insurance Costs," *Florida Times-Union*, April 8, 2002.

[45] Letter to House of Representatives, March 2001.

[46] National Governors' Association, position paper. www.nga.org.

[47] Jacob S. Hacker and Theda Skocpol, "The New Politics of U.S. Health Policy," *Journal of Health Politics, Policy and Law*, April 1997, pp. 315-38.

[48] See Nathan Miller, *Theodore Roosevelt: A Life* (1992).

[49] State of the Union address, Jan. 5, 1945.

[50] State of the Union address, Jan. 5, 1949.

[51] See Niel M. Johnson, oral history for the Harry S. Truman Library, March 30, 1989.

[52] From a speech at Truman's home in Independence, Mo., July 30, 1965.

[53] State of the Union address, Jan. 30, 1974.

[54] For background, see Sarah Glazer, "Managed Care," *The CQ Researcher*, April 12, 1996, pp. 313-336.

[55] Address to Joint Session of Congress, Sept. 22, 1993.

[56] Health Research and Educational Trust, *op. cit.* Health-cost increases reached a low in 1996, but then began rising again. Average premiums increased nearly 5 percent in 1999, more than 8 percent in 2000 and 11 percent from mid-2000 to mid-2001.

[57] Deborah Stone, "The Struggle for the Soul of Health Insurance," *Journal of Health Politics, Policy and Law* (1993), pp. 287-317. See also Rosemary Stevens, *In Sickness and in Wealth: America's Hospitals in the Twentieth Century* (1989).

[58] Robert G. Evans, "Sharing the Burden, Containing the Cost: Fundamental Conflicts in Health Care Finance," in Theodore J. Litman and Leonard S. Robins, *Health Politics and Policy* (1997).

[59] Center for Responsive Politics, April 2002.

[60] Quoted in The Associated Press, May 9, 2002.

[61] From remarks Feb. 11, 2002, at Medical College of Wisconsin in Milwaukee.

[62] Some 25 percent of the uninsured would have enough money to obtain the policy they need, and another 25 percent would be able to buy policies by adding up to $169 a year per person, according to Mark Pauly and David Song, "Tax Credits, the Distribution of Subsidized Health Insurance Premiums, and the Uninsured," National Bureau of Economic Research, Working Paper No. 8457, September 2001.

[63] Comments made in releasing the association's Fiscal Survey of States, May 16, 2002.

[64] B. Garret and J. Holahan, "Health Insurance Coverage After Welfare," *Health Affairs*, 19(1), January/February 2000.

[65] Quoted in Helen Palmer, "Marketplace," Minnesota Public Radio, May 6, 2002.

FOR MORE INFORMATION

American Medical Association, Public and Private Sector Advocacy Office, 1101 Vermont Ave., N.W., 12th Floor, Washington, DC 20005; (202) 789-7400; www.ama-assn.org. Provides information on the medical profession and health care and monitors legislation and regulations. (Headquarters in Chicago, Ill.)

Covering the Uninsured, 1010 Wisconsin Ave., N.W., Suite 800, Washington, DC 20007; (202) 572.2928; www.coveringtheuninsured.org. A national campaign funded by The Robert Wood Johnson Foundation and 15 major national organizations representing business, labor, doctors, nurses, hospitals and health-care consumers to find solutions to the problem of 41 million Americans without health insurance.

Families USA, 1334 G St., N.W., Suite 300, Washington, DC 20005; (202) 737-6340; www.familiesusa.org. Interests include health care and long-term care, Social Security, Medicare and Medicaid; monitors legislation and regulations affecting the elderly.

Federation of American Hospitals, 801 Pennsylvania Ave., N.W., Suite 245, Washington, DC 20004-2604; (202) 624-1500; www.americashospitals.com. Represents investor-owned, for-profit hospitals, monitors legislation and regulations affecting Medicaid and Medicare.

Health Insurance Association of America, 1201 F St., N.W., Suite 500, Washington, DC 20004-1204; (202) 824-1600; www.hiaa.org. Promotes effective management of health-care expenditures, provides statistical information on health-insurance issues and monitors legislation and regulations.

U.S. Chamber of Commerce, 1615 H St., N.W., Washington, DC 20062-2000; (202) 659-6000; www.uschamber.com. Develops policy on legislative issues important to American business, including covering the uninsured.

---

[66] Stephen Heffler, "Health Spending Growth Up in 1999: Faster Growth Expected in the Future," *Health Affairs*, March/April 2001, pp. 193-213.

[67] From testimony by Kathryn G. Allen, director of Health Care, Medicaid and Private Health Insurance Issues, General Accounting Office, before Senate Finance Committee, March 13, 2001, p. 8

[68] "New Rules for Managing Health Costs: Highlights from the Seventh Annual Washington Business Group on Health/Watson Wyatt Survey," May 15, 2002.

[69] The analysts at Georgia State University's Center for Risk Management and Insurance Research project the number of uninsured at 48 million with economic growth and moderate cost inflation; with a continued recession, 61 million; with rapid growth and cost inflation, 55 million. The rosiest assumptions peg the uninsured at 34 million by 2005. William S. Custer and Pat Ketsche, "The Changing Sources of Health Insurance," Health Insurance Association of America, 2000.

[70] Quoted in Robert Dodge, "Fiscal Ills Hurting Medicaid," *Dallas Morning News*, May 15, 2002, p. 1A. The White House Budget Office estimates that Medicaid costs will rise 10 percent in 2002, and nearly 7 percent annually through 2007 to $173 billion — more than triple the anticipated inflation rate. Altogether, federal and state governments are expected to spend more than $250 billion on Medicaid this year.

[71] Jennifer O'Sullivan, Hinda Ripps Chaikind, and Sibyl Tilson, "Medicare Structural Reform: Background and Options," Congressional Research Service, July 24, 2001, p. 20.

[72] For background, see Mary H. Cooper, "Retirement Security," *The CQ Researcher*, May 31, 2002, pp. 481-504.

[73] Condor, *op. cit.*

[74] Edward L. Schneider, "Aging in the Third Millennium," *Science*, Feb. 5, 1999, pp. 796-797.

[75] Steven A. Schroeder, "The medically uninsured: will they always be with us?" *The New England Journal of Medicine*, April 25, 1996; pp. 1130-1133.

[76] Quoted in Carey, *op. cit.*

Bibliography

Selected Sources

Books

Andersen, Ronald, Thomas H. Rice and Gerald F. Kominski, *Changing the U.S. Health Care System: Key Issues in Health Services, Policy and Management*, Jossey-Bass, 2001.

Three public health experts have assembled a wide-ranging collection of essays on pressing policy issues from access and costs to Medicare reform.

Litman, Theodore J., and Leonard S. Robins, *Health Politics and Policy*, Delmar Publishers, 1997.

Litman, a medical sociologist, and Robins, a professor of public administration at Roosevelt University in Chicago, describe the struggle to determine the proper role of government in developing health policy. Chapters explore politics, economics and the interplay of health interest groups and public opinion.

Rovner, Julie, *Health Care Policy and Politics*, CQ Press, 1999.

A health-policy journalist profiles government agencies, medical advances, policy proposals, the evolution of Medicare and Medicaid and children's health initiatives.

Articles

Bodenheimer, T. S., "Affordable Prescriptions for the Elderly," *Journal of the American Medical Association*, Oct. 10, 2001; Vol. 286; p. 1762.

This commentary by a professor of family and community medicine at the University of California at San Francisco assesses recent studies indicating how lack of prescription-drug coverage for Medicare beneficiaries results in less use of vital medication and increases the odds of hospitalization or placement in nursing homes.

Khan, C. N., and R. F. Pollack, "Building a Consensus for Expanding Health Coverage," *Health Affairs*, January/February 2001; Vol. 20, pp. 40-48.

The authors — traditional foes in the health-care debates — argue that extending coverage is not impossible, if only stakeholders can find common ground. Their prescription: a balance between public and private-sector approaches, and building on what works. Khan is president of the Federation of American Hospitals; Pollack is executive director of Families USA.

Saha, Somnath, "The Mirage of Available Health Care for the Uninsured," *Journal of General Internal Medicine*, October 2001; Vol. 16, pp. 714-716.

An assistant professor of medicine at Oregon Health and Science University analyzes fallacies in perceptions about the uninsured and suggests improvments in health-care access.

Tumulty, Karen, "Health Care Has a Relapse," *Time*, March 11, 2002, pp. 42-45.

This survey of the troubled health-care policy landscape and its real-world impact relates the experiences of several individuals with insurance difficulties.

Wielawski, I., "Gouging the Medically Uninsured: A Tale of Two Bills," *Health Affairs*, September/October 2000; Vol. 19, pp. 80-85.

A former health-care reporter for the *Los Angeles Times* draws an intensely personal portrait of the insured and uninsured, who, she discovers, must pay substantially more for the same medical treatment her son receives.

Reports and Studies

Institute of Medicine, "Coverage Matters: Insurance and Health Care," National Academy of Sciences, 2001.

A special committee produces a comprehensive, balanced assessment of the popular myths and underlying realities about the uninsured, including a demographic description of who they really are.

Kaiser Commission on Medicaid and the Uninsured, "Uninsured in America: Key Facts," The Henry J. Kaiser Family Foundation, March 2000.

A special commission examines who the uninsured are, why their numbers continue to grow and the consequences of lacking health coverage.

Economic and Social Research Institute, "Community-Based Health Plans for the Uninsured: Expanding Access, Enhancing Dignity," W.K. Kellogg Foundation, November 2001.

A nonprofit research organization finds lessons for policymakers in attempts by Bernalillo County, N.M., El Paso County, Texas, and four other communities to cope for themselves by relying on a variety of innovations.

Lambrew, Jeanne, "How the Slowing Economy Threatens Employer-Based Health Insurance," The Commonwealth Fund, November 2001.

A former health-policy analyst at the White House National Economic Council assesses the impact of financial conditions on private coverage.

Frogue, James, and Robert E. Moffit, "Issues 2000: The Candidate's Briefing Book, Health Care," The Heritage Foundation, 2000.

A conservative organization assesses health-care policy.

4 Medical Malpractice

KENNETH JOST

Three-year-old Forrest Bounds was born with a rare but correctible condition: a cystlike sac near his bladder that within a few weeks grew big enough to block the normal flow of urine.

Something went wrong, however, in trying to correct the problem: The urethra, the canal that carries urine away from the bladder, was ruptured. As a result, Forrest has to urinate through a hole doctors created in his scrotum. He probably will be permanently incontinent and sexually impaired.

Lawyers for Forrest's parents and the doctor who treated him disagree on who is to blame for the ghastly medical mistake. Lori and Morris Bounds, of tiny Mount Carbon, W.Va., claim in a medical-malpractice suit that Charleston urologist James Tierney nicked or tore the urethra while performing surgery to drain the sac, or ureterocele. Tierney counters that nurses probably ruptured the urethra while inserting a catheter either before or after the operation.

A West Virginia jury may decide the issue in a trial this May. If Tierney is found responsible, the jury will then have to decide how much he will have to pay in damages to Forrest and his family.

The little boy's economic losses are not the type that produce headline-grabbing malpractice awards. His medical expenses are likely to be below six figures, according to the family's lawyer, and the injury will have little, if any, effect on his income-earning potential. Instead, the bulk of any legal-

AP Photo/Tina Fineberg

Linda McDougal, 46, a Wisconsin accountant, had both her breasts removed last year after she was mistakenly told she had cancer. "The doctors who did this to me weren't held accountable, while I am permanently scarred," said the mother of three, who opposes President Bush's plan to cap non-economic medical-malpractice awards. Doctors and insurance companies say it will counter what they are calling a medical-liability crisis. Patients' advocates say it penalizes victims while not solving the problem.

ly recoverable damages will be for non-economic losses — what personal-injury lawyers call "pain and suffering."

Under current West Virginia law, a jury can award up to $1 million to compensate Forrest for the lifetime of pain and suffering he faces. In many states, a jury could award any amount, however large. But about half of the states have enacted limits — so-called damage caps — on the amount that a medical-malpractice victim can be awarded for non-economic losses.

If Congress passes legislation proposed by President Bush, such limits will protect doctors and hospitals throughout the country. Bush is calling for a cap of $250,000 on non-economic damages in medical-malpractice suits and a package of other restrictions to counter what doctors and insurance companies are calling a medical-liability crisis.

Doctors in many states are experiencing whopping increases in mal-

practice-insurance premiums. One-year hikes in 2002 for three major specialties — internal medicine, general surgery and obstetrics-gynecology — averaged 30 percent in at least eight states, according to an industry newsletter.[1] (*See table, p. 66.*) Surgeons in many states face high five-figure premiums for malpractice coverage; obstetricians in a few states pay annual premiums in excess of $100,000.

To dramatize their plight, doctors in a few states, including West Virginia and, most recently, New Jersey, have staged work stoppages — such as canceling all elective surgeries for a day or longer. Some doctors have fled rising insurance premiums by moving or commuting to low-cost states, or retiring.

Medical groups blame the rising insurance premiums on one culprit: the legal system. "The medical-liability system is broken and causing an access problem for patients in this country," says Donald Palmisano, a doctor and lawyer who is president-elect of the American Medical Association (AMA). Doctors "cannot practice in this toxic environment," Palmisano adds. "It's very sad."

Bush agrees. The problem of unnecessary costs in the health-care system does not start "in the waiting room or in the operating room," but "in the courtroom," the president said in a Jan. 16 speech in Scranton, Pa. "There are too many lawsuits filed against doctors and hospitals without merit."

Lawyer and consumer groups disagree with Bush's diagnosis of the problem and his prescription. They blame insurance companies for rising premiums, call for tighter regulations of insurance practices and oppose

From *The CQ Researcher,* February 14, 2003.

Half the States Limit Damages

Twenty-five states limit the amount a plaintiff can recover in a medical-malpractice suit for "pain and suffering," or non-economic damages. But only six states cap awards at $250,000 or less — the nationwide ceiling President Bush is seeking. At least 12 states allow awards of $500,000 or more.

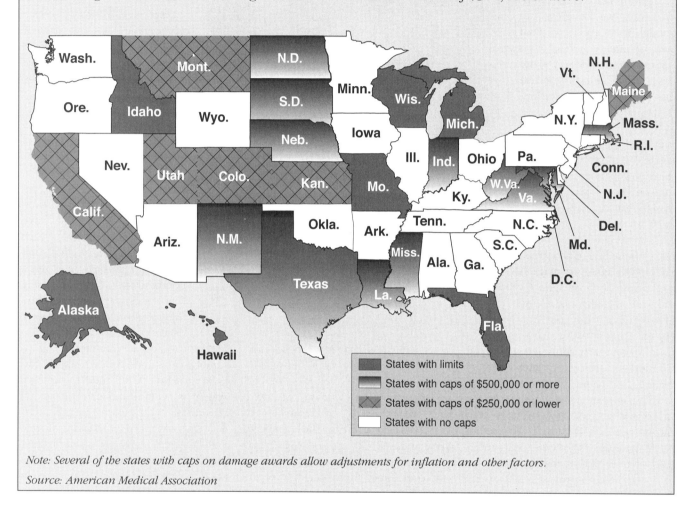

Legend:
- States with limits
- States with caps of $500,000 or more
- States with caps of $250,000 or lower
- States with no caps

Note: Several of the states with caps on damage awards allow adjustments for inflation and other factors.

Source: American Medical Association

limits on jury awards in malpractice cases.

"The problem is not in the courtroom, but appears to be in the boardrooms of our nation's insurers, where companies raise medical-liability premiums to offset low returns on investments," says Alfred Carlton, a Raleigh, N.C., lawyer and president of the American Bar Association (ABA).

"President Bush's attacks on the jury system are nothing more than a desperate attempt to divert attention away from the truth, which is that

health-care costs are skyrocketing because the insurance industry has too much control over America's health-care system," says San Francisco lawyer Mary Alexander, president of the Association of Trial Lawyers of America (ATLA). Damage caps, she says, are "an arbitrary, one-size-fits-all" solution.

The opposing interest groups make their respective cases with a welter of wrenching anecdotes and conflicting statistics. Lawyer and consumer groups cite cases like Forrest's of patients who

have been permanently disfigured, maimed or brain-damaged by grievous medical errors. They cite statistics that show plaintiffs win only 20 percent of the time and that settlements and awards in malpractice cases have been relatively stable for more than a decade.

"Forget the headline verdicts," says Joanne Doroshow, executive director of the Center for Justice and Democracy, a New York-based consumer-advocacy group. "When you look at the actual payouts, they are extremely low."

Medical and insurance lobbies cite the low success rate of malpractice plaintiffs as proof that most of the suits are — as President Bush described them — "frivolous." But they say the financial and emotional burdens of defending malpractice suits — or trying to guard against them — are too much for many doctors. And they claim that the main beneficiaries are trial lawyers, who hope to cash in on a seven-figure verdict — and take one-third or more as their contingency fee.

"Doctors and patients are enduring the tort system to give that trial lawyer his 20 percent chance to strike gold," says Lawrence E. Smarr, president of Physician Insurers Association of America, a trade association for doctor-owned mutual insurance companies. "The system truly does not work for the patients."

The debate marks the third pitched battle between doctors' and lawyers' groups over medical malpractice in 30 years. Alarms about a "crisis" in medical-malpractice insurance were first raised in the 1970s, when many carriers pulled out of the medical-liability market altogether. The episode produced the first state laws limiting pain-and-suffering damages in medical suits. Less than a decade later, a sudden spike in malpractice premiums renewed the debate and led other states to pass malpractice reforms.

Doctors paid about $7 billion for medical-malpractice insurance in 2001 — a small fraction of the country's $1-trillion plus in health-care expenditures. [2] But the Bush administration claims in a report published by the Department of Health and Human Services (HHS) in July 2002 that medical liability adds from $60 billion to $110 billion in unnecessary costs to the nation's health-care bill in the form of "defensive medicine" — unnecessary tests or procedures purportedly performed only to safeguard doctors and hospitals against potential liability. [3]

Gap Narrowed Between Premiums and Losses

Average malpractice-insurance premiums for all doctors fell by about 50 percent from 1987 through the 1990s, until turning upward after 1999 — with sharp spikes for some medical specialties. But the difference between premiums paid and losses paid narrowed during the period, creating a financial squeeze for insurers.

Premiums and Losses Per Doctor
(adjusted for health-care inflation)

Source: Americans for Insurance Reform, Oct. 10, 2002

The latest round of insurance-premium increases only adds to other pressures doctors are feeling these days. Many physicians resent the intrusive efforts of health-maintenance organizations (HMOs) to hold down health-care costs. Meanwhile, government-run health-care programs — Medicare for the elderly and disabled and Medicaid for the poor — are also trying to contain costs by reducing reimbursements for doctors and hospitals.

Bush's call for federal legislation comes at an opportune time for the groups supporting restrictions on medical-malpractice awards. Republicans, who have been the strongest supporters of tort, or liability, reform in the past, now have majorities in both houses of Congress and the White House for the first time in nearly 50 years. But Democrats have worked closely with trial-lawyers' groups in the past to bottle up tort-reform measures. Some leading Democratic senators — including North Carolina's John Edwards, a trial lawyer himself and a declared candidate for the party's presidential nomination — already have opposed the president's proposals.

As the debate continues, here are some of the major questions being considered:

Have malpractice lawsuits helped or hurt the practice of medicine?

The number of anesthesia-related malpractice suits jumped during the

1970s. In response, a consortium of hospitals and the American Society of Anesthesiologists came up with detailed standards that are now established practice, such as continuous monitoring of patients' vital signs. Those measures are widely credited with a substantial decline in anesthesia-related malpractice claims. [4]

The drop in claims illustrates what some say is the major public benefit of allowing malpractice victims to recover damages from doctors or hospitals responsible for their injuries: deterrence. "The threat of liability is what works as a deterrent to improve patient safety," says consumer advocate Doroshow.

"It is a way for doctors to be held accountable," says ATLA President Alexander. "They have to be held accountable in a courtroom for wrongdoing."

However, most doctors and medical observers believe malpractice lawsuits do more harm than good to the practice of medicine. "We see no credible evidence that litigation has improved safety," says AMA President Palmisano.

Instead, doctors complain, the fear of litigation casts an adversarial pall over the doctor-patient relationship. "Doctors talk about being much more reserved in their relations with patients and families," says Marshall Kapp, a lawyer and professor of community health at Wright State University School of Medicine in Dayton, Ohio. "They are more reluctant to paint a hopeful or optimistic picture to the patient or family because they don't want it misinterpreted as a promise that the patient will get better and then turn around and get sued because of disappointed expectations."

In addition, many doctors say, fear of litigation causes them to practice what they call "defensive medicine" — performing unnecessary tests or procedures solely to guard against being blamed later for failing to do

so. Palmisano says the practice not only adds to patient costs but also results in "more procedures, more drugs and thus more patient discomfort and risk."

As evidence, Palmisano cites surveys in which the vast majority — 79 percent — of physicians said they occasionally order more tests than they believe necessary. In addition, 74 percent of those responding said they had referred patients to specialists "just to be safe," and 51 percent had ordered biopsies to confirm diagnoses even though they believed the confirmation was unnecessary. [5]

Kapp acknowledges the doctors' concerns, but says on closer examination fear of liability often appears to be only one factor in what appears to be defensive medicine. "It's hard to say that testing was done for only defensive purposes and not because the doctor thought there was some chance that some useful information would be obtained," he explains.

Consumer advocates discount the defensive-medicine claims altogether, citing past government studies that failed to substantiate doctors' complaints on the issue. [6] In addition, the increased cost-consciousness among health insurers makes the claims even less believable, they say. "You're not going to find many people who think that's a problem any more, with the way managed care has become," Doroshow says.

In fact, say the trial lawyers, some of the more dramatic malpractice suits in recent years have resulted from doctors' failure to perform medical tests. In one case, a young California boy was alleged to have suffered permanent brain damage because a doctor failed to order an $800 CAT scan. In another, Linda McDougal, a Wisconsin accountant, underwent a double mastectomy after being incorrectly diagnosed with breast cancer — a misdiagnosis that might have been averted by a second biopsy. [7]

Critics, however, say the existing system provides little protection against malpractice, pointing out that plaintiffs lose about 80 percent of the suits filed. They also cite an influential Harvard University study, conducted a decade ago, that found most successful suits did not result from what doctors later determined to be medical negligence. [8]

In effect, the study suggested, juries sometimes approve awards plaintiffs based on sympathy for the injured plaintiff rather than on legal fault by the doctor or hospital. The existing system "does very little to deter actual medical malpractice," says Lester Brickman, a professor at Yeshiva University's Cardozo School of Law in New York City, who has written widely on liability issues. "Most medical-malpractice awards do not involve medical malpractice."

Paul Weiler, the Harvard Law School professor who directed the study, points to a second finding as more important: Most malpractice victims never even go to court. "The vast majority of actual negligent injuries never produced a lawsuit," Weiler says. Weiler calls for replacing the existing tort system with a no-fault scheme guaranteeing compensation to anyone injured as a result of medical error — whether or not legal negligence can be proven.

For their part, trial lawyer and consumer advocacy groups show no interest in alternatives to the existing tort system. "We believe in the jury system," Alexander says. Doroshow agrees: "The threat of high damage is what keeps hospitals and HMOs on their toes," she says. "This is the concept behind the tort system."

Are lawsuits to blame for rising medical-malpractice insurance premiums?

Surgeon Gary Parenteau moved from the Midwest to Wheeling, W. Va., about three years ago. He loves where he works and lives, but says he is "at wit's end" because of the high cost of malpractice insurance in the state. For the coming year, his premium is $120,000 — about four times the rate for a friend of his in a comparable practice in Michigan.

"I've never been sued," Parenteau said. "I went to medical school so I can take care of patients. Now I worry more about malpractice, and that's wrong." [9]

Rising malpractice-insurance premiums are vexing doctors in several states, sometimes prompting work stoppages or other protests. Parenteau was one of 30 surgeons in West Virginia's northern panhandle who stopped offering some surgical services in early January, saying they could no longer afford malpractice coverage.

Individual doctors and their medical associations blame jury verdicts, settlements and other malpractice expenses. Medical-liability premiums are "skyrocketing," Palmisano says, because of "large jury awards and the burgeoning costs of defending against lawsuits."

Trial lawyers and consumer groups, however, blame the insurance industry. "The culprits are the insurance companies, who have too much control of our health care — both insurance for doctors and health care for patients," says ATLA's Alexander.

The trial lawyer and consumer groups say insurance premiums are rising now because of a recurrent business cycle tied to low returns on insurers' investments rather than to high litigation costs. Malpractice premiums were generally sta-

ble — and actually fell — during the 1990s when insurers were making good returns on their investments. Now that interest rates and the stock market are down, insurance companies are raising rates to make up for the lower return they are getting on their investments, they say.

"Premiums go up and down with the cycle," says J. Robert Hunter, director of insurance for the Consumer Federation of America and a former federal and state insurance regulator. "The cycle is a well-known reality."

Demonstrators oppose caps on pain-and-suffering malpractice awards at a meeting of the governor's task force on medical-malpractice insurance in Tallahassee, Fla., on Dec. 20, 2002. Doctors say limits on awards will keep their premiums from skyrocketing, but lawyers say that will only penalize victims of malpractice who deserve compensation.

Hunter cites data in a study he authored that he says shows malpractice payouts were relatively stable through the 1990s. "Losses are not exploding," he says. "Losses are relatively flat when they're adjusted for inflation." [10]

The statistics are somewhat less salutary than Hunter depicts. The inflation adjustment is based on the increase in health-care costs — which

have been rising faster than the overall cost of living. Without the adjustment, direct losses per doctor were about 80 percent higher in 2001 than in 1991 — but only 2.3 percent higher after adjusting for health-care inflation. In addition, the industry's loss ratio — direct losses divided by premiums received — rose from 48 percent in 1991 to nearly 75 percent in 2001.

Based on Hunter's figures, an insurance-industry analyst says malpractice carriers are facing a real cost squeeze.

"Unconstrained losses" have made it "extremely difficult — if not impossible — for insurance companies to earn a profit writing medical malpractice insurance," says Raghu Ramachandran, a senior portfolio strategist with the New York-based investment firm Brown Brothers Harriman. [11]

Nonetheless, experts on both sides of the tort-reform issue agree that the insurance-industry cycle is at least partly to blame for the current round of malpractice-premium increases. "It's half true," says Victor Schwartz, general counsel to the American Tort Reform Association and co-author of one of the leading tort law casebooks. "Insurance was cheaper in the 1990s because insurance companies knew that that they could take a doctor's premium and invest it, and $50,000 would be worth $200,000 five years later when the claim came in. An insurance company today cannot do that."

Neil Vidmar, a professor at Duke University School of Law who has generally defended the existing tort system, agrees. "I don't think these things

Wide Range in Liability Premiums

Insurance premiums for doctors vary widely. Premiums in high-risk specialties rose especially dramatically in recent years in states with extra-high premiums, but remained relatively low in California, which has rigid caps on damage awards.

Professional Liability-Insurance Premiums

	2000	2001	2002
Internal Medicine (Low-risk specialty)			
Florida	$34,635	$50,774	$56,153
Nevada	15,804	15,804	23,628
Ohio	12,851	16,270	22,592
Pennsylvania	7,448	11,828	22,902
West Virginia	13,726	15,251	18,477
California	10,976	12,038	19,788
General Surgery (Moderate-risk specialty)			
Florida	$110,068	$126,599	$174,268
Nevada	56,892	56,892	85,056
Ohio	49,209	60,021	74,554
Pennsylvania	33,684	35,793	104,388
West Virginia	43,922	53,887	63,660
California	32,507	42,181	57,473
Ob-Gyn (High-risk specialty)			
Florida	$158,157	$172,634	$210,576
Nevada	94,820	94,820	141,760
Ohio	68,893	84,029	152,496
Pennsylvania	37,556	66,265	116,388
West Virginia	76,096	84,551	95,282
California	52,532	60,496	57,473

Source: Medical Liability Monitor, February 2003

dict Research showing the median jury award in medical-malpractice cases increased by 43 percent in just one year — from 1999 to 2000. The percentage of million-dollar verdicts also was shown to be increasing: They comprised more than half of the plaintiff awards in 2000. [12]

But trial lawyer and consumer groups say those figures are misleading, because the reporting service collects information on awards selectively rather than compiling comprehensive or representative data. In fact, seven-figure verdicts are extremely rare, they say. The average payout — in the small minority of cases where any payment is made — is around $200,000, they note.

Should malpractice damage awards be capped?

When the first medical malpractice "crisis" broke out in the mid-1970s, California's Democratic-controlled legislature and its liberal Democratic governor — Edmund G. "Jerry" Brown Jr. — responded by enacting a comprehensive set of restrictions on malpractice cases. The centerpiece of the Medical Injury Compensation Reform Act — widely known as MICRA — was a $250,000 cap on non-economic damages: primarily, money awarded for "pain and suffering."

California's law became the model for other state malpractice-reform efforts. The law has remained largely unchanged despite lingering questions about its impact from interest groups both inside and outside the state. And President Bush cited the California law in his Pennsylvania speech calling for federal legislation to contain malpractice costs.

Proponents say that limiting damage awards will still allow malpractice victims to recover their real costs — current and future medical expenses, as well as lost income. But damage caps for pain and suffering, they say, will hold down litigation and insurance

are due to the litigation system," he says. "The rates have gone up even when they have these caps on pain and suffering. [The increases] are independent of tort reform."

But medical groups discount the effort to blame rising premiums on cyclical factors. "Insurance premiums are determined by frequency [of payouts] and severity [size of the award], plus defense costs," says the AMA's Palmisano. "Severity is dramatically going up."

As evidence, Palmisano points to a report by Pennsylvania-based Jury Ver-

premiums while protecting doctors and hospitals from huge awards based mostly on sympathy.

"There will be fewer lawsuits nationwide," says the AMA's Palmisano. "It will certainly stabilize premiums and keep physicians from quitting medicine."

Yeshiva law Professor Brickman agrees that reducing potential awards will decrease the amount of malpractice litigation — and the contingency fees that are based on the size of the award. "It's just simple math," Brickman says. "If you want to reduce litigation, you lower the fee. If you want to increase litigation, you increase the fee."

Opponents say capping damage awards will have little overall effect on malpractice payments or insurance payments, but will hurt the victims of the most serious medical errors. "Take a little baby who comes out of an operation with half a brain or the young man who lost all four limbs because of malpractice," ATLA's Alexander says. "It's not reasonable to say $250,000 for the rest of your life for having to live like that."

Doroshow at the Center for Justice and Democracy emphasizes that big six- or seven-figure damage awards for pain and suffering are rare. "Most cases don't come anywhere near a cap," she says. The caps "are not going to have much effect on the bottom line of those [insurance] companies."

Proponents cite California's experience since enacting the $250,000 cap as evidence that damage limits will hold down malpractice-insurance premiums. "California's rates went up 167 percent over 25 years, while the rest of the country went up 505 percent," Palmisano says. He adds that the law also has helped patients: "Patients get their money more quickly, and more patients are getting compensation."

Opponents, however, contend that California's malpractice premiums are still among the highest in the coun-

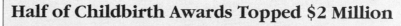

Half of Childbirth Awards Topped $2 Million

The median malpractice award in cases involving childbirth was slightly more than $2 million between 1994 and 2000 — more than double the next highest categories: erroneous cancer diagnoses or delayed treatment.*

Median Awards for Specific Liability Situations
(1994-2000)

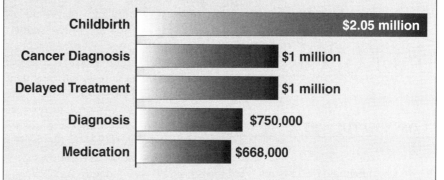

Childbirth	$2.05 million
Cancer Diagnosis	$1 million
Delayed Treatment	$1 million
Diagnosis	$750,000
Medication	$668,000

* The median is the number at which half of the sample is above and half is below.

Source: Jury Verdict Research

try and that at least one of the 13 states listed by the AMA as having a malpractice-insurance crisis — Missouri — has damage limits. Insurance expert Hunter also notes that rate filings by malpractice insurers in Florida immediately after the state enacted a damage cap in the mid-1980s said the new law would have no effect on premiums.

Some observers also question the likely effects of capping damages. "I don't think it's going to have a major impact," Duke's Vidmar says. Kapp, the Wright University lawyer and professor of community health, says that even if damage caps are enacted, "I'm not sure we wouldn't end up eight or 10 years down the road with the next malpractice crisis anyway."

Nevertheless, Kapp sees caps as a psychological benefit for doctors. "Limiting damages in malpractice cases can alleviate some of the anxiety and some of the bad effects of the anxiety."

For his part, Harvard law Professor Weiler says damage-cap proposals ignore the need to ensure fairer treatment for victims of medical errors who do not now receive adequate compensation under the existing tort system. "It is totally unethical to have a damage cap but have no such damage floor if an even more disabled patient is getting far too little money from a jury that is biased in the opposite direction," he says.

Weiler has argued for years for a no-fault system — comparable to workers'-compensation laws — that would guarantee fixed compensation to victims of medical errors even if there were no proof of negligence by the doctor or hospital. "That's the fairer way to do it," Weiler says.

In the face of opposition from both sides of the debate, the proposal has gone nowhere. Medical and insurance groups say no-fault would be too expensive. "We'd likely see more claims brought," says Smarr of the physicians' insurers group.

Plaintiffs and consumer groups also say a no-fault system would be too expensive and that in the current climate compensation levels would be set too low besides. "You would never get a no-fault system that would provide adequate benefits to victims," says Doroshow, of the Center for Justice and Democracy. ■

BACKGROUND

"Cost of Progress"

M edical-malpractice lawsuits were extremely rare in early American history and remained relatively infrequent through the first half of the 20th century. Paradoxically, the major increases in medical-malpractice litigation — in the 19th century and in the last few decades — occurred as advanced technology and increased professionalism were improving the practice of medicine. According to historian Kenneth De Ville, medical progress generates heightened expectations among patients and doctors, which combines with other legal and social changes to produce more litigation and more and larger damage awards. [13]

In Colonial and early 19th-century America, personal-injury litigation of any sort was rare. Legal rules limited the ability of most plaintiffs to recover damages. Social attitudes in rural communities and small towns and villages also deterred lawsuits. Two other factors deterred medical-malpractice lawsuits in particular. First, the medical profession was held in relatively high esteem. Second, unfavorable medical outcomes were likely to be viewed as the result of divine providence, not human error.

The country's first medical-malpractice "crisis" began in the 1830s, according to De Ville, a professor of medical humanities at East Carolina University's medical school in Greenville, N.C. Social and cultural changes played a part: Growing urbanization, along with religious and philosophical views stressing human perfectibility, weakened the inhibitions against filing lawsuits.

Medical progress also played an essential part — as seen in the sudden increase in litigation over treatment of arm or leg fractures. Before the 1830s, amputation was a common treatment for serious injuries. By the 1830s, however, doctors had developed techniques to save rather than amputate limbs — and patients and juries alike had a standard against which imperfect results could be judged. As De Ville notes, suits over orthopedic injuries were the most frequent type of medical malpractice litigation through the early 1940s.

Lawsuits against doctors continued to increase in the later 19th century. Legal barriers against plaintiffs were coming down; in addition, a growing population of lawyers and more frequent use of contingency fees made legal services more widely available. Growing urbanization and secularization also further weakened social and cultural inhibitions against lawsuits. But technological advances again played a part, De Ville says. The invention of the X-ray in 1895 was immediately recognized as an invaluable diagnostic tool. Within a year, physicians were being sued for failing to take X-rays; and plaintiffs were introducing radiological evidence in court to try to show medical negligence.

Advances in surgical techniques played a similar role in fostering more malpractice litigation in the early to mid-20th century. Invasive or so-called body-cavity surgery began to become more prevalent in the late 19th century, but it was fraught with

perils. A series of advances in the early 20th century made surgery safer and outcomes more predictable: the use of sulfa drugs to fight infection and transfusions to assuage the effects of surgical shock along with improved training, instruments and aseptic practices. By the "golden age of surgery" in the 1920s, De Ville writes, patients and doctors alike expected surgery to be successful: "When these expectations were not met, suits followed."

More recently, the effect of advances in diagnosis and treatment can be seen as a major contributing factor in the increase in obstetric litigation. Maternal and fetal risk was high as late as the mid-20th century. But they have declined significantly since then, thanks to a series of advances — including, for example, electronic fetal monitoring. Just as with X-rays, however, the improved diagnostic tools generated expectations of successful outcomes in pregnancy, labor and childbirth — and provided plaintiffs valuable evidence to try to prove negligence in cases of less-than-perfect outcomes. Obstetric claims comprised only 2 percent of all malpractice cases as late as the 1970s, but increased to 10 percent by 1985. "It's the cost of progress," De Ville says.

Despite periodic increases in litigation, medical-malpractice claims were still infrequent and insurance costs low in the mid-20th century. As of 1960, there were only about 1.3 malpractice claims per 100 physicians — compared with 15 today. Meanwhile, spending on medical-liability insurance totaled about $60 million in 1960, compared with more than $7 billion today. [14]

At the same time, legal doctrines and practices were about to be transformed in a way that would foster more personal-injury suits in several areas and result in what doctors, hospitals and medical insurers viewed as three successive crises of medical-malpractice insurance.

Chronology

Before 1960

Medical-malpractice suits are infrequent, but increase as patients' expectations rise with improved treatments; doctors periodically raise alarms, but insurance premiums remain a small fraction of provider costs.

1830s
First malpractice "crisis," with increase of suits involving orthopedic injuries.

1896
First suit charging negligence for failing to take X-rays is filed one year after the new diagnostic tool is invented.

1930s
Obstetric suits displace claims over orthopedic injuries as most frequent category of malpractice litigation.

1960s-1970s

Malpractice litigation and insurance premiums increase; commercial firms pull out of market, producing "crisis of availability."

1974
Malpractice-insurance premiums jump, nearly doubling over next two years.

1975
California enacts Medical Injury Compensation Reform Act (MICRA), limiting malpractice pain-and-suffering damages to $250,000 and imposing other restrictions on plaintiffs; California and New York medical associations become first to establish physician-owned insurance companies.

Late 1970s
New procedures adopted by anesthesiologists, hospitals to improve patient safety, curb lawsuits.

1980s *More states pass medical-malpractice reforms; new wave of insurance premium increases produces "crisis of affordability."*

1983
Malpractice-insurance premiums begin to increase sharply, doubling again by 1988.

1984
New York state legislature commissions study of medical errors, malpractice liability by Harvard group.

1990s *Medical malpractice reforms advance further in states; insurance premiums fall until end of decade.*

1991
First President Bush asks Congress to enact legislation to penalize states that do not pass medical malpractice reforms, but proposal dies with broader health-care legislation; Harvard study group blames medical errors for 150,000 deaths and 30,000 serious injuries per year, but says only small fraction of malpractice victims sue.

1993
Health care task force headed by first lady Hillary Rodham Clinton recommends broad overhaul of health insurance but does not deal with malpractice litigation.

1995-1996
With Republican majority, House twice approves legislation setting $250,000 cap on non-economic damages in medical malpractice cases; proposal killed each time by Democratic-controlled Senate.

1996
Office of Technology Assessment discounts "defensive medicine" claims; says small fraction of medical procedures are caused primarily by liability concerns.

1999
Institute of Medicine estimates 44,000-98,000 Americans die every year from preventable errors in hospitals; report urges patient-safety improvements, makes no recommendations on malpractice litigation issues.

2000-Present

New wave of insurance premium increases brings new calls for restricting malpractice suits.

2002
Health and Human Services Department unit says malpractice-litigation "crisis" threatens access to health care; Mississippi becomes 25th state to enact damage limits in medical-malpractice cases with $500,000 cap on pain and suffering; Institute of Medicine urges demonstration projects to test non-judicial compensation schemes for patients injured by medical errors.

2003
Doctors in several states stage work stoppages to demand limits on malpractice suits; President Bush urges Congress to approve $250,000 federal cap on non-economic damages and impose other restrictions on malpractice suits.

Safety Steps Overlooked in Lawsuit Debate

Medication-related errors kill thousands of patients every year and rank among the most frequent — and potentially the most expensive — of allegations in medical malpractice lawsuits. Yet they also may be among the most easily preventable of medical errors, according to a Washington-based patient-safety advocacy group.

One solution being pushed by the Leapfrog Group, a consortium of *Fortune* 500 corporations and other health-care purchasers, is computerized entry of doctors' medication orders. Software that incorporates information about side effects or contraindications of specific drugs along with the patient's medical record may be able to intercept a potential medical error before the patient is ever given the wrong medicine.

The problem — and potential solution — illustrates one point emphasized by patient-safety experts but largely overlooked by doctors and lawyers in the medical malpractice debate: Many of the medical mistakes that give rise to malpractice lawsuits result more from system failures than from individual negligence.

"There are not enough systems and processes in place to provide checks and balances for the individual human beings who are called doctors, nurses or other caregivers," says Suzanne Delbanco, Leapfrog Group's executive director. Health-care personnel "are treating people in an increasingly complex system," she says, and are often quite simply taxed beyond their individual abilities.

While plaintiffs' lawyers and consumer groups emphasize malpractice lawsuits as an important way to encourage patient safety, the Leapfrog Group takes no position on liability issues. Instead, Delbanco says the group is seeking to "harness our joint purchasing power to drive significant improvements in the quality and value of health care.

"We're trying to educate consumers about the facts that quality of care varies from institution to institution," she explains. "And we're trying to realign the incentives so that there's a reward at the end of the day for safety improvements."

Several studies over the past decade have pointed to the largely unrecognized extent of injuries and deaths resulting from medical errors. The Institute of Medicine, a branch of the National Academy of Sciences, estimated in 1999 that medical errors account for 44,000 to 98,000 deaths per year — ranking as the ninth most frequent cause of death in the United States. [1]

The Leapfrog Group decided to tackle the patient-safety issue by asking medical experts for a short list of well-researched recommendations that health-care consumers could readily understand and health-care providers could readily put into effect. They came up with a list of three, including the recommendation for computer entry of medication orders. The other two were assignment of properly trained specialists to intensive care units (ICUs) and referral of high-risk surgeries and high-risk neonatal cases to institutions best able to provide care for those conditions.

Each of the three recommendations faces significant practical obstacles. For computer entry of medication orders, the barriers include expense and the limited availability of software. So far, about 5 percent of the nation's hospitals have adopted the practice, Delbanco says. But vendors are developing more software, and more hospitals are indicating interest in the idea, she says.

For ICUs, the problem is quite simple: a shortage of doctors who have special training in critical care along with their regular specialties, Delbanco says. Only 10 percent of hospitals have properly trained critical-care specialists today, Delbanco says, but studies indicate that with proper staffing patient mortality can be reduced by nearly 30 percent.

Lack of information is the barrier to referring high-risk surgeries and neonatal cases to appropriate institutions, Delbanco says. Only a handful of states require hospitals to report patient outcomes for specified procedures. "In most states you're completely in the dark in choosing a hospital," she explains. To remedy the information gap, Leapfrog Group is establishing voluntary reporting systems — and is getting good cooperation from hospitals in many parts of the country.

Malpractice insurers can help drive patient-safety improvements by lowering premiums for hospitals that adopt recommended practices, she points out. As for malpractice litigation, the effects remain to be seen, she says. "Presumably these practices would reduce errors and one would presume fewer people would sue," she says. "But I don't know if we could perfectly correlate that."

---

[1] Linda Kohn, Janet Corrigan and Molla Donaldson, "To Err Is Human: Building a Safer Health System, Institute of Medicine" (2000), p. 1. (http://books.nap.edu). The report was released in November 1999 and formally published in 2000.

Insurance Crises

Doctors were hit with two successive malpractice crises in the 1970s and '80s. The first was a crisis of "availability," when many commercial insurance carriers pulled out of the market; the second was a crisis of "affordability," when premiums charged by both insurers and newly created physician-owned mutual companies soared. Doctors' and hospitals' groups successfully lobbied legislatures in many states — first and most significantly in California — to limit damages and impose other restrictions on medical-malpractice claims. Trial lawyers' groups and some independent experts sharply challenged the evidence of a "crisis," but their arguments did no more than slow the passage of the so-called reforms. [15]

Medical-malpractice insurance premiums suddenly spiked in the mid-1970s, nearly doubling between 1974 and 1976. More significantly, the small number of commercial insurers who offered coverage sustained large and unexpected losses. "They didn't recognize the hemorrhaging until it was too late," says Smarr of the Physician Insurers Association of America. Since medical malpractice was a small line of business for most companies, many decided to pull out of the market.

Medical groups responded to the difficulty in finding coverage by creating their own insurance companies. The new physician-owned companies — so-called "bed-pan mutuals" — were designed to provide coverage at "adequate but conservative rates," says Smarr, who helped start up Pennsylvania's company in the late 1970s. By the mid-1980s, the physician mutuals were providing coverage for 50 to 60 percent of the nation's doctors. [16]

A continuing increase in malpractice claims and payouts fueled another increase in insurance premiums in the 1980s. The number of claims more than doubled, from 7.9 per 100 physicians in 1976 to 17.8 in 1985, according to the American Hospital Association (AHA). During the same period, average payouts for successful claims against doctors quadrupled from $17,600 to $70,200, while average payouts for hospitals increased more than fivefold, from $7,500 to $40,300. [17]

Various causes were posited for the trend. Personal-injury lawyers "displayed a much stronger technical capacity for documenting [malpractice] claims in court," according to Harvard's Weiler. [18] An AHA task force suggested that jury awards were increasing partly because of jurors' knowledge of insurance coverage for doctors and hospitals. Whatever the causes, the premium increases were considerable. By the end of the 1980s, a typical New York doctor was paying about $40,000 per year, while neurosurgeons

or obstetricians faced premiums of $150,000 or more. [19]

California's MICRA law was the first to cap non-economic damages, which included "pain, suffering, inconvenience, disfigurement and other non-pecuniary damages." The law also limited attorneys' contingency fees in malpractice cases, required large damage awards to be paid over time rather than immediately and allowed defendants to introduce evidence of insurance benefits received by plaintiffs. [20]

The California law served as a model for other states. Some state laws also limited the doctrine of joint liability, which allowed a plaintiff to recover an entire damage award from any defendant even if the defendant was only partly responsible for the injury. Trial lawyers brought and won constitutional challenges to some provisions in state courts, but for the most part the laws survived judicial scrutiny.

As the decade ended, Weiler and a group of colleagues studied medical injuries and malpractice claims in New York state and found that medical injuries occurred in roughly one out of every 27 hospitalizations and that about a quarter of those injuries were due to negligence. After reviewing more than 31,000 hospitalizations from 1984, the group concluded that medical treatment caused more than 150,000 fatalities and 30,000 serious disabilities in the country each year. In a later study by the Institute of Medicine, released in November 1999, researchers projected that medical errors kill from 44,000 to 98,000 people each year — more than AIDS, breast cancer or car crashes. [21]

Somewhat surprisingly, Weiler's group found that malpractice claims were filed in only about one out of eight potentially valid cases, and only about half of those resulted in compensation. Weiler concluded that the critique of the tort system was "based largely on myth rather than fact."

Litigation critic Walter K. Olson, a senior fellow at the conservative Man-

hattan Institute, drew an opposite conclusion. Emphasizing the failure rate of malpractice claims, he said that most such suits "have nothing to do with genuine negligence." [22]

Simmering Debates

The medical-malpractice debate simmered through the 1990s, as claims, payouts and insurance premiums stabilized somewhat. States continued to tinker with restrictive reform measures, but medical and insurance groups failed in their efforts to get Congress to impose nationwide caps on damages in malpractice suits. As the decade ended, a new wave of insurance-premium increases brought new warnings of a malpractice crisis — and a renewed debate over the causes of the problem and possible solutions.

The volume of malpractice claims began to subside in the late 1980s. St. Paul Fire and Marine Insurance Co., long the largest carrier in the market, went from 16.5 claims per 100 physicians insured in 1984 to 13.0 in 1988. [23] "Frequency remained relatively flat through the 1990s," according to Jim Hurley, an actuary at Tillinghast-Towers Perrin, a leading insurance-consulting firm. While there is no authoritative national figure today, industry experts estimate the current frequency at about 15 malpractice claims filed each year per 100 physicians.

After adjusting for medical inflation, average overall losses per doctor peaked in 1989, fell sharply for three years and then fluctuated for several years before turning sharply upward again after 1999. In 2001, average losses were about $7,200.

Meanwhile, premiums fell as more companies entered the market — lured, in part, by artificially high profits reported by St. Paul Fire and Marine, which was reducing its loss reserves. Average premiums per doctor were almost the same in 2000 as in 1991, without adjusting for inflation;

Malpractice Cost $5 Billion in 2001

Medical-malpractice suits resulted in about $5 billion in court judgments or settlements in 2001 (graph at top). The average court judgment fell from $593,647 to $426,247 in the first nine months of 2002 (graph at bottom).

Payments in Medical Malpractice Cases
(includes judgments and settlements; adjusted for inflation)

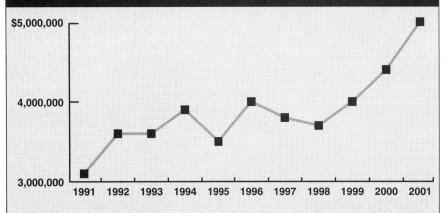

Average Judgments
(adjusted for inflation)

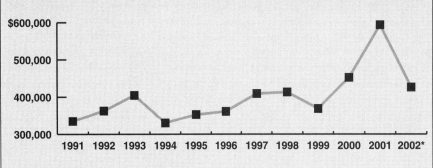

* first 9 months only

Source: National Practitioner Data Bank, Health Resources and Services Administration

after adjusting for medical inflation, the average premium had declined by 30 percent.

Yet medical and insurer groups continued to lobby for malpractice reform, even as payouts stabilized and premiums fell. The first President George Bush asked Congress in 1991 to financially penalize states that did not enact specific reforms, including a $250,000 cap on non-economic damages. The proposal died along with the broader bill. The health-care task force created by President Bill Clinton — headed by then first lady Hillary Rodham Clinton — was urged to endorse malpractice reforms, but it ducked the issue.

Restrictive medical-malpractice proposals advanced, however, after Republicans gained control of the House of Representatives in 1994. Twice, the GOP-controlled House approved malpractice reforms, including the $250,000 damage cap: first, as part of a broad tort-reform bill in 1995 and then in a health-insurance reform bill in 1996. Each time, the Democratic-controlled Senate killed the provisions. The broad tort measure died after getting through the Senate. The other measure, which made it easier for workers to keep their health insurance when changing jobs, became law in 1996.

Opposing sides in the tort-reform debate highlighted individual malpractice cases to back up their respective positions. Reform advocates ridiculed a suit brought by a Philadelphia psychic, Judith Haimes, who blamed a badly administered CAT scan for loss of her psychic powers; she won a $986,000 award. Accounts of the case, however, often glossed over the fact that she suffered permanent brain damage and the judge instructed the jury not to consider the claimed loss of psychic powers.

On the opposite side, trial lawyers and consumer groups cited cases such as the $9 million settlement won by the family of a Texas man, Benjamin Jones, who died of lung cancer in 1994, three years after doctors removed a healthy lung rather than the cancerous organ. The Osteopathic Medical Center of Texas admitted no wrongdoing in agreeing to the payout.

The upturn in premiums as the 1990s gave way to a new century brought new cries of alarms from doctors and renewed lobbying at the state level. The lobbying paid off in one state viewed as friendly to plaintiffs. Mississippi enacted malpractice damage caps after having rejected such proposals in the past. Enacted last October, the law caps non-economic damages at $500,000.

In Washington, meanwhile, the Republican-controlled House last September limited punitive damages and attorneys' fees in medical-malpractice cases — with full knowledge that it would not be taken up by the Democratic-controlled Senate, which had tabled a similar proposal in late July. [24]

The GOP takeover of the Senate last November gave doctors and insurers their best chance ever to push for a federal bill limiting malpractice suits. Bush joined the fight with his Jan. 16 speech in Pennsylvania endorsing damage caps along with other limits. "Excessive jury awards will continue to drive up insurance costs, will put good doctors out of business or run them out of your communities, and hurt communities like Scranton," Bush declared.

Four leading Democratic senators, including North Carolina's Edwards, staked out their opposition a day earlier. The proposed changes "would deprive seriously injured patients of fair compensation," Edwards and the others said in a letter to Bush. [25] ∎

CURRENT SITUATION

Striking Doctors

In early February, thousands of doctors throughout New Jersey closed their offices or deserted operating rooms in a work stoppage to dramatize their demand that the government cap rising malpractice-insurance rates. The protest — capped by a Feb. 4 demonstration by an estimated 4,000 physicians at the state Capitol in Trenton — spurred legislators toward a compromise plan, but the head of the state's medical society rejected the deal as inadequate.

The New Jersey job action — the largest of the protests staged in at least four states — caused inconvenience for many patients but no significant adverse effects, according to New Jersey health officials. Still, the head of the state's trial lawyers' association sharply criticized the tactic. "This is nothing but blatant extortion by these doctors," said Bruce Stern, president of ATLA-New Jersey. "What they did is immoral and unethical." [26]

Doctors at the Trenton protest carried placards with such messages as "Tort Reform Now" or "If your water breaks, call a lawyer." Speakers blamed malpractice suits for jeopardizing health care. "Do we want a health-care system where a small number of patients hit the jackpot?" Ruth Schulze, an obstetrician and president of the Bergen County Medical Society, asked the crowd. "Or do we want a system of quality health care for all?" [27]

The doctors were urging legislators and the state's Democratic governor, James E. McGreevey, to approve a $250,000 limit on non-economic damages imposed on doctors or hospitals in malpractice cases. As the protesters massed outside, key legislators — including the Republican and Democratic co-presidents of the Senate and the head of the chamber's health committee — unveiled a compromise.

The proposal would cap doctors' liability for pain-and-suffering damages at $300,000 but create a new catastrophic-injury fund to pay for larger awards and settlements. The fund would be financed by a $2-$3 per customer surcharge on health insurers and a $15 annual fee for the state's doctors and lawyers. A spokesman for McGreevey said the governor was "open-minded" on the proposal.

The president of the 8,500-member Medical Society of New Jersey rejected the plan, however. "It's not a good idea," Dr. Robert Rigolosi told reporters. "To pass the $2 or $3 surcharge on to the HMOs, who are just

going to pass it on, is going to make the cost of health-care insurance even higher for the insured." The $15 surcharge on doctors, he added, "is like rubbing salt into the wound because they already pay an exorbitant amount of money for the malpractice insurance." [28]

The New Jersey protest came a week after some 800 Florida doctors stayed off the job on Jan. 27 to protest their malpractice-insurance costs. A similar protest in Mississippi on the same day drew only a dozen doctors, according to news accounts, while around 30 surgeons participated in the West Virginia job action earlier in January.

The West Virginia protest opened an intense lobbying effort by the state's medical association behind legislation to lower the state's $1-million limit on non-economic damages in malpractice cases to $250,000. The measure moved quickly through the state's House of Representatives and then won approval in the state Senate on Feb. 7. A conference committee was appointed Feb. 11 to iron out differences between the two versions, and Gov. Bob Wise, a Democrat, is expected to sign the resulting bill.

In Florida, a five-member task force appointed by the state's Republican governor, Jeb Bush, is recommending a similar $250,000 cap on damages in malpractice cases. Florida's current law sets a $350,000 limit on non-economic damages in court suits and a $250,000 cap in arbitration. The legislature is expected to take up the issue when it opens its 2003 session in March.

The Mississippi protest by a dozen or so Gulf Coast surgeons came after the doctors received notices of cancellations or sharply increased malpractice premiums. The insurers acted despite legislation enacted in October — after strong lobbying by the doctors — setting a $500,000 cap on malpractice damages. Lawmakers responded to the new protests by considering a proposal they had rejected last fall, which would create a state-administered risk pool funded by doctors and hospitals to provide insurance for any providers who could not obtain coverage elsewhere.

Meanwhile, Pennsylvania's Democratic Gov. Ed Rendell is backing a different approach to taming malpractice-insurance costs. He would like to take $220 million from the surpluses of major health insurers and use the funds to reduce doctors' malpractice premiums and to subsidize trauma centers threatened with closure because of high insurance rates. The state's medical association favors the plan, but health insurers are opposed.

Dueling Lobbies

An array of powerful Republican lawmakers opened the push for medical-malpractice legislation on Capitol Hill by joining with representatives of three medical lobbies* at a press conference on Feb. 6 to decry the financial and emotional impact of litigation on doctors, hospitals and patients. The legal system "is putting a wrecking ball through our health-care system," Rep. James C. Greenwood, R-Pa., prime sponsor of the bill, declared.

Consumer groups countered by bringing some 50 victims of alleged malpractice to Washington on Feb. 11 to coincide with a joint hearing on the issue by the Senate Judiciary and Health committees. "These are the kinds of people who require compensation, these are directly the people who are affected by the cap," said Doroshow of the Center for Justice and Democracy. "It's not the lawyers, it's the patients who are affected."

---

* The groups were the American Medical Association, American Hospital Association and American College of Obstetricians and Gynecologists.

Rep. John Conyers Jr., D-Mich., the ranking member of the Judiciary Committee, also spoke out on behalf of the victims of malpractice. "The reality is, grossly negligent health-care professionals have more to do with high awards than the lawyers do," Conyers said in a Feb. 11 statement. "Whatever the reasons for the anger the president has toward lawyers, his proposal doesn't hurt lawyers nearly as much as it hurts innocent victims of medical malpractice."

House Speaker J. Dennis Hastert of Illinois underscored GOP support for the bill by giving it a single-digit bill number — HR 5 — and listing it among the top 10 legislative priorities for the 2003 session. House Majority Leader Tom DeLay, R-Texas, and Judiciary Committee Chairman James F. Sensenbrenner, R-Wis., joined Greenwood at the press conference, and both vowed to move the bill quickly through committee and on to the House floor.

The bill's centerpiece is a $250,000 cap on non-economic damages, defined to include pain and suffering, physical impairment or disfigurement and loss of companionship or enjoyment of life. Greenwood and others repeatedly stressed that the bill does not limit economic damages, including past and future medical expenses and loss of past or future earnings.

The bill would allow punitive damages only for malicious conduct or deliberate neglect and limit any punitive award to $250,000 or twice the amount of economic damages. The measure also includes a provision strongly sought by the pharmaceutical industry to bar punitive damages against drug or medical device manufacturers for products that are approved by the Food and Drug Administration (FDA).

Under the subheading "maximizing patient recovery," the bill would set a sliding-scale limit on attorneys' fees in malpractice cases starting at 40 percent of the first $50,000 in damages awarded and declining to 15 percent of any

amount over $600,000. Among other provisions, the bill would allow defendants to show that a malpractice plaintiff had received insurance benefits for injuries and would limit one defendant's responsibility for a full award if other defendants were also found liable.

Sponsors acknowledged that the bill includes no provisions relating to the insurance industry, saying they were unnecessary. "There is no industry that is more heavily regulated," explained Rep. Christopher Cox, R-Calif., who sponsored medical-malpractice bills in previous Congresses and now heads the House Republican Policy Committee.

Opponents say that without insurance reform, the measure will have no effect on malpractice premiums. "You can cap damages all you want," Doroshow says. "But unless you get control over the insurance industry's underwriting practices, this type of price gyration will go on."

Greenwood described his bill as bipartisan, but the 68 original cosponsors included only five Democrats. Still, with a disciplined 229-205 majority (with one independent), Republicans are widely expected to be able to push the bill through the House — perhaps as early as March, as Hastert envisions.

The outlook is less clear in the Senate, where the GOP holds a narrow 51-48 majority (with one independent). Republicans hope to win over some moderate Democrats — including California's Dianne Feinstein, who has supported her state's medical-malpractice limits. But some Republicans have questioned the $250,000 cap, including the two GOP senators from Greenwood's state of Pennsylvania.

"I think people have a right to sue, and they have a right to be compensated if negligent medical care was given to them," Sen. Rick Santorum told The Associated Press. The state's senior senator, Arlen Specter, also has said he opposes caps in egregious malpractice cases. [29]   ∎

At Issue:

Should Congress cap medical-malpractice damage awards?

REP. CHRISTOPHER COX, R-CALIF.

WRITTEN FOR THE CQ RESEARCHER, FEBRUARY 2003

*W*hy are doctors leaving their practices, and trauma centers closing? Why are women driving across state lines to find obstetricians who will deliver their babies? The answer, in each case, is the soaring cost of lawsuits, which has set off massive increases in the cost of medical-liability insurance. According to a 2002 study by Jury Verdict Research, the national median malpractice award is increasing 43 per cent per year.

This week's *People* magazine chronicles the devastating impact of litigation on health care in Mississippi: ob-gyn clinics closing their doors, doctors leaving the state, patients unable to get the care they need.

"The country's poorest state," reports *People*, "has become a target of jury-shopping trial lawyers. For instance, tiny Fayette . . . is known as the home of 'jackpot justice'; there are more trial lawyers registered to practice at the town's Jefferson County Courthouse than there are residents of Fayette."

Not just in Mississippi, but in at least a dozen other states as well, the costs of lawsuits are cutting off access to health care for millions of Americans.

Fortunately, as a Californian, I didn't have to look very far for the solution. The HEALTH Act (HR 5), which I co-authored with Rep. Jim Greenwood, R-Pa., is modeled after California's successful Medical Injury Compensation Reform Act — widely known as MICRA — signed into law in 1975 by Democratic Gov. Jerry Brown.

Today, HR 5 stands on the threshold of enactment, with strong support from President Bush. The bill guarantees an injured plaintiff unlimited recovery of all medical costs, lost wages, lost future income, home care, nursing, rehabilitation and anything else to which a dollar value can be attached, now and in the future. At the same time, it places reasonable limits on punitive and non-economic damages, while giving states the flexibility to raise these limits.

The MICRA reforms in the Golden State are a proven success. In fact, measured in constant dollars, the average California liability-insurance premium actually fell by more than 40 percent from 1976 to 2001.

The most important result is clear — today Californians are healthier than the national average. On average, we live longer, suffer less heart disease and have more healthy births than the rest of the country. California has proven that doctors perform better when they are NOT besieged by runaway litigation. It's time to solve America's medical crisis by extending this California success to all the people of America.

REP. DIANA DEGETTE, D-COLO.

WRITTEN FOR THE CQ RESEARCHER, FEBRUARY 2003

*L*ast year, Linda McDougal, a Wisconsin resident, received a double mastectomy because her doctor said she had cancer. The very next day, her doctor admitted that there was a mistake in the analysis of the biopsy and she, in fact, did not have cancer. Mrs. McDougal had to endure the very painful truth that she lost both of her breasts needlessly. If the congressional leadership gets its way on medical-malpractice reform, people like Linda McDougal are the ones who will suffer from limits on the amounts of damages that can be awarded by competent juries.

Those who advocate medical-malpractice reform say that capping malpractice damages will decrease doctors' insurance premiums. Reducing caps will not lower insurance for our doctors because other factors, like the cyclical nature of the insurance industry, have a much greater impact on insurance premiums. For example, since 1975, California has had a cap on pain-and-suffering damage awards of $250,000, equal to the federal proposal. Yet, the average premium for doctors in California is 8 percent higher than the average for states with no cap.

Instead, what capping damage awards will do is unfairly punish people who have legitimate malpractice claims. If the federal proposal becomes law, the most Linda McDougal will be able to recover for the loss of both of her breasts is $250,000. Some politicians seem to think they know how to judge the appropriate level of damage awards better than juries. They are wrong.

What capping damages does is punish those individuals who have already suffered horrors like paralysis, brain damage and the loss of a limb by placing an arbitrary ceiling on their compensation, regardless of the judgment of a jury, while failing to address the underlying problem of medical malpractice. Essentially, damage-award caps are Band-aids that cause bleeding.

The rising cost of medical malpractice insurance is a real concern. However, the solution is not a one-size-fits-all mandate from the federal government that unfairly limits compensation to victims of malpractice. For instance, a famous 1990 study called the Harvard Medical Practice Study found that a shockingly high number of individuals had suffered from medical malpractice. Yet, the study also found that 88 percent of doctors who committed malpractice were never sued. What the federal government must do is conduct a comprehensive review of the many factors that contribute to high insurance rates, rather than focusing solely on jury awards.

Death Accounts for Biggest Share of Verdicts

Nearly a quarter of the verdicts in favor of plaintiffs were in cases involving the death of a patient. The second highest percentage of plaintiff verdicts were for brain injuries.

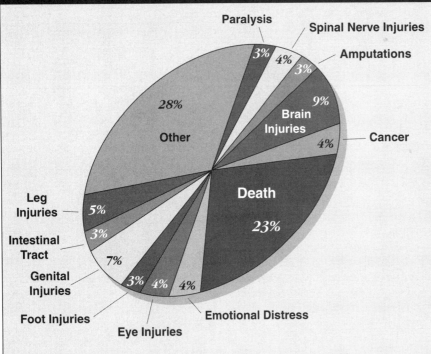

Kinds of Cases in Which Plaintiffs Won Verdicts

- Paralysis 3%
- Spinal Nerve Injuries 4%
- Amputations 3%
- Brain Injuries 9%
- Cancer 4%
- Death 23%
- Other 28%
- Leg Injuries 5%
- Intestinal Tract 3%
- Genital Injuries 7%
- Foot Injuries 3%
- Eye Injuries 4%
- Emotional Distress 4%

Source: "Statistical Trends in Medical Malpractice Litigation," Jury Verdict Research, 2002

OUTLOOK

Alternative Medicines

As a young professor in the mid-1960s, Jeffrey O'Connell helped popularize no-fault automobile insurance as a more reliable and less expensive way to compensate accident victims than negligence-based court suits. Now at the University of Virginia, O'Connell is advocating a no-fault approach to medical malpractice — with the similar purpose of providing faster, more assured compensation to victims of medical mistakes while reducing the expenses of litigation.

Under O'Connell's "early offers" proposal, a health-care provider facing a malpractice claim could offer within a 120-day deadline to pay all of the claimant's economic losses — medical expenses, lost income and so forth — along with attorney's fees based on hourly rates. [30] Accepting the offer would foreclose the claimant from seeking compensation for pain-and-suffering.

A claimant who rejected the offer could recover in court only by proving malpractice under a more rigorous standard — for example, intentional or wanton conduct with a heightened evidentiary requirement.

The scheme offers advantages to patients and doctors alike, O'Connell argues. Patients would get "rapid and essential compensation when they need it most," he says, while insurance premiums should be reduced because doctors would face "dramatically reduced" legal exposure. Moreover, O'Connell contends, the system could enhance patient safety by giving doctors and hospitals incentives to report and deal with medical mistakes quickly — within the deadline needed to foreclose open-ended lawsuits.

O'Connell's proposal is one of many ideas for changing the medical-liability system aimed at compensating victims of medical mistakes at less expense. The Institute of Medicine, part of the National Academy of Sciences, wants the federal government to give states incentives to establish demonstration projects to study non-judicial alternatives for malpractice claims. As options, the institute lists a version of O'Connell's early-offers proposal and a mandatory statewide administrative scheme. Both plans, the institute says, are "compatible" with the Bush administration's liability-reform proposals. [31]

The proposals — generally overlooked in the debate over damage caps — echo doctors' complaints that a major portion of medical-liability expenses goes to lawyers (on both sides) and other costs. Unlike the reforms backed by the medical lobbies, however, these proposals also respond to the consistent findings in several studies that most people who are injured by medical mistakes receive no compensation whatsoever — either because they do not sue or they lose when they do.

Some reform proposals also respond to doctors' complaints about rising malpractice premiums by seeking to change insurance practices. The Consumer Federation's Hunter, for example, calls for creation of a national reinsurance plan to handle large claims and spread the risk among all doctors. "That would stabilize a lot of these small areas, like West Virginia, where doctors are scarce even before you have a crisis," Hunter says. He says at least two states — Kansas and New Mexico — already have so-called health-care stabilization funds to accomplish that goal.

Trial-lawyer groups call for insurance reform, but they focus on one major recommendation: lifting insurance companies' exemption from federal antitrust law. Insurance companies say the antitrust issue is irrelevant because insurers do not collude in raising medical-malpractice premiums. In any event, medical groups — and the lawmakers who support them — have shown virtually no interest in insurance reform issues.

With little interest in modified compensation schemes or insurance reform, the debate over damage caps strikes many advocates and observers as an unenlightened repetition of previous fights. "It's a replay of the debate we last had 10 years ago," Harvard's Weiler says.

The outlook for the damage cap measure on Capitol Hill is unclear. The House seems all but certain to pass the AMA-backed bill, since Republican discipline is strong, and the same bill won approval in September 2002. The outlook in the Senate is cloudy since Republicans have a narrow 51-48 majority (with one independent), and 60 votes are needed to cut off debate by opponents.

"We're something like 15 votes shy of the 60 votes needed to get cloture," says Smarr of the Physician Insurers Association of America. "It's going to take intensive grass-roots efforts to get the additional votes."

Battles also continue in state legislatures around the country, but medical groups face daunting obstacles in gaining ground with their proposals. Of the 25 states with no damage caps, 13 have constitutional provisions that bar legislation limiting recoveries by plaintiffs in civil cases. In the other states — those without caps and those with damage limits higher than $250,000 — medical lobbies have tried in the past but failed to win enactment of their model legislation.

Trial lawyers, however, are not in an enviable position. Medical groups are working hard to exploit unfavorable perceptions of attorneys and the legal profession — apparently to some effect. Several polls indicate that most Americans do blame lawyers for increased health-care costs and do support proposals to cap medical-malpractice damages. [32]

In West Virginia, doctors' criticisms of lawyers and litigation appears to be paying off as the state legislature nears final action on a bill to cap non-economic damages at $250,000 or at $500,000 for death or certain serious injuries. The state House of Representatives approved the bill in January, and the state Senate followed suit on Feb. 7. The measure also establishes a framework for creating a physicians' mutual-insurance company in the state.

The president of the West Virginia State Medical Association says the damage cap is needed to "stabilize" malpractice insurance premiums and protect public access to health care. "If you can't keep [insurance] affordable, you're damaging access to medical care," says Douglas McKinney, a urologist in Bridgeport. "You're going to have to limit non-economic damages to a small number of plaintiffs in order to provide health care to the masses."

But Charleston lawyer Richard Lindsay says the cap will be "tremendously unfair" for people with significant injuries, like his client, 3-year-old Forrest Bounds. "I don't know how people who are for this artificial cap can sleep at night," says Lindsay, who is also a physician, "because there are going to be people like Forrest, there are going to be people who have horrible non-economic injuries, and they're not going to get adequate compensation. It's just morally wrong." ∎

Notes

[1] U.S. Department of Health and Human Services, "Confronting the New Health Care Crisis: Improving Health Care Quality and Lowering Costs By Fixing Our Medical Liability System," July 24, 2002, p. 15; (http://www.aspe.hhs.gov/daltcp/reports/litrefm.htm).

[2] Malpractice-insurance costs are from A.M. Best Co., the leading provider of information about the insurance industry. Health-care expenditures totaled $1.2 trillion in 1999, according to the Bureau of the Census, and were projected to reach $1.5 trillion in 2002. See *2001 Statistical Abstract of the United States*, Table 119 (http://www.census.gov/prod/2002pubs/01statab/stat-ab01.html).

[3] U.S. Department of Health and Human Services, *op. cit.*, p. 15. The report cites a scholarly article: Daniel Kessler and Mark McClellan, "Do Doctors Practice Defensive Medicine?" *Quarterly Journal of Economics*, Vol. 111, No. 2, (1996), pp. 353-390. The article won the 1997 Kenneth Arrow Award in Health Economics from the American Economics Association. For further discussion of defensive medicine, see Marshall B. Kapp, *Our Hands Are Tied: Legal Tensions and Medical Ethics* (1998), pp. 27-52.

[4] See Kenneth De Ville, "Medical Malpractice in Twentieth Century United States: The Interaction of Technology, Law and Culture," *International Journal of Technology Assessment in Health Care*, Vol. 14, No. 2 (1998), pp. 204-205, and sources cited.

[5] Humphrey Taylor, "Most Doctors Report Fear of Malpractice Liability Has Harmed Their Ability to Provide Quality Care: Caused Them to Order Unnecessary Tests, Provide Unnecessary Treatment and Make Unnecessary Referrals," Harris Interactive Survey, May 8, 2002 (www.harrisinteractive.com). The survey of 300 physicians was conducted March 4-20, 2002, for The Common Good, an advocacy group that favors limits on medical-malpractice suits.

[6] See U.S. Congress, Office of Technology Assessment, "Defensive Medicine and Medical Malpractice" (OTA-H0602), 1996; U.S. General Accounting Office, "Medical Liability: Impact on hospital and physician costs extends beyond insurance" (GAO/AIMD-95-169), 1995.

7 See Rob Hotakainen, "Victims of medical error testify on Capitol Hill," [Minneapolis-St. Paul] *Star Tribune*, Jan. 24, 2003, and Dana Wilkie, "California boy to be poster child for foes of Bush cap on malpractice suits," Copley News Service, Jan. 22, 2003.

8 See Paul C. Weiler *et al.*, *A Measure of Malpractice: Medical Injury, Malpractice Litigation, and Patient Compensation* (1993), p. 2.

9 Juliet A. Terry, "Wheeling Docs Stage Walkout for Rate Relief," *The State Journal*, Jan. 3, 2003, p. 1.

10 See Americans for Insurance Reform, "Medical Malpractice Insurance: Stable Losses/Unstable Rates," Oct. 10, 2002. Americans for Insurance Reform is a project of the Center for Justice and Democracy.

11 See Raghu Ramachandra, "Did Investments Affect Medical Malpractice Premiums?" Brown Brothers Harriman, Jan. 21, 2003. www.bbh.com/insurance.

12 Jury Verdict Research, "Medical Malpractice: Verdicts, Settlements and Statistical Analysis," 2002.

13 Background drawn from De Ville, *op. cit.*, pp. 197-211.

14 Paul C. Weiler, *Medical Malpractice on Trial* (1991), p. 2 (claims), p. 4 (insurance costs). See also Patricia M. Danzon, *Medical Malpractice: Theory, Evidence, and Public Policy* (1985).

15 Some background drawn from Weiler, *op. cit.*, pp. 1-16. For a more critical view, see Walter K. Olson, *The Litigation Explosion: What Happened When America Unleashed the Lawsuit* (1991), *passim*.

16 See American Hospital Association, "Medical Malpractice Task Force Report on Tort Reform," May 1986, p. 13.

17 *Ibid.*, p. 1.

18 Weiler, *op. cit.*, p. 14.

19 Weiler *et al.*, *op. cit.*, p. 2.

20 A summary of the legislation can be found on the Health Care Liability Alliance's Web site: www.hcla.org.

21 See Weiler, *op. cit.*, pp. 12-13. Weiler notes that an earlier California study reached somewhat similar results. For background on the Institute of Medicine study, see Adriel Bettelheim, "Medical Mistakes," *The CQ Researcher*, Feb. 25, 2000, pp. 137-160.

22 Olson, *op. cit.*, p. 6.

FOR MORE INFORMATION

American Hospital Association, 325 7th St., N.W., Suite 700, Washington, DC 20004; (202) 638-1100; www.aha.org.

American Medical Association, 1101 Vermont Ave., N.W., Washington, DC 20005; (202) 789-7400; www.ama-assn.org.

American Tort Reform Association, 1101 Connecticut Ave., N.W., Suite 400, Washington, DC 20036; (202) 682-1163; www.atra.org.

Association of Trial Lawyers of America, 1050 31st St., N.W., Washington, DC 20036; (202) 965-3500; www.atla.org.

Center for Justice and Democracy/Americans for Insurance Reform, 80 Broad St., Suite 1710, New York, NY 10004-3307; (917) 438-4608; www.centerjd.org; www.insurance-reform.org.

Consumer Federation of America, 1424 16th St., N.W., Washington, DC 20036; (202) 387-6121; www.consumerfed.org.

Health Coalition on Liability and Access, P.O. Box 19008, Washington, DC 20036-9008; (202) 293-4255; www.hcla.org.

Leapfrog Group, c/o Academy Health, 1801 K St., N.W., Suite 701-L, Washington, DC 20006; (202) 292-6713; www.leapfroggroup.org. Composed of more than 130 public and private organizations that provide health-care benefits.

Physician Insurers Association of America, 2275 Research Blvd., Suite 250, Rockville, MD 20850; (301) 947-9000; www.thepiaa.org.

23 Weiler, *op. cit.*, pp. 2, 6.

24 See Samuel Goldreich, "House Passes Malpractice Limits Bill," *CQ Weekly*, Sept. 28, 2002, p. 2528.

25 The other senators were Edward M. Kennedy, Mass.; Patrick J. Leahy, Vt.; and Richard J. Durbin, Ill. Quoted in Richard A. Oppel Jr., "With a New Push, Bush Enters Fray on Malpractice," *The New York Times*, Jan. 17, 2003, p. A1.

26 Quoted in "Doctors Shutter Offices," *The* [Trenton] *Times*, Feb. 4, 2003.

27 Quoted in Carol Ann Campbell and Robert Schwaneberg, "MDs Demand Tort Reform at Large Statehouse Rally," *The* [Newark] *Star-Ledger*, Feb. 5, 2003.

28 Quoted in Richard Lezin Jones and Robert Hanley, "Trenton Lawmakers Seek a Compromise for Doctors," *The New York Times*, Feb. 5, 2003.

29 Lara Jakes Jordan, "Medical Liability Reform Named Top Priority for House Leaders," The Associated Press, Feb. 6, 2003. See also Rebecca Adams and Jennifer A. Dlouhy, "Parties' Different Approaches To Medical Liability Crisis Make Quick Fix Unlikely," *CQ Weekly*, Feb. 8, 2003, p. 354.

30 See Jeffrey O'Connell and Patrick B. Bryan, "More Hippocrates, Less Hypocrisy: 'Early Offers' as a Means of Implementing the Institute of Medicine's Recommendations on Malpractice," *Journal of Law and Health*, Vol. 15, No. 1 (2000-01), pp. 23-52.

31 Janet M. Corrigan, Ann Greiner and Shari M. Erickson (eds.), "Fostering Rapid Advances in Health Care: Learning from System Demonstrations," Institute of Medicine, November 2002, pp. 81-89.

32 See, for example, "National Quorum," Health Care Liability Alliance, April 2002. The poll by Wirthlin Worldwide interviewed 1,006 adults 18 and older in the contiguous United States.

Bibliography

Selected Sources

Books

De Ville, Kenneth, *Medical Malpractice in Nineteenth-Century America: Origins and Legacy*, New York University Press, 1990.

Traces history of medical-malpractice litigation in the United States in the 1800s. DeVille is a professor at East Carolina University School of Medicine. For a shorter overview covering both the 19th and 20th centuries, see De Ville's article, "Medical Malpractice in Twentieth Century United States: The Interaction of Technology, Law and Culture," *International Journal of Technology Assessment in Health Care*, Vol. 14, No. 2 (1998), pp. 197-211.

Kapp, Marshall B., *Our Hands Are Tied: Legal Tensions and Medical Ethics*, Auburn House, 1998.

Critically examines reasons for "crisis mentality" regarding medical malpractice among U.S. physicians. Includes references after each chapter. Kapp is a professor of community health and psychiatry at Wright State University School of Medicine and adjunct professor at University of Dayton School of Law.

Sloan, Frank A., *et al.*, *Suing for Medical Malpractice*, University of Chicago Press, 1993.

Survey of malpractice claims filed in Florida at the peak of the medical-malpractice crisis in the late 1980s indicated most cases were well grounded and claimants on average were substantially under-compensated. Includes detailed notes, tabular material and 16-page bibliography. Lead author Sloan is director of the Center for Health Policy, Law and Management at Duke University.

Vidmar, Neil, *Medical Malpractice and the American Jury: Confronting the Myths about Jury Incompetence, Deep Pockets and Outrageous Damage Awards*, University of Michigan Press, 1995.

Review of medical-malpractice litigation nationally and detailed examination in North Carolina refutes critics' arguments that juries sympathize with patients over doctors or vote awards out of proportion to claimants' economic losses. Includes chapter notes, 11-page list of references. Vidmar is a professor at Duke University Law School.

Weiler, Paul C., *et al.*, *A Measure of Malpractice: Medical Injury, Malpractice Litigation and Patient Compensation*, Harvard University Press, 1993.

Study by team of Harvard scholars of hospital admissions in New York found injury-causing medical mistakes occurred in nearly 5 percent of cases, while malpractice claims were filed in a small fraction of such cases. Lead author Weiler had previewed findings in his earlier work, *Medical Malpractice on Trial* (Harvard University Press, 1991), which explicitly called for a no-fault system to ensure compensation for patients injured by medical mistakes.

Articles

"Doctor Dilemma," *The Charleston (W. Va.) Gazette*, Nov. 10, 2002-Dec. 1, 2002 (http://www.wvgazette.com).

The four-part series examined medical-malpractice issues from doctors' and patients' perspectives. An earlier series of stories pointedly challenged doctors' claims of a medical-malpractice crisis in the state. See "The Practice of Medicine," Feb. 25-27, 2001.

Reports and Studies

Americans for Insurance Reform, "Medical Malpractice Insurance: Stable Losses/Unstable Rates," Oct. 10, 2002 (www.insurance-reform.org).

Consumer coalition's analysis of medical-malpractice liability over three decades indicates payouts have been relatively stable since the 1980s, while insurance premiums have fallen or risen with the economic cycle. Web site includes separate analyses for New Jersey, Pennsylvania and West Virginia.

Corrigan, Janet M., Ann Greiner, and Shari M. Erickson (eds.), "Fostering Rapid Advances in Health Care: Learning from System Demonstrations," *Institute of Medicine*, November 2002.

Report proposes various health care improvement demonstration projects, including non-judicial compensation schemes for patients injured by medical error.

Kohn, Linda, Janet Corrigan, and Molla Donaldson, "To Err Is Human: Building a Safer Health System," *Institute of Medicine*, 1999 (http://books.nap.edu).

Medical errors result in at least 44,000 deaths and cost $17 billion to $29 billion each year, according to authors of 223-page report; comprehensive list of patient safety recommendations; no specific position on medical-liability issues. Includes detailed notes, references, appendices.

U.S. Department of Health and Human Services, "Confronting the New Health Care Crisis: Improving Health Care Quality and Lowering Costs By Fixing Our Medical Liability System," July 24, 2002 (www.aspe.hhs.gov/daltcp/reports/litrefm.htm).

Twenty-eight page report says "extreme judgments" in "small proportion" of medical-malpractice cases are creating a litigation crisis that threatens quality of and access to health care; cites proposals by President Bush to cap damages, impose other restrictions.

5 Affirmative Action

KENNETH JOST

Jennifer Gratz wanted to go to the University of Michigan's flagship Ann Arbor campus as soon as she began thinking about college. "It's the best school in Michigan to go to," she explains.

The white suburban teenager's dream turned to disappointment in April 1995, however, when the university told her that even though she was "well qualified," she had been rejected for one of the nearly 4,000 slots in the incoming freshman class.

Gratz was convinced something was wrong. "I knew that the University of Michigan was giving preference to minorities," she says today. "If you give extra points for being of a particular race, then you're not giving applicants an equal opportunity."

Gratz, now 24, has a degree from Michigan's less prestigious Dearborn campus and a job in San Diego. She is also the lead plaintiff in a lawsuit that is shaping up as a decisive battle in the long-simmering conflict over racial preferences in college admissions.

On the opposite side of Gratz's federal court lawsuit is Lee Bollinger, Michigan's highly respected president and a staunch advocate of race-conscious admissions policies.

"Racial and ethnic diversity is one part of the core liberal educational goal," Bollinger says. "People have different educational experiences when they grow up as an African-American, Hispanic or white."

Gratz won a partial victory in December 2000 when a federal judge agreed that the university's admissions

From *The CQ Researcher*, September 21, 2001.

First-year engineering students at the University of Michigan-Ann Arbor gather during welcome week last year. A federal judge ruled in December 2000 that the school's race-based admissions system in 1995 was illegal but that a revised system adopted later was constitutional. The case is widely expected to reach the Supreme Court.

system in 1995 was illegal. But the ruling came too late to help her, and Judge Patrick Duggan went on to rule that the revised system the university adopted in 1998 passed constitutional muster.

Some three months later, however, another federal judge ruled in a separate case that the admissions system currently used at the university's law school is illegal. Judge Bernard Friedman said the law school's admissions policies were "practically indistinguishable from a quota system."

The two cases — *Gratz v. Bollinger* and *Grutter v. Bollinger* — are now set to be argued together late next month before the federal appeals court in Cincinnati. [1] And opposing lawyers and many legal observers expect the two cases to reach the Supreme Court in a potentially decisive showdown. "One of these cases could well end up in the Supreme Court," says Elizabeth Barry, the university's associate vice president and deputy general counsel, who is coordinating the defense of the two suits.

"We hope the Supreme Court resolves this issue relatively soon," says Michael Rosman, attorney for the Center for Individual Rights in Washington, which represents plaintiffs in both cases. "It is fair to say that there is some uncertainty in the law in this area."

The legal uncertainty stems from the long time span — 23 years — since the Supreme Court's only previous full-scale ruling on race-based admissions policies: the famous *Bakke* decision. In that fractured ruling, *University of California Regents v. Bakke*, the high court in 1978 ruled that fixed racial quotas were illegal but allowed the use of race as one factor in college admissions. [2]

Race-based admissions policies are widespread in U.S. higher education today — "well accepted and entrenched," according to Sheldon Steinbach, general counsel of the pro-affirmative action American Council on Education.

Roger Clegg, general counsel of the Center for Equal Opportunity, which opposes racial preferences, agrees with Steinbach but from a different perspective. "Evidence is overwhelming that racial and ethnic discrimination occurs frequently in public college and university admissions," Clegg says. [3]

Higher-education organizations and traditional civil rights groups say racial admissions policies are essential to ensure racial and ethnic diversity at the nation's elite universities — including the most selective state schools, such as Michigan's Ann Arbor campus. "The overwhelming majority of students who apply to highly selective institutions are still white," says Theodore Shaw, associate director-counsel of the NAACP Legal Defense

Despite Progress, Minorities Still Trail Whites

A larger percentage of young adult African-Americans and Hispanics have completed college today than 20 years ago. But college completion rates for African-Americans and Hispanics continue to be significantly lower than the rate for whites. Today, the national college completion rate — 30 percent — is more than triple the rate in 1950.

Percentages of College Graduates, Ages 25-29

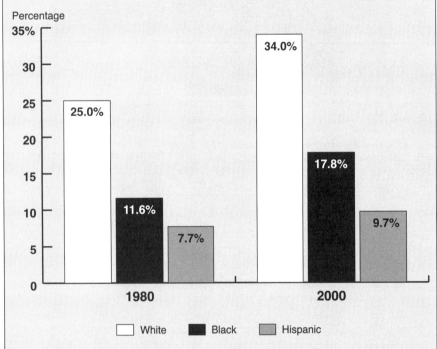

Source: U.S. Department of Education, "Digest of Education Statistics," 2001 edition (forthcoming)

Fund, which represents minority students who intervened in the two cases. "If we are not conscious of selecting minority students, they're not going to be there."

Opponents, however, say racial preferences are wrong in terms of law and social policy. "It's immoral. It's illegal. It stigmatizes the beneficiary. It encourages hypocrisy. It lowers standards. It encourages the use of stereotypes," Clegg says. "There are all kinds of social costs, and we don't think the benefits outweigh those costs."

The race-based admissions policies now in use around the country evolved gradually since the passage of federal civil rights legislation in the mid-1960s. By 1970, the phrase "affirmative action" had become common usage to describe efforts to increase the number of African-Americans (and, later, Hispanics) in U.S. workplaces and on college campuses. [4] Since then, the proportions of African-Americans and Hispanics on college campuses have increased, though they are still underrepresented in terms of their respective proportions in the U.S. population. (*See chart, p. 83.*)

Michigan's efforts range from uncontroversial minority-outreach programs to an admissions system that explicitly takes an applicant's race or ethnicity into account in deciding whether to accept or reject the applicant. The system formerly used by the undergraduate College of Literature, Science and the Arts had separate grids for white and minority applicants. The current system uses a numerical rating that includes a 20-point bonus (out of a total possible score of 150) for "underrepresented minorities" — African-Americans, Hispanics and Native Americans (but not Asian-Americans). The law school's system — devised in 1992 — is aimed at producing a minority enrollment of about 10 percent to 12 percent of the entering class.

Critics of racial preferences say they are not opposed to affirmative action. "Certainly there are some positive aspects to affirmative action," Rosman says, citing increased recruitment of minorities and reassessment by colleges of criteria for evaluating applicants. But, he adds, "To the extent that it suggests that they have carte blanche to discriminate between people on the basis of race, it's not a good thing."

Higher-education officials respond that they should have discretion to explicitly consider race — along with a host of other factors — to ensure a fully representative student body and provide the best learning environment for an increasingly multicultural nation and world. "Having a diverse student body contributes to the educational process and is necessary in the 21st-century global economy," Steinbach says.

As opposing lawyers prepare for the appellate arguments next month in the University of Michigan cases, here are some of the major questions being debated:

Should colleges use race-based admissions policies to remedy discrimination against minorities?

The University of Michigan relies

heavily on high school students' scores on standardized tests in evaluating applications — tests that have been widely criticized as biased against African-Americans and other minorities. It gives preferences to children of Michigan alumni — who are disproportionately white — as well as to applicants from "underrepresented" parts of the state, such as Michigan's predominantly white Upper Peninsula.

Even apart from the university's past record of racial segregation, those factors could be cited as evidence that Michigan's current admissions policies are racially discriminatory because they have a "disparate impact" on minorities. And the Supreme Court, in *Bakke*, said that racial classifications were constitutional if they were used as a remedy for proven discrimination.

But Michigan is not defending its racial admissions policies on that basis. "Every public university has its share of decisions that we're now embarrassed by," President Bollinger concedes. But the university is defending its use of race — along with an array of other factors — only as a method of producing racial diversity, not as a way to remedy current or past discrimination.

Some civil rights advocates, however, insist that colleges and universities are still guilty of racially biased policies that warrant — even require — explicit racial preferences as corrective measures.

"Universities should use race-conscious admissions as a way of countering both past and ongoing ways in which the admission process continues to engage in practices that perpetuate racism or are unconsciously racist," says Charles Lawrence, a professor at Georgetown University Law Center in Washington.

Opponents of racial preferences, however, say colleges should be very wary about justifying such policies on the basis of past or current discrimination against minorities. "The Supreme Court has been pretty clear that you

can't use the justification of past societal discrimination as a ground for a race-based admissions policy at an institution that did not itself discriminate," says Stephen Balch, president of the National Association of Scholars, a Princeton, N.J.-based group of academics opposed to racial preferences.

Balch defends alumni preferences, the most frequently mentioned example of an admissions policy that disadvantages minority applicants. "It's not at all unreasonable for colleges and universities to cultivate their alumni base," Balch says. In any event, he adds, "As student bodies change, the effect of that policy will change."

For his part, Rosman of the Center for Individual Rights says racial

preferences are not justified even if colleges are wrong to grant alumni preferences or to rely so heavily on standardized test scores. "If you have criteria that discriminate and are not educationally justified, then the appropriate response is to get rid of those criteria, not to use 'two wrongs make a right,'" Rosman says.

Minority students intervened in both the undergraduate and law school suits to present evidence of discrimination by the university and to use that evidence to justify the racial admissions policies. In the undergraduate case, evidence showed that the university refused to desegregate fraternities and sororities until the 1960s, allowed white students to refuse to room with black students

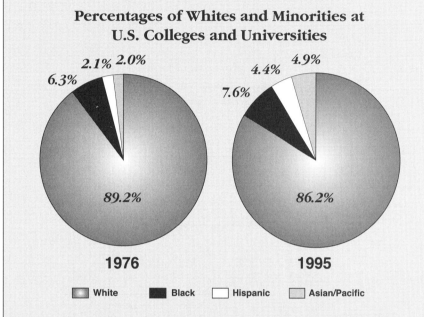

Minority Enrollments Increased

African-Americans and Hispanics make up a larger percentage of the U.S. college population today than they did in 1976, but they are still underrepresented in comparison to their proportion of the total U.S. population. Hispanics comprise 12.5 percent of the population, African-Americans 12.3 percent.

Percentages of Whites and Minorities at U.S. Colleges and Universities

1976: 6.3%, 2.1%, 2.0%, 89.2%

1995: 7.6%, 4.4%, 4.9%, 86.2%

White · Black · Hispanic · Asian/Pacific

Note: Percentages do not add to 100 due to rounding.

Source: U.S. Dept. of Education, "Digest of Education Statistics," 2001 edition (forthcoming)

and did not hire its first black professor until 1967. The evidence also showed that black students reported continuing discrimination and racial hostility through the 1980s and into the '90s.

In a Feb. 26 ruling, Judge Duggan acknowledged the evidence but rejected it as a justification for the admissions policies. The racial segregation occurred too long ago to be a reason for current policies, Duggan said. He also rejected the minority students' argument that the racial impact

"This is a social and political matter, which calls for social and political solutions," Friedman wrote. "The solution is not for the law school, or any other state institution, to prefer some applicants over others because of race."

Should colleges use race-based admissions policies to promote diversity in their student populations?

Michigan's high schools graduated some 100,000 students in 1999. Out

University officials cite that stark statistic to underline the difficulty they face in admitting a racially diverse student body — and to justify their policy of giving minority applicants special consideration in the admissions process. Without the current bonus for minority applicants, Barry says the number of African-American and Hispanic students "would drop dramatically" from the current level of about 13 percent of undergraduates to "somewhere around 5 percent."

Opponents of racial preferences dismiss the warnings. "It's certainly not inevitable that the number of students from racial and ethnic minorities will decline" under a color-blind system, Rosman says. In any event, he says that diversity is "not a sufficiently powerful goal to discriminate and treat people differently on the basis of race."

The dispute between supporters and opponents of racial admissions policies turns in part on two somewhat rarefied issues. Supporters claim to have social-science evidence to show that racial and ethnic diversity produces quantifiable educational benefits for all students — evidence that opponents deride as dubious at best. (*See story, p. 92.*) The opposing camps also differ on the question of whether the *Bakke* decision allows colleges to use diversity as the kind of "compelling government interest" needed to satisfy the so-called strict-scrutiny standard of constitutional review. (*See story, p. 86.*)

Apart from those specialized disputes, opponents of racial preferences argue simply that they constitute a form of stereotyping and discrimination. "We don't believe that there is a black outlook or an Asian outlook or a white experience or a Hispanic experience," Clegg says. "Students are individuals, and they should be treated as individuals, not as fungible members of racial and ethnic groups."

Some critics — including a few African-Americans — also say racial preferences "stigmatize" the intended

Gratz v. Bollinger: Race and College Admissions

Jennifer Gratz, a white woman, sued the University of Michigan contending she was improperly denied admission because of race. The lawsuit is shaping up as a key battle in the long-simmering conflict over racial preferences in college admissions.

"I see benefits from different opinions, different thoughts on any number of subjects. But I don't think that's necessarily race coming through. I don't think like every other white person. ... Your race doesn't mean that you're going to think this way or that way."

Jennifer Gratz, B.S., University of Michigan, Dearborn

"You get a better education and a better society in an environment where you are mixing with lots of different people — people from different parts of the country, people from different parts of the socioeconomic system, people from abroad, and people from different races and ethnicities."

Lee Bollinger, President, University of Michigan

of alumni preferences, standardized test scores and other admissions criteria justified preferences for minority applicants.

Judge Friedman rejected similar arguments in the final portion of his March 26 ruling in the law school case.

of that number, only 327 African-American students had a B-plus average and an SAT score above 1,000 — the kind of record needed to make them strong contenders for admission to the University of Michigan's Ann Arbor campus based on those factors alone.

beneficiaries by creating the impression that they could not be successful without being given some advantage over whites. "There is no way that a young black at an Ivy League university is going to get credit for [doing well]," says Shelby Steele, a prominent black critic of racial preferences and a research fellow at the Hoover Institution at Stanford University. "There's no way that he's going to feel his achievements are his own."

Supporters of racial admission policies, however, say that race plays an independent and important role in American society that colleges are entitled to take into account. "It is reasonable for educational institutions to believe that race is not a proxy for something else," Bollinger says. "It is a defining experience in American life — and therefore an important one for this goal" of educational diversity.

White supporters of affirmative action generally deny or minimize any supposed stigmatization from race-conscious policies. Some blacks acknowledge some stigmatizing effects, but blame white racism rather than affirmative action. "The stigmatizing beliefs about people of color," Professor Lawrence writes, "have their origin not in affirmative action programs but in the cultural belief system of white supremacy." [5]

The two judges in the Michigan cases reached different conclusions on the diversity issue. In his ruling in the undergraduate case, Duggan agreed with the university's argument that a "racially and ethnically diverse student body produces significant education benefits, such that diversity, in the context of higher education, constitutes a compelling governmental interest under strict scrutiny."

Ruling in the law school case, Judge Friedman acknowledged that racial diversity may provide "educational and societal benefits," though he also called for drawing "a distinction . . . between viewpoint diversity and racial

diversity." Based on his interpretation of *Bakke*, however, Friedman said these "important and laudable" benefits did not amount to a compelling interest sufficient to justify the law school's use of race in admissions decisions.

Should colleges adopt other policies to try to increase minority enrollment?

Texas and Florida have a different approach to ensuring a racial mix in their state university systems. Texas' "10 percent plan" — adopted in 1997 under then-Gov. George W. Bush — promises a spot in the state university to anyone who graduates in the top 10 percent of any high schools in the state. Florida's plan — adopted in 1999 under Gov. Jeb Bush, the president's brother — makes the same commitment to anyone in the top 20 percent.

The plans are drawing much attention and some favorable comment as an ostensibly race-neutral alternative to racial preferences. But major participants on both sides of the debate over racial admissions policies view the idea with skepticism.

"It's silly to suggest that all high schools are equal in terms of the quality of their student body," Clegg says. "And therefore it makes no sense to have an across-the-board rule that the top 10 percent of every high school is going to be admitted."

Both Clegg and Rosman also say that a 10 percent-type plan is dubious if it is adopted to circumvent a ban on explicit racial preferences. "Any neutral policy that is just a pretext for discrimination would have to survive strict scrutiny," Rosman says.

Supporters of race-based admissions are also unenthusiastic. "The only reason they work is because we have segregated high schools, segregated communities," Shaw says. "From a philosophical standpoint, I'd rather deal with race in a more honest and up-front way and make a more principled approach to these issues."

In the Michigan lawsuits, the university cited testimony from a prominent supporter of racial admissions policies in opposition to 10 percent-type plans. "Treating all applicants alike if they finished above a given high school class rank provides a spurious form of equality that is likely to damage the academic profile of the overall class of students admitted to selective institutions," said former Princeton University President William G. Bowen, now president of the Andrew W. Mellon Foundation in New York City.

Rosman looks more favorably on another alternative: giving preferences to applicants who come from disadvantaged socioeconomic backgrounds. "It's not a bad idea to take into account a person's ability to overcome obstacles," he says. "That's useful in assessing a person's qualifications."

In his testimony, however, Bowen also criticized that approach. Youngsters from poor black and Hispanic families are "much less likely" to excel in school than those from poor white families, Bowen said. On that basis, he predicted that a "class-based" rather than race-based admissions policy "would substantially reduce the minority enrollments at selective institutions."

For its part, the university stresses that its current system gives up to 20 points to an applicant based on socioeconomic disadvantage — the same number given to minority applicants. "We consider a number of factors in order to enroll a diverse student body," Barry says, "because race is not the only element that's important to diversity in education."

In their rulings, Duggan and Friedman both favorably noted a number of alternatives to race-based admissions policies. Friedman suggested the law school could have increased recruiting efforts or decreased the emphasis on undergraduate grades and scores on the Law School Aptitude Test. He also said the school could have used a lottery for all qualified applicants or admitted some

What Does *Bakke* Mean? Two Judges Disagree

The Supreme Court's 1978 decision to prohibit fixed racial quotas in colleges and universities but to allow the use of race as one factor in admissions was hailed by some people at the time as a Solomon-like compromise.

But today the meaning of the high court's famous *Bakke* decision is sharply disputed. And the disagreement lies at the heart of conflicting rulings by two federal judges in Michigan on the legality of racial preferences used at the University of Michigan's flagship Ann Arbor campus.

In upholding the flexible race-based admissions system used by the undergraduate College of Literature, Science and the Arts in December, Judge Patrick Duggan said *Bakke* means that colleges can evaluate white and minority applicants differently in order to enroll a racially and ethnically diverse student body.

But Judge Bernard Friedman rejected that widely held interpretation in a March 27 decision striking down the law school's use of race in admissions. Friedman — like Duggan an appointee of President Ronald Reagan — said that racial and ethnic diversity did not qualify as a "compelling governmental interest" needed under the so-called strict scrutiny constitutional standard to justify a race-based government policy.

The differing interpretations stem from the Supreme Court's unusual 4-1-4 vote in the case, *University of California Regents v. Bakke*. Four of the justices found the quota system used by the UC-Davis Medical School — reserving 16 out of 100 seats for minorities — to be a violation of the federal civil rights law prohibiting racial discrimination in federally funded institutions. Four others — led by the liberal Justice William J. Brennan Jr. — voted to reject Alan Bakke's challenge to the system.

In the pivotal opinion, Justice Lewis F. Powell Jr. found the UC-Davis admissions system to be a violation of the constitutional requirement of equal protection but said race could be used as a "plus" factor in admissions decisions. The "attainment of a diverse student body," Powell wrote, "clearly is a constitutionally permissible goal for an institution of higher education."

Under Supreme Court case law, it takes a majority of the justices — five — to produce a "holding" that can serve as a precedent for future cases. In a fractured ruling, the court's holding is said to be the "narrowest" rationale endorsed by five justices. But Brennan's group did not explicitly address the question of diversity. Instead, they said that race-based admissions decisions were justified to remedy past discrimination — a proposition that Powell also endorsed.

Critics of racial preferences in recent years have argued that the Brennan group's silence on diversity means that they did not join Powell's reasoning. On that basis, these critics say, Powell's opinion cannot be viewed as a controlling precedent. They won an important victory when the federal appeals court in New Orleans adopted that reasoning in the so-called *Hopwood* case in 1996 striking down the University of Texas Law School's racial preferences.

In his ruling in the Michigan law school case, Friedman also agreed with this revisionist view of *Bakke*. "The diversity rationale articulated by Justice Powell is neither narrower nor broader than the remedial rationale articulated by the Brennan group," Friedman wrote. "They are completely different rationales, neither one of which is subsumed within in the other."

But in the undergraduate case, Duggan followed the previous interpretation of *Bakke*. Brennan's "silence re-

Reporters follow Allan Bakke on his first day at the University of California-Davis Medical School on Sept. 25, 1978. The Supreme Court ordered him admitted after ruling that the school violated his rights by maintaining a fixed quota for minority applicants.

AP Photo/Walt Zeboski

garding the diversity interest in *Bakke* was not an implicit rejection of such an interest, but rather, an implicit approval of such an interest," Duggan wrote.

The two judges also differed on how to interpret later Supreme Court decisions. Duggan cited Brennan's 1990 majority opinion in a case upholding racial preferences in broadcasting — *Metro Broadcasting, Inc. v. Federal Communications Commission* — as supporting the use of diversity to justify racial policies. But Friedman said other recent rulings showed that the Supreme Court had become much more skeptical of racial policies than it had been in 1978. Among the decisions he cited was the 1995 ruling, *Adarand Constructors v. Peña* that overruled the *Metro Broadcasting* holding.

fixed number or percentage of top graduates from various colleges and universities. Friedman said the law school's "apparent failure to investigate alternative means for increasing minority enrollment" was one factor in rejecting the school's admissions policies.

For his part, Duggan noted the possibility of using race-neutral policies to increase minority enrollment when he rejected the minority students' critique of such policies as alumni preferences. "If the current selection criteria have a discriminatory impact on minority applicants," Duggan wrote, "it seems to this court that the narrowly tailored remedy would be to remove or redistribute such criteria to accommodate for socially and economically disadvantaged applicants of all races and ethnicities, not to add another suspect criteria [sic] to the list." ∎

BACKGROUND

Unequal Opportunity

African-Americans and other racial and ethnic minority groups have been underrepresented on college campuses throughout U.S. history. The civil rights revolution has effectively dismantled most legal barriers to higher education for minorities. But the social and economic inequalities that persist between white Americans and racial and ethnic minority groups continue to make the goal of equal opportunity less than reality for many African-Americans and Hispanics.

The legal battles that ended mandatory racial segregation in the United States began with higher education nearly two decades before the Supreme Court's historic ruling in *Brown v. Board of Education*. [6] In the first of the rulings that ended the doctrine of "sep-

arate but equal," the court in 1938 ruled that Missouri violated a black law school applicant's equal protection rights by offering to pay his tuition to an out-of-state school rather than admit him to the state's all-white law school.

The court followed with a pair of rulings in 1950 that similarly found states guilty of violating black students' rights to equal higher education. Texas was ordered to admit a black student to the state's all-white law school rather than force him to attend an inferior all-black school. And Oklahoma was found to have discriminated against a black student by admitting him to a previously all-white state university but denying him the opportunity to use all its facilities.

At the time of these decisions, whites had substantially greater educational opportunities than African-Americans. As of 1950, a majority of white Americans ages 25-29 — 56 percent — had completed high school, compared with only 24 percent of African-Americans. Eight percent of whites in that age group had completed college compared with fewer than 3 percent of blacks. Most of the African-American college graduates had attended all-black institutions: either private colleges established for blacks or racially segregated state universities.

The Supreme Court's 1954 decision in *Brown* to begin dismantling racial segregation in elementary and secondary education started to reduce the inequality in educational opportunities for whites and blacks, but changes were slow. It was not until 1970 that a majority of African-Americans ages 25-29 had attained high school degrees.

Changes at the nation's elite colleges and universities were even slower. In their book *The Shape of the River*, two former Ivy League presidents — Bowen and Derek Bok — say that as of 1960 "no selective col-

lege or university was making determined efforts to seek out and admit substantial numbers of African-American students." As of 1965, they report, African-Americans comprised only 4.8 percent of students on the nation's college campuses and fewer than 1 percent of students at select New England colleges. [7]

As part of the Civil Rights Act of 1964, Congress included provisions in Title IV to authorize the Justice Department to initiate racial-desegregation lawsuits against public schools and colleges and to require the U.S. Office of Education (now the Department of Education) to give technical assistance to school systems undergoing desegregation. A year later, President Lyndon B. Johnson delivered his famous commencement speech at historically black Howard University that laid the foundation for a more proactive approach to equalizing opportunities for African-Americans. "You do not take a person," Johnson said, "who, for years, has been hobbled by chains and liberate him, bring him up to the starting line of a race and then say, 'You are free to compete with all the others,' and still justly believe that you have been completely fair." [8]

Affirmative Action

Colleges began in the mid-1960s to make deliberate efforts to increase the number of minority students. Many universities instituted "affirmative action" programs that included targeted recruitment of minority applicants as well as explicit use of race as a factor in admissions policies. White students challenged the use of racial preferences, but the Supreme Court — in the *Bakke* decision in 1978 — gave colleges and universities a flashing green light to consider race as one factor in admissions policies aimed at ensuring a racially diverse student body.

The federal government encouraged universities to look to enrollment figures as the criterion for judging the success of their affirmative action policies. By requiring universities to report minority enrollment figures, the Nixon administration appeared to suggest that race-conscious admissions were "not only permissible but mandatory," according to Bowen and Bok. But universities were also motivated, they say, to remedy past racial discrimination, to educate minority leaders and to create diversity on campuses.

As early as 1966, Bowen and Bok report, Harvard Law School moved to increase the number of minority students by "admitting black applicants with test scores far below those of white classmates." As other law schools adopted the strategy, enrollment of African-Americans increased — from 1 percent of all law students in 1965 to 4.5 percent in 1975. Similar efforts produced a significant increase in black students in Ivy League colleges. The proportion of African-American students at Ivy League schools increased from 2.3 percent in 1967 to 6.7 percent in 1976, Bowen and Bok report. [9]

Critics, predominantly but not exclusively political conservatives, charged that the racial preferences amounted to "reverse discrimination" against white students and applicants. Some white students challenged the policies in court. The Supreme Court sought to resolve

President Lyndon B. Johnson signs the Civil Rights Act on July 2, 1964. Race-based admissions policies now in use around the country evolved gradually from the landmark law.

AP Photo

the issue in 1978 in a case brought by a California man, Alan Bakke, who had been denied admission to the University of California Medical School at Davis under a system that explicitly reserved 16 of 100 seats for minority applicants. The 4-1-4 decision fell short of a definitive resolution, though.

Justice Lewis F. Powell Jr. cast the decisive vote in the case. He joined four justices to reject Davis' fixed-quota approach and four others to allow use of race as one factor in admissions decisions. In summarizing his opinion from the bench, Powell explained that it meant Bakke would be admitted to the medical school but that Davis was free to adopt a more "flexible program designed to achieve diversity" just like those "proved to be successful at many of our great universities." [10]

Civil rights advocates initially reacted with "consternation," according to Steinbach of the American Council on Education. Quickly, though, college officials and higher-education groups took up the invitation to devise programs that used race — in Powell's terms — as a "plus factor" without setting aside any seats specifically for minority applicants. The ruling, Steinbach says, "enabled institutions in a creative manner to legally provide for a diverse student body."

The Supreme Court has avoided re-examining Bakke since 1978, but has narrowed the scope of affirmative action in other areas. The court in 1986 ruled that government employers could not lay off senior white workers to make room for new minority hires, though it upheld affirmative action in hiring and promotions in two other decisions that year and another ruling in a sex-discrimination case a year later. As for government contracting, the court ruled in 1989 that state and local governments could not use racial preferences except to remedy past discrimination and extended that limitation to federal programs in 1995. [11]

All of the court's decisions were closely divided, but the conservative majority made clear their discomfort with race-specific policies. Indeed, as legal-affairs writer Lincoln Caplan notes, none of the five current conservatives — Chief Justice William H. Rehnquist and Associate Justices Sandra Day O'Connor, Antonin Scalia, Anthony M. Kennedy and Clarence Thomas

Chronology

Before 1960
Limited opportunities for minorities in private and public colleges and universities.

1938
Supreme Court says Missouri violated Constitution by operating all-white law school but no school for blacks.

1950
Supreme Court says Texas violated Constitution by operating "inferior" law school for blacks.

1954
Supreme Court rules racial segregation in public elementary and secondary schools unconstitutional; ruling is extended to dismantle racially segregated colleges.

1960s-1970s
Civil rights era: higher education desegregated; affirmative action widely adopted, approved by Supreme Court if racial quotas not used.

1964
Civil Rights Act bars discrimination by federally funded colleges.

1978
Supreme Court rules in *Bakke* that colleges and universities can consider race as one factor in admissions policies.

1980s *Supreme Court leaves* Bakke *unchanged.*

1986
Supreme Court limits use of affirmative action by employers if plan leads to layoffs of senior workers, but upholds racial preferences for union admission and promotions.

1987
Supreme Court rules, 6-3, that voluntary affirmative action plans by government employers do not violate civil rights law or Constitution.

1989
Supreme Court says state and local governments can adopt preferences for minority contractors only to remedy past discrimination.

1990s *Opposition to race-based admissions policies grows.*

1995
Supreme Court, in *Adarand* case, limits federal minority-preference programs for contractors; President Clinton defends affirmative action; University of California ends use of race and sex in admissions.

1996
University of Texas law school's use of racial preferences in admissions ruled unconstitutional in *Hopwood* case; California voters approve Proposition 209 banning state-sponsored affirmative action in employment, contracting and admissions.

1997
Texas Gov. George W. Bush signs law guaranteeing admission to University of Texas to top 10 percent of graduates in state high schools.

1998
Washington state voters approve initiative barring racial preferences in state colleges and universities.

1999
Gov. Jeb Bush of Florida issues executive order banning racial preferences but granting admission to state colleges to top 20 percent of graduates in all state high schools.

2000s *Legal challenges to affirmative action continue.*

Dec. 4, 2000
University of Washington Law School's former admissions system — discontinued after Proposition 200 — is upheld by federal court.

Dec. 13, 2000
University of Michigan undergraduate admissions policies upheld by federal judge, though former system ruled illegal.

March 26, 2001
Supreme Court agrees to hear new appeal in *Adarand* case.

March 27, 2001
University of Michigan Law School admissions policies ruled unconstitutional by federal judge.

June 2001
Supreme Court declines to review conflicting rulings in *University of Washington, University of Texas* cases.

Aug. 27, 2001
Federal appeals court in Atlanta rules University of Georgia admissions system giving bonuses to all non-white applicants is unconstitutional.

October 2001
Federal appeals court in Cincinnati to hear appeals in *University of Michigan* cases on Oct. 23; Supreme Court to hear *Adarand* case Oct. 31.

Should Minority Contractors Get Preferences?

Six years ago, the Supreme Court cast doubt on the constitutionality of federal preferences for minority-owned road contractors. Now a white Colorado contractor, Randy Pech, is asking the court to rule that a revised program approved by Congress during the Clinton administration also doesn't pass constitutional muster.

The justices will hear arguments on Oct. 31 in a renewed challenge by Pech, whose company, Adarand Constructors, Inc., waged an earlier battle against a Department of Transportation (DOT) program giving contractors a 10 percent bonus for awarding subcontracts to minority-owned firms.

In a 5-4 decision in *Adarand Constructors, Inc. v. Peña*, the court in 1995 held that minority set-asides, or preferences, are constitutional only if they serve a compelling government interest and are narrowly tailored to meet that goal. [1] Applying that standard, lower courts later ruled the subcontractor-compensation clause unconstitutional.

The federal government then revised the overall program somewhat. Among other things, the revision allows white-owned businesses to apply for status as a disadvantaged company. The government dropped the subcontractor-compensation clause, but retained a provision setting aside 10 percent of federal highway contractors for "disadvantaged business enterprises." The Denver-based 10th U.S. Circuit Court of Appeals ruled last year that the revised program satisfied the "strict scrutiny" standard of constitutional review.

The new case, *Adarand Constructors, Inc. v. Mineta*, finds the Bush administration in the unanticipated position of defending an affirmative action program. President Bush was critical of racial preferences during his presidential campaign. But his newly appointed solicitor general, Theodore Olson, filed a brief in late August defending the DOT program as constitutional. Court observers note that it would have been unusual for the government to change positions after the justices agreed to review the case. [2]

In its brief, Adarand asks the court to rule that racial preferences are "intolerable, always." As an alternative, the company urges the justices to rule that the government did not have adequate evidence of racial discrimination against minority contractors to justify the program and that the mandatory presumption of disadvantage in favor of minority-owned firms was not narrowly tailored to remedy past discrimination.

In its brief, however, the government contends that Congress had "extensive evidence of public and private discrimination in highway contracting" and created the preferences system "only after race-neutral efforts . . . had proved inadequate."

---

[1] The legal citation is 515 U.S. 200 (1995). For background, see Kenneth Jost, *The Supreme Court Yearbook*, 1994-1995, pp. 27-32.

[2] The Mountain States Legal Foundation, the public interest law firm representing Adarand, has a summary of the case on its Web site: www.mountainstateslegal.org. The government's brief can be found at www.usdoj.gov/osg.

— has ever voted to approve a race-based affirmative action program. [12]

Negative Reaction

A political and legal backlash against affirmative action emerged with full force in the 1990s — highlighted by moves in California to scrap race-conscious policies in the state's university system and a federal appeals court decision barring racial preferences in admissions in Texas and two neighboring states. But President Bill Clinton rebuffed calls to scrap federal affirmative action programs. And colleges continued to follow race-conscious admissions policies in the absence of a new Supreme Court pronouncement on the issue.

In the first of the moves against race-conscious admissions, the 5th U.S. Circuit Court of Appeals in New Orleans in March 1996 struck down the University of Texas Law School's system that used separate procedures for white and minority applicants with the goal of admitting a class with 5 percent African-American and 10 percent Mexican-American students. [13] The ruling in the *Hopwood* case unanimously rejected the university's attempt to justify the racial preferences on grounds of past discrimination. Two judges also rejected the university's diversity defense and directly contradicted the prevailing interpretation of *Bakke* that diversity amounted to a "compelling governmental interest" justifying race-based policies. [14]

The ruling specifically applied only to the three states in the 5th Circuit — Louisiana, Mississippi and Texas — but observers saw the decision as significant. "This is incredibly big," said John C. Jeffries Jr., a University of Virginia law professor and Justice Powell's biographer. "This could affect every public institution in America because all of them take racial diversity in admissions." [15]

Four months later, the University of California Board of Regents — policy-making body for the prestigious, 162,000-student state university system — narrowly voted to abolish racial and sexual preferences in admissions by fall 1997. The 14-10 vote approved a resolution submitted by a black businessman, Ward Connerly, and supported by the state's Republican governor, Pete Wilson. Connerly was also the driving force behind a voter initiative — Proposition 209 — to abolish racial preferences in state government employment and contracting as well as college and university admissions. Voters approved the measure, 54 percent to 46 percent, in November 1996.

In the face of opposition from UC President Richard Atkinson, the move to scrap racial preferences was delayed to admissions for the 1998-1999 academic year. In May 1998, the university released figures showing a modest overall decline in acceptances by non-Asian minorities to 15.2 percent for the coming year from 17.6 percent for the 1997-1998 school year. But the figures also showed a steep drop in the number of black and Hispanic students in the entering classes at the two most prestigious campuses — Berkeley and UCLA. At Berkeley, African-American and Hispanic acceptances fell to 10.5 percent from 21.9 percent for the previous year; at UCLA, the drop was to 14.1 percent from 21.8 percent.

The Supreme Court did nothing to counteract the legal shift away from racial preferences in education. It declined in 1995 to review a decision by the federal appeals court in Richmond, Va., that struck down a University of Maryland scholarship program reserved for African-American students. A year later, the justices refused to hear Texas' appeal of the *Hopwood* decision; and a year after that they also turned aside a challenge by labor and civil rights groups to Proposition 209. Instead, the high court concentrated on a series of rulings beginning in June 1993 that limited the use of race in congressional and legislative redistricting. [16] And in June 1995 the court issued a decision, *Adarand Constructors, Inc. v. Peña*, that limited the federal government's discretion to give minority-owned firms preferences in government contracting. [17]

With affirmative action under sharp attack, Bowen and Bok came out in 1998 with their book-length study of graduates of selective colleges that they said refuted many of the criticisms of race-based admissions. Using a database of some 80,000 students who entered 28 elite colleges and universities in 1951, 1976 and 1989, the two former Ivy League presidents confirmed the increase in minority enrollment at the schools and the impact of racial preferences: More than half the black students admitted in 1976 and 1989 would not have been admitted under race-neutral policies, they said. But they said dropout rates among black students were low, satisfaction with their college experiences high and post-graduation accomplishments comparable with — or better than — white graduates. [18]

The Bowen-Bok book buttressed college and university officials in resisting calls to scrap racial preferences. While voters in Washington state moved to eliminate race-based admissions with an anti-affirmative action initiative in 1998, no other state university system followed the UC lead in voluntarily abolishing the use of race in weighing applications.

In Texas, then-Gov. George W. Bush sought to bolster minority enrollment in the UT system after *Hopwood* by proposing the 10 percent plan — guaranteeing admission to any graduating senior in the top 10 percent of his class. (Florida Gov. Jeb Bush followed suit with his 20 percent plan two years later.) Many schools — both public and private — re-examined their admissions policies after *Hopwood*. But, according to Steinbach, most of them "found that what they had was satisfactory."

Legal Battles

C ritics of race-based admissions kept up their pressure on the issue by waging expensive, protracted legal battles in four states: Georgia, Michigan, Texas and Washington. The cases produced conflicting decisions. The conflict was starkest in the two University of Michigan cases, where two judges both appointed in the 1980s by President Ronald Reagan reached different results in evaluating the use of race at the undergraduate college and at the law school.

The controversy in Michigan began in a sense with the discontent of a longtime Ann Arbor faculty member, Carl Cohen. [19] A professor of philosophy and a "proud" member of the American Civil Liberties Union (ACLU), Cohen had been troubled by racial preferences since the 1970s. In 1995 he read a journal article that described admissions rates for black college applicants as higher nationally than those for white applicants. The article prompted Cohen to begin poking around to learn about Michigan's system. [20]

As Cohen tells the story, administrators stonewalled him until he used the state's freedom of information law to obtain the pertinent documents. He found that the admissions offices used a grid system that charted applicants based on high school grade point average on a horizontal axis and standardized test scores on a vertical axis — and that there were separate grids or different "action codes" (reject or admit) for white applicants and for minority applicants. "The racially discriminatory policies of the university are blatant," Cohen says today. "They are written in black and white by the university. It's just incredible."

Cohen wrote up his findings in a report that he presented later in the year at a meeting of the state chapter of the American Association of University Professors. The report also found its way to a Republican state legislator, Rep. Deborah Whyman, who conducted a hearing on the issue and later held a news conference to solicit unsuccessful applicants to challenge the university's admission system. They forwarded about 100 of the replies to the Center for Individual Rights, a conservative public-interest law firm already active in challenging racial preferences.

Gratz and a second unsuccessful white applicant — Patrick Hamacher — were chosen to be the named plaintiffs in a class-action suit filed in federal court in Detroit in October 1997. The center filed a second suit against

Evidence of Diversity Benefits Disputed

The University of Michigan is defending its race-based admissions policies not only with law but also evidence of the educational benefits of having a racially mixed student body. But opponents of racial preferences dismiss the evidence as distorted and biased.

The largest of the studies introduced as evidence in the two federal court lawsuits over the university's undergraduate and law school admissions policies runs 850 pages. Written by Patricia Gurin, chairman of the Psychology Department, it contains detailed statistics derived from a national student database and surveys of Michigan students. Gurin contends that students "learn more and think in deeper, more complex ways in a diverse educational environment." [1]

In addition, Gurin says students "are more motivated and better able to participate in an increasingly heterogeneous and complex democracy." And students who had "diversity experiences" during college — such as taking courses in Afro-American studies — also had "the most cross-racial interactions" five years after leaving college.

The National Association of Scholars, which opposes racial preferences, released two lengthy critiques of Gurin's study after the trials of the two suits. The studies were included in a friend-of-the-court brief filed in the appeals of the rulings. [2]

In the major critique, Thomas E. Wood and Malcolm J. Sherman contend that the national student database actually shows "no relationship" between the proportion of minorities on campus and educational benefits. They also say that "diversity activities" had only a "trivial impact" on educational outcomes.

The university also included "expert reports" from William G. Bowen and Derek Bok, the two former Ivy League university presidents who co-authored the pro-affirmative action book *The Shape of the River.* Bowen and Bok repeat their conclusions from the 1998 book that black students admitted to the "highly selective" colleges and universities studied did "exceedingly well" after college in terms of graduate degrees, income and civic life. [3] About half of the blacks admitted to the schools would not have been admitted under race-neutral policies, Bowen and Bok say.

In their reports for the Michigan suits, Bowen and Bok briefly acknowledge that black students at the schools had lower grades and lower graduation rates than whites. In an early critique of the book, two well-known critics of racial preferences — Abigail and Stephan Thernstrom — call Bowen and Bok to task for glossing over the evidence of poor performance by black students. They note that the dropout rate for black students — about 20 percent — was three times higher than for whites and that black students' grades overall were at the 23rd percentile — that is, in the bottom quarter. [4]

The studies are the tip of a large iceberg of academic literature that has sought to examine the effects of diversity in colleges and universities. In the most recent of the studies to be published, a team of authors from Pennsylvania State University concludes that the evidence is "almost uniformly consistent" that students in a racially or ethnically diverse community or engaged in "diversity-related" activities "reap a wide array of positive educational benefits." [5] In their own study of students at seven engineering schools, the scholars found what they called "a small, if statistically significant, link between the level of racial/ethnic diversity in a classroom and students' reports of increases in their problem-solving and group skills."

University of Michigan student Agnes Aleobua speaks out against a court ruling last March that the law school's race-based admission policy is illegal.

AP Photo/Paul Sancya

[1] Gurin's report can be found on the university's Web site: www.umich.edu.

[2] Thomas E. Wood and Malcolm J. Sherman, "Is Campus Racial Diversity Correlated With Educational Benefits?", National Association of Scholars, April 4, 2001 (www.nas.org). Wood is executive director of the California Association of Scholars; Sherman is an associate professor of mathematics and statistics at the State University of New York in Albany.

[3] William G. Bowen and Derek Bok, *The Shape of the River: Long-Term Consequences of Considering Race in College and University Admissions,* 1998. Bowen is a former president of Princeton University, Bok a former president of Harvard University.

[4] Stephan Thernstrom and Abigail Thernstrom, "Reflections on The Shape of the River," *UCLA Law Review,* Vol. 45, No. 5 (June 1999), pp. 1583-1631. Stephan Thernstrom is a history professor at Harvard; his wife is a senior fellow at the Manhattan Institute and a member of the Massachusetts Board of Education.

[5] Patrick T. Terenzini *et al.,* "Racial and Ethnic Diversity in the Classroom: Does It Promote Student Learning?", *Journal of Higher Education* (September/October 2001), pp. 509-531. Terenzini is a professor and senior scientist with the Center for the Study of Higher Education at Pennsylvania State University.

the law school's admission system in December 1997. The lead plaintiff was Barbara Grutter, who applied to the law school in December 1996 while in her 40s after raising a family and working as a health-care consultant. Grutter, who is white, thought she deserved admission based on her 3.8 undergraduate grade-point average 18 years earlier and a respectable score on the law school admission test (161, or 86th percentile nationally). Since the rejection, she has not enrolled elsewhere.

The cases proved to be long and expensive. By last fall, the university said it had spent $4.3 million defending the two suits, not counting personnel costs; the center had spent $400,000, including salaries, and also received the equivalent of $1 million in pro bono legal services from a Minneapolis firm helping to litigate the suits. Among the key pieces of evidence was a long report by an Ann Arbor faculty member — psychology Professor Patricia Gurin — concluding that diversity in enrollment has "far-reaching and significant benefits for all students, non-minorities and minorities alike." The center countered with a lengthy study issued under the auspices of the National Association of Scholars that analyzed the same data and found "no connection . . . between campus racial diversity and the supposed educational benefits."

In the meantime, the university revised its undergraduate admissions system, beginning with the entering class of 1999. The race-based grids and codes were replaced by a numerical system that assigned points to each applicant based on any of a number of characteristics. An applicant from an "under-represented minority group" — African-Americans, Hispanics and Native Americans — is given 20 points. (One hundred points is typically required for admission, according to Cohen.) The same number is given to an applicant from a disadvantaged socioeconomic status, to a white student from a pre-

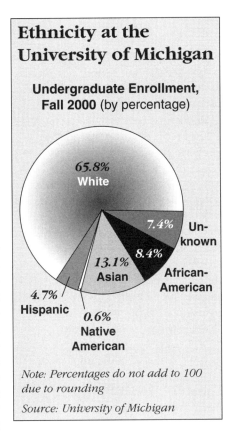

Ethnicity at the University of Michigan

Undergraduate Enrollment, Fall 2000 (by percentage)

65.8% White

7.4% Unknown

8.4% African-American

13.1% Asian

4.7% Hispanic

0.6% Native American

Note: Percentages do not add to 100 due to rounding

Source: University of Michigan

dominantly minority high school or to a scholarship athlete, according to university counsel Barry. The most important single factor, she adds, is an applicant's high school grades.

Judge Duggan's Dec. 13 ruling in the undergraduate case sustained the plaintiffs' complaint against the system used when Gratz and Hamacher had been rejected. Duggan said that the "facially different grids and action codes based solely upon an applicant's race" amounted to an "impermissible use of race." But Duggan said the revised system was on the right side of what he called "the thin line that divides the permissible and the impermissible."

Three months later, however, Judge Friedman on March 27 struck down the law school's admission system. Evidence showed that the school had used a "special admissions" program since 1992 aimed at a minority enrollment of 10 percent to 12 percent.

Friedman relied on a statistical analysis that showed an African-American applicant's relative odds of acceptance were up to 400 times as great as a white applicant's. Friedman rejected the use of diversity to justify the racial preferences, but in any event said the law school's system was not "narrowly tailored" because there was no time limit and there had been no consideration of alternative means of increasing minority enrollment.

The two Michigan cases took on added significance in June when the Supreme Court declined for a second time to hear Texas' appeal in the *Hopwood* case or to hear the plaintiffs' appeal of a ruling by the 9th U.S. Circuit Court of Appeals upholding a discontinued system of racial preferences at the University of Washington Law School. As the lawyers in the Michigan cases prepared for their scheduled appellate arguments, the 11th U.S. Circuit Court of Appeals issued a ruling on Aug. 27 striking down the University of Georgia's admissions system. With less extensive evidence in the Georgia case, however, legal observers viewed the two Michigan cases as the most likely to be accepted by the Supreme Court for its first full look at race-based admissions since *Bakke*. [21] ■

CURRENT SITUATION

Legal Confusion

A half-decade of legal and political challenges to race-based admissions policies has forced changes at some of the country's biggest state universities and produced widespread uncertainty throughout higher education.

"Colleges and universities are mystified with the confusing landscape as to what is and what is not permissible when it comes to admission practices," says Barmak Nassirian, associate executive director of the American Association of Collegiate Registrars and Admissions Officers. With the law unclear, Nassirian says, "institutions are essentially left to fend for themselves when it comes to compliance."

State universities in Texas and Florida are implementing new policies that eliminate explicit preferences for minority applicants but substitute guaranteed admission to high-ranking graduates of all high schools in the state — the top 10 percent of graduates in Texas, top 20 percent in Florida. The University of California in June approved a similar plan — guaranteeing admission to the top 12.5 percent of any high school class — that is to go into effect in fall 2003.

Both California and Texas reported significant declines in minority enrollment immediately after Proposition 209 and the *Hopwood* decision forced the state universities to eliminate racial preferences. Officials in Texas and Florida say the new policies are proving effective in minimizing the impact on minority enrollment.

Black and Hispanic enrollment dropped at the University of Texas and Texas A&M University immediately after *Hopwood*, but is now said to be back to levels immediately before the ruling. "It's maintained our course," state Rep. Irma Rangel, a Democrat and one of the authors of the 10 percent law, told the *Fort Worth Star-Telegram* earlier this year. [22]

University of Florida officials braced for reduced minority enrollment under the top 20 percent plan that first went into effect for the freshman class entering this fall. In June, university officials were projecting a drop in the number of African-American students — from 12 percent the previous year to 9 percent for the incoming class — but a modest increase in Hispanic students. "We expected we would have reductions here, but we've done everything we know how to keep it from happening," Charles E. Frazier, the university's vice provost, told The Associated Press. [23]

Public universities have the biggest problem in devising acceptable admissions policies, Nassirian says, because of the large number of applications they receive. Elite private universities have the resources to make a "very comprehensive assessment of an applicant's full portfolio," Nassirian explains. With more applications and fewer resources, he concludes, big state universities have to use less individualized ways "to make a first cut as to whose application moves up and gets reviewed."

The University of Georgia — which receives about 14,000 applications a year — defended its racial system by noting the difficulty of individual review, but the appeals court rejected the defense. "If UGA wants to ensure diversity through its admissions decisions, and wants race to be part of that calculus," Judge Stanley Marcus wrote, "then it must be prepared to shoulder the burden of fully and fairly analyzing applicants as individuals and not merely as members of groups." [24] For its part, the University of Michigan says every application is individually reviewed by one of 21 admissions counselors assigned to specific geographic areas.

Nassirian contends racial preferences are an issue only for a minority of colleges with selective admissions policies. For those schools, though, he says he hopes the Supreme Court will take up the issue soon.

"It is regrettable that the law of the land has to get so overly complicated that you need a whole team of attorneys to guess what is allowable and what is not," Nassirian says. "That is not generally a sign of health — when people cannot get definitive answers as to what the law is."

Legal Appeals

Opposing lawyers for the two major sides in the University of Michigan cases are projecting confidence as they prepare for Oct. 23 arguments in the most closely watched case on racial preferences in college admissions since *Bakke*.

The federal appeals court in Cincinnati has scheduled a total of 90 minutes to hear from lawyers representing the university, the plaintiffs and the minority intervenors in the undergraduate and law school cases — 15 minutes for each lawyer in each case. The three judges who will hear the case are to be picked at random shortly before the arguments: The court's 11 judges include five appointed by Republican presidents and six named by Democrats.

Representing the unsuccessful applicants, Rosman of the Center for Individual Rights says he is "cautiously optimistic" about the outcome. "We think we have a strong case, but you can never predict what a court will do," Rosman says. The university's attorney — John Payton, a lawyer with a prominent Washington law firm — says, "I feel very good about where we are."

Payton says *Bakke* is the key to the case, and he discounts the significance of the court rulings that have questioned its status as a precedent for using diversity to justify race-conscious admissions policies. "I don't think you can find a trend in that small group of cases," he says, "and I don't think there is a trend."

For his part, Rosman warns that justifying racial admissions policies on the basis of diversity could invite similar policies elsewhere in government. "If you think that racial diversity leads to intellectual foment that leads to new and better ideas, it's not clear why you wouldn't want to have different perspectives from different races in a lot of different areas of government," he says.

At Issue:

Should colleges eliminate the use of race in admissions?

THOMAS E. WOOD
EXECUTIVE DIRECTOR, CALIFORNIA ASSOCIATION OF SCHOLARS, CO-AUTHOR OF CALIFORNIA PROP. 209

WRITTEN FOR THE CQ RESEARCHER, SEPTEMBER 2001

colleges should eliminate the use of race in admissions. One cannot prefer on the basis of race without discriminating against others on the basis of race. Treating people differently on the basis of their race violates the Constitution's guarantee of equal protection under the laws.

There is only one national database for higher education that is in a position to adequately address this question whether, or to what extent, campus racial diversity is a necessary component of educational excellence. So far, the American Council on Education/Higher Education Research Institute database has failed to find any connection between campus racial diversity and any of the 82 cognitive and non-cognitive outcome variables incorporated in the study.

Proponents claim that the abandonment of racial classifications will result in the resegregation of higher education. Since preferences have been used to increase the number of minorities in the past, their abandonment will lead in the near term to lower numbers for minorities (though only in the most elite institutions of higher education).

But the claim that abandoning the use of race in college admissions will lead to resegregation implies that all or virtually all minorities who are presently enrolled in the most elite institutions are there only because they have been given preferences, which is both untrue and demeaning. The claim also ignores the fact that the country was making significant progress toward diversity *before* the advent of racial preferences in university admissions in the mid-to-late 1970s.

This analysis is confirmed by the experience of Texas, California and Washington, which already have bans on racial classifications in university admissions. The experience in these states has been that while there is an initial decline when racial classifications are abandoned (though only in the most elite institutions), the underlying trend toward greater diversity resumes after the initial correction.

For some, of course, any regression from the numbers that are obtainable through the use of preferences is unacceptable. At its heart, this is the view that racial diversity is a value that trumps all others. But that is a view that has clearly been rejected by the courts, and for good reason. Diversity is an important public policy goal, but there is a right way and a wrong way to pursue it. Racial classifications are the wrong way.

ANGELO ANCHETA
DIRECTOR, LEGAL AND ADVOCACY PROGRAMS, CIVIL RIGHTS PROJECT, HARVARD LAW SCHOOL

WRITTEN FOR THE CQ RESEARCHER, SEPTEMBER 2001

affirmative action policies advance the tenet that colleges, like the workplace and our public institutions, should reflect the full character of American society. Race-conscious admissions policies not only promote the integration ideal first realized in *Brown v. Board of Education* but also help create educational environments that improve basic learning and better equip students for an increasingly diverse society.

The U.S. Supreme Court upheld race-conscious admissions over 20 years ago in *Regents of the University of California v. Bakke*. Yet, affirmative action opponents, armed with the rhetoric of quotas and tokenism for the unqualified, persist in trying to undermine *Bakke*. Educators know that quotas are illegal under *Bakke* and that granting admission to the unqualified serves no one's interest. Colleges have been highly circumspect, employing carefully crafted policies that consider all applicants competitively and that use race as only one of many factors in admissions decisions.

Nevertheless, recent litigation challenging affirmative action in Texas, Washington, Georgia and Michigan portends that the Supreme Court will soon revisit *Bakke*. But the case that promoting educational diversity is, in the language of the law, "a compelling governmental interest" and that race-conscious admissions policies can best serve that interest has only strengthened in recent years.

The latest findings show that student-body diversity significantly improves the quality of higher education. Studies at the University of Michigan have found that diverse learning environments can enhance students' critical-thinking skills, augment their understanding and tolerance of different opinions and groups, increase their motivation and participation in civic activities and better prepare them for living in a diverse society. Several studies support these findings and further show that interaction across races has positive effects on retention rates, satisfaction with college, self-confidence and leadership ability.

Without race-conscious admissions, the student-body diversity necessary to advance these educational outcomes would be lost. The declining enrollment of minority students at public universities that have abandoned affirmative action strongly suggests that the "color-blind" path is not the path to equal opportunity; nor is it the path to the highest-quality education.

Affirmative action policies reflect the reality that race has always shaped our educational institutions. Justice Blackmun's admonition in *Bakke* thus remains as vital as ever: "In order to get beyond racism, we must first take account of race. There is no other way."

Payton thinks the evidence introduced by the university to defend its policies may influence the judges. "The social-science evidence confirms the consensus among educators that there is a very significant educational impact [from having] a diverse student body," he says. Rosman is dubious. "I don't think they're going to be too overwhelmingly fascinated by the social-science evidence," he says.

Both sides have drawn support from outside groups in the form of friend-of-the-court briefs, but the university rallied a more impressive list of allies. More than a dozen briefs supporting the university's position were filed by, among others, the American Bar Association, General Motors, a group of 33 other *Fortune* 500 companies, and a long roster of higher education and civil rights groups. The eight briefs in support of the plaintiffs came from such conservative groups as the National Association of Scholars, the Center for Equal Opportunity and the Independent Women's Forum.

The minority intervenors will also repeat their arguments that the race-conscious admissions policies are justified as a remedy for the university's overt discrimination in the past and the disparate impact of other admissions policies on minorities. They face an uphill fight since both judges rejected their arguments. But Miranda Massie, the Detroit lawyer representing minority students in the law school case, says pro-affirmative action groups will mount a march and rally in Cincinnati on the day of the appeals court hearing.

Whatever the three-judge panel decides, the losing parties are certain to appeal to the Supreme Court. "Eventually, the Supreme Court will decide in all probability," Univeristy of Michigan President Bollinger says. Rosman agrees: "To the extent that the Supreme Court can resolve the uncertainty, it would be appropriate." ∎

OUTLOOK

Ideals and Reality

Michigan graduate Jennifer Gratz and President Bollinger agree that someday colleges should stop using race as a factor in admissions decisions. "They can make up whatever policy they want as long as they as don't discriminate," Gratz says.

Bollinger, too, says he views color-blind admissions as an ultimate goal. "If it eventually came about that we got racial and ethnic diversity without taking race or ethnicity into account, we would no longer do so," Bollinger says.

Critics think the time for abolishing racial preferences has come. "We don't think institutionalized discrimination against African-Americans any longer exists," says Clegg of the Center for Equal Opportunity. "So institutionalized discrimination in their favor shouldn't exist."

Supporters say the critics overestimate the racial progress made since the peak of the civil rights era in the mid-1960s. "Thirty-five years — when you stack it up against 300 years — is peanuts," says Shaw of the NAACP Legal Defense Fund. "To think that we have solved all of these problems in 35 years is shortsighted and just wrong."

Public opinion and political sentiment on the issue appear to be somewhat malleable. Polls generally register support for "affirmative action" and opposition to "racial preferences." At Michigan, Cohen says he has few faculty allies in opposing race-conscious admissions. As for students, "it seems to me plain that a majority supports the university's position," he says.

Democrats in Congress have generally defended affirmative action even when the issue was hot in the mid-1990s. Republican leaders initially staked out positions against preferences after taking control of Congress

following the 1994 elections, but then put the issue on a back burner.

The Supreme Court has also charted an uncertain course on the issue. The justices are divided along ideological lines on the issue, with the five conservatives generally opposed to racial policies and aligned against the four more liberal justices: John Paul Stevens, David H. Souter, Ruth Bader Ginsburg and Stephen G. Breyer.

Two of the conservatives — Scalia and Thomas — have staked out the strongest position against considering race in government policies. But O'Connor has a pivotal vote on the subject and has consistently stopped short of flatly prohibiting the government from taking race into account in employment, contracting or redistricting.

Bollinger — a legal scholar as well as university administrator — says *Bakke* remains "a firm constitutional precedent" for the university's policy. He says he is optimistic about the outcome of the two lawsuits — and about the future course of race relations in academia and beyond.

"I really do believe people of good sense will see the importance of maintaining the course that *Brown v. Board of Education* put us on — to work very hard on issues of race and ethnicity in this society," Bollinger says. "We have much to learn, much to overcome, and our great educational institutions are one of the most meaningful ways of addressing the experience of race."

For her part, Gratz says she had a "diverse group" of friends in high school and college, but acknowledges they were predominantly other whites. Still, she believes race relations in the United States today are "pretty good."

"I think that the more emphasis that we put on race, the more people are going to look at race," she concludes. "And I would like to see that in the future we really do have equal opportunity for all, regardless of race."

Does she think that will happen? "Yes," Gratz says, "it can happen." ∎

Notes

[1] For extensive information on both cases, including the texts of the two rulings and other legal documents, see the University of Michigan's Web site (www.umich.edu) or the Web site of the public-interest law firm representing the plaintiffs, the Center for Individual Rights (www.cir-usa.org).

[2] The legal citation is 438 U.S. 265; Supreme Court decisions can be found on a number of Web sites, including the court's official site: www.supremecourtus.gov. For background, see Kenneth Jost, "Rethinking Affirmative Action," *The CQ Researcher*, April 28, 1995, pp. 369-392.

[3] See Robert Lerner and Althea K. Nagai, "Pervasive Preferences: Racial and Ethnic Discrimination in Undergraduate Admissions Across the Nation," Center for Equal Opportunity, Feb. 22, 2001 (www.ceo-usa.org).

[4] For background, see David Masci, "Hispanic Americans' New Clout," *The CQ Researcher*, Sept. 18, 1998, pp. 809-832; David Masci, "The Black Middle Class," *The CQ Researcher*, Jan. 23, 1998, pp. 49-72; and Kenneth Jost, "Diversity in the Workplace," *The CQ Researcher*, Oct. 10, 1997, pp. 889-912.

[5] Charles R. Lawrence III and Mari J. Matsuda, *We Won't Go Back: Making the Case for Affirmative Action* (1997), p. 127. Matsuda, Lawrence's wife, is also a professor at Georgetown law school.

[6] For background, see Joan Biskupic and Elder Witt, *Guide to the U.S. Supreme Court* (3d ed.), 1997, pp. 362-363. The cases discussed are *Missouri ex rel. Gaines v. Canada*, 305 U.S. 337 (1938); *Sweatt v. Painter*, 339 U.S. 629 (1950); and *McLaurin v. Oklahoma State Regents for Higher Education*, 339 U.S. 637 (1950).

[7] William G. Bowen and Derek Bok, *The Shape of the River: Long-Term Consequences of Considering Race in College and University Admissions* (1998), pp. 4-5. Bowen, a former president of Princeton University, is now president of the Andrew W. Mellon Foundation in New York City; Bok is a former president of Harvard University and now University Professor at the John. F. Kennedy School of Government at Harvard.

[8] Reprinted in Gabriel J. Chin (ed.), *Affirmative Action and the Constitution: Affirmative Action Before Constitutional Law, 1964-1977*, Vol. 1 (1998), pp. 21-26.

[9] Bowen and Bok, *op. cit.*, pp. 6-7.

[10] Description of the announcement of the decision taken from Bernard Schwartz, *Behind Bakke: Affirmative Action and the Supreme Court* (1988), pp. 142-150.

[11] The cases are *Wygant v. Jackson Bd. of Education*, 476 U.S. 267 (1986); *Johnson v. Transportation Agency of Santa Clara County* 480 U.S. 646 (1987); *City of Richmond v. J.A. Croson Co.* 488 U.S. 469 (1989); and *Adarand Constructors, Inc. v. Peña* 575 U.S. 200 (1995).

[12] Lincoln Caplan, *Up Against the Law: Affirmative Action and the Supreme Court* (1997), p. 16.

[13] The case is *Hopwood v. Texas*. Some background on this and other cases in this section drawn from Girardeau A. Spann, *The Law of Affirmative Action: Twenty-Five Years of Supreme Court Decisions on Race and Remedies* (2000).

[14] The legal citation is *Hopwood v. Texas*, 78 F.2d 932 (5th Cir. 1996). In a subsequent decision, the appeals court on Dec. 21, 2000, reaffirmed its legal holding, but upheld the lower court judge's finding that none of the four plaintiffs would have been admitted to the law school under a race-blind system. See *Hopwood v. Texas*, 236 F.2d 256 (5th Cir. 2000).

[15] Quoted in Facts on File, March 28, 1996.

[16] For background, see Jennifer Gavin, "Redistricting," *The CQ Researcher*, Feb. 16, 2001, pp. 113-128; Nadine Cahodas, "Electing Minorities," *The CQ Researcher*, Aug. 12, 1994, pp. 697-720.

[17] The legal citation is 515 U.S. 200.

[18] For a critique, see Stephan and Abigail Thernstrom, "Reflections on the Shape of the River," *UCLA Law Review*, Vol. 46, No. 5 (June 1999), pp. 1583-1631.

[19] For a good overview, see Nicholas Lemann, "The Empathy Defense," *The New Yorker*, Dec. 18, 2000, pp. 46-51. See also Carl Cohen, "Race Preference and the Universities — A Final Reckoning," *Commentary*, September 2001, pp. 31-39.

[20] "Vital Signs: The Statistics that Describe the Present and Suggest the Future of African Americans in Higher Education," *The Journal of Blacks in Higher Education*, No. 9 (autumn 1995), pp. 43-49.

[21] The Washington case is *Smith v. University of Washington Law School*, 9th Circuit, Dec. 4, 2000; the Georgia case is *Johnson v. Board of Regents of the University of Georgia*, 11th Circuit, Aug. 27.

[22] See Crystal Yednak, "Laws Meant to Boost Diversity Paying Off," *Fort Worth Star-Telegram*, Jan. 13, 2001, p. 1.

[23] Ron Word, "State Universities Have Differing Results Recruiting Minorities," The Associated Press, June 19, 2001.

[24] See Edward Walsh, "Affirmative Action's Confusing Curriculum," *The Washington Post*, Sept. 4, 2001, p. A2.

FOR MORE INFORMATION

American Council on Education, 1 Dupont Circle, N.W., Suite 800, Washington, D.C. 20036; (202) 939-9300; www.acenet.edu. The council was the lead organization in a friend-of-the-court brief filed by 30 higher-education groups in support of the University of Michigan's race-conscious admissions policies.

Center for Equal Opportunity, 14 Pidgeon Hill Dr., Suite 500, Sterling, Va. 20165; (703) 421-5443; www.ceousa.org. The center filed a friend-of-the-court brief in support of the plaintiffs challenging University of Michigan admissions policies.

Center for Individual Rights, 1233 20th St., N.W., Washington, D.C. 20036; (202) 833-8400; www.cir-usa.org. The public-interest law firm represents plaintiffs in the University of Michigan cases and others challenging race-conscious admission policies.

NAACP Legal Defense and Educational Fund, 99 Hudson St., Suite 1600, New York, N.Y. 10013; (212) 965-2200; www.naacpldf.org. The Legal Defense Fund represents the minority student intervenors in the two suits contesting admission policies at the University of Michigan.

National Association of Scholars, 221 Witherspoon St., Second Floor, Princeton, N.J. 08542-3215; (609) 683-7878; www.nas.org. The organization studies and advocates on academic issues including race-based admissions policies.

Bibliography

Selected Sources

Books

Bowen, William G., and Derek Bok, *The Shape of the River: Long-Term Consequences of Considering Race in College and University Admissions*, **Princeton University Press, 1998.**

The book analyzes data on 80,000 students admitted to 28 selective private or public colleges and universities in 1951, 1976 and 1989 to examine the impact of race-based admissions on enrollment and to compare the educational and post-graduation experiences of white and minority students. Includes statistical tables as well as a nine-page list of references. Bowen, a former president of Princeton University, heads the Andrew W. Mellon Foundation; Bok is a former president of Harvard University and now a professor at Harvard's John F. Kennedy School of Government.

Caplan, Lincoln, *Up Against the Law: Affirmative Action and the Supreme Court*, **Twentieth Century Fund Press, 1997.**

The 60-page monograph provides an overview of the Supreme Court's affirmative action rulings with analysis written from a pro race-conscious policies perspective. Caplan, a longtime legal-affairs writer, is a senior writer in residence at Yale Law School.

Chin, Gabriel J. (ed.), *Affirmative Action and the Constitution: Affirmative Action Before Constitutional Law, 1964-1977* **(Vol. 1);** *The Supreme Court "Solves" the Affirmative Action Issue, 1978-1988* **(Vol. 2);** *Judicial Reaction to Affirmative Action, 1988-1997* **(Vol. 3), Garland Publishing, 1998.**

The three-volume compendium includes a variety of materials on affirmative action from President Lyndon B. Johnson's famous speech at Howard University in 1965 to President Bill Clinton's defense of affirmative action in 1995 as well as the full text of the federal appeals court decision in the 1995 *Hopwood* decision barring racial preferences at the University of Texas Law School. Chin, who wrote an introduction for each volume, is a professor at the University of Cincinnati College of Law.

Edley, Christopher Jr., *Not All Black and White: Affirmative Action, Race, and American Values*, **Hill & Wang, 1996.**

Edley, a Harvard Law School professor, recounts his role in overseeing the Clinton administration's review of affirmative action in 1995 as part of a broad look at the issue that ends with measured support for affirmative action "until the justification for it no longer exists."

Schwartz, Bernard, *Behind Bakke: Affirmative Action and the Supreme Court*, **New York University Press.**

Schwartz, a leading Supreme Court scholar until his death in 1997, was granted unusual access to the private papers of the justices for this detailed, behind-the-scenes account of the *Bakke* case from its origins through the justices' deliberations and final decision.

Spann, Girardeau A., *The Law of Affirmative Action: Twenty-Five Years of Supreme Court Decisions on Races and Remedies*, **New York University Press, 2000.**

The book includes summaries — concise and precise — of major Supreme Court decisions from *Bakke* in 1978 to *Adarand* in 1995 Spann is a professor at Georgetown University Law Center.

Steele, Shelby, *A Dream Deferred: The Second Betrayal of Black Freedom in America*, **HarperCollins, 1998.**

Steele, a prominent black critic of affirmative action and a research fellow at the Hoover Institution at Stanford University, argues in four essays that affirmative action represents an "extravagant" liberalism that "often betrayed America's best principles" in order to atone for white guilt over racial injustice.

Articles

Lawrence, Charles R. III, "Two Views of the River: A Critique of the Liberal Defense of Affirmative Action," *Columbia Law Review*, **Vol. 101, No. 4 (May 2001), pp. 928-975.**

Lawrence argues that liberals' "diversity" defense of affirmative action overlooks "more radical substantive" arguments based on "the need to remedy past discrimination, address present discriminatory practices, and reexamine traditional notions of merit and the role of universities in the reproduction of elites." Lawrence is a professor at Georgetown University Law Center.

PBS NewsHour, "Admitting for Diversity," Aug. 21, 2001 (www.pbs.org/newshour).

The report by correspondent Elizabeth Brackett features interviews with, among others, Barbara Grutter, the plaintiff in the lawsuit challenging the University of Michigan Law School's race-based admissions policies, and the law school's dean, Jeffrey Lehman.

Thernstrom, Stephan, and Abigail Thernstrom, "Reflections on The Shape of the River," *UCLA Law Review*, **Vol. 46, No. 5 (June 1999), pp. 1583-1631.**

The Thernstroms contend that racial preferences constitute a "pernicious palliative" that deflect attention from real educational problems and conflict with the country's unrealized egalitarian dream. Stephan Thernstrom is a professor of history at Harvard University; his wife Abigail is a senior fellow at the Manhattan Institute and a member of the Massachusetts State Board of Education. An earlier version appeared in Commentary (February 1999).

6 Retirement Security

MARY H. COOPER

D eborah Perrotta was ecstatic when Enron Corp. hired her as a senior administrative assistant in 1998. The Houston energy giant was one of corporate America's shiniest stars, and its stock had reflected that success with dizzying returns.

"Enron offered tremendous compensation and benefits packages and rewarded employees who exhibited unfailing loyalty and worked hard for the company's success," Perrotta said. "I believed the company would live up to its promises, and that by working hard I would be able to secure my financial future." [1]

Perrotta's dream job disintegrated last December — together with her retirement savings and those of thousands of other Enron workers — when the company filed for bankruptcy. Their losses, estimated in excess of $1 billion from retirement accounts invested in now-worthless Enron stock, prompted widespread outrage when it became apparent that corporate leaders had quietly sold some of their own highly valued company shares long before news of the impending collapse became public knowledge. Meanwhile, Enron employees were barred from selling their shares, even after their value had plummeted. [2]

"This isn't right," Perrotta told a congressional committee investigating the Enron bankruptcy's impact on retirement savings. "We put our money in the company's stock in good faith, and Enron's leadership and the government let us down." Lawmakers are now considering legislation to limit the amount of

From *The CQ Researcher,*
May 31, 2002.

Richard Parsons, co-chairman of President Bush's Social Security Commission, speaks at a public hearing in Washington, D.C. on Oct. 18, 2001.

AP Photo/Stephen J. Boitano

company stock an employer can require workers to invest in their employer-sponsored retirement savings accounts, called 401(k) plans. *

Almost lost in the outrage over the plight of Enron employees, however, is the fact that most Americans have not saved enough to live comfortably after they retire, even if they manage to avoid working for a company with Enron-style mismanagement and fraud. Overall, Americans save less than people in every other industrialized country, except New Zealand. (*See graph, p. 100.*) To make matters worse, according to the World Bank, the personal savings rate in the United States plummeted from 4.8 percent of income in the 1980s to 0.4 percent in 1998. [3]

---

*401(k) plans are named after the section of the 1978 Revenue Act that authorized them.

Among U.S. workers nearing retirement — those ages 47 to 64 — only those with more than $1 million in assets have increased their retirement savings since the early 1980s, when 401(k) plans became popular, according to the nonpartisan Economic Policy Institute. For all other income groups, instead of raising retirees' overall wealth, as was hoped, the shift to 401(k)s — known as defined-contribution plans — has been accompanied by an average 11 percent drop in retiree wealth, which includes Social Security benefits and pension balances. [4]

"Clearly, people have not saved enough," says Michael Tanner, director of health and welfare studies at the libertarian Cato Institute, which advocates a diminished role for government. "We're moving to a real class divide between savers and non-savers, and that's worrisome because wealth comes from savings and investment these days, not from wages."

Unfortunately, few workers seem to realize just how grim their golden years may turn out to be. According to a recent survey by the nonpartisan Employee Benefit Research Institute (EBRI), 70 percent of working-age Americans are confident they will have enough savings to live comfortably in retirement, although only 67 percent say they have any retirement savings at all. [5]

One reason so many Americans appear to be in denial about the prospect of declining living standards after they retire is the sheer complexity of estimating just how much money they need to set aside for retirement. Thanks to advances in medical technology, seniors can look forward to healthier, longer retirements than their

Americans Save Less Than Most Others

Americans save less than people in every industrialized nation, except New Zealand. The U.S. household savings rate has declined from 10.6 percent in 1984 to today's record low of 1.0 percent. Savings rates are on the decline in other countries as well.

Household Savings Rates
(as a percentage of disposable income)

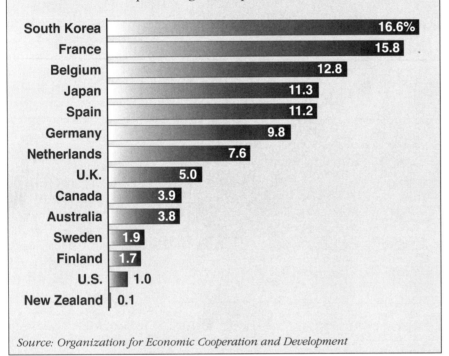

South Korea	16.6%
France	15.8
Belgium	12.8
Japan	11.3
Spain	11.2
Germany	9.8
Netherlands	7.6
U.K.	5.0
Canada	3.9
Australia	3.8
Sweden	1.9
Finland	1.7
U.S.	1.0
New Zealand	0.1

Source: Organization for Economic Cooperation and Development

parents. But increased longevity also requires a bigger nest egg to pay for those additional years, not to mention the costly medical treatments and nursing home stays that may accompany the passage to extreme old age. Workers are being asked to guess whether they will be among these survivors and to save accordingly.

"One of the most complex economic calculations that most workers will ever undertake, without doubt, is deciding how much to save for retirement," said Federal Reserve Chairman Alan Greenspan. "The difficulty in making these projections and choices is compounded by the need to forecast personal and economic events many years into the future." [6]

Financial experts used to help workers plan for their future by describing retirement savings as a three-legged stool. One leg was Social Security, the federal pension system financed by active workers. Another was the corporate pension plan, providing fixed monthly payments funded by employers who chose to offer them as a way to attract workers. The third leg was the pensioner's private savings accumulated over his or her working life. Taken together, these three sources offered the promise of a comfortable standard of living once they retired.

But today the retirement savings stool is wobbly at best. Social Security faces a financing crisis in the coming decades,

as the huge Baby Boom generation retires in droves, leaving a shrunken work force to pay for their promised benefits. Traditional corporate pensions — known as defined-benefit plans — increasingly are being replaced by the 401(k) defined-contribution plans, shifting much of the investment risk from employers to workers. Under 401(k)s workers decide how to invest their pensions. Finally, despite growing familiarity with mutual funds and stocks during the stock market boom of the 1990s, the personal savings rate in the United States has actually been declining in recent years.

"People continue to talk about a three-legged stool, but pensions don't really exist any more in a meaningful way," says Jeff Mandell, director of the 2030 Center, a public policy organization representing young adults ages 20 to 30. Because traditional pensions are giving way to worker-financed 401(k) plans, he says, the pension leg has merged into the personal savings leg. "So we've gone from a three-legged stool to a two-legged stool, and it's very difficult to balance on a two-legged stool."

To make matters worse, many people enter retirement without any personal savings at all, Mandell says, depending on Social Security as the sole source of their income. "Now we're talking about a one-legged stool, which is worse than a unicycle," he says. "It's like riding a pogo stick into your retirement."

The federal government is trying to strengthen the retirement savings system and to encourage Americans to save more. "Saving is the path to independence for Americans in all phases of life, and we must encourage more Americans to take that path," President Bush told the 2002 National Summit on Retirement Savings on Feb. 28 in Washington. "We're going to have to encourage more savings in America because people are going to live longer lives."

Shortly after entering the White House, Bush appointed a bipartisan commission to recommend ways to strengthen the Social Security system. Last December, the commission endorsed a proposal touted by Bush during his presidential campaign, which would allow workers to set up personal retirement accounts (PRAs), taking some of the money withheld from their payroll checks to pay for Social Security and investing it as they see fit.

Republicans and other supporters of PRAs say they would boost retirement savings because stocks historically have outperformed the conservative investments the Social Security trustees are required to make with payroll-tax revenues.

Democrats and other critics say the proposal would amount to "privatization" of one of the last remaining threads of the safety net set up in the 1930s for seniors and disadvantaged workers, who have little knowledge of investments.

In the wake of the Enron debacle, Congress is trying to make it harder for unscrupulous employers to clean out employees' 401(k) accounts, but it has done little to deal with the erosion of private pension coverage.

Traditional, defined-benefit pension plans were always most common in large, unionized manufacturing companies. But since the 1970s both manufacturing jobs and union membership in the United States have been declining, and companies have restricted or abandoned those pension plans in favor of 401(k)s.

Under the new plans, workers may end up with fatter payouts than they would have received in a traditional pension check, but only if they contribute generously to their accounts and happen to pick investments that pay handsome returns.

But relatively few workers are doing either. "You don't get anything out of a 401(k) unless you can afford to

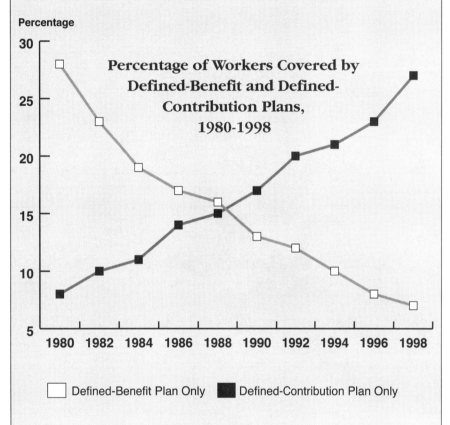

Retirement Burden Shifts to Workers

Many employers have shifted the burden of retirement savings to employees by replacing traditional, employer-financed pensions (called defined-benefit plans) with 401(k) and other "defined-contribution" plans funded primarily by employees. Participation in a 401(k) is voluntary, and the level of retirement income will depend on how well the participants invest their contributions. About half of U.S. workers have employer-sponsored pension plans.

Percentage of Workers Covered by Defined-Benefit and Defined-Contribution Plans, 1980-1998

☐ Defined-Benefit Plan Only   ■ Defined-Contribution Plan Only

Source: Bureau of Labor Statistics, U.S. Department of Labor, Pension and Welfare Benefits Administration, Private Pension Plan Bulletin, *winter 2001-2002, p. 68.*

contribute to it in the first place," says Karen Ferguson, director of the Pension Rights Center, a Washington consumer organization. According to the Census Bureau, the median annual income for full-time, year-round workers is about $32,000 a year. [7] "For people at that income level, who live paycheck to paycheck and have a lot of bills to pay, saving for retirement seems a bit remote, and understandably so."

Ferguson and other critics blame the switch to 401(k)s for Americans' inadequate retirement savings. "All of our major global competitors have a very paternalistic approach toward retirement because they recognize that it isn't really realistic to ask people in the middle of their lives, with other financial pressures, to think about retirement," she says. "But here in the United States, we're in this brave new world where do-it-yourself retirement has become all the rage."

The 401(k)s work, she says, only if an employee can afford to put money in a 401(k), keep it in, take risks on higher returns, does not work for a company like Enron and does not invest all of his retirement savings in company stock. "For the most part, however, people can't afford to contribute early enough or in large enough amounts to provide the very significant amounts that they'll need in retirement," she adds.

Some experts predict that lawmakers will go beyond the current debate over Social Security reform and consider broader policies affecting Americans' retirement security. "With the recession, the end of the stock market boom, the events of Sept. 11 and Enron, suddenly people are realizing how lousy pension coverage really is in this country," says Roger Hickey, co-director of the Campaign for America's Future, a Washington group that advocates policies to help working people. "Right now we're just in the debating and discussion phase, but it's a very, very big shift from the days during the boom when everybody assumed that if you just participate in the stock market you're going to do well."

As lawmakers and pension experts explore how to enhance Americans' retirement security, these are some of the issues they will consider:

Should workers be allowed to invest part of their Social Security payroll taxes on their own?

For several decades lawmakers have known that demographics would force them to overhaul the Social Security system if it was to survive past the early 21st century. The huge Baby Boom generation — Americans born between 1946 and 1964 — will begin retiring in 2012, when the first boomers reach the Social Security retirement age of 66.

Social Security was founded as a pay-as-you-go system. That is, current workers pay the benefits of current retirees through a special tax on all income up to $76,200. When the system was established in the mid-1930s, about 42 workers supported each retiree, so only a 2 percent payroll tax was needed to fund the system. Today, there are only 3.4 workers per retiree, and the tax now stands at 12.4 percent, half of which is paid by the worker and half by the employer. By 2030, if the boomers are to receive full Social Security benefits, the worker-to-retiree ratio is expected to be less than 2 to 1, and payroll taxes would have to increase to an estimated 19 percent.

President Bush campaigned on a promise to reform Social Security by allowing workers to open personal retirement savings accounts. Employees would be allowed to invest part of their payroll tax contributions in stocks and other securities, which historically have outperformed the lackluster, but safe Treasury bills where Social Security trust fund monies are invested.

"Today, young workers who pay into Social Security might as well be saving their money in their mattresses," Bush said after his election, as he created the President's Commission to Strengthen Social Security to recommend ways to incorporate private savings into the system. "Personal savings accounts will transform Social Security from a government IOU into personal property and real assets — property that workers will own in their own names and that they can pass along to their children." [8]

Last December the commission released its recommendations, which endorsed the president's call to partially privatize the system. "Social Security will be strengthened if modernized to include a system of voluntary personal accounts," the commission concluded. The three different models suggested by the commission for setting up personal savings accounts would allow workers to invest up to two-thirds of their payroll tax contributions. [9]

Supporters of the recommendation say it will enable less-affluent workers to enjoy the high returns of stock investing, which until now mainly have benefited wealthier Americans. "Social Security privatization . . . gives low-income people an avenue for investment because they're already paying that money now," says Tanner at the Cato Institute, adding that such an approach is more fiscally sound than the alternative: raising the payroll tax. "This will not require any additional spending on

Demonstrators support President Bush's plan for personal retirement accounts (PRAs) during a meeting of the President's Commission to Strengthen Social Security, on Aug. 22, 2001, in Washington. PRAs would permit individuals to invest some of their Social Security taxes in the stock market.

Getty Images/Shawn Thew

their part but will allow these workers to get into a form of investment."

Under Social Security, women receive lower benefits than men because of the way benefits are calculated and because women sometimes enter and exit the work force repeatedly during their childbearing years — thus contributing less to the system than men. (*See story, p. 112.*)

Some women's advocates say private accounts would overcome Social Security's inherent gender bias. "Because of their work force behavior patterns, private retirement accounts would be a very positive measure for women," says Celeste Colgan, project director for Women in the Economy at the National Center for Policy Analysis, a nonprofit organization that supports private-sector alternatives to government regulation.

"When a woman drops out of the work force, she just loses out with Social Security today because she's not making those tax payments into the system while she's not working. If she had some part of those taxes working for her and growing right along with the economy in stock index funds or other investments, she would be much farther ahead when she came back to work."

Despite President Bush's pitch to Generation X workers — boomers' kids now in their late 20s to mid-30s — not all of them are buying the promise of personal savings accounts. "We should not deviate from the fundamental principles the system was built on," says Mandell of the 2030 Center, so named both for the age group it represents and the year the Social Security trust fund was once expected to run out of money. "To privatize the system would violate the values it is built upon and weaken some of the program's most important components."

For example, privatization would not ensure continued survivors' and disability benefits, Mandell notes, which a third of Social Security beneficiaries receive, many of them young people. "Social Security provides you with an insurance

A woman in New York City demonstrates against the president's plan to create personal retirement accounts during a speech in support of PRAs by Treasury Secretary Paul O'Neill at the Coalition for American Financial Security. Critics say PRAs would amount to privatizing the federal pension plan.

policy so that if anything happens to you, you and your family will not fall into poverty," he says. "That's an insurance policy that most of us could not afford. Yet privatization completely undermines that aspect of the program."

And while Bush points to the higher potential income from private accounts, Mandell says that potential is not worth the risk of stock market investing. "Risk is antithetical to security," he says. "It is possible that for some people of my generation it would provide larger benefits in the end, but the tradeoffs would be terrible. The rhetoric of privatization is most appealing in some ways to those most in need of benefits, but the effects of the policy would be disproportionately harsh to those in need."

Finally, says Mandell, who is 26, privatization would undermine the retirement security of his and his constituents' parents, because their private accounts under the Bush proposal may not have earned enough in the 10 to 15 years before they retire. "Social Security today guarantees that our parents and grandparents won't come knocking at our doors saying it's time to move in," he says.

Critics of privatization say reform supporters have exaggerated the system's solvency problems to build support for privatization, without acknowledging the risk that change poses to retirees' financial security.

According to Ferguson of the Pension Rights Center, a payroll tax increase of only about 1 percent would suffice to ensure the trust fund's solvency, though she readily acknowledges that lawmakers are unlikely to support a tax boost of any amount during an election year.

"A lot of money has been invested in support of privatizing Social Security and the notion that everybody can be a millionaire," Ferguson adds. "It's easy for supporters of privatization to convince people to take all these risks because they won't be around to pick up the pieces."

Should employers be required to help workers fund their retirement plans?

The second leg of retirement savings, the corporate pension plan, is only as strong as an employer's will to provide it and maintain its viability. The government does not require employers to offer pension benefits of

Poorest Retirees Rely Most on Social Security

The poorest one-fifth of American retirees received 80 percent of their income in 2000 from Social Security, while the wealthiest retirees relied on it for less than 20 percent. Wealthy seniors rely on personal investments and earnings from work for most of their income, compared with 4 percent for poor people.

Sources of Retiree Income, 2000

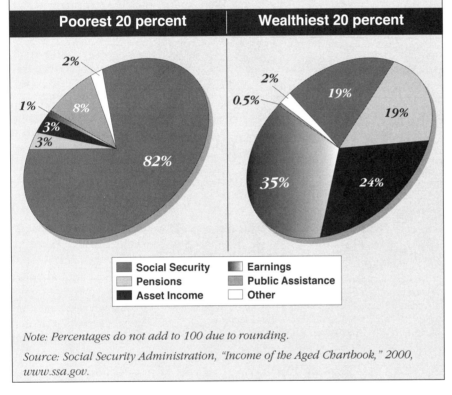

Poorest 20 percent

2%
1%
8%
3%
3%
82%

Wealthiest 20 percent

2%
0.5%
19%
19%
35%
24%

Legend:
- Social Security
- Pensions
- Asset Income
- Earnings
- Public Assistance
- Other

Note: Percentages do not add to 100 due to rounding.

Source: Social Security Administration, "Income of the Aged Chartbook," 2000, www.ssa.gov.

any kind, and the percentage of American workers who are covered by corporate pensions is declining. Today, only half of the employees of the nation's largest employers — the so-called *Fortune* 100 companies — are covered by traditional pensions, down from 89 percent in 1985. [10] Overall, only 60 percent of Americans participate in some kind of employment-based pension plan, mostly 401(k)s or other employee-funded accounts, according to the EBRI.

Colgan, of the National Center for Policy Analysis, explains that the employer-sponsored pension system is a cooperative venture among three parties:

- The government, which allows tax-sheltered savings by both employers and employees, because well-managed pension plans reduce the likelihood that retirees will be a burden on the taxpayer;

- The employee, who is expected to save responsibly by diversifying his or her 401(k) funds; and

- The employer, who uses such plans to attract and retain workers and who has the fiduciary responsibility to ensure that the employee ultimately benefits from the plan.

But defined-contribution plans are not performing as well as they should, critics say. According to the National Center for Policy Analysis, 401(k) plans have underperformed market indices — like the Dow Jones Industrial Average — by 3.2 to 10.5 percentage points since 1995, in part because companies lack incentive to help employees invest their retirement money wisely. In fact, they often choose not to educate workers, because they fear lawsuits if the investment advice proves faulty.

The center wants retirement law changed so employees would be enrolled automatically in a company's 401(k) unless they choose to opt out. In addition, it would like to see employers protected from lawsuits over any financial advice they might give employees. [11] Colgan says such reforms would both encourage companies to provide pension plans and relieve workers of some of the burden of picking investments. "If they're following the market, they're not doing the work that they should be doing for their employers," she says. "Following market trends is a full-time job."

For now, the federal government is focusing on educating workers about the need to save on their own. In July, the Labor and Treasury departments will launch a retirement savings education campaign, called "Saving Matters," designed to encourage workers to set aside more money for retirement.

Some experts say the federal government should play a stronger role in helping workers prepare for retirement. "First of all, we have to stop Social Security privatization," says Hickey of the Campaign for America's Future.

Meanwhile, he says, the recent turmoil in stock prices and Enron's bankruptcy may prompt congressional reconsideration of the trend toward defined-contribution plans. "Few of us have ever worked in a big company that still offers traditional pensions, and, especially after the collapse of Enron, a lot of Americans are looking at their own retirement situation," Hickey says.

"Enron gave people an opportunity to realize they're not in as great shape as they thought they were going to be in," he continues. "We ought to reform the way 401(k) plans are run and try to get back to more of a mix of pension sources, with a larger percentage of people covered by real pensions."

The labor movement, whose weakening led to the erosion of traditional pensions, wants lawmakers to protect workers' benefits from deteriorating still further. "Our goal is to help workers protect their retirement security, their basic rights, and to prevent them from being 'Enron-ed,'" said AFL-CIO head John J. Sweeney at one of a series of town hall meetings the labor group has held around the country this spring. "We urge [workers] to . . . Enron-proof their retirement security, make their voices heard, hold corporations accountable and join together with others for the power they need to take control of their retirement security." [12]

But efforts to introduce stricter pension laws may backfire. The Employee Retirement Income Security Act (ERISA) spells out workers' rights and the rules for running pensions, but it doesn't require employers to provide them, so making pensions mandatory may prompt some employers to scrap the plans altogether.

Indeed, many conservatives argue that tax reform is the best way to help strengthen retirement savings. "Our current tax code has a great deal of anti-saving bias," says Tanner of the Cato Institute. "If you save money, you're taxed on it when it's income, you're taxed on the interest it generates, and you're taxed on it at payout, in the form of capital gains. So our tax code is pro-consumption and anti-saving." In Tanner's view, moving toward a federal sales tax or a flat tax — key proposals during the tax-reform debate of a few years ago — would help workers save more. [13]

Some business representatives readily concede that employers should do more voluntarily to educate their employees on the need to save for their retirement. "Employers have a responsibility to their employees to do this," says Terry Neese, president and cofounder of Women Impacting Public Policy, a nonprofit group based in Oklahoma City that represents some 200,000 professional women, including business owners like herself. "Women business owners, more than their male counterparts, are very aware of the fact that they should talk with their employees about retirement, 401(k)s and long-term care. Women are natural-born nurturers, and as we nurture our businesses we also have a tendency to nurture our employees."

Neese, who owns an executive-search firm and a temporary placement service, says almost all her employees participate in the 401(k) plans she set up for them. Education is key to that high participation rate, she says.

"We're very comfortable bringing in three or four different experts to talk with our employees about their retirement savings," she says, "and I encourage them to be actively involved in the retirement program, as well as our long-term care, health and dental plans."

Can Americans afford to grow really old?

Americans are living longer than ever. Lengthening life expectancy is perhaps the most striking current demographic trend, and it will have a dramatic impact on retirement security.

For instance, in 1940, a retiring 65-year-old was expected to live another 12 1/2 years. Today, Americans can look forward to an average of 17 1/2 years of retirement. Moreover, 4.6 million Americans are members of the "old old" — those 85 and older — a group that by 2050 will range from 15.4 million to 39 million, according to demographers. [14]

At the same time, staying healthy is becoming less and less affordable, as the costs of hospital stays, prescription drugs and physician care continue to climb. For the third year in a row, the average retiree's health-care costs are increasing by 18 percent a year, prompting those employers that provide retiree health insurance to raise premiums for both current employees and retirees. Some are curtailing health insurance for retirees altogether. [15]

Lawmakers are considering extending coverage under Medicare — the federal program that helps pay for doctor visits and hospitalization for 40 million elderly and disabled — to help defray the cost of prescription drugs, a major expense for many seniors with chronic illnesses.

But health insurance and prescription drugs are not the only health-related costs of growing old. As the population ages, more and more people will need assistance with everyday activities, such as dressing and bathing, either at home or in nursing homes. Insurance companies have begun marketing long-term care insurance policies to working-age Americans to help pay for such long-term care, but relatively few employers subsidize it the way they do health insurance, since such policies are very expensive. According to EBRI, only 10 percent of workers whose employers sponsor long-term care insurance choose to participate. [16]

Without long-term care coverage, retirees must pay for such assistance out of their personal savings. But since the average annual cost of in-home care is currently $16,000 and $55,000 for nursing home care, only the wealthy can afford to spend many years with in-home caregivers or in nursing homes, unless they have insurance. [17]

Many employees assume that Medicare will cover such care, but it only covers brief nursing home stays following a hospitalization. The only government program that pays for long-term care is Medicaid, the health-care program for the poor, but it only kicks in after an individual has "spent down" nearly all his savings. And even that coverage may be in jeopardy over the long haul, because Medicaid costs have skyrocketed, straining the budgets of cash-strapped states, which foot most of the bill for the joint federal-state program. [18]

Some experts say the "longevity risk" and associated health-care costs have been overstated. The Cato Institute's Tanner points out that while life expectancy is increasing, morbidity is decreasing. "In other words, the 80-year-old of the future will be healthier than the 80-year-old of today," he says. "And while there will be more 90-year-olds, I think the costs associated with caring for the elderly are not going to increase as fast as many believe."

To deal with longevity risk, Tanner proposes offering more choices in the type and extent of health-care coverage seniors receive under Medicare, much as Social Security privatization would do for retirement income. "We're having a huge debate right now over prescription-drug costs for Medicare recipients, and no doubt prescription drugs for seniors is an important issue," he says. "But I could make a very plausible argument that nursing-home care is even more important, so why cover prescription drugs and not nursing homes? On the other hand, trying to cover both of them could break the budget. Maybe we should be giving people a choice."

But critics say "choice" is little more than a euphemism for benefit cuts. "I think most people, especially seniors, would say we can afford long-term care, and we can afford a prescription-drug benefit with price controls, like Canada and other industrialized countries have," says Hickey of the Campaign for America's Future. He blames last year's tax cut for wiping out the federal budget surplus that could have paid for such benefits. "We should be improving the way we treat the elderly, not turning our backs on them, which is what privatization is all about."

Moreover, Hickey says, broadening choice in seniors' health coverage would further undermine the quality of care available to older Americans. "A health-care system really works best when you've got a pooled system of resources, so people who need it get coverage, and those who don't need it know that if they ever do get sick they're going to be taken care of," he says. "That principle of social insurance should be the principle of our national health policy, but the corporate forces in this country want to segment the population, and they want to pick and choose who they're going to insure." ■

BACKGROUND

Birth of Pensions

The very notion of retirement is a relatively recent phenomenon. Until the advent of modern medicine, men generally died while still of working age, and many women succumbed to the rigors of childbirth. Those who survived into old age expected their grown children or other family members to house and care for them.

During the Industrial Revolution, those patterns began to disintegrate, as the promise of regular wages lured young workers away from their extended families to factory work in the cities. As employees aged and became less productive, employers began offering them limited pensions to make way for younger replacements. Industrial pensions first arose in the 1860s in Prussia, the heart of German industry, where workers who reached age 65 "retired" from work in exchange for limited pension payments for the rest of their lives.

In 1875, the American Express Co., then a transcontinental freight hauler, set up the first U.S. employer-sponsored pension plan, followed in 1880 by the Baltimore and Ohio Railroad. By the turn of the century, several banks and public utilities also provided pensions to retiring workers. [19]

Over the next several decades, pension plans continued to spread to cover retirees from large public and private employers, mostly railroads, utilities and the telephone and telegraph industry. The 1921 Revenue Act was the first U.S. law that provided tax incentives for employers to establish retirement-income benefits for workers. By 1930, 15 percent of private-sector employees were covered by pension plans. But few workers in manufacturing firms — and virtually none in the construction, mining or service industries — enjoyed pension coverage until the burgeoning labor movement took up their cause. By the end of the 1920s, 20 percent of union members were covered by corporate pension plans.

When the stock market plummeted in 1929 and the Great Depression threw millions of Americans out of work, corporate pension plans were wiped out, and there was no government safety net to protect retirees from poverty. President Franklin D. Roosevelt proposed, and Congress in 1935 approved, the Social Security Act, establishing a federal retirement plan for all Americans. The new Social Security system provided minimal payments to retired workers, age 65 and over, from a trust fund financed by a 2 percent payroll tax, shared equally between employers and employees on the first $3,000 of wages. [20]

Social Security's "pay-as-you-go" financing scheme worked well at first. Because average life expectancy was only 61, relatively few people lived long enough to receive their monthly checks. Workers who retired soon after

Chronology

1860s-1920s

Pension plans emerge from the Industrial Revolution.

1875

American Express Co. sets up the first U.S. employer-sponsored pension plan, followed in 1880 by the Baltimore and Ohio Railroad.

1921

Revenue Act provides the first tax incentives for U.S. employers to establish retirement benefits.

1930s-1960s

Widespread poverty after the 1929 stock market crash prompts Congress to create programs to ensure retirement security.

1935

Congress passes the Social Security Act, embodying President Franklin D. Roosevelt's plan for a nationwide public retirement plan. Retirees age 65 are paid from a fund financed by taxes paid by current workers and their employers.

1946

United Mine Workers of America negotiates the first industrywide union pension plan, prompting the spread of single-employer plans. By 1960, more than a third of the private work force enjoys pension coverage.

1961

Congress approves a proposal by President John F. Kennedy to boost Social Security benefits by 20 percent and provide reduced benefits for workers retiring at 62.

1965

Congress creates Medicare, which provides health insurance for citizens over 65, and Medicaid, which provides health coverage for the poor and disabled of all ages. Medicaid also covers nursing home stays for seniors whose assets fall below strict limits.

1970s-2000s

The aging work force jeopardizes Social Security's future, while employers shift the burden of retirement savings to employees.

1974

Employee Retirement Income Security Act (ERISA) sets standards for employer-sponsored plans and insures benefits against pension-plan termination if a company goes bankrupt. The law also allows workers without company pensions to save up to $2,000 a year in tax-deferred individual retirement accounts, or IRAs.

1978

Revenue Act allows employers to offer defined-contribution pension plans — also known as 401(k)s — which shift part of their pension burden to the workers themselves. The new plans appeal especially to small employers and younger, more mobile workers, who often change jobs before becoming eligible for benefits under traditional plans.

1983

As a dwindling work force and slowing economy threaten the solvency of Social Security, Congress delays cost-of-living increases and tax benefits for wealthier recipients and increases the retirement age from 65 to 67 by 2027.

1993

Omnibus Budget Reconciliation Act raises the percentage of Social Security benefits subject to taxation, to as much as 85 percent.

1997

Taxpayer Relief Act expands eligibility for deductible contributions to IRAs and creates the Roth IRA, which allows tax-free growth and withdrawals at retirement.

2001

A $1.35 trillion tax cut promoted by President Bush encourages taxpayers to boost retirement savings by relaxing rules on tax-favored IRA and 401(k) contributions.

December 2001

A Bush-appointed commission recommends allowing workers to use part of their Social Security payroll-tax contributions to set up retirement accounts that they invest themselves. Energy giant Enron Corp. goes bankrupt, wiping out thousands of workers' pension savings.

April 11, 2002

House passes Pension Security Act limiting the amount of employee 401(k) contributions that can be invested in company stock and promoting worker education concerning retirement. The measure also would bar executives from selling company stock during "blackout" periods — those times when employees are prohibited from selling their own shares.

2012

The first members of the large Baby Boom generation become eligible for Social Security benefits.

Global Aging Threatens Pension Systems

The United States is not the only country that faces financial problems stemming from a growing elderly population. Throughout the world, a combination of increased longevity and shrinking work forces is hastening a stunning global trend: By 2050, the world's population of people 60 and older will triple to 2 billion.

The implications of those demographics are beginning to come under intense scrutiny. In April, delegates from 160 nations met in Madrid for a United Nations-sponsored assembly to discuss ways to deal with global aging.

Indeed, as problematic as America's aging trend may be, it pales in comparison to what is occurring in other parts of the world. While birthrates have fallen in the United States, they have stabilized at the replacement level of around two children per couple. But in many other industrialized countries, birthrates have turned negative, meaning that native populations are actually shrinking.

"Europe's population began declining in 1998, while Japan's has leveled off and looks like it's about to decline," says Paul S. Hewitt, project director of the Global Aging Initiative at the Center for Strategic and International Studies, an independent research institute. Italy — where traditionally large families have given way in the last several decades to an average 1.2 children per couple — could face a 45 percent drop in its working-age population by 2050, he points out.

Immigration can help boost the ranks of workers, of course, and it plays an important role in the United States. But immigration is controversial in much of Europe, where fear that Third World newcomers threaten national cultures has given rise to right-wing, anti-immigrant political parties.

In any case, it would be almost impossible to maintain a stable working-age population in Europe through immigration alone. "If one were even to try to maintain a constant ratio of workers to retirees in Germany through immigration, by 2050 about 80 percent of the people living in Germany would be from foreign lands," Hewitt says. "This is immensely destabilizing."

Germany and other European countries are looking to Eastern Europe to provide needed workers, but this too has negative implications. "Western Europe is enthusiastic about opening up to the East because they really don't want to bring in the Third Worlders," Hewitt explains. "But the countries of Eastern Europe are not very well off to begin with. If all the young people leave, it would leave the East with a lot of old-age dependency and no tax base. Europe has not begun to face up to this problem."

Developing countries face potentially more daunting problems. "You're going to see a virtual explosion of dependency in poor countries that aren't prepared to handle the aging problem," Hewitt says. Falling birthrates already are jeopardizing care for the elderly in countries like China and Vietnam, where seniors traditionally depend on family members to see them through their golden years. Young people are moving to cities in search of work, leaving many elderly vulnerable.

---

the system went into effect received a windfall from the new program. The Social Security Administration often cited the case of Ida May Fuller of Ludlow, Vt., who paid just $24.75 in Social Security taxes before retiring shortly after the program became effective. Fuller collected $22,889 in benefits before she died at age 100.

Because at that time there were about 42 active workers for every Social Security recipient, the system's trust fund accumulated more than it paid out in benefits, ensuring its solvency. Indeed, the Social Security trust fund became an important source of money for myriad other federal services.

Lawmakers expanded Social Security over the next few decades, adding benefits for dependents and survivors of deceased workers in 1939. In 1950 agricultural workers were covered, as were the self-employed, members of the armed forces and disabled people 50 and older. In 1961, Congress approved a proposal by President John F. Kennedy to boost Social Security benefits by 20 percent and provide reduced benefits for workers taking early retirement at age 62.

While Social Security provided a guaranteed — albeit minimal — safety net for retirees, employers began offering private pension plans to bolster retirement income. Private pension plans took off in the 1940s, especially during World War II, when wage controls forced employers to find non-wage fringe benefits to attract workers to the booming industrial economy. In 1946, the United Mine Workers of America negotiated the first multi-employer pension, which became the model for subsequent industry-wide union pension plans. Union negotiations sparked the spread of single-employer plans as well in the late 1940s and 1950s. By 1960, more than a third of the private work force enjoyed pension coverage.

Because older people are more prone to chronic diseases like heart disease and diabetes than the rest of the population, they typically have higher medical bills, and their health insurance is often prohibitively expensive. Although many employers began offering private health insurance to active workers in the postwar years, few extended coverage past retirement, forcing many seniors to deplete their savings just to cover hospital bills.

In 1965 Congress came to their aid by creating two new federal programs that enhanced the income security of a growing elderly population —

Some critics of birth-control policies say the aging trend confirms their view that birth-control policies threaten future economic growth by reducing the labor pool. "To some of us, the wisdom of this crusade to depress birthrates around the world (and especially among the world's poorest) has always been elusive," writes Nicholas Eberstadt, a political economist at the American Enterprise Institute, a conservative think tank. "Simply put, the era of the worldwide 'population explosion,' the only demographic era within living memory, is coming to a close."[1]

But other experts say this argument ignores the negative impact of a continuing rise in global population. "Another 3 billion people on the planet in the next 50 years will put intolerable strains on the environment and quality of life," writes William B. Dickinson, director of the Biocentric Institute, a division of the International Academy for Preventive Medicine, a nonprofit organization in Warrenton, Va. "Yes, an aging population puts more pressure on the financing of social programs. But to equate more people with economic growth spells disaster for a human race that, in the end, must answer to Nature's imperatives."[2]

Hewitt sees two possible outcomes of global aging. "The implication for the developing world is potentially horrendous, and it's potentially very good," he says. "Scenario one, which results from business as usual, is that the industrial countries all melt down together, and we'll have one big [bankrupt] Argentina. Scenario two is a new global renaissance."

To survive the global aging trend, Hewitt says, industrial countries will have to stop protecting their least productive sectors, such as agriculture and textiles, and promote investment in those sectors in developing countries, which would then be able to employ their citizens instead of exporting them to industrial countries.

"Industrial countries could then focus their scarce labor resources on highly compensated activity, because the upshot of shrinking labor forces is that all growth in the future in the industrial countries will come from productivity gains," he says. "We're going to have to outsource our labor-intensive work and find very good ways to improve productivity."

Seen from this global perspective, America's retirement security cannot stand on Social Security reform or other domestic policy changes alone. "Increasingly, retirement security is going to require foreign policy," Hewitt says. "We need to be working very carefully with the developing countries to improve their ability to absorb capital."

At this point, Hewitt says, the two scenarios he cites are "equally plausible." World leaders will need to engage in "some real international cooperation and management to make sure we end up with the win-win rather than the lose-lose scenario."

---

[1] Nicholas Eberstadt, "The Population Implosion," *Foreign Policy*, March/April 2001, p. 42.

[2] From an International Academy of Preventative Medicine newsletter, April 1, 2002.

Medicare and Medicaid. Under Medicare, people age 65 and older receive health insurance benefits for hospital stays and limited physician care. Many retirees supplement that coverage with private policies called Medigap insurance. Medicaid, designed to provide health coverage for poor and disabled Americans of all ages, covers nursing homes stays for the elderly whose assets fall below the program's strict limits.

Despite the growing availability of private pension coverage, there was no law guaranteeing that the money would be there for workers after they retired. To protect pension benefits, Congress in 1974 passed the Employee Retirement Income Security Act (ERISA). The landmark measure set federal standards for employer-sponsored pension plans and created the Pension Benefit Guar-

anty Corporation (PBGC) to insure the benefits against pension-plan termination as a result of bankruptcy proceedings. By authorizing individual retirement accounts, or IRAs, ERISA also set the stage for later steps to encourage workers to save more for their own retirement and enabled workers with no company-sponsored pension plans to save up to $2,000 a year in tax-deferred retirement accounts.

Shifting the Risks

The mid-1970s marked the beginning of a gradual erosion of retirement security for working Americans, as employers began shifting responsibility for retirement savings to workers, and concerns arose over So-

cial Security's long-term viability.

After decades of robust economic growth, the nation's economy entered a period of stagflation, marked by slowed growth and high inflation. Harder times prompted corporate America to look for ways to reduce labor costs, and traditional pension coverage was targeted for cutbacks. Until then, employer-sponsored pension plans were funded entirely from company coffers, based on the workers' wages at retirement and time worked. Employers promised to pay retirees a fixed amount, with the companies bearing the risk of pension-fund investments.

In the 1978 Revenue Act, employers acquired the right to offer a new type of pension plan that shifted part of the burden of contributing to pensions, as well as some of the investment risks, to the workers themselves. These defined-contribution pension plans, or 401(k)s, were especially appealing to small companies that had never sponsored pension plans. As employment trends moved away from lifetime employment at a single firm, 401(k) plans also appealed to younger, more mobile workers, who often changed jobs before becoming vested, or eligible to receive benefits, under traditional pension plans.

For the most part, employee contributions fund defined-contribution plans, which also include 403(b)s for nonprofit organizations and simplified employee pension (SEP) plans offered by many small businesses. However, many employers also provide a small matching contribution to entice workers to save for their retirement. As the new plans grew in popularity, many larger companies curtailed their defined-benefit pension plans or replaced them altogether with the new plans. From 1985 to 1989, the number of workers covered by 401(k) plans soared, from 7.5 million to 17.3 million. Slightly more than half continued to be covered by traditional pension plans.

Meanwhile, experts began warning that the security of future Social Security benefits was in doubt. In the late 1960s the postwar population explosion that had produced the Baby Boom ended, reducing the future worker-to-retiree ratio that had ensured the success of Social Security's funding formula in its first few decades. At the same time, medical breakthroughs helped extend average life expectancy. Thus, the number of current workers supporting Social Security beneficiaries fell from 16 workers for every retiree in 1950 to 3.4 today. Automatic cost-of-living increases in Social Security benefits, introduced in 1972, added to the drain on the trust fund.

In 1977 lawmakers averted the first Social Security funding crisis by raising taxes and slowing the growth of future benefits. But an economic down-turn in 1980 threatened the trust fund's viability again, prompting President Ronald Reagan to appoint a bipartisan commission to consider reforming the system. Headed by Alan Greenspan, now chairman of the Federal Reserve, the panel suggested delaying cost-of-living increases, taxing the benefits of higher-income retirees and increasing the retirement age from 65 to 67 by 2027. Congress adopted the recommendations in 1983.

In the early 1980s, the boom in IRAs and 401(k) plans fueled investments in stocks and mutual funds, a form of investment that enabled small savers to spread their investments over a range of stocks and bonds. In 1987, Congress limited tax deductions on IRA contributions for higher-income workers who were covered by employer retirement plans, resulting in a fall in new IRA contributions. But IRAs continued to play an important role in retirement nest eggs because workers who change jobs can transfer, or "roll over," their 401(k) accounts into IRAs to avoid a tax penalty for withdrawing the funds before they reach retirement age. Familiarity with mutual-fund investing spread after 1986, when Congress created the Thrift Savings Plan as part of the retirement arrangements for federal workers, who could choose among three mutual funds. By September 2001, fully 87 percent of all federal employees were participating in the plan. [21]

Despite the popularity of defined-contribution plans, overall pension coverage has remained virtually unchanged — at less than 45 percent of all workers — since the plans were introduced in 1979. Coverage actually declined among male workers — except those in the top 20 percent income bracket — because of declines in union membership and employment at large manufacturing companies, and because many workers chose not to sign up for the new, voluntary 401(k) plans. However, pension participation among women has grown, reflecting a steady increase in their full-time employment, a prerequisite for receiving a pension and most other employee benefits. [22]

Demographic Trends

Two recent patterns are undermining the long-term viability of Social Security: People are living longer, and more people are taking early retirement. Both trends require Social Security to pay out benefits over more years, on average, than ever before.

Meanwhile, declining fertility rates reduce the number of workers available to pay into the system. Once the Baby Boomers begin retiring in 2012, the number of workers per Social Security recipient will drop from more than three in the 1990s to fewer than two by 2030. [23]

To bolster the Social Security trust fund, President Bill Clinton signed the 1993 Omnibus Budget Reconciliation Act, increasing to as much as 85 percent the portion of Social Security benefits that are subject to taxation. As a result, retirees with incomes of at least $34,000 and couples with incomes of $44,000 and up now pay taxes on part of their Social Security benefits.

In 1997, in an attempt to boost savings, Congress liberalized IRA rules. The Taxpayer Relief Act increased the amount of tax-deductible contributions each taxpayer could make. Congress also tried to encourage retirement savings by creating a new "back-loaded" type of IRA — the Roth IRA — which allows tax-free growth and withdrawals at retirement, even though contributions are not tax-deductible.

The most recent boost to retirement savings came under the 2001 Economic Growth and Tax Relief Reconciliation Act. Besides cutting taxes by $1.35 trillion over 10 years, the law increased from $2,000 to $5,000 by 2008 the annual contribution limit for both traditional and Roth IRAs. The law allowed taxpayers 50 and older to make "catch-up" contributions to their IRAs. It also increased allowable contributions to 401(k), 403(b) and SEP plans. ∎

CURRENT SITUATION

Enron Fallout

Enron's collapse prompted several legislative proposals to tighten 401(k) regulations. By mid-May, two rival approaches to pension reform had emerged along party lines. Both would tighten regulations governing auditor practices and insider stock sales and increase the budget of the Securities and Exchange Commission, the agency responsible for protecting investors and maintaining the integrity of U.S. securities markets.

The Pension Security Act, introduced by Rep. John A. Boehner, R-Ohio, would limit the amount of employee 401(k) contributions that could be invested in company stock and promote worker education concerning retirement needs and investment options. The measure, which is supported by the Bush administration, also would bar executives from selling company stock during "blackout" periods — those times when employees are prohibited from selling their own company shares. The measure passed the House April 11 and is currently under consideration in the Senate.

Another proposal would force employers who use company stock to match employees' 401(k) contributions to allow employees to move out of that stock into other investments within three months of vest-

ing in the plan. Enron employees, by contrast, were barred from selling company stock before age 50. The Pension Protection and Diversification Act, introduced by Democratic Sens. Barbara Boxer of California and Jon Corzine of New Jersey, would also encourage employers to make matching pension contributions in cash, instead of in stock. To reduce the risk of investment loss, it also would require greater diversification

of employee portfolios.

Even before Congress acts on the post-Enron measures, some companies are easing rules barring employees from selling company stock in their 401(k) plan portfolios. According to Hewitt Associates, a benefits consulting firm based in Lincolnshire, Ill., more than three-quarters of large companies that made matching contributions in the form of company stock had rules like Enron's preventing em-

How Compounding Makes Money Grow

Thanks to the "miracle of compounding," a person who starts saving regularly at an early age will amass far more money than someone who starts later in life. In the example below, four people each invested $2,000 a year for 10 years at an 8 percent interest rate and then contributed nothing more. Investor A ended up with nearly $300,000, or about $200,000 more than Investor D, who started saving 15 years later. The secret to compounding is that the interest earned is continually reinvested, and those returns earn their own returns, and so on.

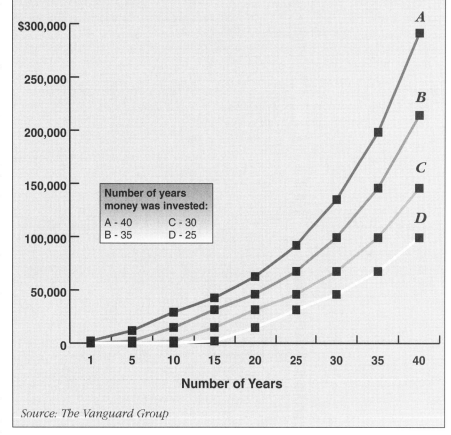

Number of years money was invested:

| A - 40 | C - 30 |
| B - 35 | D - 25 |

Source: The Vanguard Group

Women's Retirement Woes

At first glance, women should fare better than men in their golden years. After all, they can expect to live another 17 years after retiring at age 65 — four years longer than the typical man retiring at the same age. [1]

But as it turns out, the blessing of longevity is one of the few advantages a woman can claim once she retires. For starters, there's no guarantee that the quality of her life and health will match her length of life. Or, as a recent AARP report puts it, "life expectancy is not synonymous with health expectancy." [2]

The country's main advocacy group for seniors, formerly known as the American Association of Retired Persons, found that women are more likely than men to become disabled. For example, among people over 70, more women than men have difficulty with basic daily activities like dressing or eating. They also tend to have more trouble walking or climbing stairs, or doing anything that requires physical strength.

Health considerations aside, women also disproportionately face what actuaries call "longevity risk." This seeming oxymoron refers to the odds that long-lived people will outlive their savings. The longevity risk for women translates into stark statistics: For those over 65, twice as many women as men are poor, and 73 percent of the elderly poor are women. [3] As a result, many women must rely on the support of relatives or Medicaid, the federal-state program that covers nursing home and limited health costs of the poor.

In addition to longer life expectancy, women's longevity risk is compounded by the fact that they are less likely to have employer-sponsored pension benefits in old age. Of the 59 million working women in the United States, the Labor Department reports, less than half — 47 percent — participate in a pension plan. That's because they are more likely to have worked in part-time jobs that don't qualify for employee benefits like pensions or to have worked fewer years in pension-covered employment because they interrupted their working careers to care for children and other family members.

Women who do participate in so-called defined-contribution pension plans, such as 401(k) plans, tend to invest their contributions in more conservative investments like bonds, which provide lower rates of return over time and a smaller nest egg at retirement than more volatile stock investments.

"Women's roles in the workplace and family often do not provide us with the economic security to retire comfortably,"

said Rep. Nita M. Lowey, D-NY. "We earn only 72 cents of every dollar that men earn, and we frequently hold low-paying or temporary jobs."

Furthermore, Lowey points out, women spend an average of 11.5 years out of the work force, usually caring for their children, which means they earn even less over their lifetime than men." [4]

With less substantial pension benefits and personal savings than men, women are more dependent on Social Security. Although Social Security benefits alone are far from sufficient to ensure a comfortable standard of living, they remain constant for the recipient's lifetime and are thus immune to the longevity risk that jeopardizes most other income sources.

For that reason, Lowey and others oppose current Social Security "privatization" proposals, which would allow workers to invest part of their Social Security payroll taxes in personal accounts that are subject to market fluctuation. "Privatization would be devastating for women," said Rep. Robert T. Matsui, D-Calif. "Under privatization, they would have less to deposit into private accounts. They would therefore have to live on smaller benefits from smaller accounts over a longer period of time, without the protection from inflation offered by Social Security." [5]

In addition, he said, "Privatization drains trillions from the Social Security trust fund and would lead to significant benefit cuts across the board."

Supporters of privatization counter that women stand to gain from the chance to invest part of their payroll tax contributions. "I don't see that there's any conspiracy out there to keep women poor in retirement, but we just haven't gotten our public policies in harmonious connection with the way women participate in the work force," says Celeste Colgan, project director for the Women in the Economy program at the National Center for Policy Analysis.

"Even with just a historical, mean average return on interest at 5 percent, women will be tens of thousands of dollars ahead if they are allowed to invest part of the payroll tax," Colgan adds.

---

[1] U.S. Department of Labor, "Women and Retirement Savings," www.dol.gov.

[2] AARP, "Beyond 50: A Report to the Nation on Trends in Health Security, May 2002, p. 39.

[3] Vickie L. Bajtelsmit, "Women as Retirees," National Center for Policy Analysis, Women in the Economy program, February 2002.

[4] From a May 7, 2002, statement.

[5] From a May 7, 2002, statement.

---

ployees from selling their shares. Since the Enron collapse, Hewitt found, most have relaxed the rules and begun offering employees advice on their investment choices. [24]

The bright side of the Enron debacle and the emerging debate over Social Security reform, in Ferguson's view,

is the growing sense that policymakers need to address the whole universe of retirement savings. "People are finally starting to ask the hard questions," she says. "Are we moving in the right direction, and does this shift to 401(k) savings plans make sense?"

Indeed, one proposal would en-

courage companies to slow the shift to defined-contribution plans. Sponsored by Sen. Edward M. Kennedy, D-Mass., and supported by the influential seniors' lobby AARP, the 2002 Protecting America's Pension Act would make it easier for companies to provide defined-benefit pensions. "There aren't many financial

At Issue:

Should Social Security be privatized?

PRESIDENT GEORGE W. BUSH

FROM REMARKS AT THE 2002 NATIONAL SUMMIT ON RETIRE-MENT SAVINGS, WASHINGTON, D.C., FEB. 28, 2002

*a*mericans are saving too little — often, dangerously too little. The average 50-year-old in America has less than $40,000 in personal financial wealth. The average American retires with only enough savings to provide 60 per-cent of his former annual income. This problem is especially acute for women and minorities.

We must encourage for all our people the security and in-dependence provided by savings. I want America to be an ownership society, a society where a life of work becomes a retirement of independence. . . .

More than 40 million workers own 401(k) accounts totaling over $1.8 trillion in assets. Many of these assets have been contributed by employers who match their workers' own sav-ings. We know that employers contribute more when they have the option to give company stock as well as cash, and that option ought to remain as positive for American workers. But a worker should also have more freedom to choose how to invest their retirement savings. . . .

Some people like their Social Security exactly the way it is, and they'll be able to keep it exactly the way it is. But for younger workers who want to take advantage of the power of compounding interest, we should allow for personal retire-ment accounts.

The average return on Social Security is less than 2 per-cent. And in the long run, Social Security can pay retirees less than 30 percent of what they earned before retiring. And that's not good enough as we head into the 21st century.

We can do better, and a lot of people know this. Someone retiring today after 45 years of work would be entitled to a monthly benefit of $1,128 a month from Social Security. If . . . those Social Security taxes had been invested in the stock mar-ket over the last 45 years, during the same period of time, that person would now have a nest egg of $590,000, or income of more than $3,700 a month.

Because there will be an expanding number of retirees . . . in the future, we must apply the power of savings, investing and compound interest to the challenges of Social Security by introducing personal retirement accounts into the system.

Americans would own these assets. After all, it is their money. They would see more retirement income, and that's necessary as people live longer lives. And, as importantly, they would be able to pass these accounts on to their chil-dren.

REP. PETE STARK, D-CALIF.

FROM TESTIMONY BEFORE THE HOUSE WAYS AND MEANS SUBCOMMITTEE ON SOCIAL SECURITY, MARCH 6, 2002

*o*ne gimmick and falsehood promulgated by the House [Republican] majority is the idea that privatization is the savior of Social Security. The Enron debacle is a clear example of why that is not true. Just ask some of the Enron employees if they wish they had their Social Security benefits in the stock market.

Recent surveys show that people are already delaying re-tirement because of stock market losses. Dumping Social Secu-rity benefits into stocks isn't going to make retirement more secure. In fact, it may well do the opposite.

Social Security protects against the risk of death or disabili-ty, the risk of low lifetime earnings, the risk of unexpectedly long life, and the risk of inflation. Individual accounts would not accumulate enough money to protect most of those who become disabled or families who lose a provider.

All Social Security privatization proposals reduce guaranteed Social Security benefits. The president's hand-picked Social Se-curity Commission proposed cutting benefits for future retirees by 30-46 percent, reducing disability and survivor benefits, raising the retirement age and drawing on general revenues.

Because of last year's tax cut, Congress couldn't pay for the transition to a private account Social Security system even if we wanted to! All the bills that propose individual accounts and do not cut benefits end up dipping into the general rev-enue fund to pay for them. If that is what Congress needs to do to make the Social Security system solvent, then Congress should directly transfer general revenue funds into the Social Security Trust Fund. This is what I proposed in the last Con-gress. This proposal would be simpler administratively and would cut out high-priced individual account managers.

Under privatization, lower-wage workers (made up dispro-portionately of minorities and women) would trade in their progressive Social Security benefit for a regressive individual account benefit. This occurs because individual savings ac-counts, which are based on a [non-progressive] flat percentage of earnings, would be substituted for Social Security benefits, which are calculated on a progressive basis.

I ask the House majority to have a little respect for the American people and stop trying to dupe them out of their Social Security benefits with gimmicks. If President Bush and the House majority want to replace current, guaranteed Social Security benefits for some risky individual account benefit, then they should have some pride in their proposal and hon-estly share the details with the American people.

setbacks worse than having your retirement savings go up in smoke," wrote AARP Executive Director William D. Novelli. "It is important to get these much-needed pension protections passed by Congress and signed into law by President Bush." [25]

Supporters are guardedly optimistic about the prospects of substantive measures to protect pensions. "I see this as the first of many efforts to encourage companies to offer real pensions," says Hickey of the Campaign for America's Future. "But it's going to take a political movement. Government policy helped create the defined-benefit pension, and government policy could do that again. I think that if we had a Democratic president of a Democratic Congress, you'd see a whole lot more likelihood of something like that passing."

But Kennedy's bill may impose too heavy a burden on employers to garner the necessary support to gain Senate approval. An alternative measure, introduced by Sen. Charles E. Grassley, R-Iowa, resembles the House bill and may win the key support of Finance Committee Chairman Max Baucus, D-Mont., who is up for re-election this fall. [26]

Indeed, Republicans charge that Democrats are trying to exploit seniors' fears of declining living standards to gain political support. "Democrats are not only out of ideas — they're recycling tired, old attacks," said Rep. J.C. Watts, R-Okla., chairman of the House Republican Conference. "In the '90s it was 'Medi-scare.' Now their aim is to frighten all seniors in an ill-fated quest to derail the success Republicans have had on the issue of retirement security." [27]

Privatize Social Security?

The Bush-appointed Social Security Commission released its recommendations for partially privatizing Social Security last December. Enron's collapse the same month has polarized further what was already a deeply partisan debate over the federal retirement program.

"The Enron collapse shows just how foolhardy it would be to privatize Social Security," says Ferguson of the Pension Rights Center. "The only problem with Social Security from a worker's perspective is that it's not enough of a safety net. And although there are funding problems, it's not rocket science to figure those out."

Supporters of the Bush plan, however, warn that unless Social Security is partially privatized the trust fund will run out of money by 2037. The only alternative to privatization, they say, would be a payroll tax increase from the current 12.4 percent to 19 percent, a 30 percent reduction in benefits or some combination of the two.

"If forced to remain in the current Social Security system, the children and grandchildren of today's retirees face dim prospects for their own retirement years," says the United Seniors Association, a nonprofit group based in Fairfax, Va., and one of the few retiree groups that backs privatization. "The ideal solution is to create a new program that combines the best features of the current program along with private-sector investments." [28]

Privatization advocates say the change would even appeal to many seniors, who generally stick to conservative, or less-risky, investments. "A number of seniors will likely take the deal," says Tanner. "But certainly it's good for somebody who's 20 years old and has 45 years of work life ahead. We've never had a period in which you'd lose money [from stock investments] over that period of time."

The annual Social Security trustees' report, which only five years ago predicted that the trust fund would run out of money by 2030, last year pushed that estimate back to 2038. In March, it delayed that deadline by an-other three years, to 2041. [29]

Some critics of the Bush proposal say the trustees' report shows the funding problems are less serious than privatization supporters claim. "There's more revenue in the system than they had expected, which means that wages continue to grow," says Mandell of the 2030 Center. "The American economy over the last 50 years has far outpaced the trustees' moderate projections."

Moreover, he adds, if the economy continues to grow at the average rate of the past 50 years, "There will never be a funding problem."

But his group does not want to be seen as being in denial. "We're willing to say there might be a problem down the road," he says. "But we're also absolute about the fact that privatization doesn't solve the problem. It only exacerbates it."

Elder Health Care

Ever since the Clinton administration's sweeping but ill-fated attempt to overhaul the U.S. health-care system in 1994, proposals to improve the quality of health care have focused on incremental expansion of coverage. Medicare's long-term funding problems have prompted several changes, including payment cuts to doctors, hospitals and other providers under the 1997 Balanced Budget Act. [30] But the primary proposal before Congress today addresses coverage of prescription drugs under Medicare.

The program does not cover prescription drugs, one of the most burdensome health-related costs for many older Americans. Drugs also account for about half of employers' retiree health-insurance expenses. Rapidly rising drug prices, which doubled from 1995-2000, are the main cause of sky-rocketing health-care costs, especially among retirees. Their burden is becoming even heavier as retiree health coverage under employer-sponsored plans continues to shrink.

To help lighten seniors' health costs, lawmakers are considering two proposals offering prescription drug benefits under Medicare. Under a plan proposed by Sens. Bob Graham, D-Fla., and Zell Miller, D-Ga., beginning in 2004 Medicare would pay up to half of all drug costs up to $4,000 and all costs over that amount. Medicare beneficiaries would pay a maximum of $25 a month for this coverage. The measure would cost about $425 billion over eight years.

A Republican alternative still being crafted in the House would provide more limited coverage, paying all drug costs over $5,000. Monthly premiums would be $35 to $40 at most, with beneficiaries paying the first $250 in drug costs. The program, which would begin in 2005, would cost $350 billion over 10 years.

A projected quadrupling of the cost of long-term care in nursing homes and other facilities over the next 30 years has prompted several proposals to help retirees face these expenses. [31] The Long-Term Care and Retirement Security Act, introduced last year by Sens. Grassley and Graham, would provide an income-tax deduction for long-term care insurance premiums, a $3,000 tax credit for family caregivers and encourage employers to offer long-term care insurance. ∎

OUTLOOK

Election Concerns

This fall's midterm elections complicate the prospects for legislative action on nearly all pending measures addressing retirement security. As the

campaign heats up, so too has the rhetoric surrounding Social Security, Medicare and other issues dear to seniors — the segment of the population with the highest voter turnout. This is especially the case in toss-up contests that could help determine whether the Republicans will regain control of the Senate and hold onto their House majority.

The most controversial issue for seniors is the reform of Social Security, commonly known as the deadly "third rail" * of American politics because support for major benefit changes has often spelled political suicide for office-seekers. This year is no different. Democrats who oppose the Bush plan to include personal retirement accounts within Social Security are pushing Republicans to offer legislation embracing privatization before November because they want to be able to use it against the GOP in the fall elections.

"Social Security is an all-American success story, and it's something that most people don't want to see tampered with," says Hickey of the Campaign for America's Future. "The candidate who says his opponent will dismantle Social Security, cut benefits and raise the retirement age in order to privatize the system has a huge advantage, and groups like ours are going to be demanding that all politicians, Republicans and Democrats, tell the voters where they stand on privatization. We believe that question is really going to help determine a lot of elections."

Privatization advocates agree that the issue will be crucial to the outcome of the election, but they say public opinion is on their side.

"There's no doubt that the term 'privatization' doesn't resonate well with seniors," concedes the Cato Institute's Tanner. "On the other hand, the idea of individual accounts, allowing work-

---

* Named after the electrified third rail that carries high-voltage current to electric trains and can kill on contact.

ers to invest a portion of their payroll tax, is quite popular. Public opinion polls consistently show strong support for the concept. So whoever is able to define the terms of the debate is going to win this fall."

Generational Politics

As retiring Baby Boomers swell the ranks of the elderly in coming decades, some experts foresee a widening generation gap between Boomers and their successors — the so-called Generation X — as workers are asked to bear a heavier burden to support retirees. If that generational divide does emerge, it may doom efforts to expand Medicare, for example.

"[Gen-X'ers] are the first American generation that will not live as well as their parents did," writes Ann A. Fishman, president of the Generational-Targeted Marketing Corp. in New Orleans. "And they have no intention of paying unreasonably high taxes to add to Medicare, the Cadillac of health insurance plans. So aging boomers can expect a Chevrolet Medicare health plan — more basic, with fewer bells and whistles. They should start saving."

But for now, Medicare, Social Security and retirement benefits don't appear to concern many young people. "For all the talk about generational warfare on these issues, the fundamental truth is that young people don't think about Social Security," says Mandell of the 2030 Center. "It's a political debate that for the most part they're not tuned into." ∎

Notes

[1] Perrotta testified Feb. 5, 2002, before the Senate Governmental Affairs Committee.
[2] For background on the Enron debacle, see Kenneth Jost, "Accountants Under Fire," *The CQ Researcher*, March 22, 2002, pp. 241-264.

3 "Change in Household Net Worth in Relation to Income in the United States and the Personal Savings Rate," www.worldbank.org.

4 Edward N. Wolff, "Retirement Insecurity: The Income Shortfalls Awaiting the Soon-to-Retire," Economic Policy Institute, April 2002.

5 Employee Benefit Research Institute, "2002 Retirement Confidence Survey," Feb. 27, 2002.

6 From a speech at the National Summit on Retirement Savings, held Feb. 28, 2002, at the U.S. Department of Labor.

7 U.S. Census Bureau, "Money Income in the United States: 2000."

8 Bush spoke May 2, 2001, at a Rose Garden ceremony marking the commission's creation.

9 President's Commission to Strengthen Social Security, "Strengthening Social Security and Creating Personal Wealth for All Americans," December 2001, p. 11.

10 From a survey by Watson Wyatt Worldwide, a benefits consulting firm, released May 3, 2002.

11 Brooks Hamilton and Scott Burns, "Reinventing Retirement Income in America," National Center for Policy Analysis, December 2001.

12 Sweeney spoke April 3, 2002, at a town meeting on the Enron collapse held in Milwaukee, Wis.

13 For background, see Mary H. Cooper, "Tax Reform," The CQ Researcher, March 22, 1996, pp. 241-264.

14 See Robert J. Samuelson, "United in Denial," The Washington Post, April 24, 2002.

15 See Milt Freudenheim, "Companies Trim Health Benefits for Many Retirees as Costs Surge," The New York Times, May 10, 2002. For background, see Mary H. Cooper, "Retiree Health Benefits," The CQ Researcher, Dec. 6, 1991, pp. 921-944.

16 Jeremy Pincus, "Voluntary Long-Term Care Insurance: Best Practices for Increasing Employee Participation," Employee Benefit Research Institute, May 2000.

17 See Laura Parker, "Medicaid Patient Dies. Who Gets the House?" USA Today, May 1, 2002.

18 See Robert E. Pierre, "Slump Is Still Taking Toll on State Budgets," The Washington Post, May 17, 2002.

19 For background, see Mary H. Cooper, "Paying for Retirement," The CQ Researcher, Nov. 5, 1993, pp. 961-984.

20 For background, see Adriel Bettelheim, "Saving Social Security," The CQ Researcher, Oct. 2, 1998, pp. 857-880.

21 See President's Commission to Strengthen Social Security op. cit.

22 Alicia H. Munnell, Annika Sundén and Eliz-

abeth Lidstone, "How Important Are Private Pensions?" Center for Retirement Research, Boston College, February 2002.

23 Joseph J. Cordes and C. Eugene Steurle, "A Primer on Privatization," The Retirement Project, Urban Institute, November 1999.

24 Hewitt Associates, "Hewitt Survey Reveals New Trends in Companies' 401(k) Plans," press release, April 22, 2002.

25 William D. Novelli, "We Can Protect Workers' Pensions and Choices," AARP Bulletin, May 2002, p. 23.

26 See Julie Hirschfeld Davis, "Senate Unlikely to Treat Pension Changes With Bipartisan Ease of the House," CQ Weekly, April 13, 2002, pp. 960-961.

27 Quoted from a statement issued May 22, 2002.

28 United Seniors Association, "Social Security Reform," issue brief, www.unitedseniors.org.

29 "The 2002 Annual Report of the Board of Trustees of the Federal Old-Age and Survivors Insurance and Disability Insurance Trust Funds," March 26, 2002.

30 See Mary Agnes Carey, "Members Back Medicare Revamp But Are Not Unified on a Solution," CQ Weekly, May 18, 2002, pp. 1306-1307.

31 From testimony before the Senate Special Committee on Aging by Frolly Boyd, senior vice president, Aetna Life Insurance Co., April 10, 2002.

FOR MORE INFORMATION

AARP, 601 E St., N.W., Washington, DC 20049; (202) 434-2277; www.aarp.org. The leading voice of Americans over 50 (formerly the American Association of Retired Persons); monitors issues including age discrimination, Social Security, Medicaid and Medicare, pensions and retirement and consumer protection.

Center for Strategic and International Studies, 1800 K St., N.W., Suite 400, Washington, DC 20006; (202) 887-0200; www.csis.org. This nonpartisan research institute is home to the Commission on Global Aging, which studies the social and economic impact of the ongoing aging trend.

Campaign for America's Future, 1025 Connecticut Ave., N.W., Suite 205, Washington, DC 20036; (202) 955-5665; www.ourfuture.org. This project of the Institute for America's Future promotes a progressive agenda on economic issues; endorses pension rights and opposes partial privatization of Social Security.

Cato Institute, 1000 Massachusetts Ave., N.W., Washington, DC 20001-5403; (202) 842-0200; www.cato.org. A libertarian think tank that endorses President Bush's call to partially privatize Social Security.

National Center for Policy Analysis, 12655 N. Central Expressway, Suite 720, Dallas, TX 75243; (972) 386-6272; www.ncpa.org. A free-market-oriented think tank that studies a wide range of public policy issues and favors Social Security privatization. The center's Women in the Economy project studies policies affecting working women.

Pension Rights Center, 1140 19th St., N.W., Suite 602, Washington, DC 20036-6608; (202) 296-3776; www.pensionrights.org. A nonprofit advocacy group that works to preserve and expand pension rights and provides technical assistance on pensions.

2030 Center, 1025 Connecticut Ave., N.W., Suite 205, Washington, DC 20036; (202) 822-6526; www.2030.org. A public policy research and advocacy organization for young adults; supports strengthening Social Security but opposes partial privatization.

Women Impacting Public Policy, 2709 West I-44 Service Rd., Oklahoma City, OK 73112; (888) 368-5759; www.wipp.org. Represents 200,000 professional women and business owners; seeks improved Social Security benefits for women.

Bibliography

Selected Sources

Articles

Miller, Lynn, "The Ongoing Growth of Defined Contribution and Individual Account Plans: Issues and Implications," *Issue Brief*, **Employee Benefit Research Institute, March 2002.**

Although changes in last year's tax law may increase worker contributions to 401(k) plans and IRAs, it's too soon to tell whether the changes will reverse the decline in retirement savings.

Munnell, Alicia, Annika Sundén, and Elizabeth Lidstone, "How Important Are Private Pensions?" *Issue in Brief*, **Center for Retirement Research, Boston College, February 2002.**

Although employer-sponsored pensions are important for ensuring a comfortable standard of living in retirement, only about half of American workers are covered.

Novelli, William D., "We Can Protect Workers' Pensions and Choices," *AARP Bulletin*, **May 2002.**

The president of the influential seniors' lobby calls on Congress to protect private pensions from the kinds of losses suffered by Enron employees.

Uchitelle, Louis, "Do You Plan to Retire? Think Again," *The New York Times*, **March 31, 2002.**

Concern over the plight of Enron workers whose pensions were drained during the company's bankruptcy masks the more worrisome fact that few American workers are setting aside money for retirement in the first place.

Wallace, Paul, "Time to Grow Up," *The Economist*, **Feb. 14, 2002.**

From a special section on pensions, the article outlines the limitations of traditional pensions and pay-as-you-go systems like Social Security and argues that workers must assume greater individual responsibility for their retirements.

Yakoboski, Paul, "Retirement Plans, Personal Saving, and Saving Adequacy," *Issue Brief*, **Employee Benefit Research Institute, March 2000.**

Despite the introduction of voluntary retirement savings plans like IRAs and 401(k)s, the U.S. personal savings rate has been falling over the past decade. As a result, many American workers may not have a comfortable retirement.

Reports and Studies

AARP, "Beyond 50: A Report to the Nation on Trends in Health Security," May 2002.

Older Americans are living longer and leading healthier lives than their predecessors, but they face higher health-care costs amid shrinking employer-sponsored health insurance coverage.

Center for Strategic and International Studies, Commission on Global Aging, "Meeting the Challenge of Global Aging," March 2002.

The report, presented at a U.N.-sponsored meeting in Madrid, Spain, describes the impact of a global aging trend that threatens to overwhelm the social security systems of both industrial and developing countries.

Henry J. Kaiser Family Foundation, Health Research and Educational Trust and The Commonwealth Fund, "Erosion of Private Health Insurance Coverage for Retirees: Findings from the 2000 and 2001 Retiree Health and Prescription Drug Coverage Survey," April 2002.

Fewer employers are offering retiree health coverage, a trend that is likely to continue as a result of rising health-care costs and the current economic slowdown.

Organisation for Economic Co-operation and Development, "Ageing and Income: Financial Resources and Retirement in 9 OECD Countries," 2001.

The nine industrial countries reviewed in the study have adopted differing approaches to retirement security. At one extreme is Finland, where retirees depend virtually entirely on a state pension system. At the other is the United States, where Social Security provides a minimal income and retirees rely more on private pensions and savings.

President's Commission to Strengthen Social Security, "Strengthening Social Security and Creating Personal Wealth for All Americans," December 2001.

The commission endorses President Bush's call to allow workers to use a portion of the payroll taxes they contribute to the Social Security trust fund in personal retirement savings accounts and offers three plausible plans to set them up.

Wolff, Edward N., "Retirement Insecurity: The Income Shortfalls Awaiting the Soon-to-Retire," Economic Policy Institute, 2002.

Contradicting predictions that defined-contribution plans would increase retirement savings, the report finds that the only workers nearing retirement — those ages 47 to 64 — who have increased their retirement savings since 401(k) plans took off in the early 1980s are those with more than $1 million in assets. All other income groups have seen their retirement savings drop by an average of 11 percent over the same period.

7 Living-Wage Movement

JANE TANNER

Baptist Bishop Douglas Miles and other clergymen in Baltimore gave mayoral candidates an ultimatum: Endorse a proposed ordinance forcing city contractors to pay their workers at least $6.10 an hour — or lose their support.

The hard-driving activists got the raises they demanded, and more — their actions launched a powerful national movement to force municipal contractors to pay so-called living wages. That was back in 1994, when the federal minimum wage was $4.25 an hour.

Now, nearly a decade later, Miles and his colleagues are at it again: They are urging Maryland's gubernatorial candidates to back an $11-an-hour minimum wage — more than twice the federal minimum — for every business in the state that receives at least $1 million in state financing or holds a contract with the state.

"We don't shy away from politics, and we don't apologize for building power," says Robert English, a spokesman for Miles' coalition of religious and labor leaders — Baltimoreans United in Leadership Development (BUILD).

BUILD's efforts eight years ago (*see p. 128*) helped trigger a nationwide alliance of religious and labor groups that has continued pressing for better wages. So far, 98 counties and cities — including Los Angeles, San Francisco, Detroit, Chicago and Boston — have passed similar laws mandating wage floors higher than the federal minimum — now $5.15 an hour — for certain workers.

Living-wage laws require any company providing a service to a city or

Throughout the country, many educational institutions and school boards and nearly 100 cities and counties require service contractors to pay significantly above the federal minimum wage.

county, or businesses receiving a city or county subsidy, to pay wages high enough to keep a family of four above the federal poverty line without having to rely on charity or having the breadwinner work two jobs. Living wages currently in effect range from $6.75 an hour in Eau Claire County, Wis., to $12.92 in Richmond, Calif. By contrast, a family of four with a full-time worker being paid at the federal minimum actually earns 40 percent less income than the official federal poverty level for a family that size, or $18,100. *

Living-wage ordinances usually require a company to pay $1 to $2 more per hour if it doesn't offer health benefits. Many living-wage laws also require automatic annual cost-of-living increases, and some go even further. Los Angeles, for instance, requires 12 paid vacation days.

Living-wage advocates also push for higher federal, state and city minimum wages. Minimum wages are

lower than living wages and apply to all employees. Living wages usually apply only to public employees or those who work for firms that do business with public entities.

So far, the laws only cover about 100,000 workers — a tiny fraction of the nation's 134.5 million workers — but that number could rise if similar campaigns in more than 100 cities are successful.

That's a big "if." Opposition coalitions — heavily represented by hotel and restaurant owners and manufacturers that rely on low-cost labor — have launched intensive lobbying campaigns to convince state legislators to outlaw future wage laws and repeal those already in place.

The opposition groups have racked up some successes. In September, for instance, the Louisiana Supreme Court upheld a state law banning cities from setting minimum wages. [1] The decision undercut living-wage advocates' broadest victory yet: the first-ever citywide minimum wage — tagged at $1 above the federal minimum — adopted by New Orleans voters in February.

Moreover, in July, South Carolina became the seventh state to pass a so-called pre-emption law, which bars cities from establishing their own minimum wages.

Finally, a Utah law passed last year prohibits any wage requirement tied to city contracts or public financing. "Utah's law is horrific," says Jen Kern, who heads the living-wage campaign at the Association of Community Organizations for Reform Now (ACORN), a social activist network.

But living-wage advocates continue chalking up victories elsewhere. Gov. Gray Davis, D-Calif., signed legislation in August giving cities throughout the state the right to enforce wage and labor

From *The CQ Researcher,* September 27, 2002.

* To earn $18,100 a year, a worker would have to be paid $8.70 an hour.

Nearly 100 Cities Have Living-Wages Laws

At least 98 cities and counties in 26 states have passed living-wage laws, and another 75 jurisdictions are actively considering wage ordinances for the first time.*

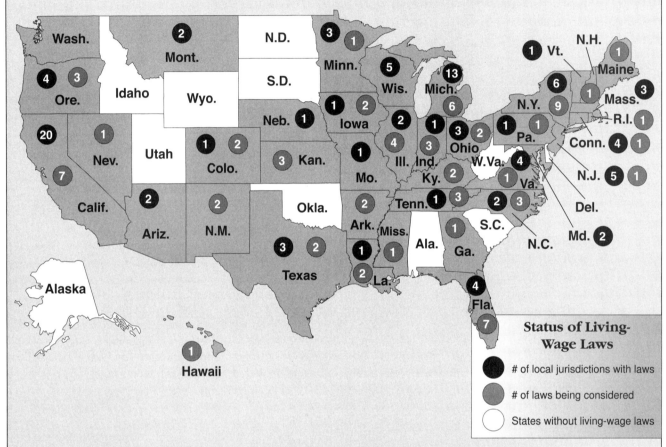

Status of Living-Wage Laws

⚫ # of local jurisdictions with laws

⚪ # of laws being considered

⚪ States without living-wage laws

* The law in Pittsburgh, Pa., is on hold; laws in Allen Park and Hazel Park, Mich., Hempstead, N.Y., and Omaha, Neb., were repealed; the New Orleans law was overturned by the state Supreme Court.

Sources: Employment Policies Institute, ACORN and city officials

standards (such as hours and benefits) on economic-development projects, in other words, private projects that get public financing as a way to lure business to cities. And on Sept. 4, Missouri's Supreme Court dismissed a challenge to St. Louis' living-wage ordinance. [2]

Now advocates are trying to push the envelope in Santa Monica, Calif. In November voters will decide if all private businesses with revenues of $5 million or more within a 1.5-square-mile posh seaside zone should pay workers at least $10.50 an hour. Like

the scuttled New Orleans law, the Santa Monica referendum would force all employers in the zone to pay the higher minimum wage, not just those with public-private financial relationships.

Not surprisingly, the campaigning has heated up on both sides. Advocates are knocking on doors all over Santa Monica, while opponents are stuffing mailboxes with literature. "Utah's ban on local wage laws is the proponents' bogey man," says Pat Sheehy, the National Restaurant As-

sociation's manager of state legislative affairs. "The Santa Monica ordinance is ours."

Opponents — who fear approval could unleash a cascade of similar laws in other cities — say living-wage laws increase unemployment because they force companies to reduce staffs or move to cities with lower employment costs. Opponents also complain that the ordinances frustrate statewide or nationwide commercial chains, which often must comply with a patchwork of local wage laws. California alone has 20 different living-wage laws on the books.

But advocates argue that living-wage laws stimulate local economies by boosting wages and lowering dependence on public welfare. And while they may cause small job losses, they also provide modest poverty relief, says a study by Michigan State University economist David Neumark. [3]

No definitive studies on outcomes exist yet, largely because most ordinances have been enacted just in the last two years. It's a big question mark, says Richard Sander, a law professor at the University of California at Los Angeles (UCLA) who is conducting the first significant analysis of post-law outcomes. "That is why we are excited about studying it."

Most laws cover city and county employees, as well as contractors' employees. Nearly half also cover businesses benefiting from public financing and economic incentives like tax breaks, loan guarantees or below-market leases. *

Yet, only a fraction of the workers in cities with a living-wage law ever see a fatter paycheck. For instance, the wage proposal pending in Eugene, Ore., would only cover 293 employees. [4] The nation's broadest law, in Los Angeles, covers 11,000 workers. [5] In addition, most cities don't appear to be enforcing their living-wage laws, says Stephanie Luce, a University of Massachusetts at Amherst researcher.

"It just gets put to the side, falls through the cracks or cities just are really dragging their feet," Luce says. "In some cases, the city does a great job, but that is unusual; usually there

---

* In the past decade, many businesses "shopped around" for a city or county that would offer them the best economic incentive package to relocate there — or to remain where they are. Such special financing deals often were justified by the company's promise to provide a certain number of new (or retained) jobs.

Cities That Pay Living Wages

Here are examples of mandated wages among the 98 cities and counties that have passed living-wage ordinances. Most cities require a higher minimum wage if employers do not offer health benefits. *

City	Per-Hour Wages	
	With Benefits	No Benefits
Richmond, Calif.	$11.42	$12.92
Burlington, Vt.	$10.93	$12.68
Boston	$10.54	
Berkeley, Calif.	$9.75	$11.37
New Haven, Conn.	$9.75	$9.75
Cleveland	$9.20	
Detroit	$8.83	$11.03
Minneapolis	$8.83	
Miami-Dade County, Fla.	$8.81	$10.06
Ann Arbor	$8.70	$10.20
Tucson	$8.58	$9.66
Rochester, N.Y.	$8.52	$9.52
Bozeman, Mont.	$8.50	$9.50
Denver	$8.50	$8.50
Durham, N.C.	$8.45	
Los Angeles	$8.27	$9.52
Charlottesville, Va.	$8.00	$8.00
Portland, Ore.	$8.00	$9.00
Chicago	$7.60	$7.60
Duluth, Minn.	$7.07	$7.88

* Only one figure is used when a city requires benefits

Source: Employment Policies Institute and city officials

---

is no political will to push forward on enforcement."

Luce says many mayors and city administrators opposed the laws during the political process and resist putting them into place. Also, some cities, such as Buffalo, say they cannot afford the personnel and other costs to monitor the law.

Meanwhile, supporters argue that living-wage laws help raise the salaries of thousands of workers who are not officially covered by them, as city contractors give raises to others on their payrolls besides city-contract workers, and competition for the best workers drives wages up. Proponents also say the heightened attention to the struggles of low-wage workers helps pressure employers to pay more. "The city laws are just one step toward raising wages nationwide," says Paul Sonn, associate counsel at the Brennan Center for Justice at New York University (NYU) Law School.

Advocates began lobbying for state and local living-wage laws because

Can a Factory Pay Fairly — and Make a Profit?

B en Cohen, the social-activist entrepreneur, has already proved that selling additive-free ice cream can turn a profit. Now he's taken on a tougher capitalistic challenge: He wants to prove that companies can provide garment workers — traditionally poorly paid — with a decent work environment and a livable wage and still generate profits.

The former co-owner of ice cream giant Ben & Jerry's threw down a gauntlet last spring in what could be called the "Sweatshop Challenge." He and long-time friend Pierre Ferrari, an heir to the Ferrari car fortune, set up a clothing factory, SweatX, in the Los Angeles garment district, an area notorious for paltry wages and sweatshop conditions.

"What's needed is to add a social, spiritual dimension to the business," Cohen said on "The Oprah Winfrey Show" last spring. [1] "When you're shopping for your next T-shirt, try thinking about these two words: 50 cents. Fifty cents is the approximate price difference between a shirt made in a sweatshop and a T-shirt that isn't."

Speed, not wages, determines profitability, Cohen said. To prove his point, he used $1.5 million from his venture-capital firm, Hot Fudge Social Venture Fund, to fill an old warehouse with high-tech, air-driven sewing machines and computerized material cutters. "Ultimately, this technology will result in fewer jobs," Cohen said in a Labor Day radio commentary. "But ignoring [advanced technology] just to maintain more miserable jobs is no solution." [2]

SweatX expects to employ about 80 workers this year, with the lowest wages pegged at $8.50 an hour (average wages are $10.58), plus benefits, pension and profit sharing. [3] Managers cannot take home more than eight times the salary of the lowest-paid worker.

The company currently only sells wholesale, mostly to unions, some colleges and faith-based nonprofits, said Ferrari, who is chairman. [4] Optimistically, it expects to turn a profit during its first year. "There are people out there who believe in the message," said Chief Financial Officer Doug Waterman, who left commercial banking and took a 50-percent pay cut to join SweatX. [5] "Are there enough to make this a successful business venture? That's the big gamble."

Ilse Metchek, director of the California Fashion Association, doubts that shoppers — including students — will pay more for a shirt because workers who made it are paid more. "Students protest," she said. [6] "But when push comes to shove, they go to Wal-Mart and buy clothing made in Saipan."

Yet, others are betting on success. "Mr. Cohen has something of a track record in balancing what appear to be contradictory business dicta and coming out on top," wrote Andrew Gumbel, a columnist with *The Independent* in London. [7]

---

[1] Quoted on "The Oprah Winfrey Show," May 23, 2002.

[2] Ben Cohen, "Commentary: Taking the sweat out of sweatshop," Marketplace, Minnesota Public Radio, Sept. 2, 2002.

[3] Nancy Cleeland, "Clothing Firm Adopts Non-Sweatshop Concept: It hopes to stay competitive and turn a profit," *Los Angeles Times*, April 9, 2002, p. C1.

[4] Winfrey, *op.cit.*

[5] *Ibid.*

[6] *Ibid.*

[7] Andrew Gumbel, "In Foreign Parts — Ice-cream tycoon turns to sweat-free clothes," *The Independent* (London), April 13, 2002, p. 18.

Congress since 1997 has refused to raise the federal minimum wage. However, tackling the issue one city at a time is inefficient and costly, says Robert Pollin, a University of Massachusetts at Amherst economist and an unabashed advocate of radical redistribution of wealth in the United States. Pollin supports revamping tax law to tilt a greater burden on the richest Americans, and says the living-wage movement in cities is a foundation "to launch more ambitious programs of egalitarian wage and employment policies."

Public pressure for living-wage laws has grown steadily in recent years because Americans are fed up with the low-paying jobs that dominate the U.S. labor market, advocates say. Indeed, living-wage laws are being adopted despite a weak economy and extremely tight state and city budgets. In fact, several living-wage laws were passed just after the Sept. 11 terrorist attacks, when thousands of layoffs occurred. "We've seen laws passed in both stagnant and booming economies," Kern says.

Nevertheless, Pollin says, while living-wage laws are popular with voters, they are not popular budget items when it comes to the cost of implementing them, even though they represent only a fraction of big-city budgets. "Projects that benefit powerful constituencies are getting taken care of even in the tight budget situation," he says.

For example, Kern of ACORN points to New York City where millions were spent attempting to lure the Olympics and other popular projects. "Why are we funding the "Big Dig" in Boston, which is costing billions of dollars to put in tunnels, and we're not even looking at why people are only making $6.50 and $7.80?" she asks.

A bill pending in Congress would boost the federal minimum to $6.65 by 2004. [6] But raising the minimum wage by $1.50 actually would provide — after adjusting for inflation — less spending power than the $3.35 minimum provided in 1981, says the liberal Economic Policy Institute.

But opponents note that wages are not based on a worker's family needs, but on an employee's skills. "If someone [lacks] skills a particular employer requires, a reasonable rate of pay is determined by what they can do," says Richard Berman, head of the Employment Policies Institute (EPI), a group representing businesses with large numbers of low-wage workers and a leading opponent of living wages.

In addition, opponents like Berman say, the labor-intensive jobs targeted by living-wage laws cannot yield more productivity. In other words, workers cannot produce more per hour, so businesses have to manage labor costs to maintain already tight profit margins, he says.

In any event, businesses should not be singled out to solve society's ills, such as dysfunctional families or poorly performing schools that produce graduates without skills, Berman says. "We've never said terribly low-skilled people who cannot justify a higher wage should be left on the streets. Welfare is an appropriate policy for them. We oppose taking a societal need and picking out a segment of society and saying 'You guys pay for it.'" [7]

On the other hand, living-wage advocates have drawn a correlation between tax breaks given to private companies and low school budgets.

As the tug of war over wages continues, here are key issues being debated:

Do living-wage laws help the working poor?

Opponents argue that living-wage ordinances not only cause job losses but also harm rather than help the least secure employees: low-skilled workers on the bottom rung of the employment ladder.

"If your goal is to help people who need the income most, you are failing on that score by imposing a living wage," says Matt Lathrop, director of the American Legislative Exchange Council, a conservative advocacy group. "They either will lose their jobs or they won't be hired."

For example, when employers are forced to raise the hourly pay for tasks that don't justify higher wages, they try to make up for the gap with superior workers, says the EPI's Berman.

A minimum-wage activist in New Orleans readies placards in support of a February referendum to establish a citywide minimum wage. Capping a six-year effort, voters approved the citywide ordinance, but in September the Louisiana Supreme Court scuttled the victory, upholding a state law banning cities from setting minimum wages.

As a result, sometimes the less-qualified workers — the most vulnerable — end up being replaced.

Richard Jackson — president of Action Janitorial, which cleans Tucson's city hall and 13 other public buildings — says he was inundated with calls after Tucson passed an ordinance two years ago requiring him to raise wages from $6 to $8.26. He soon rolled over his entire work force, cherry picking among the higher-qualified applicants. "People were lining up to get the higher wage," Jackson recalls.

Why hadn't he raised wages before? "The competition just would not allow it," he says.

The cost of implementing living-wage laws is usually higher than it appears, opponents say, because when employers raise wages for those on the bottom, they usually raise them all the way up the line to avoid dissension.

In Massachusetts, for example, KTI Recycling has refused to comply with living-wage laws in Cambridge, Somerville and Boston, claiming it would cost $1.2 million a year to raise the pay for all 160 employees beyond the few people who work on city contracts. "Any payroll increase, in order to be fair, would affect the entire KTI staff," Residential Sales Manager Greg Appleton told city officials. [8] (Cambridge and Somerville gave KTI financial-hardship exemptions from the wage rule; a waiver is under consideration in Boston.)

Moreover, living-wage laws are a scattershot approach to relieving poverty, because they often benefit many who are not poor, opponents say. For instance, they say, a low-wage city worker may have another family member who earns a hefty income. Or restaurant workers may be teenagers from comfortable homes, says Sheehy of the National Restaurant Association. Furthermore, he points out, tips often are not included in wage calculations. "Waitresses make in excess of $100 a day in tips," he says.

Some nonprofit organizations also object to the wage laws. Ready, Willing and Able places homeless people and recently released prisoners in $5.50-an-hour jobs cleaning Manhattan streets.

Federal Guidelines Determine Who Is Poor

The federal government determines which families are entitled to public aid based on whether their income is below the applicable income ceiling, or so-called poverty line. By contrast, living wages are designed to enable a full-time worker to support a family above the poverty line without having to work two jobs. A full-time worker in a family of four would have to earn $3.55 more per hour than the current $5.15-an-hour federal minimum wage just to reach the poverty line.

Family size	Annual income ceiling*	Hourly wages needed to achieve income level
1	$8,860	$4.26
2	$11,940	$5.74
3	$15,020	$7.22
4	$18,100	$8.70
5	$21,180	$10.18
6	$24,260	$11.66
7	$27,340	$13.14
8	$30,420	$14.63

* Assumes 2,080-hour full-time job

Source: Federal Register, *Vol. 67, No. 31, Feb. 14, 2002, pp. 6931-6933.*

But a New York City living-wage proposal sets base pay at $8.10. "The living-wage bill would raise the first rung of the economic ladder higher than our people should be reaching at this moment in their lives," said George McDonald, president of the Doe Fund, which runs the program. [9] "Most have been incarcerated many times and have a hard time finding any job until we hire them."

Richard Nelson, who has tracked state wage standards for a quarter of a century for the Bureau of Labor Statistics, says both sides in the debate offer support for their positions about whether living-wage laws cost jobs. "You see studies both ways," he says.

Advocates say recent studies disprove opponents' dire forecasts of high unemployment resulting from wage mandates. A study by the University of Massachusetts' Pollin shows mild job losses. "The question is, 'Are you willing to accept some small displacement effects to get a decent wage for people?'" he asks.

Opponents say a local Earned Income Tax Credit (EITC) program would

---

* According to the Internal Revenue Service, 19.4 million taxpayers received federal EITC refunds totaling $32.5 billion for tax year 2000. The average refund check was $1,678, which amounts to an 81-cent-per-hour wage supplement for a 40-hour work week.

better target the working poor. The federal EITC reduces taxes for those with very low incomes. In fact, if a taxpayer's earned income credit exceeds his tax bill, he gets a refund check for the difference. * [10]

"The EITC is a concrete way to do exactly what living-wage advocates say they want to do and avoid unemployment problems," says Sander, who heads the Empirical Research Group at UCLA's law school. Sander projects California could create a statewide EITC for $1.3 billion a year and provide checks to some 175,000 parents for as much as $2,000. By benefiting the whole household, about a half-million people would be affected, he says. [11] He also supports universal medical insurance and vouchers for housing and day care. [12]

"Things like that can dramatically change the lives of the working poor," he says.

An Employment Policies Institute report found that if the same amount of money spent on living-wage laws were spent on local EITC programs, they would provide a bigger boost to the working poor, because higher-income families would be screened out. Such programs would "give more money to the people most in need," Berman says. [13]

Living-wage advocates are quick to point out that they have long supported the tax credits. However, they say opponents are using it to avoid paying better wages, shifting the burden back to the taxpayers. "We love the EITC," says Kern of ACORN. "But they are arguing EITC instead of decent pay. Why don't they pay a dollar an hour then, and just ask the taxpayers to pick up the tab for the rest?" she asks sardonically.

Do taxpayers end up footing the bill for higher wages under living-wage laws?

Advocates promote living-wage laws as low-cost or even cost-free policies. Private companies with financial ties

How Much Does a Family Need?

Depending on where a family lives, a typical family of four needs considerably more money to make ends meet than the poverty income levels set by the federal government, according to the liberal Economic Policy Institute. In the examples below, the institute's 1999 estimates range from more than $52,000 in Long Island's Nassau and Suffolk counties to $27,005 in Hattiesburg, Miss.

Estimated Monthly Expenses for a Family of Four

City	Housing	Food	Child Care	Transportation	Health Care	Other/ taxes	Monthly Total	Annual Total
Nassau-Suffolk Cos., N.Y.	$1,105	$510	$975	$240	$273	$1,241	$4,343	$52,114
Stamford, Conn.	1,106	510	968	208	236	1,117	4,143	49,718
San Francisco	1,167	510	786	240	224	1,086	4,012	48,138
Springfield, Mass.	649	510	984	226	387	930	3,687	44,240
Manchester, N.H.	677	510	840	222	394	744	3,386	40,628
Colorado Springs	623	510	819	208	260	759	3,179	38,148
Baltimore	628	510	794	240	240	826	3,237	38,839
Miami-Dade Co., Fla.	702	510	501	240	306	642	2,900	34,796
Tucson	603	510	555	226	235	610	2,738	32,852
Columbia, Mo.	475	510	605	222	220	573	2,603	31,241
Lincoln, Neb.	525	510	539	226	229	537	2,565	30,782
Hattiesburg, Miss.	398	510	459	222	248	413	2,250	27,005

Note: Figures may not add to total due to rounding.

Sources: Economic Policy Institute, based on data from the Departments of Housing and Urban Development and Transportation, Bureau of Labor Statistics, Internal Revenue Service, Children's Defense Fund and federal "Consumer Expenditure Survey"

to government will pay the higher wages, they say. And, both companies and cities will save money, the argument goes, as worker morale improves, turnover declines and families rely less on public aid.

"What is expensive is giving a $400,000 security contract to a company that pays $5.15 and those workers then go to the food bank or homeless shelter," Kern says.

But opponents say living-wage laws simply force businesses to jack up their contract costs, forcing citizens to get fewer services as city budgets are cut to make up for the higher contract costs. And if a business can't pass the cost back to the city, it will simply re-

duce the scope of the service to lower its costs, the opponents say.

"If businesses are supposed to pay much higher rates, the city or the county is going to get bigger prices for our services," Berman says, "and then the taxpayer is going to pay for it."

That's essentially what happened in Los Angeles, according to a city-funded study by Sander's Empirical Research Group. After reviewing about two-dozen city contracts so far, it found that the private firms passed back to the city 100 percent of the added payroll costs. [14]

"Businesses were not willing to absorb the cost," Sander says. "This isn't a free lunch."

In fact, some companies charged more than the added payroll costs. E. Douglass Williams, an economics professor at the University of the South and co-author of the Los Angeles study, says some contractors may merely multiply billing rates by the percentage of the living-wage increase, raising overhead expenses, which he says should remain fixed.

Living-wage advocates are concerned the study results won't reflect the true picture. Madeline Janis-Aparicio, director of the Los Angeles Alliance for a New Economy, which led the city's living-wage campaign, says the study only considers service contracts with the city. Another 67 percent of covered employees work at businesses leasing city space, like the Staples Center stadium or the Los Angeles airport, which she says are more likely to absorb the living-wage costs than risk losing their prime lease space to another bidder. [15]

"Where there is real competitive bidding, there has been much less pass-through" of costs, Janis-Aparicio says.

But Sander disagrees. "Conceptually, there is no reason to think the dynamic is going to be any different."

June Gibson, head of Los Angeles' Contractor Enforcement Section, says the city anticipated businesses would try to charge the city for living-wage costs and expects Sander's study to determine the extent of those pass-throughs. She says a second-phase study may look at leaseholders, but so far, most have not been tested under the living-wage law because lease terms in effect before the law have not come up for renegotiation.

The Brennan Center at NYU surveyed contract administrators in 14 living-wage cities and found mixed results on pass-throughs. [16] Most cities reported only marginal cost increases — from .02 percent to .07 percent — in their operating budgets. The comptroller in Madison, Wis., for example, said the actual fiscal impact on the city "has been negligible." [17]

But some cities experienced dramatic cost increases, such as Hartford, Conn., which paid $160,392 or 30 percent more for its security guards. [18] The largest pass-throughs occurred when living-wage laws applied to nonprofit human services. In San Francisco, with a $9-an-hour wage floor, the city's human-services contract jumped $3.7 million under the living-wage law — 1 percent of the city's $312 million human-services budget. [19]

In some cases, private companies absorbed the entire payroll increase. In others, such as in Pasadena, purchasing officials decided to split the costs with the private companies. [20]

Are unions driving the living-wage movement?

No one doubts the considerable role organized labor plays in the living-wage movement. After all, social activists are focused on the same segment of the labor market that unions want to organize: those who guard office entrances, empty trash cans, make hotel beds, serve food and clear tables. But advocates and opponents of living wages disagree about whether unions are manipulating the movement or merely offering support.

Opponents allege that the movement is a union-orchestrated drive to shore up declining membership and prevent cities from outsourcing services, many of which are unionized. Besides the AFL-CIO, three of its member unions — the American Federation of State, County and Municipal Employees (AFSCME), the Service Employees International Union (SEIU) and the Hotel Employees Restaurant Employees Union (HERE) — are heavily involved.

"This is really about unionization," says UCLA's Sander.

But living-wage advocates say theirs is a grass-roots, trickle-up movement with a broad base. Certainly, the cadre of supporters is diverse. Besides labor leaders, the movement's stalwarts include religious leaders from every faith and environmental and social justice parties like the Green and New parties. Responsible Wealth, an alliance of affluent American business owners, also supports the movement. Its 700 members are among those with the top 5 percent of wealth in the United States. [21]

Nevertheless, municipal unions appear to benefit from the movement. Michigan State economist Neumark's study of 36 cities indicates wages for unionized municipal workers went up after cities passed ordinances applying only to city service contracts. Higher mandatory wages for outside contractors makes it less attractive for cities to farm out work just to save money, he said.

"Although there may be other reasons why narrow living-wage laws are passed . . . the gains these laws generate for unionized municipal workers may provide a partial explanation," Neumark said. [22]

Publicity and debate during living-wage campaigns can offer indirect benefits for unions. At the end of the summer, a local hotel workers' union was negotiating a new contract with 27 Chicago hotels. At the same time, living-wage advocates in Chicago were pushing to lift the living-wage floor beyond $10 an hour. Kern says unions were able to use that figure as leverage.

"They wanted to start their contract bargaining at $10," says Kern. "Sometimes it just helps to have a $10 figure out there in public. This is how it's part of a larger movement."

ACORN is unabashed in its support for unions as a means of protecting poor workers. Likewise, union officials are baffled that opponents find union support for living-wage laws remarkable. "Yeah, we're a labor union, and our goal is to use whatever tools we can to improve the plight of workers," says Dennis Houlihan, AFSCME labor economist. "Yes, it has a secondary effect of leveling the playing field, and it might result in less outsourcing."

However, opponents exaggerate the union role, he says. "Our efforts are traditional labor organizing," Houlihan says. But he concedes that in some cities people look upon the living-wage effort as an organizing campaign, or affiliates engage in a living-wage campaign "as part of an overall social-justice agenda."

Christine Owens, policy director for the AFL-CIO, says the umbrella organization has offered little money, only in-kind technical help: "We're very supportive, but it's not like we've gone in and launched campaigns."

Chronology

1980s-1990s
Efforts to raise the federal minimum wage stall; local wage standards emerge.

1980s
Congress leaves federal minimum wage at $3.35 an hour.

1992
Congress raises minimum to $4.25.

1994
Baltimore clergymen help pass the nation's first living-wage law.

1997
Versions of the Baltimore ordinance are enacted in St. Paul, Duluth, Minneapolis, New Haven, Los Angeles and West Hollywood, Calif. . . . Congress raises minimum wage to $5.15 (current level). . . . Louisiana and Arizona bar cities from setting local minimum wages.

1998
Two counties and nine cities pass living-wage laws, including Boston, Chicago and Detroit . . . . Missouri bans locally set minimum wages. . . . U.S. Senate rejects Democrats' effort to lift minimum wage to $6.15.

1999
Two more counties and 11 cities, including Madison, Wis., pass living-wage laws. . . . Colorado enacts ban on local minimum wages.

2000s *Living-wage movement shaped by court rulings and elections.*

2000
Another county and 12 cities, including Denver, St. Louis and San Francisco, pass living-wage laws.

Opponents go to court to challenge St. Louis ordinance, passed by 77 percent of voters. . . . Skates by the Bay restaurant, located on city property in Berkeley, Calif., challenges new ordinance requiring $9.75-an-hour base pay.

2001
Eight counties and 18 cities pass wage laws. . . . Oregon passes local minimum-wage ban. . . . Utah legislators bar city minimum-wage laws and local-wage mandates tied to contractors or public financing recipients. . . . Harvard students begin a sit-in at the president's office and remain for 21 days until administrators agree to consider wage increases for blue-collar workers . . . a circuit judge strikes down the St. Louis ordinance as unconstitutionally vague and throws out the Missouri ban on local minimum wages. . . . Wage-law advocates sue Buffalo for failing to enforce the city's living-wage law. . . . City Council in Santa Monica passes a living-wage law that applies to all companies doing business in its beach area. Hotel owners challenge the law.

February 2002
New Orleans voters approve the first-ever citywide minimum wage, pegging it to track $1 above the federal minimum wage. Opponents sue and put the law on hold pending a court ruling.

March 2002
Oakland Calif., voters extend the city's living-wage law to workers at the airport and seaport.

May 22, 2002
Sen. Edward Kennedy, D-Mass., introduces the Fair Minimum Wage Act of 2002, a bill to raise the federal minimum to $6.25 on Jan. 1, 2003, and $6.65 on Jan. 1, 2004.

July 2002
South Carolina prohibits local minimum wages. Buffalo amends its living-wage law to move enforcement from the city to workers, who must sue employers for the mandated wages.

Sept. 3, 2002
Gov. Gray Davis, D-Calif., signs a law allowing local governments to enforce local wage standards on economic-development projects.

Sept. 4, 2002
Louisiana Supreme Court upholds state minimum-wage ban, repeals New Orleans' minimum wage.

Sept. 5, 2002
Missouri Supreme Court dismisses appeal to reinstate state's ban on local minimum wages and upholds St. Louis wage ordinance for companies that get public financing.

Sept. 13, 2002
Los Angeles Mayor James K. Hahn appoints Madeline Janis-Aparicio, head of the city's living-wage coalition, to the powerful Community Redevelopment Agency, which directs public funds to private developers.

Oct. 13, 2002
Maryland's gubernatorial candidates are expected to attend the annual meeting of Baltimoreans United In Leadership Development, where the religious activists will ask for public endorsements for an $11-an-hour living wage.

Nov. 5, 2002
Voters in Santa Monica, Calif., to decide on law requiring businesses with revenues of $5 million or more within a seaside zone to pay at least $10.50 an hour.

However, union involvement is not uniform, proponents say. Some union members do not support living-wage ordinances. In some cases, local unions oppose the laws because workers make less under their union-negotiated contracts than they would under the proposed living wage. Unions worry it will make them look ineffective, Kern says.

In addition, living-wage laws also benefit non-union laborers, offering an alternative to organized labor for fighting for better pay, says the Brennan Center's Sonn. "Historically, some unions actually have opposed the minimum wage," he says. "They are thinking if the low-wage work force was assisted without unionization, they wouldn't have an incentive to unionize."

In New York City, where an expanded living-wage law is proposed, a public-employees' union initially opposed the proposal because it believed spending on the ordinance left less public money available for its future wage negotiations, Sonn says.

Today, some living-wage proponents are working to distinguish their movement from the unions. This summer the Tides Foundation — which doles out some $30 million a year to social-justice causes — specifically gave money to some living-wage campaigns that are independent of union influence.

"We are using it as a way to get beyond the skepticism that it is just a self-serving union movement," says Karie Brown, the foundation's director of programs.

Nonetheless, Tides is labor-friendly and says unions have supplied vital infrastructure to living-wage campaigns. "Unions have the resources," says Sandra Davis, who works at Tides on a fellowship. But priorities sometimes differ, she adds. In particular, she faults unions for staying out of the 1996 fight against welfare reform.

"My view is we can hold unions accountable for supporting other kinds of economic justice goals in communities," she says. ■

BACKGROUND

Low-Wage Market

The mid-1990s labor market set the stage for the emergence and swift advance of the living-wage movement. The federal minimum wage was stalled at $3.35 throughout the 1980s and didn't reach its current $5.15 until 1998. Meanwhile, its purchasing power had dropped about 36 percent. [23]

At the same time, companies moved many middle-class jobs — often union jobs held by workers without college degrees — to other lower-wage countries. The lost jobs were replaced by low-wage, low-benefit service jobs, often paying less than $10 an hour.

In addition, many downtown redevelopment projects were undertaken — like Baltimore's Inner Harbor — heavily financed either with public funds or subsidies in exchange for promised new, high-paying jobs. But in many cases, as occurred in Baltimore, the developments displaced decent industrial jobs and replaced them with lower-paying service jobs for cooks, cashiers, waiters and hotel maids in the hotels and restaurants that grew up around the new, soon-to-be popular tourist destination. Activists began demanding a new social compact. Employers who benefit from public financing, Bishop Miles and other clergymen argued, should create jobs that pay a living wage, provide benefits and offer career advancement. [24]

Meanwhile, Congress enacted dramatic welfare reforms in 1996, steering legions of unskilled former welfare recipients into the job market, raising questions about whether the former aid recipients — often single mothers —

could work full time in entry-level jobs and still raise a family. [25]

During this period, union membership was dwindling, as union members aged. In 1995, the AFL-CIO installed as president the maverick John Sweeney, former president of the SEIU. He immediately set out to reinvigorate the labor movement, specifically at the state and local level, and launched an aggressive drive to organize low-paid service workers. [26]

A budding living-wage movement provided both an organizing tool and a vehicle to align labor with community groups and a social-justice message. George Washington University Professor Jarol B. Manheim testified before a House subcommittee in July that among labors' new strategies was "building coalitions with civic and religious leaders and various progressive advocacy groups who would legitimize the union's message." [27]

Baltimore Leads

The combination of unions and religious activists worked well in Baltimore in 1994. "AFSCME saw an opportunity to perhaps unionize low-wage workers, such as janitors and bus aides, who are scattered and hard to reach," Bishop Miles recalls. "On our behalf, [they] gave us resources to hire additional organizers."

But Baltimore's living-wage law was not an entirely new concept. In 1931, Congress passed the Davis-Bacon Act, which required federal contractors to pay laborers the most common rate earned by people with similar skills in a given community — the so-called prevailing-wage rules. Many states earlier had enacted their own prevailing-wage laws, and more followed.

In 1995, Santa Clara County, Calif. (better known as Silicon Valley), passed a variation — a mandatory wage floor for private businesses receiving public economic-development financing. The same year Milwaukee passed a city-contract wage law. Then, in January the following year, the Milwaukee School Board set wage floors for its contractors and employees. Since then, the Richmond, Va., school board has followed suit.

Also in 1996, New York City enacted a limited living-wage law to cover outsourced security guards and temporary office workers, and the state of Maryland offered a new twist — a minimum-wage law aimed solely at cleaning crews in the state's World Trade Center building in Baltimore.

Los Angeles and Minneapolis were among the six cities and a county to pass living-wage laws in 1997. The next year, Boston, Chicago, Detroit, Portland, Ore., and San Antonio joined the list, along with six other jurisdictions.

Detroit's was the first living-wage measure passed by voters, and it added a new angle. It required firms with government contracts and recipients of government financing to attempt to hire city residents when creating new jobs. A 1999 Tucson ordinance had a similar requirement, but the city later dropped it, citing difficulty tracking and verifying frequently changing residences.

In 1999, 14 jurisdictions passed living-wage laws, and 14 more did so the following year. Last year, 26 cities and counties voted in laws, nearly half after the September terrorist attacks and despite a worsening recession. So far this year, 10 new laws have passed, including wealthy Montgomery County, Md., and the Port of Oakland, Calif.

About 125 living-wage campaigns are currently under way, including 75 that are new initiatives. (*See map, p. 120.*)

Meanwhile, social activists and unions — trying to be even more aggressive — were also pushing states and cities to create minimum wages higher than the federal level and applicable to all workers, often called "super-minimum wages."

Success has been modest. Today, 11 states and the District of Columbia have minimum wages exceeding the federal rate, but usually not by much. Some are fixed. Some, like the District of Columbia, set the rate at $1 over the federal minimum wage. A few, such as Alaska, index the state minimum wage to cost-of-living increases. Alaska's rate will be $7.15 starting next January, the highest state rate.

Home health-care worker Claudia Arevalo, 37, was able to stop working a second night job as a janitor after San Francisco passed a living-wage law in 2000. "I have more time for my family, for myself," says Arevalo, who now makes $10 an hour.

AP Photo/Julie Jacobson

Resistance Grows

Despite the successes, in 1996 citywide minimum-wage measures failed in Denver, Houston and Albuquerque. Those efforts, and another in New Orleans, began to rouse broader opposition.

"In the early years, most business people figured wage laws only affected city contractors," says the EPI's Berman, and so they ignored them. "They were slowly waking up to a realization that people have been pursuing this agenda for quite some time without any effective push back."

In 1997, while activists and labor coalitions were rounding up 50,000 signatures for a New Orleans minimum-wage ballot initiative, the Louisiana legislature banned city-enacted minimum wages.

The same year, Arizona passed a prohibition, followed by Missouri in 1998 and Colorado the next year. Last year, Oregon did the same, but Utah went even further. In addition to prohibiting citywide minimum wages, Utah banned local wage standards in economic-development arrangements or for city contracts. This summer, South Carolina banned local minimum wages, the latest state measure.

In late 2000, the owners of Skates on the Bay — a pricey restaurant overlooking San Francisco Bay — filed a federal lawsuit challenging the validity of a Berkeley ordinance requiring $9.75-an-hour base pay for waitresses and other workers, along with 12 paid vacation days a year. City governments

Student Showdown at Harvard

On April 18, 2001, about 50 Harvard University students slipped into venerable Massachusetts Hall, the 1720 administration building on Harvard Yard. Their game plan was simple: Hold a brief sit-in to publicize the low wages the 364-year-old Ivy League institution paid its cooks, custodians and security guards. After a few days, at most, the protesters expected the university to give in.

But 13 days later, then-President Neil Rudenstine told them: "I cannot give in. I'll resign before I give in."

Sit-in organizer Maple Razsa, a doctoral student who had captured Rudenstine's declaration on videotape, later co-produced an advocacy film on the sit-in called "Occupation," narrated by actor Ben Affleck — the son of a Harvard janitor. [1] Last spring, students and janitors showed the film at more than three-dozen universities, helping to spark living-wage campaigns on nearly 100 campuses. [2]

The sit-in was a sedate affair compared to the 1969 protest in which 300 Harvard students charged the administrative building, tossed out the deans and chained the doors, demanding that the university jettison campus military reserve training units and expand Afro-American studies programs. The next morning, hundreds of police dragged the protesters off to jail. [3]

This time, students busied themselves with e-mails and cell phone calls to outside contacts and the media. On the fifth day, organizer Aaron Bartley sat in a windowsill, calling *Boston Globe* reporter David Abel. "Just wanted to speak with you about what's happening internally at the *Globe*, trying to get a sense from you why we are being shut out since you wrote the article last Wednesday," Bartley said in a voice message. [4]

Some 400 professors declared support for the protesters. And the first night, dining hall crews — despite warnings by bosses to stay out of the fray — marched through Harvard Yard with boxes of pizzas.

"The police said, 'Nothing gets in,'" recalls dining hall worker Ed Childs. "We yelled back at them, 'Whatever it takes, it is going through the front door or the windows. We will feed our students.'" Soon, the police stepped aside, and loud cheering erupted inside as the workers handed in pizzas. [5]

Yet many other workers were reluctant to defy their bosses. "They were much more at risk than the students," recalls Razsa. "Students had much more of a sense of safety and entitlement in criticizing the university." Workers wondered if the students would lose interest but were emboldened when they realized the students were committed to staying the course.

The sit-in marked the culmination of a living-wage campaign that began in 1998, when the city of Cambridge was debating an ordinance mandating at least $10 an hour for any company with a city contract. A group of students decided that Harvard — as the largest Cambridge employer and second-wealthiest nonprofit in the world behind the Vatican — should honor the city's wage floor. They organized a living-wage campaign on campus. (Cambridge eventually passed a living-wage ordinance 9-0 on May 3, 1999.)

During the next three years, students staged several protests. In March 1999, students presented Rudenstine with their "Worst Employer in Boston" award while he was addressing high-school students. Later that year, during commencement, a student-chartered airplane pulled a sign overhead that read: "Harvard Needs a Living Wage."

By spring 2001, the students had garnered strong support. On May 2 — day 15 of the sit-in — Cambridge's mayor, City Council members and other sympathizers marched from city hall to Harvard Yard to support the sit-in. [6]

Supporters continued to arrive. Many camped nightly outside the building in dozens of tents, a scene broadcast by television stations around the world. During the second week, three-dozen Harvard Divinity School students joined the vigil, chanting: "Where's your horror? Where's your rage? Div School wants a living wage." [7]

Meanwhile, about 100 alumni held a mock sit-in at the posh Harvard Club in Manhattan. [8] Sen. Edward M. Kennedy, D-Mass., and former labor Secretary Robert Reich, then running for governor, weighed in with support. "These movements represent a new moral consciousness," Reich said. [9]

Yet, not all of their classmates supported the protest. A *Harvard Crimson* poll showed that only 53 percent of Harvard students supported a living wage, while nearly half the respondents opposed the sit-in. [10]

To Razsa, who spent this summer in Slovenia and Croatia doing dissertation fieldwork in social anthropology, economic segregation of low-wage U.S. workers is the new Civil Rights

have no right to require paid vacation days, argued R. Zachary Wasserman, an attorney representing the restaurant's parent company. [28]

Also in 2000, St. Louis voters approved a living-wage ordinance by a decisive 77 percent margin. Missouri lawmakers earlier had banned citywide minimum wages, after a ballot initiative calling for a higher statewide minimum wage failed in 1996. At that time, proponents noted that a majority of St. Louis voters favored the higher state minimum. So, they pursued a living-wage law setting base wages at $8.84 (with health benefits) to $10.76 (without benefits) for service contracts of $50,000 and up and for companies receiving at least $100,000 in city financing.

Opponents challenged the St. Louis

movement. "The workers affected are, by and large, people of color and especially recent immigrants," Razsa says. "It is precisely the kind of work that Martin Luther King was moving toward at the end of his life."

On May 9, Rudenstine capitulated. The occupation had lasted 21 days. The president formed a work-and-pay issues committee which, for the first time, included Harvard students and labor representatives. "That composition added many perspectives not included [before]," says Merry Touborg, university Human Resources Department spokeswoman.

Among the compelling insights that administrators gained during the committee meetings, Touborg says, was the sense of "isolation and marginalization" felt by the blue-collar workers at Harvard.

"When you are custodial, nobody sees you, nobody hears you, people don't want to talk to a custodian," says Jean Phane, a union steward for Harvard Medical School custodians, who works three jobs. Last spring, Phane traveled with Razsa to present the film at universities in Southern California. He also spoke to a group of international personnel executives at the Los Angeles Wilshire Hotel.

In the end, the work-and-pay panel agreed that outsourcing had pushed wages too low. The university agreed to negotiate higher wages with unions and to hold outside contractors to the same wage and benefit standards. Yet students were not satisfied, because the university failed to index a wage floor to inflation. "The university hasn't fundamentally been reformed on that point," Razsa says. "Their attitude remains the same."

Newsmakers/Darren McCollester

Harvard University students picket on May 3, 2001, during a 21-day sit-in for living wages for custodians and other blue-collar workers at the school.

Phane says the university has yet to fulfill its promise to create more full-time jobs for medical school custodians, except at undesirable hours.

But Touborg says, "There has been an enormous amount of work done to correct inequities. I don't know that everyone will be completely satisfied.

"No one is arguing that their situation isn't difficult," Touborg says. "We never said that Harvard didn't have the money." But the university did not agree that a living-wage law was the best solution to the pay issue.

Meanwhile, student demonstrations continued. In March, police arrested nine students blocking Cambridge traffic to protest what they said were slow negotiations between Harvard and janitors. [11]

[1] "Occupation," directed by Maple Razsa and Pacho Velez, EnMasseFilms, 2002.

[2] ACORN Living Wage Resource Center.

[3] "Ex-Student Radicals to Commemorate Harvard Sit-In," The Associated Press, March 16, 1989.

[4] "Occupation," op. cit.

[5] Ibid.

[6] Joanna Weiss, "A Life of its own: Harvard Sit-In, Now in Day 16, Goes Far Beyond Protesters' Expectations," The Boston Globe, May 3, 2001, A1.

[7] Quoted in ibid.

[8] "A Brief History of the Living Wage Debate at Harvard," The Harvard Living Wage Campaign, www.hcs.harvard.edu/~pslm/livingwage/originalpage/timeline.html.

[9] Quoted in Chris Colin, "Welcome to the Occupation," Salon.com, June 3, 2002.

[10] Pamela Ferdinand, "Harvard Sit-in for 'Living Wage' Divides Campus; Many Back Raise for Workers; Some Question '60s-Era Tactics," The Washington Post, May 5, 2001, p. A3.

[11] Arlene Levinson, "Across U.S. Campus Employees Getting Organized: Wage and Workload Issues Spur Unionization; Many Universities Fighting Bargaining Efforts," The Associated Press, March 24, 2002.

measure, citing the state ban. Advocates argued that the St. Louis law was more limited in scope than a citywide minimum and challenged the legality of the state ban, citing procedural errors.

In July 2001, St. Louis Circuit Judge Robert Dierker struck down the city ordinance, ruling it unconstitutionally vague because it did not specify the level of public benefits that would trigger the wage standard. For instance, would a store or restaurant that was a tenant in a publicly financed development have to comply? The judge also threw out the state ban on local minimum wages.

Living-wage advocates began rewriting the ordinance. Meanwhile, opponents immediately appealed the case to the Missouri Supreme Court. [29] ∎

CURRENT SITUATION

Action by Voters

This November, Santa Monica's 60,000 registered voters will add their strong imprint to the living-wage movement. They'll either hand advocates a huge victory by sanctioning a law that reaches private businesses without direct financial ties to government, or they will boost opponents' confidence in holding the line.

"It's not a slam dunk," says Janis-Aparicio of the Los Angeles living-wage movement.

Actually, the Santa Monica City Council had already passed the ordinance in July 2001, but hotel owners garnered enough signatures to suspend imposition of the law, forcing the matter before the voters.

Berman says a win for advocates would serve as a loud wake-up call for dormant business opposition that doesn't fully appreciate the advance of the living-wage movement. "If the Santa Monica proposal becomes law, it will get the attention of a lot of people," he says.

But the Santa Monica vote is not the only living-wage election action this November. Support for higher state minimum wages and local living-wage laws has become a litmus test in several U.S. Senate and gubernatorial races. For instance, in Texas, a network of nonpartisan groups has pressed candidates vying to replace GOP Sen. Phil Gramm to commit to its six priorities, one of which is living-wage jobs. [30]

In Michigan, the *Detroit Free Press* asked candidates for governor to declare publicly their positions on local living-wage laws. All the Democratic candidates said they support the local measures, while all the Republicans opposed them. [31]

However, in Massachusetts, the Republican gubernatorial candidate, venture capitalist Mitt Romney, has pledged to boost the state minimum wage. "I have proposed indexing the minimum wage to inflation to provide annual cost-of-living adjustments, which is certainly out of step with most members of my party," Romney said. [32]

But Massachusetts labor leaders were not impressed. They refused to let Romney attend a Labor Day breakfast that served as a schmoozing ground for other candidates. [33]

In Florida, gubernatorial candidate Bill McBride, who defeated former Attorney General Janet Reno for the Democratic ticket, several years ago instituted a $12-per-hour living wage for all employees at Holland & Knight, the 1,300-lawyer firm where he was managing partner. McBride, who enjoys strong support in Florida's business community, includes living wages in his platform. [34] Republican Gov. Jeb Bush opposes wage mandates.

In Louisiana with its high-profile minimum-wage battles, former U.S. Rep. Claude Leach, the second announced contender for governor next year, has prominently endorsed a state minimum wage higher than the federal level. "Louisiana will not keep its best workers by continuing to pay low wages and salaries," Leach said. [35]

While opponents are lobbying for bans in many states, activity is most likely in Florida, Michigan and Virginia, where living-wage bans have been introduced, but have failed or stalled. Action is more likely in those states because they've already got the momentum from previous attempts to get the bills passed.

Meanwhile, a proposed federal living-wage law that could cover as many as 200,000 contract workers is going nowhere, Kern says. ACORN, the key engine behind the measure when it was introduced several years ago, has backed off to devote its attention to campaigning for a higher federal minimum wage.

The proposal to increase the federal minimum wage remains on Congress' back burner. A spokeswoman for Sen. Edward Kennedy says he may try to tack it onto another bill in the three weeks remaining before Congress ends its session.

Even so, Kern and others say that even if the federal minimum wage were lifted to $6.65 by 2004, it would not have much impact. While about 9 million workers would likely get a raise, it does little to remedy the vast decline in purchasing power overall, she says.

"That's the reason living-wage organizing is so important," she adds. "There hasn't been much trickle up [to the state and federal levels] on the living-wage movement."

Legal Challenges

Besides lobbying for new living-wage laws, advocates have been defending laws already on the books. They are not only battling legal challenges but are also pushing for enforcement of laws being resisted or ignored.

"The real action only starts after a law passes," says the University of Massachusetts' Pollin. "That is when the armies of lawyers come in and fight about the details."

ACORN's Kern says the outcome of court action is solidly lopsided in favor of living-wage laws. "In eight years, 98 laws and only three lawsuits," she says. "It's not surprising that the moneyed opposition, unable to mount effective ground campaigns, has taken to the air, filing lawsuits and lobbing pre-emptive bombs."

In August, Berkeley city officials insisted that Skates on the Bay begin paying the higher wages after U.S. District Judge Susan Illston sided with the city.

At Issue:

Do living-wage laws help poor workers?

MAUDE HURD
**PRESIDENT, ASSOCIATION OF COMMUNITY
ORGANIZATIONS FOR REFORM NOW (ACORN)**

WRITTEN FOR THE CQ RESEARCHER, SEPTEMBER 2002

*i*n nearly 100 cities and counties, living-wage laws do what the federal minimum wage used to do: enable workers to provide for their basic needs without relying on charity and without neglecting their families by working long hours at multiple jobs.

- A retail worker at the Los Angeles airport quits her second job and enrolls in a class to advance her career.
- A home health-care worker in Chicago pays back medical bills and buys herself a new pair of work shoes.
- A parking-lot attendant in Alexandria, Va., quits one of his three jobs and is able to spend more time with his family.

Not only have hundreds of thousands of workers and their families enjoyed the benefits of a living wage, but countless others have benefited indirectly. Companies paying living wages find they have reduced turnover and increased productivity. Local retail businesses benefit from the increased circulation of money.

When workers earn enough to support themselves, taxpayers spend less on food stamps, housing assistance, Earned Income Tax Credits and other handouts. Communities benefit from less crime, more homeownership and increased time for parents to spend with their kids. When workers quit second and third jobs, it opens up positions for others to find employment. By requiring that companies receiving major public contracts or subsidies pay a living wage, the new laws also help hold accountable local governments that spend tax dollars on corporate welfare.

Many living-wage laws further benefit workers by including additional provisions, such as health benefits, paid days off and local hiring. Most important, the grass-roots coalitions that have arisen to win these laws often score additional victories for the working poor, such as unionization, statewide minimum-wage increases, improved access to child care and laws to protect renters' rights and prevent predatory lending.

Proponents of low wages continue to claim that wage standards cause unemployment, despite an utter lack of evidence. Others claim that low-skilled workers will be "displaced" by higher-skilled workers. But just where are these high-skilled would-be janitors waiting in the wings?

Big businesses also say they prefer to let the government pick up the tab for poverty through Earned Income Tax Credits, but when was the last time you saw them out lobbying for government assistance to the working poor? Don't patronize us. Pay us!

RICHARD BERMAN
**EXECUTIVE DIRECTOR,
EMPLOYMENT POLICIES INSTITUTE**

WRITTEN FOR THE CQ RESEARCHER, SEPTEMBER 2002

*l*iving-wage laws are an inefficient way to help the poor. They are blunt tools that target everyone to get at the few in need. By requiring employers to pay a much higher wage for positions once considered entry-level, higher-skilled workers will enter that end of the labor pool, displacing the very low-skilled workers that living-wage laws promise to help.

Researchers at San Francisco State University found that "there will be significant new competition for these (relatively) well-paying jobs from others in the labor market. Thus, currently employed low-wage workers may be displaced by better-qualified workers."

This conclusion is echoed in a national survey of labor economists conducted by the University of New Hampshire Survey Center. Nearly eight in ten (79 percent) believe that a typical living-wage law would cause employers to hire entry-level employees with greater skills or experience than the applicants they previously hired. Seven out of ten labor economists (71 percent) believe that even modest living-wage proposals would cause employers to reduce the number of entry-level employees.

Even the most die-hard living-wage proponents agree that the displacement effect is an unintended consequence. Living-wage campaigner and union organizer David Reynolds says the living wage helps businesses "attract and retain the best workers" — and not necessarily those lower-skilled workers who currently have the jobs.

University of Massachusetts Professor Robert Pollin, considered the father of the living-wage movement, has reported: "The other possible effect on employment policies would be through labor substitution — i.e., firms replacing their existing minimum-wage employees with workers having better credentials. . . . Openings for the covered New Orleans jobs would likely attract workers with somewhat better credentials, on average, than those in the existing labor pool."

Proponents often cite a Public Policy Institute study as evidence that living-wage laws are effective in fighting poverty. However, a closer look at the study finds author David Neumark stating, "In particular, the estimates indicate that a 50 percent increase in the living wage would reduce the employment rate for workers in the bottom tenth of the skill distribution by 7 percent." This is a huge hit for those with the least employment opportunities.

Living-wage proponents employ the conceit that one can suspend the "skills-equals-wages" formula of real-world economics. The only certainty in this debate is that the wage proponents won't lose their jobs once their ideas are proved wrong.

But restaurant owners appealed the ruling and have set aside retroactive wages they've agreed to pay if their appeal fails. [36]

The Missouri Supreme Court dismissed the opponents' appeal in September, and the St. Louis Board of Alderman passed the revised living-wage ordinance, which goes into effect this fall. The high court also dismissed opponents' appeal to reinstate Missouri's ban on local minimum wages, which means St. Louis or other Missouri cities could go further than the limited living-wage laws and pursue citywide minimum wages.

"It leaves us wide open," said state Rep. Gary Marble, R-Neosho, who is president of Associated Industries of Missouri, a large coalition of businesses. [37]

However, in Louisiana the Supreme Court sided decisively with opponents in early September, ending a six-year drive for the New Orleans minimum wage. "It's dead," says Sonn, of NYU's Brennan Center. "If the legislature forbids it, it's over."

The 6-1 ruling emboldens opponents as they push for legislation in other states to ban or repeal the laws. "It validated an argument the business community has been making all along," says Sheehy at the National Restaurant Association. "Policies on labor and employment are most appropriately made at the state level."

He says most state lawmakers understand complex economic issues like tax incentives or loan guarantees better than city council members.

Resisting Raises

A hundred living-wage advocates protested in front of Buffalo's city hall in July, some waving signs that read "Shame on you." The city had passed a wage ordinance two years ago, but never put it into place. [38]

Activists and labor representatives sued the city in July 2001, alleging city officials had not notified vendors of the new wage rule. City officials insisted they didn't have the manpower to put the law into place or to track compliance. The 1999 ordinance requires city vendors with contracts of $50,000 or more to pay at least $8.08 an hour.

This summer, the City Council and mayor changed the ordinance to require individual workers to sue employers for the living wage, taking compliance responsibility off the city's shoulders. "This is the perfect way to have a living-wage law on the books without ever seeing a single person earn a living wage," said Maria Whyte, executive director of the Coalition for Economic Justice, which sued the city.

After transferring compliance responsibilities to the employees, the city asked the court to dismiss the lawsuit. "We thought the judge would see the issue was clearly moot," says City Attorney Darryl McPherson.

But state Supreme Court Justice John Lane instead ordered the city to provide city contract documents for the period from July 2000 — when the law was set to go into effect — to this past July.

In Boston, a dozen child-care agencies requested economic-hardship waivers in July when the city's living wage went from $10.25 to $10.54. Robert Coard, president of the largest group, Action for Boston Community Development, said parents would lose jobs if agencies had to give the raises. [39] Coard argued agencies like his would have to cut down staff and services, leaving parents high and dry.

For the Action for Boston group, however, the raises amount to 29-cents-an-hour increases for 23 child-care workers, or just over 1 percent of the $4.7 million it receives in state funding. [40]

"Child care is an industry primarily staffed by women, many women of color," said Monica Halas, an attorney with Greater Boston Legal Services, who wrote a memo objecting to the waivers. "They should not be relegated to jobs that don't pay enough to live in the city of Boston."

A decision on the exemptions is still pending.

In Chicago, researchers at the University of Illinois found that city officials were not tracking whether city contractors were complying with the city's wage mandate. Similarly, a study of Cleveland's living-wage law found that while 100 city workers received raises to $8.70 an hour, city enforcement was generally weak. "The city has focused very little time and effort on monitoring enforcement," the report said, noting that a "loophole" in the law's wording had excluded all but one recipient of loan guarantees, tax abatements and other financial-assistance programs. [41] ∎

OUTLOOK

New Initiatives

C ampaigns for new or expanded living-wage laws continue in several other cities. This fall, advocates in Baltimore will press for the $11-an-hour wage measure to cover all state employees, contractors and workers at companies that receive state economic aid. [42]

However, the next step for national advocates is to boost wages for child-care and home health-care workers who serve low-income families that rely on publicly subsidized programs. Getting these low-wage providers covered under the laws will be a tough fight, they acknowledge. As the Brennan Center study shows, successful efforts often require cities and counties to come to the table with money.

Most care providers who work in the homes of elderly and disabled people or watch over children in day-care programs work for nonprofit agencies funded through state and federal grants. While advocates have argued the private sector carries a big share of the costs of other living-wage laws, they acknowledge that broad wage increases for these jobs will require public appropriations.

"The first generation of living-wage laws didn't even try to cover these human-services jobs," says NYU's Sonn. "Politically, they didn't have the clout to get the city to provide extra funding."

But pressure, if not clout, is likely to intensify, since demand for home health aides is growing faster in the U.S. labor market — by 62 percent by the end of the decade — than all the job categories except computer specialists. [43]

"The caregiving professions are shamefully, chronically, underfunded," Kern says. "There are 60-year-old women taking care of very elderly, very sick citizens in their homes. We're keeping them out of nursing homes, which saves us money, but the caregivers are getting paid $5.30 an hour."

Local officials, especially those in human services, are acutely aware that low wages create chronic staffing shortages and poor care. Cities and counties are looking to the federal government for money. In Chicago, where the city is pushing for more federal funding, available infant care only meets 19 percent of demand, according to a city report. [44] Child-care programs, also in short supply, don't meet the work schedules of many parents.

The report says that children in subsidized programs go to mediocre programs and blames low wages and scarce benefits for teachers. Of the 36,000 child-care workers in Illinois, two-thirds have no health coverage, it

said. "The average salary for a child-care teacher in Chicago is $7.40 per hour, less than half what a dog walker earns," the report said. [45]

Meanwhile, ACORN continues to press for additional local funding. In June living-wage proponents assembled child-care and home-health representatives from around the country to brainstorm in New York City. Besides, higher wages, they want career ladders and pay scales based on education and seniority.

Similar elements are part of a living-wage law proposed for affluent Westchester County, N.Y, which may come up for a vote this fall. In addition, a proposed New York City ordinance would provide raises for some 50,000 human-services workers, but Mayor Michael Bloomberg opposes it.

"We are launching campaigns to make an argument that new public investment needs to be made," Kern says.

However, opponents predict that the living-wage movement's momentum will soon slow, because many socially liberal communities or cities with strong union influence — where it's easiest to get such measures enacted — have already passed such laws. "The rate of passage will go down after all the low-lying fruit is picked off," says Berman of the Employment Policies Institute.

But Berman and other opponents are most worried about the potential for broader laws that would impose wage rules on private businesses within a geographic area, regardless of whether they have financial ties to local governments. "The elephant in the living room is the geographic application," he says.

Opponents assume living-wage advocates will have a harder time getting broader laws passed, especially as they move up to the state level. "In cities, it is easier to gerrymander a more liberal constituency," Berman says. "You've got too many different political constituencies at the state level." ∎

Notes

[1] Supreme Court of Louisiana, No. 02-CA-0991, Sept. 4, 2002.

[2] Missouri Supreme Court, Case No. SC84107, Sept. 5, 2002.

[3] David Neumark, "How Living-wage laws Affect Low-Wage Workers and Low-Income Families," Public Policy Institute of California, March 2002.

[4] Greg Bolt, "Living Wage Campaign Starts at Eugene, Ore., City Hall Rally," *The Register-Guard*, March 5, 2002.

[5] City of Los Angeles Contract Enforcement report, Sept. 11, 2002.

[6] The Senate bill is S 2538.

[7] For background see Kathy Koch, "Living-Wage Movement Gaining Strength . . . As Grass-Roots Groups Seek Economic Justice," in "Child Poverty," *The CQ Researcher*, April 7, 2000, pp. 281-304.

[8] Letter to the City of Cambridge Recycling Department from Greg Appleton, Residential Sales Manager, KTI Recycling of New England Inc., Nov. 21, 2000.

[9] Quoted in John Tierney, "Puzzling Out The Logic In Living Wage," *The New York Times*, May 10, 2002, Section B, p.1.

[10] Department of the Treasury, Internal Revenue Service "Earned Income Credit," Publication 596, Cat. No. 15173A.

[11] Richard Sander, *et. al.*, "Living Wages and the Problem of Inequality in California," *California Policy Options 2001*, University of California at Los Angeles, 2001.

[12] For background, see Mary H. Cooper, "Tax Reform," *The CQ Researcher*, March 22, 1996, pp. 241-264; Keith Epstein, "Covering the Uninsured," *The CQ Researcher*, June 14, 2002, pp. 521-544; Jane Tanner, "Affordable Housing," *The CQ Researcher*, Feb. 9, 2001, pp. 89-112 and Karen Lee Scrivo, "Child-care Options," *The CQ Researcher*, May 8, 1998, pp. 409-432.

[13] Richard S. Toikka, "The Case for a Targeted Living Wage Subsidy," Employment Policies Institute, June 2001.

[14] "Inside the Living Wage: A Study of the Los Angeles LWO in Operation, 1997-2002" (Working Title), Empirical Research Group; a final report will be available later this fall.

[15] The Los Angeles Contract Enforcement Section reports that 3,573 workers affected by the living-wage ordinance work on city contracts and 7,265 work for leaseholders, Sept. 11, 2002.

[16] Andrew Elmore, "Contract Costs and Economic Development in Living Wage Localities,"

Working Draft, Brennan Center for Justice, Sept. 9, 2002.

[17] *Ibid*, p.11.

[18] *Ibid*.

[19] *Ibid*, p. 13.

[20] *Ibid*, p. 16.

[21] Karen Kraut, *et. al.*, "Choosing the High Road: Businesses that Pay a Living Wage and Prosper," Responsible Wealth (affiliated with United for a Fair Economy) 2000.

[22] Neumark, *op. cit.*, p. 133.

[23] Department of Labor site for minimum wage tracking: www.dol.gov/esa/min-wage/chart.htm. See also Jarad Bernstein and Jeff Chapman, "Time to Repair the Wage Floor," *EPI Issue Brief No. 80*, Economic Policy Institute, May 22, 2002.

[24] James Bock, "BUILD Prods City's Social Conscience: Fairer Share of Jobs Sought for Blacks," *The Baltimore Sun*, June 30, 1993, p. B1.

[25] For background, see Christopher Conte, "Welfare, Work and the States," *The CQ Researcher*, Dec. 6, 1996, pp. 1057-1080, and Sarah Glazer, "Welfare Reform," *The CQ Researcher*, Aug. 3, 2001, pp. 601-632.

[26] Kenneth Jost, "Labor Movement's Future," *The CQ Researcher*, June 28, 1996, pp. 553-576.

[27] Testimony before House Education Subcommittee on Workforce Protections, July 23, 2002.

[28] Quoted by Jason Hoppin, "Eatery Gags on Berkeley's Living Wages," *The Recorder*, March 4, 2002, p.1.

[29] Missouri Supreme Court, SC84107, Missouri Hotel and Motel Association, etc., *et al.*, *Associated Industries of Missouri v. City of St. Louis, et al.*

[30] "Kirk, Cornyn promise to meet with network if elected," Associated Press Newswires, Sept. 9, 2002.

[31] "Election 2002: Priorities of the candidates for governor," *Detroit Free Press*, May 28, 2002.

[32] Quoted by Jeff Jacoby, "Pop Quiz for Gubernatorial Candidates," *The Boston Globe*, Sept. 5, 2002, p. A15.

[33] Elisabeth J. Beardsley, "Labor to Romney: Get lost; GOP hopeful turned away from breakfast," *Boston Herald*, Sept. 3, 2002.

[34] Michael Peltier, "Florida lawyer challenging Reno for Democratic nod," Reuters English News Service, Sept. 6, 2002.

FOR MORE INFORMATION

Association of Community Organizations for Reform Now (ACORN), 739 8th St., S.E., Washington, DC 20003; (202) 547-2500; www.livingwagecampaign.org. A network of social-activist groups that maintains a Living Wage Resource Center, which tracks local legislation.

Economic Policy Institute, 1660 L St., N.W., Suite 1200, Washington, DC 20036; (202) 775-8810; www.epinet.org. Analyzes income distribution, minimum-wage laws and other economic data.

Empirical Research Group, UCLA School of Law, 405 Hilgard Ave., Box 951476, Los Angeles, CA 90095-1476; (310) 206-2675; www1.law.ucla.edu/~erg. A policy analysis firm studying the impact of a Los Angeles living-wage ordinance.

Employment Policies Institute, 1775 Pennsylvania Ave., N.W., Suite 1200, Washington, DC 20006-4605; (202) 463-7650; www.EPIonline.org. Sponsors research on issues affecting companies with large proportions of entry-level jobs, such as living-wage ordinances.

Employment Policy Foundation (EPF), 1015 15th St., N.W., Suite 1200, Washington, DC 20005; (202) 789-8685; www.epf.org/LWsite/factsheets/adopted.asp. Posts copies of adopted living-wage ordinances on its Web site.

Good Jobs First, 1311 L St., N.W., Washington, DC 20005; (202) 737-4315; www.ctj.org/itep/gjf.htm. An Institute on Taxation and Economic Policy project that studies corporate subsidies and catalogs accountability outcomes for state and local governments.

Political Economy Research Institute, 10th floor Thompson Hall, University of Massachusetts, Amherst, MA 01003-7510; (413) 545-6355; www.umass.edu/peri. Researches and advises on policy issues, such as living-wage laws.

Responsible Wealth, 37 Temple Place, Boston, MA 02111; (617) 423-2148; www.responsiblewealth.org. Nonprofit alliance of 700 affluent American business owners devoted to highlighting dangers of excessive inequality of income and wealth in the United States; focuses on tax fairness, corporate responsibility and living wages.

[35] Marsha Shuler, "Claude 'Buddy' Leach to seek governorship," *The Advocate*, Aug. 11, 2002.

[36] Chip Johnson, "Restaurant tries to skate past wage law," *The San Francisco Chronicle*, Aug. 2, 2002, p.1.

[37] Quoted in David A. Lieb, "Supreme Court Dismisses Appeal in Living Wage Case," Associated Press Newswires, Sept. 5, 2002.

[38] Brian Meyer, "Protesters say Revisions Nullify Living Wage Law," *Buffalo News*, July 10, 2002, p. B3.

[39] Quoted in Sarah Schweitzer, "'Living Wage' in Boston Threatens Child-Care Programs," *The Boston Globe*, July 22, 2002.

[40] "Memorandum in Opposition to Hardship Waiver," filed with the Living Wage Division, Office of Jobs and Community Services, City of Boston, filed by ACORN and UAW Local 1596, July 22, 2002.

[41] David Focareta, "Minimal Enforcement: The Cleveland Living Wage Law's First Year," Policy Matters Ohio, March 2002.

[42] 2002 Agenda, Baltimoreans United In Leadership Development.

[43] "Occupational Employment Projections to 2010," U.S. Bureau of Labor Statistics, November 2001.

[44] "Federal Agenda 2001," City of Chicago.

[45] *Ibid*.

Bibliography

Selected Sources

Books

Pollin, Robert, and Stephanie Luce, *The Living Wage: Building a Fair Economy*, The New Press, 2000.

The authors challenge critics' claims that living-wage laws harm low-wage workers and are prohibitively costly.

Articles

Bailey, Steve, "Brushing Off the Janitors," *The Boston Globe*, Aug. 14, 2002, p. D1.

The reporter outlines the plight of janitors in downtown Boston, where 75 percent of 15,000 custodians work part-time jobs with no health benefits.

Greenhouse, Steven, " 'Living Wage' Roulette: Bigger Check, or Will it Be a Pink Slip?" *The New York Times*, May 19, 2002.

The author points to both improvements in the lives of low-wage workers because of the laws and harm to businesses and workers at the labor market's bottom rung.

Herbert, Bob, "Paying People to Work, but Not Enough to Live," *The New York Times*, Sept. 16, 2002.

The columnist outlines ongoing labor strife over wages for home health-care workers.

Romney, Lee, "Community, Developers Agree on Staples Plan," *Los Angeles Times*, May 31, 2001, A1.

Romney outlines a compromise deal between developers in Los Angeles and living-wage activists and environmentalists that is being called a model for public-private partnerships.

Tejada, Carlos, "Swelling Ranks? Living wage supporters push to expand current laws," *The Wall Street Journal*, May 22, 2002, B14.

Tejada describes efforts by living-wage advocates to cover more private employers and points to growing opposition.

Reports and Studies

"Living Wage Policy: The Basics," Employment Policies Institute, 2000.

This manual outlines job losses and adverse affects of the ordinances.

Baiman, Ron, *et. al.*, "A Step in the Right Direction: An Analysis of Forecasted Costs and Benefits of the Chicago Living-Wage Ordinance," Center for Urban Economic Development, University of Illinois at Chicago, July 2002.

The authors dispute a 1996 study that predicted high costs and dire economic consequences of a proposed Chicago ordinance (it was passed in 1999).

Elmore, Andrew, "Contract Costs and Economic Development in Living-Wage Localities," (Working draft), Brennan Center for Justice, New York University, Sept. 9, 2002.

A survey of city contract administrators and economic-development officials offers a mixed cost experience under living-wage laws.

Focareta, Dave, "Minimal Enforcement: The Cleveland Living-Wage Law's First Year," Policy Matters Ohio, March 2002.

The author reports Cleveland weakly implemented a wage law enacted in 2001. He recommends active monitoring and removing an exemption for publicly financed developments of limited liability investors.

Kraut, Karen, "Choosing the High Road: Businesses that Pay a Living Wage and Prosper," *Responsible Wealth*, 2000.

The report outlines business advantages from higher payrolls and offers anecdotal accounts from a variety of businesses.

Neumark, David, "How Living-Wage Laws Affect Low-Wage Workers and Low-Income Families," Public Policy Institute of California, 2002.

A study of 36 communities with living-wage laws reports a drop in urban poverty but also job losses among low-wage workers.

Reynolds, David, and Jen Kern, "Living Wage Campaigns: An Activist's Guide to Building the Movement for Economic Justice," Labor Studies Center, Wayne State University and Association of Community Organizations for Reform Now, 2000.

The authors offer a detailed blueprint for creating a living-wage campaign and provide clear insight into advocates' point of view. Reynolds is professor of labor studies at Wayne State and Kern directs ACORN's Living Wage Resource Center.

Sander, Richard, *et. al.*, "Living Wages and the Problem of Inequality in California," California Policy Options, School of Public Policy and Social Research, University of California at Los Angeles, 2001.

The authors outline political and labor shifts and wage-inequality trends at the outset of the movement. They raise unemployment and taxpayer cost concerns and offer an alternative policy.

Toikka, Richard, "The Case for a Targeted Living-Wage Subsidy," Employment Policies Institute, June 2001.

The report outlines arguments for local Earned Income Tax Credits as better policy than living-wage laws, such as: Wage laws raise hiring costs and destroy jobs; tax credits don't increase labor costs and promote hiring limited-skill workers.

8 SUV Debate

MARY H. COOPER

S tan Bishop got so upset about the controversy surrounding his wife's car that he started up a Web site to defend her purchase. Bishop's wife drives a $117,000 Hummer H1, a civilian knockoff of the military Humvee.

"She'd been talking about one for two years, and that's what she wants to drive," says Bishop, an Atlanta developer. "She bought it because she thinks it's cool, it's top of the food chain, it's big and it's strong and she likes it."

The H1 is indeed big and strong. Equipped with a 195-horsepower, V8 diesel engine, the three-ton behemoth can ford a stream two-and-a-half-feet deep and conquer the most rugged terrain. It's also 15 feet long and wider than any passenger vehicle on the road. Humvees are great for Army patrols. But does a suburban mom need one to fetch a quart of milk?

That's not the point, say Hummer drivers. "We live in America," says David Harris, Hummer sales manager at Moore Cadillac Hummer, in the Northern Virginia suburbs of Washington, D.C. "Are we not allowed to choose what we drive?"

Harris says his customers don't blink at the H1's price tag — the cheaper H2 goes for around $50,000 — for a variety of reasons. "A lot of soccer moms are willing to pay the cost for that added protection," he says. "The extremists want to get out into the woods, and not many other SUVs can do that without expensive modifications. And then there are the wealthy guys who just want a new toy."

Sport-utility vehicles are, perhaps, the quintessential icon of the 1990s. Ex-

From *The CQ Researcher*, May 16, 2003.

The three-ton, $117,000 Hummer H2 counts actor Arnold Schwarzenegger among its biggest fans. SUVs like the Hummer are seen as the ultimate escape vehicle and safe commuter car but also despised as gas-guzzling polluters that threaten their own occupants and everyone else on the road. But there's no disputing their popularity: SUVs account for 25 percent of all new-car sales.

Liaison/Chris Weeks

tolled as the ultimate escape vehicle and safe commuter car, they also are despised by critics as gas-guzzling, turnover-prone polluters that, contrary to widespread belief — are not safer than cars. Indeed, critics say, SUVs threaten the lives of both their own occupants and everyone else on the road.

"To buy a Hummer, you'd have to have an ego as big as the car," says Joan B. Claybrook, president of Public Citizen, a nonprofit safety-advocacy group. But the Hummer is only the most blatant expression of the "wasteful" and "dangerous" excess she and other critics attach to all SUVs.

A growing anti-SUV backlash has united an unlikely coalition against the big vehicles. The activists include such disparate forces as columnist and socialite Arianna Huffington, whose television ads blame SUVs for increasing U.S. dependence on Middle Eastern oil; religious leaders, whose "What Would Jesus Drive?" campaign makes fuel efficiency a moral issue; and environmental and safety activists, who plaster tickets and bumper stickers on SUVs "charging" owners with endan-

gering lives and befouling the planet. [1]

The recent invasion of oil-rich Iraq — which some critics said was motivated by America's dependence on foreign oil — helped turn SUVs into a moral issue for some. "America needs a line of cars that can get us to work in the morning without sending us to war in the afternoon," Huffington said in launching her latest TV ad, on May 7. "It's time to make sure our military and economic strength are never held captive to the politics of petroleum. We need cars and trucks that meet our transportation and safety needs without sacrificing our freedom, security or prosperity." [2]

The anti-SUV campaign is unprecedented in American society, pitting as it does advocates of one consumer item against another. "When was the last time that you saw people almost come to blows over the Apple vs. the PC, or the cell phone vs. the regular old telephone?" asks Daniel Becker, director of the Sierra Club's global warming and energy program. [3] "There is a level of divisiveness about SUVs and the selfishness that some people attribute to their drivers that causes enormous friction in our society."

Several key attributes set sport-utility vehicles apart from traditional sedans and coupes. Most noticeably, they're taller and boxier. Because they typically are built on a pickup-truck chassis, with higher clearance between the road and the undercarriage, SUVs are higher than cars. The higher center of gravity also explains the often choppy ride and truck-like feel of a typical SUV, despite the addition of such creature comforts as power accessories, leather seats and advanced sound systems usually associated with sedans.

SUV Sales Leveled Off

Since SUV sales peaked in 1998, they have leveled off at around 3 million vehicles per year — about 25 percent of the U.S. new-car market. Meanwhile, sales of sport wagons and other carlike "crossover" vehicles topped the million mark just six years after their introduction.

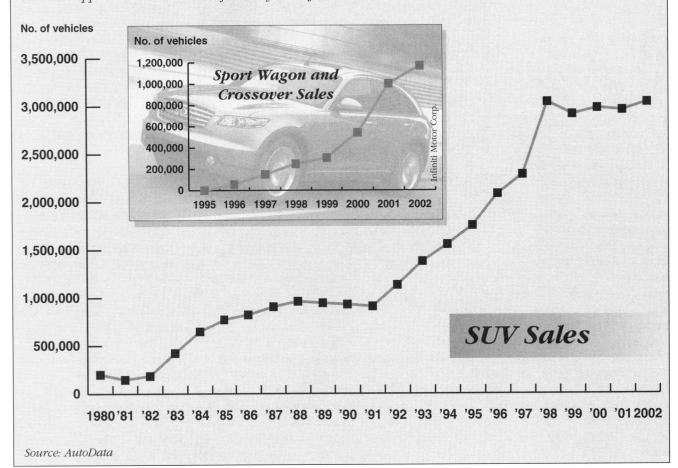

Source: AutoData

Moreover, like minivans, SUVs are categorized by the government as light trucks, so they are held to less stringent fuel-efficiency and safety standards than cars. [4] Since they are heavier than most cars, SUVs generally get much poorer gas mileage. In fact, the largest SUVs are so heavy they don't fall under federal fuel-economy standards at all. The Hummer, for example, gets only around 10 miles per gallon. The average car gets 27.5 miles per gallon. [5]

SUVs have been around for decades, but until the early 1990s they appealed mostly to outdoor enthusiasts who wanted the four-wheel drive capability typically offered in SUVs to access remote destinations. But after Ford Motor Co. introduced its popular Explorer in 1991, sales of SUVs skyrocketed, from less than a million a year to 3 million in 2002. In the past decade, SUVs — along with minivans — have essentially replaced the station wagon as the suburban car of choice in America. Today, there are 73 different models of SUVs, and they account for 25 percent of all new-car sales. [6]

"The SUV has evolved from a very spartan, unrefined, not accessorized, primarily two-door configuration with almost exclusively four-wheel drive to the point where today's SUVs in many households are the family car," says George Pipas, Ford's manager of sales analysis. "And they come in all sizes, from quite small vehicles all the way to the very large SUVs."

It's the largest SUVs — which account for only about 5 percent of new-vehicle sales — that have become "the poster children for the SUV controversy," Pipas notes.

Many drivers of the larger SUVs say they like the vehicle's massive size and high profile because it gives them better visibility over traffic and more safety. "We have two children, and my wife wants them wrapped up in an envelope of safety," says Bishop of the family Hummer. "We don't speed, we don't take chances and we don't get tickets. We just motor around and pick up our kids from school like everybody else. It's just that she's driving a little bit bigger car than anybody else."

But critics say the safety advantages of SUVs are illusory. In fact, the very attributes that SUV owners think make them safer — their heavier weight and higher center of gravity — make them more dangerous in certain circumstances. The higher profile makes them more likely to roll over, endangering their occupants. The SUV's greater size and weight also put passenger-car occupants at a disadvantage in case of collision.

It is the illusion of greater safety for the SUV's occupants that galls many critics, who see SUV drivers as selfish bullies willing to put their own personal safety above that of their fellow drivers. "One of the things they taught us in driver's ed. was to look ahead so we could anticipate what's going on in traffic several cars ahead," says Becker. "Well, if you're stuck behind an SUV, you can't see several cars ahead."

There is also the intimidation factor, he says. "It's literally designed into the SUV, with its growling front end, which is clearly designed to intimidate," he says. Indeed, one of the Hummer's latest ad campaigns touts the vehicle as a way women can "threaten men in a whole new way." [7]

SUVs do look different from their light-truck cousin, the minivan. "Minivan ads tend to emphasize themes like protection, togetherness and helping others," writes Keith Bradsher, a former *New York Times* Detroit bureau chief and author of *The High and Mighty*, a new book about the rise of SUVs. "SUV ads celebrate a more individualistic, sybaritic and even sometimes epicurean vision of life."

Like many critics, Bradsher attribut-

SUV Rollover Deaths Increased Most

The biggest increase in vehicle rollover deaths from 2001 to 2002 — nearly 10 percent — occurred among occupants of SUVs. The number who died in car crashes increased by only 4.3 percent, while deaths in vans dropped 11 percent. Overall, the number of people killed in rollover accidents in the one-year period jumped nearly 5 percent nationwide.

Percent Change in Rollover Deaths
(By vehicle type, 2001 to 2002)

Type of vehicle	Deaths in 2001	Deaths in 2002	Percent change
SUV	2,142	2,353	9.9%
Pickup truck	2,643	2,819	6.7
Passenger car	4,549	4,746	4.3
Van	784	695	-11.4
Total killed*	10,130	10,626	4.9%

* Includes occupants of all light trucks

Source: National Highway Traffic Safety Administration

es the SUV's explosive popularity in part to a cynical calculation by the auto industry. [8] "In marketing SUVs, automakers also try to capitalize on motorists' fear of crime or violence. In the process, the manufacturers have subtly raised the stakes in the highway arms race by making it appear unsafe to drive anything but an SUV." [9]

Indeed, SUV advocates say drivers of smaller vehicles are irresponsibly endangering the lives of their loved ones. And they insist that SUVs meet a legitimate need. "The public has a need for vehicles beyond what even large sedans can offer," says Ron Defore, spokesman for the Sport Utility Vehicle Owners Association. "SUVs let you carry four or five passengers safely when the in-laws are in town or when you're picking up the soccer team. Many Americans do their own home improvements, so on weekends they're hauling mulch and lumber,

things you just can't do very easily in most sedans. That's why SUVs have become so popular."

As long as consumers continue to buy SUVs, the controversy will likely continue to rage. As many Americans go shopping for a new vehicle to take on the road this summer, these are some of the questions they may wish to consider:

Are SUVs more dangerous than cars?

In the late 1990s, a spate of fatal accidents involving Ford Explorers equipped with defective Firestone tires revealed the vehicles' propensity to roll over. The accidents focused intense scrutiny on the widely held perception that SUVs are safer than cars because they are heavier. Automakers often reinforced that perception in congressional testimony, arguing that they could not make SUVs more fuel-efficient because that would

SUVs Fall Through Safety Loopholes

Sport-utility vehicles (SUVs) are not only held to less-stringent fuel-economy and pollution regulations than cars, they also enjoy far less stringent federal scrutiny when it comes to safety.

"When the safety, fuel-economy and emissions laws were originally passed in the 1960s and '70s, it was unimagined that SUVs and other light trucks would become nearly half of all new vehicles sold," said Joan B. Claybrook, president of Public Citizen, a safety-advocacy group. "Most safety standards and emissions rules are more than 30 years old, and relentless industry lobbying has killed off interim attempts to update them or pass badly needed new ones on rollover or vehicle crash compatibility."[1]

The gap in safety regulations for SUVs became apparent in the late 1990s, when 271 people died and more than 700 were injured in rollover accidents involving Ford Explorers fitted with defective Firestone tires. In the scandal that followed, nearly 20 million tires were recalled, and Congress passed the 2000 Transportation Recall Enhancement, Accountability and Documentation (TREAD) Act.

The new law required vehicle and equipment manufacturers to promptly report potential safety defects to the National Highway Traffic Safety Administration (NHTSA), increased penalties for safety violations and imposed criminal penalties for misleading the government about dangerous defects.

But the new law did not mandate that the government establish minimum rollover standards for SUVs — which safety experts have advocated for years — even though nearly 13,000 people died in SUV rollover accidents between 1994 and 2001, according to Claybrook. Instead, the TREAD law only required that by November 2002 NHTSA begin rating new cars on their propensity to roll over. While the agency already rates vehicles for their rollover propensity in a single-car crash, it has yet to comply with the TREAD Act's requirement to assess vehicles' rollover risks under emergency steering maneuvers in the absence of a crash. NHTSA Administrator Jeffrey W. Runge recently said the agency would finalize such a test "in the near future."[2]

But critics say it really doesn't matter, because the propensity ratings will be meaningless without a minimum standard by which to judge them. "Congress should require crash protections that will protect occupants in rollovers," Claybrook said. "Rollovers are primarily dangerous due to poor vehicle design. Safety belts and seat structures are not made to keep occupants in place during a crash, and vehicle roofs are so flimsy they crush into occupants' heads and spines, inflicting very serious injuries."

Despite the lack of a federal standard, most automakers voluntarily began taking steps to reduce the rollover tendency of SUVs. They lowered the center of gravity of some models and introduced new "crossover" SUVs — such as the Subaru Forester and the Lexus RX 300. Built on a car chassis and designed to resemble SUVs, crossovers blend the attributes of cars and SUVs and are held to the same safety regulations as cars.

With their higher bumpers and heavier weight, sport-utility vehicles also pose a major safety hazard to lower-riding vehicles. According to NHTSA, although SUVs and other light trucks represent 36 percent of all registered vehicles, they are involved in about half of all fatal two-vehicle crashes with passenger cars. Over 80 percent of the fatalities from such accidents are to occupants of passenger cars. Moreover, the Insurance Institute for Highway Safety has found that when an SUV collides with a car, occupant deaths in the car are about 50 percent more likely in side impacts than in frontal impacts.

Automakers have taken steps in recent years to improve their SUVs' safety records and reduce crash incompatibility with passenger cars. Ford, for example, now installs side airbags that protect the head and chest areas of occupants in its Escape and Excursion models. Ford Excursions now include "Blocker Beams" that lower the point of impact with a car in a frontal collision, helping prevent the SUV from riding over the car.

"The automotive industry in general, and Ford in particular, will continue to build vehicles with the utility and safety that our customers require," said Susan M. Cischke, Ford vice president for environmental and safety engineering.[3]

Nevertheless, Claybrook lists several other safety loopholes enjoyed by SUVs, including:

- **Side-impact protection:** SUVs heavier than 6,000 lbs. are held to a weaker standard than cars.
- **Roof strength:** SUVs over 6,000 lbs. need not meet any crash-protection standard for roof strength.
- **Child-restraint anchors:** Unlike cars, the biggest SUVs (above 8,500 lbs. carrying weight) are not required to provide anchorage systems to accommodate child restraints.
- **Brake lights:** Unlike cars, SUVs are not required to provide a center, high-mounted brake light.

Meanwhile, the Explorer continues to outsell all other SUVs, even though hundreds of lawsuits against both Ford and Bridgestone/Firestone are still pending. So far, all cases have been settled before going to a jury, and the U.S. Supreme Court handed the companies a victory in January by refusing to hear a case on whether Explorer owners qualified for class-action status.[4]

But Ford and Bridgestone/Firestone are not out of the woods on the rollover issue. In February, federal prosecutors in southern Illinois subpoenaed documents from both companies in a possible criminal investigation of tire failures.[5]

---

[1] Claybrook testified Feb. 26, 2003, before the Senate Commerce, Science and Transportation Committee.

[2] Runge testified Feb. 26, 2003, before the Senate Commerce, Science and Transportation Committee.

[3] Cischke testified Feb. 26, 2003, before the Senate Commerce, Science and Transportation Committee.

[4] See Davis Lazarus, "Greed Takes Class out of Class Action," *The San Francisco Chronicle*, Jan. 17, 2003.

[5] United Press International, "UPI News Update," Feb. 28, 2003.

require a decrease in vehicle weight, making them more dangerous. [10]

"SUVs are among the safest vehicles on the road and have contributed dramatically to the decline in the nation's fatality rate over the last decade," General Motors said recently. [11]

However, as the Ford scandal revealed, most mid-size SUVs have a much narrower and somewhat taller profile, making them more prone to roll over in a blowout, or when the driver takes a corner too fast.

Critics claim deceptive advertising campaigns continue to draw consumers to the perceived safety advantages of SUVs. "The auto industry has duplicitously created a false impression that you're safer in an SUV because you're surrounded by so much steel," says Becker of the Sierra Club. "The reality is that you are no safer than in a car because of the design flaws built into SUVs that make them just as dangerous to their occupants as they are to the occupants of the vehicles they hit. These vehicles have a higher center of mass, and they drive like trucks. They are unforgiving, and people roll over at a fairly alarming rate."

In fact, the National Highway Traffic Safety Administration (NHTSA) reported in April that between 2001 and 2002 total traffic fatalities increased by 1.7 percent nationwide — to 42,850 — but that SUV rollover deaths jumped almost 10 percent. [12] Jeffrey W. Runge, an emergency-room physician who now heads the agency, said that since SUVs and other light trucks account for an increasing portion of total passenger-

vehicle sales, "Deaths and injuries in rollover crashes will become a greater safety problem unless something changes." [13]

Runge shocked automakers in January when he told them he would never allow his daughter to drive an SUV that flunked his agency's rollover tests, even "if it was the last one on Earth." [14]

Defenders of SUVs concede they are more prone to roll over than cars but still offer greater protection for their occupants than cars do. "It's true that SUVs have a higher center of gravity and therefore a higher propensity to roll over," says Defore of the SUV Owners Association. "But when you get into your car today, if you're going to be in a crash, you don't know what kind of crash you're going to be in."

The best measure of a vehicle's safety, Defore says, is the overall fatality rate of its occupants. "The largest of the SUVs have the lowest fatality rate of all," he says. According to association figures, rollovers account for only 2.5 percent of crashes, and SUVs are more protective of their occupants in rear and side collisions, which make up the other 97.5 percent of crashes. [15]

"What the critics do is very cleverly point you to rollovers, but rollovers are very rare events," Defore says. "When you look at the overall risk, the largest of the SUVs come out the best."

But critics point out that while rollovers may account for less than 3 percent of accidents, they cause 30 percent of vehicular deaths. [16]

In addition, they cite two recent studies — including one by the industry itself — that have cast doubt on the bigger-is-safer assumption. The first study, conducted jointly by scientists at the University of Michigan and the Lawrence Berkeley National Laboratory, found that SUV drivers are not necessarily safer than those in smaller cars.

"On average, [SUVs] are as risky as the average midsize or large car," the study concluded, "and no safer than many of the most popular compact and subcompact models." The report was the first to analyze both the risk to SUV drivers and to drivers of other vehicles on the road — which the authors called combined risk. "If combined risk is considered," the report said, "most cars are safer than the average SUV." [17]

"We need to move away from the idea that bigger and heavier vehicles are automatically safer," said Marc Ross, a University of Michigan physicist. "Quality is a bigger predictor of safety than weight." [18]

Responding to the study, Priya Prasad, a senior technical fellow for safety at Ford Motor Co., insisted that in all Ford's studies, "Heavier is better, especially when you get into two-way accidents." [19]

One person died and four were injured in Indianapolis when a Chevrolet Trailblazer hit a Volkswagen Beetle head-on. SUVs are held to weaker safety standards than passenger cars, but automakers have voluntarily begun taking steps to make SUVs safer, including reducing their rollover tendency.

AP Photo/The Indianapolis Star, Steve Healey

Toyota SUVs Are Most Fuel-Efficient

The Japanese-made Toyota Rav4 sport-utility vehicle gets twice the mileage of the least-efficient SUVs.

Fuel Efficiency of 2003 SUVs and Vans
(by city and highway mpg)

Make/Model Drive train/Engine/Transmission	MPG	
	City	Hwy
Most-Efficient		
Sport-Utility Vehicles		
Toyota Rav4, 2WD, 4 cyl, Manual	25	31
Toyota Rav4, 2WD, 4 cyl, Automatic	24	29
Minivans		
Chrysler Voyager/Town & Cntry, 2WD, 4 cyl, Automatic	21	27
Dodge Caravan, 2WD, 4 cyl, Automatic	21	27
Passenger Vans		
Chevrolet Astro 2WD, 6 cyl, Automatic	16	20
GMC Safari 2WD, 6 cyl, Automatic	16	20
Least-Efficient		
Sport-Utility Vehicles		
Cadillac Escalade, AWD, 8 cyl, Automatic	12	16
GMC K1500 Yukon, AWD, 8 cyl, Automatic	12	16
Land Rover Discovery Series II, 4WD, 8 cyl, Automatic	12	16
Minivans		
Kia Sedona, 6 cyl, Automatic	15	20
Passenger Vans		
Chevrolet H1500 Express, AWD 8 cyl, Automatic	13	17
Ford E150 Club Wagon, RWD 8 cyl, Automatic	13	17
GMC H1500 Savana, AWD 8 cyl, Automatic	13	17

Source: Environmental Protection Agency

A week later, the Alliance of Automobile Manufacturers released figures conceding for the first time that SUV occupants are 3.5 percent more likely to die in crashes than sedan occupants. The automakers' analysis found that while SUV occupants were less likely to die in front-end, side and rear-end collisions than passenger-car occupants, they are nearly three times more likely to be killed in rollovers.

The alliance's vice president for safety, Robert Strassburger, said, "At a minimum, SUVs are as safe as automobiles." He noted that 72 percent of those killed in SUV rollovers were not wearing their seat belts.

Safety advocates said the alliance's Feb. 25 press briefing marked the first time automakers have acknowledged that SUVs overall are not as safe as cars. "They are recognizing that there are safety issues that are unique to SUVs," said Brian O'Neill, president of the Insurance Institute for Highway Safety (IIHS). [20]

In addition to the rollover danger, Becker says, SUVs are more dangerous to their own occupants because they use a solid-steel beam that extends from bumper to bumper to make the vehicle strong enough to sustain heavy off-road use. "When that vehicle hits something else, the beam doesn't absorb the impact of the crash and dissipate it over the vehicle like a car, which crumples and dissipates the force of the impact around the occupants," he says. "If a Ford Expedition SUV and a subcompact GM Saturn hit the same bridge abutment at the same speed, the occupants of the Saturn will come out better in that crash than the occupants of the Expedition because the Saturn has crashworthiness built into it, and the Expedition does not."

In addition to endangering their own occupants, say critics, SUVs threaten smaller vehicles. Drivers of passenger cars can't see around SUVs to observe traffic ahead, and cars are likely to incur greater damage in collisions with the heavier, taller vehicles. (*See "At Issue," p. 153.*)

According to studies by the IIHS, a passenger car is at a significant disadvantage in a collision with an SUV, especially if hit from the side. In a side crash, according to a 1998 IIHS "crash-incompatibility" study, the car's occupants are 25 times more likely to die than the SUV's occupants. [21]

"The theory that I'm going to protect myself and my family even if it costs other people's lives has been the operative incentive for the design of these vehicles, and that's just wrong," NHTSA's Runge said. "That's not compassionate conservatism." [22]

During his Jan. 14 speech to automakers, Runge told automakers that he had appointed a NHTSA panel to consider new safety regulations for SUVs and challenged the industry to solve the problems of rollovers and disproportionate crash damage to smaller vehicles.

Faced with the threat of new regulations, the automakers alliance quietly signaled that they are willing to work with Runge to make SUVs less lethal. In a Feb. 13 letter to Runge, they pledged to work with the IIHS to develop short- and long-term measures to deal with SUV safety hazards. [23]

Indeed, some manufacturers already have begun making voluntary changes. Ford and GM have lowered bumper heights or the center of gravity on some models to reduce the risk of rollover and bumper override. Others have introduced new "crossover" SUVs. Built on a car chassis and designed to resemble SUVs, crossovers look like SUVs but are subject to most of the same safety regulations as cars.

"Crossovers are much more humane, both for their occupants and other people on the road," says Claybrook of Public Citizen. "They're easier to see around, they have shorter stopping distances and they're not as high up as SUVs."

Yet SUV advocates like Defore — who calls SUV critics like Claybrook "social nannies" — dismisses the compatibility issue. "There has always been a disparity in size of vehicles, and I hope there always will be," he says. "You're always going to have a wide variety of needs, from 18-wheelers to dump trucks to municipal buses to small compact cars."

Other SUV advocates blame the compatibility problem on small-car owners themselves. "By choosing to buy a smaller vehicle because they want to save a few hundred dollars

a year, [small car owners] put their families in jeopardy," says Atlanta developer Bishop. "That is a personal choice."

But David M. Nemtzow, president of the Alliance to Save Energy, responds: If all car drivers were to trade in their small cars for SUVs, "We'd end up with a kind of arms race, where you trade in your small car for something bigger, and the other guy gets an SUV that's bigger still."

Should SUVs be held to stricter fuel-economy standards?

When Arab oil producers imposed an embargo on exports to the United States in 1973, skyrocketing oil prices plunged the country into its first energy crisis. Congress responded in 1975 with a flurry of energy regulations, including Corporate Average Fuel Economy (CAFE) standards requiring automakers to improve fuel efficiency in new cars. Automakers were allowed to continue manufacturing gas-guzzlers, but they had to make enough fuel-efficient models to keep their overall mileage within the required federal limits. [24]

At the time, light trucks were a relatively small segment of the auto market, mostly pickups and cargo vans used by farmers and small-business owners for work-related transportation. So Congress set a more lenient mileage standard for these vehicles — currently 20.7 miles per gallon, as opposed to the 27.5 mpg required of passenger cars. The looser standard has continued to apply to minivans and SUVs — essentially modified pickup trucks — even as they became best-selling alternatives to passenger cars. Light trucks also are exempt from the "gas-guzzler tax," a separate levy imposed on the sale of new cars whose fuel economy falls below 22.5 mpg.

Nemtzow, of the Alliance to Save Energy, recalls that when the CAFE standards went into effect, then-Chrysler Corp. Chairman Lee Iacocca lament-

ed that within a decade everyone in America would be driving a subcompact Ford Pinto, one of the few cars that met the standard at that time.

"That was duplicitous," Nemtzow says. "It's a time-honored tradition for auto industry lobbyists to always undersell their own engineers. The lobbyists say it can't be done, it's fabulously expensive; then if they're forced to do it, the engineers always come through and figure out inexpensive ways to make cars more fuel-efficient. Luckily, American ingenuity is more successful than American lobbying."

Indeed, the Big Three Detroit automakers — General Motors, Ford and Chrysler — made rapid gains in fuel efficiency during the 1970s by reducing vehicle size and weight. Then they implemented more innovative technological changes during the 1980s, such as radial tires, aerodynamic body design and four-cylinder engines, which enabled them to meet the CAFE standards and improve performance.

"The technology revolution has been very helpful for fuel efficiency as well as environmental performance because cars now are much better at taking the available gasoline and combusting it accurately in the cylinder using sensors and control technology," Nemtzow says. "As a result, they waste less gas and emit less unburned hydrocarbon."

But critics of fuel-economy regulations trace the phenomenal popularity of SUVs to the standards themselves. "As CAFE standards rose for cars, it became increasingly difficult for vehicle manufacturers to satisfy the demand of many Americans who wanted the utility of larger and more powerful vehicles," says the SUV Owners Association's Defore, a former official at NHTSA, which administers the standards. "Thirty years ago, those needs were met by the station wagon, which was built on a passenger-car platform. But it just became too difficult for the manufacturers to keep building them in any great number and still comply with CAFE standards." To fill the need for utility vehicles, automakers started making minivans and SUVs, built on truck platforms. "SUVs, minivans and pickups are the last remaining vehicles that can meet those needs," Defore says.

But industry critics say the SUV was less a response to pent-up consumer demand for bigger vehicles than the product of a cynical effort to cut production costs by sidestepping federal fuel and safety regulations. "The American manufacturers discovered, and have taught the Japanese manufacturers, that you can make a lot of money — $8,000 to $20,000 per vehicle — by creating a gas-guzzling behemoth that poses safety threats to its own occupants and others, consumes prodigious amounts of gas and pollutes too much," says the Sierra Club's Becker.

The critics say Detroit created demand for SUVs by aggressively marketing what were essentially inexpensive trucks as "safer," high-end cars. "SUVs are basically gussied-up pickup trucks, and most have never been comprehensively redesigned to be safely used as passenger vehicles," said Claybrook of Public Citizen. "In the SUV, the industry found and developed a broad market that allowed it to rake in cash while taking every step to avoid spending money to fix the unstable and threatening vehicle that resulted." [25]

In 1996, automakers repeated their earlier arguments against proposals to tighten CAFE standards, this time covering SUVs. Under pressure from the automakers, Congress actually prohibited NHTSA from even studying the possibility of raising the CAFE standards.

Lawmakers later lifted the ban and required the agency to issue a new, tighter standard for the 2004 model year of SUVs, vans and other light trucks. In July 2001 the National Academy of Sciences released a long-awaited review of fuel-economy standards stating that existing technology allowed for fuel-efficiency improvements in SUVs. However, industry representatives put a dif-

ferent spin on the report, claiming that it proved their argument that it would not be feasible to improve SUV fuel efficiency. [26] NHTSA announced last year that it would maintain the current light-truck standard of 20.7 mpg through 2004, saying it would be too hard for the industry to make the needed improvements by the deadline.

Responding to complaints that the 2004 standard was too lenient, the U.S. Department of Transportation (DOT) announced on April 1 that it was raising the CAFE standard for SUVs and other light trucks. Automakers will now have to increase light-truck mileage by a total of 1.5 mpg to 22.2 mpg during the 2005-'07 model years.

However, the new standard seems unlikely to end the debate. "The administration thought it could take the fuel-economy issue off the table forever by making a minuscule improvement in fuel-economy standards," Becker says. "Fortunately, no one bought their argument that they've dealt with this issue by calling for a 1.5 mpg improvement. The reality is that we could save 3 million barrels of oil a day if our cars, SUVs and other trucks averaged 40 mpg — and we have the technology right now to do that."

Indeed, former Ford CEO Jacques Nasser promised in July 2000 that his company would reduce fuel consumption in its new SUVs by 25 percent by 2005. Though his successor, William Clay Ford Jr., recently recanted that promise, Ford still plans to introduce next summer a hybrid version of its small Escape SUV that will get 40 mpg. [27] Hybrid vehicles run on a combination of gas and electricity.

"Beyond a shadow of a doubt, automakers are perfectly capable of building SUVs with greater mileage," said Rep. Sherwood Boehlert, R-NY. "In fact, they crow about it every place but Washington, D.C. GM and Ford have both announced plans to bring out an SUV that gets 40 miles per gallon in the next model year. What we're

told is impossible on the House floor turns out to be perfectly possible on the auto-assembly floor."

Boehlert concedes that the 1.5-mile-per-gallon change is better than nothing. "The administration should be congratulated for at least acknowledging the need to improve fuel economy," he said. "But the 1.5 mile per gallon increase over three years sought by the administration is minuscule — far less than what is needed, and far less than what is possible." [28]

Boehlert and Rep. Edward J. Markey, D-Mass., have sponsored a measure that would eliminate the fuel-economy disparity between cars and light trucks and require automakers to achieve an average of 30 mpg across their product lines by 2010. "The automakers can decide whether they want to reach these levels by improving the mileage of cars or SUVs or both," Boehlert said. "It does not set a specific standard for SUVs."

On April 11, the House defeated the Boehlert-Markey proposal, 268-162. The same fate may await another effort, by Sens. Dianne Feinstein, D-Calif., and Olympia J. Snowe, R-Maine, to require SUVs to meet the same fuel standards as cars by 2011. [29]

It appears unlikely, in fact, that Congress will require additional changes to CAFE standards so soon after the administration's regulatory action on SUVs, a fact that some supporters of stricter regulations now concede. "Improvements in fuel-economy standards have worked before," Becker says. "They will likely work again if either Detroit will stop fighting it or the Congress will stop listening to Detroit's siren song."

Do Americans have a moral duty to conserve energy?

Hostility toward SUV drivers also stems from their use of more gasoline than many other vehicles on the road. SUVs get less than 18 mpg, compared to 22.5 mpg for the average passenger car. [30] Because Americans

Chronology

1930s-1960s
Early SUVs draw limited numbers of outdoors enthusiasts.

1935
General Motors Corp. introduces the Suburban Carryall, an eight-passenger vehicle combining a passenger-car body with a light-truck chassis.

1946
Responding to heavy post-war demand, Willys-Overland introduces a civilian version of the four-wheel drive Jeep.

1956
Congress authorizes construction of the Interstate Highway System. Detroit automakers indulge Americans' passion for cars with powerful, V8-driven behemoths.

1966
The National Traffic and Motor Vehicle Safety Act and Highway Safety Act establish federal safety standards for cars and tires — including padded dashboards, outside mirrors and impact-absorbing steering columns — and require states to establish highway-safety programs or lose highway-construction funds.

1970s
Energy crises spark regulations to curb fuel consumption.

1970
Congress creates the National Highway Traffic Safety Administration (NHTSA) to administer auto-safety regulations and set new ones to address design flaws that pose an "unreasonable risk" to public safety.

Oct. 29, 1973
Arab oil producers impose an embargo on exports to the United States, hiking oil prices and plunging the country into its first energy crisis.

1975
As part of the 1975 Energy Policy and Conservation Act, Congress authorizes Corporate Average Fuel Economy (CAFE) standards requiring automakers to improve fuel efficiency in new cars. Light trucks, used mainly by farmers and small-business owners, are held to less-stringent standards.

1980s
Regulation-driven technological changes improve auto mileage and safety.

1984
Chrysler Corp.'s minivan quickly displaces the station wagon as the Baby Boom generation's standard family car.

1900s
SUVs are among the nation's most popular passenger vehicles.

1991
Ford Motor Co. introduces the Explorer, which becomes the best-selling SUV.

1996
Under pressure from automakers, Congress prohibits NHTSA from even studying the possibility of raising CAFE standards.

February 1999
Ford introduces its largest SUV to date, the four-ton, "super-duty" Excursion. The Sierra Club blasts Ford for producing a "sport-utility vehicle that guzzles enough gas to make Saddam Hussein smile."

2000s
A string of rollover crashes highlights SUV safety flaws.

Aug. 9, 2000
Defective Firestone tires are implicated in dozens of Explorer rollover accidents; Firestone recalls 17.9 million tires.

Nov. 1, 2000
President Bill Clinton signs the Transportation Recall Enhancement, Accountability and Documentation (TREAD) Act aimed at forcing auto companies and their suppliers to more promptly recall defective products. It also mandates that within two years NHTSA test new cars for rollover propensity.

2001
SUVs, minivans and pickup trucks capture 52 percent of total vehicle sales.

February 2003
Federal prosecutors in southern Illinois subpoena documents from Bridgestone/Firestone and Ford in a possible criminal investigation of tire failures.

April 2003
NHTSA reports that 42,850 people died in traffic accidents in 2002, the most since 1990. Most of the increase in fatalities was in pickup trucks, SUVs and vans; SUV rollover deaths were almost 10 percent higher than in 2001.

SUV Rates Pollution 'Loopholes'

Environmentalists have long complained that sport-utility vehicles (SUVs) pollute more than passenger cars, largely because they are held to weaker mileage and emissions standards.

Defined as "light trucks," most SUVs are held to less stringent fuel-economy standards than cars: currently 20.7 miles per gallon (mpg), compared with 27.5 mpg required for cars under the Corporate Average Fuel Economy (CAFE) standards passed in 1975 to curb gasoline consumption.

The higher a vehicle's gas mileage, the less carbon dioxide it emits as a byproduct of the fuel-combustion process. The United States is by far the world's biggest emitter of carbon dioxide — the main "greenhouse" gas believed responsible for global warming — and almost a third of America's carbon dioxide emissions come from cars and trucks.

Bowing to pressure from the public and environmentalists, the Bush administration recently tightened CAFE standards for light trucks, including the majority of SUVs, by 1.5 mpg — to 22.2 mpg by 2007. But even with the new standard, most SUVs, pickups and minivans will continue to consume more gasoline than automobiles.

The Mercedes G500 and other big SUVs don't have to meet fuel-economy standards because they're classified as medium-duty trucks.

Courtesy Daimler Chrysler

"The auto companies have been using the loophole that allows SUVs and other trucks to guzzle more gas and pollute more," says Daniel Becker, director of the Sierra Club's Global Warming and Energy Program. The really big SUVs — like General Motors' Hummer series, the Ford Excursion and Lincoln Navigator — don't have to meet any fuel-economy standards at all because they're classified as medium-duty trucks, a category that once consisted almost exclusively of commercial haulers. "By using the loophole, the auto industry has increased our gas guzzling, increased our dependence on OPEC [Organization of Petroleum Exporting Countries] and increased the emissions spewing from these vehicles," Becker says.

In referring to emissions, Becker and other environmental advocates include carbon dioxide, because of its impact on global climate, as well as the traditional tailpipe pollutants that cause urban smog and ground-level ozone. But SUV advocates reject that definition, saying carbon dioxide is not an officially designated pollutant like nitrogen oxides and sulfur dioxide, which are regulated under the 1970 Clean Air Act.

"The Environmental Protection Agency (EPA) does not classify carbon dioxide as a pollutant," says Ron Defore, a spokesman for the Sport Utility Vehicle Owners Association and a former official at the National Highway Traffic Safety Administration (NHTSA). "As for the so-called loophole in the [Clean Air Act] emissions standard, EPA has already promulgated rules that are going to require all vehicles in the light-truck category to meet the same strict emissions standards as passenger cars. So end of story."

Defore was referring to a Clean Air Act "loophole" that allowed light trucks — because they were used chiefly as farm and commercial vehicles at the time — to meet less stringent tailpipe emissions standards than cars. All vans and most SUVs and pickups were allowed to emit up to 47 percent more carbon monoxide and 175 percent more nitrogen oxides than passenger cars.

But in November 1998, in order to meet its overall Clean Air Act goals, California ruled that all light trucks would have to meet the same emissions standards as cars no later than the 2004 model year. On Feb. 10, 2000, the EPA followed California's lead and required that all light trucks and passenger cars — as well as medium-duty SUVs and passenger vans — meet the same emissions standards by the 2009 model year, which will arrive in showrooms in 2008. [1]

But that doesn't close the emissions loophole for SUVs on the road today.

---

[1] See Brent D. Yacobucci, "Sport Utility Vehicles, Mini-Vans, and Light Trucks: An Overview of Fuel Economy and Emissions Standards," *CRS Report for Congress*, Congressional Research Service, Feb. 28, 2003.

import more than half the oil they consume, higher fuel consumption means greater dependence on foreign oil, as well as more carbon-dioxide emissions, considered a primary cause of global warming. The United States is the world's largest emitter of carbon dioxide — a third of which comes from burning transportation fuels. [31]

Environmentalists say these statistics alone constitute a moral indictment against the use of SUVs for most personal transportation.

"The United States uses 25 percent

of the world's oil, and we sit on 3 percent of the world's known reserves," says the Sierra Club's Becker. "Being dependent on others for the natural resources that we don't have when we use a disproportionate share of those resources causes problems for the United States. I believe the war we just fought in Iraq had something to do with oil. A bunch of U.S. soldiers just died, and a bunch of Iraqis died, too, in part because we needed to secure oil for SUVs."

Becker's group estimates that switching from an average car to a 13-mpg SUV for one year would waste more energy than leaving your refrigerator door open for six years. [32] "Making cars go further on a gallon of gas is the biggest, single step we can take to curb our oil dependence and cut global-warming pollution," Becker says.

Some religious leaders echo the call for improved fuel economy and cleaner-running engines. "The cars that we buy represent probably the single, largest expenditure with ecological impact that most of us will make," says Paul Gorman, director of the National Religious Partnership for the Environment. "People should learn a little about why this represents a moral choice."

Last November, the Partnership spearheaded the widely publicized "What Would Jesus Drive?" campaign to encourage people to consider the environmental impact of their car-purchasing decisions. Though Gorman denies that the campaign was intended to vilify SUVs or any other specific vehicle type, heeding its call would undoubtedly result in fewer SUV sales in favor of more fuel-efficient cars. "Our goal is not to become another environmental advocate," Gorman says, "but to bring issues of environmental sustainability and justice to the heart of religious life. Caring for God's creation has got to be central to every tradition that cares about God."

SUV advocate Bishop says Americans are unlikely to shun big vehicles on moral or religious grounds alone. "America is a car-centric society, and

you can't mandate that a person drive a car that's too small," he says. "Can we continue to improve safety? Yes. Can we improve fuel economy? Absolutely. But you're not going to get Americans into physically smaller vehicles on the basis of a perception of whether there's a hole in the ozone layer or whether we have an insufficient amount of oil."

In the past, energy conservation has figured high on the list of efforts expected of patriotic Americans. During the energy crises of the 1970s, President Jimmy Carter called conservation "the moral equivalent of war." Later administrations also placed conservation and environmental protection high on their policy agendas.

But SUV buyers have received little discouragement from President Bush. The administration's energy policy, laid out in 2001, focuses more on increasing domestic oil drilling, including in Alaska's Arctic National Wildlife Refuge (ANWR) and other protected lands, than on reducing fuel consumption. Bush also renounced the Kyoto Protocol, an international agreement to curb emissions of carbon dioxide and other greenhouse gases contributing to global warming. [33] And critics say the administration's recent tightening of fuel-efficiency standards for SUVs will have little impact on fuel consumption or auto emissions.

"Many Americans just don't want to think they're trashing the environment," says Nemtzow of the Alliance to Save Energy. In his view, it is to this group that Bush is appealing with his new SUV fuel-economy standard, as well as a recent tightening of diesel-emission standards for off-road vehicles and the administration's recent call for a $1.2 billion program to develop non-polluting hydrogen cars by 2020. [34] "These actions show the Bush administration's new thinking as they look forward to 2004. They recognize they won't be able to persuade those Americans who want them to lead on the environment, but they're trying to reach out to Middle-American swing voters by saying we're

not so bad on the environment."

But SUV advocates say the administration's approach is in tune with Americans' views on energy and environmental issues. "Nobody wants to be anti-environment," says Defore of the SUV Owners Association. "But when it comes to the most expensive consumer product that most people buy, second to a house, people act a lot differently. Many people are willing to pay extra for safety advantages, but when it comes to environmental advantages — which are more societal and less personal — the majority are not willing to pay much, if anything, for that." ∎

BACKGROUND

Station-Wagon Era

S port-utility vehicles trace their ancestry back to 1935, when, in the midst of the Great Depression, General Motors (GM) introduced the Chevrolet Suburban Carryall. The eight-passenger vehicle lacked four-wheel drive, but like SUVs it combined a passenger-car body with a light-truck chassis. The next year, GM used the same combination to produce the first station wagon with a body made entirely of steel instead of wood.

The first car with off-road capabilities typical of modern SUVs was the classic, open-sided Jeep used in World War II. [35] Willys-Overland churned out more than 700,000 of the small, versatile workhorses during the war. Ford also produced Jeeps under license for the military.

After the war, farmers and sportsmen snapped up decommissioned Jeeps for their off-road capability and inexpensive upkeep. They were in such great demand that Willys introduced a nearly identical, four-wheel-drive "civilian Jeep" in 1946. The original Jeep's appeal proved so enduring that an updated but visually similar model, the Wrangler, continues to sell.

Willys produced the first SUV forerunner in 1949, with the Jeep All-Steel Station Wagon, equipped with four-wheel drive. Farmers, ranchers and sportsmen were the main consumers of both the civilian Jeep and the new wagon, which remained popular through the early 1950s. Britain's Land Rover, a similarly rugged, off-road vehicle used extensively in Africa, was no match in the U.S. market for the Jeep.

Development of Jeep station wagons continued apace during a post-war economic boom in the late 1950s and '60s that enabled more and more Americans to buy vehicles of all types. But the biggest focus in automotive design was on passenger sedans suited for travel on the country's expanding roadway network. With seemingly unlimited gasoline supplies, Americans' love affair with the car blossomed, and Detroit indulged their passion with powerful, V8-driven behemoths with dramatic tailfins, three-tone paint jobs and convertible tops. Comfort and convenience were the order of the day, as automatic transmissions gradually replaced the standard gearshift, and air-conditioning, power steering and power brakes became popular options.

The station wagon was Detroit's answer to the postwar Baby Boom, with its burgeoning families. The elongated version of a standard passenger car, with a large, windowed, rear storage area accessed by a separate door, the wagon became the family car of the 1950s. By decade's end, one in every six vehicles made in Detroit was a station wagon.

Compact Cars

During the 1960s, small, zippy, sports cars made by foreign automakers like MG, Triumph and Alfa

Romeo began to claim a small share of the U.S. market. With rising incomes, more and more American households opted for a second car, often a smaller model made by Japan's Datsun (now Nissan) and Toyota, as well as European Volkswagens, Renaults and Saabs.

Detroit, which continued to account for 90 percent of U.S. auto sales, followed suit with "compact" cars such as the Ford Falcon and Chevrolet Corvair (1960). Toward the end of the 1960s, as the first Baby Boomers reached driving age, Detroit turned out "muscle cars" like the Dodge Charger and sporty models like the popular Ford Mustang (1964).

Throughout the 1950s and '60s, utility vehicles continued to serve a limited but growing niche in the auto market. In 1956, Chevrolet equipped the Suburban with four-wheel drive, producing the first model of what would become its later SUV prototype. Farm-equipment maker International Harvester introduced the Travelall, a four-wheel-drive passenger vehicle, and a smaller model, the Scout. Jeep came out with a similar vehicle, the Wagoneer, in 1962. Toyota, then an obscure Japanese manufacturer, sent its first Land Cruiser SUVs to the United States. Ford entered the SUV market in 1966 with the Bronco, a two-door passenger vehicle mounted on a full-size pickup chassis. Three years later, GM followed with the similarly built Chevrolet Blazer and GMC Jimmy.

In the 1960s, concern arose about the number of cars, which doubled from 49 million in 1950 to 102 million in 1968. Congress passed the Clean Air Act in 1963 to improve air quality and reduce auto-induced urban smog. Later amendments required automakers to reduce exhaust emissions, starting with 1968 models.

Deaths from auto accidents also rose, from 35,000 in 1950 to 55,000 in 1968. Although Swedish automaker Volvo had first introduced three-point safety belts as early as 1959, U.S. au-

tomakers resisted installing anything more than lap belts, despite mounting highway deaths and injuries.

In 1965, consumer advocate Ralph Nader's scathing criticism of the industry's safety record, *Unsafe at Any Speed*, called for safer cars. Congress responded with the National Traffic and Motor Vehicle Safety Act and the Highway Safety Act, signed in 1966 by President Lyndon B. Johnson. The laws established federal safety standards for cars and tires and required states to set up highway safety programs or lose part of their federal highway-construction funds. The newly created DOT administered the programs. [36] By 1968, automakers were required to install front seat lap-and-shoulder safety belts in all new cars.

Energy Crunch

The age of the large passenger vehicle abruptly ended after the 1973 Arab oil embargo. [37] The national energy policy that emerged from the resulting gas shortage — embodied in the 1975 Energy Policy and Conservation Act — required automakers to improve fuel efficiency. Manufacturers were required to meet a company-wide average threshold on all new cars of 18 mpg by 1978, 20 mpg by 1980 and 27.5 mpg by 1985. [38]

But the CAFE standards contained a loophole that would prove critical to the later development of SUVs. Congress set more lenient mileage standards for "light trucks," a special category of vehicles that included pickups (and later vans and sport-utility vehicles) weighing 8,500 pounds or less. Average light-truck mileage, originally mandated at 17.5 mpg for 1982, gradually rose to 20.7 mpg in 1996. [39]

While automakers could continue selling the popular station wagons, SUV precursors and other gas-guzzlers, they also were required to produce more fuel-efficient vehicles in order to meet their fleetwide average. Japanese and European automakers specializing in small, energy-efficient cars — like Toyota, Honda and Volkswagen — quickly stepped in to meet America's sudden demand for more economical vehicles. Detroit responded with subcompacts like the AMC Gremlin, Chevrolet Vega and Ford Pinto, but they were no match for the foreign competition. By 1980, Japanese manufacturers had captured 20 percent of the U.S. auto market.

Detroit soon gained a reputation for producing inferior vehicles, especially after a sensational 1980 trial confirmed that a design flaw caused the gas tank of the subcompact Ford Pinto to explode when rear-ended.

Meanwhile, in an effort to improve fuel efficiency and reduce highway deaths, Congress in 1973 enacted a nationwide speed limit of 55 mpg. And in 1975 and 1976, lawmakers tightened emission standards for passenger vehicles. Automakers responded with new technology, including catalytic converters to capture pollutants released during fuel combustion.

Enter the SUV

B y the 1980s, new sources of oil had been discovered in the North Sea and Africa, contributing to a decline in worldwide oil and gasoline prices. Interest in SUVs — albeit smaller and lighter models — resumed. In 1983, GM introduced the Chevy S-10 Blazer and GMC S-15 Jimmy, relatively compact SUVs powered by four-

Ford says its 2004 Hybrid SUV Escape will get 40 mpg. Hybrids run on a combination of gas and electricity.

Getty Images/Stephen Chernin

cylinder and six-cylinder engines instead of the V8s of earlier models. Ford followed with another "compact" SUV, the Bronco II.

In 1984, Jeep came out with smaller versions of its 1960s-era Cherokee and Wagoneer. Like modern SUVs, the Jeep models were marketed as peppier, sportier alternatives to the station wagon.

Building on their reputation as makers of superior-quality, energy-efficient compacts, Japanese carmakers made further inroads into the U.S. auto market in the 1980s with truck-based models of their own, including the Mitsubishi Montero (1982), Isuzu Trooper (1984), Nissan Pathfinder (1987) and Toyota 4Runner (1985).

Detroit continued to market station wagons, but the 1980s saw a revolution in family-car design. Ford, tarnished by the Pinto controversy, made a speedy comeback in 1986 with the Ford Taurus and Mercury Sable. The aerodynamic, jellybean shape of the midsize cars and wagons marked a departure from the boxy profiles typical of earlier models; it also improved fuel efficiency by cutting down on wind resistance. Consumers turned the Taurus into a best-seller for several years, even as Japanese brands captured 30 percent of total U.S. vehicle sales.

Chrysler Corp., which had been saved from bankruptcy in 1979 by a federal loan bailout, also scored a major success in the 1980s family-car market. Chrysler's bulbous, new Dodge Caravan minivan, introduced in 1984, became a favorite among Baby Boomers, many of whom jettisoned their parents' stodgy wagons. The carpooling, Baby-Boomer "soccer mom" behind the wheel of a minivan became a ubiquitous symbol of the times.

The 1990s booming economy boosted the SUV from a niche product to an industry standard. Buoyed by a bullish stock market, declining interest rates, low unemployment and low gasoline prices, American consumers discarded their concerns about fuel economy (the 55-mph speed limit was repealed in 1995) and sought vehicles reflecting their optimism. SUVs fit the bill.

Ford's hugely popular Explorer led the way. Introduced in 1991, it combined the lure of the outdoors through its rugged, truck-like appearance with power windows and locks, leather seats, advanced sound systems and other passenger-car refinements. The Explorer's four-wheel drive capability made it appealing not only to outdoor enthusiasts but also to suburban wannabes anxious to shed their domesticated wagons and minivans. With Explorers dominating the best-seller charts for both cars and trucks, the SUV as hip commuter car was born.

Reflecting the Explorer's phenomenal popularity, sales figures rose from 187,000 units in 1982 to 900,000 in 1992, the year after the Explorer appeared. For the rest of the 1990s, SUVs continued to be the industry's fastest-growing segment. To satisfy a broader range of consumers, carmakers in the mid-1990s began introducing a variety of smaller, car-based models, combining all-wheel drive and the SUV look with carlike handling and comfort, such as Toyota's RAV4 and Highlander, the Honda CR-V and the Subaru Forester.

Luxury SUVs also made their entrance with the unveiling of the Lexus RX 300. Continued low fuel prices helped boost sales of the biggest SUVs, such as the Chevy Suburban and its new competitor, the Ford Expedition. By 2000, SUV sales reached a record 3.3 million vehicles; by 2001, SUVs, minivans and pickups captured 52 percent of total vehicle sales. ■

CURRENT SITUATION

Anti-SUV Backlash

As SUV sales have mounted, America's streetscape has changed. A decade ago, a typical line of suburban traffic consisted of traditional passenger cars of approximately the same height. Today, the passenger car is often in the minority; SUVs ranging from the small Subaru Forester to the massive Hummer H1 make up about half the vehicles on the road.

The rise of a backlash among non-SUV drivers was only a matter of time. Frustrated by what they saw as aggressive, intimidating behavior by SUV drivers who cut them off and barred their visibility, angry sedan drivers began filling the traffic columns of newspapers around the country.

Then, as automakers introduced ever-larger models, environmental groups stepped up their criticism of SUVs as gas-guzzling polluters. In February 1999, when Ford introduced its largest model to date, the four-ton,

"super-duty" Excursion, the Sierra Club awarded the automaker with its "Exxon Valdez Award" for producing a "a rolling monument to environmental destruction." [40]

It wasn't long before activists began taking matters into their own hands. In 2000, Robert Lind of San Francisco launched an anti-SUV Web site — changingtheclimate.com — and began posting bumper stickers on SUVs that read, "I'm Changing the Climate! Ask Me How." [41] Others left fake traffic citations on SUV windshields chiding owners for polluting the environment. Reports of vandalism against SUVs, including slashed tires and broken windshields, also mounted. [42]

Last fall, the anti-SUV backlash gained national attention after Huffington launched the Detroit Project, a full-blown anti-SUV campaign complete with a Web site and television ads excoriating SUV buyers. Some of the ads were modeled on anti-drug commercials charging marijuana users with funding terrorists who profit from the illegal drug trade. One Huffington ad pictures masked, armed men in the desert and warns, "These are the terrorists who get money from those countries every time George fills up his SUV. Oil money supports some terrible things. What kind of mileage does your SUV get?" [43]

Huffington's campaign rankled SUV owners. [44] "Excuse me, Arianna, I didn't realize that black smoke billowing out the back of your Lear jet doesn't pollute the environment," Atlanta developer Bishop scoffs. "You're flying from rally to rally on your private jet, and that kind of fuel consumption doesn't seem to irritate you, but Middle Americans driving their little SUVs really tick you off!"

Last Nov. 20, Christian and Jewish religious leaders belonging to the Interfaith Climate and Energy Campaign went to Detroit to ask automakers to produce cleaner, more fuel-efficient vehicles. GM responded with a statement affirming consumers' right to

pick the car of their choice: "GM embraces a strong ethic of environmental and social responsibility. Ultimately, this issue is rooted in vehicle choice, and GM respects the rights of all people to make those choices."

The Evangelical Environmental Network also launched its controversial "What Would Jesus Drive?" campaign, which sparked a heated response from conservative religious leaders such as Jerry Falwell, who staunchly defended the right to drive an SUV.

"I believe that global warming is a myth," Falwell said. "Therefore, I have no conscience problems at all, and I'm going to buy a Suburban next time." Falwell also chided his fellow evangelicals involved in the campaign. "If you spent as much time winning people to Christ and building soul-winning churches and sending missionaries around the world as you're worrying about God being unable to take care of his creation, we would get a lot more done. I urge everyone to go out and buy an SUV today." [45]

Still the King

Recent sales figures suggest that many Americans share Falwell's sentiments. Although the overall market for new vehicles is slow — with April sales 6.1 percent below last year at this time — SUVs continue to pull consumers into the auto showrooms. Honda, for example, saw sales of its SUVs, pickups and minivans soar by 55 percent over last year, even as its passenger-car sales fell by half.

Indeed, current trends suggest that the anti-SUV backlash has largely fallen on deaf ears. The hottest-selling SUVs today are the very behemoths that are the targets of the strongest criticism. Ford enjoyed record sales of its big Lincoln Navigator in April, while sales of Cadillac's comparable Escalade were up 18.6 percent. [46]

At Issue:

Are SUVs a safety threat to occupants of other vehicles?

JOAN B. CLAYBROOK
PRESIDENT, PUBLIC CITIZEN

**FROM TESTIMONY BEFORE SENATE COMMERCE, SCIENCE AND
TRANSPORTATION COMMITTEE, FEB. 26, 2003**

*t*he criticism of SUVs is richly deserved. SUVs are basically gussied-up pickup trucks, and most have never been comprehensively redesigned to be safely used as passenger vehicles. In a crash, the high bumper, stiff frame and steel-panel construction of SUVs override crash protections of other vehicles. Due to their cut-rate safety design, SUVs often fail to adequately absorb crash energy or to crumple, as they should, so they ram into other motorists and shock their own occupants' bodies. . . . Overall, SUVs are less safe on average for their occupants than large or midsize cars, yet they inflict far greater costs in both lives and money for the dangers they inflict on other motorists.

The SUV is a bad bargain for society and a nightmare for American roads. The switch from midsize and large passenger cars to SUVs has endangered millions of Americans, without any recognizable benefits. One former NHTSA [National Highway Traffic Safety Administration] administrator estimated in 1997 that the aggressive design of light trucks (a category including SUVs, pickup trucks, vans and minivans) has killed 2,000 additional people needlessly each year. Yet automakers continue to exploit special-interest exemptions and safety loopholes, while creating consumer demand and shaping consumer choice with a multibillion-dollar marketing campaign because SUVs bring in maximum dollars for minimal effort. . . .

Manufacturers have known for decades about the tendency of SUVs to roll over, and about the damage incurred when the vehicles' weak roof crushes in on the heads and spines of motorists. . . . They've also unblinkingly faced the carnage inflicted on other motorists from high SUV bumpers and menacing front grilles, building ever-more heavy and terrible SUVs over time and continuing to market them militaristically, such as the ads calling the Lincoln Navigator an "urban assault vehicle. . . ."

Although many Americans purchase SUVs because they believe that they will safely transport their families, the truth is that SUVs are among the most dangerous vehicles on the road. They are no more safe for their drivers than many passenger cars and are much more dangerous for other drivers who share the highway, making them a net social loss for society. Yet this cycle is perpetuated by industry-spread myths that heavier vehicles are safer per se, so consumers believe that they must continue to "supersize" their own vehicle in order to remain safe. The self-reinforcing nature of this growing highway arms race makes the notion that SUVs are safe for their occupants one of the more harmful myths of our time.

SUSAN M. CISCHKE
*VICE PRESIDENT, ENVIRONMENTAL AND SAFETY
ENGINEERING, FORD MOTOR CO.*

**FROM TESTIMONY BEFORE SENATE COMMERCE, SCIENCE AND
TRANSPORTATION COMMITTEE, FEB. 26, 2003**

*c*ars, as well as motorcycles and bicycles, have always shared the road with large commercial trucks, buses, cargo vans and pickup trucks. Historically, size differences among vehicles were more pronounced in the 1970s than they are today.

While the vehicle fleet in the U.S. is changing to include more and more light trucks and vans . . . the number of vehicle miles traveled has continued to increase, [but] the total number of crash fatalities has stayed relatively constant.

Ford continues to be a leader in researching the factors that contribute to crash safety and compatibility, including weight, geometry and stiffness and in translating that research into enhancements to vehicle design. Ford is working with NHTSA [National Highway Transportation Safety Administration] to assess whether vehicle compatibility can be predicted by measuring average height of force, to evaluate not just "bumper alignment" but also the load path that would transmit force by the striking vehicle. By aligning the load path, it is possible to reduce harm to the struck vehicle. . . .

Ford has been working to improve the safety of cars in collisions with SUVs by adding structure and lowering rail heights of SUVs. For example, in the 2003 Expedition and Navigator, the bumper beam is attached directly to the front of the frame rail, instead of being bracketed to the top. This allows the rails to more directly engage a struck object and manages the crash forces more efficiently. For example, the Expedition bumper beam and rail are compatible with the height of the bumper on a Ford Taurus or Mercury Sable. Also, the frame of the 2003 Explorer and Mountaineer was lowered to be more compatible with other vehicles on the road.

In addition, Ford introduced on the 2000 Excursion Ford's BlockerBeam that offers front-bumper underside protection for crash compatibility with smaller vehicles. The BlockerBeam lowers the point of engagement for a frontal impact with an SUV to the same level as a Taurus. This helps prevent the SUV from riding over the passenger car, and transfers crash forces to engineered crumple zones on both the striking and the struck vehicles, where they can be best managed.

The automotive industry in general, and Ford in particular, will continue to build vehicles with the utility and safety that our customers require. Nevertheless, we view vehicle safety as a partnership, and where vehicle design ends, customer responsibility begins.

Comparing David and Goliath

The Toyota Prius, a compact hybrid, gets nearly four-times better gas mileage than the GMC Yukon, which is four feet longer and weighs twice as much.

Comparing the Toyota Prius and GMC Yukon

	Toyota Prius	GMC Yukon
Base Price (suggested retail)	$20,450	$35,552
Mileage rating: city/hwy/combined	52/45/48	12/16/14
Weight	2,765 lbs.	5,839 lbs.
Height	57.6"	75.7"
Width	66.7"	78.8"
Length (inches)	169.6"	219.3"
Seating capacity	5	9
CO_2 production (tons)*	36	124

* Over the vehicle's 124,000-mile lifetime

Source: Sierra Club

Ford analyst Pipas attributes the enduring popularity of SUVs to the same demographic phenomenon that made the muscle cars, station wagons and minivans such hot sellers in earlier decades, the 65-million-strong Baby Boom generation. "Throughout the 1990s, most of the growth in the SUV segment was in traditional, truck-based models," he says. "There's an element of toughness to them that appeals to the Baby Boomers. In the 1990s, they had mature households, with adolescent children, they were pretty affluent after benefiting from the stock market's go-go years, and they led very active lifestyles. The SUV ideally suited that go-anywhere, do-anything approach to life."

But most of these boomers are buying an adventure-seeking image that few will put into practice. "Only a little over half of all SUVs are four-wheel drive, and while some people do take them hunting and boating, less than one-fifth of the people who drive them actually go off-road," Pipas says.

"You can get an interesting view of Americana at a Home Depot parking lot on a Saturday morning," Pipas adds. "It will be filled with pickups and SUVs because, while a Ford Taurus or a Toyota Camry may be appropriate for bringing home a can of paint, they aren't particularly well suited for bringing home plywood, flats of flowers and other kinds of landscaping materials."

Energy Prices

A spike in gasoline prices earlier this year also failed to dampen Americans' enthusiasm for SUVs. Due in part to a cutoff in oil exports from Venezuela during an oil-industry strike and fears that Iraq would destroy its oilfields during the recent war to oust Saddam Hussein, prices peaked at $1.76 a gallon on March 21, up from $1.45 a year earlier. But sales of fuel-guzzling SUVs were seemingly unaffected.

That doesn't surprise analysts. Unlike the 1970s, when high gas prices resulted from a true shortage of oil, prompting consumers to trade their gas-guzzlers for smaller cars, no one predicts a permanent oil shortage today. Though the 11-member Organization of Petroleum Exporting Countries (OPEC) tries to keep oil prices stable through production quotas, it controls only about a third of the world's oil production, and thus cannot interrupt oil supplies to the United States; non-members such as Canada, Russia and Britain ensure a plentiful supply to the United States. "In the 1970s, there was no fuel, and people were totally panicked," says Claybrook of Public Citizen. "Today it's just a matter of price, and because SUV owners are wealthy, they will pay more than $2 a gallon. It will have to go to $5 before it will change their behavior."

As a result, many consumers ignore gas prices when car shopping today. "There was a 50 percent increase in gas prices several years ago, and it made not one whit of difference in people's driving patterns or car-purchasing patterns," says Becker of the Sierra Club. "People will pay whatever they need to pay for gas. They may drive an extra two miles to go to the cheaper pump and save 25 cents, but they aren't going to buy a different kind of vehicle or drive less because prices go up 50 cents a gallon."

The rising price of new cars, including SUVs, also helps explain why consumers ignore gas prices. Many SUVs cost upward of $30,000, and the most expensive more than $50,000. "The price of gas only accounts for about 10 percent of annual operating costs," says Pipas. "Once you've decided to spend whatever it is you're going to spend on a vehicle, it really doesn't make too much difference whether the price of gas is a buck or two-fifty." ∎

OUTLOOK

New Kid on the Block

There are signs that consumers' love affair with SUVs, at least with the biggest models, may be cooling. Citing poor sales, Ford will discontinue its jumbo-sized Excursion in 2004. Even the Hummer — the only GM model that doesn't need financing incentives to lure buyers — may be in for a bumpy ride. According to a recent customer-satisfaction survey, the new Hummer H2 ranked last among 36 brands. [47]

Surprisingly, the biggest complaint about the $50,000 H2 was its poor gas mileage. Apparently Hummer buyers were surprised that their 6,400 lb., six-liter V8 truck got less than 10 mpg. As gas prices inched toward the $2 mark during the Iraq war, they were hit with sticker shock when it came time to fill the 32-gallon tank.

Gas mileage rarely figures among car buyers' top complaints, presumably because fuel-efficiency information stickers are required on most new cars. But because the Hummer and other big SUVs are classified as commercial vehicles, the manufacturers don't have to post that information. GM reportedly is considering voluntarily putting mileage stickers on its Hummers anyway to avoid future complaints. [48]

It's too soon to write off mega-SUVs as a relic of the booming 1990s, however. Last year alone, Americans bought more than 787,000 large SUVs, including Hummers, Chevy Tahoes and Ford Expeditions. [49] But the best-selling SUVs continue to be the midsize models, such as the ever-popular Explorer, Trailblazer and Grand Cherokee, which accounted for almost two-thirds of the 3 million truck-based SUVs sold in 2002.

SUV advocates cite these figures in dismissing critics' complaints. "People are moving away from the really big SUVs," says Defore of the SUV Owners Association. "Even over the past five years, the predominance of SUV sales is not in the behemoths, but rather in the small to midsize SUVs. So what's the problem? It's not like it's an epidemic or something."

Indeed, the spring auto shows in Detroit and New York City featured several so-called crossover vehicles designed to appeal to a broader swath of consumers by incorporating some of the design features more commonly found in cars into slightly downsized SUV profiles. In addition to the usual safety and fuel-efficiency advantages incorporated into cars, many crossovers offer safety features that go beyond federal requirements. The popular Lexus RX series, for example, contains an air-suspension system that automatically lowers the vehicle's height at high speeds, reducing rollover risk. The new Volvo XC90 SUV features a stability-control system designed to detect an impending rollover and help the driver maintain control, as well as head-protection airbags for occupants in all three rows of seats. [50]

Once again, it appears that Baby Boomers are driving automotive-design trends. The oldest boomers reach 57 this year, and while they aren't quite ready to give up the adventurous self-image that draws them to SUVs, many are looking for a little more comfort and additional safety.

"We at Ford still see SUVs outperforming other segments in the coming year, but over the next decade most of the growth is going to come from crossover SUVs," Pipas says. Environmentalists may welcome the trend because crossovers — which technically are classified as cars rather than light trucks — are smaller, consume less gas and pollute less than traditional SUVs. "But the popularity of crossovers has little to do with the environment or fuel consumption," Pipas says. "These Baby Boomers are seeking vehicles that suit their needs.

"The SUV was unquestionably the vehicle of the 1990s," Pipas continues. "When we look back, we'll find that the crossover SUV is going to be the vehicle of the 21st century." ∎

Notes

[1] For background, see Mary H. Cooper, "Energy and the Environment," *The CQ Researcher*, March 3, 2000, pp. 161-184.

[2] Huffington launched her latest TV ad on May 7, 2003, www.detroitproject.com.

[3] For background, see Mary H. Cooper, "Global Warming Update," *The CQ Researcher*, Nov. 1, 1996, pp. 961-984; Mary H. Cooper, "Global Warming Treaty," *The CQ Researcher*, Jan. 26, 2001, pp. 41-64.

[4] Kathy Koch, "Truck Safety," *The CQ Researcher*, March 12, 1999, pp. 209-232.

[5] See Warren Brown, "It's Rugged, and They're Cross," *The Washington Post*, April 24, 2003, p. G7.

[6] Autodata Corp.

[7] See www.hummer.com.

[8] For background, see David Masci, "Auto Industry's Future," *The CQ Researcher*, Jan. 21, 2000, pp. 17-40.

[9] Keith Bradsher, *High and Mighty: SUVs: The World's Most Dangerous Vehicles and How They Got That Way* (2002), pp. 110-111.

[10] For background, see Brian Hansen, "Auto Safety," *The CQ Researcher*, Oct. 26, 2001, pp. 873-896.

[11] Ricardo Alonso-Zaldivar, "Automaker Data Say SUVs Are Riskier," *Los Angeles Times*, Feb. 26, 2003, p. A1.

[12] NHTSA, April, 2003 statistics. Also, see Greg Schneider, "Deadly Driving Trend Alters Safety Focus; Fatalities Turn Attention to SUVs, Crash-Avoidance Technology," *The Washington Post*, May 3, 2003.

[13] Testifying April 3, 2003, before the House Appropriations Subcommittee on Transportation and Treasury.

[14] From comments before an automotive group in Detroit, Jan. 14, 2003. See Cindy Skrzycki, "Regulator Assails Safety of SUVs," *The Washington Post*, Jan. 16, 2003.

[15] Insurance Institute for Highway Safety, "Status Report," Feb. 14, 1998.

[16] Quoted in Myron Levin, "Study Questions Safety of SUVs," *Los Angeles Times*, Feb. 18, 2003, p. A1.

[17] Marc Ross and Tom Wenzel, "An Analysis of Traffic Deaths by Vehicle Type and Model," Lawrence Berkeley Laboratory/University of Michigan, with funding from the Department of Energy, March 2002.

[18] Quoted in Levin, *op. cit.*

[19] *Ibid.*

[20] Alonso-Zaldivar, *op. cit.*

[21] Insurance Institute, *op. cit.*

[22] Quoted in Danny Hakim, "A Regulator Takes Aim At Hazards of S.U.V.'s," *The New York Times*, Dec. 22, 2002, p. C1.

[23] Levin, *op. cit.*

[24] For background, see Mary H. Cooper, "Energy Security," *The CQ Researcher*, Feb. 1, 2002, pp. 73-96.

[25] From testimony before the Senate Commerce, Science and Transportation Committee, Feb. 26, 2003.

[26] National Academy of Sciences, "Effectiveness and Impact of Corporate Average Fuel Economy Standards," July 31, 2001. For the industry response, see Alliance of Automobile Manufacturers, "NAS Report Confirms Need for Reform of CAFE Program," July 30, 2001.

[27] See Danny Hakim, "Ford Backs Off Efficiency Pledge for Its S.U.V's," *The New York Times*, April 18, 2003, p. C1.

[28] From a statement to the House floor, April 10, 2003.

[29] Richard Simon, "House Stalls Bid to Increase Fuel Standards for SUVs," *Los Angeles Times*, April 11, 2003, p. 38.

[30] As of 2001. See Energy Information Administration, *Monthly Energy Review*, March 2003, p. 17.

[31] See Cooper, "Global Warming Treaty," *op. cit.*

[32] See "Driving Up the Heat: SUVs and Global Warming," www.sierraclub.org.

[33] See Mary H. Cooper, "Transatlantic Tensions," *The CQ Researcher*, July 13, 2001, pp. 553-576.

[34] Bush announced the fuel-cell initiative during his State of the Union speech, Jan. 28, 2003. The off-road diesel rule, which would curb particulate-matter emissions, was announced by the Environmental Protection Agency on April 16, 2003.

[35] Information in this section is based on "SUV Heritage: From Carryalls to Crossovers,"

FOR MORE INFORMATION

Alliance to Save Energy, 1200 18th St., N.W., Suite 900, Washington, DC 20036; (202) 857-0666; www.ase.org. Monitors energy legislation and provides information on energy conservation.

Insurance Institute for Highway Safety, 1005 North Glebe Road, Suite 800, Arlington, VA 22201; (202) 247-1500; www.hwysafety.org. An independent research organization funded by auto insurers.

National Religious Partnership for the Environment, 49 South Pleasant St., Suite 301, Amherst, MA 01002; (413) 253-1515; www.nrpe.org. A coalition of faith groups that launched the "What Would Jesus Drive?" campaign to spur consumers to drive fuel-efficient vehicles.

Public Citizen, 1600 20th St., N.W., Washington, DC 20009; (202) 588-1000; www.citizen.org. A consumer-advocacy organization founded by Ralph Nader that calls for more stringent safety standards for SUVs.

Sierra Club, 408 C St., N.E., Washington, DC 20002; (202) 547-1141; www.sierraclub.org. An environmental organization that provides information about the impact of fuel-inefficient vehicles on global warming.

Sport Utility Vehicle Owners Association, One Thomas Circle, N.W., 10th floor, Washington, DC 20005; (877) 447-8862; www.suvoa.com.

www.cars.com; and "Looking Back: Special 50th Anniversary Section," *Consumer Reports*, April 2003, pp. 21-26.

[36] For background on early legislation on auto safety, see Congressional Quarterly, *Congress and the Nation: Volume II, 1965-1968*, (1969).

[37] For background, see Mary H. Cooper, "Energy Policy," *The CQ Researcher*, May 25, 2001, pp. 441-464.

[38] The standard was tightened to 26 mpg from 1986-88, but loosened to 26.5 mpg in 1989 and restored in 1990 to 27.5 mpg, where it has remained ever since.

[39] For more information on CAFE standards, see www.fueleconomy.gov. See also Robert Bamberger, "Automobile and Light Truck Fuel Economy: The CAFE Standards," Congressional Research Service, March 12, 2003.

[40] Sierra Club, "Sierra Club Awards Ford Motor Company the 'Exxon Valdez Environmental Achievement Award,'" Feb. 25, 1999, www.sierraclub.org.

[41] See Ann Grimes, "SUV-Driver Alert: Steer Clear of This Guy at Cocktail Parties," *The Wall Street Journal*, Oct. 13, 2000, p. B1.

[42] "Madison Police Suspect Environmentalists Slashed SUV Tires," The Associated Press, April 23, 2003.

[43] The ads can be seen at www.detroitproject.com.

[44] See, for example, Woody Hochswender, "Did My Car Join Al Qaeda?" *The New York Times*, Feb. 16, 2003, p. D11.

[45] Speaking on CNN, "Inside Politics," Nov. 20, 2002.

[46] See Danny Hakim, "Auto Sales Dropped 6.1 percent During April," *The New York Times*, May 2, 2003, p. C1.

[47] J.D. Power and Associates,

[48] See Danny Hakim, "Whether a Hummer or a Hybrid, The Big Complaint Is Fuel Use," *The New York Times*, May 7, 2003, p. C1.

[49] Sales statistics from Autodata Corp., Woodcliff Lake, N.J.

[50] See *Consumer Reports, op. cit.*

Bibliography

Selected Sources

Books

Bradsher, Keith, *High and Mighty: SUVs — The World's Most Dangerous Vehicles and How They Got That Way*, Public Affairs, 2002.

A former Detroit bureau chief for *The New York Times* traces the auto industry's successful marketing strategy for SUVs, which are cheaper to build than cars because of loopholes in federal fuel and safety regulations.

Penenberg, Adam, *Tragic Indifference: One Man's Battle with the Auto Industry Over the Dangers of SUVs*, Harper-Business, 2003.

A business reporter chronicles the legal battles that have ensued from a spate of SUV rollover accidents in the late 1990s involving the Ford Explorer equipped with defective Firestone tires. Scheduled for publication in October.

Articles

"Annual Auto Issue," *Consumer Reports*, April 2003.

A respected annual review of the current auto lineup provides safety, customer-satisfaction, resale and fuel-economy data for 2003 models as well as a history of auto trends and regulations over the past half-century.

"Roadroller," *The Economist*, Jan. 16, 2003.

The belief among SUV owners that their vehicles are safer than cars is "nonsense," in light of government statistics showing that SUV rollover accidents are responsible for a third of all highway deaths.

Brown, Stuart F., "Dude, Where's My Hybrid?" *Fortune*, April 28, 2003, p. 112.

Cars with hybrid engines, which run on a combination of gasoline and electricity, have sold out in the United States, but analysts question whether Americans will demand enough of them to ensure their future viability.

Hakim, Danny, "Whether a Hummer or a Hybrid, The Big Complaint Is Fuel Use," *The New York Times*, May 7, 2003, p. C1.

A recent customer-satisfaction survey placed the giant Hummer at the bottom of the list — with its roughly 10 mpg mileage the biggest complaint.

Mateja, Jim, "System Makes Volvo SUV Anti-Roll Model," *Chicago Tribune*, March 27, 2003, p. CARS 1.

Volvo has taken the lead in voluntarily installing new technology to reduce the safety threat SUVs pose to their occupants and those of other cars on the road.

Salkever, Alex, "Where High-Tech Cars Still Sputter," *Business Week Online*, May 1, 2003.

While Ford Motor Co. plans to introduce a new version of its popular hybrid SUV, the Escape, it has backed away from an earlier pledge to boost the fuel efficiency of all its SUVs by 25 percent by 2005.

Reports and Studies

Bamberger, Robert, "Automobile and Light Truck Fuel Economy: The CAFE Standards," *Issue Brief for Congress*, Congressional Research Service, March 12, 2003.

The author reviews the history and current status of fuel-efficiency standards in place since 1975 and how they differ for passenger cars and SUVs.

Insurance Institute for Highway Safety, "Special Issue: Incompatibility of Vehicles in Crashes, Status Report," April 26, 2003.

The study focuses on the crash incompatibility of passenger cars and SUVs and the safety risks posed by SUVs to occupants of smaller, lower-profile vehicles.

Insurance Institute for Highway Safety, "Status Report," Feb. 14, 1998.

This early study on crash incompatibility between SUVs and cars concluded that the occupants of cars struck in the side by pickups or SUVs are more than 25 times more likely to die than the occupants of the striking vehicle.

National Academy of Sciences, "Effectiveness and Impact of Corporate Average Fuel Economy Standards," July 31, 2001.

Although fuel-economy standards have helped reduce U.S. dependence on imported oil and lowered emissions of carbon dioxide, tightening the standards for SUVs and light trucks would make the regulations more effective.

Ross, Marc, and Tom Wenzel, "An Analysis of Traffic Deaths by Vehicle Type and Model," American Council for an Energy-Efficient Economy, March 2002.

Ross, a University of Michigan physicist, and Wenzel, a researcher at the Lawrence Berkeley National Laboratory, conclude that most cars are safer than most SUVs.

Yacobucci, Brent D., "Sport Utility Vehicles, Mini-Vans, and Light Trucks: An Overview of Fuel Economy and Emissions Standards," *CRS Report for Congress*, Congressional Research Service, Feb. 28, 2003.

This brief summarizes the latest developments related to SUVs, which are held to more lenient emission and fuel-economy standards than passenger cars.

9 Reforming the Army Corps of Engineers

DAVID HOSANSKY

I n Arkansas, the U.S. Army Corps of Engineers wants to spend $50 million diking and dredging the White River to expand shipping — even though local officials want to preserve the waterway that draws bird watchers and other outdoor enthusiasts as it flows through two national wildlife refuges.

In Louisiana, the Corps is working on a congressionally mandated $1.5 billion study to extend its Red River Navigation Channel, despite complaints that the original $2 billion navigation channel has failed to generate the barge traffic that was forecast.

And in the mid-Atlantic, the Bush administration is trying to kill a $311 million project to dredge the Delaware River, after the General Accounting Office (GAO) found that the Corps inflated the project's potential economic benefits by 300 percent. [1]

These questionable Corps of Engineers projects and others have provoked a storm of criticism in Congress and the White House in recent years. The venerable agency — once hailed for its role in opening up inaccessible areas in the young nation by straightening navigable rivers, filling in wetlands, preventing floods and deepening harbors — is under fire by the Bush administration and veteran lawmakers for wasting tax dollars on pork-barrel projects, devastating the environment and misleading policymakers. Unlikely partners like environmentalists and fiscal conservatives are joining together to demand top-to-bottom reforms.

"The way the Corps plans, studies and develops civil works programs

From *The CQ Researcher,* May 30, 2003.

The Delta Queen *riverboat steams down Mississippi's Red River. Keeping river traffic flowing is a major responsibility of the Corps of Engineers. But the huge, 35,000-employee public works agency is also responsible for protecting the nation's dwindling wetlands. Critics say the Corps uses faulty economic assumptions to press for costly, pork-barrel water projects that damage the environment while providing little benefit to society.*

Corps of Engineers/Alfred Dulaney

does not serve the interests of this country in either an economic way or an environmentally sustainable way," says Kate Costenbader, coordinator for the National Wildlife Federation's (NWF) Greening the Corps of Engineers campaign, which seeks to make the Corps more environmentally friendly. "Until these problems are addressed, we have no business authorizing new water projects."

Peter J. Sepp, vice president for communications at the conservative National Taxpayers Union (NTU), agrees: "There will simply have to be a reckoning of the Corps' priorities."

Although the Corps has been attacked sporadically since the rise of the environmental movement 40 years ago, it is facing an especially powerful group of adversaries this time around. Last year President Bush — who wants to cut some controversial water projects — fired Corps chief Mike Parker, who had publicly pressed for more spending on projects. A bi-

partisan group of lawmakers insists on overhauling Corps procedures before approving any new projects. Weighing in, both the GAO and the Army's inspector general have sharply rapped the agency for the way it goes about justifying expensive projects, and the National Academy of Sciences (NAS) last year called for independent reviews of Corps projects. [2]

The reform camp includes such powerful lawmakers as Senate Minority Leader Tom Daschle, D-S.D., who is so disillusioned with the Corps he wants to shift the management of all large-scale water projects to another agency. "I'm convinced it's one of the most incompetent and inept organizations in all the federal government," Daschle said. [3]

But the agency's many congressional supporters adamantly oppose many of the reforms or scaling back its projects, which provide lawmakers with a high-profile way to steer federal funds to their home districts and states. They praise the Corps' efforts to support commercial development by dredging waterways and building dikes and other structures to protect low-lying areas from flooding. "Every year, billions of tons of commerce move over the navigable waterways the Corps maintains," said Rep. Bill Pascrell Jr., D-N.J., a member of the House Transportation and Infrastructure Committee. "This creates jobs and assures our leadership in the global economy." [4]

Lawmakers are so evenly divided on the issue that last year they deadlocked on passing either reforms or a biennial measure authorizing new Corps water projects. Reformers essentially are holding new water projects hostage until they can get Congress to require independent reviews

Half of U.S. Wetlands Have Disappeared

More than half the wetlands in the Lower 48 states have been lost to development during the past two centuries. The biggest losses were in the Midwest, where more than 80 percent of the wetlands were lost in Indiana, Illinois, Missouri, Kentucky, Iowa and Ohio.

Wetlands in the 1780s

Percentage of wetlands	
	1-5%
	5-12%
	12-25%
	25-50%
	50-55%

Wetlands in the 1980s

Source: Department of the Interior, Fish and Wildlife Service, 1990

world's largest hydraulic pumping plant on Mississippi's Yazoo River to prevent periodic flooding — at an estimated cost of $191 million. Authorized in 1941, the project was left on the back burner until powerful Mississippi lawmakers, including Republican Sen. Trent Lott, the former majority leader, recently took up the cause again. Meanwhile, other political leaders, including Bush, want to eliminate the project, which the Environmental Protection Agency (EPA) says could destroy massive areas of wetlands, wiping out habitat for deer, bear, and migratory waterfowl. (*See sidebar, p. 168.*)

Corps officials acknowledge they can do a better job of projecting the economic benefits of proposed projects and reducing environmental impacts. But they contend they are merely taking their orders from Congress, which has consistently approved costly projects even when they appear to offer little economic justification.

"There's certainly an awareness that we need to make some changes in our processes and procedures," says Lt. Col. Gene Pawlik, a Corps spokesman. He points out, however, that the Corps' job is to do the nation's work "as expressed by the people through their elected representatives. That is our mission."

In recent years, however, that mission has zigzagged as erratically as an untamed river prior to a Corps canalization project. During the Clinton administration, the Corps was told to emphasize environmental protection — sometimes to the point of undoing past projects and restoring fragile ecosystems. [5] For instance, the Corps has begun a multibillion-dollar initiative to restore the Florida Everglades to its natural state, 60 years after building a series of locks, levees and canals to drain the low-lying area to produce arable farmland free from periodic flooding. (*See sidebar, p. 174.*)

Bush's positions on the Corps have zigzagged as well. While he supports

of proposed water projects. But traditional pork-barrel politics has such sway on Capitol Hill that neither Bush nor reform-minded lawmakers have yet been able to overpower loyal Corps supporters in Congress, including many

on the Transportation and Appropriations committees.

In a particularly closely watched tug-of-war between traditional supporters and reformers, the Corps is drawing up plans to build what may be the

the Everglades restoration, a pet project of his brother, Florida Gov. Jeb Bush, the president has directed the Corps to back off some other environmental initiatives. For instance, the administration opposes removing four dams on the Snake River in Washington that are preventing populations of endangered salmon from spawning.

Further roiling the waters, the Corps is under mounting political pressure to allow private developers to dredge and fill wetlands. The agency's permit process, established under the 1972 Clean Water Act, is supposed to be the government's foremost line of defense in protecting wetlands, which play a vital role in absorbing floodwaters and removing pollutants from watersheds. Yet even under the more environmentally minded Clinton administration, the Corps approved more than 99 percent of permit applications nationwide to develop wetlands. [6]

As evidence of the Corps' pro-development leaning, critics cite a revealing e-mail sent to the agency's nationwide staff by John Studt, chief of the Corps' regulatory branch, after the Sept. 11, 2001, terrorist attacks. "The harder we work to expedite issuance of permits," it said, "the more we serve the Nation by moving the economy forward." [7]

Now the Bush administration appears to be taking steps that could further erode wetland protection. [8] The administration is drafting a rule to allow developers to fill in so-called isolated wetlands — those not directly connected to navigable waterways — without first getting a permit from the Corps. Depending on how broadly the administration structures the rule, such wetlands may include wet depressions in the ground, known as prairie potholes in the upper Midwest and vernal pools in California, that house numerous rare plant and animal species and rank as some of the most biologically diverse habitat in the United States. [9] (*See sidebar, p. 164.*)

Spending Cut on Several "Wasteful" Projects

Congress appropriated more than $58 million in 2003 for the 10 Corps projects that Taxpayers for Common Sense, a government-watchdog group, considers unnecessary. The Bush administration's proposed 2004 budget would reduce or eliminate funding for seven of the projects.

Project	2003 Funding	Proposed 2004 Funding
Eastern Arkansas Irrigation Projects	$1,150,000	$0
Delaware River Deepening, N.J.	$2,000,000	$300,000
Upper Mississippi River Lock Expansions, Ill.	$3,000,000	$3,216,000
Big Sunflower River Dredging/ Yazoo Pumps, Miss.	$11,400,000	$890,000
Oregon Inlet Jetties, N.C.	$150,000	$0
Apalachicola River Navigation, Ga.	$4,709,000	$1,500,000
Lower Snake River Navigation, Wash.	$14,868,000	$13,190,000
Savannah Harbor Expansion, Ga.	$500,000	$0
Beach Replacement, N.J.	$17,076,000	$25,513,000
Beach Replacement, Long Island, N.Y.	$3,500,000	$3,800,000

Source: Taxpayers for Common Sense and National Wildlife Federation, "Troubled Waters: Congress, the Corps of Engineers, and Wasteful Water Projects," March 2000

Developers praise the administration for reducing unnecessary bureaucratic requirements. For decades, they have complained about seemingly arbitrary Corps decisions to require permits for bulldozing drainage ditches, wet fields or other geographic features that are miles from any significant body of water. "If you get to the level of absurdity, everything's connected — including the puddle in the middle of the parking lot," says Susan Asmus, vice president for environmental policy at the National Association of Home Builders. "Should the federal government now regulate the puddle in the middle of the parking lot? I don't think so."

But environmentalists are up in arms. "It's going to be devastating to all the progress we've made in the last 30 years," warns Julie Sibbing, a NWF wetlands specialist.

In recent years, the Corps has taken on new and increasingly ambitious

tasks — some praised by environmentalists and some abhorred. But as the public's understanding of nature and the environment has changed, the agency's view of nature as something that needed to be tamed to spur economic development was increasingly seen as environmentally destructive and economically wasteful.

Scientists now view natural river flows as vital for preserving populations of fish and other species, and wetlands are seen as nature's way of cleansing runoff and controlling flooding. Meanwhile, barge traffic is becoming something of an anachronism in the era of interstate trucking and jet planes. Only 8 percent of the nation's freight is now carried on inland waterways. [10] In Alabama and Mississippi, only one barge churned along the Corps' channelized Pearl River in 1997.

"Years later the Corps realizes they've cut their own throats" with some large-scale projects, says Larry Larson, executive director of the Association of State Floodplain Managers.

The Corps' chief of engineers, Lt. Gen. Robert Flowers, recently told a congressional panel: "The Corps does need to change, and we have been changing over time." [11]

However, the Corps cannot switch to more economical and environmentally friendly projects without a congressional mandate to do so. As Congress prepares to debate the Corps' future and wetlands protection in general, it will be debating these questions:

Should the Corps be reformed?

In 2000, an Army Corps of Engineers economist named Donald Sweeney caused an uproar when he revealed that his superiors had ordered him to make it look as though the benefits of a project to expand locks on the upper Mississippi River would outweigh the costs. The rigged study spurred the Corps' inspector general to rebuke the agency and the NAS to propose several reforms. [12]

Although Corps officials subsequently stated they had restructured their study, Sweeney assailed the agency again in late 2002, saying it was using an antiquated economic model that overstated the case for lock expansion because it failed to weigh alternatives to shipping grain on barges. "What the Corps has done is actually make the study even worse than it was with cooked numbers," he said. [13]

Such allegations have spurred many in Congress — along with an unusual coalition of interest groups ranging from environmentalists to fiscal conservatives — to take a hard look at the agency they entrust with high-priority hometown projects. They have demanded guarantees that the benefits of Corps projects significantly outweigh the costs, and they predict that national outrage at the agency will force lawmakers to pass that and other reforms.

"There's a critical mass of support, because there are numerous bipartisan reasons among the interest groups for pursuing reform," says the National Taxpayers Union's Sepp. "There's great potential that the two-pronged approach between fiscal conservatives on the one hand and environmental liberals on the other could finally be enough to move the process forward." [14]

At the top of nearly everyone's list of proposed reforms is requiring independent cost-benefit analyses of big-ticket projects. "[Outside experts] could help insure the most-needed and worthwhile projects while eliminating those of dubious value," says former University of Virginia professor James Mitchell, chairman of an NAS panel that looked at potential ways of reforming the Corps.

In addition, some reformers want Corps projects to only be funded if their benefit-to-cost ratio is at least 1.5 to 1, compared to the ratio required now: anything better than 1:1. They also want to change cost-sharing formulas so local communities must shoulder more than the approximately 33 percent of the cost of major projects they currently pay.

Reformers also worry that the Corps has more than $50 billion worth of projects on the drawing boards — approved by congressional authorizing committees over the years but not yet funded by appropriators through the agency's annual $1.8 billion civil-works budget. Critics want the projects reviewed, with only the most important ones receiving funding. "If you continue to add on project after project after project, then existing, proven projects that are essential to commerce and jobs suffer," warned Trent Duffy, a spokesman for the White House Office of Management and Budget. [15]

Even Corps officials acknowledge they have stumbled badly in some of their economic analyses, approving unnecessary or inefficient projects. Flowers acknowledged in Senate testimo-

ny last year that the agency's internal planning and oversight procedures had "eroded over time." [16]

But many Corps-watchers worry that the proposed reforms may make a bad situation worse. For example, Howard Marlowe, a lobbyist for the American Shore and Beach Association, warns that an independent review of Corps projects — while fine in theory — might do little more than slow down an already lengthy approval process. Corps projects already go through numerous rounds of technical and environmental reviews and typically take 10 to 15 years from conception to completion.

"We go through a heck of a lot of reviews," says Marlowe, whose group represents city and county governments, engineers and planners who favor the sound development of coastal lands. "We don't want any more. The proposals to provide more review are time-consuming. Slowing a project down in my judgment is only another way to kill it."

Marlowe also objects to suggestions that communities pick up more of the tab for local projects. Renourishing beaches, dredging harbors and similar projects generally favored by the association help the economy as a whole, he says, so it is unfair and unrealistic to expect a single community to pay for that. "There is no way on this Earth that any community can possibly nourish a beach and keep it maintained for the 50-year period that the federal program [typically] provides for," he says.

Marlowe does favor some reforms, however, such as requiring the Corps to take a regional approach to projects, rather than viewing each project on a case-by-case basis. For example, rather than handling similar projects in adjacent counties separately, the Corps could use the same workers and equipment for regional projects. It could also take sand from a dredging project and use it for beach renourishment instead of simply dumping the dredged material.

Such an approach would be more economically efficient and environmentally friendly, he says.

Others differ sharply over whether the problems are so severe that Congress needs to step in. In fact, they say Congress is the problem. Reforming the Corps will not do any good until Congress staunches its appetite for "pork," they say. Often politicians will authorize money for large projects to please powerful commercial constituents and then pressure the Corps into coming up with the economic justification for them.

"You can talk about reforming the Corps until you're blue in the face, but until Congress stops saying, 'We don't care about the cost-benefit analysis; you're going to build it,' we've got a problem," says Larson of the Association of State Floodplain Managers. "Congress really feels that the Corps of Engineers is its own construction agency."

Edward Dickey, former chief of planning for the Corps, says top Corps officials in Washington must set clear standards for the agency's 41 districts and take a firmer line when lawmakers press for unworthy projects. "Congress all too many times has sent the message that they're not interested in good analysis," he says. "Congress is a big part of the problem, sending signals that they want the projects undertaken one way or another."

Dickey asks: "Is the Corps going to be run on a parochial basis, a pork-barrel basis, or is it going to be run according to national criteria?"

"Reform legislation in and of itself won't change a politically problematic process overnight," the National Taxpayers Union's Sepp says. "But what it will do is put the tools into place so we can chip away at some very flawed foundations.

"If we can even change some of the inputs into the process, insist on tougher benefit-cost standards, at least some lawmakers' consciences might be nagged into submission," he says.

Can the Corps safeguard the environment?

When the Corps of Engineers was authorized in 1945 to build four dams on the lower Snake River in Washington state, public officials hailed the project for supplying the Pacific Northwest with power and irrigation water, and for opening up river navigation to Idaho.

More than 50 years later, critics say the dams provide only marginal economic benefits while decimating valuable salmon populations, which are prevented by the dams from swimming upriver to spawn. But in 2000 the Corps defended the dams, claiming they helped salmon populations by cooling river water. The report was so controversial the EPA blasted it as "false and misleading." [17]

Critics point to the Snake River dams as typifying the Corps' handiwork. In the 20th century, critics say, the Corps spent more than $100 billion (in 1999 dollars) to straighten and tame America's rivers — and billions more to dredge harbors, fill in wetlands and renourish beaches — while downplaying the environmental impact of such projects.

National Wildlife Federation President Mark Van Putten has labeled the Corps "one of the most environmentally destructive agencies in United States history" — a view shared by many other conservationists. [18]

"Everywhere there's a big river, the Corps is there," says Melissa Samet, senior director of water resources for American Rivers, a river-conservation organization. "They have 1,400 projects now under construction, so they have an enormous impact on the nation's ecological health and rivers. They have that Old World, antiquated view: that a river is something to control, to manage and to change, rather than a natural system with enormous ecological and economical value. They don't strive to work with the river's system; they're always fighting it."

American Rivers calculates the Corps has built more than 500 dams and al-

tered more than 30,000 miles of rivers. Although the agency's intent is to safeguard low-lying settlements from floods and boost economic growth, Samet and other conservationists say the projects have scarred the nation's environment. Hundreds of species are threatened with extinction because their habitat has been dramatically changed or destroyed; vast expanses of former wetlands are covered with concrete; some floodplains are more hazardous than ever because storm water has been redirected into narrow channels instead of being allowed to overflow the land; and pollution is accumulating in stagnant canals instead of being washed out by flowing rivers, according to American Rivers. [19]

Corps defenders argue the agency has merely responded to the desire for economic expansion expressed by Congress and the public. But Corps officials now concede that they could have been more sensitive to the environmental havoc caused by their projects. Flowers said the time has come for the Corps to consider a more holistic, watershed-wide approach. "The current approach narrows our ability to look comprehensively and . . . leads to projects that solve one problem but may inadvertently cause others," he told Congress last year. [20]

Many doubt whether the Corps, whose primary mission is to alter nature, can switch its emphasis toward conservation. "An awful lot of it has do with the culture of the Corps and the way they conduct business," Samet says.

Although in the last decade the Corps has taken steps toward better environmental stewardship — and indeed is restoring ecologically damaged areas from the Everglades to San Francisco Bay — conservationists worry the agency continues to push projects that have major environmental repercussions.

For example, the Corps has recommended spending $108 million to

The Nature of Wetlands

Scientists define landforms that are wet for at least part of the year and feature particular soils and vegetation as wetlands. The continental United States has about 105 million acres of wetlands — roughly half the wetlands that existed prior to the Revolutionary War. Every region of the country contains wetlands, even the arid Southwest.

Wetlands are vital components of a healthy watershed. They regulate the flow of surface water, absorb flood waters, retain suspended and dissolved materials that could affect water quality and provide shelter for animals and plants — many of them rare — that have adapted to a specialized habitat.

The United States contains many types of wetlands, including:

Non-tidal marshes — More prevalent than any other form of wetlands, they tend to form in depressions in the ground near streams or along the boundaries of lakes and rivers. Although some dry out completely at times during the year, they rank among the Earth's most productive ecosystems because of their mineral-rich soils and high level of nutrients. Non-tidal marshes include prairie potholes in the upper Midwest, playa lakes in the southern High Plains and vernal pools on the West Coast.

Tidal marshes — Found along coastlines, saltwater and freshwater tidal marshes are influenced by the ebb and flow of ocean tides. They help protect the coast from storms, slow shoreline erosion and absorb excessive nutrients, such as fertilizer that runs off from farms. They also provide crucial habitat for shellfish and many juvenile fish species, as well as nesting sites for migratory waterfowl.

Swamps — Trees or other woody plants dominate this broad category of wetlands. Swamps range from red maple forests in the Northeast to bottomland hardwood forests that flourish along slow-moving rivers in the Southeast. Their thick, organic soils provide habitat for freshwater shellfish such as shrimp and crayfish, as well as rare species such as the American crocodile. Swamps absorb pollutants and help control flooding.

Bogs — Formed atop spongy peat deposits and often carpeted by sphagnum moss, bogs are home to unusual species, including carnivorous plants, which can adapt to low nutrient levels and acidic water. Bogs prevent downstream flooding by absorbing rain and also store large amounts of carbon in peat deposits — an important role in regulating global climate.

Fens — Also formed atop peat deposits, fens are less acidic and contain more nutrients than bogs. Covered by sedges, rushes, grasses and wildflowers, fens help control floods and improve water quality.

Most Wetlands Are Freshwater

About 95 percent of the 105.5 million acres of wetlands in the contiguous United States are freshwater. From 1986 to 1997, about 58,500 acres of wetlands were lost per year.

Makeup of Freshwater Wetlands

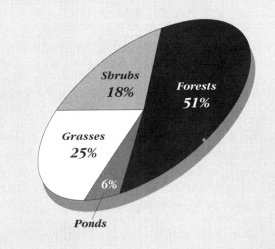

Shrubs 18%
Forests 51%
Grasses 25%
Ponds 6%

Source: Thomas E. Dahl, "Status and Trends of Wetlands in the Coterminous United States 1986 to 1997," U.S. Fish and Wildlife Service

construct two jetties at popular Oregon Inlet along the North Carolina coast. Corps officials say they would stabilize a channel used by fishing boats to reach the ocean, but the National Park Service (NPS) and U.S. Fish and Wildlife Service worry the jetties would encourage overfishing and erode nearby beaches.

The NWF's Costenbader says Congress should overhaul the agency's principles and guidelines. Formulated in 1983, they direct the Corps to recommend projects that maximize national economic development, provided it is consistent with protecting the environment.

Such criteria tend to favor large-scale projects that promise economic benefits. When faced with a flooding problem, for example, the Corps tends to make the case for building levies or other structures — which could pave the way for more development in a floodplain. An alternative approach, such as restoring the floodplain's natural function of absorbing water — which could cost far less, avoid environmental harm and potentially minimize downstream flooding — is rarely taken because it delivers no direct economic benefit.

Moreover, Costenbader says, the

principles and guidelines do not require the Corps to select the most sustainable or cost-efficient alternative, so it frequently misses some of the benefits provided by the natural environment.

Larson, of the floodplain managers' association, agrees, pointing out that the Corps is directed to base its recommendations on its economic-development quidelines. "You get convoluted results off that," Larson says. "Building a levy to protect a set of buildings will [produce] a higher benefit-cost analysis than buying the buildings and moving them, although the total bottom-line cost is higher. Congress needs to say to the Corps: 'You will give the environmental approach as high a value as the economic plan.'"

Such an approach, of course, would run smack into the interests of those who favor managing rivers for navigation purposes. For example, the agency is in the middle of a particularly fierce dispute over the Missouri River that pits not just environmentalists against business interests but also one state against another. To keep enough water in the river to sustain barge traffic and satisfy agricultural interests, the Corps drains water from reservoirs in the Dakotas and Montana — which angers upper Midwesterners who want the reservoirs full during the summer recreation season. Keeping the river's flow relatively constant also has wiped out almost all of the river's sandbars and most of its aquatic food, devastating the populations of fish and other creatures.

But powerful agribusiness and farm groups downstream want access to barges to haul grain, thereby holding down shipping costs. [21] "We're all sick of this Mother Nature cultism," said Ron Blakely, a Missouri farmer who is leading efforts to build a new port near St. Joseph. "Yeah, I'd like to save the fish. But . . . who's going to save me?" [22]

Should the Corps do more to protect wetlands?

To Jeffrey Potter, director of outreach and education at the Wisconsin Wetlands Association, there's no such thing as an "isolated" wetland. A small pond might seem to be unimportant from an environmental point of view, but in fact it may help store water when a nearby stream overflows, or reach other ponds through an underground aquifer, or serve as an important resting stop for migratory waterfowl.

"It's an archaic term," Potter explains. "The concept of 'isolated' makes it sound like they exist in a whole other world and not in the natural landscape. But, scientifically speaking, they are part of an overall ecosystem that uses them."

Whether a wetland can be defined as "isolated" might seem like a trivial question. But it has critical ramifications for the Corps of Engineers, which is helping to develop new rules for the types of wetlands it can protect.

Under the 1972 Clean Water Act, the Corps is charged with protecting the nation's wetlands, known as the Earth's "kidneys" because of their essential role in filtering pollutants. They also absorb runoff during heavy rains and harbor rare species of animals and plants. Developers wanting to pave over wetlands must first get a permit from the Corps — a sometimes-lengthy process that requires them to prove they have no other viable alternative and are minimizing the environmental damage. Typically, they also must "mitigate" the damage by taking such steps as constructing an artificial wetland nearby.

Responsibility for the nation's wetlands has put the Corps in the middle of a fierce tug-of-war between developers, who want access to more land, and environmentalists, who believe wetlands merit the strictest possible protection. The debate became much more heated after a 2001

Supreme Court decision removing some isolated wetlands not connected to interstate commerce from the Corps' jurisdiction. (*See "At Issue," p. 173.*)

The decision in *Solid Waste Agencies of Northern Cook County v. U.S. Army Corps of Engineers* was one of those complex judicial rulings that could be construed in a variety of ways. The high court ruled that the Corps could not use its longstanding so-called migratory bird rule to regulate an isolated pond in Illinois. The rule had said the federal government (whose regulatory reach is typically limited to matters that involve interstate commerce) could regulate ponds not connected to interstate waterways because migratory birds that use such ponds are significant to interstate commerce.

The ruling was issued in the final days of the Clinton administration, which interpreted it as removing federal oversight only from completely isolated waters where the only justification for federal oversight was the migratory bird rule. But the Bush administration has signaled that it will interpret the ruling much more broadly. In January, it invited public comment on possible new wetlands-protection rules that the Corps and the EPA said would "clarify" the government's authority "over a vast majority of the nation's wetlands." [23] A new rule is expected this summer or fall.

Developers want to end government oversight of all isolated wetlands — many of which, they say, serve little ecological function. "What we on the development side are generally talking about when we are talking about isolated wetlands are little puddles in the middle of vacant land, a low spot that was created by a dump truck or tractor," says Asmus at the home builders' association. "For those low-quality wetlands created incidental to other activities, there has got to be a balance between environmental benefits and economic activities."

Environmentalists, however, worry that the ruling would cause the Corps to lose authority over as much as 20 million acres of wetlands — or 20 percent of the remaining 105 million acres of wetlands in the contiguous United States. Individual states could still protect such potentially environmentally sensitive areas, but many of them lack the funding or inclination to do so — leaving the lands vulnerable to bulldozers.

"The very day [the decision] hit the press, I was driving from Galveston to Houston, and I counted no less than six huge tracts of land where bulldozers were knocking everything down," said James Jones, a consultant and former wetlands regulator. "And they hadn't been developed [prior to the decision] because there were isolated wetlands in them." [24]

Isolated wetlands aside, critics say the Corps approves an unconscionable number — more than 99 percent — of permit applications to develop wetlands, even though the Clean Water Act states that permits should be issued only when proposed developments cannot be reconfigured to prevent wetlands damage.

"It's extremely unlikely to see a Corps permit denied," says Carlton Dufrechou, executive director of the Lake Pontchartrain Basin Foundation, a citizens' organization dedicated to restoring the big Louisiana lake. "The process we have right now is not a wetland-preservation process — it's a wetland-destruction process."

Corps officials, however, say it is misleading to judge the agency by how many permits it issues, because developers often are forced to scale back their projects in order to get the permits, minimizing environmental harm. "[The percentage] doesn't address how much work goes into those permits before they're submitted in their final form," Pawlik says.

Environmentalists are also skeptical about the efficacy of mitigation rules requiring developers who destroy wetlands to build or restore other wetlands. The first Bush administration adopted a wetlands policy of "no net loss" — meaning that any destroyed wetlands should be balanced by the creation of new ones. But the nation is still losing about 60,000 acres of wetlands a year, although environmentalists say the number may be higher.

A National Academy of Sciences (NAS) advisory council concluded in 2001 that the continuing loss is partly due to the fact that many artificial wetlands projects are delayed or never completed. Even those that are finished often fail to function as true wetlands, often because the site is too dry or the soil is not right, the council said.

"Many of these projects fail because nature never intended for there to be a wetland there, or a particular type of wetland there," said Suzanne van Drunick, director of the study for the NAS' National Research Council. [25]

In addition, the Bush administration loosened mitigation rules somewhat last year, giving developers options other than building wetlands near ones that had been destroyed. Developers can now create wetlands at a greater distance from the old ones (although still within the same watershed) or take other steps designed to help the environment, such as planting trees along streambeds.

Developers hail the increased flexibility as a common-sense approach to minimizing environmental harm. As Asmus of the home builders' association puts it: "They've expanded it out to say, 'Let's go and do the best kind of mitigation we can do and not put artificial limits on it.'"

However, the environmentalists are afraid the new policy will accelerate wetlands destruction. "These things have nothing to do with replacing what was there and will absolutely lead to a loss of wetlands," says the NWF's Sibbing. "But they're enshrining these things as acceptable policies." ■

BACKGROUND

Civil-Engineering Role

The Corps of Engineers traces its history to the Revolutionary War. On June 16, 1775, the Continental Congress organized an army with a chief engineer and four years later formed a separate engineering corps for the duration of the war. In 1802, it formally established the U.S. Army Corps of Engineers. [26]

Since its inception, the Corps has had a dual mission — building both military fortifications and civil projects. Civilian responsibilities initially included building lighthouses, helping to develop jetties and piers for harbors and mapping navigation channels — as well as much of the American West.

In the early 19th century, federal officials eschewed funding canals, roads and other "internal improvements," for fear of undercutting states' authority. However, in 1824, the Supreme Court ruled in a landmark case, *Gibbons v. Ogden*, that the federal government's authority extended into interstate commerce, including riverine navigation.

Congress subsequently passed two laws that year instituting the Corps' continuous involvement in civil projects. The General Survey Act authorized surveys of potential routes for roads and canals that could have national importance for commercial or military uses. A month later, lawmakers appropriated $75,000 to improve navigation on the Ohio and Mississippi rivers by removing sandbars and other obstacles — a measure considered by many to be the first rivers and harbors legislation.

Throughout the 19th century and into the 20th, the Corps became

Chronology

Late 1700s
The Colonial government establishes the precursor of a military engineering corps during the War of Independence.

1824
The Supreme Court, in *Gibbons v. Ogden*, establishes the federal government's authority over interstate commerce, clearing the way for the Corps to oversee river navigation.

1890s
Congress approves two Rivers and Harbors acts, which require dams to be approved by the Corps and the secretary of war and allow the Corps to regulate waste dumping into waterways.

1926
Flooding in the Mississippi River Delta kills more than 500 people. Congress responds with the 1929 Flood Control Act, which makes flood protection a federal responsibility.

1928
A devastating hurricane in South Florida kills 1,300 people and prompts the construction of a vast drainage and flood-control system in the Everglades.

1930s
The Corps helps build major hydropower projects.

1936
Congress expands the Corps' responsibilities to include building reservoirs and establishes the principle that a project's economic benefits must exceed its costs.

1940s-1960s
Congress again expands the Corps' mission.

1944
Congress directs the Corps to build dams for flood control, recreation and other purposes.

1956
Congress gives the Corps responsibility for renourishing beaches to protect coastal developments.

1970s
Growing environmental awareness leads to questions about the negative impact of Corps water projects.

1972
The landmark Clean Water Act gives the Corps responsibility to regulate development of wetlands.

1977
President Jimmy Carter tries to delete funding for major water projects, sparking a decade-long battle between the executive and legislative branches over Corps budgets.

1980s
After a decade of executive-branch resistance, Congress adopts a scaled-back water-projects bill.

1986
Reauthorization of the Water Resources Development Act enables President Ronald Reagan to strike a compromise with lawmakers over water projects. Although the law authorizes $20 billion for projects, it requires local governments to pay more of the costs.

1989
President George W. Bush pursues a "no net loss" of wetlands policy, requiring developers who destroy wetlands to create new ones.

2000s
News reports indicate flawed economic analyses enable the Corps to build inefficient and environmentally destructive projects.

February 2000
Corps economist Donald Sweeney alleges he and other Corps economists were pressured by superiors to inflate the benefits of a locks-expansion project on the Mississippi River.

Dec. 11, 2000
President Bill Clinton signs the Water Resources Development Act reauthorization, directing the Corps to begin restoring the Everglades.

2001
Mounting reports of Corps mismanagement prompt a bipartisan group of lawmakers to form a Corps Reform Caucus.

Jan. 9, 2001
The Supreme Court limits federal oversight of "isolated" wetlands.

Oct. 7, 2002
With lawmakers deadlocked over Corps reforms, House leaders withdraw a biennial bill authorizing new water projects. Similar legislation dies in the Senate.

Feb. 3, 2003
President Bush's budget proposes spending cuts on several controversial Corps projects while encouraging independent reviews of the agency's proposals.

Controversy Along the Yazoo

Mississippi's Yazoo River is an unlikely place for national controversy — but it's the focus of one of the most fiercely contested Army Corps of Engineers projects. The agency is proposing to build a massive hydraulic pumping facility — possibly the largest in the world — to protect the low-lying region of black-earth farms and small towns from surging floodwaters. Locals still talk about the great flood of 1927 that ravaged the Mississippi Delta, killing more than 500 people and leaving tens of thousands homeless.

To guard against such floods, the Yazoo pump would force some 6 million gallons of water a minute over an existing levee to redirect excess water into the Mississippi River. Powerful backers, including Mississippi's congressional delegation, agricultural interests, and the Corps' Vicksburg district, say it would spare residents from the trauma of floods and help revitalize an area that has been losing population. "Year after year, these people who live in this area are threatened with floods, as are their homes and businesses and hospitals," Sen. Trent Lott, R-Miss., said during a Jan. 23 Senate debate on funding for the project. "It is a very dangerous situation."

To environmentalists, fiscal conservatives and even some Delta residents, the project would waste taxpayers' money, damage fragile ecosystems and aid just a few large landowners. The Environmental Protection Agency (EPA) warns the project would destroy some 200,000 acres of wetlands — more than the Corps allows developers across the country to destroy in a single year.

"Everything that could be wrong with a project is wrong with this project," says Melissa Samet, senior director of water resources at American Rivers, an environmental group. "The environmental and economic studies supporting this proposal are flawed at levels that are shocking."

Samet and other critics say the Corps has oversold the project by relying on highly questionable assumptions. For example, the agency based its estimate for the flood-control benefits of the project — $1.47 for every $1 expended — on projections of a population increase, even though south Delta counties have lost population steadily since World War II. And the Corps appeared to minimize the environmental costs, estimating no more than 24,000 acres of wetlands would be destroyed, which is vastly less than the EPA assessment.

The debate even has reached into the issue of whether the pumps would do much to protect residents. Supporters say the project would diminish floodwaters even though it would not prevent flooding altogether. "We like to say [the pumps] would take four to four-and-one-half feet off any given flood," Mississippi Levee Board chief engineer Jim Wanamaker said. "If you had three feet of water in your house in 1973, you wouldn't have any with the pumps." [1]

But some in the region say floods rarely pose a threat to residents. In an editorial, the *Deer Creek Pilot* warned: "Let's not fool either ourselves or anybody else that what has always been a project proposed as one to protect against back-

increasingly proficient at managing inland waterways. After using wooden wing dams to control currents, the engineers experimented successfully with steam-powered boats to jar loose snags, hydraulic dredges to deepen river channels and locks and dams to regulate river flows. The Corps eventually dammed and channelized numerous rivers, including the Missouri, Rio Grande and Columbia. But in the process of aiding navigation the corps devastated once-pristine wetlands, estuaries and floodplains.

Over the years, Congress called upon the Corps to perform increasingly challenging tasks, including building a series of levees to prevent flooding along the Mississippi River and — when floods persisted — creating an unprecedented system of controlled

outlets and floodways to disperse water. They did the same thing in the South Florida Everglades in the 1940s after devastating hurricanes and floods killed thousands of residents who live around Lake Okeechobee.

As the federal government grew during the Great Depression, the Corps took on significantly more responsibilities. Tackling the dual demands for flood protection and job creation, Congress passed the Flood Control Act of 1936, which for the first time declared that flood control was the province of the federal government. The law also established the principle that the economic benefits of a proposed project should exceed its costs. Meanwhile, the administration of President Franklin D. Roosevelt sought the Corps' help building hy-

droelectric dams in order to provide rural residents with electricity.

In 1944, Congress again expanded the Corps' reach, passing a new Flood Control Act. The sweeping law gave the Corps oversight over multipurpose projects, such as Missouri River dams that would provide flood control, irrigation, navigation, water supply, hydropower and recreation. After World War II, lawmakers continued to authorize major hydroelectric projects, despite concerns by some critics — including President Dwight D. Eisenhower — that they were too costly.

Then, amid concerns about eroding coastlines and vanishing beaches, Congress in 1956 gave the Corps a new task: beach replenishment. [27]

water flooding of agricultural land and enhance agricultural production has suddenly turned into one which would protect old ladies and babies from flooding in their homes every year. Because at least in Sharkey and Issaquena counties, [people aren't] threatened by the kinds of rapidly rising floodwaters which take lives." [2]

The idea for the project can be traced back to the 1929 Flood Control Act, when Congress, responding to the catastrophic 1927 flood, made flood protection in the Mississippi River Valley a federal responsibility. Congress authorized the actual pumping station in 1941 as the final piece of a flood-control system that includes levees and the widening and connecting of the Big and Little Sunflower rivers. Until recently, the project languished because of cost concerns, especially as the region lost population after World War II. But farmers now are pressing for it as a way of reclaiming land that is often flooded.

President Bush, in his fiscal 2004 budget request, declined

Corps of Engineers/Alfred Dulaney

Supporters say a proposed major pumping facility along the Yazoo River in Mississippi will alleviate dangerous flooding; critics say it will damage the environment and mainly aid big landowners.

to provide any money for the pumping system. And Sen. John McCain, R-Ariz., a vocal critic of wasteful government spending, has repeatedly urged eliminating the $191 million project. "The pumps are specifically designed to drain wetlands so that large landowners can increase agricultural production on marginal lands," he said on the Senate floor in January.

Nonetheless, Congress included about $10 million for the project in a recent omnibus appropriations bill. And environmentalists worry that unless the political calculus shifts suddenly, the pulses of flooding each spring that sustain animals and plants in the Delta will be disrupted permanently.

"It's a really unbelievable level of impact," Samet says. "They're destroying an entire ecosystem."

---

[1] Ray Mosby, "Yazoo Pump: Protecting people or political pork?" *Deer Creek Pilot*, Feb. 20, 2003, p. A1.

[2] Editorial, "Our agenda is finding the truth," *Deer Creek Pilot*, March 6, 2003.

Environmental Role

T oward the end of the 19th century, the Corps had become involved in a task far removed from civil engineering and waterway management: protecting the environment. In the 1880s and '90s, Congress charged the Corps with preventing companies from illegally dumping waste into the nation's waterways. To some extent, the enforcement activity was a natural outgrowth of maintaining navigable waterways. In 1893, for example, the Corps forced an Ohio town to burn its waste instead of dumping it into a river and obstructing navigation.

Congress expanded the Corps' role as an environmental watchdog with the landmark Rivers and Har-

bors Act of 1899, which gave the agency regulatory authority over any waste dumping that could obstruct navigation.

Not surprisingly, the Corps' early environmental actions spurred lawsuits. In 1910, for example, the Corps failed to block a proposed sewer in New York City because of a court ruling that pollution control was a state prerogative. By the 1920s, according to an official history of the agency, Corps officers were failing to aggressively use their anti-pollution powers, both due to limited staffing and because the agency did not concern itself with pollution unless it impacted navigation.

By the time the modern environmental movement blossomed in the 1960s and '70s, the nation's major wa-

terways were so polluted that floating debris on Cleveland's Cuyahoga River actually caught fire, and Lake Erie was regularly closed to swimmers because of sewage contamination. In 1970, President Richard M. Nixon issued an executive order — based on the largely forgotten 1899 Rivers and Harbors Act — requiring industries to obtain a permit from the Corps before dumping certain wastes into waterways.

Two years later, Congress overwhelmingly passed the Clean Water Act, which sought to dramatically reduce water pollution. [28] Section 404 authorized the Corps to administer a permit program to regulate wetlands dumping, signaling a new determination to protect wetlands, which traditionally had been regarded as little more than breeding grounds for mosquitoes. The Lower 48 states had lost almost half their original wetlands because developers, not realizing their ecological functions, had filled them in.

Although Section 404 caused little comment when passed, it soon placed the Corps in the middle of a furious debate between environmentalists and industry. The Corps had angered environmentalists by construing its permitting authority to cover only wetlands linked to navigable waters. Then a federal court in 1975 ruled that Congress intended the permitting program to cover all U.S. waters.

But environmentalists worried the Corps would prove a lukewarm protector of wetlands; Sen. Edmund Muskie, D-Maine, a chief sponsor of the 1972 law, said later that he wished the EPA had been designated to protect wetlands instead.

Budget Concerns

In the 1970s, the Corps began attracting criticism on another front: its construction of huge dams and other large water projects. Dams can interfere with natural river flows, damaging wetlands and other important habitats, and block annual fish migrations.

President Jimmy Carter — concerned about mounting budget deficits as well as the potential environmental harm posed by dams — set off a 10-year battle with Congress when he tried to cut some two-dozen dams and other water projects from the budget. [29] He temporarily deleted funding for some, but appropriators continued year after year to try to restore the funding.

A Corps of Engineers dredge deepens a stretch of the Missouri River near Bellevue, Neb. Critics say many Corps dredging projects damaged wetlands or were based on faulty economic assumptions and didn't deliver the promised economic benefits.

Corps of Engineers/Harry Weddington

Ronald Reagan, Carter's White House successor, continued the campaign against costly water projects. The battle finally ended with a compromise in 1986, when lawmakers passed the first major water-projects bill in a decade, authorizing $20 billion for port development, locks and dams, flood control and other projects. But Congress raised local governments' share of the costs from 5-10 percent to about 25 percent.

The Corps, however, was left vulnerable to both environmental groups and fiscal conservatives. On the environmental front, it was whipsawed between liberals and conservatives over wetlands protection in the late 1980s and early '90s. In an effort to minimize the loss of wetlands, then-Pres-

ident George Bush declared a goal of "no net loss" of wetlands. But at the same time, he sought to narrow the Corps' oversight of wetlands, setting off a storm of criticism from environmentalists.

Meanwhile, the Corps faced continuing criticism over its efforts to re-nourish beaches. Environmentalists and fiscal conservatives alike condemned such projects as futile because erosion is a natural process that cannot be easily prevented. Instead of spending millions of dollars dredging sand and dumping it on disappearing beaches, critics said the government should bar development along exposed coastal areas and allow nature to take its course. But wealthy coastal communities successfully demanded such projects year after year.

President Bill Clinton sought to improve the Corps' environmental record by stiffening wetlands protection and seeking the engineers' expertise to restore degraded waterways. Typical of this new direction was the $16 million restoration of the Yolo Basin wetlands in California — a major stop for migrating waterfowl along the Pacific Coast. Flood-control projects designed to protect Sacramento had begun to dry out the area. But in the more environmentally conscious 1990s, the Corps sought to bring back wildlife by restoring drained wetlands, forested areas and grasslands.

But the agency soon found itself embroiled in perhaps the worst controversy of its history — over both its fiscal oversight of water projects and its wetlands policies. In 2000, a series of scathing articles in *The Washington Post* alleged the agency had based costly projects on optimistic barge-traffic projections that never materialized. In some cases, only a single barge a year, or none at all, steamed along the dammed, diked and dredged rivers. *The Post* also revealed the Corps approved more than 99 percent of developers' requests to drain, dredge and fill wetlands even in ecologically sensitive areas. [30]

More embarrassments and scandals came to light. The same year, a whistle-blower alleged that the Corps had rigged a study to overstate a proposed project's economic benefits. *The Post* revealed that the Corps had secretly launched a program to boost its $4 billion annual budget by 50 percent without the knowledge of military higher-ups. [31] And over the following couple of years, studies by the Pentagon, the NAS and the GAO questioned the Corps' accounting procedures.

Lawmakers were so outraged they formed the Corps Reform Caucus in 2001, vowing that this time the agency would change. As Rep. Tom Tancredo, R-Colo., put it: "We cannot allow the Army Corps of Engineers to recklessly spend taxpayer funds on bloated and wasteful projects." [32] ■

CURRENT SITUATION

Reform Efforts

E nvironmental groups have criticized the administration for favoring the interests of industry over conservation, but President Bush won kudos from them for the Corps budget he released in February. His plan, part of a larger initiative to restrain non-military government spending, would cut funding for several projects favored by lawmakers from $171 million in this year's budget to just $1.8 million.

Among the controversial projects that were cut was the Devil's Lake flood-control project in Mississippi, which would build an outlet on the lake's western shore despite EPA warnings that it could cause pollution problems downstream. The budget also eliminated funds for a dredging project on the Delaware River, which had drawn GAO criticism amid indications that the Corps was overstating its benefits.

With his plan, Bush signaled that he is serious about limiting pork-barrel spending. But powerful members of Congress say they'll find a way to restore funding for the projects. Former Senate Majority Leader Lott, who maintains considerable influence as a member of the Commerce, Science and Transportation Committee, had this to say in response to Bush's budget: "We're going to provide the funding like we do every year." [33]

By seeking to cut water projects, Bush could be setting up the biggest battle over the Army Corps of Engineers since the late 1970s and early '80s, when the Carter and Reagan administrations squared off against Capitol Hill, tying up new water-project authorizations for a decade.

This time, however, Congress is split. For example, members who have recently formed the Army Corps Reform Caucus are so troubled by reports about agency mismanagement they are vowing to block authorizations of new water projects until their colleagues agree to overhaul the agency. "Congress simply cannot continue to ignore the evidence that significant problems exist within the Corps," said Rep. Wayne Gilchrest, R-Md. [34] Appropriators could still provide annual money for construction of previously approved projects, but with his budget, Bush has thrown his weight squarely behind the forces for reform. Besides deleting questionable projects, the administration would:

- Require independent reviews of large Corps projects.
- Fund only projects that yield "a very high net economic or environmental return to society relative to their cost" and that "meet current economic and environmental standards and that address contemporary needs."
- Deauthorize certain projects authorized decades ago that were never built.
- Require local entities to pay a higher share for Corps projects that benefit them.
- Require the Corps to explore options other than building or expanding existing navigational and flood-control systems.

Last year, lawmakers battled to a draw over such issues. Reformers such as Sens. Russell D. Feingold, D-Wis., and Robert C. Smith, R-N.H. (who has since left the Senate), coalesced behind legislation that included many of the reforms Bush is seeking.

Knowing they could not win approval of a stand-alone bill with such provisions, they sought to attach the reforms to the Water Resources Development Act (WRDA) — a multibillion-dollar bill typically passed every other year authorizing politically popular dams and other water projects. But lawmakers from the coasts, the Mississippi Delta and other regions that benefit from Corps projects assailed the proposed reforms as an indirect way to slow or even stop economically important projects. Rather than swallow the reforms, key Corps supporters, such as House Transportation Committee Chairman Don Young, R-Alaska, allowed the entire measure to die.

"I didn't pick this fight," said Sen. Christopher Bond, R-Mo., an outspoken Corps proponent. "But I am ready and anxious, with energy and enthusiasm, to join it." [35]

Some lawmakers are trying to bridge the divide. But so far, they have failed.

In the House, for example, James L. Oberstar, D-Minn. — a veteran Transportation Committee member who is sympathetic to the Corps — has suggested a comparatively modest series of reforms. His plan would require independent reviews of projects over $30 million or that were for some reason controversial, and would direct the Corps to accept more public input. But before he could propose such amendments to WRDA last year, House leaders pulled the bill from floor consideration.

It remains uncertain when lawmakers will return to the fray. The House and Senate Transportation committees are consumed with reauthorizing a massive surface-transportation measure, which would provide funding for roads and highways. The daunting task may spill over into next year, delaying consideration of a water bill.

As a result, the battle over water projects may be fought this year in annual-spending bills. Corps supporters appear to have the advantage in such skirmishing between seasoned appropriators who like to spend money on water projects and the president, who lacks line-item veto authority to delete a single project from a multibillion-dollar bill. Demonstrating their muscle, Senate appropriators in February slipped a provision into an omnibus spending bill that prohibits the privatization or restructuring of the Corps. The provision makes the Corps the sole agency exempt from Bush's continuing efforts to outsource hundreds of thousands of federal jobs.

Wetlands Protection

While lawmakers on Capitol Hill may stand up to the administration on water projects, there are few signs it will try to interfere with Bush's attempts to scale back wetlands protection.

The administration is trying to clarify the 2001 Supreme Court decision that limited the federal government's authority over some isolated wetlands. Environmentalists worry that the administration's new rule, expected to be issued this summer or fall, could undermine the 1972 Clean Water Act and lead to widespread water pollution.

If the administration pares back federal oversight of isolated wetlands, states could still step into the breach. The Wisconsin legislature in 2001, for example, responded to the Supreme Court decision by setting up a program to regulate isolated wetlands. But states are facing their worst budget crisis since the 1930s, and few are in a position to protect wetlands.

The issue has attracted relatively little attention in Congress, which has refused to expand or reaffirm many environmental laws. Last year, Sens. Feingold and Oberstar and Rep. John D. Dingell, D-Mich., introduced legislation that would have allowed the Corps of Engineers to regulate all wetlands in the United States, regardless of their relevance to interstate commerce. But Congress took no action on the proposals.

In the end, the issue is likely to spark court battles — as have previous attempts to define the Corps' role in regulating wetlands. "No matter how the rule turns out," says the National Wildlife Federation's Sibbing, "there's going to be litigation on one side or the other." ∎

OUTLOOK

Restoration Efforts

Environmentalist Marc Holmes is getting help from the Corps for a wetlands project in California — but it has nothing to do with expanding development.

Instead, Holmes wants to restore some 100,000 acres of marshlands diked and drained in the San Francisco Bay area over the past 150 years to permit development. And the Corps — which has spent much of its history filling in wetlands — is playing a key role in the ambitious effort.

"The restoration of those wetlands is important for restoring the ecological vitality of San Francisco Bay," explains Holmes, who manages the Baylands Restoration Project for the Bay Institute. "The impact will be first on wildlife that depend on the wetlands and secondly on water quality and flood protection." The project is a high priority for conservationists, some of whom refer to Bay Area wetlands as the Everglades of California.

The San Francisco project is only one of numerous restoration projects involving the Corps. About 20 percent of the agency's budget now goes toward environmental restoration, as policymakers seek to repair the damage caused by past projects. Restoration projects generally enjoy broad political support because hunters, birdwatchers and other outdoor enthusiasts welcome the prospect of expanded wildlife habitat. Some even predict that environmental restoration may be the primary thrust of the Corps in the new century.

"The Corps has the engineering expertise, the project management

At Issue:

Should the federal government protect "isolated" wetlands?

JULIE SIBBING
WETLAND LEGISLATIVE REPRESENTATIVE,
NATIONAL WILDLIFE FEDERATION

FROM TESTIMONY BEFORE WATER RESOURCES AND THE ENVI-
RONMENT SUBCOMMITTEE OF THE HOUSE TRANSPORTATION
AND INFRASTRUCTURE COMMITTEE, SEPT. 20, 2001

Our nation's wetlands provide numerous valuable services to society, including floodwater storage, water-
quality improvement, groundwater recharge, moderation
of stream flows, wildlife habitat and recreation. Yet, already the
Lower 48 states have lost more than 53 percent of their historic
wetlands. While [the] U.S. Fish and Wildlife Service and Natural
Resources Conservation Service estimate annual acreage losses
of wetland have declined in recent years . . . our remaining
wetlands . . . are more vulnerable to destruction and degradation than at any time in the past 25 years.

On Jan. 9, 2001 . . . the U.S. Supreme Court in *Solid
Waste Agency of Northern Cook County v. U.S. Army Corps
of Engineers* held that Clean Water Act protections did not
extend to non-navigable, "isolated," wholly intrastate waters.
This decision left a significant portion of America's valuable
wetlands vulnerable, not only to unrestricted drainage and destruction but also to unrestricted discharges of pollutants. . . .
Overly broad interpretations of the Clean Water Act loophole
have resulted in the unrestricted drainage of more than 25,000
acres of wetlands and the degradation of many hundreds of
miles of streams across the country.

The risk posed by these gaps in the Clean Water Act is
staggering. The vast majority of "prairie pothole" wetlands of
the Northern Great Plains, which provide breeding habitat for
more than half of the North American population of migratory
waterfowl, are left without Clean Water Act protection — as
are the playa lakes and rainwater basin wetlands relied upon
by millions of migratory water birds, including sandhill and
whooping cranes, ducks, geese and shorebirds. Vernal pools,
which provide critical habitat for many species of declining
amphibians [also] are at risk.

The loss of "isolated" wetlands will also have profound impacts on human populations. Many areas that already suffer serious flooding problems — and even areas that have not yet experienced flooding — will suffer much greater problems with
the loss of additional upstream water-storage capacity. Areas that
rely upon wetlands for groundwater recharge may suffer greater
depletion of their aquifers if "isolated" wetlands are destroyed.

Perhaps most shocking is the risk posed to our groundwater supplies from unregulated discharges of pollutants, including mine wastes, human and animal wastes, petroleum and
other chemicals. Since wetlands are frequently groundwater-
recharge areas, discharges of pollutants into such waters pose
an especially great risk to groundwater supplies.

VIRGINIA S. ALBRECHT
ATTORNEY REPRESENTING THE NATIONAL MULTI
HOUSING COALITION AND OTHER REAL ESTATE
TRADE ASSOCIATIONS

FROM TESTIMONY BEFORE THE ENERGY POLICY, NATURAL RE-
SOURCES AND REGULATORY AFFAIRS SUBCOMMITTEE OF THE
HOUSE GOVERNMENT REFORM COMMITTEE, SEPT. 19, 2002

In ruling in *SWANCC* [*Solid Waste Agency of Northern
Cook County v. U.S. Army Corps of Engineers*] . . . the
Supreme Court set forth several principles which require
[federal] agencies to cease their attempts to claim jurisdiction
over areas and features that are only remotely related to "navigable waters" and that are better managed under the traditional
authorities of the states over land and water use.

Rather than reassess their jurisdiction in light of this disposi-
tive Supreme Court decision, the agencies have failed to give direction to their staff or the regulated community. The result is
that some in the agencies have been able to work to retain as
much jurisdiction as they can through novel and creative theories concerning the meaning of such terms as "tributary" and
"isolated," neither of which is defined by existing regulations.

For example, the Corps and EPA have claimed jurisdiction
over remote ditches and wetlands on the theory that any "sur-
face-water connection," or any potential that a molecule of
water could eventually mix with a downstream navigable
water, created federal jurisdiction. These attempts to replace
the invalidated "Migratory Bird Rule" with a new "Migratory
Molecule Rule" are unauthorized by the CWA [Clean Water
Act], violate the letter and spirit of *SWANCC*, impose significant burdens on the regulated public (not to mention the
Corps' regulatory staff and budget), and provide little or no
environmental benefit. . . .

The current approach of regulating on a case-by-case, dis-
trict-by-district, region-by-region, basis is untenable and patent-
ly unfair to applicants as it leads to inconsistent jurisdictional
determinations. For example, in Florida we have seen clients
advised by one section of the Corps' Jacksonville District that
no permit was required in light of the *SWANCC* decision for
a wetland that was 50 feet from a man-made drainage canal.
Yet, another section within the same Corps district required
the applicant to obtain a permit for a wetland that was over
150 feet away from a similar man-made drainage canal. The
field regulator made this determination even though hydrological data showed that the wetland did not have a hydrological
connection with the canal, even in a 100-year storm event,
and was over a mile away from navigable water. . . .

The agencies should focus their scarce resources on regulating those waters that are truly "federal" in nature such as
the traditional navigable waters and adjacent wetlands, thus
maximizing federal environmental protection.

Environmentalists Question Plan to Restore Everglades

After a horrific hurricane in 1928 blew most of Lake Okeechobee onto the surrounding lowlands — drowning 1,300 South Floridians — and a 1947 flood again devastated the region, the Army Corps of Engineers waded into the Everglades in a big way in 1948.

Congress authorized a vast network of canals and dikes including 1,700 miles of levees and canals, 150 flood-control structures and 16 pumping stations. They were so successful in diverting floodwaters that some 1.7 billion gallons of water are flushed daily into the Atlantic Ocean and Gulf of Mexico. The massive flood control and water-supply project drained more than a half-million acres of marshland that today supplies 25 percent of the nation's sugar and provides enough water to support dozens of new housing developments. [1]

But in the process, the project ravaged the area's unique and fragile ecosystem. Today, the storied "River of Grass" covers barely half its 1948 expanse; 90 percent of its wading birds are gone and 69 percent of its plant and animal species are endangered. [2] The nation's largest wetland area — home to dozens of rare species, including the Florida panther and American crocodile — is beset by poisonous agricultural runoff, aggressive, non-native species and lack of water. Some biologists also warn that destruction of the famed wetlands threatens the vast underground Biscayne Aquifer — water source for millions of South Floridians.

To avert the crisis, Congress in 2000 gave the Corps a very different mission: help spearhead the largest environmental project in U.S. history — a 38-year, $7.8 billion plan to build dozens of water projects to capture a trillion gallons of rainwater and distribute it to farmers and residents and to rehydrate the area's shrinking marshes. "The Everglades [is] a very environmentally sensitive region, and clearly is a treasure," said then-Sen. Robert C. Smith, R-N.H., who sponsored the landmark bipartisan legislation authorizing the joint federal-state project. [3]

However, many scientists and hydrologists working on the project have grave doubts about the multipronged restoration effort. "We have no idea if this will work," said Stuart J. Appelbaum, the Corps official who is in charge of the project. [4]

"I don't see a shred of evidence that all this money will help the environment," said Fish and Wildlife Service biologist Bob Gasaway. [5]

Moreover, last year, a National Academy of Sciences study warned that the project could have devastating effects — killing sea grasses and causing algal blooms in Florida Bay, a popular, 1,000-square-mile recreation destination at the state's southern tip. [6]

And there's another problem. Critics warn that the Corps appears to be falling short in its new role as environmental steward. Under pressure from Florida business interests, the Corps has redesigned the restoration plan, turning it into what critics call a local water-supply and flood-control boondoggle designed to support a doubling of South Florida's population. Benefits for developers and farmers far outweigh efforts to restore the Everglades, say environmentalists, who have threatened to withdraw their support.

"We're just very worried that this project is setting itself up for failure," says Alan Farago, Everglades chair for the Florida chapter of the Sierra Club. "There is no lack of vision within the staff at the Corps, but there's a very pronounced lack of institutional strength to counter political interference by special interests."

Powerful Florida commercial interests are continuing activities that could threaten the restoration efforts. Sugar growers — whose fertilizer runoff has contributed to the decline of the fragile wetlands — successfully lobbied state lawmakers this year to scale back a 1994 state Everglades clean-up law. Angered by the move, Congressional GOP appropriators took the unprecedented step of urging Republican Gov. Jeb Bush to veto the bill, but he signed it on May 20, saying it would not undermine the project. [7]

And last year, in a decision that particularly outraged environmentalists, the Corps allowed limestone-mining companies

expertise and the budget to engage in a restoration of America's waterways," says Costenbader of the National Wildlife Federation. "That's the real need of the 21st century."

Corps restoration work blossomed under the Clinton administration. In 1997, Clinton hailed the agency's wetlands-restoration work near Sacramento as signaling a new direction for the engineers. "They have not only changed their image, they've changed their reality," he said at the dedication of the Yolo Basin Wetlands Project. "They're working hard not only to give us water

projects, but to give us the kind of environmental conservation that we need for the long run." [36]

President Bush has continued the emphasis on restoration. His 2004 budget would fund several large restoration projects, including a fish-recovery effort on the Columbia River and fish and wildlife programs along the Missouri and upper Mississippi rivers.

In some cases, such projects seek to return wetlands to their natural state by removing dikes and other structures that impede river flow. In other cases, the Corps is using materials from dredg-

ing projects to build parks and new habitat areas for wildlife. In California, for example, the Corps is taking dredged material from Oakland Bay and using it to create a park and shallow-water wetlands near Oakland Harbor.

Although the Corps has traditionally been on the other side — manipulating nature in order to spur development — Holmes and others say the Corps has tremendous expertise when it comes to environmental restoration. "You can restore a degraded environment, and the Corps is just as capable of doing it as any agency," says Dickey, the former

to destroy 5,400 acres of wetlands on the Everglades' eastern flank. The Corps eventually will use the resulting mining pits as reservoirs for water to replenish the marshes, but critics fear the reservoirs could leak and contaminate the Biscayne Aquifer. "We're committing an act of environmental cannibalism of really historic proportions," said Brad Sewell, senior attorney for the Natural Resources Defense Council. [8]

Environmentalists also warn that the Corps' record of caving in to developers elsewhere in South Florida does not bode well. "Environmentalists have very good reason to worry that the political influence on the Corps is going to result in an unmanageable process that will work in the end to benefit special interests," Farago says.

Housing developments and strip malls, which have already eaten up much of the Atlantic Coast's wetlands, are cropping up in fast-growing retirement communities on Florida's Gulf Coast. In almost every case, the Corps permits developers to destroy wetlands — sometimes hundreds of acres at a time. A frustrated Florida Corps regulator, who says his bosses refuse to sign denials, told a *Washington Post* reporter: "All we do is document the destruction of the aquatic environment. If we have no denial power . . . I am wasting my time and your money." [9]

In addition, the U.S. Fish and Wildlife Service (FWS) and the Environmental Protection Agency accused the Corps of rubber-stamping projects that destroy habitat and pollute pristine bays. The FWS last year accused the Corps of illegally permitting "sub-

The Florida panther survives deep in the Everglades, but critics say changes in restoration plans could harm the rare cat.

So. Fla. Water Management District

stantial and unacceptable adverse impacts to aquatic resources of national import." [10]

Corps officials say they will be sued if they deny permits, and miners did successfully sue the agency in a permit dispute several years ago.

The Corps' conflicting responsibilities in Florida and across the nation — enabling development while protecting the environment — means it will be criticized by environmentalists or developers no matter what it does, says Corps spokesman Gene Pawlik. "It's very difficult to make everybody happy on any single issue that we're responsible for."

[1] See Michael Grunwald, "A Rescue Plan, Bold and Uncertain; Scientists, Federal Officials Question Project's Benefits for Ailing Ecosystem," *The Washington Post*, June 23, 2002, p. A1.

[2] Sierra Club

[3] *Congress and the Nation*, Volume X, 1997-2001, p. 373.

[4] Grunwald, *op. cit.*

[5] *Ibid.*

[6] Michael Grunwald, "Everglades Restoration May Affect Florida Bay; Report Cites Algae Growth, Sea Grass Loss," *The Washington Post*, Aug. 9, 2002, p. A 21.

[7] For background, see "Jeb Bush signs bill delaying Everglades cleanup deadline," at http://www.cnn.com/2003/ALLPOLITICS/05/20/bush.everglades.ap/

[8] David Fleshler, "Mining, Recovery Collide in Everglades; As Restoration Moves Ahead, Industry Wins OK to Tear up Acres," *Orlando Sentinel*, Aug. 4, 2002, p. A1.

[9] Quoted in Michael Grunwald, "Between Rock and a Hard Place; Wetlands Shrink Before Growing Demands of Industry, Consumers," *The Washington Post*, June 24, 2002, p. A1.

[10] Michael Grunwald, "Growing Pains in Southwest Fla.; More Development Pushes Everglades to the Edge," *The Washington Post*, June 25, 2002, p. A1.

chief of planning for the Corps. "The engineers in the Corps are the experts at manipulating hydrology. If you want environmentally sensitive solutions, the Corps can deliver it."

Some warn, however, that many Corps projects fall short of restoring natural habitat. Samet of American Rivers cites Corps efforts to create fish habitats by constructing side channels off the Missouri and other rivers. In some cases, however, fish failed to populate the channels because water did not flow naturally through them. She also raps the Corps for planning dredging

activities to shelter rare species in California's Bolinas Lagoon — a project that could result in "fetid ponds" that would disrupt species instead of helping them.

"It's a $133 million restoration plan that actually destroys stuff and doesn't restore it," she warns.

Corps spokesman Pawlik acknowledges the agency has made mistakes. But, he says, the agency's scientists are learning more about natural systems with each project they undertake. As he puts it, "It's an evolving science." ■

Notes

[1] "Delaware River Deepening Project: Comprehensive Reanalysis Needed," GAO-02-604, General Accounting Office, June 7, 2002.

[2] "Review Procedures for Water Resources Project Planning," National Academy of Sciences, 2002, available at www.nap.edu/books/030908508X/html/.

[3] Kevin Murphy, "Senators want reform at Corps of Engineers," *The Kansas City Star*, June 27, 2002, p. A1.

[4] "What is the future of the Army Corps of Engineers?" *Roll Call*, June 17, 2002.

[5] For related article, see Mary H. Cooper,

"Saving Open Spaces," *The CQ Researcher*, Nov. 5, 1999, pp. 953-976.

[6] Michael Grunwald, "Reluctant Regulator on the Slope, Corps of Engineers Bends to Pressure on Alaska Wetlands Issues," *The Washington Post*, Oct. 1, 2000, p. A1.

[7] Michael Grunwald, "Between Rock and a Hard Place; Wetlands Shrink Before Growing Demands of Industry, Consumers," *The Washington Post*, June 24, 2002, p. A1.

[8] For background, see Mary H. Cooper, "Bush and the Environment," *The CQ Researcher*, Oct. 25, 2002, pp. 865-896.

[9] For background, Mary H. Cooper, "Endangered Species Act," *The CQ Researcher*, Oct. 1, 1999, pp. 849- 872; Kenneth Jost, "Protecting Endangered Species," *The CQ Researcher*, April 19, 1996, pp. 337-360, and Mary H. Cooper, "Environmental Movement at 25," *The CQ Researcher*, March 31, 1995, pp. 273-296.

[10] For related report, see Kathy Koch, "Truck Safety," *The CQ Researcher*, March 12, 1999, pp. 209-232.

[11] Damon Franz, "Corps Partners with Enviro Groups," *Land Letter*, Aug. 1, 2002.

[12] A synopsis of the Army Inspector General's report can be found on the Office of Special Counsel Web site, at www.osc.gov/documents/press/2000/pr00_36.htm.

[13] *Ibid.*

[14] Vernon Loeb, "Whistle Blows Again at Corps; Economist Says Locks Project Still Based on Flawed Model," *The Washington Post*, Nov. 15, 2002, p. A31.

[15] Jim Barnett, "Congress, Administration Intensify Scrutiny of Corps," *The [Portland] Oregonian*, April 7, 2002, p. A8.

[16] Michael Grunwald, "Army Corps Overhaul Gets a Boost," *The Washington Post*, June 19, 2002, p. A19.

[17] Quoted in Robert McClure, "EPA says that Snake River dams must come down," *Seattle Post-Intelligencer*, April 29, 2000.

[18] Quoted in "Public and political pressure for reform of the Army Corps of Engineers," "All Things Considered," National Public Radio, May 17, 2002.

[19] See www.amrivers.org/corpsreformtoolkit/whoisthecorps.htm.

[20] Quoted in Damon Franz, "Talk of Corps Reform Dominates First Senate WRDA Hearing," *Environment and Energy Daily*, June 19, 2002.

FOR MORE INFORMATION

American Rivers, 1025 Vermont Ave., N.W., Suite 720, Washington, DC 20005; (202) 347-7550; www.americanrivers.org. The group issues an annual report on the most endangered rivers, many of which are threatened by Corps projects.

National Association of Home Builders, 1201 15th St., N.W., Washington, DC 20005; (202) 266-8200; www.nahb.org. This major national trade association seeks to pare back Corps oversight of wetlands to give developers more opportunities to build.

National Wildlife Federation, 11100 Wildlife Center Dr., Reston, VA 20190-5362; (703) 438-6000; www.nwf.org. The conservation group contends the Corps is far too permissive in allowing developers to pave over wetlands.

Taxpayers for Common Sense, 651 Pennsylvania Ave., S.E., Washington, DC 20003; (202) 546-8500; www.taxpayer.net. The government-watchdog group has established a "Corps watch project."

U.S. Army Corps of Engineers, 441 G St., N.W., Washington, DC 20314; (202) 761-0008; www.usace.army.mil. The Pentagon agency employs about 35,000 people and probably undertakes more major water projects than any other organization in the world.

---

[21] For related report, see Brian Hansen, "Crisis on the Plains," *The CQ Researcher*, May 9, 2003, pp. 417-449.

[22] Michael Grunwald, "Army Corps of Engineers Caught in Crosscurrents," *The Washington Post*, Jan. 10, 2000, p. A1.

[23] Quoted in Douglas Jehl, "U.S. Plan Could Ease Limits on Wetlands Development," *The New York Times*, Jan. 11, 2003, p. A10.

[24] Quoted in Traci Watson, "Developers rush to build in wetlands after ruling," *USA Today*, Dec. 6, 2002, p. 15A.

[25] Quoted in Marshall Wilson, "Wetlands protection lagging, study says; Many developers not replacing habitat," *The San Francisco Chronicle*, June 27, 2001, p. A1. A summary of the 2001 National Academy of Sciences study, "Compensating for Wetland Losses Under the Clean Water Act," can be found at: http://www.nap.edu/catalog/10134.html?onpi_newsdoc062601.

[26] Except where noted, background is drawn from a history produced by the Army Corps of Engineers, available at http://www.hq.usace.army.mil/history/brief.htm.

[27] For background, see Rodman D. Griffin, "Threatened Coastlines," *The CQ Researcher*, Feb. 7, 1992, pp. 97-120.

[28] For background, see Mary H. Cooper, "Water Quality," *The CQ Researcher*, Nov. 24, 2000, pp. 953-976.

[29] For background, see *Congress and the Nation*, 1980. See www.amrivers.org/corpsreformtoolkit/whoisthecorps.htm.

[30] The influential articles, by Michael Grunwald, can be found at http://www.washingtonpost.com/wp-dyn/nation/specials/aroundthenation/corpsofengineers/

[31] Michael Grunwald, "Generals Push Huge Growth for Engineers," *The Washington Post*, Feb. 24, 2000, p. A1.

[32] Brad Knickerbocker, "On Earth Day, water policy floods the ecodebate," *The Christian Science Monitor*, April 22, 2002, p. 2.

[33] Alexander Bolton, "Bush wants Corps of Engineers Curbed," *The Hill*, Feb. 12, 2003, p. 6.

[34] Damon Franz, "House Leadership Seeks to Dodge Corps Reform Vote," *Environment and Energy Daily*, Oct. 7, 2002.

[35] Damon Franz, "Reform Fight May Continue to Block New Water Projects," *Environment and Energy Daily*, Dec. 2, 2002.

[36] Jason Fanselau, "President Clinton dedicates wetlands project," *Engineer Update*, Vol. 21, No. 12, December 1997; published by the Army Corps of Engineers.

Bibliography

Selected Sources

Books

Pilkey, Orrin H., and Katharine L. Dixon, *The Corps and the Shore*, **Island Press, 1996.**

Using several case studies, coastal geologist Pilkey and activist Dixon examine the often-harmful impact of Corps of Engineers projects on the nation's coastlines.

Articles

Barnett, Jim, "Congress, Administration Intensify Scrutiny of Corps," *The* **[Portland]** *Oregonian*, **April 7, 2002, p. A8.**

The paper, which had raised questions about Corps projects in the Pacific Northwest, provides a good overview of the debate over reforming the agency.

Fleshler, David, "Mining, Recovery Collide in Everglades; As Restoration Moves Ahead, Industry Wins OK to Tear up Acres," *Orlando Sentinel*, **Aug. 4, 2002, p. A1.**

This in-depth examination suggests that Corps-sanctioned limestone mining in South Florida threatens to undo the government's landmark initiative to restore the Everglades.

Franz, Damon, "Corps Partners With Enviro Groups," *Land Letter*, **Aug. 1, 2002.**

This article looks at cases in which the Corps has teamed up with environmental groups to restore wildlife habitat.

Grunwald, Michael, "A Rescue Plan, Bold and Uncertain; Scientists, Federal Officials Question Project's Benefits for Ailing Ecosystem," *The Washington Post*, **June 23, 2002, p. A1.**

In the first of a lengthy, four-part series, Grunwald explores the questions and concerns being raised about plans by the Corps to restore the Everglades.

Grunwald, Michael, "Corps' Taming of Waterways Doesn't Pay Off," *The Washington Post*, **Jan. 9, 2000, p. A1.**

The first of an influential, two-part series showing that the Corps spends billions of dollars rechanneling rivers to make them more economical for use by barges — even though the barges rarely show up. The series blames both the Corps, which produces overly optimistic economic forecasts, and powerful lawmakers, who want the government to fund major projects in their states.

Grunwald, Michael, "Norton Closes Everglades Renewal Office," *The Washington Post*, **Nov. 7, 2001, p. A3.**

Interior Secretary Gale A. Norton announced that she is closing the federal Office of Everglades Restoration in an effort to slash costs. Environmentalists denounced the decision.

Jehl, Douglas, "Chief Protector of Wetlands Redefines Them and Retreats," *The New York Times*, **Feb. 11, 2003, p. A1.**

Jehl provides dramatic instances of the Corps ceding its regulatory authority over wetlands development during the first two years of the Bush administration, often paving the way for wetlands-damaging construction.

Smith, Bob, and Bill Pascrell, "What is the future of the Army Corps of Engineers?" *Roll Call*, **June 17, 2002.**

Then-Sen. Robert C. Smith, R-N.H. and Rep. Bill Pascrell Jr., D-N.J., debate reforming the Corps. Smith argues the agency "has spiraled out of control." Pascrell defends the embattled agency for performing economically important tasks, such as dredging harbors and protecting floodplains.

Watson, Tracy, "Developers rush to build in wetlands after ruling," *USA Today*, **Dec. 6, 2002, p. 15A.**

A sobering look at the reaction by developers to a 2001 U.S. Supreme Court decision that pared back government oversight of wetlands. The article highlights numerous instances in which shopping centers, offices and other structures were quickly constructed in ecologically sensitive areas following the decision.

Reports and Studies

***Delaware River Deepening Project*, General Accounting Office, June 2002.**

Congress' watchdog agency raised alarm bells on Capitol Hill with this highly critical analysis of a proposed $287 million Corps project to deepen a Delaware River shipping channel. The GAO warned that the Corps' economic analysis contained so many "miscalculations, invalid assumptions, and . . . significantly outdated information" that it overstated the project's benefits by a factor of three.

***Review Procedures for Water Resources Project Planning*, National Academy of Sciences, 2002, available at www.nap.edu/books/030908508X/html/.**

The academy's Water Science and Technology Board and Ocean Studies Board called for impartial, highly qualified independent reviews of Army Corps of Engineers projects.

***Troubled Waters: Congress, the Corps of Engineers, and Wasteful Water Projects*, Taxpayers for Common Sense and the National Wildlife Federation, March 2000.**

This blistering look at the Corps cites about two-dozen projects that it claims are particularly wasteful and harmful, such as creating an irrigation district in Arkansas that would benefit local rice farmers at a cost of more than $1 billion.

10 Civil Liberties in Wartime

DAVID MASCI AND PATRICK MARSHALL

As a Republican senator from Missouri, Attorney General John Ashcroft served on the Judiciary Committee. So when he testified on Capitol Hill on Dec. 6 before his old panel, the camaraderie was palpable as he joked and reminisced with his former colleagues.

But the smiles quickly disappeared when the hearing — on civil liberties following the Sept. 11 terrorist attacks on the World Trade Center and the Pentagon by Middle Eastern airplane hijackers — began in earnest. Democrats and Republicans alike closely questioned and even criticized Ashcroft on some of the tough, new policy changes made by the Bush administration in the name of national security — changes that critics say restrict cherished freedoms.

In particular, committee members worried that the Justice Department's continued detention of more than 600 mostly Muslim men may infringe on their rights. They also questioned Ashcroft's recent order permitting federal agents to eavesdrop on conversations between inmates and their attorneys. Until now, such communications have been considered privileged, or protected by law from disclosure. In addition, many senators worried that the president's plan to try foreigners charged with terrorist acts in secret military tribunals might lead to "victor's justice" at the expense of due process.

"The Constitution does not need protection when its guarantees are popular," said Committee Chairman Patrick Leahy, D-Vt. "But it very much

From *The CQ Researcher,* December 14, 2001.

Attorney General John Ashcroft defends the administration's tough, new policies as vital to combating terrorism, but civil libertarians say they undermine cherished American freedoms.

needs our protection when events tempt us to, 'just this once,' abridge its guarantees of our freedom."

Ashcroft repeatedly dismissed panel members' concerns. "Our efforts have been crafted carefully to avoid infringing on constitutional rights, while saving American lives," he said.

In fact, the attorney general turned the tables and criticized his critics, arguing that they help the enemy when they oppose efforts to give the government more tools to fight terrorism. "To those who scare peace-loving people with phantoms of lost liberty, my message is this: Your tactics only aid terrorists — for they erode our national unity."

The impulse to restrict liberties has always been and still is especially strong during wartime, and not just among the military and law enforcement com-

munities. Polls show that the American people generally support the steps taken by the administration since Sept. 11, just as they backed the last great raft of security measures — President Franklin D. Roosevelt's internment of Japanese-Americans and other restrictions enacted during World War II. [1]

For instance, according to a recent *Washington Post*/ABC News survey, 73 percent of Americans favor allowing the federal government to eavesdrop on normally privileged conversations between suspected terrorists and their attorneys. The new rules — which so far affect only 16 suspects — would be used in cases where the attorney general believed the person might be passing information to his lawyer that would further a terrorist act by their co-conspirators still at large. Ashcroft claims that discussions not involving terrorist plans will still be privileged and will not be used against the suspect.

But civil libertarians and others counter that lawyers and their clients need absolute privacy in order to speak freely when planning defense strategy. "An inmate won't feel like there is privacy, since the people who are prosecuting you are also the people who are listening into the conversation and deciding what is and isn't privileged," says Irwin Schwartz, executive director of the National Association of Criminal Defense Lawyers. Moreover, Schwartz says, there is an existing process — which involves acquiring a warrant from a judge — that allows officials to breach attorney-client privilege, but it at least requires the approval of a third, independent party.

Public Attitudes Toward Censorship

Public support for military censorship is almost as high as it was during the 1991 Persian Gulf War. By a 53 percent to 39 percent margin, respondents in late November said it is more important for the government to be able to censor stories than for the media to be able to report news it sees as in the national interest.

	1985	1991	Nov. 2001
What is more important:	Percent Responding		
Government censorship of news it believes a threat to national security?	38%	58%	53%
Media's ability to report news it believes is in national interest?	50	32	39
In covering war news:			
Give military more control?	29	57	50
Media should decide how to report?	64	34	40
News coverage should be:			
Pro-American	--	--	20
Show all points of view	--	--	73

Source: The Pew Research Center For The People & The Press, Nov. 28, 2001

Schwartz and others also have strongly criticized the Justice Department's initial arrest of more than 1,200 immigrants — mainly from predominantly Muslim countries — in the weeks following the attacks and the continuing detention of about half of them. Most are being held on immigration violations, but a small number are also being detained as possible material witnesses to terrorist acts.

Critics charge that in its efforts to prevent another attack, the department has essentially gone on a fishing expedition, rounding up Arabs and others without giving any real reasons that justify such a mass detention. "The federal government needs to explain what it's doing here, needs to publicly show that these people are planning criminal activity or have engaged in criminal activity, instead of just throwing them in jail and not saying any-

thing," says James Zogby, president of the Arab American Institute, an advocacy group for Americans of Arab descent. * The secrecy surrounding the detentions is causing loyal Arab-Americans to feel threatened and disillusioned in their own country, he adds.

Zogby and others are also disturbed by charges that some detainees have been held for weeks or even months with little or no evidence to link them

---

* On Dec. 11, a federal grand jury indictment charged that Zacarias Moussaoui, a French Moroccan, conspired with terrorist Osama bin Laden in the Sept. 11 attacks — the first U.S. charges in the case. Moussaoui had sought pilot training in Minnesota last summer, but school officials became suspicious when he only wanted to learn to steer a plane. He was arrested shortly afterward on immigration charges. Moussaoui had trained in bin Laden terrorist camps in Afghanistan, the indictment alleges.

to terrorist acts or groups. They point to Al Bader al-Hazmi, a San Antonio physician who was held for 13 days before being cleared, and Tarek Abdelhamid Albasti, an Arab-American and U.S. citizen from Evansville, Ind., who was detained for a week because he has a pilot's license. [2] His detention came at the time authorities were investigating reports that Middle Eastern men were taking flying lessons in the United States, or seeking to rent crop-duster planes.

But Ashcroft has argued that his strategy of "aggressive detention of lawbreakers and material witnesses" has very possibly prevented new attacks. [3] "This is an entirely appropriate reaction," agrees Kent Scheidegger, legal director at the conservative Criminal Justice Legal Foundation. "Given what happened on Sept. 11 and the shadowy nature of the perpetrators, we need to look at a lot people in order to effectively stop future acts of terrorism."

The Justice Department also says that none of the detainees have been denied their rights. "All persons being detained have the right to contact their lawyers and their families," Ashcroft told the Judiciary Committee.

At the same hearing, Ashcroft was called on, repeatedly, to explain and defend the administration's plan to possibly use military courts to try high-ranking, foreign terrorism suspects. The attorney general and other defenders of the proposal say that such courts may be needed because much of the evidence presented against defendants may be highly classified and not appropriate for use in an open court. In addition, they say, using traditional courts to try terrorists may endanger the lives of all of those involved, including the jury, prosecutors and judges. (*See sidebar, p. 184.*)

But military courts, with their lower standards of due process, might not guarantee defendants a full and fair trial, says Ralph Neas, president of People for the American Way, a liberal civil liberties advocacy group. "This looks like a star chamber to me," he says. In particular, Neas worries that defendants may not be allowed to confront all of the evidence presented against them and that juries, made up of military officers, will be able to convict someone with a two-thirds vote rather than the usual unanimous verdict.

Civil libertarians also are concerned about some of the provisions of the USA Patriot Act, which cleared the Congress and was signed into law by President Bush just six weeks after the Sept. 11 attacks. The new law creates new terrorist-related offenses as well as giving the federal government new powers to conduct surveillance and detain non-citizens (*see p. 194*).

Opponents say the new law's provisions allowing the detention of immigrants are particularly worrisome because non-citizens can be held indefinitely so long as the attorney general believes they threaten national security. "They've gone way overboard here because the government can hold someone as long as they like. Period," says Stephen Henderson, an assistant professor of law at Chicago's Kent Law School.

But Clifford Fishman, a professor of law at Catholic University, says the new law is necessary to protect the country in a time of war. "This is not some great expansion of government authority," he says. "And besides, people who come here are still going to be much freer here than where they came from."

The performance of the news media also has been swept up in the raging post-9/11 civil liberties vs. security debate. Media-watchers of all political stripes have complained that some editors and reporters at times have acted more like patriots than journalists and thus have failed in their "free-press" mission to keep the public fully informed, especially since the war in Afghanistan began.

The debate over the proper balance between liberty and security is as old as the American Republic. In

Evaluating the War on Terrorism

In early November, the vast majority of Americans approved of the way top administration officials and major governmental institutions were handling the war on terrorism, but they gave a low rating to the performance of the news media.

Do you approve or disapprove of the way the following people and institutions are handling the war on terrorism since September 11?

Percent who approve

President Bush	89%
Secretary of State Colin Powell	87
Defense Secretary Donald Rumsfeld	80
Attorney General John Ashcroft	77
Congress	77
U.S. Postal Service	77
Vice President Dick Cheney	75
Centers for Disease Control and Prevention	71
Homeland Security Director Tom Ridge	60
The news media	43

Source: The Gallup Organization, Nov. 8-11, 2001

1798 President John Adams' Federalist Party passed the Alien and Sedition Acts, which restricted free speech and the rights of immigrants. Enactment of the law produced a storm of criticism and it was largely overturned during the first term of Adams' successor in the White House, Thomas Jefferson. Similar questions were raised during the Civil War and during both world wars, when the federal government curtailed certain liberties in the name of protecting the nation. (*See "Background," p. 188.*)

As the United States prepares to enter the fourth month of its latest war, here are some of the questions lawyers, national security experts and others involved in the debate over civil liberties and security are asking:

Should the Justice Department monitor conversations between lawyers and defendants in the interest of preventing further terrorist attacks?

For defense lawyers, the ability to communicate confidentially with clients is tantamount to a sacred right. The "attorney-client privilege," as it is known, "is one of the most significant and oldest rules governing" what is and isn't admissible in court, says Schwartz of the criminal defense lawyers association. "It's one of our most cherished and long-recognized rights."

On Oct. 30, though, the Department of Justice instituted new rules, which took effect immediately, that limit the attorney-client privilege for certain criminal defendants in federal custody. The changes permit the department to listen in on communications between inmates and their lawyers when "reasonable suspicion exists . . . that a particular inmate may use the communications with attorneys or their agents to further or facilitate acts of terrorism." [4]

The inmate and attorney would be notified of the monitoring, which would be conducted by a special "taint team" that would disclose only information that might be used to prevent future attacks. Other information, such as discussions of the inmate's guilt or innocence and defense strategy, would remain confidential and would not be made available to federal prosecutors, the department said. [5]

In explaining the new procedure, Attorney General Ashcroft said that given the threats currently facing the nation, the new rules were needed to "thwart future acts of violence or terrorism." [6] He gave assurances that the power to eavesdrop would be used sparingly, noting that only 16 out of 158,000 federal prisoners are now subject to the special monitoring. [7]

Still, many lawyers, lawmakers and civil libertarians immediately condemned the new rule as unnecessary and unconstitutional. They contend that by eliminating the attorney-client privilege for some suspected terrorists the Justice Department has denied inmates both their Sixth Amendment right to an attorney and their Fourth Amendment right to unreasonable search and seizure. *

"A client in a criminal case can't trust his lawyer and really can't work with him unless he believes that whatever he's saying is being said in confidence," Schwartz says. "So we're taking away one of the fundamental rights of criminal defendants."

---

* Notably, recent polls have shown that Americans overwhelmingly believe that U.S. citizens charged with terrorism, like Oklahoma City bomber Timothy McVeigh, should be afforded constitutional rights, while non-citizens should not.

"It's absolutely impossible to defend someone if you can't speak to them in private," agrees Henderson at Kent Law School. "If someone is listening in, you simply can't speak your mind, which of course is crucial when planning your defense."

Opponents also worry that the so-called taint team won't be able to adequately protect inmates because it may reveal more to Justice Department officials than is proper under the disclosure guidelines. "Look, the problem with this is that the team is made up of Justice Department officials," Henderson says. "How can an inmate feel confident when the people who are listening work for the same organization as the people who are prosecuting the case?"

In addition, Henderson and others say, there is a means, under the old rules, by which prosecutors can break the attorney-client privilege while still affording constitutional protections. "If you have 'probable cause' to believe that the [attorney-client] privilege is being exploited to further criminal ends," says David Cole, a law professor at Georgetown University, "then you can go to a judge and get a warrant to listen in to the conversation."

Requiring the government to show "probable cause" is more demanding than the "reasonable suspicion" standard required under the new anti-terrorist rule, but it makes it more likely that a breach of the attorney-client privilege will be justified, Cole says.

More important, the old rules give final authority to an independent judge while the new procedure puts the entire decision in the hands of the attorney general, says Neas of People for the American Way. "This change gives the attorney general unbridled powers because he's become the only real arbiter in this process," Neas says. "We've cast off the role of the judiciary and in doing so have cast off the checks and balances given to us by the founders."

But supporters of the new powers echo the attorney general, arguing that they are needed to prevent another major terrorist attack. "One thing that we know for sure is that the enemy is planning more and worse attacks," Fishman says. "The other thing we know is that we didn't do enough to prevent the Sept. 11 attacks."

Indeed, supporters of the new rules say, there are many examples of inmates directing criminal activity from prison, making the possibility that terrorists would do the same quite high. "Violent criminals — especially gang members — order murders and attacks from prison all the time," Scheidegger of the Criminal Justice Legal Foundation says.

Scheidegger, Fishman and others say that the taint team and other safeguards built into the new rules are adequate to protect a client's right to consult with his attorney in confidence. "We know that there's always a possibility for abuse or mistakes because there are people involved, and people aren't perfect," Fishman says. "But I think that, in general, everything that doesn't involve plotting a new attack" will still be confidential.

Supporters also argue that the less rigorous "reasonable suspicion" standard is needed because Justice Department officials should have the authority to follow hunches when the fate of the nation is at stake.

"One could imagine a legitimate situation where important information discovered because of a 'reasonable suspicion' would not have been discovered using 'probable cause,'" Fishman says. "I'm not happy that the government has to [lower the standard], but I'll sleep better at night knowing they have more tools to prevent the next attack."

Is the detention of hundreds of terrorism suspects an overreaction to the events of Sept. 11?

Following the attacks on New York City and the Pentagon, the Justice Department rounded up more than 1,700 people possibly connected to terrorist acts or groups. And while many were released in subsequent weeks, more than 600 remained in custody in early December. [8] In addition, the department is currently engaged in questioning an additional 5,000 recent immigrants who could also be detained. (*See sidebar, p. 189.*)

The current detainees are mostly male, foreign born and from predominantly Muslim countries like Egypt, Saudi Arabia and Pakistan. According to figures cited by the attorney general on Dec. 7, 563 people are being held for violations of their immigration status and another 60 are in federal custody for other reasons. Of these 60, roughly two dozen are being detained as "material witnesses," indicating that investigators believe they may have some information about past or future terrorist attacks.

Critics of the detentions say the government initially prevented the detainees from contacting defense attorneys, often for several days. In addition, the government has not revealed the identities of some of those being held, what they are being charged with or where they are being detained.

While polls show that most Americans support the detentions, many civil libertarians and Arab-American advocates point to the stories of those who have been released, as proof of the haphazard and heavy-handed nature of the operation. Countless Arab-Americans now out of prison have told of spending weeks or even months in jail, often based on very tenuous evidence. For instance, two Palestinian-Americans were held for more than two months because a federal agent at an airport in Houston determined that their passports looked like they could have been tampered with. Tests later showed that nothing had been altered and the men were finally released.

But Fishman defends the policy as a necessary element in the government's efforts to bring those respon-

sible for past attacks to justice and to stop future terrorist acts. Indeed, Fishman and other detention supporters say, the fact that some innocent people may have to spend weeks or even months in jail is a price worth paying, since the detentions may prevent future terrorist activity.

"It's clearly better to err on the side of sweeping too broadly than not sweeping broadly enough," Fishman says. "The worst that will happen is that someone will be wrongfully detained for a few weeks or months, and frankly that pales in comparison with the consequences of not detaining legitimate suspects."

Attorney General Ashcroft alluded to this argument recently when he compared the current detention strategy to Attorney General Robert F. Kennedy's efforts to snuff out organized crime in the early 1960s.

"Robert Kennedy's Justice Department, it is said, would arrest mobsters for spitting on the sidewalk if it would help in the battle against organized crime," he said. "It has been and will be the policy of the Department of Justice to use the same aggressive arrest and detention tactics in the war on terror." [9]

Supporters also point out that the net is not cast as wide, or as carelessly, as it might at first seem. "It's important to remember that there are hundreds of thousands of young Arab men in this country right now," says Orin Kerr, an associate professor at the George Washington University School of Law. "Sure, the government has made mistakes — detaining people they have since let go — but this idea that they're pulling all of them off the street is incorrect. They've arrested only a very small fraction of them."

Finally, defenders of the policy argue that it is dangerous to second-guess the Justice Department — especially at this early stage in the investigation. "Frankly, it's hard to know what is and isn't appropriate because we don't

know what Ashcroft and the others know," Kerr says.

Fishman agrees. "At this stage we have to trust the people in charge because they have the best information available to make these decisions. The way I see it, we really don't have a choice."

But opponents argue that lack of information about the nature of the threat the United States faces is not an excuse for trampling on the civil liberties of hundreds of possibly innocent people.

"Everyone knows we're going through a troubled and tense time and that the situation is very difficult," says Neas of People for the American Way. "But that doesn't mean that we can't bring some standards and accountability to the process."

"There needs to be more transparency here," agrees the Arab American Institute's Zogby. "The government needs to start showing probable cause for keeping those people they decide to detain."

Neas and Zogby find the secrecy surrounding the detentions especially troubling. Not only are names and locations not being revealed, they point out, but also no one is really sure that the rights of the detainees are being respected.

"It's not good enough for the Department of Justice to say, 'Trust us,' " Neas says. "Right now, all of the big decisions are essentially being made by the attorney general, and we don't know what those decisions are. It's as if there were only one branch of government."

"We've heard a lot of troubling stories," Zogby adds, "like some people are being denied access to their lawyer, or detainees have no idea why they're being held."

Opponents also contend that the detentions are reinforcing negative stereotypes that all Arab-Americans cannot be trusted and might be terrorists. "This kind of behavior on the part of the federal government is feeding the impression that if someone's young, Arab and male, they're guilty," Zogby says. "I think the Justice Department

Military Tribunals Play by Different Rules

"These are extraordinary times," President Bush said after authorizing the creation of secret military tribunals to try suspected terrorists. "And I would remind those who don't understand the decision I made that Franklin Roosevelt made the same decision in World War II. Those were extraordinary times, as well."

Military tribunals have a long history in the United States as well as in other countries. Most countries typically try members of the armed forces in a different court system than civilians. And, in times of war, military tribunals have judged civilians and military personnel of other nationalities. Military courts have also substituted for domestic civilian courts in the United States under conditions where the civilian court system could not function.

Neither international nor U.S. law sets procedures for military tribunals. Historically, however, U.S. military courts have provided fewer protections for the accused than civilian courts. Generally, military courts do not require a presumption of innocence, nor do they require a jury of one's peers or proof of guilt "beyond a shadow of a doubt." In recent history, U.S. military courts have required only a two-thirds vote of the officers on the tribunal to convict, and there are no provisions for appeal.

Revolutionary War

The first and most notable instance of an American military court passing judgment on a foreign national occurred during the Revolutionary War. Officers chosen by Gen. George Washington convicted British secret agent Major John Andre of collaborating with Benedict Arnold and sentenced him to be hanged. The British government did not object to the use of a military tribunal in judging Andre.

Civil War

During the Civil War, not only was the right of habeas corpus suspended by President Lincoln but also many civilians were judged by military courts. Accused civilians, thus, were denied their constitutionally protected right of a trial by jury, and there was no procedure available for them to challenge the legality of the proceedings.

In 1866, the attorney general of the United States argued that the legal protections established in the Bill of Rights were "peacetime provisions." But the Supreme Court ruled that the Lincoln administration had no authority to take away civilians' right to a trial by jury: "[U]ntil recently no one ever doubted that the right to trial by jury was fortified in the organic law against the power of attack. It is now assailed; but if ideas can be expressed in words, and language has any meaning, this right — one of the most valuable in a free country — is preserved to every one accused of crime who is not attached to the army, or navy, or militia in actual service. The Sixth Amendment affirms that 'in all criminal prosecutions the ac-

cused shall enjoy the right to a speedy and public trial by an impartial jury,' language broad enough to embrace all persons and cases." [1]

World War I

In a case recalling that of Major Andre, a German spy caught near the Mexican border in 1918 was tried in secret by the U.S. Army. Lothar Witzke, a lieutenant in the German Navy, was found guilty and sentenced to hang. In 1920, with the war over, President Woodrow Wilson commuted his sentence to life imprisonment. As it happened, in 1923 Witzke rescued a number of fellow inmates during a prison fire. He was then set free and returned to Germany.

World War II

Two particularly notable uses of military tribunals occurred during the Second World War. In 1942, eight German saboteurs were tried in a secret by a military commission. German submarines had landed them on beaches in Long Island and Florida, and they were captured after one of their party, George Dasch, turned himself in. The government may have used military trials both to ensure conviction and to apply the death penalty, a punishment not available in civilian courts. Six of the eight were convicted and electrocuted on Aug. 8, 1942. Dasch and another defendant who cooperated received prison terms and were released after the war.

Lawyers for the defendants did manage to get their case before the Supreme Court on the grounds that one of the defendants was the son of naturalized American citizens. In its decision, however, the Court held that both citizens and non-citizens lose the protection of the American legal system when they become agents of the enemy in time of war. [2]

Military tribunals also judged foreign nationals at Nuremberg, Germany, after the war. The International Military Tribunal, established by the United States, Great Britain, the Soviet Union and France, indicted and tried 24 former Nazi leaders for a variety of war crimes. Three were acquitted, eight received long prison sentences and the rest were sentenced to death.

While the International Military Tribunal reflected the tradition of Anglo-American civil law, it differed from civilian courts in several critical areas. Most notably, the tribunal did not offer trial by jury. Also, hearsay evidence — evidence provided by those not available for questioning by the defense — was admissible. And there was no way to appeal the tribunal's judgment.

A similar postwar tribunal in Tokyo tried 25 Japanese nationals for war crimes. Seven were sentenced to hang — including General Hideki Tojo, the prime minister from 1941-44; 16 were sentenced to life imprisonment.

---

[1] *Ex Parte Milligan*, 71 U.S. (4 Wall.) 2 (1866).

[2] *Ex Parte Quirin*, 317 U.S. 1 (1942).

wants to look like they're doing something, so they detain a lot of people and go to the American people and say, 'We have 600 Arabs in jail, so you can feel safer.'"

Finally, opponents argue that in a large, open society, the detention — even of several hundred people — is not a very effective way of preventing future terrorist attacks.

"With more than 4 million aliens who have overstayed their visas currently residing in the country, and 5,000 miles of largely unprotected borders, detaining a thousand people probably isn't making too much of a dent in the threat," says Michael Ratner, a lecturer at the Columbia University School of Law and vice president of the Center for Constitutional Rights in New York City. "On top of this, we don't really know if any of these people we've detained are dangerous."

Zogby goes so far as to say the department's strategy is probably backfiring, since it is alienating an ethnic community that might be able to offer all kinds of help in tracking down the real terrorists. "We are loyal Americans, and we want to cooperate with the investigation," he says. "But when you do this, you create so much ill will that people are much less inclined to help."

But Kerr cautions that it is unrealistic to expect that no one will be unjustly detained during what has become the largest criminal investigation in U.S. history. "Look, they've been trying to prevent another attack, using sketchy information, so they're bound to make mistakes," he says. "But that's the price of doing business when you're trying to save thousands, maybe tens of thousands of lives."

Should the federal government try suspected terrorists in a military court?

In 1996, Sudan offered to arrest Osama bin Laden and hand him over to Saudi Arabia for eventual extradition to the United States. The suspected mastermind of the terrorist actions of Sept. 11, 2001, ultimately left Sudan a free man, in part because the United States could not convince Saudi Arabia to take him.

But even if the Saudis had cooperated, another obstacle prevented bin Laden's extradition to the United States. "The FBI did not believe we had enough evidence to indict bin Laden [in a civilian court] at that time, and therefore opposed bringing him to the United States," said then deputy national security adviser Samuel R. "Sandy" Berger. [10]

The failure to nab bin Laden in 1996 is often cited as a reason for supporting President Bush's plan to set up military tribunals to try foreigners suspected of terrorism. Bush has not said that he will use military courts, only that he wants the option. In addition, the administration has yet to explain how the courts will operate, since the Pentagon hasn't finished drafting operational guidelines for the tribunals, according to William J. Haynes II, the Defense Department's general counsel. [11]

Still, if military tribunals are established, they probably would require less rigorous evidentiary standards than a civilian court, allowing prosecutors to offer information against a defendant that would be barred from a traditional trial. For example, the secondhand recounting of a conversation, or "hearsay" evidence, could be used against a defendant in a military court, though such evidence is generally prohibited in federal criminal judicial proceedings

In addition, evidence culled from classified information could be offered in secret in a military trial in order to protect national security — and defendants could be prevented from challenging the information, even if it led to their conviction.

Moreover, in a military trial, defendants would be denied judgment by a jury of their peers and instead would face a panel made up of American military officers. The usual requirement of a unanimous jury verdict for conviction also would be set aside. Defendants could be convicted and sentenced on a two-thirds jury vote. Appeals would also be limited: Only the Supreme Court could review a verdict.

In the face of domestic and international criticism, President Bush has defended the use of military tribunals as "the absolute right thing to do." [12] Even as the government of Spain announced that it would not hand over terrorist suspects to the United States without assurances that they would be tried in civilian courts, the president insisted that he "must have the option of using a military tribunal in times of war." [13]

Douglas W. Kmiec, dean of the Catholic University School of Law, agrees with Bush that revealing classified information at a public trial could severely compromise national security.

"Frankly, we can't always reveal how and what we know and the identities of the people who help provide us with this information in open court," he says.

In addition, Kmiec says, trying terrorists in federal court could put the lives of judges, prosecutors, jurors and others at risk.

"I'd be concerned for my safety if I were on a jury that convicted an Al Qaeda member," he says. "These trials would even endanger the cities they were held in because they might be bombed in retribution for the conviction of a terrorist."

Beyond practical considerations, tribunal supporters say, terrorists simply are not entitled to civilian trials, and the president has complete authority to use military tribunals.

"Foreign terrorists are unlawful combatants, and they do not have a right to civilian trial," says Todd Gaziano, director of the Center for Legal and Judicial Studies at the Heritage Foundation, a conservative think tank. "The Constitution gave Congress the authority to set up a military justice system to deal with military personnel and others in the theater of war, and Congress has delegated the president the authority to use this military justice system."

Supporters also point out that the United States has a long history of using military tribunals during past conflicts to try foreign nationals and that the Supreme Court has upheld their use.

"I would remind those who don't understand the decision I made that Franklin Roosevelt made the same decision in World War II," Bush said, referring to the use of military courts to try German nationals who had been caught on U.S. soil in 1942 trying to commit acts of sabotage. [14]

But opponents counter that using military tribunals against certain defendants runs counter to American notions of justice and is completely unnecessary. "In no way does this comport with our idea of due process," says Columbia University's Ratner. "If we go forward on this, we'll look back on it as a dark day in American history."

Ratner is troubled by the fact that much evidence that is inadmissible in a regular court could be used against a defendant in a military trial. "People say that such and such a conversation wouldn't be admissible in a regular court," he says. "There's a reason why it wouldn't be admissible: It's unreliable. All of a sudden that doesn't matter anymore?"

Ratner says it is possible to present classified evidence in open court without jeopardizing national security. "In the 1993 [World Trade Center] bombing case, we used a lot of classified information to help convict the defendants," he says. "In cases like this, you enter or present the evidence in private and then present a non-classified version of the evidence to the jury."

In fact, Georgetown's Cole says, the public trials and convictions of the bombers of the World Trade Center, the two American embassies in East Africa as well as the federal building in Oklahoma City show that it is possible to effectively try domestic and even foreign terrorists in an open, non-military court. "Have we shown that we can't try terrorism suspects in

open court?" Cole asks. "No. The opposite is true, because we've already tried horrendous crimes of terrorism in open court, and on more than one occasion."

Finally, opponents argue that trying terrorism suspects in military courts will make any convictions suspect. "When you have a trial where people are being tried in secret and they are unable to confront the evidence against them, they lack the kind of legitimacy that an open court would give," Cole says.

This lack of legitimacy will tarnish America's moral standing in the world and erode its reputation as a nation that respects human rights and the rule of law, according to Judiciary Committee Chairman Leahy. In his view, President Bush's order "sends a message to the world that it is acceptable to hold secret trials and summary executions, without the possibility of judicial review, at least when the defendant is a foreign national."

But supporters counter that if handled properly, military courts will not hurt America's reputation, nor deny defendants their most basic rights.

"This is not going to be some sort of barbaric process, like you see in countries like Peru," Kmiec says. "Our military has a history of following fair guidelines and procedures, and I think that anyone who appears before one of these tribunals will have a fair chance to defend himself."

Has the press bowed to patriotic fervor and not reported critically on U.S. efforts to fight terrorism?

Some conservatives have joined liberals in complaining that journalists have failed to fulfill their responsibility to properly inform the public. Other media analysts argue that the system is working just as it should.

Critics of the media's performance point to three major issues. First, the general compliance, and lack of an outcry, when the government asked

TV networks to broadcast only limited portions of speeches by bin Laden. Second, critics cite the firings of journalists who have criticized President Bush's behavior immediately following the incidents of Sept. 11. Third, critics complain of the limited attention paid by the press to policies and legislation, such as the USA Patriot Act, that would potentially infringe on Americans' civil liberties.

Marvin Kalb, executive director of the Joan Shorenstein Center on the Press, Politics, and Public Policy at Harvard University, believes that some press failings are explained by the fact that immediately after the terrorist attacks, the press responded with patriotic emotion, like the rest of the country.

"Right after Sept. 11, everyone was caught up in a rush of patriotism," Kalb says. "The idea of criticizing your country was something that most reporters didn't want to do. And they didn't. It was a patriotic press."

Soon, however, Kalb says that the press returned to its proper, questioning role. "Once the bombing began and the Taliban began to fall apart, the coverage changed," he says. "Before, the reporters were almost totally dependent upon whatever [Defense Secretary Donald H.] Rumsfeld told them. Now reporters are in the field covering the story, seeing it and being exposed to terrible danger."

Far from being uncritical of the government, reporters are doing their jobs vigorously, some observers say. "I don't think the press is being too submissive," says Neil Hickey, editor-at-large at the *Columbia Journalism Review.* "I've talked to eight or nine Pentagon correspondents, and they're mutinists down there over the problem they're having of penetrating the Pentagon. The curtain has come down, and the word has gone out that nobody is supposed to talk to them except Rumsfeld, [Pentagon spokesman Rear Adm. John] Stufflebeam and Gen. Meyers, the chairman of the Joint Chiefs of Staff."

Chronology

1776-1864 *The new nation struggles to define and protect citizens' rights, but the government clamps down on civil liberties during the Civil War.*

Dec. 15, 1791
The Bill of Rights is ratified.

1798
Congress passes the first Alien and Sedition Act, which restricts immigrants' free speech and other rights.

April 27, 1861
President Abraham Lincoln suspends the right of habeas corpus, allowing the government to hold arrested persons indefinitely without explaining the reasons for detention to the courts.

September 1862
Lincoln orders citizens suspected of disloyal practices to be tried under military jurisdiction.

———— • ————

1870-1922 *Economic problems and waves of labor unrest plague the country and state and local officials, often aided by federal resources, use their power to break the unions. World War I brings the threat of foreign influence and domestic agitation.*

1886
Labor protests in Chicago lead to the Haymarket bombing and riots in which seven policemen are killed and 70 wounded, along with many civilian casualties. The affair marks the beginning of new actions curtailing the rights of domestic labor and radical groups.

1894
A strike at the Pullman railway car factory in Chicago is broken up by 16,000 federal troops.

March 1917
War Department authorizes Army officers to repress acts committed "with seditious intent."

1918
Congress passes the Sedition Act, making virtually all criticism of the government and the war effort illegal.

November 1919
In America's first "Red Scare," Attorney General A. Mitchell Palmer begins cracking down on individuals and organizations suspected of communist leanings. The so-called Palmer raids reach their climax on Jan. 2, 1920, when federal agents in more than 30 cities arrest 5,000 to 10,000 alien residents.

———— • ————

1941-1945 *World War II offers new challenges for domestic and international law.*

1941
Japan attacks Pearl Harbor on Dec. 7. Hawaii's governor places the territory under martial law for three years.

1942
In February, President Franklin D. Roosevelt interns ethnic Japanese on the West Coast.

1945
House Un-American Activities Committee (HUAC) becomes a standing committee.

1950-1975 *Red scares return, and America tries to protect itself.*

1950
Sen. Joseph R. McCarthy, R-Wis., launches a series of investigations into alleged communist sympathizers in the federal government.

1954
Congress censures McCarthy.

1956
FBI launches COINTELPRO, a secret program of intelligence gathering and disruption of legal organizations in the United States.

———— • ————

2001 *Terrorism strikes on U.S. soil.*

Sept. 11
Middle Eastern terrorists hijack four civilian airliners. Two crash into the World Trade Center; a third hits the Pentagon and the fourth crashes in rural Pennsylvania.

Oct. 26
President Bush signs the USA Patriot Act, aimed at deterring terrorist acts.

Oct. 30
New Department of Justice rules limit the attorney-client privilege for certain criminal defendants.

Nov. 13
President Bush authorizes military tribunals to try suspected terrorists.

Dec. 6
Attorney General John Ashcroft appears before lawmakers on Capitol Hill to defend the crackdown on terrorism.

Hickey complains that similar restrictions on access to information are in place overseas. "Foreign editors and newspaper executives are extremely irate that their reporters have been excluded from contact with those in the staging areas in Pakistan," he says. Hickey says most reporters also have been excluded from the aircraft carrier *Kitty Hawk*, from which many of the commando raids have been launched. The exception, he says, was "a tiny [media] pool that is with the Marines in Kandahar — and that consists of an AP guy, a Reuters guy, a still photographer, a TV cameraman and, of all things, a reporter from the *Marine Times*."

Other observers criticize the press for being too lax in covering potential threats to civil liberties at home, especially the antiterrorism legislation and the proposed military tribunals.

"Rumsfeld, Ashcroft and Powell keep saying, 'We are going to protect our basic values,' while they're really shredding them," columnist Nat Hentoff says. "Well, most people don't see the contradiction. And the press is not illuminating that contradiction."

Hentoff blames two factors for the limited coverage. First, he says, the pressure of deadlines and the 24-hour news cycle cause reporters to rush material to print without doing as much research as they should. Secondly, he says, "Many reporters and editors don't know that much about the Constitution, about past precedent."

Reed Irvine, director of Accuracy in Media, a conservative watchdog group, generally agrees with Hentoff's assessment. "There's a tendency on the part of journalists today to accept the word of the government as being the word of God," Irvine says. "They don't challenge it. One of the reasons for that, I believe, is that most of the reporters that cover these things are beat reporters. If you're assigned to cover aviation, for example, you'd better be on good terms with the FAA. You'd better not make people mad at you by revealing that they've been lying."

Hentoff also points to the firing of two journalists — Tom Guthrie of the *Texas City* (Texas) *Sun* and Dan Guthrie of the *Grants Pass* (Ore.) *Daily Courier* — over columns critical of President Bush as signs of an overly submissive press.

"In both cases, publishers appeared to be responding to furious reader reaction to criticism of the commander in chief in time of war," Hentoff wrote in a recent column. "Fear had conquered freedom of the press." [15]

Daily Courier Editor Dennis Roler says that Guthrie's criticism of Bush for flying around the country instead of immediately returning to the White House in the wake of the Sept. 11 attacks wasn't the only reason he was fired. Still, Roler felt compelled to write an editorial apologizing for Guthrie's column, stating, "Criticism of our chief executive and those around him needs to be responsible and appropriate. Labeling him and the nation's other top leaders as cowards as the United States tries to unite after its bloodiest terrorist attack ever isn't responsible or appropriate." [16]

Most press observers, however, disagree with the proposition that controversial columns should be vetted. "The antidote to controversial speech is not less controversial speech, it's more controversial speech," Hickey says. "Let the public be exposed to a whole range of ideas and let them make up their own minds. The public doesn't need protection." ∎

BACKGROUND

Lincoln's Action

The greatest dangers to liberty lurk in insidious encroachment by men of zeal, well meaning but without understanding," wrote Supreme Court Justice Louis Brandeis in a court decision in 1928. [17]

Indeed, throughout America's history, with the notable exception of racist acts, the greatest challenges to civil liberties have come at the hands of well-meaning politicians and government officials during wartime or in response to other perceived dangers to national security.

The first such acts by federal officials that attracted significant attention were during the Civil War. Southern states began seceding from the Union shortly after, and partly due to, the election of Abraham Lincoln as president in 1860. On April 12, 1861, Confederate forces began firing on Fort Sumter, a Union garrison near Charleston, S.C.

Fully aware that the nation's capital was surrounded by states sympathetic to the Confederacy — Lincoln even had to enter Washington surreptitiously for his inauguration to avoid the violence of pro-South mobs — the president felt it necessary on April 27 to issue a proclamation suspending the right of habeas corpus. The carryover from English common law requires the government to explain to the court why it is detaining a prisoner and, if the court decides the reason is not sufficient, to free the prisoner.

In one of the more notable incidents, in the fall of 1861 the suspension of habeas corpus was used to detain more than a dozen Maryland legislators who the federal government thought favored secession. They were arrested to prevent them from voting their sentiments. [18]

Lincoln knew the step was of questionable legality. "Are all the laws, but one, to go unexecuted and the government itself go to pieces, lest that one be violated," Lincoln asked Congress in a special message on July 4, 1861, in an attempt to quiet critics.

Is Questioning Immigrants Fair?

The government's plan to prevent future terrorist attacks on American soil relies to a large extent on the Justice Department's ongoing efforts to interview thousands of recent immigrants from the Middle East. But critics charge the plan is unconstitutional and racist.

When the Bush administration began conducting the interviews in early November, it portrayed the operation as an effort to gather information, not a massive dragnet intended to arrest thousands of suspects. "Terrorist activity rarely goes entirely unnoticed," Attorney General John Ashcroft said on Nov. 29. "Non-citizens are often ideally situated to observe the precursors to, or early stages of, terrorist activity." [1]

Some 5,000 people who have arrived in the U.S. since Jan. 1, 2000, mostly Middle Eastern men between the ages of 18 and 33, have been asked to voluntarily submit to questioning at their homes.

"We're being as kind and fair and gentle as we can in terms of inviting people to participate," Ashcroft said. [2] Indeed, on Nov. 29, the attorney general tried to sweeten the pot by announcing that the government would help those who provide useful information to remain in the country and even become citizens. [3]

The Fifth Amendment to the Constitution protects a suspect's right against self-incrimination, including the right not to answer questions from police. In addition, the Fourth Amendment protects privacy by prohibiting "unreasonable searches and seizures."

"The government has the right to ask questions," said Norman Dorsen, former president of the American Civil Liberties Union. "But people have a right not to answer questions." [4]

In 1973, the Supreme Court fleshed out the Constitution's protections against self-incrimination, stating that consent to be searched or answer questions must be "voluntarily given and not the result of duress or coercion, express or implied."

But some civil liberties advocates worry that a number of factors could make those interviewed feel compelled to cooperate, regardless of their legal protections. For instance, they argue that since all the interviewees are recent immigrants, many could be concerned that the Immigration and Naturalization Service would detain or even deport them depending on whether and how they decide to cooperate. "My sense is that many of these people will only talk to the government because they think they'll be arrested or deported if they don't," says Michael Avery, an associate professor of law at Suffolk University in Boston. "That sounds like coercion to me."

Others might be intimidated because they feel like they are one of the targets of what has become a massive investigation in the wake of the Sept. 11 attacks, Avery says. "The government is already holding a lot of people, and these folks know it," he says. "That fact has to be in the back of their minds when they talk to federal officials."

Opponents also say that targeting Middle Eastern immigrants amounts to racial profiling on a mass scale. "You're stigmatizing a whole community when you do this," says James Zogby, executive director of the Arab American Institute.

But others defend the administration's efforts as well-directed and within the bounds of the law. "Look, we need to cast a wide net and suck in as much information as possible, and these people could be well suited to help us do that," says Kent Scheidegger, legal director for the Criminal Justice Legal Foundation, a conservative think tank in Sacramento, Calif. "Asking people to come in voluntarily and answer questions is not unconstitutional. It's what police investigators do."

Scheidegger also defends the decision to focus on people from Middle Eastern countries. "The terrorist threat is from the Middle East, so you don't want to waste your time interviewing recent immigrants from Norway," he says. "It's appropriate to look a certain group when, as in this case, there's a substantial connection between national origin and the threat."

---

[1] Quoted in Neil A. Lewis, "Immigrants Offered Incentives to Give Evidence on Terrorists," *The New York Times*, Nov. 30. 2001.

[2] Quoted in William Glaberson, "Legal Experts Question Legality of Questioning," *The New York Times*, Nov. 30, 2001.

[3] Lewis, *op. cit.*

[4] Quoted in Glaberson, *op. cit.*

Perhaps surprisingly, Lincoln's suspension of habeas corpus provoked little public outcry. Today, Chief Justice William Rehnquist suggests that this may be because the court opinion that held Lincoln did not have the authority to do so was authored by Chief Justice Roger B. Taney, who was also the author of the infamous Dred Scott decision. Rehnquist notes that the case "inflamed the North and would cast a cloud over the High Court for at least a generation." [19]

Suspending habeas corpus was not the only violation of citizens' civil rights. First Amendment protections were also abused. Newspapers that were not sufficiently sympathetic to the Union cause were banned from the mails, which was the major means of delivery at the time.

The New York News tried to fight the policy by hiring newsboys to deliver it locally. The government ordered U.S. marshals to seize copies of the paper and one newsboy was arrested for selling it.

"Remarkably, other New York papers did not rally round the sheets that were being suppressed," writes Rehnquist. "Instead of crying out about an abridgement of First Amendment rights — as they would surely do today — their rivals simply gloated." [20]

Worse still, President Lincoln went much farther than suspending habeas corpus in September 1862 — just a month after the Emancipation Proclamation. He issued a proclamation holding that citizens found "discouraging volunteer enlistments, resisting militia drafts, or guilty of any disloyal practice affording aid and comfort to rebels," would be subject to trial and punishment under military law. Rehnquist commented that, "Such people faced, in other words, stringent penalties for actions that were often not offenses by normal civilian standards, and faced them, moreover, without the right to jury trial or other procedural protections customarily attending a criminal trial in a civil court." [21]

Attacks on Labor

In the years after the Civil War, periodic economic crises were the occasion for federal actions against what were perceived to be radical labor unions that threatened the economic stability of the country.

"Union organization depended on the constitutional freedoms of speech, press and assembly, but employers consistently abridged these rights. Their reliance on espionage, blacklisting, strikebreakers, private police and, ultimately, armed violence, nullified the Bill of Rights for those workers who had the temerity to resist their employers' unilateral exercise of power," a historian wrote. [22]

Not only did the federal government not do anything to defend the constitutionally protected rights of workers, but on a number of occasions it actually took action against workers.

"During the 1870-1900 period, all of the various techniques used to repress labor were gradually developed and institutionalized by business and governmental elites: the company town, the use of private police, private arsenals and private detectives, the deputization of private police, the manipulation of governmental police agencies, the revival of conspiracy doctrine and the labor injunction,"

writes Robert Justin Goldstein, professor of political science at Oakland University in Rochester, Mich. [23]

During a strike against the Pullman railway car company in 1894, for example, federal troops were sent to Chicago to quell the strike. "Federal troops were also sent to Los Angeles; Sacramento; Ogden, Utah; Raton, New Mexico, and many other areas, especially in the West, and often on the thinnest of excuses," writes Goldstein. In all, 16,000 federal troops were sent.

"In a number of cases the actions of the troops were so reckless that local officials protested bitterly," Goldstein notes. "Thus, the Sacramento Board of City Trustees adopted a resolution condemning the 'tyranny and brutality which has characterized the conduct of the U.S. soldiers who have wounded and assaulted unoffending persons upon the streets,' and condemned troops for free and unprovoked use of their bayonets and guns and for the reckless wounding of innocent citizens." [24]

The Palmer Raids

The threat of world war brought the next wave of federal erosions of civil liberties.

"The story of civil liberties during World War I is a dreary, disturbing and, in some respects, shocking chapter out of the nation's past," writes Paul L. Murphy, professor of history and American studies at the University of Minnesota. "Americans, committed through their president, Woodrow Wilson, to 'make the world safe for democracy' — a phrase which implied that the nation and its allies bore a responsibility to free the world to adopt America's traditional 'liberal' commitment to liberty and justice — stood by on the domestic scene and saw liberty and justice prostituted in ways more extreme and

extensive than at any other time in American history." [25]

As early as March 1917, the War Department authorized Army officers to repress acts committed with "seditious intent." The guidelines were so vague that abuses were widespread. "Military intelligence agents participated in a wide range of dubious activities, which involved a wholesale system of spying on civilians that would be unmatched in scope until the late 1960s. Military intelligence activities included surveillance of the International Workers of the World (IWW), the Pacific Fellowship of Reconciliation and the National Civil Liberties Bureau, forerunner of the American Civil Liberties Union." [26]

The Sedition Act, passed in May 1918, made illegal virtually all criticism of the government or of the war effort.

The Wilson administration also helped organize the American Protective League, a privately funded organization that was intended to help the government with, among other things, food rationing and investigating the loyalty of soldiers and government personnel.

"The organization quickly became a largely out-of-control, quasi-governmental, quasi-vigilante agency which established a massive spy network across the land," writes Goldstein. [27]

The assault on civil liberties didn't end with the armistice. The Bolshevik Revolution and the Red Scare that ensued in the United States resulted in a series of further measures.

Under pressure from Congress to take steps against anarchists and communists, Attorney General A. Mitchell Palmer launched a series of raids, which came to be known as "Palmer Raids," against groups with suspected communist leanings, such as the Union of Russian Workers, the Communist Party and the IWW. Alien residents associated with the groups were arrested and detained while deportation proceedings were conducted. The raids, which began in November 1919, reached their climax on Jan. 2, 1920, when federal agents raided organizations in more than 30 cities and arrested between 5,000 and 10,000 alien residents.

Japanese Internment

During World War II, barely more than two months after Japanese forces bombed Pearl Harbor on Dec. 7, 1941, President Roosevelt signed Executive Order 9066, which authorized the removal of ethnic Japanese — many of them U.S. citizens — from West Coast communities.

At the time, at least, the action seemed understandable to many. There was widespread fear of Japanese attacks on the coast and of sabotage of critical facilities. And, unlike ethnic Italian and German populations in the United States, ethnic Japanese were not seen as integrated into American society.

"Both federal and state restrictions on the rights of Japanese emigrants had prevented their assimilation into the Caucasian population and had intensified their insularity and solidarity," writes Rehnquist. "Japanese parents sent their children to Japanese-language schools outside of regular school hours, and there was some evidence that the language schools were a source of Japanese nationalistic propaganda. As many as

10,000 American-born children of Japanese parentage went to Japan for all or part of their education. And even though children born in the United States of Japanese alien parents were U.S. citizens, they were under Japanese law also viewed as citizens of Japan." [28]

While the internment of Japanese-Americans during World War II has since come to be seen as an injustice, the Supreme Court decided in several cases in 1943 and 1944 that the internment was justified, given the threats facing the country.

Internment was the most dramatic

Sen. Joseph R. McCarthy, R-Wis., made unsubstantiated accusations against suspected communists in the movie industry and the U.S. and foreign governments in the early 1950s, giving rise to the term "McCarthyism." Here he holds up a picture of former British Prime Minister Clement Attlee and suggests that his communist salute during the Spanish Civil War 20 years earlier marked him as a sympathizer.

AP Photo

civil rights issue during World War II, but it was not the only issue. In the wake of the attack on Pearl Harbor, the governor of Hawaii placed the islands under martial law and suspended habeas corpus. At the same time, and with Gov. Poindexter's blessings, Lt. Gen. Walter Short, com-

mander of the Military Department of Hawaii, declared himself military governor of Hawaii.

Short issued a series of ordinances, and violations could and did land many civilians in military rather than civilian courts. The military rule of Hawaii continued for three years until President Roosevelt ordered it revoked.

Cold War McCarthyism

At the end of World War II, civil liberties advocates were hopeful that the climate was improving. "In July 1945," writes Goldstein, "the ACLU reported that its caseload had 'markedly declined' and that it foresaw its post-war activities as revolving much less around court cases that involved challenges to individual civil liberties. Instead it looked forward to building 'institutional arrangements to protect civil liberties' such as fighting monopolistic practices in communications and promoting 'the wider participation of faculties and students in educational control.'" [29]

By August 1947, however, the ACLU reported "the national climate of opinion in which freedom of public debate and minority dissent functioned with few restraints during the war years and after, has undergone a sharply unfavorable change." [30]

Historians credit two factors with the turnaround. First, there was a wave of labor strikes in 1946, which resulted in a rise of anti-labor sentiment. Secondly, and even more significantly, it became

Limiting Free Speech Online

When terrorists crashed two airliners into the World Trade Center on Sept. 11, Stuart Biegel tried to reach friends in Manhattan. He couldn't get through using a telephone or a cell phone, but he was able to reach them via e-mail.

"So much for the Internet being a vulnerable medium," says Biegel, a professor at the University of California-Los Angeles (UCLA) who specializes in cyberspace law. "The Internet is like water flowing. If it's blocked from one direction it goes around."

And it's not just e-mail that's circulating on the Web. Americans following events in Afghanistan and the nation's war on terrorism can find a wealth of information. Neither Osama bin Laden nor the now-deposed Taliban regime have Web sites, but at www.rawa.org readers can read about the heroic efforts of the Revolutionary Association of the Women of Afghanistan (RAWA). In addition to a calendar of protests and press conferences and a history of the organization, a pop-up window on the site hawks RAWA T-shirts and coffee mugs.

Online visitors also can participate in a chat with a journalist just back from Afghanistan on CNN's Web site. (http://www.cnn.com/2001/COMMUNITY/08/24/shah/.)

The Internet is coming into its own, much like talk radio, as a public medium for citizens to voice their opinions on the issues. The lively chat rooms maintained by America Online, Yahoo and Microsoft Network feature strong opinions on all sides — but only up to a point.

"Certainly, there were a lot of very strong emotions that were expressed in the days after Sept. 11, which is exactly what our service is designed for," says Nicholas Graham, a spokesperson for AOL.

Biegel agrees that people seem more inclined to speak their minds on the Internet than in other places, including his classroom. "People tend to feel more comfortable because they perceive anonymity when they take a screen name, and also because they're doing it in the privacy of their own home," he says. "I even see this with my students in on-line discussion forums. Some who may not speak out in class are suddenly very articulate in an online discussion forum. They're not sitting there in a room with everybody around, so they feel more relaxed."

Discussions have been so lively, in fact, that online services have stepped in to moderate the language in some chat room conversations. "We draw a very, very fine line between expressing heartfelt emotions and hate speech," Graham says. "When we are made aware of hate speech online, or if we see it ourselves, we take immediate action ranging from a disciplinary warning to termination of service."

But some chat-room visitors say the censoring isn't even-handed. "We have had several cases reported to us of postings by people with Arab-sounding names being taken down because they expressed a different point of view," said Laila Al-Qatami, a spokeswoman for the Arab-American Anti-Discrimination Committee. "Likewise, we've been told of harassing messages against people of Arab descent not being taken down." [1]

Indeed, according to *The Washington Post*, "Yahoo has deleted a note calling someone a "Zionist Israeli [expletive]." But the following message has remained up for weeks despite several complaints lodged by users and copied to *The Washington Post*: "Muslims are against the Jews because Muslims are too greedy. They want to take Israel's teeny-weeny land. That's how greedy and parasitic these Muslims are. America should wipe them all out." [2]

Biegel notes that while the Internet is a public medium and people can says just about anything they want on their own Web site, the online services actually are private.

"Companies such as AOL and Yahoo are private companies and are not subject to the First Amendment in the same way that public entities are," Biegel says. "AOL can restrict speech and make rules that would not withstand First Amendment scrutiny."

Online services generally rely on staff "chaperones" to screen out overly offensive messages. They visit chat rooms to check on what's going on. "Our guides are trained very carefully to deal with discrimination, whether it's religious, ethnic or whatever," Graham says. "They're very familiar with terms that might be offensive to a given community."

Given the large number of chat groups and messages, however, chaperones or moderators find it very difficult to keep up with the huge flow of messages. Accordingly, most actions by the online services are initiated in response to a user complaint.

Since chat rooms take place in real time, however, monitoring and controlling content is very difficult, as indicated by a Dec. 10 spot check of AOL's chat room on the World Trade Center. In addition to several instances of extremely vulgar language, there was even a user proposing to drive an armored tank to Washington, D.C.

---

[1] Quoted in Ariana Eunjung Cha, "Screening Free Speech? Online Companies Draw Fire for Removing 'Offensive' Postings," *The Washington Post*, Nov. 18, 2001, p. H01.
[2] *Ibid.*

---

apparent that America was involved in a new kind of war, a Cold War with the Soviet Union. The United States now had global responsibilities, and it had an enemy with global reach. Espionage was a major fear.

The House Un-American Activities Committee (HUAC) was made a standing committee of the House in January 1945. Soon after, a series of spy scares rattled the American public, including the case of Alger Hiss, a State Department employee accused, and eventually convicted, of spying for the Soviet Union. Then, in 1951, Julius and Ethel Rosenberg were convicted of spying for the Soviet Union and electrocuted at Sing Sing Prison in New York state.

On March 21, 1947, President Harry S Truman announced the creation of

At Issue:

Should airports use racial profiling to screen passengers?

CLIFFORD S. FISHMAN
PROFESSOR OF LAW, THE CATHOLIC UNIVERSITY OF AMERICA

WRITTEN FOR THE CQ RESEARCHER, DEC. 6, 2001

*a*irport and airline security in this country — or more accurately, the lack of it — has been an open scandal for decades. On September 11, we paid the price.

Now it is proposed that airport security personnel should "profile" airline passengers from Moslem and Middle Eastern countries for special scrutiny.

To target an entire ethnic group, the overwhelming majority of whom are good, decent, innocent people, because of the crimes committed by a tiny handful of them, is immoral, in most instances illegal and violates fundamental American values.

Nevertheless, in the aftermath of September 11, airport security officials are temporarily justified in doing so, for three reasons:

First, because since 1993, the perpetrators of every terrorist act committed or attempted by foreigners within the U.S. — the World Trade Center car bomb, September 11 and several unsuccessful conspiracies in between — have been from the Middle East, Algeria or Pakistan.

Second, September 11 taught us that failing to prevent terrorists from boarding an airliner can cost thousands of lives and significantly disrupt our way of life.

Third, because we do not yet have in place the resources or personnel to properly scrutinize every individual who boards and every package loaded onto a plane, it would be irresponsible not to focus most of our attention on people who fit the "profile" of those most likely to attempt another September 11.

This justification is temporary, for two reasons: Permanently profiling any group violates our ideals and values. And the next group of hijackers might not fit the profile. They might be from Somalia or Indonesia (where allegedly there are Al Qaeda cells in each country). Or they could be members of Aum Shinrikyo, the Japanese sect that a few years ago released a deadly chemical in the Tokyo subway.

Or they might be "all-American guys" like Timothy McVeigh and Terry Nichols, who blew up the federal building in Oklahoma City. Until adequate security resources are put in place to properly screen everyone, we can only hope that security personnel who "profile" Middle Easterners will act professionally and courteously. Inevitably, though, thousands of innocent, decent people will be singled out unfairly, and many will be harassed and humiliated — and that is an outrage, even though it is temporarily necessary.

Let us pray that those who are singled out or mistreated will have the grace to understand, and to forgive us for the wrongs that will be done to them.

JEAN ABINADER
MANAGING DIRECTOR, ARAB AMERICAN INSTITUTE

WRITTEN FOR THE CQ RESEARCHER, DEC. 10, 2001

*i*n poll after poll taken after September 11, Arab Americans indicated their overwhelming desire to cooperate with the authorities to improve airline security. This desire to cooperate, however, does not justify the rude and abusive behavior by airline crews, ground personnel and security staff.

Many of the improvements in procedures and technology can be implemented in a non-discriminatory fashion. Recommendations ranging from baggage matching to better equipment and training for security personnel can be applied to all passengers equally, thus ensuring greater security without the need to single out passengers because of perceived ethnic origin, or other characteristics such as clothing or accents.

There is a continuing need for airlines to restate their policies against racial profiling, especially to inform and advise passengers and crew that federal and state statutes do not permit "vigilantism," particularly if the person in question has passed the common screening procedures for all passengers. Perhaps a variation of the "passenger bill of rights" regarding profiling needs to be included in the materials available to passengers in their seat pockets.

Finally, racial profiling presents more complications than solutions. Based on testimony by security officials, profiling does not make a measurable difference in the prevention of crimes, although it is helpful in investigating criminal activities once there has been a crime. This is not to suggest that law enforcement officials should be passive because of ethnic or racial considerations. Rather, it requires that great caution be exercised if racial or ethnic factors are to be included as one of a number of variants that may warrant that a security person investigate further.

Basing security procedures solely on racial or ethnic characteristics leads to discriminatory behaviors by the officials involved and reinforces stereotypes that damage the government's ability to reach out and coordinate its efforts with the affected communities.

We recommend that the government work diligently to improve its screening of all travelers and their belongings. Equally applied procedures and reminders that racial profiling is unhelpful can also be useful in reducing the potential for disruptive behavior by passengers intent on independently assuming the role of air police.

Efforts should also be made to hire more Arab-Americans and American Muslims. Qualified and trained Arab-Americans can be resources to the security services and to the airlines by validating non-discriminatory practices and helping to deal with passengers from Arab and Muslim countries who may feel overwhelmed by enhanced security procedures.

a new government-loyalty program, under which all current or prospective government employees were to undergo loyalty investigations.

It was in an environment of fear, then, that Sen. Joseph R. McCarthy of Wisconsin rose to public prominence when, beginning in early 1950, he warned of rampant communist influence in government.

The anti-communist hysteria resulted in extensive hearings over the next two years by HUAC and its Senate counterpart, the Permanent Investigations Subcommittee. By the time McCarthy was finally censured by his colleagues in 1954, countless careers and reputations had been needlessly ruined.

COINTELPRO and the Vietnam War

It wasn't much of a step from the anti-communist hysteria and blacklistings of the early 1950s to federal actions against suspected domestic radical opponents of the Vietnam War in the 1960s and early '70s. In fact, the most dramatic federal violation of citizens' civil rights actually began in 1956 when the FBI launched COINTELPRO, a counterintelligence program designed to disrupt what remained of the Communist Party in the United States.

The initial FBI memo that formalized COINTELPRO indicated that the agency would explore a number of tactics to combat communist influences in domestic organizations, including using the Internal Revenue Service to investigate suspected citizens, planting informants and attempting to create dissention within the groups and to disrupt their activities. [31]

Between 1964 and 1968 alone, the FBI conducted more than 1,000 undercover operations against antiwar, white supremacy, civil rights and other domestic groups. ∎

CURRENT SITUATION

USA Patriot Act

Within hours of the Sept. 11 attacks, lawmakers and commentators were calling for Congress to give new powers to the federal government to fight terrorism. And in spite of warnings by civil libertarians and some members of the House and Senate to tread carefully, Congress quickly complied, sending legislation to the president six weeks after the attacks.

Attorney General Ashcroft had asked for a variety of new powers in the weeks after the tragedy. In particular, Ashcroft requested new authority to conduct searches and detain suspects.

Exactly a month after the attacks, the Senate easily passed an anti-terrorism bill that had been crafted by Republican and Democratic leaders that encompassed many of Ashcroft's proposals. The following day, the House passed its own tougher version. Less than two weeks later, on Oct. 25, the Senate cleared a compromise bill, 98-1. President Bush signed the USA-Patriot Act the next day.

Although the bill was tempered somewhat by more liberal members of Congress, especially Senate Judiciary Committee Chairman Leahy, it gave Ashcroft much of what he had asked for, including provisions that:

- Allow "roving wiretaps" that follow suspects no matter what telephone they use. Old rules required law enforcement officers to acquire a new warrant each time a

suspect used a different phone. The provision "sunsets" in 2005.
- Give law enforcement the authority to conduct "secret searches" of a suspect's residence, including computer files. Authorities can delay telling the suspect of the search for "a reasonable time" if such information would adversely affect the investigation. Previously, law enforcement had to inform suspects of any search.
- Allow the attorney general to detain any non-citizen believed to be a national security risk for up to seven days. After seven days the government must charge the suspect or begin deportation proceedings. If the suspect cannot be deported, the government can continue the detention so long as the attorney general certifies that the suspect is a national security risk every six months.
- Make it illegal for someone to harbor an individual they know or should have known had engaged in or was about to engage in a terrorist act.
- Give the Treasury Department new powers and banks and depositors new responsibilities in tracking the movement of money.
- Allow investigators to share secret grand jury information or information obtained through wiretaps with government officials if it is important for counterintelligence or foreign intelligence operations.
- Allow authorities to track Internet communications (e-mail) as they do telephone calls.

While not entirely happy with the new law as written, many civil libertarians and others applauded Congress for not including all of the provisions requested by the attorney general. For instance, under Ashcroft's

> **"Under this law, we impose guilt by association on immigrants. We make them deportable not for their acts but for their wholly innocent associations."**
>
> — *Professor of Law David Cole, Georgetown University*

> **"It's a gross overreaction to say that this new law is going to take away vital freedoms. It gives the government a bit more power than it had."**
>
> — *Professor of Law Clifford Fishman, Catholic University*

initial proposal, evidence obtained overseas in a manner that would be illegal in the United States would still have been admissible in an American court if no laws had been broken in the country where the evidence was gathered.

"So if you had a wiretap in Germany that would have been illegal here, but is legal there, the evidence would have been admissible here," law Professor Henderson says. "Congress said 'no way' and tossed that out."

And yet, Henderson and Georgetown's Cole argue, even though it doesn't contain some of the most troubling provisions proposed by the Justice Department, the bill still goes too far. They particularly object to those parts of the law that allow the government to detain and deport or hold immigrants.

"I think the most radical provisions are those directed at immigrants," Cole says. "Under this law, we impose guilt by association on immigrants. We make them deportable not for their acts but for their associations, wholly innocent associations with any proscribed organization and you're deportable."

But George Washington University's Kerr argues that the Patriot Act does not, as critics contend, go too far. "Overall, I think this is a very balanced act, giving the government just what it needs in this fight," Kerr says. "I'm actually impressed at how narrowly tailored this language is. The administration could have gotten even more authority, but they asked just for what they needed."

"It's a gross overreaction to say that this new law is going to take away vital freedoms," agrees Catholic University's Fishman. "It gives the government a bit more power than it had. And remember, this is a government that has generally shown that it can be trusted with power." ■

OUTLOOK

Back to Normal Soon?

On more than one occasion, President Bush has warned the American people that the struggle to defeat Al Qaeda and other terrorist groups will last years, even decades.

But some critics of the administration predict that many of the tough steps taken to prevent terrorism domestically will be short-lived. They base their prediction on past actions, when the American people reacted to curtailments of civil liberties by eventually reasserting their rights.

"We have a long history of overreacting during times of crisis, whether it be the Alien and Sedition Acts or the internment of the Japanese during World War II," says Neas of People for the American Way. "After a while, we usually look back on those actions and realize that they were a mistake, and I think that's what will happen here.

"Congress put sunset provisions in the Patriot Act for a reason. But I wouldn't be surprised if popular pressure forced the government to sunset the law and some of these other changes before five years passed."

Schwartz of the criminal defense lawyers' association agrees that after the initial shock of the attacks wears off, Americans will want the government to relinquish the new powers it has acquired. "The American people are not going to let the government burn the Constitution in the name of fighting terrorism," he says. "Look at the Congress and the press: They're already challenging the administration on many of its policies. This, only three months after attacks."

But others, on both sides of the civil liberties debate, say that the terrorist attacks on New York and Washington have thrust the United States into a long struggle, similar to the Cold War, and that new limits on freedoms could remain in place for years.

"Everything is different now," says Columbia University's Ratner. "The fact that serious people are now talking about using torture means that the [civil liberties] bar has been lowered dramatically since Sept. 11, and I don't see it being raised any time soon."

"Unless there are very visible abuses of this new authority, I doubt there will be a groundswell of support for repeal of these new powers any time soon," agrees Catholic University's Fishman. He points out that most people supported giving the government more crime-fighting authority even before Sept. 11, because they don't see the changes as a direct threat to their personal freedom. "They say, 'I'm not a criminal so I have no problem with the government taking more power to get the bad guys.'"

In addition, Fishman says, new terrorist attacks would make Americans even more supportive of tough, new measures to fight terrorism. "Another great disaster would further solidify opinion behind these changes."

But Scheidegger of the Criminal Justice Legal Foundation predicts only modest changes in future U.S. civil liberties. "There's always this great push for new authority when something dramatic happens," he says, "and then things always settle down and we take it back a little. While I don't think we'll go back to where we were before Sept. 11, I also don't think the long-term changes will be as far-reaching as it might appear they'll be right now." ∎

Notes

[1] Cited in Richard Moran and Claudia Deane, "Most Americans Back U.S. Tactics," *The Washington Post*, Nov. 29, 2001.

[2] Amy Goldstein, "A Deliberate Strategy of Disruption," *The Washington Post*, Nov. 4, 2001, and Deborah Sontag, "Who Is This Kafka That People Keep Mentioning?," *The New York Times Magazine*, Oct. 21, 2001.

[3] Quoted in "Disappearing in America," *The New York Times*, Nov. 10, 2001.

[4] Quoted in George Lardner Jr., "U.S. Will Monitor Calls to Lawyers," *The Washington Post*, Nov. 9, 2001.

[5] *Ibid.*

[6] Quoted in David G. Savage and Robert L. Jackson, "Response to Terror Defendants: Ashcroft Eavesdropping Rule Assailed Law,"

Los Angeles Times, Nov. 10, 2001.

[7] Cited in *Ibid.*

[8] Christopher Drew and William K. Rashbaum, "Opponents' and Supporters' Portrayals of Detentions Prove Inaccurate," *The New York Times*, Nov. 3, 2001.

[9] Goldstein, *op. cit.*

[10] Quoted in Barton Gellman, "U.S. Was Foiled Multiple Times in Efforts to Capture Bin Laden or Have Him Killed," *The Washington Post*, Oct. 3, 2000.

[11] Vernon Loeb and Susan Schmidt, "U.S. Wants Custody of Enemy Leaders," *The Washington Post*, Dec. 1, 2001.

[12] Quoted in Mike Allen, "Bush Defends Order for Military Tribunals," *The Washington Post*, Nov. 20, 2001.

[13] Quoted in "Taking Liberties," "The News Hour with Jim Lehrer," Nov. 27, 2001, www.pbs.org/newshour.

[14] Quoted in *Ibid.*

[15] Nat Hentoff, "Between Freedom and Fear: A Self-censored Press?" *Editor & Publisher*, Nov. 6, 2001.

[16] Reprinted in The Associated Press wire,

Sept. 26, 2001.

[17] *Olmstead v. United States* (1928), 277 U.S. 438 at 479:

[18] Rehnquist, William H., *All the Laws But One: Civil Liberties in Wartime*, Vintage Books, 1998, p. 45.

[19] *Ibid.*, p. 45.

[20] *Ibid.*, p. 47.

[21] *Ibid.*, p. 60.

[22] Jerold S. Auerbach, "The Depression Decade," in Alan Reitman, (ed.), *The Pulse of Freedom* (1975), p. 73.

[23] Robert Justin Goldstein, *Political Repression in Modern America: From 1870 to 1976* (1978), p. 23.

[24] *Ibid.*, p. 55.

[25] Paul L. Murphy, *World War I and the Origin of Civil Liberties in the United States* (1979), p. 15.

[26] Goldstein, *op. cit.*, p. 110.

[27] *Ibid.*, p. 111.

[28] Rehnquist, *op. cit.*, p. 107.

[29] Goldstein, *op. cit.*, p. 287.

[30] American Civil Liberties Union, "Annual Report, 1946-1947," p. 4.

[31] Goldstein, *op. cit.*, p. 407.

FOR MORE INFORMATION

Accuracy in Media, 4455 Connecticut Ave., N.W., Suite 330, Washington, D.C. 20008; (202) 364-4401; www.aim.org. AIM analyzes print and electronic news media for bias.

American Civil Liberties Union, 1333 H St., N.W., Washington, D.C. 20005; (202) 544-1681; www.aclu.org. The ACLU initiates court cases and lobbies for legislation with the aim of protecting civil liberties.

Arab American Institute, 1600 K. St., N.W., Suite 601, Washington, D.C. 20006; (202) 429-9210; www.aaiusa.org. An advocacy group concerned with issues affecting Arab-Americans.

Criminal Justice Legal Foundation, P.O. Box 1199, Sacramento, Calif. 95816; (916) 446-0345; www.cjlf.org. Advocates victims' rights and a strengthening of the ability of law enforcement to fight crime.

The Heritage Foundation, 214 Massachusetts Ave., N.E., Washington, D.C. 20002; (202) 546-4400; www.heritage.org. A think tank that advocates the promotion of individual freedom and strong law enforcement.

National Association of Criminal Defense Lawyers, 1150 8th St., N.W., Suite 950, Washington, D.C. 20036; (202) 872-8600; www.nacdl.org. Represents the interest of criminal-defense attorneys.

People for the American Way, 2000 M St., N.W., Suite 400, Washington, D.C. 20036; (202) 467-4999; www.pfaw.org. Promotes the protection of civil liberties.

Bibliography

Selected Sources

Books

Goldstein, Robert Justin, *Political Repression in Modern America: From 1870 to 1976*, **University of Illinois Press, 1978.**

Goldstein, a political science professor at Oakland University, details the history of repressive actions against U.S. citizens, especially the little-covered actions against labor unions in the late 1800s and the early 1900s. Includes extensive footnotes and a lengthy bibliography.

Linfield, Michael, *Freedom Under Fire: U.S. Civil Liberties in Time of War*, **South End Press, 1990.**

Linfield, a Los Angeles attorney, chronicles the dangers to civil liberties during wartime, with special focus on actions during the Revolutionary War.

Murphy, Paul L., *World War I and the Origin of Civil Liberties in the United States*, **W. W. Norton, 1979.**

A professor of history and American studies at the University of Minnesota readably explores the severe erosion of Americans' civil rights during World War I and the Red Scare afterwards.

Rehnquist, William H., *All the Laws But One: Civil Liberties in Wartime*, **Vintage Books, 1998.**

This readable work by the chief justice of the United States deals heavily with the Civil War and its aftermath and the Japanese internments during World War II, paying close attention to Supreme Court actions.

Articles

Glaberson, William, "Use of Military Court Divides Legal Experts," *The New York Times*, **Nov. 14, 2001, p. A1.**

Glaberson details the debate over the administration's proposed use of military tribunals.

Goldstein, Amy, "A Deliberate Strategy of Disruption," *The Washington Post*, **Nov. 4, 2001, p. A1.**

Goldstein looks in detail at the government's detention of potential terrorism suspects.

Lane, Charles, "Liberty and the Pursuit of Terrorists," *The Washington Post*, **Nov. 25, 2001, p. B1.**

A Supreme Court reporter argues that President Bush's recent steps in the war against terrorism are consistent with those taken by his predecessors in similar situations.

Lardner, George Jr., "U.S. Will Monitor Calls to Lawyers," *The Washington Post*, **Nov. 9, 2001, p. A1.**

Lardner explains the Justice Department decision to monitor attorney-client communication when the defendants are suspected terrorists.

Palmer, Elizabeth A., "Terrorism Bill's Sparse Paper Trail May Cause Legal Vulnerabilities," *CQ Weekly*, **Oct. 27, 2001, p. 2533.**

The article chronicles the legislative course of the U.S.A. Patriot Act and details its provisions.

Posner, Richard A., "Security Versus Civil Liberties," *The Atlantic*, **Dec. 2001, p. 46.**

A noted federal judge urges Americans not to overreact to possible curtailing of freedoms as the government gears up to combat terrorism.

Safire, William, "Seizing Dictatorial Power," *The New York Times*, **Nov. 15, 2001, p. A31.**

The conservative columnist argues that military tribunals are a tragic mistake. "Intimidated by terrorists . . . we are letting George W. Bush get away with the replacement of the American rule of law with military Kangaroo courts," he writes.

Thomas, Evan, *et al*, **"Justice Kept In the Dark; Closed military tribunals,"** *Newsweek*, **Dec. 10, 2001, p. 37.**

In the past few weeks, Ashcroft has led such an aggressive campaign to stamp out subversion that even old-time G-men are wondering whether the attorney general is trying too hard to fill the shoes of the late J. Edgar Hoover.

Toner, Robin, "Civil Liberty vs. Security: Finding a Wartime Balance," *The New York Times*, **Nov. 18, 2001, p. A1.**

Toner examines recent steps to strengthen government authority in the fight against terrorism in light of historical precedent as well as popular attitudes.

Willing, Richard and Toni Locy, "U.S. Now a Less-Forgiving Host to Illegal Immigrants," *USA Today*, **Nov. 30, 2001, p. A1.**

More than 1,200 people have been detained in the probe into the attacks on the World Trade Center and the Pentagon, and 548 of them are illegal aliens, most of them young Muslim men, who likely never would have come to the attention of immigration officials had they not been scooped up by the FBI.

Reports and Studies

"Bringing Al-Qaeda to Justice: The Constitutionality of Trying Al-Qaeda Terrorists in the Military Justice System," Heritage Foundation, Nov. 5, 2001.

The conservative think tank argues that military tribunals make sense and are probably constitutional.

11 Cyber-Crimes

BRIAN HANSEN

Carlos Salgado Jr. walked into San Francisco International Airport carrying a tote bag containing an ordinary CD-ROM disk and Mario Puzo's popular Mafia novel *The Last Don*. He passed through security without incident and strolled down the concourse to a passenger lounge near Gate 67. But Salgado, 36, wasn't there to catch a plane.

The freelance computer technician had stolen more than 100,000 credit-card numbers by hacking into several e-commerce databases on the Internet. It was an easy heist for Salgado, who simply used a ready-made computer-intrusion program that he found on the Web. Using a pirated e-mail account to conceal his identity, Salgado arranged to sell the information to an online fence for $260,000. The exchange was set for May 21, 1997.

As a precaution, Salgado put the stolen data on a CD-ROM, but with Hollywood-like flair he encoded the information based on a passage in Puzo's novel. Salgado's story, too, would someday make good reading: He was about to pull off one of the largest cyber-crimes in the Internet's short history. All told, the bank data that Salgado had electronically liberated from the Internet had a combined credit line of more than $1 billion.

Unfortunately for Salgado, he was walking into an FBI sting operation. The bureau had started monitoring Salgado's online machinations after being tipped off by an alert technician at one of the companies Salgado had pilfered. Initially, the FBI knew Salgado only as "SMACK," his online "handle." But when he handed over the encrypted

From *The CQ Researcher,*
April 12, 2002.

Onel de Guzman, a 23-year-old hacker from the Philippines, has been tied to the "Love Bug," an Internet "worm" that caused an estimated $10 billion in damage worldwide in 2000. Guzman, pictured with his sister, claims he did not know the bug would be so devastating.

CD to an undercover agent, the feds finally had their man. Salgado pleaded guilty to breaking into a computer network and trafficking in stolen credit cards. He was sentenced to two and a half years in prison.

Few cyber-attacks are as serious as Salgado's. Nonetheless, experts say unauthorized incursions into government and private computer systems are part of a larger — and growing — cyber-crime trend.

"This is the 21st-century equivalent of the armored-car robbery," says Computer Security Institute (CSI) Editorial Director Richard Power. "Why should the bad guys bother dealing with armored cars and police with machine guns when they can knock off a [network] server and get tens of thousands of live credit cards? This is happening all the time now. The Salgado case was just the beginning."

Riptech, Inc., an Internet security firm in Alexandria, Va., verified 128,678 cyber-attacks on just 300 of the companies it serves in the last six months of 2001. [1] To be sure, only a small fraction of these attacks successfully breached the organizations' front-line security measures. Still, 41 percent of

Riptech's clients had to patch holes in their computer-security systems after "critical" attacks. And nearly one in eight suffered at least one "emergency" attack requiring some form of data-recovery procedure. (*See graph, p. 205.*)

"Our findings strongly suggest that once companies connect their systems to the Internet, they are virtually guaranteed to suffer some form of attack activity," Riptech recently reported. "The Internet security threat is real, pervasive and perhaps more severe than previously anticipated." [2]

An annual survey conducted by the FBI and CSI confirms the explosion of cyber-crime to epidemic proportions. More than 91 percent of the corporations and U.S. government agencies that responded reported a computer-security breach in 2001, and 64 percent acknowledged financial losses because of the attacks. [3]

Some cyber-crimes, like Salgado's caper, are committed primarily for money. Others are "inside" jobs perpetrated by disgruntled employees like Timothy Lloyd, a revenge-minded network administrator in New Jersey. After being demoted and reprimanded in 1996, he wrote six lines of malicious computer code that caused $10 million in financial losses for the Omega Engineering Corp.

Lloyd was convicted of sabotaging the company's computer network and last February was sentenced to 41 months in prison and ordered to pay more than $2 million in restitution. At Lloyd's trial, an Omega executive said the firm "will never recover" from the attack. [4]

Many computer attacks are essentially online vandalism. Hackers have defaced countless Web pages, greatly embarrassing major corporations and government agencies. Hackers sometimes

How to Avoid Internet Scams

Con artists have been quick to seize upon the Internet for new ways to separate consumers from their money. According to the Federal Trade Commission (FTC), the nation's chief consumer-protection agency, the best way to avoid getting taken is to buy with a credit card from a reputable Web site, and to use common sense. The following list of the most popular scams is based on more than 285,000 fraud complaints filed last year on a centralized database utilized by hundreds of law-enforcement agencies. To report Internet scams to the FTC, call 1-877-FTC-HELP (1-877-382-4357), or use the online complaint form at www.ftc.gov/ftc/consumer.htm.

The Scam	The Bait	The Catch	The Safety Net
Internet Auctions	Shop in a "virtual marketplace" that offers a huge selection of products at great deals.	You receive an item that is less valuable than promised, or, worse yet, you receive nothing at all.	When bidding through an Internet auction, particularly for a valuable item, check out the comments about the seller and insist on paying with a credit card or through a reliable payment service such as PayPal or BillPoint.
Internet Access Services	Free money, simply for cashing a check.	You get trapped into long-term contracts for Internet access or another Web service, with big penalties for cancellation or early termination.	If a check arrives at your home or business, read both sides carefully for the conditions you're agreeing to if you cash the check. Monitor your phone bill for unexpected or unauthorized charges.
Credit-Card Fraud	View adult images online for free, just for providing your credit-card number to prove you're over 18.	Fraudulent promoters make charges using your credit-card number, or sell your card number to other online hucksters.	Share credit-card information only with a company you trust. Dispute unauthorized charges on your credit-card bill by complaining to the bank that issued the card. Federal law limits your liability to $50 in charges if your card is misused.
Modem Hijacking	Get free access to adult material and porno-graphy by downloading a "viewer" or "dialer" computer program.	The program you download surreptitiously disconnects your computer's modem from your local Internet Service Provider and reconnects you to a high-priced service overseas. You don't find out until you get a huge phone bill in the mail.	Don't download any program in order to access a so-called "free" service without reading all the disclosures carefully for cost information. Just as important, read your phone bill carefully, and challenge any charges you didn't authorize or don't understand.

Source: Federal Trade Commission

act to advance social or political views. Last year, Chinese hackers defaced a host of U.S. government Web sites after a Chinese pilot died in a collision with an American spy plane over the South China Sea. American hackers retaliated by defacing 2,500 Chinese sites. Similar cyber-warfare broke out between American and Middle Eastern hackers after the Sept. 11 terrorist attacks.

To be sure, not all hackers are viewed as criminals. So-called ethical or white-hat hackers who try to break into computer systems at the behest of security-conscious companies are often lauded for advancing the state of computer technology. But "black-hat" hackers, or "crackers," seek to wreak havoc or illegally profit from their cyberspace forays.

"Gray-hat" hackers occupy a shadowy niche somewhere in between these two extremes. While they have no qualms about illegally breaking into computer systems, gray hats generally don't pilfer or damage assets but inform their victims about the security flaws they discover.

Many hackers embrace a controversial philosophy: They show the general public how they compromised particular computer systems by posting their hacking codes, or "scripts," to public areas of the Internet. The hackers say this forces careless companies and slipshod software

The Scam	The Bait	The Catch	The Safety Net
Web Cramming	Get a free, custom-designed Web site for a 30-day trial period, with no obligation to continue.	Charges appear on your telephone bill, or you receive a separate invoice, even if you never accepted the offer or agreed to continue the service after the trial period.	Review your telephone bills, and challenge any charges you don't recognize.
Multilevel Marketing Plans/ Pyramid Schemes	Make money through the products and services you sell as well as those sold by the people you recruit into the program.	After paying to join the program and purchase inventory, you learn that your "customers" are other distributors, not the general public. Some multilevel marketing programs are actually illegal pyramid schemes. When products or services are sold only to distributors like yourself, there's no way to make money.	Avoid plans that require you to recruit distributors, buy expensive inventory or commit to a minimum sales volume.
Travel and Vacation Scams	Get a luxurious trip with lots of "extras" at a bargain-basement price.	You get lower-quality accommodations and services than advertised, or no trip at all. Or, you get hit with hidden charges or additional requirements after you've paid.	Get references on any travel company you're planning to do business with. Then, get details of the trip in writing, including the cancellation policy, before signing on.
Bogus Business Opportunities	Be your own boss and earn big bucks.	You get scammed in any number of ways. The bottom line: If it looks too good to be true, it probably is.	Talk to other people who started businesses through the same company, get all the promises in writing, and study the proposed contract carefully before signing. Get an attorney or an accountant to look at it, too.
Online Investment Scams	Make an initial investment in a day-trading system or service, and you'll quickly realize huge returns.	Big profits always mean big risk. Consumers have lost money to programs that claim to be able to predict the market with "100 percent accuracy."	Check out the promoter with state and federal securities and commodities regulators, and talk to other people who invested through the program to find out what level of risk you're assuming.
Health-Care Products/ Services	Items sold over the Internet or through other non-traditional suppliers that are "proven" to cure serious and even fatal health problems.	You put your hopes — and your money — on a marketing company's "miracle" product instead of getting the health care you really need.	Consult a health-care professional before buying any "cure-all" product that claims to treat a wide range of ailments or offers quick cures and easy solutions to serious illnesses.

manufacturers to take computer security more seriously.

Not surprisingly, many organizations don't like having their vulnerabilities publicized in this manner. Law-enforcement agencies typically don't endorse the philosophy, either.

"Thanking hackers who violate the privacy of networks or network users [by] pointing out our vulnerabilities is a little bit like sending thank-you notes to burglars for pointing out the infir-mity of our physical alarms," said Martha Stansell-Gamm, chief of the Department of Justice's Computer Crime and Intellectual Property division. [5]

Many of the hacker-crafted scripts that circulate in cyberspace are viruses or worms — programs that can corrupt computer files and spread themselves across the Internet. (*See glossary, p. 211.*) Novice hackers known as "script kiddies" unleash thousands of viruses and worms every year, often without

realizing the potential impact of their actions. Onel de Guzman, the 23-year-old Filipino hacker who has been tied to the "Love Bug," claimed he had no idea the worm would be so devastating. It caused an estimated $10 billion in damage worldwide in May 2000. [6]

Con artists, meanwhile, are using the Web to perpetrate various types of fraud schemes in record numbers, according to law-enforcement officials. "The number of [fraud] complaints has increased steadily over the last two or three years," says Timothy Healy, director of the Internet Fraud Complaint Center (IFCC), operated by the FBI and the National White Collar Crime Center.

Internet auction fraud was the most frequently reported type of complaint handled by the IFCC last year, according to Healy. Fraudsters can rig Internet auctions in a number of ways, such as using shills to drive up the bidding process. Con men also use the Internet to perpetrate a wide variety of investment scams, bogus e-commerce opportunities and confidence rackets. "It's amazing what's out there," Healy says.

One of the most prevalent and insidious Internet-assisted scams is identity theft — stealing credit card and Social Security numbers and other personal information. Some identity thieves hack into e-commerce Web sites to pilfer such data. Others set up bogus Internet sites of their own to dupe unwitting consumers into revealing their credit-card numbers.

Armed with stolen identities, thieves can perpetrate a variety of crimes, from opening bogus bank accounts and writing bad checks to taking out car loans and mortgages in their victims' names.

Under federal law, consumers who use credit cards are liable only for the first $50 of fraudulent charges made on their accounts, and many credit-card companies even waive that amount. Still, identity-theft victims typically incur more than $1,000 in out-of-pocket expenses trying to restore their mangled credit ratings, according

FBI agent Doris Gardner heads the bureau's computer crimes unit in Charlotte, N.C., one of several throughout the country. The unit focuses on both e-commerce fraud and cyber-predators who target children.

AP Photo

to the Federal Trade Commission. (Debit-card purchases do not receive automatic fraud protection.) [7]

Lenders are hit even harder. Identity theft cost financial institutions some $2.4 billion in direct losses and related mopping-up expenses in 2000, according to Celent Communications, a Boston consulting firm. [8]

Controversies abound over how best to deal with Internet hucksters, hackers and virus writers. Some policymakers, wary of Internet-facilitated terrorist attacks, are calling for tough new laws to prevent computer crimes — including life sentences for some offenses (*see p. 214*). Others fear that such initiatives will trample on civil liberties. Still others want legislation to

make software companies such as Microsoft liable for damages caused by computer-security failures.

As the debate rages, here is a closer look at some of the key questions being asked:

Is it safe for consumers and merchants to do business online?

Only about 40 percent of all adult Internet users in the United States use the Web to shop or pay bills, according to the Census Bureau. [9] Many Americans eschew online shopping, banking and other types of Internet commerce because they fear having their credit card or Social Security numbers stolen, numerous studies have found. For example, 85 percent of the Internet users polled recently by Washington-based SWR Worldwide cited security as the biggest deterrent to e-commerce. A poll by GartnerG2, a Stamford, Conn., firm, put the number worried about security at 60 percent. [10]

According to Gartner, U.S. e-commerce fraud losses in 2001 exceeded $700 million, constituting about 1.14 percent of the $61.8 billion in total online sales. That ratio was 19 times higher than the fraud rate for traditional in-store transactions, which hovered at less than one-tenth of 1 percent during the same time period, Gartner said. Since the e-commerce era began in the mid-1990s, Gartner estimates that one in every six online consumers has been victimized by credit-card fraud, and one in 12 has been hit with identity theft.

"We're not going to see low fraud rates like we have in the brick-and-mortar world until we make some serious changes in the way that online business is conducted," says Avivah Litan, Gartner's vice president for research.

"There are some big issues to deal with."

For merchants, the Internet is a double-edged sword. While they can broaden their customer bases and increase their revenues by going online, merchants also expose themselves to cyber-criminals.

Some law-enforcement officials concede that they can't keep pace with the number of e-commerce fraud scams already on the Internet. "There's no way that we can police the entire Web with the small staff that we have at this agency," says an official at the FTC, which investigates Internet fraud. "We go after things that are particularly egregious or pernicious, but we really have to strategically target our limited resources."

Other experts downplay the risks associated with online commerce. "I think we're doing quite well in terms of protecting buyers and sellers in the virtual marketplace," says Emily Hackett, executive director of the Internet Alliance, a Washington-based trade group. "The vast majority of online transactions are carried out without any problems at all."

Consumers can protect themselves when shopping online (as well as in traditional brick-and-mortar stores) by using a credit card. Under federal law, consumers are liable for only the first $50 of fraudulent charges made on their credit-card accounts, and many card issuers waive that amount. Users of debit cards, checks or other payment methods are not necessarily protected. Consequently, more than 95 percent of all e-commerce transactions are made with credit cards, Gartner says.

Credit-card companies are liable for fraudulent in-store transactions accompanied by signed (albeit forged) receipts. However, merchants are typically on the hook for any transactions they process without validating the purchaser's signature — which is rarely done over the Internet. Consequently, merchants — not consumers or

Internet Fraud Complaints

Auction and communications fraud and non-delivery of merchandise are the most common fraud complaints reported to the Internet Fraud Complaint Center (IFCC.) Losses were especially high with identity theft and investment fraud.

Complaint Type	% of Complainants Who Reported Dollar Loss	Average (median) $ Loss per Typical Complaint
Auction fraud	78.4%	$230
Non-delivery (of purchases or payment)	73.8	225
Credit card/debit card fraud	58.3	207
Confidence fraud	63.1	339
Nigerian letter scam	01.1	3,000
Investment fraud	69.1	469
Check fraud	56.4	194
Business fraud	55.8	192
Identity theft	14.4	520
Communications fraud	78.7	145

Source: "IFCC Annual Internet 'Fraud Report,'" National White Collar Crime Center and FBI

credit-card companies — bear most of the costs of e-commerce fraud.

Most Internet merchants utilize a fraud-prevention program. But programs vary widely in effectiveness and customer convenience. Many small merchants screen their online orders manually, flagging those with unusually high dollar volumes, suspicious billing information or other indicators of fraud. Large merchants often use sophisticated computer software programs to identify potentially fraudulent transactions. Best Buy Co., a consumer electronics retailer, can program its system to red-flag or automatically reject any online orders that originate from countries with high fraud rates.

Many Internet merchants also protect their online sales through the Secure Socket Layer protocol, or SSL. This technology encrypts consumers' credit-card numbers and other personal information so that it can be safely transmitted to merchants' databases. But

while SSL allows consumers and merchants to exchange payment information through a secure "electronic pipe," the technology does not protect the database. And since all merchants don't encrypt their customers' data, they provide juicy targets for ill-intentioned hackers. Meredith Outwater, an e-commerce fraud expert at Celent Communications, says fraud-minded hackers constantly surf the Internet looking for these kinds of opportunities.

"Merchants aren't securing their servers enough," Outwater says. "There are merchants who have their [customers'] credit-card data just sitting on servers, waiting to be hacked. That happens more often than data getting intercepted in transmission."

Nonetheless, Kenneth Kerr, a senior analyst at Gartner, does not consider e-commerce to be riskier than shopping in traditional brick-and-mortar stores. "It takes a sophisticated thief to hack into a Web server," Kerr said. "It is a lot simpler to steal identity information in a physical environment like a restaurant." [11]

Many computer-security experts say that consumers should avoid doing business with small e-commerce merchants. "Stay away from the mom-and-pop e-tailers, because they typically don't have the resources to implement a comprehensive, layered approach to security," says Victor Keong, a Toronto-based business consultant at Deloitte & Touche. "Merchants that rely only on one layer of security are very vulnerable."

Alfred Hunger, vice president of engineering at SecurityFocus, in San Mateo, Calif., agrees that there is a wide range of security among Internet merchants. "The publicly held e-tailers take [security] much more seriously than the mom-and-pop shops," Hunger says. "The small shops still represent a significant risk."

Should computer network security problems be publicly disclosed?

Hackers and virus writers regularly cause problems in cyberspace by exploiting flaws, or "bugs," in software programs. The computer-security community has long debated the wisdom of informing the general public about these vulnerabilities. Some experts argue that software security bugs should be publicly disclosed as soon as they are detected. Advocates of "full disclosure" say that by publicizing software vulnerabilities immediately, computer users can protect themselves against hackers and cyber-criminals who will inevitably discover and exploit the flaws. Full disclosure also compels vendors to promptly engineer and disseminate software "patches" to fix computer-security problems engendered by their flawed products, these advocates say.

"I'm very big on disclosure because it advances the security posture of everyone," Keong says. "The earlier that [software vendors] get the patches out there, the better."

Salt Lake City-based BugNet is one of several firms that hunts for software flaws and posts warnings about vulnerable systems on its Web site. Eric Bowden, BugNet's general manager, says that such disclosures get software companies to address computer security problems. Bowden denies that his bug hunters are out to embarrass, vilify or extort money from software giants such as Microsoft, as some critics contend.

"BugNet is very solutions-oriented," Bowden says. "We're not in it to point fingers or play the blame-game with [software] developers as much as we're trying to find solutions to serious problems."

Unlike other bug-hunting organizations, BugNet does not immediately publicize detailed information about every software vulnerability it finds. Depending on the type of the bug at hand, BugNet may or may not give a vendor time to engineer a patch before posting a vulnerability warning, Bowden says. Bugs that pose only minor problems usually get posted immediately, he concedes. However, BugNet typically delays publicizing serious security flaws if vendors agree to develop workable patches, he says.

"It's important to get [vulnerability] information out there early, but I also believe in giving vendors enough time to develop some kind of work-around for security bugs," Bowden says. "You can cause a lot of damage by calling attention to a security bug before a patch is available."

Moreover, unlike some other bug-hunting organizations, BugNet does not publish "exploit scripts" — step-by-step instructions that hackers can use to exploit security vulnerabilities. Indeed, novice hackers known as "script kiddies" often download these ready-made scripts and run them without realizing the consequences of their actions, Bowden notes.

"There are millions of script kiddies out there, and I don't want to arm

them with the tools to do all kinds of destructive things," Bowden says.

Microsoft couldn't agree more. Scott Culp, manager of Microsoft's security response center, blasted the full-disclosure policy in an essay published last October.

"It's simply indefensible for the security community to continue arming cyber-criminals," Culp wrote. "We can and should discuss security vulnerabilities, but we should be smart, prudent and responsible in the way we do it." [12]

Microsoft advocates a policy of full disclosure but not full exposure. "Our policy on disclosure of security problems is intended to keep our customers safe," a spokesperson says. "If we were to publicize a problem without being able to offer a solution, that would make potential attackers aware of the hole but not give our customers a way to protect themselves."

Last fall, in a controversial move, Microsoft formed an alliance with several bug-hunting firms in an effort to curtail the publication of software-security flaws. At Microsoft's request, the firms agreed to wait at least 30 days before publicizing detailed information about any security-related bugs they discover.

"We want to create an atmosphere where people are more responsible with the disclosure of vulnerability information," said Eddie Schwartz, an analyst at Guardent Inc., a Waltham, Mass., firm that joined the alliance. "Right now, it is way too ad hoc." [13]

Other security experts are less enthusiastic about the alliance's efforts.

"I think the 30-day grace period is just another way for Microsoft and others to once again remove themselves from their responsibility for developing quality software before it hits the streets," said John Cowan Jr., of Louisville, Ky.-based Caldwell Industries Inc. [14]

Bruce Schneier, chief technology officer at Counterpane Internet Security Inc., in Cupertino, Calif., agrees.

"Microsoft's motives in promoting bug secrecy are obvious: It's a whole lot easier to squelch security information than it is to fix problems or design products securely in the first place," Schneier said. "Disclosure doesn't create security vulnerabilities — programmers create them, and they remain until other programmers find and remove them." [15]

Should software companies be liable for Internet security breaches?

Hackers and virus writers frequently launch attacks over the Internet by exploiting security flaws in commercial software. The Boston consulting company @Stake found that 70 percent of the security gaps that plagued its customers' computer networks last year were due to software bugs. [16]

Many computer-security experts say that software manufacturers know about most of these flaws before they put their products on the market. Mark Minasi, an investigative journalist who specializes in technology issues, claims that 90 percent of the bugs that consumers report to software vendors were already known to the vendors at the time of release. [17] Yet, many studies have found that businesses and government agencies that have been attacked via these types of software security gaps have incurred billions of dollars in damages. [18]

There are no laws requiring software vendors to manufacture hack-proof or virus-resistant products. Likewise, no software company has ever been held responsible for damages stemming from a known security flaw in a product. Software vendors have long avoided this type of liability by inserting disclaimers in the so-called end-user licensing agreements (EULAs) that customers must consent to before using a product. In general, EULAs require users to assume all risks associated with the product. The EULA for Microsoft's Windows 2000 operating

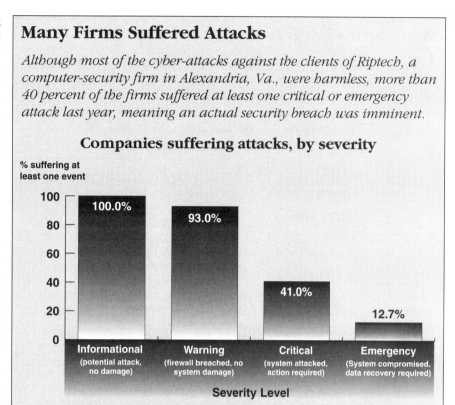

Many Firms Suffered Attacks

Although most of the cyber-attacks against the clients of Riptech, a computer-security firm in Alexandria, Va., were harmless, more than 40 percent of the firms suffered at least one critical or emergency attack last year, meaning an actual security breach was imminent.

Companies suffering attacks, by severity

% suffering at least one event

- Informational (potential attack, no damage): 100.0%
- Warning (firewall breached, no system damage): 93.0%
- Critical (system attacked, action required): 41.0%
- Emergency (System compromised, data recovery required): 12.7%

Severity Level

Source: "Riptech Internet Security Threat Report," January 2002

system is typical of this type of liability waiver. It states, in part:

"In no event shall Microsoft or its suppliers be liable for any damages whatsoever . . . arising out of the use of or inability to use the software product, even if Microsoft has been advised of the possibility of such damages." [19]

Given the crucial role that software plays in the modern world, many computer-security experts say it's high time that software companies take responsibility for producing hack-prone products.

"Software is deployed in places where it's absolutely critical for safety, like in much of our infrastructure," says Hunger of SecurityFocus. "It's totally unreasonable to give software vendors immunity from liability when every other industry — the Fords and the Boeings of the world — are held to a much, much higher standard."

Some legal experts predict that consumers will use the courts to force

software vendors to accept liability for unsafe products, as occurred with the tobacco industry. "I think where you're going to see reform come is through lawsuits," said Jeffrey Hunker, dean of the H. John Heinz III School of Public Policy and Management at Carnegie Mellon University in Pittsburgh. "So much of our economic structure depends on computers that it's unsustainable to hold software companies blameless." [20]

Michael Erbschloe, vice president for research at Computer Economics, in Carlsbad, Calif., says the modern world "doesn't have any choice economically" not to require secure software. "People are getting very tired of the hack attacks and the lax security," Erbschloe adds. "The economic consequences of this run very high, and go to many levels."

Since 1995, computer viruses and worms have caused more than $54 billion in economic damages, Erbschloe

Many Firms Keep Mum About Attacks

A significant percentage of the firms and organizations that suffer security incidents don't report them because they fear negative publicity, according to a recent survey.

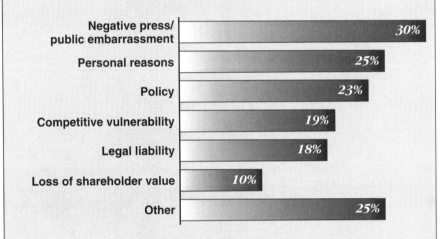

Why security incidents are not reported
(by percentage of firms reporting)

Negative press/public embarrassment	30%
Personal reasons	25%
Policy	23%
Competitive vulnerability	19%
Legal liability	18%
Loss of shareholder value	10%
Other	25%

Note: Includes multiple responses; 4,500 security professionals were polled.

Source: InformationWeek, "Global Information Security Survey, 2001," September 2001

estimates. That figure, he notes, does not include the damages inflicted by other types of cyber-crimes, such as computer-facilitated credit-card theft. [21]

A recent National Academy of Sciences report declares that the state of the nation's cyber-security is "far worse than what known best practices" could provide. The report says that "market incentives" have failed to push software companies and other private-sector interests toward creating a secure computing climate. Consequently, the report recommends that policymakers consider "legislative responses" to improving cyber-security, including making vendors liable for security breaches. [22]

But Mark Bohannon, general counsel and vice president for government affairs at the Software and Information Industry Association, says it would be impossible to hold software vendors responsible for security breach-

es, because software programs must interact with myriad other computer network systems.

"The notion of holding software vendors liable for security breaches when their products must interoperate with other things that they don't even control just boggles my mind," Bohannon says. "The people who are making these proposals really need to carefully examine how the industry really works."

Microsoft continues to oppose efforts to make software vendors liable for security breaches. However, CEO Bill Gates says security is now the company's highest priority. In a Jan. 15 e-mail to all Microsoft employees, Gates launched the company's "trustworthy computing" initiative, which he described as "more important than any other part of our work. Our products should emphasize security right out of

the box, and we must constantly refine and improve that security as threats evolve. Eventually, our software should be so fundamentally secure that customers never even worry about it." [23]

Gates acknowledged that in the past, Microsoft's biggest priority was adding new features and "functionality" to its products. That can no longer be the case, Gates wrote. "All those great features won't matter unless customers trust our software," he declared. "So now, when we face a choice between adding features and resolving security issues, we need to choose security." [24]

To that end, Microsoft sent every one of its more than 9,000 software developers through advanced security-training courses earlier this year. But many security experts question whether Microsoft will follow through.

"Issuing a statement doesn't solve any problems," said Schneier of Counterpane Internet Security. "Microsoft is notorious for treating security as a public-relations problem. Gates said all the right words. If he does that, it will be a sea change. I'd like to believe him, but I need proof. [25]

BugNet's Bowden offered a similar assessment. "It may or may not be lip service," Bowden said. "But it's obvious that they have been bloodied up enough by critics who claimed that their products were too insecure." ■

BACKGROUND

Early Hackers

Many of today's computer-facilitated crimes were inspired, in part, by a technology-centered counterculture that emerged in the United States in the late 1950s. Led by ambitious students at the Massachusetts Institute of Technology and other top

Chronology

1960s-1970s
The first hackers advance computer technology, sometimes with illegal activities.

1961
Hackers at MIT known as the Tech Model Railroad Club write advanced programming code for an early minicomputer.

1971
Esquire magazine publishes detailed instructions for "phone-phreaking," or making free long-distance calls.

1972
California phone-phreaker John Draper ("Captain Crunch") uses a toy whistle from a cereal box to produce the 2,600-hertz tone needed to make free long-distance calls.

1975
Hackers produce one of the first personal computers, the Altair 8800.

1977
Hackers Stephen Wozniak and Steven Jobs form Apple Computer.

1980s
Hackers help launch the personal computer revolution. Congress cracks down on computer criminals.

1981
Philadelphia hacker Pat Riddle ("Captain Zap") uses a pre-Internet computer network called ARPANET to break into computer systems at the Pentagon and White House.

1983
"War Games," a movie about a teenage hacker who nearly starts a nuclear war, is released. Real-life hacker Kevin Mitnick, 17, is arrested in Los Angeles for hacking into the Pentagon.

1984
2600: The Hacker Quarterly, is founded.

1986
The Computer Fraud and Abuse Act (CFAA), the first federal computer-crime law, makes it a felony to enter computer systems operated by the government or federally insured financial institutions.

1988
Cornell University graduate student Robert Morris creates an experimental computer program, later dubbed a "worm," that cripples thousands of computer systems. The Computer Emergency Response Team (CERT) is formed.

1989
Mitnick is arrested again and convicted of stealing software and long-distance access codes from two corporations. After a year in prison, he resumes hacking.

1990s
Cyber-crime explodes with the development of the Internet.

1993
Hackers discover myriad vulnerabilities in Microsoft's new Windows NT Web server operating system.

1994
Music student Richard Price ("Datastream Cowboy") is charged with hacking into NASA and Korean Atomic Research Institute computers.

1994
Russian hacker Vladimir Levin breaks into Citibank's computer system and steals more than $10 million from customers' accounts. Levin is eventually convicted of bank and wire fraud.

1995
Tsutomu Shimomura helps the FBI track down Mitnick, who is imprisoned for four years while he awaits trial. Hackers deface popular Web sites, including *The New York Times*, to protest Mitnick's imprisonment. He eventually pleads guilty to seven counts and is released in January 2000 but prohibited from using computers and mobile phones.

1999
The "Melissa" virus shuts down computers around the world. David L. Smith, a New Jersey programmer, gets five years in prison for releasing the malicious code.

2000-Present
Hackers and virus writers continue to cause billions in damages. The Sept. 11 attacks against the United States spark fears of cyber-terrorism.

2000
A 15-year-old hacker known as "Mafiaboy" cripples popular e-commerce sites. The attacks cost some $1.7 billion in lost sales and damages. Hackers access Microsoft's proprietary source code.

2001-2002
Hackers deface pro-Muslim Web sites in the wake of the Sept. 11 terrorist attacks. The White House orders government agencies to remove certain information from public Web sites, fearing it could aid cyber-terrorists.

A Tale of Two Hackers

K evin Mitnick called himself the "Condor," after the 1975 thriller about a man on the run. It was a suitable alias: At the time of his arrest in 1995, he was the most wanted computer hacker in cyberspace history.

Mitnick, now 38, is out of prison and living in California. His hacking spree cost his victims tens of millions of dollars over the course of two decades. It all began in 1981, when Mitnick and two other "phone phreakers" stole passwords and operating manuals for the Pacific Bell telephone company's computer system and used the information to hack into the system and get free calls. The three were arrested after a jilted girlfriend turned them in to the police. Mitnick, then 17, was placed on probation.

In 1983, Mitnick gained national notoriety by hacking into a Pentagon computer via the ARPNET, a pre-Internet computer network operated by the Defense Department. This time, he was sentenced to six months in a juvenile detention facility. After his release, Mitnick put custom license plates on his car that read "X HACKER." But his hacking days were far from over.

In 1988, he and a friend, Lenny DiCicco, hacked into the Digital Equipment Corp., a Palo Alto, Calif., software company. The company discovered the incursion immediately, but the FBI couldn't pinpoint the source of the attacks. Anticipating the surveillance, Mitnick had hacked into the phone system and scrambled the source of his computer's modem calls.

The electronic subterfuge worked — until DiCicco, under pressure, confessed to the FBI. Mitnick was accused of stealing $1 million worth of proprietary software and causing $4 million in damages. He eventually pleaded guilty to two charges and was sentenced to a year in prison. Under the terms of his release, he was told to stay out of trouble. He didn't.

The FBI came looking for Mitnick in 1992 in conjunction with yet another computer break-in. But before they could arrest him, he vanished. Still, it didn't take long for the FBI to pick up his trail. Later that year, a caller purporting to be a law-enforcement officer asked the California Department of Motor Vehicles (DMV) office in Sacramento to fax a photograph of a confidential police informant to a non-government phone number in Los Angeles. A suspicious DMV official traced the number to a Kinko's copy shop. Police rushed to the shop, but the suspect bolted across a parking lot and disappeared around the corner, dropping the documents as he fled. Fingerprints confirmed it was Mitnick.

Mitnick's undoing began on Christmas Day in 1994, when he broke into files belonging to Tsutomu Shimomura, a scientist at the San Diego Supercomputer Center. Shimomura began monitoring Mitnick's movements through cyberspace as the outlaw hacker broke into myriad computer systems around the world. Shimomura eventually traced Mitnick to an apartment in Raleigh, N.C. The FBI moved in on Feb. 15, 1995.

After more than two years on the run, the Condor was again in custody. Mitnick faced a multitude of charges, including 23 counts of computer and wire fraud. He pleaded guilty to one count and was extradited back to California, where he was hit with an additional 25 charges. Prosecutors argued that Mitnick had cost his victims more than $290 million during his two-year hacking spree. [1]

To prepare his defense in the complicated case, Mitnick waived his right to a speedy trial. As a result, he sat in prison for four years awaiting trial. The hacker underground protested Mitnick's long pre-trial detention by defacing some of the most popular Web sites on the Internet, including Yahoo! and *The New York Times*.

On March 16, 1999, Mitnick pleaded guilty to five felony counts of computer and wire fraud and was sentenced to 46 months in prison, with time off for months served. He received an additional 22 months for crimes committed in North Carolina. To date, Mitnick's composite 68-month prison sentence is the longest yet imposed on a computer hacker.

Mitnick was released from California's Lompoc federal penitentiary on Jan. 21, 2000. Under his unusually stringent parole conditions, he is prohibited from using a computer or cell phone until Jan. 20, 2003.

universities, it was grounded in a belief that technology should be liberated from the control of governments and private industry.

The technology junkies who spearheaded this revolution were known as "hackers." Back then, the term was a laudatory moniker bestowed on people who were skilled at improving the capabilities of computer systems.

To be sure, the early hackers sometimes ran afoul of the law. However, they were motivated primarily by the promise of new technologies, not the pursuit of ill-gotten gains. The early hackers wanted to advance computer technology beyond the level of hulking, room-sized machines and punch cards. They often carried out their electronic experiments surreptitiously and without authorization. Then as now, they justified their unlawful actions on the grounds that they were working for the betterment of everyone.

Steven Levy, chief technology writer for *Newsweek*, dubbed this no-tion the "hacker ethic." In a seminal book on the subject, Levy described the mindset of the hacker community in the late 1950s:

"Access to computers should be unlimited and total. All information should be free. You can create art and beauty on a computer. Computers can change your life for the better." According to Levy, bona fide hackers "believe that essential lessons can be learned . . . from taking things apart, seeing how they work, and using this knowledge

Testifying before a Senate committee hearing on cyber-crime shortly after his release from prison, Mitnick sounded an ominous warning: "My motivation was a quest for knowledge, the intellectual challenge, the thrill and the escape from reality," he said in March 2000. "If somebody has the time, money and motivation, they can get into any computer." [2]

Adrian Lamo: Hero or Criminal?

Adrian Lamo has hacked into some of the largest corporations in the world, but unlike Kevin Mitnick, he's never been arrested. After he breaches a computer network, Lamo, 21, informs his "victims" and offers to help fix the flaws he finds for free. Some computer-security experts praise so-called ethical hackers like Lamo.

"Ethical hackers who don't do damage and push the state of the art in security [provide] a valuable service," said Jonathan Couch Sr., a network security engineer at Sytex Inc., a Doylestown, Pa., technology-consulting firm. "The government needs to have the discretion not to prosecute." [3]

But Marcus Ranum, chief technology officer at NFR Security, in Rockville, Md., calls Lamo a "sociopath" whose behavior is indefensible.

"It's against the law — how much more cut and dried can you get?" said Ranum. "If society was comfortable with what he's doing, they'd change the law." [4]

Lamo himself doesn't put much stock in society's norms and conventions. He lives largely out of a backpack, spending most of his time in San Francisco and the suburbs of Washington, D.C. Sometimes he stays with friends; other times he sleeps in abandoned buildings. Armed with his laptop, he does much of his hacking from Web kiosks at all-night copy shops and Internet cafes.

Adrian Lamo, left, and Kevin Mitnick

WBG Links

Lamo prefers the vagabond lifestyle because he likes to put himself in situations where "interesting things" can happen. "All the interesting things that have happened to me have been the result of synchronicity and organized chaos," he said. "I do what I do; there's no particular motive I can describe." [5]

Although Lamo has yet to be prosecuted for his unauthorized forays, one of his recent victims hasn't been so quick to thank him. Earlier this year, Lamo hacked into a cache of confidential information at *The New York Times*, but the newspaper has not sought Lamo's assistance in plugging the hole in its network. On the contrary, the company is contemplating pressing charges. "We're still investigating and exploring all of the options," *Times* spokesperson Christine Mohan says.

Lamo acknowledges that it's illegal to hack into a computer system without permission. But unauthorized hacking is not necessarily wrong, he says.

Obviously, [no organization] wants to be compromised and it's never a one-hundred-percent pleasant experience," he said. "But I'd like to see more receptivity to processing compromises that don't result in damage, without necessarily destroying the life of the person involved." [6]

---

[1] Cited in Richard Power, *Tangled Web: Tales of Digital Crime From the Shadows of Cyberspace*, Que/MacMillan, 2000.

[2] Quoted in John Schwartz, "Hacker Gives a Hill How-To," *The Washington Post*, March 3, 2000. Mitnick testified before the Senate Committee on Governmental Affairs.

[3] Quoted in Kevin Poulsen, "Panel Debates Hacker Amnesty," *SecurityFocus*, March 25, 2002.

[4] *Ibid.*

[5] Quoted in Kevin Poulsen, "Lamo's Adventures in WorldCom," *Security-Focus*, Dec. 5, 2001.

[6] *Ibid.*

---

to create new and even more interesting things." Hackers also "resent any person, physical barrier, or law" that stands in the way of this objective, a philosophy that continues to thrive in the hacker community today. [26]

"As long as the human spirit is alive, there will always be hackers," said Eric Corley, a.k.a. Emmanuel Goldstein, an editor at *2600: The Hacker Quarterly*.* "We may have a hell of a fight on our hands if we continue to be imprisoned and victimized for exploring, but that

will do anything but stop us. I'm the first to say that people who cause damage should be punished, but I really don't think prison should be considered for something like this unless the offender is a true risk to society." [27]

---

* Corley borrowed his computer handle from the name of a character in George Orwell's futuristic novel *1984*, which warned that the government, or "Big Brother," would take over society if permitted. The character Emmanuel Goldstein fought the system.

But computer-security experts generally reject such reasoning. "Hacking is a felony — for good reason," said Charles C. Palmer, of IBM. "Some [hackers] . . . think it's harmless [if they] don't do anything besides go in and look around. But if a stranger came into your house, looked through everything, touched several items, and left — after building a small, out-of-the-way door to be sure he could easily enter again — would you consider that harmless?" [28]

Phone "Phreaks"

The early hackers did not limit their technological forays to computers. In the 1960s and '70s, many hackers tried to exploit telephone systems. Known as phone "phreaks," they made devices known as "blue boxes" that allowed them to make free long-distance calls. The boxes could duplicate the high-pitched, 2,600-hertz tone that AT&T used to control its long-distance switching system.

Blue boxes quickly became hot commodities in the United States. Two enterprising phone phreaks, Stephen Wozniak and Steven Jobs, the future founders of Apple Computer, pedaled blue boxes in college dormitories. Another phreak, John Draper, discovered that he could hack into the phone system using a toy whistle from a box of Cap'n Crunch breakfast cereal.

"Cap'n Crunch," as Draper was called, quickly became a legend in the phreaking community. He outfitted his Volkswagen van with a high-tech blue box and roamed the highways in California in search of isolated telephone booths from which he could practice his craft. He spent hours at these booths, "sending calls around the world, bouncing them off communications satellites, leapfrogging them from the West Coast to London to Moscow to Sydney and then back again." [29]

The phone-phreak community was never very large, numbering a few hundred die-hards, at most. In 1971, they formed an alliance with the Yippies, an anarchist, anti-capitalist, anti-Vietnam War group. The Yippies' chief agitator, Abbie Hoffman, believed that phreaking could play an important role in fomenting a social revolution. Together, the groups published an underground newsletter that provided detailed phone-phreaking instructions to about 1,000 subscribers around the world.

Several widely circulated magazine articles brought the phone-phreaking craze to the attention of the general public — and the police. In June 1972, *Ramparts* magazine printed schematic diagrams for ripping off the Bell Telephone Co. Police seized copies of the magazine from newsstands, which helped to drive it out of business.

The *Ramparts* article and a similar piece in *Esquire* sparked a crackdown on phone phreakers. The police were especially eager to take down "Cap'n Crunch," who was convicted on federal wire-fraud charges and sentenced to four months in prison. He made good use of his time.

"Jails are the perfect venue for transferring hacking knowledge," Draper later wrote. "Inmates have a lot of spare time on their hands, and a patient teacher can teach just about anyone anything, given enough time." [30]

Hacking With PCs

The personal computer revolution of the early 1980s ushered in a new hacking era. Hackers equipped their PCs with modems and began communicating via a rudimentary electronic bulletin-board system, the precursor to modern e-mail. Hackers used bulletin boards to gossip, trade tech tips and exchange software — and also to traffic stolen computer passwords and credit-card numbers.

Hackers also began to break into online computer systems. Pat Riddle, a hacker in Philadelphia, used the ARPANET — a pre-Internet computer network — to hack into computers at the Pentagon, the White House and other high-profile institutions. At the time, the ARPANET was still controlled by the government. Riddle, whose online handle was "Captain Zap," also used his PC to pilfer more than $500,000 in merchandise from several large computer companies.

The FBI caught up with Riddle in 1981. There was no comprehensive computer-fraud law at the time, so Riddle, then 24, was indicted for stealing property and telephone service. Incredibly, he plea-bargained his way to a $1,000 fine and probation after the high-priced legal team retained by his prominent family warned prosecutors that "no jury will ever understand" the technical evidence needed to convict him. [31]

Meanwhile, hacking groups began to pop up everywhere. The U.S-based Legion of Doom and a German group, Chaos Computer Club, were started in 1984 along with *2600: The Hacker Quarterly.*

Anti-Hacking Law

The proliferation of hacker clubs, the Captain Zap incident and several other high-profile computer-intrusion cases caused great trepidation among policymakers and law-enforcement officials. The media and the entertainment industry did much to fuel — or exaggerate, according to some critics — the hacker threat and mystique. The 1983 movie "War Games," for example, portrayed a teenage hacker who nearly triggered a nuclear war by breaking into Defense Department computers. The movie led to a spike in modem sales — as well as a congressional inquiry to see if the Hollywood scenario could really happen.

In Washington, lawmakers scrambled to address the threats posed by computer crime, although some critics said they overreacted because of the hyped media coverage. In 1986, Congress passed the Computer Fraud and Abuse Act, the first federal computer-crime law. The CFAA made it a felony, punishable by up to five years in prison, to enter computer systems operated by the federal government or federally insured financial institutions.

Speaking the Language of Cyber-Crime

Black Hat — a hacker who breaks into a computer system to steal or destroy information. White Hat, or "ethical," hackers are hired by corporations or government agencies to look for vulnerabilities in computer systems. Somewhere in between are Gray Hats, who unlawfully break into systems and then tell their victims how they did it. Black Hats and Gray Hats are sometimes called crackers.

Bug — an unintended design flaw in a software program that may cause a computer to malfunction or crash. A security bug, according to software giant Microsoft, is "a flaw in a product that makes it infeasible — even when using the product properly — to prevent an attacker from usurping privileges on the user's system, regulating its operation, compromising data on it, or assuming ungranted trust."

Distributed Denial of Service (DDoS) Attack — an attack that renders a Web site unavailable to Internet users by overloading it with high volumes of data.

Firewall — a hardware or software device designed to keep hackers from accessing a computer system.

Hacker — originally, a laudatory term used to describe highly skilled computer programmers. Today, it usually describes people who break into computer systems to steal or destroy data.

Password Cracker — a software program that helps hackers gain access to a computer system by automatically sending thousands or millions of words — usually taken from dictionaries — against password fields.

Phreak — someone who hacks into telephone systems, usually to make free long-distance calls.

Script — A computer code used by a hacker.

Social Engineering — a method by which hackers trick or coerce gullible computer users into revealing their passwords or other confidential information that can be used to gain access to their systems. Often done with a phone call to an unsuspecting administrative aide.

Trojan Horse — a seemingly innocuous program containing code designed to damage, destroy or alter files in an unsuspecting user's computer; normally spread by e-mail attachments.

Virus — a self-replicating computer program that spreads itself across a network, usually via an e-mail attachment. Some viruses are designed to damage files or otherwise interfere with normal computing functions, while others don't do anything but spread themselves around. Computer worms differ from viruses in that they do not spread through e-mail attachments, but rather by exploiting software flaws common to individual computers linked to a network.

The law also made it a crime to exchange computer passwords with the intent of committing interstate fraud. The provision was designed to outlaw the "pirate" bulletin boards that hackers often used to exchange pilfered confidential information.

The first hacker prosecuted under the new measure was Robert T. Morris, a 22-year-old graduate student at Cornell University. Morris wrote an experimental, self-replicating computer program called a "worm" and on Nov. 2, 1988, injected it into the newly launched Internet. A flaw in the program allowed the worm to reproduce itself far faster than Morris had anticipated, and it shut down or seriously crippled thousands of computer systems at universities, military installations and medical research facilities, mainly in the United States.

Dealing with Morris' worm cost millions of dollars. Morris was convicted, fined $10,050 and sentenced to three years of probation and 400 hours of community service. Critics said he got off too easily, but the trial judge maintained the light sentence was appropriate because he had only been experimenting and meant no harm.

The Morris worm demonstrated that the Internet had several gaping security flaws. Over the next few years, it was inundated by worms and viruses, another type of malicious computer code. By 1992, some 1,300 computer viruses existed — a 420 percent increase from just two years earlier. While the vast majority were harmless, a few caused tremendous damage. [32]

One of the worst was unleashed on March 26, 1999. The virus spread over the Internet through an e-mail attachment that, when opened, forwarded itself to 50 other people in a victim's e-mail address book. The multiplying effect of the virus shut down thousands of e-mail systems around the world. It was dubbed "Melissa," a name that investigators found embedded in the malicious code.

Federal authorities quickly tracked Melissa to David L. Smith, a 30-year-old computer programmer in New Jersey who did contract work for AT&T and Microsoft. Smith admitted that he created and unleashed the virus, named after an exotic dancer he had met in Florida.

Smith pleaded guilty to federal and state charges in December 1999 and was sentenced to five years in prison. Experts estimated that Melissa had inflicted $400 million in actual damages.

At Smith's sentencing, Robert J. Cleary, the U.S. attorney who prosecuted the case, said the virus "demonstrated the danger that business, government and personal computer users everywhere face in our technological society."

Hackers and malicious code writers have continued to vandalize cyberspace. In February 2000, a hacker crippled Yahoo! and several other popular e-commerce Web sites by bombarding them with thousands of simultaneous data requests. The so-called distributed denial of service (DDoS) attacks prevented customers from accessing the sites for several hours. Experts estimated that the attacks cost more than $1.7 billion in lost sales and damages.

Law-enforcement officials eventually linked the attacks to a 15-year-old Canadian who called himself "Mafiaboy." On Jan. 18, 2001, the teen hacker pleaded guilty to 56 charges, including mischief and illegal use of a computer service. He was sentenced to eight months in a youth detention center and ordered to donate $250 to charity. Under Canadian law, the maximum sentence he could have received was two years detention.

"The [Mafiaboy] case demonstrates . . . that the entire Internet is vulnerable to the machinations of a 15-year-old kid," said Mark Rasch, vice-president for cyber-law at Global Integrity Corp., in Reston, Va. "It demonstrates that the Internet, for security purposes, is only as strong as its weakest link." [33] ∎

CURRENT SITUATION

Cyber-Crime and FOIA

Many companies are tight-lipped about attacks on their computer systems. For example, only 36 percent of the firms and organizations that responded to the latest CSI/FBI computer-crime survey called the police after being victimized by hackers. The secrecy is understandable, says CSI Director Patrice Rapolus.

"They didn't want to make themselves more of a target, and they don't want the publicity," Rapolus said. [34]

In addition, says Patricia McGarry, a prosecutor in the Justice Depart-

ment's Computer Crime and Intellectual Property division, companies often don't disclose cyber-attacks for fear of hurting their bottom lines.

"There are some companies that have been reluctant to report, especially those that have publicly traded stock, because they have a perception that it may affect their standing in the stock market and their economic growth," McGarry says. "We try to encourage them to come forward no matter what, but there are many that choose not to."

Some experts argue that companies would be more willing to report attacks if the government would better protect the information from public disclosure. At present, however, computer attack information reported to the FBI or other federal law-enforcement agencies is subject to release to the general public through Freedom of Information Act (FOIA) requests.

The Bush administration and some lawmakers on Capitol Hill want to exempt from FOIA laws any organization that shares computer-attack information with the government. Advocates of exemptions say they are necessary because the entire nation is at risk when companies fail to report cyber-attacks.

One such proposal would exempt from FOIA disclosure any information about computer attacks waged against companies that form the nation's "critical infrastructure." The measure, sponsored by Sen. Robert Bennett, R-Utah, and Jon Kyl, R-Ariz., defines critical infrastructure as the "physical and cyber-based systems and services essential to the national defense, government, or economy of the United States."

The bill notes that much of the nation's critical infrastructure — such as power plants, communications companies and the banking and finance industry — is owned and operated by the private sector. The government, Bennett said, must give these organizations an incentive — in the form of a FOIA

exemption — to report cyber-attacks. "No company is going to voluntarily provide information in a forum where competitors, critics and attackers can get hold of it," Bennett said. [35]

The Bennett/Kyl measure also would exempt participating companies from antitrust laws so they could legally work together to develop technologies for stemming future cyber-attacks. Reps. Thomas M. Davis III, R-Va., and James P. Moran, D-Va., have introduced similar legislation in the House.

Richard A. Clarke, the president's special adviser on cyber-security, says a FOIA exemption might entice companies to report more computer attacks to the FBI. "Companies might not immediately start telling the [FBI] what they need to tell them, but at least they won't have that excuse anymore," Clarke told a Senate Judiciary subcommittee in February.

Several of the nation's largest industries are lobbying in favor of the exemption — including energy, manufacturing and pharmaceutical firms.

Critics dismiss the measure as unnecessary because other laws already protect the disclosure of sensitive information. Moreover, the critics say, the proposed exemption could prevent citizens from obtaining information completely unrelated to cyber-security, such as environmental data.

"This [FOIA exemption proposal] goes way beyond cyber-attacks," said Rena Steinzor, an academic fellow at the Natural Resources Defense Council, an environmental group. "It's basically nothing more than an avenue for industry to receive amnesty for voluntarily giving the government information about blatant law violations."

Eric Sobel, general counsel at the Electronic Privacy Information Center, agrees. "It seems like the industry is trying to use this issue as a basis for closing down a whole range of public disclosure," he said. "The people on [Capitol Hill] don't understand the unintended consequences." [36]

At Issue:

Are e-tailers doing enough to make online shopping safe?

EMILY HACKETT
EXECUTIVE DIRECTOR, INTERNET ALLIANCE

WRITTEN FOR THE CQ RESEARCHER, APRIL 2002

*t*he Internet is a safer place for shopping than the neighborhood mall or downtown department store. And online retailers are working to improve consumer confidence so the Internet can become the marketplace of the 21st century.

In online transactions, there are no carelessly discarded or duplicate credit-card receipts for thieves to pull from the trash can; no sales clerks or waiters to steal your name and credit-card numbers and no pickpockets lurking in crowded department store elevators. The online marketplace is secure because merchants have invested in technology, like VeriSign's verification and encryption systems and eBay's charge-back protection guarantee.

Internet transactions increasingly are paid with credit cards, the most secure method of online payment. Consumers are right to be concerned about protecting credit-card information. But while fraud has occurred online, identity theft primarily remains an offline crime. An identity stolen offline is often used online to defraud a consumer and a marketer. It is this fraudulent online activity with data stolen offline that retailers are working hard to combat.

Merchants are doubly motivated: They need to calm consumer fears, and they themselves are the ultimate victims of credit-card fraud. The major credit-card companies, by law, never expose the consumer to more than a $50 loss. In fact, VISA and MasterCard guarantee zero liability for consumers.

Technology is just the first step. Education is critical. An informed consumer, armed with the latest technology, is a powerful weapon against online fraud. Here is how smart consumers shop online:

- Shop with vendors whose reputation is sound.
- Shop only with vendors who use a secure server.
- Use a credit card.
- Use the secure payment mechanisms offered online.
- Report problems to the FTC at http://www.consumer.gov/idtheft/.

Industry has supported the passage of identity-theft legislation in an effort to give states the tools they need to capture online criminals. Internet companies have supported tough spam laws that make it illegal to fraudulently sell in the rapidly growing online marketplace. Industry has established a tough set of guidelines for ethical behavior on the Internet.

Technology is the key to solving the problems of Internet security and safety, but common sense and thoughtful legislation also have their roles to play.

EDMUND MIERZWINSKI
CONSUMER PROGRAM DIRECTOR,
U.S. PUBLIC INTEREST RESEARCH GROUP

WRITTEN FOR THE CQ RESEARCHER, APRIL 2002

*p*olls do show some increases in online shopping, but I'm sure that e-tailers are disappointed in its modest growth. Why? Consumers don't trust the Internet. And, they shouldn't.

First, consumers don't always get what they paid for. A recent "secret shopper" survey conducted by Consumers International found that too many sites failed to deliver — goods ordered failed to arrive, sites charged for goods that never turned up and where goods were returned, the retailer never sent a refund. Credit-card company data support these findings — chargebacks are much higher when consumers shop cyber-sites than when they shop stores or catalogs. Many chargebacks are refund requests when merchandise is shoddy or doesn't arrive.

Second, consumers are wary of card fraud. While the notion that hackers might nab your numbers as they hurtle through space is largely false, the problem of hackers or thieving employees breaking into poorly designed Web-merchant computers is real.

Worse, if I only have a debit card, I don't have the same legal $50-fraud limit as I do when I use a credit card, nor do I have the same legal rights to dispute goods that are shoddy or don't arrive. When I go on the radio or television to talk about debit cards, my advice is: "Never use these risky cards on the Internet." Why shouldn't consumers have the same billing-dispute protection and $50-fraud limit when they use a debit card?

Third, consumers have a real fear that e-tailers will share or sell their secrets to the highest bidder. I can shop in a store, and pay cash, if I want to be anonymous. Why not on the Net? Instead, everyone's business model is designed around capturing customer information. Consumers have a right to shop without giving up their privacy.

I'm encouraged by some Internet ideas — trusted third-party escrow systems show some potential, for example — but more needs to be done to make the Internet a safe place to shop. Advocates want the Internet to offer innovative small companies low-cost-of-entry opportunities to compete with the big boys. We want consumers to have more choices. To get there, we need help from e-tailers.

Join our call for strengthened consumer rights when we use any payment card — credit, debit or even stored value. Second, strengthen alternative-dispute resolution and Internet trusted-seal programs by basing them on laws. Third, change business models to respect our privacy.

Terrorism by Computer?

Since the Sept. 11 terrorist attacks on New York City and the Pentagon, computer-security experts and government officials have feared another type of attack: cyber-terrorism. White House cyber-security adviser Richard A. Clarke said terrorists could use the Internet to snarl the air-traffic control system, open floodgates on dams, cripple power grids or sabotage nuclear power plants.

"When I look at the vulnerabilities of the Internet, I lose sleep," Clarke said. "Why is any of that stuff connected to the Internet in the first place?" [1]

The Bush administration has ordered a number of federal departments to remove certain information from their Web pages, on the theory that terrorists could use the data to plan additional attacks. The White House also has asked for the cooperation of several private organizations — a move that has drawn fire from civil liberties groups.

Testifying before a Senate panel earlier this year, Clarke acknowledged that the United States had yet to catch a foreign government or terrorist group using Internet warfare. Still, Clarke said, several nations are gearing up to wage Internet warfare, including Iraq, Iran, North Korea and China. He warned that any nation or terrorist group that launches a cyber-attack against the United States should expect serious repercussions.

"We reserve the right to respond in any way appropriate: through covert action, through military action, [or] any one of the tools available to the president," Clarke told lawmakers. [2]

Clarke would not say what level of cyber-attack might provoke a military response. "That's the kind of ambiguity that we like to keep intentionally to create some deterrence," he said.

The Bush administration has budgeted about $4.2 billion for cyberspace security in 2003, a 64 percent increase over the present spending level. The private sector must also dramatically increase its computer-security budget in order to keep the U.S. economy on solid ground, Clarke said.

"The Internet . . . was not designed to have the entire economy of the United States built onto it," Clarke said. "We need to be hardened against attack." [2]

---

[1] Quoted in Thomas Peele, "Web Called Vulnerable to Terror," *The Contra Costa Times*, Feb. 20, 2002.
[2] Clarke testified before the Senate Judiciary Committee on Feb. 13, 2002.
[3] Quoted in Alan Goldstein, "U.S. Attorney General, Others Discuss Fragile Nature of Computer Networks," *The Dallas Morning News*, Feb. 13, 2002.

Tougher Sentences

Washington lawmakers also are debating a bill that would curb cyber-crime by punishing hackers and virus writers with longer prison terms — including life sentences for some crimes. Under current laws, sentences for computer crimes are capped at a maximum of 10 years in prison and are determined primarily by calculating the actual economic damages caused by each incident — which is difficult to prove in most cases.

The proposed Cyber Security Enhancement Act would require judges to consider several factors when sentencing computer criminals, including the judicial system's need to provide an "effective deterrent" to the "growing incidence" of cyber-crime. Under the measure, sponsored by Rep. Lamar Smith, R-Texas, judges could impose life sentences on any hacker or virus writer who "knowingly causes or attempts to cause death or serious bodily injury."

The Justice Department favors an even broader measure. Earlier this year, Deputy Assistant Attorney General John G. Malcolm told a House panel that hackers should be imprisoned for life for acting in a "reckless" manner — not just in a knowingly dangerous fashion. Malcolm said an example of such "reckless" behavior would be hacking into a telephone company and knocking out a community's 911 emergency system.

"It is easy to envision . . . that somebody might die or suffer serious injury as a result of this conduct," Malcolm told lawmakers. "Although the hacker might not have known that his conduct would cause death or serious bodily injury, such reckless conduct would seem to merit punishment greater than the 10 years permitted by the current statute." [37]

Microsoft, which is frequently accused of putting product functionality ahead of security concerns, also favors tougher sentences for cyber-criminals. Susan Kelley Koeppen, a Microsoft lawyer, told the House panel that society must stop coddling hackers and virus writers.

"Cyber-crime will never be effectively curbed if society continues to treat it merely as pranksterism," Koeppen said. "While our society does not tolerate people breaking into brick-and-mortar homes and businesses, we inexplicably seem to have more tolerance for computer break-ins. Computer attacks need to be treated as the truly criminal activities that they are." [38]

Jennifer Stisa Granick, a San Francisco attorney who has represented several well-known hackers, says harsher sentences won't curb cyber-crime. Like all criminals, people who commit computer crimes don't think they're going to get caught, Granick says. Tougher sentencing laws would only induce "false guilty pleas" by innocent defendants who don't want to risk trial, she says.

Granick is especially concerned that tougher sentencing laws would be unjustly applied to all types of computer crimes — no matter how minor.

"I think the punishment should fit the crime, and not all computer crimes are equal," Granick says. "Some are the equivalent of vandalism, and some could be the real-world equivalent of terrorism. We shouldn't paint all computer-intrusion incidents with the same brush."

Power, of CSI, agrees that tougher laws won't cut down on computer attacks. Indeed, Power says that throwing the book at hackers whose only crime is curiosity would diminish — not bolster — Internet security.

"It's crazy to indict somebody for pointing out the vulnerabilities of a supposedly secure [computer] system," Power says. "We're in an era where everybody's experimenting, including the people who write the laws. And some of these laws are not going to work very well." ∎

OUTLOOK

Losing Battle?

Police never will keep up with hackers and virus writers, in the view of some computer security experts.

"I don't think that law enforcement will ever have the upper hand," says BugNet's Bowden. "Hackers are researching new ways of doing things that law enforcement can't even imagine how to protect against at this point."

But the police do have one thing going for them, according to Bowden: Once hackers do launch attacks, their methods can be scrutinized so that organizations can protect themselves the next time around.

"There's a pretty small window that [any one particular] hack can be used," Bowden says.

Power concedes Bowden's point. But he notes that the argument is only true if computer-users make use of the latest security technology — which he says many are not doing.

"Companies are not doing enough to defend themselves," Power says. "They're not staffing for information security, they're not dedicating enough resources for information security and they're not organized in the right way to make information security effective."

A recent *InformationWeek* survey of some 4,500 private and public-sector organizations around the world bears out Power's argument. It concludes that "few businesses have taken the necessary steps to guard themselves adequately against break-ins and espionage." Moreover, at most companies, spending on computer security falls far short of business objectives, the report found. [39] It recommends increased spending on security.

Many security experts say law-enforcement agencies, too, must boost spending if they want to keep pace with hackers and virus writers. Hunger, of SecurityFocus, says law enforcement has been, and will continue to be, hindered by "brain drain."

"When people in law enforcement become technically apt enough to be on par with the game, they're able to get jobs in the civilian world that pay significantly more," Hunger says. "That's a hurdle they need to overcome if they want to get up to speed and stay up to speed."

The Justice Department's McGarry concedes that cyber-crime is "only going to grow to be a larger problem" in the future. But she rejects the notion that the federal law-enforcement community is losing the battle, noting that Justice maintains specialized cyber-crime units in New York, Los Angeles and Washington — cities with high incidences of computer-facilitated crimes.

"I don't think we are behind the eight ball in any fashion," she says. "We're devoting a great amount of resources in terms of manpower and technical expertise, so I don't think we're lagging in any respect." ∎

Notes

[1] "Internet Security Threat Report," *Riptech, Inc.*, February 2002. For related coverage, see Brian Hansen, "Cyber-Predators," *The CQ Researcher*, March 1, 2002, pp. 169-192, and Ellen Perlman, "Digital Nightmare," *Governing*, April 2002, pp. 20-24.

[2] *Ibid.*

[3] "Computer Crime and Security Survey 2001," Computer Security Institute (CSI) and Federal Bureau of Investigation (FBI), January 2002.

[4] Quoted in Sharon Gaudin, "Computer Sabotage Case Back in Court," *Network World Fusion*, April 4, 2001.

[5] Quoted in Linden MacIntyre, "Hackers," PBS "Frontline," Feb. 13, 2001.

[6] For background, see Richard Power, *Tangled Web: Tales of Digital Crime from the Shadows of Cyberspace* (2000), pp. 150-151.

[7] Top 10 Consumer Fraud Complaints of 2001, Federal Trade Commission, Jan. 23, 2002.

[8] "Identity Theft and its Effect on the Financial Services Industry," Celent Communications, September 2001.

[9] U.S. Census Bureau, *Current Population Survey*, September 2001.

[10] GartnerG2, "Privacy and Security: The Hidden Growth Strategy," August 2000.

[11] Quoted in Mark W. Vigoroso, "Online Mugging a Threat, but no Showstopper," *E-Commerce Times*, Feb. 1, 2002.

[12] Scott Culp, "It's Time to End Information Anarchy," Microsoft Security Response Center white paper, October 2001.

[13] Jaikumar Vijayan, "Vendors Lead Effort to Delay Reporting of Security Vulnerabilities," *Computerworld*, Nov. 19, 2001.

[14] *Ibid.*

[15] Bruce Schneier, "Is Disclosing Vulnerabilities a Security Risk in Itself?" *Internetweek*, Nov. 19, 2001.

[16] From "The Injustice of Insecure Software," @Stake white paper, February 2002.

[17] Mark Minasi, *The Software Conspiracy: Why Companies Put Out Faulty Software, How They Can Hurt You and What You Can Do About It* (1999).

[18] See, for example, CSI and FBI, *op. cit.*, and "Security Review 2002," Computer Economics Inc., 2002.

[19] From "End-User License Agreement for Microsoft Software," as posted on Microsoft's Web site.

[20] Quoted in Dennis Fisher, "Software Liability Gaining Attention," *Eweek*, Jan. 14, 2002.

21 Computer Economics, *op. cit.*

22 From "Cybersecurity Today and Tomorrow: Pay Now or Pay Later," The Computer Science and Telecommunications Board of the National Research Council (a branch of the National Academy of Sciences), January 2002.

23 Bill Gates, "Trustworthy Computing" memo, Jan. 15, 2002, as posted on Microsoft's Web site.

24 *Ibid.*

25 Quoted in Kristi Helm and Elise Ackerman, "Gates Makes Security Top Focus," *The San Jose Mercury News*, Jan. 17, 2002.

26 Steven Levy, *Hackers: Heroes of the Computer Revolution* (1984).

27 CNN special report on hackers, May 1999.

28 *Ibid.*

29 Paul Mungo and Bryan Clough, *Approaching Zero: The Extraordinary Underworld of Hackers, Phreakers, Virus Writers and Keyboard Criminals* (1992).

30 Quoted in Winn Schwartau, *Cybershock: Surviving Hackers, Phreakers, Identity Thieves, Internet Terrorists and Weapons of Mass Destruction* (2000).

31 Quoted in Mungo and Clough, *op. cit.*, p. 67.

32 For background, see *Security of the Internet*, Froehlich/Kent Encyclopedia of Telecommunications, Vol. 15, Marcel Dekker, New York, 1997, pp. 231-255. Also available online at www.cert.org/encyc_article/tocencyc.html.

33 Quoted in "Canadian Internet Hacker 'Mafiaboy' Pleads Guilty," Reuters, Jan. 19, 2001.

34 Quoted in Randy Barett, "Trust Me!" *Eweek*, Aug. 20, 2001.

35 Quoted in Matt Richtel, "In an Era of Tighter Security, How Much Cyberfreedom Are We Willing to Surrender?" *The New York Times*, Dec. 3, 2001.

36 *Ibid.*

37 Malcolm testified before the House Judiciary Subcommittee on Crime on Feb. 12, 2002.

38 *Ibid.*

39 "Global Information Security Survey," *Information Week*/PricewaterhouseCoopers, 2001.

FOR MORE INFORMATION

BugNet, 391 South 520 West, Lindon, UT 84042; (801) 443-4000; www.bugnet.com. A division of Key Labs Inc. that finds flaws in commercial software and posts vulnerability warnings on its Web site.

Business Software Alliance, 1150 18th St., N.W., Suite 700, Washington, DC 20036; (202) 872-5500; www.bsa.org. A membership group representing personal computer software publishing companies. Operates toll-free anti-piracy hotline (888) 667-4722.

Computer Emergency Response Team (CERT), Software Engineering Institute, Carnegie Mellon University, Pittsburgh, PA 15213; (412) 268-7090; www.cert.org. Collects and distributes detailed technical information about computer security breaches and posts information for computer neophytes on its Web site.

Computer Security Institute, 600 Harrison St., San Francisco, CA 94107; (415) 947-6320; www.gocsi.com. An organization for computer-security professionals that works with the FBI to produce an annual report cataloging the cost of computer-facilitated crimes.

Cult of the Dead Cow, 1369 Madison Ave., N.Y., NY 10128; www.cultdeadcow.com. A quasi-underground computer-security organization that publishes hacking techniques on its Web site. Created "Black Orifice," a computer program that allows users to remotely take control of computers with certain Microsoft operating systems.

Federal Trade Commission, 600 Pennsylvania Ave., N.W., Washington, DC 20580; (202) 326-2222; www.ftc.gov. The federal agency responsible for preventing fraudulent, deceptive and unfair business practices in the marketplace, including Internet fraud and identity theft.

FBI National Infrastructure Protection Center (NIPC), 935 Pennsylvania Ave., N.W., Washington, DC 20535; (202) 323-3205; www.nipc.gov. Now part of the Dept. of Homeland Security, investigates intrusions into government, educational and corporate computer networks and provides information on major computer-crime investigations on its Web site.

Information Technology Association of America, 1401 Wilson Blvd., Arlington, VA 22209; (703) 522-5055; www.itaa.org. A trade organization for IT professionals that works to advance Internet and e-commerce security.

2600: The Hacker Quarterly, P.O. Box 752, Middle Island, NY 11953; (631) 751-2600; www.2600.com. A magazine written by hackers, for hackers, that publishes techniques for hacking computer and telephone systems. Online version provides archived speeches and presentations from the annual Hackers on Planet Earth (HOPE) conference.

Bibliography

Selected Sources

Books

Levy, Steven, *Hackers: Heroes of the Computer Revolution*, Anchor Press/Doubleday, 1984.

Many experts consider this the most complete account of the personal-computer revolution in the late 1950s. Packed with anecdotes and scientific details about the hacker clubs at top schools. Levy is chief technology writer for *Newsweek*.

Mungo, Paul, and Bryan Clough, *Approaching Zero: The Extraordinary Underworld of Hackers, Phreakers, Virus Writers, and Keyboard Criminals*, Random House, 1992.

This anecdotal, non-technical overview of computer-facilitated crimes provides good detail about the evolution of computer hacking in Europe. Mungo is a British journalist, Clough an accountant who specializes in international computer-security issues.

Power, Richard, *Tangled Web: Tales of Digital Crime from the Shadows of Cyberspace*, Que/Macmillan, 2000.

This comprehensive study of cyber-crimes includes more than 50 tables, charts and diagrams, a glossary and the full text of major U.S. computer-crime laws. Power is editorial director of the Computer Security Institute in San Francisco.

Shimomura, Tsutomu, with John Markoff, *Takedown: The Pursuit and Capture of Kevin Mitnick, America's Most Wanted Computer Outlaw*, Hyperion, 1996.

Shimomura, a senior fellow at the San Diego Supercomputing Center, began tracking Mitnick in 1994 after he stole files from his work station. Shimomura outsmarted Mitnick, leading the FBI to his doorstep. Markoff covers computer crime and technology for *The New York Times*.

Stephenson, Peter, *Investigating Computer-Related Crime*, CRC Press, 2000.

A fairly technical account of how police catch cyber-criminals. An excellent resource for students interested in careers in law. The author is a network consultant and lecturer.

Articles

Bettelheim, Adriel, "Emerging Players: Sen. Robert F. Bennett, R-Utah," *CQ Weekly*, Jan. 5, 2002.

A profile of one of Washington's leading cyber-security advocates.

Bettelheim, Adriel, and Rebecca Adams, "Threats and Priorities," *CQ Weekly*, Oct. 20, 2001.

Examines how Congress is dealing with the fact that much of the national infrastructure is vulnerable to computer-facilitated attacks.

Cohen, Adam, "The Identity Thieves are Out There — and Someone Could be Spying on You," *Time*, July 2, 2001.

A journalist who specializes in science and technology issues provides a non-technical overview of how personal and financial information can be compromised on the Internet.

Docherty, Neil (producer and director), and Linden MacIntyre (correspondent), "Hackers," PBS "Frontline," Program No. 1910, Feb. 13, 2001.

This public television program offers a good overview of hackers and cyber-crime. Printer-friendly transcripts of the program are at www.pbs.org/wgbh/pages/frontline/shows/hackers.

Mandelblit, Bruce D., "Clicks & Crime: The Inside Story of Internet Fraud," *Security*, Sept. 1, 2001.

A computer-security professional warns readers about the most common Internet fraud scams.

Vigoroso, Mark W., "Online Mugging a Threat, but No Showstopper," *E-Commerce Times*, Feb. 1, 2002.

A technology writer reports that e-commerce continues to grow despite the public's security concerns.

Vijayan, Jaikumar, "Vendor Led Effort to Delay Reporting of Security Vulnerabilities," *Computerworld*, Nov. 19, 2001.

A technology writer reports on Microsoft's effort to prevent the disclosure of flaws in its software.

Studies and Reports

Computer Emergency Response Team (CERT) Coordination Center, *2001 Annual Report*, Feb. 19, 2002.

A technical overview of the Internet-security vulnerabilities reported in 2001 to CERT, a federally funded organization based at Carnegie Mellon University.

Computer Security Institute/San Francisco FBI Computer Intrusion Squad, *2001 Computer Crime and Security Survey*, January 2002.

The annual CSI/FBI survey is based on data reported by 538 U.S. corporations, government agencies, financial and medical institutions and universities. Annotated with charts, graphs and tables; an executive summary is at www.gocsi.com/prelea/000321.html.

Riptech, Inc., "Internet Security Threat Report," January 2002.

A broad analysis of Internet-based attacks on hundreds of organizations during the last six months of 2001. Annotated with numerous charts, graphs and tables; discusses technical aspects of virus attacks and computer-intrusion events. Executive summary is at www.riptech.com/newsevents/release020127.html.

12 Abortion Debates

KENNETH JOST

Armed with prayer book, rosary and anti-abortion literature, Christine Walsh takes up her post on a chilly Saturday morning recently outside a Planned Parenthood clinic within sight of the White House. As women approach, the teenage college student rushes to their side and tries with soft-spoken insistence to dissuade them from having an abortion.

Invariably, the women quickly turn away and are shepherded inside by volunteer "escorts" from the Washington Area Clinic Task Force. Wearing orange vests, they lock arms to block Walsh or her fellow "sidewalk counselors" from going farther once the patients reach the clinic's grounds.

Thirty years after the Supreme Court's landmark *Roe v. Wade* decision allowing abortions, the abortion wars continue — in Congress and state legislatures, in the courts and outside women's clinics across the country.

The sidewalk confrontations are usually orderly, but the potential for violence lurks in the background. The clinic has bullet-resistant windows and a 600-pound steel door; doctors often wear bulletproof vests. [1]

The number of protesters and clinic escorts grows on special occasions — notably, every Jan. 22, the anniversary of the *Roe* decision. Sometimes, the two sides get into shoving matches. "It's like a war zone," Walsh comments as two motorcycle police officers set up watch across the street in case of a disturbance.

Walsh says she simply wants prospective patients to "take a step back" and

From *The CQ Researcher,*
March 21, 2003.

Anti-abortion militant James Kopp faces up to life in prison after being found guilty on March 18 of second-degree murder in the 1998 shooting of Barnett Slepian, a Buffalo, N.Y., doctor who carried out abortions. Violence directed against abortion providers and clinics has ebbed over the past few years, but legislative and judicial fights between anti-abortion and abortion-rights groups continue unabated 30 years after the Supreme Court's landmark Roe v. Wade *decision establishing a constitutional right to abortion.*

Getty Images

think about their choices. "They're killing children here," she explains, "and we're here trying to offer alternatives."

Rebecca Fox, 24, the leader of a team of 10 escorts, says the "anti-choice harassers," as she calls them, never succeed. In four years, she says, she has never seen a sidewalk change-of-mind. "The women know what their choices are," Fox says, "and they've made their decision."

The arguments are no less fervent for being well worn. [2] Abortion-rights advocates praise *Roe v. Wade* as a landmark guarantee of what they call a woman's "right to choose." Anti-abortion groups bitterly assail the 1973 ruling and defend what they call the "right to life" of the "unborn child." Public opinion polls generally favor a woman's right to choose an abortion but also favor certain restrictions on that right, many of which have been enacted at the state and fed-

eral levels in recent years. (*For state laws, see chart, p. 224; public opinion polls, p. 222.*)

Today, with Congress and the White House in Republican hands, anti-abortion groups see their best chance in more than a decade of winning federal passage of parts of their agenda. The GOP has been closely aligned with anti-abortion forces since 1980, when the party platform first supported a "right-to-life" constitutional amendment.

"We're in better shape as pro-lifers than we have been in a while," says Connie Mackey, vice president for government affairs at the Family Research Council, a Christian-oriented family-advocacy group. Republican control "should give us a leg up that we haven't had in a while."

"Abortion rights are in great peril," says Elizabeth Cavendish, legislative director for the newly named NARAL Pro-Choice America — formerly, the National Abortion Rights Action League. "We're likely to see a renewed assault on a woman's right to choose."

At the top of the right-to-life agenda is a bill to ban so-called partial-birth abortions — in which a fetus is brought partly outside a woman's body before being aborted, usually after 20 weeks gestation. "This is closer to infanticide than it is to abortion," Sen. Rick Santorum, R-Pa., told a March 10 news conference, three days before the Senate voted 64-33 to ban the procedure.

The bill is expected to win easy House approval and be signed into law by President Bush, but still faces legal hurdles. The Supreme Court in 2000 struck down a Nebraska ban on the procedure, but supporters of the measure say it was rewritten to meet the court's objections. [3]

Number of Abortions Has Been Dropping

The number of abortions performed in the United States each year increased through the 1970s, leveled off in the 1980s and has been falling since 1990. The decline is attributed to a decline in sexual activity by adolescents and increased use of contraceptives, including the "morning-after" pill. Anti-abortion groups also note a public-opinion shift against abortion except under limited circumstances.

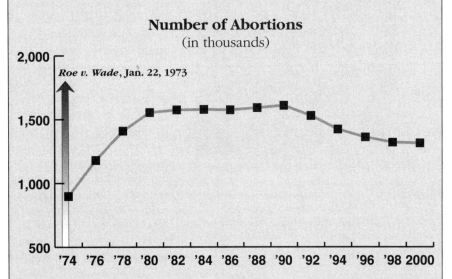

Number of Abortions
(in thousands)

Roe v. Wade, Jan. 22, 1973

Source: Lawrence B. Finer and Stanley K. Henshaw, *"Abortion Incidence and Services in the United States in 2000,"* Perspectives on Sexual and Reproductive Health, *January/February 2003, The Alan Guttmacher Institute.*

But abortion-rights groups say the new bill suffers from the same constitutional defects cited in the Supreme Court's Nebraska decision. "Make no mistake," says NARAL President Kate Michelman, "this bill goes directly to the heart of a woman's constitutional right to choose."

Anti-abortion groups are pushing three other bills to regulate abortion practices in the United States. The measures would:

- Make it a federal crime to help a minor cross state lines to get an abortion without parental notification or consent;
- Allow hospitals and doctors to refuse to perform, and health insurers to refuse to cover, abortions without risking loss of federal funding; and

- Make it a federal crime to injure or kill a fetus during the commission of any one of a specified list of other violent offenses.

Anti-abortion groups will also continue to try to block any international aid for groups that promote abortion. And they have strongly backed legislation to ban any form of human cloning — a measure the House approved, 241-155, on Feb. 27.

Some of the bills were approved previously in the House, where anti-abortion groups have held narrow but secure majorities for several years. But they stalled in the Democratic-controlled Senate. Now — as evidenced by the Senate's March 13 ban on partial-birth abortions — the Republican-controlled Senate is expected to be more hospitable to anti-abortion measures, even

though it is still considered more abortion-rights-minded than the House.

Most important, anti-abortion groups believe they have a strong and reliable ally in President Bush. On his first workday in office, he reinstated a Reagan-era ban on U.S. funding of overseas groups that promote abortions. He has also appointed well-known abortion foes to key agency positions dealing with abortion policy, and his administration has instituted a laundry list of what abortion-rights advocates call "anti-choice" executive orders, regulatory policies and legal briefs championed by anti-abortion groups.

"On every pro-life legislative measure [the administration] has been effectively involved," says Douglas Johnson, director of federal legislation for the National Right to Life Committee (NRLC). "And on matters of administrative discretion, they have come down on the side of a culture of life."

In addition, Bush has nominated conservatives to federal judgeships — some of them openly critical of abortion rights — and endorsed anti-abortion measures in Congress, including the partial-birth abortion ban. Pro-choice groups are also bracing for a full-scale confrontation over a Bush Supreme Court appointee if one or more vacancies arise — as many political and legal observers expect to happen as early as this summer.

"It's very possible that President Bush will have the opportunity to reshape the court," Cavendish says. If one of the "pro-choice" justices is replaced, she says, the court could end up approving some "draconian" restrictions on abortion, including a revised partial-birth abortion ban. With two new appointments, she warns, the court might formally overrule *Roe*.

The political situation is mixed in the states, although anti-abortion groups appear to have the upper hand. NARAL estimates that 335 anti-choice measures have been enacted by state legislatures since 1995. Moreover, the NRLC claimed "critical gains" in state legislative races in the November 2002 elections. "We're in a better position than we were last year," said Mary Balch, NRLC's director of state legislation. [4]

In its annual state-by-state report, NARAL counts 23 states with anti-abortion majorities in both houses, but claims the number of "pro-choice" governors increased from 15 to 22 after the November elections. [5] Cavendish predicts that at least 12 and as many as 17 states might ban abortion altogether if the Supreme Court overturns *Roe* and gives states discretion to regulate abortions with minimal constitutional constraints.

As the abortion debates continue, here are some of the major questions at issue:

Should Roe v. Wade be overturned?

As he was completing his opinion for the Supreme Court in *Roe v. Wade*, Justice Harry A. Blackmun cautioned his colleagues that the decision "will probably result in the Court's being severely criticized." [6] Thirty years later, the ruling indeed remains controversial: praised by abortion-rights advocates, bitterly opposed by anti-abortion groups and held in some disrepute among legal scholars.

Anti-abortion groups want to overturn the decision, even though they have failed to nullify the ruling by constitutional amendment or to persuade the high court to overrule the decision itself. "It's been an enormous tragedy," says Johnson of the National Right to Life Committee.

For their part, abortion-rights groups say *Roe* has survived only in a weakened state — and could be overruled if President Bush gets the chance to name one or more new justices to the Supreme Court. "*Roe* is in jeopardy," says NARAL's Cavendish.

Criticisms of *Roe* stem not only from its outcome but also from the structure of the opinion. Legal critics have long said Blackmun based his opinion

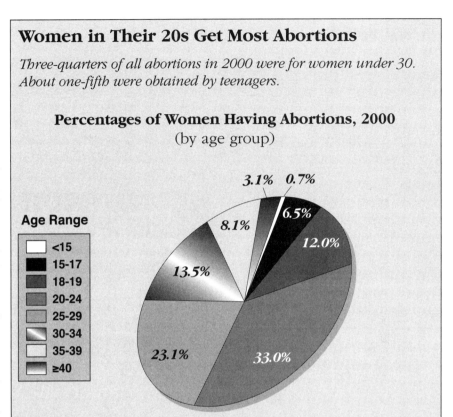

Women in Their 20s Get Most Abortions

Three-quarters of all abortions in 2000 were for women under 30. About one-fifth were obtained by teenagers.

Percentages of Women Having Abortions, 2000
(by age group)

Age Range

☐	<15
■	15-17
▨	18-19
▨	20-24
▨	25-29
▨	30-34
☐	35-39
▨	≥40

3.1%   0.7%   6.5%   12.0%   8.1%   13.5%   23.1%   33.0%

Source: Rachel K. Jones, et al., "Patterns in the Socioeconomic Characteristics of Women Obtaining Abortions in 2000-2001," Perspectives on Sexual and Reproductive Health, September/October 2002, p. 228, The Alan Guttmacher Institute.

more on medical policy than constitutional law. They also contend that the decision's trimester approach — allowing unregulated abortion during the first three months of pregnancy, some regulations up to the point of fetal viability and a near-ban except to save the life of the mother during the final trimester — amounts to what Johnson calls "the apex of judicial legislation."

"There is consensus within the legal academy, whether one is pro-life or pro-abortion, whether one is liberal or conservative, that *Roe* had no grounding in the Constitution or in constitutional jurisprudence," says Douglas Kmiec, dean of the Columbus School of Law at the Catholic University of America in Washington, D.C.

"That's just not true," counters Louis Michael Seidman, a constitutional-law

expert at the Georgetown University Law Center in Washington. "If you did a survey of constitutional-law professors, I'd be pretty confident that a majority think *Roe* was correctly decided."

Seidman acknowledges the criticism of the trimester approach, but says such line-drawing is common in constitutional decisions. "To give meaning to constitutional rights, it's sometimes necessary for justices to draw what may seem like arbitrary lines," he says. "You have to draw them someplace."

In a showdown case two decades after the 1973 decision, the Supreme Court reaffirmed what three of the justices — Sandra Day O'Connor, Anthony M. Kennedy and David H. Souter — called, in an unusual joint opinion, *Roe's* "essential holding." Their ruling in *Planned Parenthood v. Casey*

Public Favors Abortion Rights

More Americans favor a woman's right to have an abortion than oppose it. But a majority of Americans also approve of placing some restrictions on abortions.

Would you describe yourself as being more pro-choice — supporting a woman's right to have an abortion — or more pro-life — protecting the rights of the unborn children?

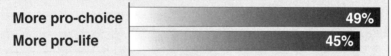

More pro-choice	49%
More pro-life	45%

Do you favor the Supreme Court ruling that women have the right to an abortion during the first three months of their pregnancy?

Favor	55%
Oppose	40%

Do you favor or oppose the following proposals?

	Favor	Oppose
Law requiring women seeking abortion to wait 24 hours	78%	19%
Law requiring doctors to inform patients about alternatives	88	11
Law requiring women under 18 to get a parent's consent	73	24
Law to make it illegal to perform an abortion procedure in the last six months of pregnancy, known as a partial-birth abortion, except to save the mother's life	70	25

Sources: Time/CNN poll conducted Jan. 15-16, 2003 (questions 1-2); Survey Research Center, University of California-Berkeley, fall 2002 (questions 3-6).

rebuffed repeated calls from the Justice Department under Presidents Ronald Reagan and George Bush to overturn *Roe*. But the decision also appeared to discard the trimester approach and to allow states to regulate abortion unless the laws imposed an "undue burden" on women's rights. [7]

The three justices sought to strengthen the constitutional basis of the ruling by explicitly tying the abortion right to the "liberty interest" protected by the 14th Amendment's Due Process Clause.

They also defended the decision not to overrule *Roe*, in part on the legal doctrine of *"stare decisis"* — Latin for let the decision stand.

Johnson calls that part of the decision especially unjustifiable. "They didn't try to defend the constitutional analysis," Johnson says. "They just said, 'That's what we did. If we changed it now, people would be upset.' "

Some critics also fault the *Roe* court for taking the issue out of the hands of state legislatures — several of which

were moving in the early 1970s to liberalize abortion laws. Today, though, Johnson says most Americans support more restrictions on abortion than are allowed under the Supreme Court's decisions.

"There is a great gulf between the policy that is supported by the majority of Americans and the regime that has been imposed by judicial decree," Johnson says.

Abortion-rights advocates, however, note that polls show most Americans agree that the abortion decision should rest with women rather than the government. In any event, they say women's reproductive freedom should not be subject to the legislative process. "It would be a terrible thing for women to have to lobby for their liberty state by state, year by year, and legislature by legislature," Cavendish says.

Indeed, abortion-rights advocates say the court itself has already undermined *Roe*. "It's already been eroded by cases like *Casey*," Cavendish says.

Johnson disagrees. "The notion that *Casey* was a rollback of *Roe* is pure fiction," he says.

As for a direct overruling of *Roe*, anti-abortion groups are hopeful and abortion-rights groups fearful. But experts on both sides of the issue discount the likelihood.

"It's just not going to happen," says Ronald Rotunda, a conservative professor at George Mason University Law School in Fairfax, Va., outside Washington. "It's just like asking whether we should change the speed of light."

Seidman agrees: "In my lifetime, *Roe* will not be overruled."

Should Congress ban so-called "partial-birth" abortions?

Anti-abortion groups describe the procedure in stark terms: a late-stage fetus is brought through the woman's dilated cervix feet first; then — because the head is too big to pass through — the skull is pierced, the contents suctioned out and the skull finally

Anti-Abortion Tactics Test Free-Speech Limits

The Web site opened by a militant anti-abortion group in January 1997 sent a chilling message. The site listed the names of some 200 physicians identified as "abortionists." Some of the names were grayed out. "Wounded," the home page explained. Other names had a horizontal strikethrough — for "fatality."

Among the doctors named on the site were four Oregon physicians who also had been pictured two years earlier on a Wild West-style poster released by the American Coalition of Life Activists. The poster bore the headline "Guilty" and identified the 13 physicians shown as "baby butchers."

At a time when abortion clinic violence was at a peak, the Oregon doctors viewed the Web site and poster as threats on their lives. Along with taking security precautions, the physicians also filed a federal court suit hoping to take down the postings and collect damages from the groups and individuals responsible.

A jury in Oregon awarded $107 million to the four doctors and two women's clinics that joined as plaintiffs. A federal appeals court upheld the award in May 2002, but dissenting judges in the 6-5 decision strongly argued that the anti-abortion messages were constitutionally protected speech. [1]

Now, the anti-abortion groups' appeal is presenting the Supreme Court with another in a series of difficult cases testing the limits of free speech in the context of anti-abortion activities that entail violence or disruption, actual or threatened. The Bush administration also appears to be struggling with the case. The court asked the Justice Department's solicitor general's office to submit a brief on the case in mid-December, but as of mid-March nothing had been filed. The justices would normally wait for the government's brief before deciding whether to hear the appeal.

The closely watched case comes against the backdrop of a decade of abortion-related violence that included shootings, bombings, arson and clinic blockades. At least seven people have been killed: three physicians, two clinic employees, a clinic escort and an off-duty police officer who died in a Birmingham, Ala., clinic bombing in 1998. [2]

James Kopp, the defendant in the most recent of the shootings, went on trial in Buffalo, N.Y., on March 17. Kopp has admitted shooting Barnet Slepian at his home in Amherst, N.Y., in 1998, but claimed he meant only to wound the doctor. Kopp was convicted of second-degree murder on March 18; he faces a minimum prison term of 15 years and a maximum of 25 years to life.

Violence and disruption have been ebbing for the past three years. For 2002, the National Abortion Federation (NAF), which represents abortion clinics, counted 265 incidents of "violence," but almost all were in the least serious categories of trespassing, vandalism or stalking. The federation listed one arson and one "invasion" for the year. It also counted four clinic blockades, with no arrests.

NAF President Vicki Saporta attributes the decline in violence to federal law enforcement. She notes that former Attorney General Janet Reno put Kopp and another anti-abortion fugitive — Eric Rudolph — on the FBI's "Ten Most Wanted" list. Kopp was arrested in France and extradited to the U.S. Rudolph, charged in the Birmingham bombing, is still at large.

Operation Rescue, once the largest of the militant anti-abortion groups, is now bankrupt and defunct; none of the existing groups matches its size or visibility. Major anti-abortion organizations routinely condemn violence. The National Right to Life Committee says it prohibits any violence or illegal activity by its members. Still, Saporta says she fears trials such as Kopp's give militant organizations "the chance to recruit the next assassin."

The Supreme Court has bolstered clinics' legal efforts against violence with a series of divided rulings over the past decade. [3] Three rulings in 1994, 1997 and 2000 allow court injunctions or state laws to establish "buffer zones" requiring protesters to keep some minimum distance from clinic entrances or clinic personnel and patients as they enter or leave the premises. Dissenting justices in each of the decisions argued the rulings infringed on free speech.

A separate ruling in 1994 allowed women's clinics to sue demonstrators for damages under the federal anti-racketeering law commonly known as RICO. Under that ruling, women's clinics later won a $250,000 verdict in the case, but the Supreme Court on Feb. 26 threw out the award. The court ruled, 8-1, that the demonstrators' conduct did not amount to extortion for purposes of the racketeering law. [4]

---

[1] *Planned Parenthood v. American Coalition of Life Activists*, 290 F.3d 1058 (CA9 2002). Plaintiffs included Robert Crist, James Hern, Elizabeth Newhall and James Newhall; defendants included two organizations — American Coalition of Life Activists and Advocates for Life Ministries — and 15 individuals. For coverage, see Henry Weinstein, "Abortion Foes Are Ruled a Threat," *Los Angeles Times*, May 17, 2002, p. B1.

[2] Summary information on the cases can be found on the National Abortion Federation's Web site: www.naf.org.

[3] For a summary, see Claire Cushman (ed.), *Supreme Court Decisions and Women's Rights* (2001), pp. 204-206.

[4] The case is *Scheidler v. National Organization for Women, Inc.*

---

crushed or collapsed. "A partial-birth abortion brutally and painfully takes the life of a human baby who is inches away from being born alive," the NRLC's Johnson says.

Abortion-rights groups bristle at the terminology, which they call medically inaccurate and politically inflammatory. In fact, the medical term is "dilation and extraction" — short-

ened to "D&X" — or, alternatively, an "intact D&E" for "dilation and evacuation."

The opposing groups also disagree over the frequency of the procedure.

Abortion-rights advocates generally depict the procedure as relatively rare and used only when medically necessary. Anti-abortion groups insist the procedure is more common than acknowledged and never medically justifiable.

Public opinion polls that use the term partial-birth abortion indicate substantial public support for banning the procedure: 70 percent in the most recent Gallup survey in January. [8] When a state law banning the procedure reached the Supreme Court, however, the justices voted 5-4 to strike it down on the ground that the statute interfered with women's abortion rights.

The court's 2000 decision in *Stenberg v. Carhart* said the Nebraska law was defective because it could be construed to apply to the more common D&E procedure, where the fetus is dismembered while still in utero. The court also held that the law failed to include a constitutionally required exemption to permit the procedure necessary to protect the woman's health. [9]

Now, anti-abortion groups are celebrating the March 13 Senate passage of a measure banning the procedure nationwide. Family Research Council President Ken Connor said the Senate's action would help "put an end to this unnecessary and grisly procedure which has taken the lives of thousands of partially born children and hurt so many women."

Abortion-rights groups assailed the bill as unnecessary, ill-advised and constitutionally flawed. "It's pretty much flagrantly unconstitutional," says NARAL's Cavendish. She contends that anti-abortion groups are pushing the proposal in the hope that by the time the issue reaches the Supreme Court again, there will be one or more new justices who will vote for a different outcome.

The Nebraska law defined a partial-birth abortion as a procedure performed after "delivering into the vagina a living unborn child, or a substantial portion thereof." To narrow the defi-

nition, the new bill pending in Congress prohibits an abortion in which "the entire fetal head" or "any part of the fetal trunk past the navel" is "outside the mother."

Johnson says the new phrasing meets the Supreme Court's objection that the Nebraska law covered commonly used techniques. "By no stretch

of the imagination could it be subject to that construction," he says.

Abortion-rights advocates, including abortion providers, disagree. "The law is not what they say it is," says Vicki Saporta, president of the National Abortion Federation (NAF), an organization of abortion clinics and physicians. "It's a pre-viability ban, with a definition

Most States Limit Abortion Rights

Forty-three states required parents to be notified before an abortion is performed on a minor child in 2002, and more than 30 states had informed-consent, TRAP laws or measures banning "partial-birth" abortion or other procedures.

Selected State Abortion Rates and Limits, 2002
(x = state has such a law)

States	Rate (per 1,000 women)	Informed Consent	Parental Notification	Waiting Period	Abortion Methods Banned*	TRAP Laws**
Alabama	14.3	x	x	x	x	x
Alaska	11.7	x	x		x	x
Arizona	16.5		x		x	x
Arkansas	9.8	x	x	x	x	x
California	31.2	x	x			x
Colorado	15.9	x				
Connecticut	21.1	x			x	
Delaware	31.3	x	x	x		
Dist. of Columbia	68.1					
Florida	31.9	x	x		x	x
Georgia	16.9		x		x	x
Hawaii	22.2					x
Idaho	7.0	x	x	x	x	x
Illinois	23.2		x		x	x
Indiana	9.4	x	x	x	x	x
Iowa	9.8		x		x	x
Kansas	21.4	x	x	x	x	
Kentucky	5.3	x	x	x	x	x

Continued ⟶

* *Includes partial-birth abortions and certain other procedures.*

** *So-called TRAP (targeted regulations of abortion providers) laws govern what an abortion doctor must do before performing an abortion, such as requiring a woman to first undergo an ultrasound procedure.*

Sources: "Who Decides: A State-by-State Review of Abortion and Reproductive Rights, 2003," NARAL, pp. iii-xxv; rates are from Lawrence B. Finer and Stanley K. Henshaw, "Abortion Incidence and Services In the United States in 2000," Perspectives on Sexual and Reproductive Health, *January/February 2003, The Alan Guttmacher Institute.*

Selected State Abortion Limits, 2002
(x = state has such a law)

States	Rate (per 1,000 women)	Informed Consent	Parental Notification	Waiting Period	Abortion Methods Banned*	TRAP Laws**
Louisiana	13.0	x	x	x	x	x
Maine	9.9	x	x			
Maryland	29.0		x			
Massachusetts	21.4	x	x	x		x
Michigan	21.6	x	x	x	x	x
Minnesota	13.5	x	x			x
Mississippi	6.0	x	x	x	x	x
Missouri	6.6	x	x		x	x
Montana	13.5	x	x	x	x	
Nebraska	11.6	x	x	x	x	x
Nevada	32.2	x	x		x	x
New Hampshire	11.2					
New Jersey	36.3		x		x	x
New Mexico	14.7		x		x	
New York	39.1					x
North Carolina	21.0	x				x
North Dakota	9.9	x	x	x	x	x
Ohio	16.5	x	x	x	x	x
Oklahoma	10.1		x		x	x
Oregon	23.5					
Pennsylvania	14.3	x	x	x		x
Rhode Island	24.1	x	x		x	x
South Carolina	9.3	x	x	x	x	x
South Dakota	5.5	x	x	x	x	x
Tennessee	15.2	x	x	x	x	x
Texas	18.8		x			x
Utah	6.6	x	x	x	x	x
Vermont	12.7					
Virginia	18.1	x	x	x	x	x
Washington	20.2					
West Virginia	6.8		x		x	
Wisconsin	9.6	x	x	x	x	x
Wyoming	1.0		x			
		31	**43**	**22**	**31**	**35**

Congress put the issue on hold immediately following the Supreme Court's 2000 decision, but the House again passed a ban in 2002. With the Democrats in control of the Senate, however, then-Majority Leader Tom Daschle of South Dakota blocked consideration of the measure.

The major legislative fight in the Senate turned on failed amendments sponsored by Democratic senators who wanted to add a health exception to the bill. A health exception "would ban no abortions at all," argued Sandy Rios, president of the Concerned Women for America, a conservative policy group.

NARAL's Cavendish countered that the proponents' refusal to agree to a health exception "just reveals that they really want to shackle doctors and have the government inserted squarely into medical decision-making."

Whatever happens in Congress, both sides expect the issue to be settled again in the courts — eventually, at the Supreme Court. Catholic University's Kmiec, a leading constitutional scholar on the anti-abortion side, doubts the bill will be upheld. "Not unless the Supreme Court changes its mind," he says.

The more explicit definition of the procedure "may convince five justices," he says, "especially if there's a new justice looking at it for the first time." But the law will be struck down, he predicts, if it does not allow the procedure when necessary to protect the woman's health. "I don't think you get around the health exception," Kmiec concludes.

Should Congress and the states enact additional restrictions on abortion?

State legislatures have adopted hundreds of laws regulating or limiting abortions in recent years. One type of anti-abortion law — requiring parental notification or consent before an abortion can be performed on a minor — has been adopted by at least 20 states,

so vague as to encompass more than one procedure," she says.

The new bill seeks to meet the Supreme Court's insistence on a health exception with a series of "congressional findings" that the procedure is "never medically indicated to preserve the health of the mother," is "unrecognized as a valid procedure by the mainstream medical community" and "poses additional health risks for the mother."

"The court has recognized in the past that Congress has a fact-finding role of its own that's entitled to deference," Johnson says.

But Saporta calls the findings "nonsense," with "no basis in scientific medical evidence."

and 15 others are considering similar measures.

But anti-abortion groups say Planned Parenthood and other abortion-rights organizations help teenagers get around these laws by referring them to women's clinics in states without parental-involvement statutes.

To counteract the practice, anti-abortion groups are urging Congress to make it a federal crime punishable by up to a year in prison for anyone other than a parent to transport a minor from a parental-consent state to a non-parental-involvement state in order to obtain an abortion. Abortion-rights groups strongly oppose the bill, saying it would endanger girls in dysfunctional families and expose relatives, such as aunts or grandmothers, to prosecution.

Twice approved by the House, the proposal is one of several abortion-related measures sought by anti-abortion groups, girded with greater confidence now that Republicans also control the Senate.

Meanwhile, state legislatures are engaged in pitched battles over other abortion measures. NARAL Pro-Choice America counts 23 states as considering either informed-consent measures — which require that women be given certain information about fetal development and the procedure itself before an abortion can be performed — or bills requiring that a woman wait at least 24 hours before an abortion. Nine states are considering measures to ban most or all abortions.

Both sides in the debate agree the restrictions already on the books have reduced the number of abortions. "The states that have passed pro-life legislation have had a significant impact on their abortion rates, birth rates and the number of abortions generally," says the NRLC's Balch. "They've all gone down."

Abortion-rights groups point in particular to waiting-period laws, which in some states require a woman to make two trips to a clinic before undergoing an abortion. One study suggested such laws reduced the number of abortions by 10 percent or more in two states: Mississippi and Utah. [10] "It definitely has an impact," says Erica Smock, legislative counsel for the Center for Reproductive Rights, a national litigation center based in New York City. "It increases burdens for women who already face obstacles."

Anti-abortion groups say the proposed federal Child Custody Protection Act will strengthen state parental-involvement laws by making it illegal to take a minor to another state for an abortion if state law requires parental-involvement in a minor's abortion. "Parental-notification laws are being systemically evaded by organized activity," Johnson says. "Elements of the abortion industry set up systems for shunting girls across state lines to get abortions without notifying their parents."

Abortion-rights groups say young women with abusive or unsupportive parents need to be able to turn to other relatives or other "trusted adults" in the event of an unwanted pregnancy. "This bill would endanger young women and isolate them when confronted with a crisis pregnancy," says NARAL's Cavendish. "The government cannot force healthy family communication where it doesn't already exist."

Among other bills pending in Congress, the Unborn Victims of Violence Act would make harming or killing a fetus a federal crime if the injury or death resulted from any one of 68 existing federal offenses, whether or not the assailant knew the woman was pregnant or intended to harm the fetus. Many states already have such laws.

Abortion-rights advocates say such laws are unnecessary. "The crime is on the pregnant woman who loses a wanted fetus or a wanted embryo," Cavendish says. She says the bill is "part of a strategy to undermine the foundations of *Roe* by weaving throughout the law a fabric of fetal personhood or embryonic personhood."

Anti-abortion groups say the bill simply recognizes that crimes that result in injury or death to a fetus have "two victims, not one." And Johnson denies any intention of using the bill to undercut *Roe*. "Pro-abortion groups try to enforce a policy that the unborn child must be invisible," he says. "Most Americans, whatever their views on abortion, don't think of it that way."

A so-called right-to-refuse bill — passed by the House in September 2002 — is designed to prevent health-care providers with religious or moral objections to abortion from being forced to perform the procedure. Supporters say it merely clarifies a "conscience clause" inserted into federal public-health law after the 1973 *Roe* decision. But opponents say the bill expands existing law by allowing hospitals, as well as health insurers, to prevent physicians or others from performing abortions or providing referrals to abortion counseling.

The child custody, right-to-refuse and fetal-protection bills all passed the House during the past (107th) Congress but failed to come to a vote in the Democratic-controlled Senate. Today, even with Republican control, the Senate is still regarded as a difficult hurdle for anti-abortion groups. Johnson counts 53 senators — a majority — on the record in support of *Roe v. Wade*. Nonetheless, he says, "some of those senators will support specific pro-life legislation." ∎

BACKGROUND

Road to *Roe*

Abortion laws — adopted by nearly all the states by the end of the 19th century — came under strong attack from a reform movement beginning in the 1950s. It was slowly gaining ground when the U.S.

Chronology

Before 1970
Most states enact laws in 19th century generally prohibiting abortions; movement to reform or repeal statutes forms in 1950s, advances slowly through 1960s.

1970s
Abortion-reform movement gains in state legislatures, then wins constitutional ruling from U.S. Supreme Court; decision spawns "right-to-life" movement.

1970
New York and three other states pass abortion "repeal laws."

1973
Supreme Court's *Roe v. Wade* decision establishes a woman's qualified constitutional right to abortion during most of pregnancy; "right-to-life" groups seek to limit or overturn ruling.

1977
Supreme Court allows states to deny abortion funding under Medicaid; three years later, court similarly upholds Hyde amendment barring use of federal funds for abortion for poor women.

1980s
Presidents Reagan and Bush support anti-abortion initiatives; Supreme Court, in conservative shift, upholds some abortion regulations.

1983
Parental consent for abortion for minors upheld by Supreme Court

if law allows "judicial-bypass" procedure; court invalidates "informed consent" and waiting-period provisions.

1984
Reagan adopts "Mexico City" policy to bar U.S. funds to groups that promote abortion overseas.

1989
Missouri abortion law upheld by Supreme Court in 5-4 vote; four justices criticize *Roe*, one short of majority.

1990s
Supreme Court reaffirms Roe's "essential holding," with modification; President Clinton adopts abortion-rights stands on several issues.

1991
Supreme Court upholds rule barring abortion counseling at federally funded family-planning clinics.

1992
Three-justice plurality provides key votes for Supreme Court to reaffirm *Roe* while giving states leeway to regulate abortion unless laws impose "undue burden" on women's rights; ruling upholds most provisions of Pennsylvania law, including waiting period and informed consent.

1993
President Clinton reverses several Reagan-era anti-abortion policies on *Roe's* 20th anniversary. . . . First killing of doctor who performs abortions.

1994
Congress approves Freedom of Access to Clinic Entrances Act to establish criminal and civil penal-

ties for use of force to intimidate abortion-clinic staff, patients.

1996, 1997
Clinton vetoes bills passed by Congress to ban "partial-birth abortions."

2000-Present
President Bush supports anti-abortion initiatives in Congress, controlled by Republicans after midterm elections.

2000
Supreme Court on June 28 strikes down Nebraska statute banning "partial-birth" abortions. . . . Food and Drug Administration in September approves the "abortion pill" RU-486. . . . Texas Gov. George W. Bush soft-pedals anti-abortion views during presidential campaign, wins disputed election.

2001
President Bush re-establishes "global gag rule" on his first workday, barring federal funds for international organizations that promote abortions; draws fire from abortion-rights groups on judicial nominations.

2002
Bush signs Born-Alive Infants Protection Act on Aug. 5. . . . Health and Human Services regulation approved Sept. 27 allows states to define fetus as "unborn child" for purposes of prenatal care under federal health-insurance program.

2003
Roe's 30th anniversary marked by demonstrations by both sides. . . . Partial-birth abortion ban approved by Senate March 12, with House expected to follow and send to Bush to become law subject to certain court test.

Supreme Court in 1973 dramatically invalidated all existing abortion laws with its landmark decision in *Roe v. Wade*. The ruling triggered a bitter fight between opposing forces now in its fourth decade.

The common law that the United States carried over from the Colonial period generally permitted abortion until "quickening," or the first movement of the fetus. [11] Connecticut became the first state to pass an abortion statute with an 1821 law prohibiting the inducement of abortion through dangerous poisons. By 1900, almost all the states had passed anti-abortion laws, largely in response to urgings from doctors. The laws typically permitted abortions when necessary in a doctor's opinion to preserve the life of the woman.

The laws remained on the books through the mid-20th century, but enforcement was uneven at most. Middle- and upper-class women often found ways to circumvent the laws by finding doctors willing to certify the procedure as medically necessary. Low-income women resorted to illegal abortions performed figuratively, if not literally, in the back alleys of metropolitan areas, often by people with little, if any, formal medical training. As of the late 1960s, the number of illegal abortions performed annually in the United States was variously estimated at between 200,000 and 1.2 million. In 1965, an estimated 200 women died from botched abortions, some of them crudely self-administered. [12]

The abortion-reform movement of the 1950s and '60s drew from the work of family-planning groups such as Planned Parenthood, anti-poverty organizations and the nascent women's-liberation movement. The movement gained ground despite strong opposition from the Roman Catholic Church and public ambivalence about what were then termed "elective" abortions.

Colorado in 1967 became the first state to liberalize its abortion law; by 1970, a dozen states had passed laws generally legalizing abortion in cases of rape, incest or to protect a woman's health or life. Then, in early 1970, New York dramatically became the first of four states to pass a "repeal law," virtually eliminating any barriers to abortion.

Reformers also had challenged abortion laws in courts, but with little success at first. In 1971, however, the justices agreed to hear challenges to laws in two states: Texas' 1857 ban on abortions except to save the woman's life and Georgia's 1968 "reform" statute allowing abortions if approved by a hospital committee after examination by two physicians other than the woman's personal doctor. The plaintiffs sued under the pseudonyms Jane Roe and Mary Doe, but years later identified themselves as Norma Jane McCorvey and Sandra Race Cano. Both women gave birth in 1970 after they were unable to obtain abortions in their states.

The Supreme Court struggled with the case, hearing arguments twice: once in December 1971 and then again in October 1972 after Justice Blackmun's initial draft of a decision failed to satisfy colleagues. Blackmun's second draft — strengthened by a summer's worth of research at the Mayo Clinic in Minnesota — eventually won concurrence from six other justices, including Chief Justice Warren Burger. Blackmun relied heavily on medical history, but based the decision on a "personal-liberty interest" protected under either the Ninth Amendment's "unenumerated rights" provision or the 14th Amendment's Due Process Clause. In a short dissent, then-Associate Justice William H. Rehnquist said the court's "conscious weighing of competing factors" was "far more appropriate to a legislative judgment than a judicial one."

From *Roe* to *Casey*

Anti-abortion forces responded to *Roe v. Wade* first with protests and then with well-organized campaigns that failed to overturn the decision but won enactment of a host of restrictive state and federal laws. Over the next two decades, the Supreme Court struck down some of the restrictions but upheld others. The court rejected pleas during the 1980s to reconsider the *Roe* decision, but significantly modified the ruling with its 1992 decision in *Casey* fortifying the states' discretion to regulate abortion procedures. [13]

The court fights played out against a political backdrop that became increasingly polarized over time. At the national level, President Ronald Reagan decisively aligned the Republican Party with the anti-abortion movement by such steps as prohibiting abortion counseling at federally funded family-planning clinics (the so-called "gag rule"), cutting off federal funds for international family-planning organizations promoting abortions (the "Mexico City policy") and barring the importation of the so-called abortion pill RU-486.

The first President George Bush continued the policies in his four years in the White House. Both Reagan and Bush also appeared to be choosing federal judges — including Supreme Court justices — likely to be skeptical at best of expanding abortion rights. As the GOP stance hardened, the Democratic Party equally committed itself to supporting abortion rights and opposing legislated restrictions or judicial efforts to overturn *Roe*.

Along with political organizing and lobbying, some elements of the anti-abortion movement turned to civil disobedience and violence. The National Abortion Federation counted some 161 incidents of arson or bombings against abortion clinics from 1977-1992. There were more than 100 clinic blockades each year in 1988 and 1989, resulting in more than 10,000 arrests per year. Most ominous were death threats and actual killings. Anti-abortion activists killed five people in 1993 and 1994: a physician at a Pensacola, Fla., clinic in

March 1993; a second physician and a volunteer escort outside another Pensacola clinic in July 1994; and receptionists at separate Brookline, Mass., clinics on Dec. 30, 1994. [14]

The Supreme Court, meanwhile, gave anti-abortion forces major victories with decisions in 1977 and 1980 that permitted first the states and then the federal government to deny abortion funding under the Medicaid program for the indigent. Through the 1980s, the so-called Hyde amendment — named after Rep. Henry J. Hyde, R-Ill. — barred federal funding of abortions except to save the life of the woman. The court, on the other hand, struck down provisions requiring spousal consent, waiting periods or informed consent before an abortion could be performed.

After some wavering, the court in 1990 ruled that states could require parental notification for a minor to obtain an abortion, but only with a judicial procedure to bypass the requirement under certain circumstances. The court in 1991 also upheld the "gag rule" on family-planning clinics.

By the end of the 1980s, Reagan had appeared to shift the high court in a conservative direction with four appointments: Rehnquist's elevation to chief justice in 1986 and the selection of Justices O'Connor in 1981, Antonin Scalia in 1986 and Kennedy in 1987. The shift encouraged anti-abortion groups to view a challenge to a Missouri abortion law as a vehicle for overturning Roe. In fact, the court in 1989 upheld the law by a 5-4 vote, with four of the justices explicitly criticizing Roe: Rehnquist, Scalia, Kennedy and Byron R. White. But O'Connor declined to reconsider Roe and instead upheld the Missouri law because it did not create what she had described in previous opinions as an "undue burden" on a woman's right to an abortion.

The first President Bush appeared to shift the court further to the right with his appointments of Justice Souter in 1990 and Clarence Thomas in 1991.

A new showdown came in a case challenging a Pennsylvania law that required a waiting period, informed consent and spousal consent — provisions seemingly barred by previous decisions. The Bush administration defended the law and expressly urged the court to overturn Roe. In an unusual move, however, three of the Republican-appointed justices — O'Connor, Kennedy and Souter — filed a pivotal joint opinion that reaffirmed what they called Roe's "essential holding" but nonetheless upheld all of the Pennsylvania law except the spousal consent portion, arguing that the measure met O'Connor's "undue burden" test.

Blackmun praised the three for "personal courage" while lamenting the apparent narrowing of Roe. From the opposite side, four justices — including Thomas — said abortion regulations should be permitted if "rationally related to a legitimate state interest."

Abortion-Rights Gains

The election of Democrat Clinton as president in 1992 brought an abortion-rights supporter to the White House for the first time in 12 years. Clinton reversed several Reagan-Bush abortion policies, supported abortion-rights measures in Congress and — perhaps most significantly — fortified the Supreme Court's abortion-rights bloc with his appointments of Justices Ruth Bader Ginsburg and Stephen G. Breyer. Those appointments helped produce a pivotal victory for abortion-rights forces with the court's 5-4 decision in 2000 striking down a state ban on "partial-birth abortions." [15]

Clinton cheered abortion-rights groups by changing three Reagan-Bush policies on his second day in office: Jan. 22, 1993 — the 20th anniversary of Roe. By executive order, Clinton ended enforcement of the "gag rule" on family-planning clinics and over-

turned the Mexico City policy on aid to international family-planning organizations. He also lifted a ban on abortions at overseas military facilities and directed the Department of Health and Human Services (HHS) to study whether to allow the importation of RU-486.

With Democratic majorities in the House and the Senate, Clinton also won enactment in 1994 of a law aimed at countering blockades of women's clinics. The Freedom of Access to Clinic Entrances Act — dubbed FACE — provided criminal and civil penalties for anyone using force or the threat of force against clinic workers or patients. In addition, Congress eased the Hyde amendment by allowing federal funding for abortions in cases of rape, incest or to protect the life of the mother. Abortion-rights supporters also won House and Senate committee approval of the "Freedom of Choice Act," aimed at writing the Roe decision into federal law. Neither bill was brought up for a floor vote, however, and anti-abortion forces gained the upper hand when Republicans won control of the House in the 1994 elections.

Ginsburg, a pioneer in women's-rights litigation before her appointment to the federal bench in 1980, and Breyer, a one-time aide to abortion-rights supporter Sen. Edward M. Kennedy, D-Mass., have both supported abortion rights after their appointments to the high court in 1993 and 1994, respectively. For several years, however, the court dealt with abortion issues only tangentially. In two decisions in 1994, the court ruled that judges could restrict anti-abortion demonstrations by setting up "buffer zones" around abortion-clinic entrances and that abortion clinics or patients could sue anti-abortion protesters for damages under the federal anti-racketeering law. Dissenting justices said the rulings limited anti-abortion groups' free-speech rights.

Beginning in 1995, anti-abortion groups were lobbying for laws to ban

Abortion Rates Higher for Low-Income Women

Abortion rates have been increasing dramatically among low-income women while declining among wealthier women.

Woman's Economic Status	Abortion Rate (No. of abortions per 1,000 women)	
	1994	2000
Income below poverty level	36	44
Income up to twice poverty level	31	38
Income two to three times poverty level	25	21
Income more than triple poverty level	16	10

Source: Rachel K. Jones, et al., "Patterns in the Socioeconomic Characteristics of Women Obtaining Abortions in 2000-2001," Perspectives on Sexual and Reproductive Health, September/October 2002, pp. 226-235, The Alan Guttmacher Institute.

the procedure that they provocatively termed "partial-birth abortion." A federal ban won approval in the GOP-controlled House and the Democratic-controlled Senate in 1996, but Clinton vetoed the measure in a White House ceremony on April 10, attended by several women who insisted the procedure had saved their lives and their future ability to bear children. A second legislative push also ended with a veto in 1997. Anti-abortion groups were more successful with state legislatures; by the end of the decade, some 30 states had banned the procedure.

A challenge to one of those state laws — Nebraska's — reached the high court in 2000. In an opinion by Breyer, the court ruled that the measure created "an undue burden on a woman's right to make an abortion decision." First, he said, the law could be construed to prohibit the commonly done dilation and extraction (D&E) procedure. In addition, Breyer said, the law conflicted with *Roe* and subsequent cases because it did not include an exception for the procedure if necessary to protect the woman's health. In a pivotal concurring opinion, O'Connor suggested a more carefully drawn statute might pass constitutional muster.

For the dissenters, Thomas likened the procedure to "infanticide." [16]

As the presidential campaign unfolded later that year, the Supreme Court's composition became a proxy for the opposing views of Republican George W. Bush and Democrat Al Gore. [17] Bush said he would appoint future justices in the mold of the court's strongest abortion opponents: Thomas and Scalia. Gore countered by pledging his support for abortion rights and warning of a likely reversal of *Roe v. Wade* if Bush made good on his pledge.

The two candidates staked out contrasting positions on other abortion issues, including partial-birth abortions and RU-486, but they also appeared to play down the issue to avoid alienating swing voters. For his part, Bush said he supported a constitutional amendment to ban abortions, but cautioned that it would not be adopted "until a lot of people change their minds."

Anti-Abortion Advances

During his first two years in office, President Bush has cheered anti-abortion groups with an array of policy moves and appointments. Anti-abortion bills won approval in the Republican-controlled House but stalled in the Senate after the Democrats gained control in May 2001. The GOP's recapture of the Senate in the 2002 midterm congressional elections improved the chances for the anti-abortion agenda, including the ban on partial-birth abortions. But abortion-rights advocates vowed to continue opposing the bills — and immediately to challenge the partial-birth abortion measure if it became law.

Bush touched off fierce fights before his inauguration by naming determined abortion opponents to two key Cabinet posts: John Ashcroft, a former Missouri governor who had been defeated for re-election to the Senate, as attorney general; and Wisconsin Gov. Tommy G. Thompson as HHS secretary. Then two days after his inauguration, Bush marked *Roe's* 28th anniversary by sending greetings to the annual "March for Life" and, more tangibly, by reinstating the Mexico City policy of barring U.S. funds to international family-planning organizations that promote abortion.

Abortion-rights supporters had no leverage to try to block the reinstated funding policy. They tried hard but failed to block Ashcroft's confirmation. In his confirmation hearings, however, Democratic senators secured Ashcroft's promise to enforce federal laws protecting abortion rights — including the access-to-clinic-entrances act. He also said he would not try to overturn *Roe v. Wade*. Despite the concessions, anti-abortion groups hailed the Senate's 58-42 vote to confirm him on Feb. 1. Thompson had won easier confirmation earlier, after initial opposition to the nomination failed to harden.

Abortion politics also shaped the reaction to Bush's judicial nominations, including his first batch of 11 nominees for federal appeals courts, announced on May 9, 2001. [18] Abortion-rights groups criticized several of the nominees for taking anti-abortion stands as academics, lawyers or judges. Under Democratic control, the Senate held up many of Bush's nominees in 2001 and 2002, including the most controversial. Priscilla R. Owen, a Texas Supreme Court justice chosen for the federal appeals court in New Orleans, failed to win approval by the Judiciary Committee last September after being criticized for arguing in a dissenting opinion for a restrictive interpretation of the state's parental-notification law. (Owen is expected to be approved by the committee, now under Republican control, in the next two weeks.)

As Bush began his second year in office, he renewed his anti-abortion credentials with a more detailed message to the annual "March for Life" on Jan. 22. In an eight-paragraph statement read by telephone, Bush promised his administration would oppose partial-birth abortion and public financing of abortions and support teen abstinence, crisis-pregnancy centers and parental consent and notification laws. He also vowed to support "a comprehensive and effective ban on all forms of human cloning." [19] Some abortion opponents believe cloning human embryos to extract the cells for biomedical research is the equivalent of murder.

The administration also won praise the same month from anti-abortion groups — and strong opposition from abortion-rights organizations — with a proposed rule to define a fetus as a child eligible for government-subsidized health care under the Children's Health Insurance Program. Congress created the program in 1997 to benefit children in near-poverty families ineligible for Medicaid. Thompson said the proposed rule would allow states to increase insurance coverage for prenatal care and delivery. But abortion-rights advocates said the proposal was really a back-door attempt to establish a legal precedent for recognizing the fetus as a person; they called for simply adding

pregnant women to the program's coverage.

The debate continued through the administrative rulemaking process. Nearly 7,800 comments were received on the proposed rule before Thompson gave final approval on Sept. 27 for the regulation to go into effect 30 days later. [20] The fight then shifted to the states. Abortion-rights advocates said they would urge states to reject the option and instead ask HHS for permission to include pregnant women in the program. Two states had already taken that approach: New Jersey and Rhode Island.

In the meantime, Bush had signed into law a bill sought by anti-abortion groups to guarantee legal protection to babies born alive at any state of development. The Born-Alive Infants Protection Act defined a child as born alive if he or she has been expelled from the mother; is breathing; and has a beating heart, a pulsating umbilical cord or muscle movement, even if the expulsion occurred during an abortion. The bill included a disclaimer that it was not intended to infringe on abortion rights. Abortion-rights supporters in Congress called the measure unnecessary but did not oppose it. Bush signed the measure on Aug. 5, saying that it would give legal rights to "every infant born alive — including an infant who survives an abortion procedure."

As midterm elections approached, the House on Sept. 25 passed by a comfortable 229-189 margin the right-to-refuse bill, exempting health-care providers with religious or moral objections from being forced to perform abortions. But the anti-abortion agenda remained blocked in the Democratic-controlled Senate. The GOP gains in the midterm elections immediately buoyed the anti-abortion forces, who counted eight of the 10 newly elected senators as "pro-life." Three of those took seats previously held by Democrats who had supported abortion rights. The election results helped clear one logjam when

the Senate shifted to GOP control, with the early swearing in of two of the new Republicans. The move allowed confirmation of one of Bush's judicial nominees: Michael McConnell, a conservative law professor named to the federal appeals court in Denver, who had been opposed by abortion-rights groups because of writings critical of *Roe.*

On the 30th anniversary of the decision, Bush again spoke to the anti-abortion march by telephone. [21] "You and I share a commitment to building a culture of life in America," the president said, "and we are making progress."

The crowd numbered in the tens of thousands, leading abortion-rights groups to sound urgent alarms. "Pro-choice America has to wake up," NARAL's Cavendish declared. ∎

CURRENT SITUATION

"Abortion-Pill" Controversy

For more than a decade, American women waited to learn whether a new drug developed in Europe — the so-called abortion pill — would be approved for use in the United States. Finally, in August 2000, the Food and Drug Administration (FDA) gave the official green light for doctors who wanted to prescribe the drug, known most commonly as RU-486. [22]

Some observers speculated that use of the drug — now called mifepristone — could defuse the abortion controversy. But today RU-486 remains a source of contention between the opposing camps. Anti-abortion groups call it unsafe and are asking the FDA to rescind its approval, while abortion-rights groups are actively promoting what they prefer to call the "early-option pill."

The dispute underscores the chasm that continues to separate the opposing camps in the abortion debate on virtually every issue relating to women's reproductive health. Occasional efforts to find common ground appear to make little headway, as the rhetoric remains hot and accusatory. Anti-abortion groups call their opponents "the abortion industry" or more provocatively "baby killers," while abortion-rights organizations label their adversaries not just "anti-choice" but sometimes "anti-woman."

Whatever its political impact, RU-486 appeals to abortion-rights advocates as an additional and, at first blush, more convenient option for women to terminate unwanted pregnancies. Two years after FDA approval, the drug had been used to complete more than 100,000 abortions in the United States, according to Danco Laboratories, the New York-based company that markets the drug here. [23] The Alan Guttmacher Institute — a nonprofit research center affiliated with Planned Parenthood — estimates that pill-induced, or medical, abortions comprised about 6 percent of all abortions in the first half of 2001, the most recent period covered in its survey.

Abortion providers insist RU-486 is both safe and effective. "This has been a very acceptable method for women," says the National Abortion Federation's Saporta. Medical abortion can be completed earlier than surgical procedures — an important advantage, Saporta says. "Earlier abortion by any method is safer," she explains.

Anti-abortion groups, however, say RU-486 can cause hemorrhaging, or even death, and its approval was the result of political pressure in the last year of the Clinton administration. "The evidence would seem to show that it is not safe for the woman and obviously not safe for the baby," says Wendy Wright, senior policy director for Concerned Women for America (CWFA). The Christian-oriented orga-

nization petitioned the FDA in August 2002 to rescind its approval of RU-486 because of safety complaints and alleged procedural flaws in the approval process.

The National Abortion Federation is working on a response to correct what it calls the "medical misinformation" in CWFA's petition. "There isn't any question that mifepristone is safe and effective," says Saporta. "We don't believe the FDA will change its approval."

Anti-abortion groups emphasize — and an NAF fact sheet acknowledges — that use of RU-486 is not so simple as some news coverage might suggest. The drug works by blocking the body's production of progesterone, a hormone crucial to the early progress of pregnancy. The treatment requires at least two visits to a clinic or medical office, can take anywhere from three days to three to four weeks and fails about 5 percent of the time — necessitating a surgical procedure. Anti-abortion groups also say that a pill-induced abortion has a greater emotional impact on the woman because she is likely to see the aborted fetus when it is expelled.

For abortion-rights advocates, on the other hand, RU-486 helps to circumvent the persistent problem of limited availability of abortion providers. "Access is probably the biggest problem facing women who choose to have an abortion," Saporta says. The number of abortion providers has declined by more than one-third since 1982, according to the Guttmacher Institute. More than one-third of American women live in a county without an abortion provider. [24]

Doctors today often are not trained in how to perform an abortion. Fewer than half of the obstetrics-gynecology residency programs require or even offer abortion training, Saporta says. To remedy the problem, NAF and other abortion-rights groups are calling for laws — like an executive order issued by New York City Mayor Michael Bloomberg in April 2002 — to require

abortion training in residency programs at public hospitals. Anti-abortion groups say such requirements run afoul of existing federal law that prohibits discrimination against any health-care entity for refusing to provide abortion training.

In another fight, opposing camps have squared off on the question of whether women who have abortions have a heightened risk of developing breast cancer. Although most cancer experts doubt any link, the National Cancer Institute — part of the National Institutes of Health within the HHS Department — acceded to lobbying from anti-abortion lawmakers last summer and changed its Web site to describe the research on the subject as "inconsistent." [25]

Abortion-rights groups strongly criticized the revision. The institute responded by convening a closed-door conference on the issue in February that ended by reverting to the previous position. In a conference summary posted on its Web site, the institute now states flatly: "Induced abortion is not associated with increased breast cancer risk."

Legislative Battles

Anti-abortion groups are exulting in the Senate's quick approval of legislation to ban so-called partial-birth abortions and predicting easy passage in the House in April en route to being signed into law by President Bush. Meanwhile, other parts of the anti-abortion groups' agenda are progressing in Congress and in some state legislatures.

The Senate's March 13 ban on partial-birth abortions came after two days of debate and unsuccessful efforts by opponents to soften the measure. With some Democratic votes, the Republican majority rejected by margins of more than 20 votes each of two Democratic-sponsored amendments to add a health exception to the bill.

At Issue:

Should Congress ban so-called partial-birth abortions?

REP. CHRISTOPHER H. SMITH, R-N.J.
*CHAIRMAN, BIPARTISAN CONGRESSIONAL
PRO-LIFE CAUCUS*

WRITTEN FOR THE CQ RESEARCHER, MARCH 2003

a society is measured by how well — or poorly — it treats the most vulnerable in its midst, and partial-birth abortion, like all abortions, is horrific violence against women and children.

Justice Clarence Thomas accurately described the procedure in his *Stenberg v. Carhart* (2000) dissent: "After dilating the cervix, the physician will grab the fetus by its feet and pull the fetal body out of the uterus into the vaginal cavity. At this stage of development, the head is the largest part of the body. . . . the head will be held inside the uterus by the woman's cervix. While the fetus is stuck in this position, dangling partly out of the woman's body, and just a few inches from a completed birth, the physician uses an instrument such as a pair of scissors to tear or perforate the skull. The physician will then either crush the skull or will use a vacuum to remove the brain and other intracranial contents from the fetal skull, collapse the fetus' head, and pull the fetus from the uterus."

Most partial-birth abortions are committed between the 20th and 26th week of pregnancy. At this stage, a prematurely delivered infant is usually born alive. These are babies who are extremely sensitive to pain — whether inside the womb, fully born or anywhere in-between.

An overwhelming majority of Americans are outraged that this procedure is legal in our country. A January Gallup Poll found that 70 percent favored and 25 percent opposed "a law that would make it illegal to perform a specific abortion procedure conducted in the last six months of pregnancy known as 'partial birth abortion,' except in cases necessary to save the life of the mother."

In a January speech, President Bush agreed: "Partial-birth abortion is an abhorrent procedure that offends human dignity."

I have written two torture-victims relief laws and many other pieces of human-rights legislation including a law to stop exploitation of women by sex traffickers. Partial-birth abortion is torture of baby girls and boys, and I am ashamed of my colleagues who stand on the House floor to defend it.

Abortion methods are violence against children. There is absolutely nothing compassionate or benign about dousing a baby with superconcentrated salt solutions or lethal injections or hacking them to pieces with surgical knives, and there is absolutely nothing compassionate or caring about sucking a baby's brains out.

REP. LOUISE SLAUGHTER, D-N.Y.
CO-CHAIR, PRO-CHOICE CAUCUS

WRITTEN FOR THE CQ RESEARCHER, MARCH 2003

i do solemnly swear that I will support and defend the Constitution of the United States against all enemies, foreign and domestic. . . ." Before taking office, Members of Congress pledge these words to uphold the Constitution. Yet, again this year, anti-choice legislators introduce legislation that disregards the Constitution and the precious rights it guarantees.

The right to privacy as recognized in *Roe v. Wade* and reaffirmed in *Planned Parenthood v. Casey* is a fundamental American value. Opponents of a woman's right to choose have failed in their efforts to eliminate this constitutionally protected right, so they have changed tactics. Their strategy now is to whittle away at a woman's right to choose until all that remains are hollow guarantees in a faded court opinion.

The legislative centerpiece of this strategy is misleadingly titled Partial Birth Abortion Ban Act of 2003. Three years after the Supreme Court addressed this issue in the landmark *Stenberg v. Carhart* decision overturning Nebraska's prohibition of so-called "partial-birth" abortions, opponents of reproductive freedom want to force through Congress legislation that contains the same serious constitutional flaws as the Nebraska ban.

The court ruled that the Nebraska law was unconstitutional because it did not provide an exception to protect a woman's health. Further, it ruled that the law was an undue burden on women's rights to privacy, because the vague description of partial-birth abortions covered multiple procedures, including the most common form of second trimester abortion.

The legislation's authors could have drafted a bill that complies with constitutional standards, yet they have not done so. This bill does NOT include an exception for the health of the woman, and it does NOT prohibit a specific abortion procedure.

Congress should not invade the doctor-patient relationship. These intensely personal choices must be made by women, their doctors and their families — not by politicians. We should praise doctors who care for women faced with this difficult decision, not make them federal criminals. This legislation is an attack on the power of the Supreme Court, the Constitution and women's health and dignity.

Forcing members of Congress year after year to consider a bill that is clearly unconstitutional is a waste of taxpayers' money. Instead of continually reintroducing unconstitutional legislation, proponents of this measure should put their energies and resources into promoting women's health by improving access to contraception and supporting comprehensive family-planning programs.

Seeking Common Ground

Cristina Page and Amanda Peterman are both thirty-something college graduates and self-described feminists with a common interest in promoting women's health and family welfare. Since they first met a little over two years ago, they have become fast friends. They happen to disagree, however, on one major issue: abortion.

Page works as program director for the New York affiliate of NARAL Pro-Choice America, while Peterman serves as life media director for Right to Life of Michigan. Nonetheless, Page and Peterman marked the 30th anniversary of *Roe v. Wade* in January with a jointly bylined op-ed article in *The New York Times* calling for the opposing camps in the abortion debate to find common ground on such issues as pregnancy prevention, high-quality child care and "family friendly" workplace policies.

"If the pro-choice and pro-life movements work together to support legislation to expand the social safety net for low-income mothers, and to lobby for more family-friendly policies for working parents, their power would be formidable," Page and Peterman wrote. "But sadly, they are issues that often get lost in the larger debate." [1]

Since they met on the eve of the 2000 election, Page and Peterman have traveled together and talked at length. Page took Peterman to an abortion clinic in Pittsburgh to try to dispel the image of counselors rushing women to have the procedure. For her part, Page says she better appreciates that many people in the right-to-life movement are turned off by violence and harsh rhetoric.

Together, Page and Peterman are now working to raise money for a new organization to collaborate on what Page calls "the surprising number of important issues on which we agree."

The project is both ambitious and delicate. Page says her abortion-rights colleagues have been supportive for the most part, but Peterman bowed out of a scheduled interview in March because of what she called "stuff inside my ranks. It's a very slow process to educate both sides," Peterman said apologetically.

"There's a lot of distrust, there's been a lot of violence," Page says. "We can retrace the disagreements, but that's what we've been doing for 30 years."

---

[1] Cristina Page and Amanda Peterman, "The Right to Agree," *The New York Times*, Jan. 22, 2003, p. A21.

Abortion-rights advocates scored a symbolic victory with a 52-46 vote on March 12 adding a "sense of the Senate" amendment in support of *Roe v. Wade*, but the language is certain to be rejected by the House and stripped out in conference. More substantively, abortion-rights advocates suffered a narrow loss on March 11 with a failed amendment to require health insurance plans to provide coverage for birth control pills. The measure was approved, 49-47, but under Senate rules needed 60 votes to overcome a point of order because it would have raised federal spending.

On final passage, 16 Democrats joined 48 of the chamber's 51 Republicans in voting for the ban. Democrats voting aye included Minority Leader Daschle. The three GOP "no" votes came from moderate New Englanders: Lincoln Chafee of Rhode Island and Maine's Olympia J. Snowe and Susan Collins. Sen. James M. Jeffords, I-Vt., also voted no. The three non-voting senators were all Democrats,

including two declared presidential candidates — John Kerry of Massachusetts and John Edwards of North Carolina — and Delaware's Joseph Biden, Jr.

President Bush issued a statement commending the Senate for voting to outlaw what he called "an abhorrent procedure that offends human dignity."

Opponents continued to insist, however, that the bill will not survive a court test. "Anti-choice senators simply ignored Supreme Court precedent," said NARAL's Michelman, referring to the 2000 decision striking down Nebraska's partial-birth ban. But the NRLC's Johnson noted that four justices had voted to uphold the Nebraska law and voiced hope for a different outcome when a case testing the federal law reaches the high court.

Meanwhile, anti-abortion groups are also advancing a variety of restrictive bills in state legislatures around the country. But the only major bills to win final legislative approval by mid-March were a package of measures in

Virginia that faced a possible veto from the state's Democratic governor, Mark Warner. Abortion-rights groups, however, are having some success with bills designed to reduce the need for abortions by easing women's access to emergency contraception — so-called morning-after bills.

The bills approved by the Virginia legislature include a new ban on so-called "partial-birth infanticide" to replace the state's previous law that was invalidated following the Supreme Court's decision in the Nebraska case. The bill prohibits "any deliberate act that is intended to kill a human infant (or that does kill an infant) who has been born alive but who has not been completely extracted or expelled from its mother." A second measure would require a minor to obtain the consent from one parent before an abortion; current state law only requires notice.

Warner says he may veto the measures, which he calls "a frontal assault on a woman's right to choose." But both bills originally passed with veto-proof majorities; the legislature is to return on April 1 to consider any gubernatorial vetoes. Opponents vow to challenge the partial-birth abortion bill in court if it does become law. [26]

Some of the other bills gaining in state legislatures are examples of what abortion-rights groups call "TRAP laws" — for "targeted regulation of abortion providers." A Kansas House committee has approved a bill setting safety standards for abortion clinics; opponents say the bill is unnecessary and designed to impose unaffordable costs. [27]

Some other bills are largely symbolic. A Georgia lawmaker is proposing to require a judge to issue a death warrant before an abortion can proceed. In South Carolina, a legislator has a bill to erect a six-foot statue of a fetus outside the statehouse as a memorial to "unborn children who have given their lives because of legal abortion."

For their part, abortion-rights advocates won legislative approval in two states — Hawaii and New Mexico — requiring hospitals to inform sexual-assault survivors about emergency contraception. Hawaii also passed a bill to allow women to obtain emergency contraception from pharmacists without an individual prescription from a physician; similar proposals were pending in other states, including New York, Oregon and Texas. ■

OUTLOOK

Unabated Conflict

The abortion wars show no signs of abating.

The dueling press releases issued after the Senate passed the partial-birth abortion bill carried forward the harsh debates from the Senate floor. The

NRLC accused opponents of "extremism in defense of abortion," while NARAL said the bill took "direct aim at a woman's right to choose."

The bill's ultimate fate rests with the courts — most likely, the Supreme Court itself. The justices have shied away from abortion disputes since their 2000 decision striking down the Nebraska ban. In February, for example, the court declined to hear a women's-clinic challenge to an Indiana waiting-period law upheld by the federal appeals court in Chicago. The justices are likely to feel obliged to take up a case testing a new federal law, but any legal challenge will take more than a year to reach them.

By then, the court may have one or more new justices, but its tilt on abortion issues depends on who retires. The court's three oldest members are Rehnquist, 78, who opposes abortion rights; and Justices John Paul Stevens, 82, a strong abortion-rights supporter, and O'Connor, nearly 73, who helped preserve *Roe v. Wade* in 1992 but has voted to uphold most state restrictions on abortion.

Rehnquist's retirement would not give President Bush the chance to shift the court's balance toward the anti-abortion side; Stevens' or O'Connor's departure might. Any vacancy, however, will result in a likely confirmation fight between liberals and conservatives in the narrowly divided Senate.

The opposing abortion-related groups are both using a fight over one of Bush's judicial nominees as a rehearsal of sorts for a potential Supreme Court fight. Anti-abortion groups are strongly supporting and abortion-rights organizations strenuously opposing confirmation for Miguel Estrada, a Washington lawyer and former assistant U.S. solicitor general, to the federal appeals court in Washington. Republicans say they have sufficient votes — 54 — to approve the nomination, but they have been unable to muster the 60 votes needed to overcome a Democratic filibuster.

Legislatively, anti-abortion lawmakers enjoy the upper hand on Capitol Hill, but they still face significant hurdles. As the new Congress convened, NARAL estimated that it had only prevailed in 25 out of 148 votes on reproductive rights issues since 1996. With the newly strengthened GOP hold in Congress, abortion-rights advocates already have been on the losing end of two major votes — the House's ban on human cloning in February and the Senate's partial-birth abortion ban in March. Abortion-rights advocates are likely to face more rough sledding over the next two years.

Meanwhile, the debates continue not only in legislative chambers but also on the sidewalks outside women's clinics, where abortion-rights advocates appear determined but beleaguered. "I don't think *Roe v. Wade* will be overturned," clinic escort Fox says. "But it's going to continue to be broken down until we only have a right to abortion under very limited parameters."

For her part, "sidewalk counselor" Walsh is equally determined and seemingly more hopeful of eventual victory in the fight against *Roe v. Wade*. "With the way our society is, our government is, it would take a miracle" to overturn *Roe*, Walsh says. "But God does do miracles. The most effective thing we can do is pray. So with God's grace, one day it will happen." ■

Notes

[1] For background, see Charles S. Clark, "Abortion Clinic Protests," *The CQ Researcher*, April 7, 1995, pp. 297-320.

[2] For background, see Sarah Glazer, "Roe v. Wade at 25," *The CQ Researcher*, Nov. 28, 1997, pp. 1033-1056.

[3] See *1996 CQ Almanac*, pp. 6-42 to 6-45; *1997 CQ Almanac*, pp. 6-12 to 6-18.

[4] Mary Balch, "Pro-Lifers Celebrate Gains in State Legislative Elections," *NRLC News*, December 2002 (www.nrlc.org/news/2002).

[5] NARAL Pro-Choice America Foundation, "Who Decides? A State-by-State Review of Abortion and Reproductive Rights," January 2003 (www.naral.org/mediaresources/publications.html).

[6] "Memorandum to the Conference," Nov. 21, 1972, cited in Barbara Hinkson Craig and David M. O'Brien, *Abortion and American Politics* (1993), p. 21.

[7] *Planned Parenthood of Southeastern Pennsylvania v. Casey*, 505 U.S. 833 (1992). For accounts of the case, see David J. Garrow, *Liberty and Sexuality: The Right to Privacy and the Making of Roe v. Wade* (1998), pp. 681-701; N.E.H. Hull and Peter Charles Hoffer, *Roe v. Wade: The Abortion Rights Controversy in American History* (2001), pp. 249-258.

[8] *Time*/CNN/Gallup Poll conducted Jan. 15-16, 2003, among 1,010 adult Americans age 18 or older.

[9] *Stenberg v. Carhart*, 505 U.S. 833 (2000).

[10] The studies are discussed in a recent federal appeals court decision upholding Indiana's waiting-period law. See *A Woman's Choice-East Side Women's Clinic v. Newman*, 7th U.S. Circuit Court of Appeals, 01-2107, Sept. 16, 2002.

[11] For historical background, see Hull and Hoffer, *op. cit.*, pp. 11-88; James C. Mohr, *Abortion in America: The Origins and Evolution of National Policy, 1800-1900* (1978).

[12] The Alan Guttmacher Institute, "Trends in Abortion in the United States, 1973-2000," January 2003.

[13] For a compact summary of Supreme Court decisions from *Roe* through the partial-birth abortion decision in *Stenberg v. Carhart* (2000), see "Abortion" in Claire Cushman (ed.), *Supreme Court Decisions and Women's Rights* (2001), pp. 188-206.

[14] See Dallas A. Blanchard, *The Anti-Abortion Movement and the Rise of the Religious Right: From Polite to Fiery Protest* (1994), pp. 53-60; Garrow, *op. cit.*, p. 705.

[15] For summaries, see *Congress and the Nation, Vol. IX, 1993-1996* (1998), pp. 536-541, 563-565; *Congress and the Nation*, Vol. X, 1997-2000 (2002), pp. 455-459, 472-475.

[16] For an account, see Kenneth Jost, *Supreme Court Yearbook 1999-2000* (2000), pp. 34-41.

[17] Account drawn from Mary Leonard, "Both Candidates Keep Quiet on Abortion," *The Boston Globe*, Nov. 1, 2000, p. A23.

[18] For background, see Kenneth Jost, "Judges and Politics," *The CQ Researcher*, July 27, 2001, pp. 577-600.

[19] The complete text can be found on *National Right to Life News*, February 2002 (www.nrlc.org/news).

[20] See Robert Pear, "Bush Rule Makes Fetuses Eligible for Health Benefits," *The New York Times*, Sept. 28, 2002, p. A13; Laura Meckler, " 'Unborn Child' Coverage Rule Set," The Associated Press, Sept. 29, 2002.

[21] See Robin Toner, "At a Distance, Bush Joins Abortion Protest," *The New York Times*, Jan. 23, 2003, p. A16.

[22] Some background drawn from interest-group Web sites: National Abortion Federation (www.naf.org); National Right to Life Committee (www.nrlc.org). For a journalistic account, see Sharon Bernstein, "Persistence

Brought Abortion Pill to U.S.," *Los Angeles Times*, Nov. 5, 2000, p. A1.

[23] Marc Kaufman, "Abortion Pill Sales Rising, Firm Says," *The Washington Post*, Sept. 25, 2002, p. A3.

[24] Stanley K. Henshaw and Lawrence B. Finer, "The Accessibility of Abortion Services in the United States, 2001," *Perspectives on Sexual and Reproductive Health*, Vol. 35, No. 1 (January/February 2003), pp. 15-24 (www.agi-usa.org/journals).

[25] See Daniel Costello, "An Enduring Debate: Cancer and Abortion," *Los Angeles Times*, March 10, 2003.

[26] Warner quoted in Warren Fiske, "Now, the Vetoes," *The* (Norfolk) *Virginian-Pilot*, Feb. 28, 2003, p. A1. See also Tammie Smith, "Lawmakers Focus on Abortion," *The* (Richmond) *Times-Dispatch*, Feb. 23, 2003, p. A11.

[27] See David Crary, "Abortion Foes Step Up Efforts Nationally," The Associated Press, March 11, 2003.

FOR MORE INFORMATION

Alan Guttmacher Institute, 120 Wall St., New York, NY 10005; (212) 248-1111; www.agi-usa.org. Nonprofit research center on reproductive issues; "special affiliate" of Planned Parenthood Federation.

Center for Reproductive Rights, 120 Wall St., New York, NY 10005; (917) 637-3600; www.crlp.org.

Concerned Women for America, 1015 15th St., N.W., suite 1100, Washington, DC 20005; (202) 488-7000; www.cwfa.org. Opposes abortion.

Family Research Council, 801 G St., N.W., Washington, DC 20001; (202) 393-2100; www.frc.org. Opposes abortion.

NARAL Pro-Choice America, 1156 15th St., N.W., Suite 700, Washington, DC 20005; (202) 973-3000; www.naral.org.

National Abortion Federation. 1755 Massachusetts Ave., N.W., Suite 600, Washington, DC 20036; (202) 667-5881; www.prochoice.org. Represents abortion clinics.

National Right to Life Committee, 512 10th St., N.W., Washington, DC 20004; (202) 626-8800; www.nrlc.org.

Bibliography

Selected Sources

Books

Blanchard, Dallas A., *The Anti-Abortion Movement and the Rise of the Religious Right: From Polite to Fiery Protest*, Twayne Publishers, 1994.

Critically examines the movement from *Roe* through *Casey* (1992). Blanchard is professor emeritus at the University of West Florida. Lists major anti-abortion publications and organizations.

Cook, Elizabeth Adell, Ted G. Jelen and Clyde Wilcox, *Between Two Absolutes: Public Opinion and the Politics of Abortion*, Westview Press, 1992.

Detailed analyses of public opinion on abortion with extensive statistical information over 20-year period. Cook is now an editor at the *American Political Science Review*; Jelen teaches at the University of Nevada-Las Vegas, and Wilcox at Georgetown University. Jelen is also editor or co-editor of *Abortion Politics in the United States and Canada* (with Marthe A. Chandler), Praeger, 1994; *Perspectives on the Politics of Abortion*, Praeger, 1995.

Craig, Barbara Hinkson, and David M. O'Brien, *Abortion and American Politics*, Chatham House, 1993.

Analyzes the politics of the abortion issue from *Roe* through *Casey*. Craig is a professor emerita at Wesleyan University, O'Brien teaches at the University of Virginia. Includes major statutes and case index.

Garrow, David J., *Liberty and Sexuality: The Right to Privacy and the Making of Roe v. Wade*, Macmillan, 1994 [updated edition, University of California Press, 1998].

Definitive history of Supreme Court decisions on reproductive rights. Historian Garrow, an abortion-rights advocate, is a professor at Emory Law School. Includes voluminous notes, 30-page bibliography.

Gorney, Cynthia, *Articles of Faith: A Frontline History of the Abortion Wars*, Simon & Schuster, 1998.

Details the personalities and issues in the "abortion wars" by focusing on one of the most contentious battleground states: Missouri. Gorney is associate dean at the University of California's Graduate School of Journalism in Berkeley. Includes long source list.

Hull, N.E.H., and Peter Charles Hoffer, *Roe v. Wade: The Abortion Rights Controversy in American History*, University Press of Kansas, 2001.

Compactly traces history of abortion law from 19th-century state laws through *Casey*. Hull teaches at Rutgers University, Hoffer at the University of Georgia. Includes lengthy chronology and bibliographical essay.

Tribe, Laurence H., *Abortion: The Clash of Absolutes*, W.W. Norton, 1990.

The prominent Harvard Law School professor, an abortion-rights advocate, tries to look at the issue anew. In a 1992 edition, Tribe describes the *Casey* decision as watering down *Roe* by permitting states new powers to restrict abortion.

Articles

Savage, David, "As Roe vs. Wade Turns 30, Ruling's Future Is Unsure," *Los Angeles Times*, Jan. 21, 2003, p. A1.

Analyzes possible impact on abortion-rights ruling if President Bush gets to fill one or more Supreme Court vacancies.

Tumulty, Karen, and Viveca Novak, "Under the Radar," *Time*, Jan. 27, 2003, pp. 38-41.

Examines the White House strategy to undercut abortion rights legalized by *Roe v. Wade*.

Zernike, Kate, "Thirty Years After Abortion Ruling, New Trends but the Old Debate," *The New York Times*, Jan. 20, 2003, p. A1.

Discusses views on abortion among women, activists and others against backdrop of decline in abortion rate to lowest level since 1974. Package includes sidebar by same reporter: "An Abortion Doctor's View."

Reports and Studies

Finer, Lawrence B., and Stanley K. Henshaw, "Abortion Incidence and Services in the United States in 2000," *Perspectives on Sexual and Reproductive Health* (January/February 2003) (www.agi-usa.org/journals).

Documents a decline in U.S. abortions; a second article in the issue details information about abortion providers: Stanley K. Henshaw and Lawrence B. Finer, "The Accessibility of Abortion Services in the United States, 2001." The authors are researchers at the Alan Guttmacher Institute, a research center affiliated with Planned Parenthood but accepted as reliable by both sides in abortion debates.

NARAL Pro-Choice America, "Who Decides? A State-by-State Review of Abortion and Reproductive Rights," January 2003 (www.naral.org/mediaresources/publications/2003).

The advocacy group's 12th compendium of state abortion laws details what it calls the "further erosion" of *Roe v. Wade*.

National Right to Life Committee, "NRL News," monthly series (www.nrlc.org/news).

The anti-abortion group's monthly newsletter provides up-to-date information and perspective on legislative and legal developments.

13 Stimulating the Economy

KENNETH JOST

Democrats had been sharpening their knives well before President Bush strode confidently to the podium at the Economic Club of Chicago on Jan. 7 to lay out a bold — and controversial — economic-recovery plan.

As North Carolina Democrat Sen. John Edwards put it three days before the speech, Bush is trying "to put money in the pockets of the richest Americans . . . while providing very little help for regular people."

Then in about 15 minutes, the president sketched out his plan. In his first major policy address since the midterm elections, Bush urged the new Republican-controlled Congress to swiftly approve a $674 billion "jobs and growth" package centered on one of the most sweeping tax changes proposed in recent years: eliminating the taxes investors pay on corporate dividends.

"We cannot be satisfied until every part of our economy is healthy and vigorous," Bush said. "We will not rest until every business has an opportunity to grow and every person who wants to work can find a job."

Bush's plan also calls for speeding up tax breaks already approved as part of his 2001 tax cut, including rate cuts for higher-income brackets due to take effect in 2004 and 2006 and provisions favoring married couples and families with children. The plan also would give small businesses a faster write-off for new investments.

But Bush's plan has raised skeptical questions from many economic experts. And congressional Democrats say it does less than their own pro-

Laid-off workers at the Wabash National Corp., a trailer-truck maker in Lafayette, Ind., gather information about unemployment benefits in early 2002. President Bush says his $674 billion tax-cut plan will boost the nation's sluggish economy. But congressional Democrats are offering a rival plan they say will cost less and provide more immediate relief for average taxpayers.

posal to stimulate the economy in the short run, while risking fiscal ruin in the long run.

"The president's plan is too little, too late and much too irresponsible," Rep. Robert Menendez of New Jersey, chair of the House Democratic Caucus, told a crowded news briefing at the Capitol on Jan. 6.

In contrast to Bush's plan, Democrats are centering their proposals on one-time, across-the-board relief to perk up consumer spending. House Democrats are calling for a tax rebate of $300 for individuals or $600 for couples. The Senate's leading Democrat on tax-writing issues — Montana's Max Baucus — is proposing similar tax relief in the form of a one-year Social Security payroll-tax holiday.

Meanwhile, Democrats vigorously denounced Bush's proposal to eliminate the tax on corporate dividends. Bush says the plan eliminates "double taxation" on dividends — first as a tax on corporate profits and then on in-

dividuals when they receive the profits as dividends. Democrats say eliminating the tax on individuals will disproportionately benefit wealthy Americans, who are the biggest stock investors.

The tax-cut debate arrives as the economy appears to be moving out of recession — but only gradually. Major economic indicators give a mixed picture of the likely pace and extent of the rebound.

Bush began talking up a possible economic-stimulus package last fall. The discussions grew bolder after Bush defied political logic by leading the GOP to gains in the midterm congressional elections that gave the party control of both houses of Congress.

At the same time, business groups were seeking tax cuts to give consumers more money to spend and encourage businesses to invest more to meet new demand. "Our economy needs an injection of consumer demand to break through its temporary sluggishness and achieve the strong growth that it's poised to deliver," said Stephen Sanger, chairman and CEO of General Mills and chairman of The Business Roundtable's fiscal policy tax force.

"We have an uneven and momentumless economy," said R. Bruce Josten, executive vice president of the U.S. Chamber of Commerce. "We need stimulus." [1]

Liberal advocacy groups are unconvinced, arguing the economy may be on its way to recovery without any new tax cuts. In any event, they say business tax cuts may have little stimulative effect and that any individual tax relief should be targeted at middle- and low-income individuals — for example, through a holiday on Social Security taxes.

From *The CQ Researcher*, January 10, 2003.

Republican and Democratic Stimulus Packages

President Bush proposed an economic-stimulus package on Jan. 7, 2003, in Chicago, one day after House Democrats released their own proposal. Here are the details and costs of each plan for this year and over the coming decade:

	Costs in billions			
	2003	2003-12	2003	2003-12
	Bush's Plan		House Democrats' Plan	
Individuals				
Eliminate tax on dividends	20	364	--	--
Accelerate income tax cuts due in 2004-2006	29	64	--	--
Income tax rebate ($300/person, $600/couple)	--	--	55	58
Accelerate child tax-credit increase	16	91	--	--
Extend unemployment benefits	--	--	18	10
Accelerate marriage-penalty relief to 2003	19	58	--	--
Accelerate expansion of the lowest tax bracket	5	48	--	--
Create $3,000 re-employment accounts for the jobless	4	4	--	--
Increase the alternative minimum tax through 2005	8	29	--	--
Businesses				
Tax breaks for new investments	2	16	32	1
Aid for States and Localities				
One-time homeland security grants	--	--	10	10
New highway construction and delayed state share	--	--	5	5
One-year increase in federal Medicaid payments	--	--	10	10
One-time special support for needs of the unemployed	--	--	6	6
Total	**102**	**674**	**136**	**100**

* *Dashes indicate no proposal is offered on that issue.*

** *Numbers may not add to exact total due to rounding.*

*** *Sen. Max Baucus, D-Mont., ranking minority member of the Senate Finance Committee, has proposed a $160 billion economic-stimulus package that somewhat parallels the House Democrats' proposal. However, it would provide a $45 billion Social Security payroll-tax holiday and give states $75 billion in general-revenue sharing — a proposal not included in either the president's or the House Democrats' plans.*

The anti-deficit Concord Coalition echoes those concerns while also warning that any additional tax cuts will worsen the country's fiscal health, just as the federal government has gone back into red ink after three years of budget surpluses. "It is very possible that the new tax-cut proposals and the new spending proposals will dig the deficit hole much deeper than it is currently, and the deficits will persist longer and be bigger than is fiscally prudent," says Executive Director Robert Bixby. [2]

Tax cuts have been viewed as a way for the federal government to counter a recession since the 1930s, when the theories of the British economist John Maynard Keynes first gained a foothold in academic circles in the United States. Keynesian economics preached using tax cuts to boost flagging consumer demand — even if they led to budget deficits.

Those views conflicted with traditional conservative principles that treated a balanced budget as an essential of economic health. In the 1970s, however, some conservative economists began advocating tax cuts — even at the expense of deficits — to provide more incentives for work and investment. They called themselves "supply-siders" because they looked to increase production ("supply") in contrast to Keynesian economists' emphasis on boosting demand. Critics — including Bush's own father when he ran for president — derided the theory as "voodoo economics."

President Ronald Reagan adopted much of the supply-siders' argument in pushing through a big tax cut in 1981, his first year in office. Supply-siders claim the tax cuts helped the economy grow through the '80s; critics say they jeopardized the country's economic health by creating mammoth deficits and triggering a deep recession in the late 1980s.

The debate over tax cuts vs. deficits continues today. Richard Kogan, a budget expert at the liberal Center for Budget and Policy Priorities, says the groups pushing tax cuts as economic stimuli are driven more by ideology than economic policy. "They're trying to do their preferred ideological long-term policy under the guise of short-term fiscal stimulus, even when their proposals do little or nothing or may even be harmful as a short-term stimulus," Kogan says.

In fact, some supply-side economists acknowledge that their calls for renewed tax cuts are not linked to current economic conditions. "There are things that should be fixed whether the economy is growing at 4 percent or 2 percent or in a recession," says Daniel Mitchell, a senior fellow at the conservative Heritage Foundation.

"We're not talking about just a stimulus package," says Wayne Brough, chief economist at the conservative Citizens for a Sound Economy. "We're talking about long-term economic growth."

Meanwhile, state and local governments are suffering under what the National Governors Association estimated as a $50 billion budget shortfall in 2002. [3] State tax revenues naturally decline with a sagging economy — just as federal revenues do. Unlike the federal government, though, all

but one of the states are required by their constitutions to maintain balanced budgets.

As a result, states are going through painful budget cuts — even releasing prisoners early to save money. Liberal advocacy groups say any economic-stimulus plan should include substantial help for the states. But some conservatives oppose any relief at all. Bush's proposal includes no direct aid to states. House Democrats propose about $30 billion in "targeted" assistance to states and localities, while Baucus is calling for a one-time appropriation of $75 billion. (*See sidebar, p. 248.*)

The debate on cutting taxes to stimulate the economy is likely to be the first major issue for the new Congress that convened on Jan. 7. As lawmakers in both parties stake out their positions, here are some of the major questions being considered:

Are tax cuts needed to stimulate the economy?

Alan Greenspan gave a mixed assessment of the U.S. economy when the longtime chairman of the Federal Reserve testified before Congress' Joint Economic Committee last fall. Citing the 3 percent growth rate over the previous four quarters, Greenspan said the economy had proved to be "remarkably resilient." But slow spending by consumers and businesses alike provided what he called "increasing evidence" that the economy "has hit a soft patch." [4]

Tax cuts in 2002 had helped boost disposable income, Greenspan told the lawmakers, but he was noncommittal on the need for additional reductions. If "the outlook is exactly what the most probable path is, then I would say no additional stimulus is necessary," Greenspan said in response to questions. "But then you get to the question of what happens if you're wrong." [5]

Major business groups entertain no similar doubts about the need to give

the economy a boost by cutting taxes for individuals and, in particular, for business. "The economy still seems to be missing a spark in the manufacturing sector," says Martin Regalia, chief economist for the U.S. Chamber of Commerce. "It's an economy that's not hitting on all cylinders yet."

"There is a need for a short-term stimulus to get the economy started," says David Heuther, chief economist at the National Association of Manufacturers.

Economists outside the business lobbies are less convinced. "The evidence is that the economy is recovering," says Leonard Burman, an economist at the liberal-leaning Urban Institute in Washington and co-director of the joint Urban-Brookings Center on Tax Policy. Spending is at "reasonably high levels," while unemployment is at "low levels, historically speaking."

"There really is a concern that we could be overstimulating, that we could be setting the stage for higher inflation or higher interest rates a year or two from now," continues Burman, who served as deputy assistant Treasury secretary for tax analysis in the Clinton administration. "I think it would be very dangerous for the government to engage in a new rush of fiscal stimulus."

Anti-deficit advocacy groups echo his tentativeness about the need for an economic stimulus, while cautioning against tax cuts that would increase the government's red ink over the long term. "My own guess is that the economy probably doesn't need a stimulus," says Bixby of the Concord Coalition. "If they're going to do a stimulus, it ought to be quickly implemented and have a lot of bang for the buck in the short term with virtually no long-term consequences."

An economic stimulus "probably wouldn't hurt in the short run," says Robert McIntyre, executive director of the liberal advocacy group Citizens for Tax Justice, "but the danger is that they pass something temporary and it never goes away. Then we'd be up a creek."

Many economists believe tax cuts are rarely helpful in stimulating the economy. "The history of fiscal stimulus measures suggests that they are often mistimed, taking effect after the economy has begun growing rapidly again," says William Gale, a liberal economist at the Brookings Institution and co-director with Burman of the Urban-Brookings center. Eric Engen, a conservative economist at the American Enterprise Institute, agrees. "We're poised to debate this over the next six months and put it into effect exactly when we don't need it," he says.

Instead of fiscal measures, many economists say monetary policy is more effective for managing the economy — in part because the Federal Reserve can raise or lower interest rates more quickly than Congress can act on tax matters. The Fed is generally credited with helping perk up the economy over the past year by lowering interest rates.

Tax-cut advocates, however, say with the Fed's most recent interest-rate reduction in November it may have exhausted its ability to boost the economy. The Fed approved a larger-than-expected half-percentage-point cut in its key interest rate to 1.25 percent — the lowest figure in 41 years. "I don't think there's

an awful lot more juice we can add with monetary policy," says Stephen Moore, chairman of the Club for Growth, a low-tax and low-spending advocacy group.

Kogan at the Center for Budget and Policy Priorities agrees that monetary policy offers little additional opportunity to stimulate the economy. With signs of recovery, he says there may be no need for a fiscal stimulus ei-

President Bush formally unveils his $674 billion tax-cut plan at the Economic Club of Chicago on Jan. 7, 2003. "We cannot be satisfied until every part of our economy is healthy and vigorous," he said. "We will not rest until every business has a chance to grow and every person who wants to find work can find a job."

Getty Images/Tim Boyle

ther. In the end, however, he bluntly confesses uncertainty on the issue.

"There's a mainstream consensus that we don't know," Kogan says. "Any economist who tells you that he knows for sure is suffering from a considerable overestimate of what the profession can tell us."

Should taxes for individuals be cut to stimulate the economy?

President Bush scored his biggest legislative victory to date in May 2001 when Congress approved an across-the-board income tax cut for individuals estimated to cost $1.35 trillion over 10 years. Rate cuts for the lowest bracket went into effect immediately. To trim the overall cost, however, reductions for higher-income taxpayers were to be phased in gradually in 2004 and 2006.

With the economy now sagging, many Republicans and conservative tax-cut advocates say that speeding up — or accelerating — the previously deferred rate reductions would rev up a slow-moving recovery. But many Democrats, liberals and anti-deficit advocacy groups disagree. They argue that the move would tilt the benefits of the tax cuts further toward upper-income taxpayers and worsen the deficit problem, while having little stimulative effect on the economy.

Business groups are at the forefront of the issue. "Accelerating the tax cuts will increase consumer spending and ensure consumer confidence," says Dorothy Coleman, NAM vice president for tax policy. "We need to do something as quickly as possible."

"The tax cuts that we had were good as far as they went," says Regalia at the Chamber of Commerce. But, he adds, "they weren't permanent, and they were phased in over a long period of time."

Accelerating the cuts, Regalia says,

"would certainly put more money in the hands of consumers." In addition, Regalia says the tax cuts — now scheduled to expire in 2010 — should be made permanent. "As we get closer, you have more and more of a problem because people are going to anticipate a decline in disposable income," he says.

Liberal advocacy groups say moving up the cuts would just pass on more benefits to higher-income taxpayers. "The rate cuts passed last year, plus the repeal of the estate tax, are going to make the tax system less progressive than before," says the Urban Institute's Burman. "I don't see any justification for that."

"High-income people have done very well over the last 20 years, our tax rates overall are among the lowest in the developed world and we have all these social needs that are unmet or ignored," Burman continues. "It makes sense to try to meet those needs by taxing high-income individuals at higher rates than those with low incomes."

Liberal groups also say higher-income taxpayers are more likely to save than to spend the money — diluting any potential stimulative effect. "The vast majority of that money will go to people who will basically save all of it," says Kogan at the Center for Budget and Policy Priorities. "The focus should be on the middle class."

Accelerating the cuts would be "fairly expensive for the next couple of years," says the Concord Coalition's Bixby. "You may make the short-term deficit worse without providing more long-term stimulus." In any event, he adds, "We're in favor of re-examining those tax cuts. If you accelerate them, it would be much more difficult to change them."

Some Democrats and liberal advocates have looked to reducing the Social Security payroll tax as a more effective economic stimulus on the ground that such a move would pass more benefits to lower-income taxpayers. But because of Social Securi-

The Deficit See-Saw

President Bill Clinton presided over an eight-year economic boom that transformed the record federal budget deficit into a huge surplus in 2000, his final year in office. But during President Bush's term, the economy has declined, worsened by the Sept. 11, 2001, terrorist attacks and the resulting war in Afghanistan and the efforts to beef up homeland defense.

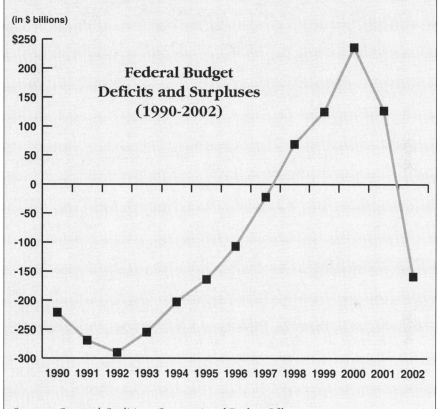

Sources: Concord Coalition, Congressional Budget Office

ty's long-term financial problems, the idea often took the form of a temporary "holiday" rather than a permanent reduction.

There was only muted enthusiasm for the idea, however, even in that form. "There are worse things, but it's awfully expensive," says McIntyre at Citizens for Tax Justice.

Burman calls the proposal "probably the least dumb idea I've heard." But, he adds, "If they have to do something, that would be in the category of something that doesn't do any long-term harm."

Business groups, however, say a payroll tax holiday would be an administrative burden for employers, especially small businesses. "It could be a real nightmare," says Coleman. In addition, conservatives warn against reducing Social Security taxes when the system faces the prospects of long-term deficits as the Baby Boomers start to retire a decade or so from now.

"If we know that there's a part of the budget that's fiscally imbalanced, it's Social Security," says the AEI's Engen. "Every April, we see that this is a system that can't go on with the

Dividend Tax Break Favors the Rich

The president's plan to eliminate individual taxes on stock dividends would save Americans earning over $1 million an average of about $45,000, or nearly a quarter of all the dividend tax cuts. Those earning under $10,000 would get an average tax break of $6.

Annual Income	Percent of Tax Break Received	Average Tax Reduction
<$10,000	0.4%	-$6
$10,000-20,000	1.0	-18
$20,000-30,000	1.7	-39
$30,000-40,000	2.1	-65
$40,000-50,000	3.3	-135
$50,000-75,000	8.9	-208
$75,000-100,000	8.2	-336
$100,000-200,000	20.9	-885
$200,000-$500,000	19.8	-3,463
$500,000-1 million	9.3	-9,372
>$1 million	24.3	-45,098

Source: Urban Institute-Brookings Tax Policy Center, Jan. 5, 2003

current level of taxes and the current level of promised benefits."

Business groups discount concerns that accelerating the scheduled tax cuts would add to the deficit problems. "Tax relief is critical" to getting the economy moving again, Coleman says. "The only way we're going to have surpluses is to have economic growth. The end result will be that you end up reducing deficits."

The proposal also offers a tactical advantage for tax-cut advocates, by putting Democratic lawmakers who voted for the tax cuts earlier in a bind. "Some of the people who voted for the Bush tax cuts would have a problem arguing against accelerating them," says Moore at the Club for Growth.

Should taxes on businesses and investors be cut to stimulate the economy?

To simplify the politics of his first tax cut, President Bush made a de-liberate decision that businesses would have to wait till later for tax relief. After getting some modest tax relief in a measure passed in Bush's second year in office, business lobbies are now pushing hard for tax cuts for companies and investors — and using the need to invigorate a sluggish economy as the major justification.

"We feel strongly that we need some additional tax relief to give the economy some oomph and get it back on track," says the NAM's Coleman. "There's a recovery under way," she adds, "but it is very slow going."

Bush's proposal adopts the two major goals that business groups had settled on while the president was readying his plan: reducing taxation on corporate dividends and allowing faster write-offs for investments in plant and equipment. Anti-deficit and liberal advocacy groups say Bush's proposals — as well as less ambitious alternatives discussed earlier — are too

costly, benefit only higher-income taxpayers and provide little stimulus.

"Business would not be high on my priority list for short-term economic stimulus," says Joel Friedman, a tax expert at the Center for Budget and Policy Priorities. "There are other things that are better suited to get the economy moving again."

Proposals to reduce taxes on corporate dividends reflect the longtime complaint from business and investor groups that dividends are subject to taxation twice — first as profits earned by a company and then as income for individual taxpayers. In the current debate, business groups contend that the tax treatment of dividends discourages investment. "Reducing the tax on dividends would lower the cost of capital, spur investment and strengthen equity markets," Coleman says.

Business groups offer different ways to reduce taxation of dividends. The manufacturers' group favors allowing companies to take deductions for dividends, but says it is open to other alternatives — including a rate cut on dividends for either companies or individuals. The Business Roundtable instead would retain taxation of dividends at the corporate level and allow individuals receiving the payouts to take a deduction.

Bush had reportedly considered a plan to cut in half the tax paid by investors on dividends, but he opted instead to call for completely eliminating the levy. In a meeting with his Cabinet on the day before formally unveiling the plan, Bush said his proposal would encourage investment and eliminate what he described as the unfairness of taxing dividends twice.

Liberal experts and advocates interviewed offer no theoretical defense of the current tax treatment of dividends. "Virtually all economists" agree on the need to change the current system, The Urban Institute's Burman says. But he says the rules should be changed only as part of a broad corporate-tax reform.

"There are huge loopholes," Burman says. "Right now when the corporate income tax is falling apart, we should not spend more scarce dollars to give a tax benefit to corporations."

Liberal experts also say easing the tax treatment on dividends would disproportionately favor high-income taxpayers. "That's just another tax break for extremely wealthy individuals," says Kogan at the Center for Budget and Policy Priorities. "Taxable dividends are concentrated very, very much at the top end of the income spectrum."

New depreciation rules to allow faster tax write-offs for the cost of new investments were being pushed by NAM and the Chamber of Commerce, though not by The Business Roundtable — an organization of CEOs from major corporations. "One of the most effective ways to spur business investment is through an enhanced capital-cost-recovery system," NAM leaders said in their Nov. 25 letter to Bush.

Tax laws require companies to write off the cost of long-term investments over time rather than taking the deduction for the entire amount in the year of the expenditure. Typically, companies can take 20 percent of the cost as a current deduction, but the 2002 tax measure created a "bonus depreciation" allowance of 30 percent of the cost for the year the money was spent. The provision was to expire after 2004.

Business groups wanted the allowance increased to as much as 60 percent. Bush chose a more limited step: to increase to $75,000 from $25,000 the new investments that small businesses are allowed to deduct immediately. In their plan, House Democrats propose to let small businesses take an immediate deduction for up to $50,000 in new investment; the Democrats' plan also would increase the bonus depreciation allowance to 50 percent for 2003, but cut it to 10 percent in 2004.

Liberal advocates contend that the bonus depreciation is failing to spur new investment. Last year's bill "was a big corporate failure," says McIntyre at Citizens for Tax Justice. "Businesses said, 'Now we will invest,' but there are stories all over the newspapers that they're not investing. They didn't deliver."

In any event, liberal experts argue that neither liberalized depreciation rules nor reduced taxation of dividends will do much to stimulate the economy at a time of excess business capacity and insufficient consumer demand.

"Businesses are suffering because not enough people are buying their products," Kogan says. "If you give them a tax cut, it increases their bottom line, so that they can give greater dividends and capital gains to their owners. But it doesn't do anything to stimulate business demand. It doesn't change business activity." ■

BACKGROUND

The Government's Hand

The federal government's recognized responsibility for managing the national economy dates only from the Great Depression of the 1930s. Before then, classical economics had taught that the boom-and-bust business cycle would right itself through natural economic forces — Adam Smith's so-called "invisible hand." President Franklin D. Roosevelt's New Deal policies combined with an intellectual revolution in economics to produce a new conventional wisdom: that the government can and should try to keep the economy on track through some combination of fiscal and monetary policies. [6]

Roosevelt was a pragmatic politician who adopted pump-priming policies to get people and businesses back to work without the benefit of any well-thought-out economic theory. But he came to office in 1933 in the early days of what came to be called the Keynesian revolution — after the English economist John Maynard Keynes. First in his 1930 book, *Treatise on Money*, and then in his larger 1936 work, *The General Theory of Employment, Interest and Money*, Keynes argued that the government could boost employment and production by increasing government spending and/or the monetary supply — or, conversely, control inflation by reducing spending and/or the monetary supply.

Keynes' views gained a foothold among some U.S. economists — and eventually with FDR himself — but remained controversial through the decade and beyond. The economy's partial recovery in the mid-'30s gave Keynesians (as supporters of Keynes' theory were called) some evidence for their arguments. But the strongest proof, according to economic historians Charles Wilber and Kenneth Jameson, came during and after World War II, when the government's wartime demands on the economy generated a production boom that put enough money into workers' pockets to fuel significant economic growth for several years after the war. [7]

Keynesian economics fell out of favor under President Dwight D. Eisenhower, who supported balanced budgets and laissez-faire policies, but regained influence in the 1960s under President John F. Kennedy. Facing sizable budget deficits, Kennedy acceded to arguments from Keynesians on his Council of Economic Advisers to propose a tax cut in 1962 to boost economic activity. The cut, enacted in 1964, "had all the appearances of a smashing success," according to Wilber and Jameson. "Output rose, unemployment fell, inflation was negligible, and the deficit did not worsen, but actually improved by 1965." [8]

Keynes' prescription to raise taxes to combat inflation proved less politically appealing under Kennedy's successor, Lyndon B. Johnson. As spending on the Vietnam War increased the federal budget deficit, Johnson resisted his Keynesian advisers' recommendation to raise taxes lest the move weaken popular support for the war or for his Great Society social programs. When Johnson finally proposed a tax hike in 1967 — enacted in 1968 — it was "too late to stem the tide of rising inflation," the historians say. [9]

The economic malaise of the 1970s challenged government policymakers and Keynesian academics alike. In 1971 the Republican president, Richard M. Nixon, sought to curb inflation not by raising taxes but by adopting the most un-Republican of policies: wage and price controls. The policies — unpopular and ineffectual — were being phased out just as the Organization of Petroleum Exporting Countries (OPEC) imposed an oil embargo in 1973. The embargo set the stage for a series of spikes in oil prices that rolled through the U.S. economy for the rest of the decade producing double-digit inflation.

As President Jimmy Carter struggled to right the economy he inherited in the late '70s, he found his policies at odds with those of the independent Federal Reserve System, headed by Chairman Paul Volcker. The Fed tightened the money supply — contrary to a Keynesian prescription — and thereby may have worsened a recession even as prices were still rising:

so-called "stagflation." The sagging economy helped sink Carter's bid for re-election in 1980. The new president — Republican Ronald Reagan — promised during the campaign "to get the economy moving again."

"Supply-Side" Economics

President Reagan sought individual tax cuts to stimulate productivity and spending cuts to reduce the size of the federal government. Taxes were cut — twice — along with spending on social services. However, a sus-

New Yorkers shop for the December holidays. Consumers jittery about jobs and the economy disappointed major retailers, but many other economic indicators were upbeat in December and early January.

tained military buildup caused overall federal spending to continue to rise, and budget deficits soared as a result. Reagan's admirers claimed his policies spurred economic growth without inflation through the 1980s. His critics claimed that he had whipped inflation at the cost of deep recession and contended that the overall growth rate was unimpressive compared to the '60s or even to the '70s. [10]

Reagan's policies reflected the view of so-called "supply-side" theorists, who

challenged the Keynesian emphasis on manipulating government policies to shape consumer demand. They argued instead that the government should focus on increasing supply by lowering marginal tax rates, thereby increasing incentives for work and investment. Supply-siders also contended that increased economic production would generate sufficient new revenues to offset the effect of lower tax rates — as famously depicted in the so-called Laffer curve, named after economist and low-tax crusader Arthur Laffer.

When it passed the Economic Recovery Tax Act in 1981, Congress gave Reagan most of what he had sought. The law cut marginal tax rates for individuals by 25 percent over three years, indexed income-tax brackets, lowered rates on investment income, and gave business accelerated depreciation allowances.

Estimated total cost: $750 billion over five years. Congress again lowered individual tax rates in the Tax Reform Act of 1986, which reduced the number of income tax brackets to three — with a maximum marginal rate of 28 percent — while eliminating a variety of tax preferences in the name of simplification. The five-year savings for individuals was put at $120 billion — ostensibly offset by an equal amount of business tax hikes.

But contrary to the supply-siders' assurances, budget deficits ballooned from $78.9 billion in fiscal 1981 to a record high of $221.2 billion in 1986 before falling to $155.1 billion in 1988 — Reagan's last full year in office. The inflation rate was cut in half: from 9.3 percent from 1973-1980 to an average of 4.7 percent for 1981-1988. However,

Chronology

Before 1930
Federal government plays limited role in managing the national economy; budget typically balanced except in wartime.

———•———

1930s *President*
Franklin D. Roosevelt uses federal spending to boost economy, but Great Depression ends only due to World War II boom.

1930
British economist John Maynard Keynes argues government can boost employment and production by increasing government spending.

———•———

1950s *President*
Dwight D. Eisenhower returns to balanced-budget politics.

———•———

1960s-1970s
U.S. economy buffeted by Vietnam War, oil embargo.

1964
Congress approves tax cut first proposed by President John F. Kennedy in 1962 to boost economy.

1965
President Lyndon B. Johnson starts Vietnam buildup but refuses to raise taxes or cut Great Society programs; as war continues, deficits grow.

1971
President Richard M. Nixon imposes unpopular and ineffective wage-price controls to limit inflation.

1973
Oil embargo by petroleum exporting countries produces price hikes that reverberate through the U.S. economy.

Late 1970s
President Jimmy Carter struggles with "stagflation" — high unemployment with high inflation; Federal Reserve tightens monetary supply.

———•———

1980s *President Ronald*
Reagan wins two major tax cuts; budget deficits balloon, but "supply-side" advocates discount importance as inflation subsides.

1981
Congress approves the cuts sought by Reagan, cutting marginal tax rates and indexing income-tax brackets.

1986
Tax Reform Act reduces number of income-tax brackets, cuts taxes for individuals by $120 billion; budget deficit hits record $221 billion.

———•———

1990s *Economy booms;*
budget achieves a large surplus.

1990
President George Bush accepts deficit-reduction package with tax hike, reneging on no-new-taxes pledge.

1992
Democrat Bill Clinton wins election after linking recession to Bush.

1993
Democratic-controlled Congress approves deficit-reduction package urged by Clinton.

1997
Congress lowers capital-gains tax from 28 percent to 20 percent; approves new deficit-reduction package.

1998
Federal budget has $69 billion surplus in fiscal 1998; surplus grows to $236 billion in Clinton's last year in office.

———•———

2000-Present
President Bush pushes major tax cut through Congress, then calls for more cuts to stimulate economy despite new deficits.

2000
Gov. George W. Bush, R-Texas, promises a major tax cut during the presidential campaign; narrowly defeats Vice President Al Gore.

2001
Just as economy falls into recession, Congress approves Bush's $1.35 trillion tax cut, lowering tax rates across the board and phasing out the estate tax over 10 years; terrorist attacks on Sept. 11 prompt increased federal spending for homeland security, war against terrorism.

2002
Federal revenues dive due to recession, Bush tax cuts; deficits return; Congress passes minor stimulus plan in March.

Jan. 7, 2003
New Bush stimulus plan calls for ending tax on stock dividends for individuals, accelerating scheduled rate cuts and easing rules on tax write-offs for business investments; Democrats say plan primarily benefits wealthy taxpayers, offer their own proposal.

States Face Massive Budget Crises

Democrat Gray Davis and Republican George Pataki have had little time to celebrate after winning re-election in November as governors of the country's two most populous states — California and New York, respectively. Instead, both are grappling with gargantuan budget problems: a $35 billion shortfall in California over the next 18 months and at least an $8 billion deficit in fiscal 2004 in New York.

Davis and Pataki have plenty of company. States overall experienced a $50 billion budget shortfall in fiscal 2002, according to the National Governors Association — a gap expected to reach at least $60 billion in fiscal 2003 and perhaps higher in 2004.

"Nearly every state is in fiscal crisis," the association warned in its annual fiscal survey in November 2002. [1] Raymond Scheppach, the group's executive director, says the fiscal problems are "the worst budget crisis the states have faced since World War II."

The causes of the problems are multiple — and somewhat disputed between conservative and liberal advocacy groups. Scheppach says state revenues have fallen with the slumping economy. States also depend heavily on sales taxes, which are levied on goods but not on the economy's increasingly important services sector. In addition, the federal tax cuts that President Bush pushed through Congress in 2001 cost states billions of dollars because some state taxes are tied to federal levies.

Meanwhile, Scheppach says, states face hard-to-control financial pressures in administering Medicaid — the joint state-federal health insurance program for the indigent — as well as new federally imposed spending demands in homeland security, education and election reform.

Conservative advocacy groups maintain that states overspent during the booming 1990s and should have saved more for the economic downturn that has now materialized. Liberal groups counter that states imprudently cut taxes during the boom times and are now paying the price: an estimated $40 billion revenue loss, according to the Center for Budget and Policy Priorities in Washington. [2]

Whatever the causes, the effects of the fiscal problems are evident: difficult, often painful budget cuts in states all across the country. "We've seen virtually every state program affected by spending cuts," says Corina Eckl, a budget expert with the National Conference of State Legislatures in Denver. Many states have increased tuition or cut enrollment at state-run colleges. Health-care services are being cut or expansion plans dropped. Kentucky's governor freed some 567 low-level felons from prison to save money. Oregon prosecutors will stop handling some minor crimes. [3]

For fiscal 2002, some 26 states enacted across-the-board cuts or dipped into so-called rainy day funds, according to the governors' association. Fifteen states laid off employees, five used early retirement and 13 reorganized programs to trim spending.

For the current and future years, the group's report warned, available solutions are "increasingly dire." More spending cuts are expected, and many governors — Republicans and Democrats alike — are likely to seek tax increases.

The anti-recession medicine many mainstream economists usually prescribe, cutting taxes and increasing government spending, will not work for states because — except for Vermont — all state constitutions prohibit deficit spending. Thus, governors must balance their budgets each year.

Nevertheless, California and New York are among eight states facing budget deficits in fiscal 2004 of at least 20 percent, according to the Center for Budget and Policy Priorities. The others include Alabama, Alaska, Nevada, Oregon, Texas and Wisconsin.

In early December California's Davis proposed budget cuts for fiscal 2003-04 that would slash school spending by $3.1 billion, health and social services by $2 billion, government operations by $1.9 billion and transportation by $1.7 billion. Later in the month, he signaled that his budget — due to the legislature by Jan. 10 — would likely also call for tax increases. Democratic lawmakers are complaining about the cuts, Republican legislators about the possible tax hikes. [4]

In New York, Pataki imposed a freeze on hiring in 2002, trimmed agency spending and asked the legislature to authorize billions in new bonds. As of his Jan. 1 inaugural, however, Pataki had yet to indicate how he would meet the state's expected $8 billion shortfall. [5]

All told, the 50 states spent about $491 billion from their general funds for fiscal 2002, according to the governors' association's

the economy suffered the worst recession since the Great Depression: unemployment peaked at 10.3 percent in 1983 and averaged 7.4 percent for the period 1981-1987. And the 2.7 percent average growth rate for Reagan's eight years was only slightly higher than the 2.2 percent average of the late '70s and significantly below the 3.9 percent growth rate of 1960-1973.

Supply-siders contended that — despite the larger-than-anticipated deficits — the economic expansion during Reagan's last years in office vindicated their theories. They blamed the recession in large part on Volcker's continuing tight-money policies at the Fed. Mainstream economists, however, insisted that the tax cut failed to generate the promised investment boom, be-

stowed disproportionate benefits on the well-to-do, and created huge deficits that jeopardized the social safety net.

In successfully campaigning to be Reagan's successor, Vice President George Bush vowed in 1988 to resist calls to raise taxes to reduce the deficits. Two years later, however, he went back on his 1990 "no new taxes" pledge to accept a deficit-reduction measure

report. That represented a modest 1.3 percent increase over the previous year, but it followed an 8 percent increase for fiscal 2001. Total state spending — including federal funds, special state funds, and bonds — went past $1 trillion for the first time in fiscal 2001.

Conservative groups say the states have themselves to blame for their budget problems. "Today's record cumulative state budget . . . did not just happen," said Jason Thomas, a staff economist with the group Citizens for a Sound Economy in Washington. "It is the product of irresponsible budgeting and overly sanguine revenue forecasts." [6]

Scheppach and Eckl disagree. "The states didn't engage in any mass spending," says Scheppach. "If you trace back spending through 1995-2000, the growth was about 6.5 percent per year — just about exactly what it's been for the last 20 years."

"States certainly were shoring up some programs, like health care for children and the elderly," says Eckl. "But they were also cutting taxes and putting record amounts of money into their rainy day funds."

Whatever the history, liberal groups like the Center for Budget and Policy Priorities complain that the cuts already enacted or those being considered are falling disproportionately on low- and moderate-income people. "Cuts of unprecedented depth in vital basic services — and especially in health insurance for working poor and near-poor families lie ahead," says Robert Greenstein, the group's executive director. [7]

Both state groups and liberal organizations are calling for federal aid to the states as part of any economic-stimulus package that President Bush proposes to Congress. Fiscal relief for the states is "probably the most powerful short-run economic stimulus the federal government could do," Scheppach says. "Plus, it could give the states time to work out something with the federal government on Medicaid and time for the states to restructure."

"They should put the money into the hands of people who will almost certainly spend it," says Robert McIntyre, executive director of Citizens for Tax Justice. "One way to do that is to send it out to the states."

But Stephen Moore, president of the tax-cut advocacy group Club for Growth, dismisses talk of major federal aid to the states as "a pipe dream."

"The states are victims of their own policies," Moore says. "This argument that the federal government owes the states money to help them with their budget problems just isn't valid."

States were sorely disappointed with the president's plan, which not only failed to provide any direct assistance but also added to their fiscal woes. Since state income taxes are tied to federal taxes, states would stop taxing dividends as well. In addition, exempting dividends from taxation makes tax-exempt state or municipal bonds less attractive as investment vehicles — possibly forcing state and local governments to pay higher interest.

Support for state aid is likely to be stronger among Democrats. Sen. Max Baucus of Montana, the party's ranking member on the Senate Finance Committee, is calling for a one-time expenditure of $75 billion in general revenue-sharing with the states as part of an overall $160 billion economic-stimulus package. States "would use almost all of these funds to avoid implementing many of these counter-cyclical [budget cuts]," Baucus said, "thereby preventing the exacerbation of the economy's weakness that would otherwise occur."

[1] National Governors Association/National Association of State Budget Officers, "The Fiscal Survey of States," November 2002 (www.nga.org). See also National Conference of State Legislatures, "State Budget Update," November 2002 (www.ncsl.org).

[2] See Nicholas Johnson, "The State Tax Cuts of the 1990s, the Current Revenue Crisis, and Implications for State Services," Center for Budget and Policy Priorities, Nov. 18, 2002 (www.cbpp.org).

[3] See Stephanie Simon, "Many States Face Gloomy Budget Choices," Los Angeles Times, Dec. 29, 2002, p. A1.

[4] See Gregg Jones, Davis Says Tax Hikes Likely as Shortfall Soars," Los Angeles Times, Dec. 19, 2002, p. A1.

[5] See James C. McKinley Jr., "Pataki's Challenge," The New York Times, Jan. 1, 2003, p. A1.

[6] Jason M. Thomas, "It's Spending, Stupid! Or Why There's No State Budget Quagmire," Citizens for a Sound Economy, Nov. 20, 2002 (www.cse.org).

[7] Center for Budget and Policy Priorities, "State Budget Deficits Loom Larger Than Previously Thought, Signaling Deep Cuts in Health Insurance, Other Programs," Dec. 23, 2002 (www.cbpp.org).

from Congress that promised to raise $137 billion in new taxes over five years and hiked the top tax rate from 28 percent to 31 percent.

Bush's reversal on taxes weakened his hold on his conservative base, while a moderate recession in the second half of his term gave Democrats an issue that helped carry Bill Clinton to victory in the 1992 campaign.

The Booming '90s

President Clinton presided over an eight-year-long economic boom that transformed the record federal budget deficit into a $236.4 billion surplus in 2000, his final year in office. The good times were attributed to multiple causes — some of them policy decisions by Clinton or Congress, but many of them not. As Clinton left the White House in 2001, economists and policymakers were forecasting budget surpluses for years to come — and debating what to do with the largely unanticipated windfall. [11]

Fiscal policy played a major part in the turnaround. At Clinton's urging, the Democratic-controlled Congress enacted a deficit-reduction package in August 1993 projected to cut the red ink by $433 billion over five years through a combination of tax increases and spending cuts. Pressure on Clinton to contain spending intensified after Republicans gained control of the House in the 1994 midterm elections. In 1997 a second deficit-reduction package called for $210 billion in spending cuts — more than offsetting a projected $92 billion in tax cuts.

Federal spending was also constrained by procedural barriers enacted in the Budget Enforcement Act, part of then-President Bush's 1990 deficit-reduction package. The law established caps on so-called discretionary spending, which were to be enforced by the Office of Management and Budget (OMB) if exceeded by Congress. A separate so-called pay-as-you-go mechanism required that the combined effects of fiscal and mandatory legislation approved in any year could not increase the deficit. The two provisions "proved remarkably effective," according to economists Robert Reischauer and Henry Aaron of the Brookings Institution. Inflation-adjusted discretionary spending was reduced by 11 percent from 1990 to 1998, they wrote, and Congress made only limited use before 1999 of its power to override the limits with "emergency" spending actions. [12]

The fiscal turnaround also benefited from what Reischauer and Aaron called "serendipitous" developments. Abroad, the collapse of the Soviet Union permitted significant reductions in defense spending. At home, a slowdown in the growth of employer health-care costs contributed to higher profits and wages, boosting federal revenues because — unlike health-care premiums — wages and profits are taxable. Spending for Medicare and Medicaid, the federal health-insurance programs, also increased more slowly in the last years of the decade.

Above all, though, the budget surpluses of the late '90s resulted from what Reischauer and Aaron call the "superlative" performance of the economy. By the end of the decade, the gross domestic product (GDP) was $700 billion higher than had been projected at the start of Clinton's presidency. The deficit shrank to $22 billion in fiscal 1997 and then produced back-to-back-to-back surpluses of $69.2 billion, $125.2 billion, and $236.4 billion for Clinton's last three years in office. Budget forecasters projected surpluses extending through the first decade of the new century.

During the presidential campaign of 2000, the budget surplus — and what to do with it — became a pivotal issue. As the Republican nominee, Bush proposed an across-the-board tax cut with a projected price tag of $1.3 trillion over 10 years. "I want to send one-quarter of the surplus back to the people who pay the bills," Bush repeatedly declared. Democrat Al Gore — who had served as Clinton's vice president for eight years — told voters that Bush's plan would "squander your surplus on tax cuts for the wealthiest of the wealthy" and jeopardize Social Security and other government programs. Despite the narrowness of his victory, Bush claimed a mandate for his proposed tax cuts and presented it to lawmakers in his first address to a joint session of Congress on Feb. 27, 2001.

Return of Deficits

President Bush won speedy congressional approval of his tax cut in late May 2001, after agreeing to increase the benefits for middle- and lower-income taxpayers. Republicans were touting their role in approving the cuts through the summer while Democrats fretted about the effects on long-term fiscal solvency. But the 2001

terrorist attacks and a moderate recession dramatically changed the fiscal landscape by triggering higher federal spending as revenue was declining sharply. By early 2002, the promised budget surpluses had vanished. But the economic downturn led Bush and Republican lawmakers to turn again to tax-cut proposals — this time, primarily to help a sagging economy. [13]

In its final form, the tax cut was projected to reduce federal revenues by $1.35 trillion through 2011 by lowering tax rates across the board and giving individuals several other breaks, including immediate rebates of $300 for individuals and $600 for married couples — a late addition aimed at stimulating the economy. [14] The measure also would phase out and eventually repeal estate taxes — a long-sought GOP goal that constituted about 10 percent of the overall cost. The final 10-year projection of the cost was shaved by including a sunset provision repealing the cuts in 2010. The measure included no significant breaks for businesses; a separate economic-stimulus bill with business tax cuts passed the House in October 2001 but died in the Senate. [15]

By fall 2001, however, the fiscal picture had changed dramatically. The terrorist attacks of Sept. 11 moved federal spending into a wartime and homeland-securing mode, even as unemployment rose, revenues plunged and corporate scandals were making daily headlines. [16]

In early 2002, Congress revived the same debates that had stalled the 2001 stimulus package. Republicans wanted to jump-start the economy with broad tax relief, specifically acceleration of the 2001 tax cuts. Democrats insisted on aid for the unemployed, infrastructure improvements and homeland security. [17]

Unable to get either plan to the Senate floor, senators compromised in February and passed a stripped-down bill containing only a 13-week extension of unemployment benefits. House Republican leaders fired back by attaching a broad stimulus plan to the bill and returning it to the Senate. The Senate responded by sending back a bill containing only the unemployment benefits.

The deadlock was broken with a deal combining $43 billion in business tax cuts with 13 additional weeks of unemployment benefits for those who lost jobs after Sept. 11. The House passed the $94 billion, five-year bipartisan package on March 7, 2002; the Senate cleared it the next day. Neither side was particularly happy with the final product.

By summer 2002 Congress had approved $40 billion in additional spending to combat terrorism, even as the economy had fallen into a recession that was shrinking government revenue. The recession dates from March 2001, according to the private National Bureau of Economic Research, the recognized authority on business-cycle dating.

The slump — which continues despite signs of recovery in early 2003 — is being blamed for a record-setting drop in federal revenue. In 2002, federal revenues fell $131 billion, the largest yearly percentage decline since the rollback of World War II taxes in 1946. About $43 billion of that is attributed to the Bush tax cut. [18]

White House and congressional budget forecasters alike acknowledged the change first in January and again over the summer by projecting budget deficits for at least the next three years. In July the OMB forecast a $165 billion deficit in fiscal 2002 and $109 billion in 2003. A month later, the Congressional Budget Office (CBO) forecast $157 billion of red ink in 2002 and $145 billion in 2003. For the 10-year period, OMB and CBO project cumulative surpluses of $2.3 trillion or $1 trillion, respectively, but both predictions depend on the uncertain assumption that the tax cuts due to expire in 2010 will not be extended. [19]

Democrats hoped to use the troubling economic news to political ad-

vantage in the midterm congressional elections, but Bush and his advisers succeeded in focusing the campaign instead on terrorism, homeland security and presidential leadership. Sweeping the South and winning key races elsewhere, Republicans regained control of the Senate and increased their numbers in the House — emerging with absolute majorities in both chambers for the first time since 1954.

A month after the election, however, Bush sacked the principal members of his economic team: Treasury Secretary Paul O'Neill, a maverick who had minimized the tax-cut issue, and Lawrence Lindsey, viewed by many as a disappointment as head of the National Economic Council. As their successors, Bush turned on Dec. 9 and 10 to two corporate executives: John Snow, chairman of the railroad company CSX Corp., for Treasury; and Stephen Friedman, former co-chairman of the investment firm Goldman Sachs, for the economic council. Some conservative tax-cut advocates viewed both men with suspicion because of their records as anti-deficit activists. In accepting the nomination to the Treasury post, however, Snow vowed to support a "pro-growth, pro-jobs" agenda — phrasing used by conservatives to denote tax cuts. [20] ∎

CURRENT SITUATION

Economic Indicators

People in Washington and much of the Northeast celebrated a white Christmas in 2002 thanks to an unanticipated snowstorm, but the nation's retailers found the holiday season was short on their favorite color: green. Major retailers reported disappointing sales for

the all-important December holidays. The giant Wal-Mart Corp., for example, reported right before Christmas that sales were at the lower end of the projected 3 percent to 5 percent increase over the previous year. [21]

Despite the lackluster retailing report, many other economic indicators were upbeat in December and early January. Consumer spending was rising, along with personal income and consumer confidence. New-home sales hit a record high in November. And an unexpectedly positive report on manufacturing released on Jan. 2 helped spark a 3 percent rise on the nation's stock markets on the first trading day of the new year.

Still, some economic signals were not so promising. Most importantly, unemployment remained at recession levels. The jobless rate rose in November to 6 percent — equal to the highest rate since 1994. Ominously, the Labor Department reported on Jan. 2 that new jobless claims filed in the last week of December rose unexpectedly — indicating that job creation remains sluggish at best.

On balance, though, the economy seems to be heading upwards — casting a new light on the debate in Washington over Bush's economic-stimulus package. *The Wall Street Journal* led its Jan. 3 editions with a story proclaiming "signs of a rebound." Tellingly, the newspaper noted that despite a downbeat prediction in November of future business investment, the company headed by one of the major advocates for an economic stimulus is planning to boost capital spending in 2003 by a hefty 10 percent to 15 percent.

"During hard times, you cut back on capital [improvements]," John Dillon, CEO of International Paper Co. and chairman of The Business Roundtable, told the newspaper. "But over time you have to spend to improve your competitiveness." [22]

NAM's chief economist Heuther acknowledges the encouraging signs but still believes the nation needs an economic stimulus — in the form of business and individual tax cuts. "The ingredients are there for a modest recovery," he says. But, he adds, "Without any stimulus package, the recovery we're going to see in 2003 is going to be fairly gradual."

For his part, the Urban Institute's Burman says whatever the economy's current trends are, Bush's proposed tax cuts would do little to perk it up. "The numbers that have come out recently have been contradictory," he says. "It doesn't change my opinion that the kind of stimulus that we're talking about is not well timed and wouldn't do any good in any event."

On the consumer side, rising spending and confidence figures for November fueled further optimism. Consumer spending rose a healthy 0.5 percent, according to the Commerce Department. Heuther estimates that even with modest growth in December, spending for the fourth quarter of 2002 is likely to be up by 3 percent — higher than projected earlier in the year. At the same time, the University of Michigan's benchmark monthly consumer sentiment index rose in November, reversing a downward trend that had started in May. [23]

On the business side, the favorable harbinger came with a report on a key gauge of manufacturing activity: the Institute for Supply Management's December factory index. Based on a survey of purchasing managers — the index jumped unexpectedly in December to 54.7 from the previous month's level of 49.2. A figure above 50 means the manufacturing sector is expanding; a figure below 50 indicates contraction.

Experts quoted in news reports were offering differing assessments of the report, however. "This is a hugely strong report," said Ian C. Shepherdson, chief U.S. economist at the market research firm High Frequency Economics.

But Richard Rippe, a Prudential Securities economist, was more downbeat. "It is an encouraging sign," he said, "but the overall array of information on the industrial sector is still mixed." [24]

News on the job front was less encouraging, though. Unemployment stood at 6 percent in November — up from the 4 percent range at the start of the Bush presidency in 2001. And the Labor Department's Employment and Training Administration reported Jan. 2 that new claims for unemployment benefits for the week ended Dec. 28 totaled 403,000 — an increase of 13,000 over the previous week. The 12 states reporting increases of 1,000 or more new jobless claims attributed the jump to layoffs in a variety of sectors — including construction, transportation, communications, manufacturing and public administration.

Earlier, Labor Secretary Elaine Chao had acknowledged that the November unemployment figures were "disappointing." The report, she said, "indicates that the economy is soft and stable and underscores the need to encourage economic growth." [25]

Political Strategies

President Bush is trying to sell his tax-cutting proposals as a "jobs and growth" package that will let working Americans keep more of their paychecks and encourage investment and job creation by boosting the stock market. Democrats say their rival plan does more to help the economy right now while containing no long-term tax cuts that will add to the budget deficit.

The focal point of the debate appears likely to be the dividend-taxation issue. Bush and the Democrats sharply disagree over both the fairness of the plan and the likely effects of eliminating the taxes that investors pay on dividends.

Bush insists that eliminating "double taxation" of dividends would provide broad tax relief to some 35 million households, especially senior citizens. He also says the plan would pump about $20 billion into the economy "this year."

Democrats counter that Bush's plan would primarily benefit higher-income taxpayers. "This is for the wealthiest people in the country," House Minority Leader Nancy Pelosi of California says. In addition, Democrats say it provides no immediate fiscal stimulus — since the benefits would be realized only in 2004.

A range of experts and policy advocates lend support to the Democrats' critique on the issue. Calculations by the Urban-Brookings Center for Tax Policy and the more avowedly liberal Citizens for Tax Justice both show that the change would give only a nominal tax reduction to people with low-to-moderate incomes, while affluent taxpayers would reap the lion's share of the benefits. Taxpayers earning more than $1 million would see their taxes reduced on average by more than $45,000, according to the Urban-Brookings study.

Economists, meanwhile, are generally skeptical of White House claims that eliminating taxation of dividends will do much to increase consumer spending or business investment. "It is not at all clear how the plan is going to stimulate the economy in the near term," Diane Swonk, chief economist at Chicago's Bank One Corporation, told *The New York Times.* [26]

The administration's supporters counter by depicting taxation of dividends as unfair and illogical. "The dividend tax is inefficient and punishes savings and capital formation," says Paul Beckner, president of Citizens for a Sound Economy. Supporters also contend that eliminating the tax will give a psychological boost to the stock market at a time when more and more moderate-income workers own stocks.

At Issue:

Should Congress adopt President Bush's stimulus package?

STEPHEN MOORE
PRESIDENT, CLUB FOR GROWTH

WRITTEN FOR THE CQ RESEARCHER, JANUARY 2003

*p*resident Bush has proposed a $674 billion tax cut to help pull the economy out if its two-year rut. This bold and ambitious plan is being criticized as fiscally unaffordable, but it is the right fiscal medicine at the right time.

What we cannot afford is letting the economy continue to underperform to the detriment of workers, investors, states and cities — all victims of anemic growth.

The centerpiece of the president's plan is elimination of the double taxation of dividends. This can result in effective tax rates on dividends up to 70 percent. These punitive tax rates, in turn, reduce stock values, capital investment and savings.

By some estimates, elimination of the dividend tax could cause stock values to rise by as much as 10 percent — good news for the 85 million American shareholders. It could also increase U.S. gross domestic product by at least $5 for every $1 of reduced tax receipts.

The other major feature of the Bush plan is to fast-forward the tax cuts from the president's 2001 plan. Phased-in tax cuts are always of questionable economic wisdom. Would you go to the store today to buy a product if the store advertised that tomorrow the price will be marked down by another 20 percent?

Delayed tax cuts delay economic activity — they de-stimulate the economy.

The rhetoric from the Democrats about curtailing the tax cuts only ensures that they will have no effect today. Would you buy a car with the promise of zero financing if the dealer was threatening to change the terms of the deal next year?

A symptom of the ailing U.S. economy is the dormant U.S. venture capital industry. Costs are too high for new businesses, thanks to government meddling; payoffs are too meager, thanks to excessive taxes on capital investment.

President Bush would accelerate his earlier tax cut. I would prefer to see the entire 2001 Bush tax cut effective immediately. A majority of House and Senate members voted for the tax cut two years ago. Why not provide the full economic bang of the tax cut now, when the economy desperately needs a shot of steroids.

The idea behind this plan is to replicate the supply-side tax-cut successes of Presidents Reagan and Kennedy. Deficit hawks in both parties will no doubt squeal that this tax plan will run up the national debt. They are wrong. What JFK and Reagan and now George W. Bush understand clearly is that it is the absence of economic growth that causes runaway budget deficits.

ROBERT BIXBY
EXECUTIVE DIRECTOR, CONCORD COALITION

WRITTEN FOR THE CQ RESEARCHER, JANUARY 2003

*t*he president's new economic plan is built around an ambitious mix of tax-rate reductions. To ask whether these reductions make sense right now, we need to ask three questions.

First, are the reductions justified by a more favorable reassessment of the budget's long-term outlook? Absolutely not. All of the recent reassessments have gone dramatically in the opposite direction. Partly due to the recession, the crashing of the equity price bubble and last year's tax cuts, revenue projections have plunged. And with America's new war on terrorism heating up, we may be facing an urgent, long-lasting demand for new national defense and homeland-security spending. Two years ago, we were looking at a $5.6 trillion surplus over 10 years. Today, we may be looking at a 10-year deficit as high was nearly $3 trillion.

Second, are the reductions advisable as a short-term stimulus? The experts are uncertain. Many believe that the economy is recovering and will continue to do so with or without additional stimulus. Even the president has stated that the economy is "pretty darn strong." To the extent that there is a problem, it is with near-term business and consumer confidence. This suggests that any new stimulus plan, if needed at all, should be capable of swift implementation and targeted to have an immediate bang for the buck with minimal long-term costs. The president's plan does not meet these criteria.

Finally, do the reductions improve the tax code's overall efficiency? There is much to be said for the president's desire to impose fewer tax penalties on savings and investment — especially his plan to reduce or eliminate the "double taxation" of corporate dividends, which many economists have long criticized.

Such structural reforms, however, would only be beneficial as part of a revenue-neutral package. Reducing the taxation on dividends may marginally improve savings behavior — but not nearly enough to compensate for the loss in federal revenue, which adds directly to the federal debt and — in the long run — subtracts dollar-for-dollar from national savings.

In short, the president's proposed tax cuts must be evaluated in the context of long-term spending needs and revenue realities — and that means looking at everything from Social Security, Medicare and Medicaid to home-equity loan deductions and corporate expense loopholes.

How we resolve the balance of priorities will ultimately determine our long-term tax burden — not whether Congress can muster the "courage" to hand voters another tax cut.

Different Assumptions, Different Outcomes

The Congressional Budget Office (CBO) projects that over the next decade, assuming current policies remain unchanged, the country will achieve a total surplus of $1 trillion. But the anti-deficit Concord Coalition projects a nearly $2 trillion deficit, assuming current tax cuts are made permanent and Congress enacts a low-cost Medicare drug benefit.

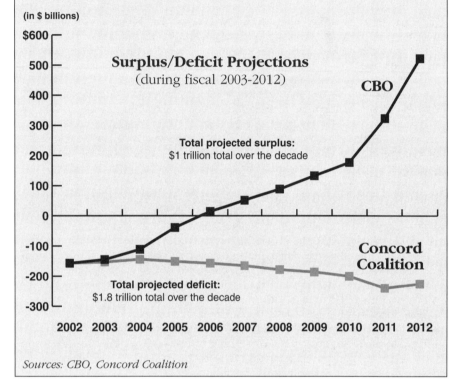

(in $ billions)

Surplus/Deficit Projections
(during fiscal 2003-2012)

CBO

Total projected surplus:
$1 trillion total over the decade

Concord Coalition

Total projected deficit:
$1.8 trillion total over the decade

2002 2003 2004 2005 2006 2007 2008 2009 2010 2011 2012

Sources: CBO, Concord Coalition

The potential impact of the dividend tax cut is complicated by the fact that many dividends are not taxed on a current basis because workers or retirees hold stock in tax-deferred retirement accounts. Moreover, an administration official acknowledged after the president's speech that the money eventually withdrawn from retirement accounts — personal contributions, dividends and interest — would still be taxed as ordinary income under the president's plan. [27]

Bush is pushing the other tax breaks for individuals by arguing that his proposals would merely speed up changes already approved in the 2001 law. "The time to deliver the tax-rate reductions is now, when they can do the most good for American businesses," Bush said in his Chicago speech.

The plan calls for lowering the rates for higher-income taxpayers to levels now set to take effect in 2004 and 2006; changes would be retroactive to Jan. 1, 2003, and withholding adjustments would be made immediately. In addition, Bush wants to increase the child tax credit to $1,000 from $600 — a phased-in change due to be completed in 2010. He also would immediately reduce the so-called marriage penalty by setting the deduction for married couples at twice that for single filers — a change now due to be completed in 2009.

Democrats instead are offering what they call "front-loaded" tax relief for 2003 only. Under their plan, the House Democrats say, "virtually all costs fall in 2003, allowing the budget to recover as the economy recovers." Bush's plan would produce "enormous deficits and endless debts," says Rep. John M. Spratt Jr. of South Carolina, ranking Democrat on the House Budget Committee.

In his Chicago speech, Bush called for quick action on his plan. "I proposed a bold plan because our need is urgent," the president said. One day earlier, House Democrats had also called for "early enactment" of their stimulus package to provide "up-front help for the sagging economy now." With partisan lines so sharply drawn, however, congressional observers were girding for a fight more likely to be both long and loud. ■

OUTLOOK

"It's the Economy"

The first President Bush started the 1992 campaign year with approval ratings still elevated by voters' memories of the U.S. victory in the Persian Gulf War. By November, though, voters in the sagging economy were more concerned with pocketbook issues. Bush went down to defeat by Bill Clinton in a campaign famously encapsulated by Clinton adviser James Carville: "It's the economy, stupid."

As his bold tax-cut plan makes clear, George W. Bush has no intention of repeating his father's miscalculation of overlooking economic issues. A slow recovery "is the greatest threat overhanging the Republicans and President Bush for the next two years," says GOP strategist Ed Gillespie. [28] By laying out a "jobs and growth" package well in advance of the 2004 campaign year, Bush is evidently trying to show voters he wants to get the economy on track before he stands for re-election — and to be in a position to claim credit for the recovery.

Bush startled even some of the administration's supporters with the size of his proposal — $674 billion, more than double the $300 billion figure that had been widely reported as late as the weekend before the president's Chicago speech. White House Press Secretary Ari Fleischer insisted to reporters, however, that Bush had actually decided on the size of the package in November. He also claimed that Bush had early decided to call for completely eliminating the tax on corporate dividends for investors — despite reports that a 50 percent cut had been under consideration when the new year began.

Democrats face a difficult political calculus in opposing the president's package. They sought to claim the high road — offering a constructive alternative rather than simply criticizing the president's plan — by laying out an alternative package. But as the minority party in both the House and the Senate, they have little chance to win approval of major parts of their proposals. And tax-cutting proposals have an easier time winning popular acclaim than the kind of calls for fiscal responsibility that Democrats are using to criticize the Bush plan.

Despite the scope of the Bush plan, experts on both sides of the issue expect a stimulus package to emerge from Congress. "It's pretty inevitable that some kind of plan is going to go through," says conservative economist Engen at the American Enterprise Institute. Kogan at the liberal Center for Budget and Policy Priorities agrees: "I expect to see something that they will call economic stimulus but will provide a low or

failing grade in terms of the stimulus that it actually provides."

The effects of any stimulus package remain much in doubt. Both Bush and the congressional Democrats acknowledge that their plans will have only a modest effect given the overall size of the U.S. economy. The slow pace of the legislative process further militates against any substantial short-term stimulative effect. And the economy may already be trending upward, according to some indicators.

On the other hand, enactment of major parts of Bush's plan could have significant, long-term effects — for better or worse. If the administration's supporters are right, the plan would bolster the economy by giving individuals and businesses incentives to spend and invest not only in 2003 but also in what economic policymakers call "the out years."

If the critics are to be believed, the plan would jeopardize the country's economic health by adding to a federal budget deficit already at more than $150 billion — and widely expected to grow to as much as $250 billion or more if the United States goes to war against Iraq later this year. The continuing war on terrorism, and even the growing cost of health-care, will only add to the red ink.

Taxpayers interviewed by reporters immediately after the president's speech had differing reactions. Cleve Baker, a California retiree who lives primarily off dividend and interest income, voiced approval. "Taking the tax off dividends will certainly help with my cash flow, which is welcome," he told the *Los Angeles Times*.

But Bee and Robert Moorhead, an Austin, Texas, couple with good jobs but virtually no dividend income, saw little to praise. "They're trying to sell this once again as trickle-down economics," Robert Moorhead told *The New York Times*. "I have my doubts." ∎

Notes

[1] Sanger and Josten are both quoted in David Cay Johnston, "Key Questions on Tax Breaks: How Big? Who Gets Them?" *The New York Times*, Dec. 16, 2002, p. C4.

[2] For background, see Mary H. Cooper, "Budget Surplus," *The CQ Researcher*, April 13, 2001, pp. 297-320.

[3] See National Governors Association/National Association of State Budget Officers, "Fiscal Survey of the States," November 2002.

[4] For background, see David Masci, "The Federal Reserve," *The CQ Researcher*, Sept. 1, 2000, pp. 673-688, and Christopher Conte, "Deflation Fears," *The CQ Researcher*, Feb. 13, 1998, pp. 121-144.

[5] Quoted in Greg Ip, "Greenspan Raises Possibility Rate Cut May Be Reversed," *The Wall Street Journal*, Nov. 14, 2002, p. A2. For other coverage, see Edmund L. Andrews, "Fed Chief Says He Supports Bush Tax Cut," *The New York Times*, Nov. 14, 2002, p. A1; Jonathan Weisman, "Greenspan Throws Damper On Permanent Tax-Cut Plan," *The Washington Post*, Nov. 14, 2002, p. A6. Greenspan's prepared testimony can be found on the Federal Reserve's Web site: www.federalreserve.gov.

[6] Some background drawn from Charles K. Wilber and Kenneth P. Jameson, *Beyond Reaganomics: A Further Inquiry into the Poverty of Economics* (1990), pp. 30-63. See also David C. Colander and Harry Landreth (eds.), *The Coming of Keynesianism to America: Conversations with the founders of Keynesian Economics* (1996), pp. 1-34.

[7] Wilber and Jameson, *op. cit.*, pp. 43-44.

[8] *Ibid.*, p. 45.

[9] *Ibid.*, pp. 46-47.

[10] For background, see *ibid.*, pp. 92-121; Mary H. Cooper, "Economics After Reaganomics," *Editorial Research Reports*, Aug. 27, 1987, pp. 425-440.

[11] Some background drawn from Robert D. Reischauer, "The Dawning of a New Era," in Henry J. Aaron and Robert D. Reischauer, *Setting National Priorities: The 2000 Elections and Beyond* (1999), pp. 1-16. See also Cooper, "Budget Surplus," *op. cit.*, pp. 310-311.

[12] Reischauer and Aaron, *op. cit.*, pp. 4-5. Reischauer was director of the Congressional Budget Office from 1989-1995. He is now president of The Urban Institute.

[13] See The Concord Coalition, "Budget Update: The Return of Deficits," September 2002.

[14] See 2001 *CQ Almanac*, pp. 18-3-18-14.

[15] *Ibid.*, pp. 18-15-18-20.

[16] For background, see *2001 CQ Almanac*, "Stimulus Bill Dies in Senate," p. 18-15.

[17] For background, see Julie Hirschfeld Davis, "Unemployment Benefits Provide Catalyst to Pass Recovery Bill," *CQ Weekly*, March 9, 2002, p. 633.

[18] Jill Barshay, "Stock Market Tumble, Tax Breaks Blamed for Federal Revenue Drop," *CQ Weekly*, Aug. 31, 2002, p. 2240.

[19] See Daniel J. Parks, "Revenue Decline a Tepid Issue for Voters Despite Democratic Finger-Pointing," *CQ Weekly*, Aug. 31, 2002, p. 2238.

[20] See Richard W. Stevenson, "Nominee Tackles His First Day as Economic Salesman," *The New York Times*, Dec. 10, 2002, p. A30; Bob Davis and Jeanne Cummings, "Fight Brews Over New Tax Cuts," *The Wall Street Journal*, Dec. 10, 2002, p. A4. As evidence of Snow's and Friedman's views, conservatives noted that Snow endorsed deficit reduction and balanced budgets in an op-ed article in 1995 and that Friedman was a member of the anti-deficit Concord Coalition and served with the Clinton administration's Treasury secretary, Robert Rubin, as Goldman Sachs co-chairman.

[21] See Dina ElBoghdady, "Shopping Binge Falls Short of Stores' Hopes," *The Washington Post*, Dec. 24, 2002, p. E1.

[22] Greg Ip, "Inside a Shaky Economy, Signs of a Rebound Emerge," *The Wall Street Journal*, Jan. 3, 2002, p. A1.

[23] See John M. Berry, "Consumer Data Show Economy Stirring," *The Washington Post*, Dec. 24, 2002, p. E1.

[24] Shepherdson was quoted in Anitha Reddy, "Stocks Start With Big Rally," *The Washington Post*, Jan. 3, 2002, p. E1; Rippe in Jon E. Hilsenrath, "Manufacturing-Activity Gauge Increases More Than Expected," *The Wall Street Journal*, Jan. 3, 2002, p. A2.

[25] Quoted in John M. Berry, "Jobless Rate Rose to 6% in November," *The Washington Post*, Dec. 7, 2002, p. E1.

[26] Edmund L. Andrews, "White House Aides Launch a Defense of Bush Tax Plan," *The New York Times*, Jan. 7, 2003, p. A1.

[27] See Edward L. Andrews, "Plan Gives Benefits to Wealthy and Families," *The New York Times*, Jan. 8, 2003, p. A17.

[28] Quoted in Howard Gleckman and Richard S. Dunham, "How Bush Will Stoke the Engine," *Business Week*, Nov. 25, 2002, p. 32.

FOR MORE INFORMATION

The Business Roundtable, 1615 L St., N.W., Suite 1100, Washington, DC 20036; (202) 872-1260; www.brtable.org. Examines issues that concern big business, such as taxation and antitrust law.

Center on Budget and Policy Priorities, 820 1st St., N.E., Suite 510, Washington, DC 20002; (202) 408-1080; www.cbpp.org. Liberal research group that analyzes government policies affecting low- and moderate-income Americans.

Citizens for a Sound Economy, 1900 M St., N.W., Suite 500, Washington, DC 20036; (202) 783-3870; www.cse.org. Conservative advocacy group that promotes reduced taxes, free trade and deregulation.

Citizens for Tax Justice, 1311 L St., N.W., Suite 400, Washington, DC 20005; (202) 626-3780; www.ctj.org. Coalition that promotes progressive taxation.

Club for Growth, 1776 K St., NW, Suite 300, Washington, DC 20006; (202) 955-5500; www.clubforgrowth.org. A conservative research and fundraising group that supports free-market candidates.

Concord Coalition, 1011 Arlington Blvd., Suite 300, Arlington, VA 22209; (703) 894-6222; www.concordcoalition.org. A liberal, grass-roots organization advocating preservation of Social Security, Medicare and Medicaid.

National Association of Manufacturers, 1331 Pennsylvania Ave., N.W., Suite 600, Washington, DC 20004; (202) 637-3000; www.nam.org. Lobbies for industry on national and international issues.

National Conference of State Legislatures, 444 N. Capitol St., Suite 515, Washington, DC 20001; (202) 624-5400; www.ncsl.org. Lobbies Congress and conducts research on issues of interest to the states. (Headquarters in Denver, Colo.)

National Governors Association, Hall of States, 444 N. Capitol St., Washington, DC 20001-1512; (202) 624-5300; www.nga.org. Recommends policy on economic development and other issues important to the states.

U.S. Chamber of Commerce, 1615 H St., N.W., Washington, DC 20062-2000; (202) 659-6000; www.uschamber.org. Federation of businesses and trade and professional associations that develops policy on issues important to U.S. business, including tax policy.

The Urban Institute, 2100 M St., N.W., Washington, DC 20037; (202) 833-7200; www.urban.org. Liberal public policy research organization focusing on social and economic problems.

Bibliography

Selected Sources

Books

Krugman, Paul, *Peddling Prosperity: Economic Sense and Nonsense in the Age of Diminished Expectations*, W.W. Norton, 1994.

A *New York Times* columnist recounts — from an avowedly liberal perspective — the rise of conservative economic policies under Presidents Reagan and Bush in the 1980s, and the formation of new policies on President Clinton's watch. Krugman taught economics at MIT when writing the book.

Roberts, Paul Craig, *The Supply-Side Revolution: An Insider's Account of Policymaking in Washington*, Harvard University Press, 1984.

A columnist and senior fellow at the Hoover Institution at Stanford University traces the history of "supply-side" economics from its genesis in the mid-1970s.

Wilber, Charles K., and Kenneth P. Jameson, *Beyond Reaganomics: A Further Inquiry into the Poverty of Economics*, University of Notre Dame Press, 1990.

Traces the origins and ascension of Keynesian economics from the 1930s into the 1970s and the birth of the rival "supply-side" school of economics; includes detailed notes. Wilber is professor emeritus, University of Notre Dame; Jameson is a professor of economics at the University of Utah.

Woodward, Bob, *The Agenda: Inside the Clinton White House*, Simon & Schuster, 1994.

The Washington Post associate editor and famed Watergate investigator recounts the formation of economic policy during President Clinton's first year in office.

Articles

Barshay, Jill, with Alan K. Ota, "With Economy Still Lagging, Everyone Has a Stimulus Plan," *CQ Weekly*, Nov. 16, 2002, pp. 2990-2999.

Cover story details various economic-stimulus proposals.

Cooper, Mary H., "Budget Surplus," *The CQ Researcher*, April 13, 2001, pp. 297-320.

Report covers debate over President Bush's proposed tax cut at a time when the federal budget was still in surplus.

Nekirk, William, "Bloated Industries Put Economy in Bind," *The Chicago Tribune*, Dec. 15, 2002, p. A1.

Recounts challenges faced by U.S. economy at a time of widespread overcapacity. First of four-part series.

Simon, Stephanie, "Many States Face Gloomy Budget Choices," *Los Angeles Times*, Dec. 29, 2002, p. A1.

Recounts budget cuts that states have instituted or considered to avert looming deficits.

Reports and Studies

Brough, Wayne T., "Taxes, Spending, and Deficits," *Citizens for a Sound Economy*, Dec. 18, 2002.

Critique of Keynesian economics and support for tax cuts by the conservative group's chief economist. For other pro-tax cut commentary, see www.cse.org.

Congressional Budget Office, "The Budget and Economic Outlook: An Update," August 2002.

Updated economic and budget projections by the nonpartisan office that advises Congress on economic policy.

Gale, William G., and Peter R. Orszag, "A New Round of Tax Cuts?" Urban Institute-Brookings Tax Policy Center, August 2002.

Argues against various tax-cutting proposals put forth at President Bush's economic summit in August 2002, including the reduction in or elimination of the so-called double taxation of corporate dividends.

National Conference of State Legislatures, "State Budget Debate, November 2002."

Details the continued deterioration of state fiscal conditions at the end of 2002.

National Governors Association/National Association of State Budget Officers, "The Fiscal Survey of States," November 2002.

Details budget cuts adopted because of "fiscal crisis" in states and calls for federal legislation to help; includes more than 20 tables.

> ### On the Web
>
> The White House includes substantial information about the president's "jobs and growth" package on its Web site, including the text of the president's Jan. 7 speech (www.whitehouse.gov). Information on the House Democrats' economic-stimulus plan is being posted on the House Minority Leader's Web site, http://democraticleader.house.gov. The nonpartisan Tax Foundation has a fact-sheet on both major plans along with several analyses: www.taxfoundation.org. Useful interest-group sites include the Center for Budget and Policy Priorities (www.cbpp.org), Citizens for a Sound Economy (www.cse.org), Citizens for Tax Justice (www.ctj.org), the Club for Growth (www.clubforgrowth.org), the Concord Coalition (www.concordcoalition.org), and the Urban-Brookings Center on Tax Policy (www.urban.org).

14 Accountants Under Fire

KENNETH JOST

Enron Corp. was flying high in October 2000 as the company's employees gathered for a rousing annual meeting at its gleaming Houston headquarters and in more than a dozen satellite offices around the world.

The huge energy-trading company's stock had doubled over the past year to $80 per share. Earnings per share were reported to be up 26 percent. And the company had just signed a promising deal with Blockbuster to deliver movies on demand to home viewers. "We're in great shape," Enron President Jeffrey Skilling proclaimed.

One of the Houston employees, however, had a question. What about a *Wall Street Journal* article claiming that, if not for its accounting techniques, Enron would have had a loss in the second quarter?

Skilling debunked the story without skipping a beat. The article has "absolutely no merit, no substance," he told the crowd. The company properly recognizes income from energy trades when the contracts are signed, he explained, and properly discloses the methodology in its financial reports.

"Our accounting policies are not only appropriate, in my opinion, they're conservatively executed," Skilling concluded. "So, we're in a strong position from an accounting basis." [1]

Ten months later, however, an Enron executive reached a different conclusion. Sherron Watkins, a vice president for corporate development, had become alarmed by the accounting of several complex transactions. The deals used Enron stock to set up separate companies of unclear purpose and uncertain financing.

From *The CQ Researcher*,
March 22, 2002.

Enron Vice President Sherron Watkins has been hailed by congressional committees as a courageous corporate whistle-blower for her warnings to Enron CEO Kenneth Lay about accounting procedures used to hide losses.

Accountants from Arthur Andersen LLP — the firm that audits Enron's books — had approved the transactions. But Watkins, a former Andersen employee, thought the deals simply hid Enron losses by keeping red ink off the company books.

When Skilling abruptly resigned on Aug. 14, 2001 — ostensibly for personal reasons — Watkins could contain her suspicions no longer. She poured out her concerns in an anguished seven-page letter to Enron Chief Executive Officer Kenneth Lay.

"I am incredibly nervous that we will implode in a wave of accounting scandals," Watkins wrote. Others in the company have similar concerns, she said. "We're such a crooked company," she quoted an unidentified manager as saying. [2]

Seven months later, Watkins' warnings have come true. Enron, on paper the nation's seventh-largest corporation, has been forced into bankruptcy. And Andersen — one of the "Big Five" accounting firms that dominate the auditing of public corporations in the U.S. and abroad — has suffered so much damage that its survival is in doubt.

Not only have Andersen's big audit clients and top employees begun jump-

ing ship, but on March 14 a federal grand jury indictment charged the company with obstruction of justice for its admitted destruction of Enron-related documents. To make matters worse, the firm faces the likelihood of hundreds of millions of dollars in liability for purported accounting malpractice, and merger talks with other accounting firms appear to have gone up in smoke.

Enron's collapse already has had tangible political impact. The company's active program of political contributions and lobbying helped spur the House of Representatives to approve a sweeping campaign finance reform measure on Feb. 14. [3] More broadly, though, Enron's fate has cast an unflattering light on the accounting profession and the way it performs its role under federal law in protecting investors by auditing the books of publicly held corporations.

Suddenly, corporate auditors seem neither especially competent nor particularly trustworthy. And the financial information that companies regularly report to the Securities and Exchange Commission (SEC), stock analysts and the business press seems not only less than exact, but also less than honest.

"The really different thing about Enron is that ordinary people — non-accountants — now realize that something has gone amiss with accounting," says J. Edward Ketz, an associate professor of accounting at Pennsylvania State University in College Station.

Accounting-industry leaders put a more positive light on the story. Enron's collapse "highlights the important role that the accounting profession plays in our capital market," says James Castellano, a St. Louis accountant and chairman of the 336,000-member American Institute of Certified Public Accountants

ACCOUNTANTS UNDER FIRE

The 'Big Five'

The five largest American accounting firms netted nearly $25 billion in 2001. The two biggest firms make nearly half of their U.S. revenue from non-audit services; Ernst & Young and KPMG have recently shed their consulting services

Name	U.S. Revenue ($ millions, net)	% of Revenue by Type of Work		
		Acctg/Audit	Tax	Consulting
PricewaterhouseCoopers	$8,057	34.9	20.3	44.8
Deloitte & Touche	5,578	32.5	21.5	45.9
Ernst & Young	4,095	57.1	38.0	4.8
Arthur Andersen	3,971	42.0	32.0	26.0
KPMG	3,171	61.7	38.3	0

Percentages do not add up to 100% due to rounding.

Source: Bowman's Accounting Report

(AICPA). "We're interested in making whatever changes are necessary to restore public confidence in the capital markets and in our profession."

Public confidence, in fact, has slipped. Accounting traditionally ranks among the most trusted of professions and occupations. A recent *USA Today*/CNN/Gallup poll, however, shows that fewer than one-third of those surveyed rate accountants high for honesty and integrity, down from two-fifths last year. [4]

Proposals for change abound. Members of Congress from both parties are pushing various proposals — including moves to limit the purported conflict of interest from accountants providing consulting services to corporations whose books they audit. SEC Chairman Harvey Pitt — a lawyer who once represented the Big Five as well as the AICPA — is talking of revamping the profession's system of self-regulation. President Bush weighed in on March 7 with a multipart package that includes a proposal to force corporate executives to return bonuses based on bogus earnings reports.

Both Congress and the administration are also eyeing changes in federal laws governing private pension plans — so-called 401(k) plans. Last fall, as the price of Enron stock tumbled, many Enron employees whose pension plans were heavily invested in the stock saw their nest eggs plummet in value. (*See sidebar, p. 268.*)

Amid the firestorm over the company's collapse and the millions of dollars in stock sales by Enron executives, the general public is paying less attention to the obscure but important issue of accounting standards for accurately reporting the financial consequences of increasingly complex corporate transactions.

"The Enron story exposes a whole raft of problems relating to accounting rules and the ability of companies to mislead investors about their overall financial health without necessarily violating [those] rules," says Barbara Roper, director of investor protection at the Consumer Federation of America.

Some observers note, however, that Enron appears to have violated existing accounting rules in some of the controversial transactions — including the separate business entities Watkins warned about in her letter. Andersen accountants eventually reached the same conclusion — forcing Enron to take a

$1 billion write-off in October that started the company on a downward spiral ending with its Dec. 2 bankruptcy filing. (*See timeline, p. 266.*)

Indeed, Enron's collapse stems as much from a failure of corporate governance as from any shortcomings of the accounting profession, some experts say. They say Enron's top management got away with sham accounting only because of negligence or complicity by the corporation's board of directors and its supposedly independent audit committee. "Corporate governance and leadership stand between great triumph and natural disaster," says Michael Useem, a professor of management at the University of Pennsylvania's Wharton School of Finance in Philadelphia.

As accountants, lawmakers and others continue to sort through the fallout from Enron's implosion, here are some of the questions being debated:

Are questionable accounting practices common among major U.S. companies?

Enron CEO Lay tried to put a positive spin on the stunning announcement last fall that the company had sustained a third-quarter loss of $618 million after writing off $1 billion for "asset impairments" and losses related to "certain structured financing arrangements." The company "decided to take these charges," Lay explained in an Oct. 16 press release, "to clear away issues that have clouded the performance and earnings potential of our core energy businesses."

A second shoe fell the next day as Lay acknowledged to analysts and reporters that the company was reducing shareholder equity by $1.2 billion. The reduction was caused by the repurchasing of 55 million shares of stock issued in connection with some "special purpose partnerships" connected to Chief Financial Officer Andrew Fastow. Those complex transactions, it is now clear, were part of aggressive ef-

Complex Web Oversees Auditors

Various industry and government bodies oversee auditors of publicly held companies. While state boards license public accountants and stock exchanges supervise them, the private Financial Accounting Standards Board writes accounting standards. Discipline generally is handled by the SEC, the private Public Oversight Board and American Institute of Certified Public Accountants panels.

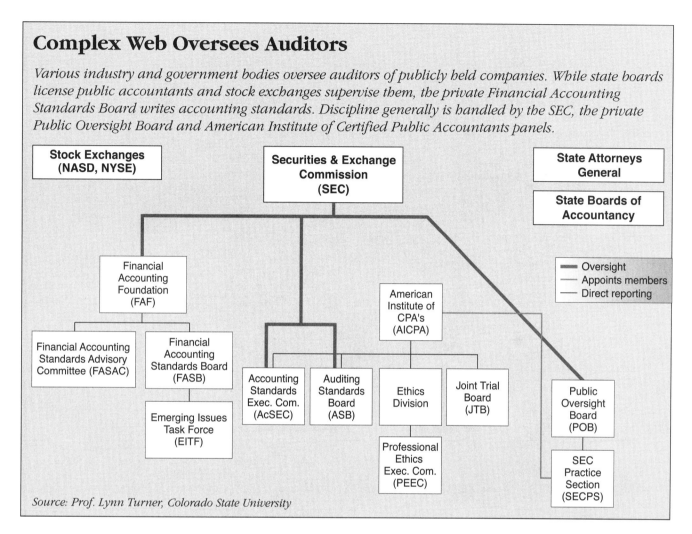

Source: Prof. Lynn Turner, Colorado State University

forts by Fastow and others to conceal a true picture of Enron's financial performance. Fastow was replaced on Oct. 24, 2001.

"These partnerships were intended evidently to disguise indebtedness and pump up earnings," Useem says. "They served no other purpose."

Enron's collapse called into question not only its own accounting techniques but also the methods used by other major U.S. companies to report their financial performance. Investor advocates, former regulators and other critics say the collapse reveals corporate America's dirty secret — that companies routinely use dubious accounting gimmicks to cook their books, or, in more academic terms, engage in "earnings management."

"Earnings management is like dirt," says Walter Schuetze, who served in two of the SEC's top accounting posts during the 1990s and continues as a consultant to the agency. "It is everywhere." [5]

But business leaders take issue with the picture of rampant chicanery by managers and their accountants. "Some companies can be found that maybe did one of those things," says Ronald Bernebeim, a business-ethics expert at the Conference Board, a New York-based organization of major U.S. corporations. "But when you talk about the size, scale, variety and pervasiveness [of Enron's accounting problems], Enron is pretty much in a class by itself."

In fact, Enron foundered over an issue faced by many — but by no means most — companies: how to account for joint ventures with other investors, unrelated to the company's main business. Accounting standards — now under review by the private-sector Financial Accounting Standards Board (FASB) — set guidelines for when the separate entity must be "consolidated" with the company's books and when it can be reported "off balance sheet."

"In some cases, the separate reporting of a special-purpose entity is the best way to report it," says Mark Cheffers, a former partner with the Big Five accounting firm Pricewaterhouse-Coopers and now chief executive officer of AccountingMalpractice.com, which provides risk-management advice to accountants.

Who Takes the Fall for Enron's Collapse?

Enron Corp.'s descent into bankruptcy stemmed in large part from the unraveling of shaky financing arrangements crafted by Enron executives with extensive accounting help from Arthur Andersen LLP.

Three Enron board members who investigated the collapse issued a scathing, 218-page report that found much to fault within the company itself: self-enriching executives, inattentive directors and a corporate culture of "overreaching."

But the three-member investigating committee also had stinging criticism for the company's accounting firm. Andersen "failed to meet its responsibilities," they said, to ensure the accuracy of Enron's financial statements or to establish proper safeguards for Enron's "related-party" transactions with its own executives — including Chief Financial Officer Andrew Fastow.

Andersen — its reputation already tattered by the admission that its lead Enron auditor had destroyed documents — fired back by blaming the collapse on Enron itself. "Poor business decisions on the part of Enron executives and its board ultimately brought the company down," C. E. Andrews, a managing partner, said in a prepared statement. [1]

The financing arrangements consisted of a series of so-called "special-purpose entities" (SPEs) created by Enron — ostensibly with outside parties as investors — but reported off the

Former Enron CFO Andrew Fastow declined to answer questions before the House Committee on Energy and Commerce on Feb. 7, 2002.

AFP Photo/Stephen Jaffe

company's main balance sheet. Accounting rules generally require companies to show their financial position and report profits and losses on a "consolidated" basis, but allow for "off-balance sheet" reporting for SPEs if outside investors put in and maintain at least 3 percent of the equity, and the company itself does not exercise control.

The web of special entities that Enron constructed was of daunting complexity. [2] The first step seems to have been innocent enough: a $500 million investment fund formed in 1993 on a 50/50 basis by Enron and the California Public Employee Retirement System (Calpers). The fund — known by its "Star Wars" acronym Jedi (joint energy development investment) — met accounting standards for off-book reporting.

After making a profit, Enron wanted to do it again, but Calpers wanted to cash out its Jedi profits first. So, in fall 1997, Enron helped form a new SPE — called Chewco after the "Star Wars" character Chewbaca — to buy out Calpers' share of Jedi. Chewco now became Enron's partner in Jedi. But Chewco's formation and operation skirted corporate governance and accounting rules. [3]

Fastow — depicted in the committee report as the prime mover in the arrangements — found some investors, but the total outside equity was eventually determined not to have met the 3 percent guideline for off-book reporting. Two of the investors were Michael Kopper, a friend of Fastow's and man-

Corporate managers and their auditors face a variety of other accounting issues that are subject to reasonable disagreement and capable of significantly changing the reporting of current earnings. For instance, research-and-development costs either may be booked as they are incurred or amortized over a period of years. Conversely, revenue from installment contracts can be booked as a lump sum or over time. "Companies can comply with the accounting rules and still present a misleading picture of their financial condition," Roper says.

With so much discretion, managers may naturally opt for the accounting

methods that maximize current earnings. "There are so many incentives for them to use aggressive accounting," Ketz says. Those incentives are increasing, he says, in part because of the now common practice of paying top executives in stock options, which increase in value as stock prices rise.

Auditors are expected to exercise independent judgment over a corporation's accounting practices. If they disagree, auditors can decline to give an "unqualified opinion" as to the accuracy of the financial statements — a red flag to investors and regulators. Andersen auditors questioned Enron's special partnerships in internal discussions on

Feb. 5, 2001, but a week later they raised no concerns when questioned by the company's audit committee.

"The auditors have not been doing quite the job they used to do," Ketz says, partly because the major accounting firms have increased their dependence on work other than corporate auditing, such as consulting. "It's basically changed their focus."

Even in the best of circumstances, though, auditors can go only so far in vouching for a company's financial statements. "Audits are not designed to ferret out fraud," says Roman Weil, a professor of accounting at the University of Chicago's Graduate School

aging director of an Enron subsidiary, and Kopper's domestic partner, William Dodson. Fastow effectively arranged for Kopper to control Chewco — circumventing a disclosure rule that would have applied if Fastow had assumed that role.

Enron made out well: Jedi agreed to pay a five-year "management fee" to the company that Enron booked in one lump in March 1998 — seemingly in violation of accounting practices. Kopper and Dodson made out extremely well: They eventually shared a $10.5 million payout for their $125,000 investment. And Chewco was used — in what Andersen later determined to be in violation of accounting rules — to enable Enron over a period of years to claim $405 million in profits and conceal more than $600 million in debt.

A later set of separate entities — a series of partnerships formed by Fastow, the last of them dubbed "Raptors" — is even harder to sort out. In brief, Enron used the off-book entities to lock in gains on stocks it held in other companies — and report the gains as current earnings — while the partnerships absorbed subsequent losses. Fastow served as general partner only after getting a waiver from the board of the rules limiting the company from entering into business arrangements with its senior executives.

In the first such deal, Enron invested $10 million in a start-up Internet service provider, Rhythms Net Connections, Inc., in March 1998. In the volatile world of dot.com stocks, the value of Enron's holding rose to $300 million a year later. Enron booked the gains. When the stock fell later, the off-book partnership took the hit.

Enron itself had financed the partnerships with its own stock, taking what amounted to an IOU in return. When Enron stock began to decline, however, the partnerships' solvency was threatened and the house of cards began to collapse.

Andersen auditors questioned the arrangements internally in early February 2001, but did not voice their concerns to the Enron board's audit committee in a meeting a week later. Only in September — after Enron Vice President Sherron Watkins' warning in August of looming accounting "scandals" — did Andersen auditors conclude the separate entities should have been "consolidated" — that is, reported on Enron's own balance sheet. The result: Enron reported a loss of $544 million for the third quarter and, a month later, restated its earnings for 2001 and three prior years to reverse the Chewco transactions, resulting in another huge write-off.

Enron's three-member investigating committee — headed by William Powers, dean of the University of Texas Law School — concluded that Andersen bore part of the blame. "There is abundant evidence that Andersen, in fact, offered Enron advice at every step, from inception through restructuring and ultimately to terminating the Raptors," the committee wrote.

In its statement, Andersen called the committee report "an attempt to insulate the company's leadership and the Board of Directors from criticism by shifting blame to others." Andersen "fully communicated with the audit committee," and the Enron board "was aware of the issues."

"We have said all along that we will take responsibility for any errors we may have made," Andersen's statement concluded. "But, we firmly believe our audit of Enron was conducted with rigor and in full accord with the standards of our profession."

---

[1] "Report of Investigation by the Special Investigative Committee of the Board of Directors of Enron Corp.," Feb. 1, 2002. The report can be found on the House Energy and Commerce Committee Web site: http://energycommerce.gov. Andersen's statement is on its Web site: www.arthurandersen.com.

[2] Among the many stories explaining the transactions, one of the clearest is Matt Krantz, "Peeling Back the Layers of Enron's Breakdown," *USA Today*, Jan. 22, 2002, p. 1A, with an accompanying sidebar: "Trouble Grew in Enron's Interlinking Partnerships," p. 2A.

[3] Some background parallels the account in Peter Behr, "How Chewco Brought Down an Empire," *The Washington Post*, Feb. 4, 2002, p. A1.

---

of Business. "If management sets out systematically to fool you, they're going to succeed part of the time."

Should the government take a more active role in regulating the accounting profession?

Twice within the past three years, Andersen settled major suits by shareholders alleging Andersen misled them about overstated profits: a $110 million settlement to Sunbeam shareholders last May and $75 million as part of a total $220 million payout to Waste Management Inc. shareholders in December 1998. [6] But when one of the other Big Five firms conduct-ed a "peer review" of Andersen as part of the accounting profession's self-regulatory system, it gave the firm a clean bill of health.

The review by Deloitte Touche Tohmatsu, covering a 12-month period through Aug. 30, 2001, certified that Andersen had been found "to provide reasonable assurance of compliance with professional standards." While the review cited three areas needing improvement, Andersen felt sufficiently confident to issue a news release about the finding in early January, even as it was defending itself against charges of accounting misfeasance while auditing Enron's books. [7]

Critics say the contrasting pictures of Andersen's professionalism demonstrate that the accounting industry's self-regulatory system is a failure. "Basically, there's no effective regulatory oversight of auditors right now," says the Consumer Federation of America's Roper. "The mechanisms that exist are under the control of the industry."

Calls to revamp the system are now being voiced nearly across the board. SEC Chairman Pitt says he wants greater public participation in the system, but is still working on details. Two former top SEC officials urged Congress to create a new, government regulatory body within the agency to oversee the profession. Some academic experts and investor advocates say the SEC itself could do the job if given more money.

For its part, the AICPA promises to work with Congress and the SEC to "improve" and "go beyond" the existing self-regulatory process. "We strongly support moving from public oversight to public participation and increasing the transparency, effectiveness and timeliness of the process," AICPA Chair Castellano told the House Energy and Commerce Subcommittee on Commerce, Trade and Consumer Protection last month.

But AICPA president Barry Melancon told the House Financial Services Committee on March 13 that shifting regulation to a public body would be "a radical change in the accounting profession's landscape."

The existing system of licensing and regulating accountants is a confusing crazy quilt of industry bodies and state and federal agencies. (*See diagram, p. 261.*) State boards of accountancy are responsible for licensing CPAs, but the AICPA requires anyone involved in auditing a publicly held company to be a member of its SEC Practice Section. The SEC itself has the power to bar an accountant from auditing a publicly held company.

Meanwhile, a five-member Public Oversight Board (POB) — an ostensibly independent, industry-funded unit established in 1977 — is charged with overseeing the peer-review process. The POB voted to disband following Pitt's call for revamping it. The outgoing head, former Comptroller General Charles Bowsher, told the Senate Banking Committee on March 19 that he favors a new, government body with members appointed by the SEC, the Federal Reserve Board and the secretary of the Treasury.

Discipline of auditors involved in corporate oversight is notoriously weak, according to regulators quoted in a comprehensive report by The Washington Post's David S. Hilzenrath. [8]

Over a decade-long period, Hilzenrath reported, the SEC disciplined only 280 accountants — about half of them public auditors and half corporate officers. SEC officials told the *Post* the agency only has the personnel to investigate the most egregious cases.

For its part, the AICPA took action in fewer than a fifth of the cases in which the SEC imposed sanctions, the newspaper said, while the New York Board of Accountancy acted in about a third of its cases. The story quoted Dennis Spackman, a former president of the National Association of State Boards of Accountancy, as saying that many state boards lack the resources to pursue disciplinary actions against members of the big accounting firms.

The self-regulatory peer-review process has built-in limitations. The POB has no subpoena power and cannot take any action regarding a matter in litigation until all legal action is completed. Still, Castellano calls the process "incredibly valuable" in helping firms improve their procedures. "It was never intended to be punitive," he explains.

In his testimony to Congress last month, however, Lynn E. Turner, a former SEC chief accountant and now a business professor at Colorado State University, sharply criticized the peer-review process. "The system of firm-on-firm reviews by the large firms reminds one of grade school where the rule was, 'I won't tell on you if you won't tell on me,' " Turner told the Senate Banking Committee on Feb. 14. He also said that the AICPA had cut off the POB's funding in 2000 when it undertook an investigation of auditors' compliance with rules aimed at safeguarding independence. [9]

Turner urged lawmakers to create an independent regulatory oversight body for the accounting profession under the SEC's supervision. He said the new body should be "adequately funded," with members "drawn from the public rather than the profession," and should be charged with taking "action against

those who fail to follow the rules, regardless of whether they are small or large firms."

Some industry observers oppose creating a new government agency. "Putting accountants under the microscope will disturb the delicate balance between informed risk-taking and accountability," says Douglas M. Branson, a law professor at the University of Pittsburgh.

Others are uncertain. "I don't know if we need anything other than more bucks for the SEC if we want them to do more discipline," says the University of Chicago's Weil.

Charles Elson, director of the Center for Corporate Governance at the University of Delaware, says the accounting firms themselves have the main responsibility for improving the profession's ethics. "They have to realize that getting too close to a client is dangerous," he says. "That has to come internally, not from the SEC."

Should accounting firms be barred from providing consulting services to companies that they audit?

Arthur Andersen received a hefty $25 million for auditing Enron's books during 2000. But it received even more — $27 million — for other, non-auditing services it provided for Enron.

That kind of breakdown between audit and non-audit fees is typical for the major accounting firms today. Over the past 25 years, all five have increased the percentage of their revenues from services other than public auditing — such as giving tax advice or helping design internal audit procedures.

The increased importance of consulting fees raises fears about compromising auditors' ability to conduct an objective evaluation of a company's books while other employees from their firm are providing non-audit services to the same company. "It doesn't look good," says Elson. "It never has. It's always had a funny smell."

Andersen officials initially tried to deflect the criticism. "I do not believe the fees we received compromised our independence," Chief Executive Officer Joseph Berardino told the House Financial Services Committee on Dec. 12. He minimized the conflict by noting that after separating tax and audit-related work, the firm received only about $13 million from Enron for consulting services.

The accounting industry earlier appeared to be ready to accept proposals that it long opposed to limit the ability of firms to provide consulting services to the companies that they audit. "It's become apparent that it doesn't matter whether auditors are in fact independent when they provide [non-audit services]," AICPA Chairman Castellano said in a March 1 interview. "The public believes that they aren't. We've acknowledged that, and we need to move beyond that."

But AICPA President Melancon had a different tone in his March 13 appearance before the House Financial Services Committee. "We believe any proposal that results in the creation of audit-only firms will inevitably prevent the audit from keeping pace with changes in business models, market dynamics and the overall economy."

Efforts to ban dual auditing and consulting roles date to the 1970s. The SEC in 1978 required accounting firms to disclose any non-audit services they provided to audit clients, but it rescinded the rule after what it called "unexpectedly severe" criticism from the industry. In 2000, then-SEC Chairman Arthur Levitt Jr. revived the idea, only to back off after strong criticism from the industry again, as well as from members of Congress from both parties. Instead, the agency adopted a milder rule requiring companies to disclose all fees paid to auditing firms, including fees for non-audit work. [10]

The AICPA itself issued a cautionary guideline in 1988, urging accounting firms to exercise "sound judgment" in providing non-audit services to their clients. But association leaders have

always maintained that there is no evidence of actual conflicts. "We don't believe that independence is, in fact, impaired when proper safeguards are deployed," Castellano says.

A recent study by three professors provides the first statistical evidence of an adverse effect on audit quality from simultaneously providing auditing and consulting services to a client. After examining reports from some 3,000 companies, the scholars found that firms that paid higher non-audit fees were more likely to be using accounting devices to manipulate their income. [11]

"Firms that purchase a lot of non-audit services from their auditors are more likely to engage in 'earnings management,' or what some people call 'cooking the books,' " says Karen Nelson, a professor at Stanford's Graduate School of Business in Palo Alto, Calif., and one of the study's three authors.

Surprisingly, though, the three scholars stop short of calling for a ban on dual auditing/consulting roles. Richard Frankel, the lead author and a professor of business at the Massachusetts Institute of Technology in Cambridge, says a company sometimes may have good reasons for turning to an auditor already familiar with its operations for other services. "Economically, it's difficult to make the argument that there's a benefit to [the auditing/consulting ban]," he says, "and it's easy to make the argument that there's a cost."

Other experts disagree. "Using your auditor as your consultant should be done under very limited — very, very narrow — circumstances," Elson says. Ex-SEC official Turner calls for allowing auditors to provide non-audit services only if a company's audit committee — appointed by the board of directors — certifies that the other services are in shareholders' best interests and will improve the quality of the company's financial reporting.

Consumer and investor advocacy groups call for strictly banning the dual roles, but say additional changes are

needed to strengthen auditor independence. Prohibiting auditors from providing consulting services is only "the most minimal step" to take, says the Consumer Federation's Roper.

More fundamentally, she says, auditors should be hired and fired by the audit committees established by corporate boards of directors rather than by a company's management. "The conflict starts with the fact that the auditor is hired, fired and paid by the audited client," Roper says. "They're supposed to be working for investors, but they have to please the management." ∎

BACKGROUND

Birth of a Profession

The modern public accounting profession emerged during the 19th century's Industrial Revolution, first in Britain and then in the United States. [12] The history of the organized profession in the United States has been marked by recurrent controversies stemming from business failures blamed on misleading or fraudulent financial disclosures to investors. As with the collapse of Enron, the business failures elicited calls for tighter government regulation of companies and their accountants. But the profession typically deflected the pressure by promising to solve the problems through self-regulation.

Simple bookkeeping techniques date from Roman times or earlier. Double-entry bookkeeping — invented by an Italian mathematician in the 1400s — represented a critical advance by introducing the principle that for every credit, the accounts must show a corresponding debit. The new method facilitated the creation of more complex business

Enron's Year of Living Dangerously

Feb. 5, 2001 *Arthur Andersen LLP accountants privately discuss concerns about Enron's off-book partnerships; consider dropping Enron as client.*

Feb. 12 *Andersen audit team voices no concerns about special partnerships when questioned by Enron audit committee; Jeffrey Skilling is named chief executive officer (CEO), replacing Kenneth Lay.*

Aug. 14 *Skilling suddenly resigns; Lay becomes CEO again.*

Aug. 15 *Sherron Watkins, Enron vice-president, writes to Lay expressing concern about "alarming" accounting practices; shares concerns few days later with one of Andersen auditors; meets with Lay Aug. 22.*

Aug. 21 *Andersen audit team meets to discuss Watkins' concerns.*

Late September *Andersen auditors conclude accounting for special partnerships was improper.*

Oct. 16 *Enron reports $618 million third-quarter losses, due in part to terminating special partnerships.*

Oct. 17 *Lay acknowledges $1.2 billion loss in shareholder equity.*

Oct. 22 *SEC opens inquiry into Enron's accounting; upgraded to formal investigation Oct. 31.*

Oct. 23 *Lay seeks to reassure investors in conference call; Andersen team begins document-shredding after urgent meeting called by chief auditor, David Duncan.*

Oct. 24 *Andrew Fastow replaced as Enron's chief financial officer.*

Oct. 27 *Andersen auditors question another off-book partnership.*

Nov. 8 *Enron acknowledges overstating profits for previous years by $586 million.*

Nov. 9 *Dynergy agrees to acquire Enron by merger.*

Nov. 28 *Dynergy calls off merger after reviewing Enron books.*

Nov. 29 *SEC expands investigation to include Andersen.*

Dec. 2 *Enron files for Chapter 11 bankruptcy protection; stock closes Dec. 3 at 26 cents per share.*

January 2002 *Andersen admits destruction of documents Jan. 10, fires Duncan Jan. 15; Enron fires Andersen Jan. 17.*

Feb. 1 *Enron board committee says profits were manipulated and senior executives enriched through accounting schemes.*

organizations financed by investment capital, such as the joint stock companies of pre-industrial Europe.

Without financial reporting and auditing, however, investors had few protections against fraud or excessive speculation. In one famous episode — the so-called South Sea Bubble — thousands of British investors faced ruin after the collapse in 1720 of a failed venture to develop trade with the South Sea Islands.

A century later, Britain in 1845 legally established the modern corporation, with protections for shareholders against improper actions by promoters and directors. Directors were required to compile a "full and fair balance sheet" for review by independent auditors. A decade later, accountants in Edinburgh organized the first Society of Accountants, and societies quickly developed in other financial centers, including London. By 1880, "chartered accountants" constituted an established profession. Their role was to review a company's balance sheet and verify whether it showed "a true and correct view of the state of the company's affairs."

In the late 19th century, Britain exported capital to help finance U.S. industrialization, and British accountants came along to help evaluate the investment possibilities. Among the British firms that came to America at the time was Price Waterhouse & Co., the dominant part of the merged PricewaterhouseCoopers, today's largest American accounting firm.

In 1887, the first U.S. professional organization was established: the American Association of Public Accountants (AAPA), the predecessor of today's AICPA. Nine years later, New York enacted the first state licensing law — giving birth to the American terminology "certified public accountants." And in 1902, U.S. Steel, the industrial powerhouse forged by the financier J.P. Morgan, set a precedent for American corporations by voluntarily selecting Price Waterhouse to audit its books for a report to shareholders. [13]

Chronology

Before 1900

Public accounting profession forms in Britain, United States.

1887
American Association of Public Accountants (AAPA) — predecessor of today's American Institute of Certified Public Accountants (AICPA) — established in U.S.

1896
New York passes first state licensing law for "certified public accountants."

1901-1930s

Accountants given expanded responsibilities under federal laws.

1913
Sixteenth Amendment authorizes federal income tax, creating new demand for accountants' services; Arthur Andersen firm founded.

1917
Federal Reserve Board prescribes AAPA-written standards for banks.

1933, 1934
Securities Act of 1933 and Securities Exchange Act of 1934 require independent auditing of publicly held companies, authorize suits against accountants for false or misleading financial disclosures.

1937
SEC policy defers to standard-setting by accounting profession group.

1970s *Congressional hearings bring calls for major reforms in accounting industry.*

1973
Financial Accounting Standards Board (FASB) established as autonomous standard-setting group.

1976, 1977
Moss and Metcalf subcommittee reports link business failures to flawed audits by major accounting firms; call for auditor independence, improved financial reporting.

1977
Public Oversight Board (POB) established as independent, private-sector body to oversee accountants; AICPA establishes SEC practice section.

1980s *Accounting firms take share of blame for savings and loan crisis.*

1989
Two pairs of "Big Eight" firms merge to form Ernst & Young and Deloitte, Touche, Ross — reducing to six the number of major national firms; Arthur Andersen spins off Andersen Consulting as separate, but financially tied, unit.

1990s-2000

Accounting industry prospers in decade-long boom

1995
Private Securities Litigation Reform Act limits accountants' liability in shareholder suits.

1996
General Accounting Office (GAO) credits accounting profession with some improved auditing and financial reporting practices, but says auditor independence, other major issues remain unresolved.

1998
PricewaterhouseCoopers merger takes effect July 1, reducing "Big Six" to "Big Five."

1999
Ernst & Young agrees to pay record $335 million in shareholder suit for inflated profits in corporate audit.

2000
SEC backs off plan to limit non-audit work for audit clients; Andersen Consulting gets green light from arbitrator to separate completely from Arthur Andersen under new name: Accenture.

2001-Present

Accounting industry faces pressure for overhauls after Enron bankruptcy.

2001
Enron in behind-the-scenes accounting crisis; CEO Kenneth Lay is warned in August of "accounting scandals"; company reports third-quarter loss in October after big write-down, later restates earnings for previous years; files for bankruptcy Dec. 2.

2002
In congressional hearings Enron, Arthur Andersen executives swap blame for Enron's collapse; Andersen struggles to survive civil litigation, SEC and criminal investigations; lawmakers offer bills to revamp accounting profession oversight and discipline, limit non-audit work; SEC studies regulatory overhaul; President Bush targets corporate officers, directors for tighter regulation.

Debacle Spurs Pension-Protection Proposals

The collapse of Enron Corp. decimated many of its employees' retirement savings, raising new questions for policymakers in Washington about how to better protect workers' investments. In the process, party-line divisions have erupted over potential solutions.

Enron's 21,000 employees had invested most of their 401(k) retirement-plan assets in company stock — 62 percent of the $2.1 billion they had collectively saved. As the share price plummeted, and executives from CEO Kenneth L. Lay to Human Resources Director Cindy Olson sold millions of dollars of their personal holdings, rank-and-file workers were left with essentially worthless stock in their retirement accounts.

In fact, at a key moment last October, as Enron's accounting irregularities were being discovered and its stock price was falling, managers of the firm's 401(k) plan imposed a temporary "lockdown" — a period during which plan participants cannot access their assets to buy or sell stock — because they were switching administrators.

Even if the freeze had never occurred — and Enron officials say the stock lost only $3.83 in value during the 11-day 401(k) lockdown — Enron employees would not have been allowed to sell many of their shares. Like many firms that choose to match their employees' 401(k) contributions with company stock, Enron had rules prohibiting workers from selling those stock matches until they reached age 50.

Pension experts say the structure of Enron's 401(k) plan was not the only factor that ultimately doomed workers' funds; another key force was the company's ability to convince employees — along with the rest of the world — that Enron stock was a good buy. According to a Congressional Research Service report, 89 percent of the 401(k) assets Enron employees held in company stock were there because employees chose to allocate them that way. [1] In fact, internal documents show, top Enron officials — including Lay and Olson — were actively encouraging employees to invest in the company's stock even after they became aware of the firm's internal problems.

Trend Toward Flexibility

Congress first created tax incentives for Americans to invest in 401(k) plans in 1978, in order to foster voluntary participation in private pension plans. The years since then have witnessed a distinct shift by employers and workers away from traditional "defined benefit" pension plans to "defined contribution" plans.

In a defined benefit plan, a company guarantees a set level of specifically defined benefits to be paid upon the worker's retirement, and the government insures the so-called "defined benefits." Defined contribution plans, such as 401(k) plans, emphasize individual choice and investment flexibility, and are subject to far less regulation. Traditional pensions, for example, may not invest more than 10 percent of their total assets in employer stock; 401(k) plans have no such restriction.

Rank-and-file employees have flocked to 401(k) plans, and in many cases, thanks to a bull market, made millions by investing their funds in stocks. In fact, the rules for stock savings plans that left Enron employees so vulnerable to loss are the same regulations that encourage employers to be more generous and employees to save in the first place.

"It's almost indigenous in the system," says David Wray, the president of the Profit Sharing/401(k) Council of America, a trade association representing 1,200 companies that sponsor such plans. "You really are up against a philosophical issue

---

The federal government played a critical role over the next three decades in stimulating the accounting profession's growth — both in size and responsibility. The federal income tax, authorized by the 16th Amendment in 1913, created a new demand for accounting services. The Federal Reserve Board in 1917 prescribed AAPA-written standards as uniform accounting methods for member banks. Some calls were heard in the 1920s for broader federal regulation to deal with misleading financial statements, but it took the stock market crash of 1929 and the ensuing Great Depression finally to force Congress and a new president — Franklin D. Roosevelt — to act.

Two centerpieces of FDR's New Deal — the Securities Act of 1933 and the Securities Exchange Act of 1934 — established the basic framework of today's stock registration and financial-disclosure system. Taken together, the laws required companies issuing stock to file financial statements certified by independent public accountants under uniform principles to be prescribed by the newly established SEC. Along with their expanded responsibilities, accountants — as well as companies and their directors — also were liable to lawsuits by investors if a stock registration statement contained any "untrue statement of material fact" or omitted any required material fact.

The new laws began restoring confidence in U.S. stock markets. But the mandatory audit provision failed to prevent a massive business failure at the end of the decade: the bankruptcy of the McKesson Robbins pharmaceutical firm due to massive fraud by the company's president. [14]

Auditors from Price Waterhouse — the firm retained by the company's president — failed to discover a $19 million overstatement in the company's accounts receivable and inventory balances. Hearings by the SEC and the New York attorney general's office later established that the firm had failed to confirm the accounts-receivables balance with customers or to observe a physi-

here: You either want to have employee [stock] ownership, or not."

Conflicting Proposals

Those close to the issue agree any solution will require a bipartisan compromise involving Congress and President Bush. But for now, Republicans and Democrats are deeply split over whether the government should limit the amount of company stock workers can hold in their 401(k) accounts.

The leading Democratic proposal, sponsored by Sen. Edward M. Kennedy of Massachusetts, does not impose specific caps on the amount of company stock workers can hold in their 401(k) accounts, but it indirectly limits their ability to acquire it. The bill would force employers who do not offer a traditional pension plan to choose between offering company stock as a matching contribution and allowing employees to invest their own contributions in company stock. If a firm made its matching contribution with stock instead of cash, it could not give employees the option of investing in company stock with their own contributions. If workers were given the option to invest in company stock themselves, the employer would have to make its 401(k) contribution in cash.

"If we know, as a matter of policy, that it's a mistake, or bad policy, or bad under any kind of prudent investment rule, to have people's assets concentrated all in one place, we need to

AFP Photo/James Nielsen

Retired Enron worker Charles Prestwood of Conroe, Texas, saw the value of his company retirement account drop from $1.3 million months ago to virtually nothing.

close off that option," says David Certner, director of federal affairs for the American Association of Retired Persons.

Most Republicans vehemently oppose investment limits or specific caps, arguing they will prompt companies to be less generous with their 401(k) contributions or stop offering the plans altogether. "Over-regulation could kill the golden pension goose," says Russell J. Mueller, a pension expert at the Washington law firm of Verner, Liipfert, Bernhard, McPherson and Hand. "No one has to have a pension plan."

President Bush and congressional Republicans prefer an approach that leaves employers free to contribute company stock, but allows employees to sell it once they have participated in a 401(k) plan for three years. Many Democrats also back the provision.

"Enron was a message that something was terribly wrong with this system, and we don't want to see that happen again," said Democratic Rep. Benjamin L. Cardin of Maryland, who has — with Republican Rob Portman of Ohio — cosponsored a bill similar to a plan introduced by President Bush.

Said Portman, "We think this is something that ought to be addressed this year. We want to be aggressive about it."

— Julie Hirschfeld Davis

[1] Patrick J. Purcell, "The Enron Bankruptcy and Company Stock in Retirement Plans," Congressional Research Service, March 11 2002.

---

cal count of inventories. The SEC's final report on the episode recommended that auditors be chosen in the future not by company management, but by the board of directors.

"Traumatic" Decades

By the 1960s, a rapidly growing accounting profession had established itself as an integral component of an expanding national economy and an increasingly complex financial reporting system. The enlarged responsibilities brought increased visibility and increased exposure to scrutiny and criticism for auditors' roles in major financial scandals and business failures. Meanwhile, the industry had become highly concentrated. Eight major firms dominated national practice by the 1970s; but the urge to merge reduced the number to six by the end of the '80s and then to five in the late '90s.

The number of certified public accountants increased more than fivefold, from barely 20,000 in 1940 to more than 100,000 by the mid-1960s. Nonetheless, a leading business magazine in 1960 described the profession's growth as "almost unnoticed by most Americans." [15]

Within a few years, however, accountants began to face what *The Wall Street Journal* termed "an unprecedented attack." [16] Critics in the financial press and law journals faulted the profession for imprecise standards and uncertain independence. Meanwhile, courts began to entertain, and in some cases sustain, shareholder lawsuits holding accounting firms liable for false or misleading financial disclosures. Even more jarring, a federal appeals court in 1969 upheld the criminal convictions of three partners in a leading accounting firm for fraudulent financial disclosures in a corporate audit. [17]

The pressures on the profession only increased during what the author of a history of one of the big accounting firms called the "traumatic decade" of the 1970s. [18] The SEC and courts continued to examine auditors' roles in the business failures of the previous decade, even as new ones emerged, including the bankruptcy of the Penn Central Railroad in 1970 and the collapse of the National Student Marketing Corp. In both of those cases, Peat, Marwick & Mitchell — the largest of the "Big Eight" at the time, now part of KPMG — faced accusations of having been, at the least, inattentive to signs of impending financial disaster. [19]

The string of business failures prompted two congressional subcommittees — one headed by Sen. Lee Metcalf, D-Mont., and the other by Rep. John Moss, D-Calif. — to hold extensive hearings on accounting-industry practices and to recommend increased auditor independence and improved financial reporting. [20] Among the recommendations: mandatory rotation of auditors for publicly held corporations and divestment of management advisory services by accounting firms. None of the changes was enacted. But Congress did — in the Foreign Corrupt Practices Act of 1977 — strengthen internal auditing controls, primarily in response to disclosures of widespread bribes paid by U.S. firms operating overseas.

The profession responded, but in limited ways. To improve standard writing, the AICPA replaced the Accounting Standards Board in 1973 with a broader-based, autonomous body: the Financial Standards Accounting Board (FASB). The new board's seven members were to sever any links to accounting firms, and a separate Financial Accounting Foundation was to raise funds for its operations. Then in 1977, the AICPA created the new Public Oversight Board (POB) to bring a measure of public accountability to its self-discipline system. In addition, the association created a new SEC Practice Section, with membership mandatory for auditors of publicly held companies.

S&L Scandals

Any benefits from the modest changes were obscured by a new round of attacks on accountants, stemming from the collapse of dozens of savings and loan (S&L) institutions in the 1980s. Among the prominent thrifts that went belly up: Andersen client Lincoln Savings & Loan, whose chief executive, Charles Keating, became a symbol of the decade's combination of financial risk-taking and political influence-peddling.

S&L executives bore the primary responsibility for the reckless and sometimes fraudulent practices that brought down so many thrift institutions, but many critics depicted accountants as negligent or complicit. "The S&L crisis . . . has led people to question the auditors' words," Rep. Ron Wyden, D-Ore., declared. [21]

Both the General Accounting Office (GAO) and the AICPA responded with new studies calling for strengthening auditors' roles and responsibilities in detecting and reporting financial fraud. [22] A decade later the GAO said in a report that the profession had been "responsive in making changes to improve financial reporting and auditing of public companies." But the agency also said that the profession had not been "totally effective in resolving several major issues," including auditor independence, auditor responsibility for detecting fraud, public participation in standard setting, the timeliness and relevancy of accounting standards and maintaining the FASB's independence. [23]

In fact, hundreds of lawsuits were filed against accountants for failed S&Ls, and in the 1990s the big firms paid $1 billion in penalties and fines to the government. The payouts apparently spurred the industry to increase the amount of money it was sending to Washington. From 1989 to 2001, according to the Center for Responsive Politics, the accounting industry funneled some $50 million through individuals, political-action committees and soft-money contributions. [24]

Amid the regulatory and political pressures, the accounting industry continued to become ever more concentrated. Conventional wisdom among the "Big Eight" firms that came to dominate accounting practice by the 1970s held that bigger was better. Each of the firms scrambled to open more offices and hire more accountants to better serve national and multinational firms — and to compete with other members of the exclusive club. Two of the giants — Price Waterhouse and Deloitte Haskins & Sells — agreed to merge in 1984, only to see the union vetoed by Price Waterhouse's British contingent. Price Waterhouse later eyed a merger with Arthur Andersen, but the courtship came to naught.

In 1989, however, two mergers reduced the Big Eight to the Big Six: Ernst & Whinney and Arthur Young & Co. combined to form Ernst & Young, while Deloitte found a willing partner in eighth-ranked Touche Ross & Co. to form Deloitte, Touche Ross — now Deloitte Touche Tohmatsu.

While the firms trumpeted the benefits of the mergers, Arthur Bowman, editor of *Bowman's Accounting Report*, was skeptical. The mergers, Bowman remarked at the time, "are done more for the betterment of the partners than for the betterment of the clients." [25]

Today, he remains critical. "There are so few choices," Bowman says. "In 1989, if you were going to change from one giant firm to another, you had at least seven choices. Today, if Arthur Andersen cannot survive this crisis, a firm changing from one giant firm to another would have only three choices."

What about industry claims that mergers enhance productivity and synergy? "All we've really seen," he answers, "is that bigger makes them bigger."

Prosperous Times

The accounting industry continued to grow and prosper during the 1990s as stock prices soared and record numbers of new public offerings were filed. The boom times put pressure on corporate managers to meet or beat financial earnings estimates — and pressures on auditors to go along with accounting methods to brighten the financial picture. By decade's end, SEC officials were complaining of increasing instances of accounting abuses or outright fraud. But the industry flexed its political muscles by lobbying Congress to limit damage awards against accountants in shareholder suits and by thwarting some SEC initiatives to tighten auditing regulations.

Revenues for the 100 largest U.S. accounting firms grew throughout the decade, according to *Bowman's Accounting Report*. The growth rate dipped slightly with the 1992 recession, but rebounded the next year. Starting in 1996, revenues saw double-digit growth for five consecutive years. AICPA membership rose gradually through the decade, peaking at 337,405 in 2000, before dipping slightly last year to 335,914. The association estimates that about three-fourths of all CPAs are members.

For the biggest firms, consulting practices grew in comparison to their corporate auditing work. The firms saw that consulting services were "quite profitable" and started bidding against each other for auditing contracts to get a foot in the door for the non-audit services, Bowman says.

In a dramatic example of the importance of consulting work, Andersen suffered through a decade-long civil war between the core firm and the separate Andersen Consulting unit, created in 1989. Partners in the consulting unit, resentful of sharing their profits, eventually emerged as the de facto winner of an arbitrator's decision in August 2000.

The decision allowed the consulting unit to spin off as a new company — Accenture — after paying about $1 billion to the former firm. [26]

Politically, accounting firms sought to safeguard their profitability by taking the lead role in lobbying Congress to pass legislation limiting shareholder lawsuits. The Private Securities Litigation Reform Act of 1995 — enacted with bipartisan majorities over President Clinton's veto — included a variety of provisions making it harder for shareholders to recover stock losses blamed on inaccurate or misleading financial information. For accountants, the most important provision established a rule of "proportionate liability," under which any defendant would be responsible only for a share of any award based on its degree of responsibility for the fraud. Accountants claimed that under the previous rule of "joint and several liability," they were liable for a disproportionate share of any award because they had deeper pockets than other defendants. [27]

Although plaintiffs' lawyers said the law made shareholder lawsuits more difficult, it did not completely shut off litigation. In December 1999, Ernst & Young set a record by agreeing to a $335 million settlement in a suit by shareholders of the franchise conglomerate Cendant, Inc. The shareholders blamed the accounting firm for overstated profits by one of the companies that merged to form Cendant in 1997. Ernst & Young claimed it had been the "victim of intentional, collusive fraud" by the company's management. [28]

Meanwhile, an aggressive SEC chairman, Levitt, was complaining of what he called an increasing practice of "accounting hocus-pocus" by corporate managers and their auditors. In a widely noted speech at New York University in 1998, Levitt blamed "an erosion in the quality of earnings" on a variety of dubious accounting techniques practiced by auditors and managers in-

tent on making earnings estimates at whatever cost. He called for tighter rules on several accounting issues, but left office at the end of the Clinton administration with few concrete changes to show for his remarks. [29]

For Levitt's successor, President Bush in May 2001 turned to Pitt, who had served as the SEC's general counsel during the Carter administration in the late 1970s and then went on to a lucrative law practice in New York, representing, among others, the major accounting firms and the AICPA. [30] Speaking to the association's governing council last fall, Pitt appeared to promise a "kinder and gentler" attitude from the agency toward the profession. "We will do everything in our power to evidence a new era of respect and cooperation," Pitt said in the Oct. 22 speech.

Today, Pitt says critics who faulted him for cozying up to the profession took his words out of context; he also claims — wrongly — that the speech came "well before Enron had reared its ugly head." [31] In fact, Enron had announced the accounting-related write-down six days earlier, and the SEC itself opened an inquiry into Enron's accounting practices on the very day of Pitt's speech.

In any event, Pitt is now taking a more critical stance toward the profession. "We have had far too many financial and accounting failures," Pitt told reporters at the SEC's headquarters Jan. 17. [32] He called for revamping the system of self-discipline and peer review and speeding FASB standard setting. He also promised to improve the agency's reviews of financial disclosure and reporting and to continue "actively and aggressively" investigating the reasons for Enron's collapse.

"Significant work remains to be done," Pitt concluded, "but we are confident that with input from all sectors we can erect a system that will restore public confidence in the integrity of the accounting profession." ∎

CURRENT SITUATION

Rival Plans for Reform

Four months of congressional hearings have produced dramatic scenes of finger pointing by top Andersen and Enron executives and detailed proposals from a range of advocates and experts to reform accounting and corporate governance. [33] Republican and Democratic lawmakers developed parallel but competing legislative proposals, while President Bush offered his own measures earlier this month — all but one of which could be adopted by the SEC without congressional action. Meanwhile, SEC Chairman Pitt began filling in details on what he promised would be "comprehensive reform proposals" — most of them calling for regulatory rather than legislative action.

Andersen CEO Berardino was the star witness at one of the first congressional hearings, voluntarily going before two House Financial Services subcommittees on Dec. 12 to defend the firm's handling of Enron's accounts. While acknowledging an "error in judgment" in accounting for one of Enron's off-book partnerships, Berardino also blamed Enron executives for keeping some "critical information" from Andersen auditors. In any event, auditors were in no position, he insisted, to verify all the complex transactions.

Some of Enron's top executives — including Lay and Fastow — declined to testify, citing the Fifth Amendment privilege against self-incrimination. But Skilling twice appeared before congressional panels last month to combatively defend both Enron and himself. "I had no

reason to think there was a problem with Enron's accounting practices," Skilling told the Senate Commerce Committee on Feb. 26.

Legislatively, lawmakers in both parties focused on two major issues in measures proposed to improve auditing and accounting practices: regulatory oversight of the profession and restrictions on consulting services to audit clients. House Financial Services Committee Chairman Michael Oxley, R-Ohio, and the committee's ranking Democrat, Rep. John LaFalce of New York, introduced competing bills in February. Two Democratic senators — Connecticut's Christopher Dodd and New Jersey's Jon Corzine — joined in March to offer a measure somewhat parallel to LaFalce's.

Both Democratic bills call for a new government body, under SEC supervision, to have disciplinary and oversight powers over public accountants. By contrast, Oxley's bill calls for a private-sector regulatory organization under SEC auspices. All three bills specify that a majority of members be non-accountants. Dodd's bill calls for funding the new body through assessments on accounting firms; LaFalce's would impose fees on publicly audited companies. Oxley's measure specifies that accounting firms would not be assessed to pay for the board.

The Dodd-Corzine bill includes the toughest prohibition against accounting firms performing non-audit work for their audit clients. The measure would require advance determination by a company's audit committee that any non-audit work — including tax advice — for an auditing client would not "adversely affect" the auditors' independence. Oxley's bill would effectively bar accounting firms from providing audit clients with internal audit or financial-system design services, but would permit tax advice.

Bush moved into the debate on March 7 with a 10-point package fo-

cusing more on corporate officers and directors than on accountants. Unveiled in a speech that never mentioned Enron by name, the package calls for the SEC to require speedier disclosure of insider stock trading and to adopt a rule forcing executives to surrender bonuses or other compensation based on erroneous financial statements resulting from misconduct.

The Bush plan also asks Congress to authorize the SEC to bar corporate directors or senior officers who engage in "serious misconduct" from serving in such positions in the future. Under current law, the agency must seek a court order to impose such a ban. Pitt had already included such a proposal in his recommendations.

On accounting issues, Bush's plan calls for the SEC to establish "guidelines" for audit committees to use in limiting non-audit work by accounting firms. It also calls for an "independent" regulatory body and stronger SEC supervision of standard setting by the FASB.

For his part, Pitt elaborated on his proposals in a Feb. 22 speech at the SEC headquarters to a securities industry audience. Pitt continues to back a private-sector regulatory body for accountants, to be funded by "involuntary assessments" imposed on all those who benefit from the public auditing services. He also wants the SEC to have "greater influence" over the FASB, including the power to require the board to adopt standards "in a short time frame."

The speech did not address the issue of limiting non-audit work by accounting firms.

Andersen's Troubles

Arthur Andersen is teetering on the edge of financial extinction in the wake of its role in the Enron collapse, but struggling to survive

At Issue:

Should the government establish a new federal agency to oversee accountants?

LYNN E. TURNER
DIRECTOR, CENTER FOR QUALITY FINANCIAL REPORTING, COLORADO STATE UNIVERSITY; FORMER CHIEF ACCOUNTANT, SECURITIES AND EXCHANGE COMMISSION

WRITTEN FOR THE CQ RESEARCHER, MARCH 2002

*a*merican investors — one out of every two adults in this country — have suffered through a litany of corporate earnings restatements, massive financial frauds, billions of dollars in losses and a daily parade of financial-reporting issues. Today they wonder if their hard-earned savings would be just as safe on a card table in 'Vegas, given stories of greed, accountants who are equally good at manipulating both numbers and Congress, and criminal indictments of members of a once trusted and proud profession.

In my view, it is well past time for Congress to establish a new public-accounting oversight board overseen by the Securities and Exchange Commission (SEC). The organizations that currently oversee the accounting profession are neither efficient nor effective at quality control. The American Institute of Certified Public Accountants' (AICPA) own Professional Ethics Executive Committee is weak, if not totally ineffective. It conducts meetings behind closed doors, often defers action for years, lacks subpoena power and has failed to act in several instances after the SEC has acted.

The current Public Oversight Board (POB), a private-sector, self-regulatory organization funded by voluntary industry assessments, is a well-intentioned group that has been outgunned by the profession. Two years ago, the AICPA cut off the board's funding when it tried to investigate accounting firms' lack of compliance with auditor independence rules. The POB also cannot ensure that auditing standards are written based on meeting the needs of the public, as opposed to the needs of auditors' attorneys.

The new disciplinary body must be adequately funded and independent. It should draw members from the public rather than the profession. It should impose timely and effective disciplinary actions against those who break the rules, whether they are from small or large firms. The new body should also issue auditing and quality-control standards that protect investors, as opposed to the profession. And it should inspect auditors' work to ensure that the investing public — not the consulting fees auditors can generate — is their No. 1 priority.

Amazingly, accountants are singing their old tune — "Beware of unintended consequences" — and continuing to vehemently oppose fundamental reforms. Americans now have seen the "unintended consequences" from the lack of reform. Now I hope they see reforms adopted before they watch more Americans suffer.

DOUGLAS M. BRANSON
W. EDWARD SELL CHAIR IN LAW, UNIVERSITY OF PITTSBURGH; MELTON PROFESSOR OF LAW, WILLAMETTE UNIVERSITY

WRITTEN FOR THE CQ RESEARCHER, MARCH 2002

*w*e do not need a new regulatory body to oversee public accounting. The SEC has a chief accountant with a staff. The Financial Accounting Standards Board and the SEC chief accountant will be extra vigilant in the Enron aftermath.

Enron is the rare case in which all monitoring systems failed. The auditors did not catch it. A capable audit committee failed to ask the right questions. A prestigious law firm missed it. Analysts did not catch it. Credit-rating agencies failed to examine explicit Enron disclosures about its off-balance-sheet debt. A board of 10 upstanding independent directors (and only two insiders) was not able to ferret it out. Even CEO Jeffrey Skilling and Chairman Ken Lay say they themselves failed to detect anything amiss.

Never say "never," but an Enron is a rare occurrence in our governance system. That system is a finely tuned one that induces an optimal amount of informed risk-taking. Putting directors, and other monitors of corporate performance, such as accountants, too, under the microscope will disturb the delicate balance between informed risk-taking and accountability.

Our scheme of corporate governance is a central component of an economic system that, in the '90s, was the goose that laid golden egg after golden egg. Remedial steps should be surgical. Congress, however, and to a lesser extent President Bush, are waving Texas-size Bowie knives in the air. They just may cut one of the goose's main arteries, or slit its throat altogether. They should curtail the grandstanding.

On the other hand, I do agree that Congress should mandate separation of auditing and consulting services.

Many people do not realize that public accounting firms do not prepare financial statements. Instead, through random checks and examination of accounting principles, auditors merely "audit" financial statements prepared by corporations' own accountants. That division of labor represents an important check and balance in our corporate governance system.

However, in the last decade, large accounting firms have offered a menu of "consulting services," including internal accounting services. The result? In the annual audit, the accountants are reviewing their own work. In one recent year, a major accounting firm derived 70 percent of its income from consulting, and only 30 percent from auditing. Enron paid Arthur Andersen $29 million for the annual audit but $31 million in consulting fees. Congress and the executive branch should undertake post-Enron reform slowly, one step at the time.

with an aggressive defense. In addition to its March 14 indictment, the 88-year-old accounting firm faces a strong chance of hundreds of millions of dollar in liability for purported accounting malpractice. More immediately, Andersen has lost more than two-dozen auditing clients — and suffered such damage to its professional reputation that the exodus may continue, dooming any prospect for the firm to survive. [34]

Andersen is responding by denouncing the criminal investigation as "a gross abuse of government power" and trying to cut the civil suit short with an offer of a $750 million settlement to Enron shareholders. As for the loss of business, Andersen notes that most of its 2,300 audit clients are still with the firm. "We regret the loss of any client, but we are gratified that the vast majority of Andersen's clients in the U.S. remain with the firm," a spokesman told reporters.

Nonetheless, the criminal indictment shook the firm's confidence. Paul Volcker, a former Federal Reserve Board chairman heading up a special internal oversight committee Andersen created early in the crisis, conceded to *The Wall Street Journal* after the grand jury's action that Andersen's future is "in jeopardy." [35]

The criminal prosecution stems from the devastating disclosure in January that Andersen employees destroyed thousands of e-mails and trunkfuls of paper records last fall after learning on Oct. 23 of the SEC's inquiry into Enron. Andersen first informed government investigators of the document shredding on Jan. 10; CEO Berardino followed with a statement on Jan. 15 blaming the episode on — and firing — Andersen's lead Enron auditor, David Duncan. Congressional investigators, however, claimed that up to 80 Andersen employees were involved.

By March, Justice Department prosecutors told Andersen officials that they had drawn up an indictment charging the firm with obstruction of justice. Andersen faced a deadline of 9 a.m., March 14, to plead guilty or face indictment and possible trial. On the eve of the deadline, Andersen lawyers sent a strongly worded letter arguing against the charges. The letter — as reported by the *New York Times* and *Washington Post* — acknowledged "poor judgment" by some "partners and employees," but contended that "a criminal prosecution against the entire firm . . . would be both factually and legally baseless."

The one-count indictment by a federal grand jury charges that during a one-month span in October and early November, "Andersen . . . did knowingly, intentionally and corruptly persuade" employees to "alter, destroy, mutilate and conceal" documents. Pointing to top executives, the indictment said that shortly before the destruction began, Andersen's high-level management held a conference call to discuss the SEC inquiry. The maximum penalty is a five-year term of probation and a $500,000 fine.

As for civil liability, Andersen and some 29 current or former top Enron executives face consolidated suits by dozens of shareholders who blame the officials for hundreds of millions of dollars in stock losses. The lead lawyer in the suit, filed in Houston, is William Lerach, a nationally known class-action attorney representing the University of California, which put its losses at $144.9 million.

Andersen was reported in late February to have offered to settle all claims for $750 million, including $250 million from its own insurance coverage, both to resolve the civil suit and pressure the Justice Department to drop the criminal prosecution. No quick settlement emerged, however, and plaintiffs' lawyers were taking depositions in mid-March from some of the key players — including Duncan.

Meanwhile, Andersen agreed on March 1 to pay $217 million to settle an unrelated civil suit stemming from its work for the Baptist Foundation of Arizona, which declared bankruptcy in 1999. Investors claimed Andersen auditors failed to spot evidence of massive fraud by foundation officials. [36]

The legal troubles contribute to Andersen's loss of more than two dozen audit clients since the beginning of the year. The list includes Andersen's two biggest clients — Enron itself and pharmaceutical giant Merck & Co. — along with such other major companies as Delta Air Lines, Federal Express and the Federal Home Loan Mortgage Corp., or Freddie Mac.

The loss of two dozen clients does not threaten the survival of a company with 85,000 employees worldwide and $9.3 billion in revenues. But the exodus further damages Andersen's reputation and contributes to a loss of morale within the firm — with some partners and employees reportedly looking to leave before the firm's feared demise.

With the firm's prospects so cloudy, Andersen executives were trying in mid-March to avoid extinction by enticing one of the other Big Five firms into a merger or purchase of all or part of Andersen's assets. News of the discussions with Deloitte Touche Tohmatsu and Ernst & Young surfaced on Monday, March 11. By week's end, however, both firms had spurned the overtures.

Meanwhile, the SEC was talking with the other four big firms on how to deal with Andersen's possible demise — which could leave more than 2,000 corporate clients searching for auditing services. And Andersen faced the prospect of further congressional scrutiny as a House committee prepared to open an investigation into another of the firm's clients, the start-up telecommunications company Global Crossing, for using questionable accounting techniques to inflate its revenues; the company filed for bankruptcy on Jan. 28. ■

OUTLOOK

"Transparent" Accounting

Former Federal Reserve Chairman Volcker added his voice last month to the chorus of criticism about the current state of corporate America's account books. Enron's collapse, Volcker told the Senate Banking Committee on Feb. 14, was only one symptom of a crisis in the accounting profession that had been building for years.

"We have had too many restatements of earnings, too many doubts about 'pro forma' earnings, too many sudden charges of billions of dollars to 'good will,' too many perceived auditing failures accompanying bankruptcies to make us at all comfortable," Volcker said. "Fundamental changes and reforms will be required," he concluded, "to provide assurance that our financial reporting will be accurate, transparent, and meaningful." [37]

A full year has passed since Andersen accountants looked at Enron's accounting methods and, despite misgivings, decided to stick with the lucrative client. Andersen — its reputation already damaged by several audit failures in the '90s — is paying a huge price for its missteps. But the rest of the Big Five, and the profession as a whole, are paying some part of the price for losing sight of the public responsibilities of public accountants.

"Any business in the pursuit of profit gets off track," says the University of Delaware's Elson. "I don't think it's a profession that's corrupt, but it's a profession that needs to recommit itself to some of its fundamental standards."

Other industry observers say corporate America shares the blame for the aggressive accounting that benefits company executives while misleading public investors. "We have cor-porations rewarding management for meeting quarterly expectations, and then we have the accountants who are helping companies reach those expectations — all under the rules," says industry observer Bowman. "They're not breaking the rules. They're just using them to the utmost extreme."

Prospects for passage are uncertain for the two major legislative proposals to emerge from the Enron collapse — strengthening oversight of the accounting profession and limiting the dual roles of auditor and consultant to the same corporation. After professing support for "meaningful" reforms, AICPA leaders are now pushing hard to keep accounting-industry oversight in the private sector and to block any mandate that firms shed their consulting services. The association is also resisting any efforts to undo provisions of the 1995 law that limits accountants' liability in shareholder suits.

Some advocacy groups expect Congress once again will bow to the accountants' arguments. "Despite all the statements of outrage, Congress seems inclined to let the auditors define the solution," says the Consumer Federation's Roper.

Some broader proposals have also been put forth — such as requiring corporations to periodically rotate auditors on corporate accounts or shifting corporate auditors from private firms to the SEC or perhaps the stock exchanges. But, Roper concedes, "I'm not naive enough to think that even in the face of Enron Congress is going to wipe out the private-sector audit function."

Other critics say additional changes are needed in other areas: stronger corporate boards and audit committees and tougher enforcement by federal prosecutors and a better-funded SEC. "The safety nets that are supposed to protect corporations from disappearing from the face of the Earth are the board of directors, the auditors, the regulators and the prosecutors," says Sarah Teslik, executive director of the Coun-cil of Institutional Investors. "They all failed, completely."

Despite the obstacles to broad reform, many observers say they expect a significant measure of change to emerge both from regulators and the profession itself. "You will see regulation on the consulting issue, some movement to narrow [accounting rules], and some movement in the [firms] themselves to limit conflicts," Elson says.

For his part, the Wharton School's Useem thinks Enron's demise may prove to be a "benchmark" that leads to more fundamental changes both for accountants and for corporations. "The Enron collapse is going to be on a par with the 9/11 disaster," he says. "It's a wake-up call about corporate governance and corporate leadership."

"In the case of 9/11, U.S. security was quite good, but now we have to redouble our efforts," Useem concludes. "Corporate governance was actually pretty good, and the wakeup call is to strengthen it all that much more." ∎

Notes

[1] Videotape and transcript of the Oct. 3, 2000, meeting were released by Rep. Henry Waxman, D-Calif., ranking minority member of the House Government Reform Committee (www.house.gov/reform/min). *The Wall Street Journal's* story was carried only in its Texas edition. See Jonathan Weil, "Energy Traders Cite Gains, but Some Math Is Missing," Sept. 20, 2000, p. T1. For background on the Enron-Blockbuster agreement, see Rebecca Smith, "Blockbuster, Enron Agree to Movie Deal," *The Wall Street Journal*, July 20, 2000, p. A3.

[2] The letter, released by the House Energy and Commerce Committee on Jan. 14, can be found at www.energycommerce.house.gov. For a profile of Watkins, see Jennifer Frey, "The Woman Who Saw Red," *The Washington Post*, Jan. 25, 2002, p. C1.

[3] See David Nather with Jill Barshay, "Campaign Finance Outcome Now in Daschle's Hands," *CQ Weekly*, Feb. 16, 2002, p. 440. For background, see Mary Cooper, "Campaign Finance Reform,," *The CQ Researcher*,

March 31, 2000, pp. 257-280.

[4] Cited in Bill Sternberg, "Accounting's Role in Enron Crash Erases Years of Trust," *USA Today*, Feb. 22, 2002, p. A1.

[5] Schuetze testified before the Senate Banking, Housing and Urban Affairs Committee on Feb. 26. He served as the SEC's chief accountant from January 1992 to March 1995 and as chief accountant of the agency's enforcement division from November 1997 to February 2000.

[6] Robert Manor, "Arthur Andersen Settles Sunbeam Earnings Lawsuit," *Chicago Tribune*, April 28, 2001, p. N2; James P. Miller, "Waste Management, Andersen Agree to Settle Holder Suits for $220 Million," *The Wall Street Journal*, Dec. 10, 1998, p. B22.

[7] See Jonathan Weil and Scot J. Paltrow, "Peer Pressure: SEC Found Accounting Flaw," *The Wall Street Journal*, Jan. 29, 2002, p. C1; Kirstin Downey Grimsley, "Scandals Put Andersen's Future at Risk," *The Washington Post*, Jan. 16, 2002, p. E1. Peer review documents can be found on the AICPA's Web site: http://peerreview.aicpaservices.org; Andersen's press release, dated Jan. 2, can be found at www.arthurandersen.com.

[8] David S. Hilzenrath, "Auditors Face Scant Discipline," *The Washington Post*, Dec. 6, 2001, p. A1.

[9] See Carrie Johnson, "Audit Oversight Board Urged," *The Washington Post*, Feb. 27, 2002, p. E1.

[10] See Jackie Spinner, "'You Were Right,'" *The Washington Post*, Jan. 25, 2002, p. E1.

[11] Richard M. Frankel, Marilyn F. Johnson, and Karen K. Nelson, "The Relation Between Auditors' Fees for Non-Audit Services and Earnings Quality," January 2002. The paper is to be published in a forthcoming issue of *Accounting Review*, journal of the American Accounting Association, and is available at http://aaahq.org/qoe/tarAcceptedPapers.htm.

[12] Some background drawn from John L. Carey, *The Rise of the Accounting Profession* (Vol. I): *From Technician to Professional, 1896-1936* (1969). See also Paul J. Miranti Jr., *Accountancy Comes of Age: The Develop-ment of an American Profession, 1886-1940* (1990); Gary John Previts and Barbara Dubis Merino, *A History of Accountancy in the United States: The Cultural Significance of Accounting* (1998).

[13] For the text of Price Waterhouse's certificate, see *ibid.*, pp. 28-29.

[14] See John L. Carey, *The Rise of the Accounting Profession* (Vol. 2): *To Responsibility and Authority, 1937-1969*, pp. 35-38; Miranti, *op. cit.*, pp. 175-176.

[15] Tom Wise, "The Auditors Have Arrived," *Fortune*, November/December 1960, cited in Carey, *op. cit.* (vol. 2), pp. 386-387.

[16] The article is cited without author or date in *ibid.*, p. 136. Other background drawn from pp. 135-138.

[17] The case is *United States v. Simon*, 425 F.2d 796 (CA2 1969), but is commonly known as the Continental Vending case after the name of the company involved. See Floyd Norris, "An Old Case Is Returning to Haunt Auditors," *The New York Times*, March 1, 2002, p. C1. The accounting firm was Cooper, Ross Brothers & Montgomery — which later merged into Coopers Lybrand and then into the present-day PricewaterhouseCoopers.

[18] T.A. Wise, *Peat, Marwick, Mitchell & Co. — 85 Years* (1982).

[19] *Ibid.*, pp. 61-63.

[20] "Federal Regulation and Regulatory Reform," Report by the Subcommittee on Oversight and Investigations of the House Committee on Interstate and Foreign Commerce (Moss subcommittee), October 1976; "Improving the Accountability of Publicly Owned Corporations and Their Auditors," Report of the Subcommittee on Reports, Accounting and Management of the Committee on Governmental Affairs, U.S. Senate (Metcalf subcommittee), November 1977. For details on recommendations from these and other investigations 1972-1995, see U.S. General Accounting Office, *The Accounting Profession: Major Issues: Progress and Concerns* (1996), Appendixes.

[21] Quoted in Mark Stevens, *The Big Six: The Selling Out of America's Top Accounting Firms* (1991), p. 102.

[22] U.S. General Accounting Office, *loc. cit.*

[23] *Ibid.*, pp. 4-5.

[24] See "Accountants Long-Term Contribution Trends," Center for Responsive Politics, www.opensecrets.org (visited March 15, 2002).

[25] Cited in Stevens, *The Big Six*, p. 223.

[26] See Ken Brown, "Andersen Consulting Wins Independence," *The Wall Street Journal*, Aug. 8, 2000, p. A3.

[27] See *1995 CQ Almanac*, pp. 2-90 to 2-92.

[28] See Mitchell Pacelle and Elizabeth MacDonald, "Ernst & Young Settles One Suit in Cendant Scandal," *The Wall Street Journal*, Dec. 20, 1999, p. B9.

[29] Arthur Levitt, "The 'Numbers Game,'" Sept. 28, 1998 (www.sec.gov; click on speeches). For coverage, see Jube Shiver Jr., "Wall Street, California Seek Crackdown on Inflated Earnings," *Los Angeles Times*, Sept. 29, 1998, p. D1.

[30] See Michael Schroeder, "Bush Is Expected to Name Pitt, Securities Lawyer, to Head SEC," *The Wall Street Journal*, May 7, 2001, p. A24.

[31] See Harvey L. Pitt, "Remarks Before the AICPA Governing Council," Oct. 22, 2001 (www.sec.gov). For Pitt's later remarks, see Jackie Spinner, "Harvey Pitt's Recalculation," *The Washington Post*, Feb. 13, 2001, p. E1.

[32] Harvey L. Pitt, "Regulation of the Accounting Profession," Jan. 17, 2002 (www.sec.gov).

[33] Coverage drawn in part from testimony transcripts on CQ.com On Congress (www.oncongress.CQ.com).

[34] The Andersen Web site has a time line with a history of the firm since its founding on Dec. 1, 1913: www.arthurandersen.com.

[35] "Indictment of Andersen in Shredding Case Puts Its Future in Question," *The Wall Street Journal*, March 15, 2002, p. A1.

[36] For background, see Jonathan Weil, "Beset Over Enron, Anderson Faces Trial in Church-Group Case," *The Wall Street Journal*, Feb. 20, 2002, p. A1.

[37] The text of Volcker's statement is on the Senate Banking Committee's Web site (http://banking.senate.gov) and the Arthur Andersen site (www.arthurandersen.com).

Bibliography

Selected Sources

Books

Carey, John L., *The Rise of the Accounting Profession: From Technician to Professional, 1896-1936* (Vol. 1); *To Responsibility and Authority, 1937-1969* (Vol. 2), American Institute of Certified Public Accountants, 1969, 1970.

Comprehensively covers the rise of the accounting profession to "a position of crucial importance in the American economy." Carey served a quarter-century as executive director of the AICPA. Illustrated; no bibliography.

Miranti, Paul J. Jr., *Accountancy Comes of Age: The Development of an American Profession, 1886-1940*, University of North Carolina Press, 1990.

Covers the critical period from the birth of the profession through the passage of federal securities laws significantly expanding accountants' role in protecting investors. Miranti is associate dean for academic affairs at Rutgers University Graduate School of Business Administration. Includes detailed notes and 34-page bibliography.

Previts, Gary John, and Barbara Dubis Merino, *A History of Accountancy in the United States: The Cultural Significance of Accounting*, Ohio State University Press, 1998.

Traces history of accountancy from Colonial times through the contemporary global era; updates 1979 work. Previts is a professor at Case Western Reserve University, Merino a senior professor at the University of North Texas, Denton. Includes detailed notes and 78-page bibliography.

Stevens, Mark, *The Big Six: The Selling Out of America's Top Accounting Firms*, Simon & Schuster, 1991.

Critically relates several accounting controversies just after mergers had reduced the "Big Eight" firms to the "Big Six."

In an epilogue, Stevens says auditing had "taken a back seat to consulting in terms of growth, glamour and profitability." No source notes or bibliography. Stevens also authored *The Accounting Wars* (MacMillan, 1985) and *The Big Eight* (MacMillan, 1981).

Wise, T. A., *Peat, Marwick, Mitchell & Co.: 85 Years*, 1982.

Traces the birth and growth of what once was the world's largest accounting firm as of its 85th anniversary — seven years before its merger into the Big Five firm of KPMG. Business journalist Tom Wise brought a measure of objectivity and analysis into the authorized history. Illustrated.

Articles

Nather, David, and Adriel Bettelheim, "Enron Inquiry Likely to Be Broader Than Response," *CQ Weekly*, Feb. 9, 2002, pp. 354-357.

Provides a good overview of legislative prospects as congressional committees stepped up the pace of investigations. For an earlier overview, see Keith Perino, "An Industry Called to Account," *CQ Weekly*, Jan. 19, 2002, pp. 172-175.

Reports and Studies

U.S. General Accounting Office, *The Accounting Profession: Major Issues: Progress and Concerns*, September 1996.

Issues of concern cited by the congressional watchdog agency in the 139-page report include detecting fraud and the timeliness and relevancy of accounting standards. The appendices to the report, printed as a second volume, include a listing of major studies of the accounting profession from 1972 to 1995 and major recommendations and actions taken to improve auditing and financial reporting during that period.

FOR MORE INFORMATION

American Institute of Certified Public Accountants, 1455 Pennsylvania Ave., N.W., 4th floor, Washington, D.C. 20004-1081; (202) 737-6600; www.aicpa.org. Trade association with 336,000 members.

Consumer Federation of America, 1424 16th St., N.W., #604, Washington, D.C. 20036; (202) 387-6121; www.consumerfed.org. Provides information and advocacy on investor protection issues.

Council of Institutional Investors, 1730 Rhode Island Ave., N.W., Suite 512, Washington, D.C. 20036; (202) 822-0800; www.cii.org. Represents public, union and corporate pension funds.

Financial Accounting Standards Board, 401 Merritt 7, P.O. Box 5116, Norwalk, Conn. 06856-5116; (203) 847-0700; Fax: (203) 849-9714; www.fasb.org. Autonomous, private-sector organization founded in 1973 to establish standards of financial accounting and reporting.

Securities and Exchange Commission, 450 5th St., N.W., Washington, D.C. 20549; (202) 942-8020; www.sec.gov. Independent federal agency established in 1934 to administer system of stock registration and corporate financial disclosure.

15 North Korean Crisis

MARY H. COOPER

The bombs dropping in Iraq this week are real. But Pentagon planners also worry about the fictional scenario known as Operation Plan 5027:

Along the heavily guarded demilitarized zone (DMZ) between North and South Korea, deadly chemicals released by a barrage of North Korean artillery shells doom 630 South Korean and American soldiers to a grisly death. Other rounds pound South Korea's capital, Seoul, 30 miles to the south. Then tanks — carrying North Korean soldiers clad in chemical-protection gear — roll into Seoul.

The invasion would be over within hours — but the victory short-lived. Superior U.S. and South Korean firepower would drive the invaders back across the DMZ in a day or two. But an estimated 1 million people, mostly civilians in Seoul, would be killed.

While American troops in Iraq move into Baghdad, the Pentagon's nightmare scenario for the Korean Peninsula may be inching closer to reality. And because North Korea may already possess at least one nuclear weapon, in the event of war it likely would prove a more dangerous adversary than Iraq.

"The situation in Korea is infinitely more serious than in Iraq right now," says Kurt Campbell, program director for international security at the Center for Strategic and International Studies (CSIS). "It is probably one of the most serious foreign-policy crises that the United States has faced in a decade."

The Korean crisis has been building since March 2001, when President

From *The CQ Researcher,*
April 11, 2003.

President Bush looks through bulletproof glass across the demilitarized zone into North Korea during a visit to South Korea in February 2002. Bush has condemned the North for abusing its people and trying to build nuclear weapons. But North Korean leader Kim Jong Il says Bush's statements and policy changes amount to a policy of aggression.

AFP Photo/Luke Frazza

Bush repudiated the policy of engagement toward North Korea crafted by his predecessor, Bill Clinton. Under the Agreed Framework signed by Clinton and North Korean leader Kim Jong Il in 1994, the North agreed to freeze its program to develop nuclear weapons in exchange for vitally needed fuel and food and construction of two nuclear power plants. Clinton's policy of engagement, coupled with South Korea's "sunshine policy" of gradual reconciliation with the North, eased the tensions that had gripped the peninsula since the Korean War ended in 1953. [1]

At about the same time the negotiations were being completed, however, U.S. intelligence agencies began receiving new evidence that North Korea had developed one, perhaps two, nuclear bombs in violation of its commitments under both the Framework and the 1985 Nuclear Non-Proliferation Treaty (NPT). Clinton decided to rely on diplomacy to convince the North to abandon its nuclear ambitions, a po-

sition Bush has emphatically rejected.

"The Bush administration thought the Clinton approach to North Korea was servile," says Selig S. Harrison, chairman of a group of Korea experts who recommend changes to current U.S. North Korea policy and director of the Asia program at the Center for International Policy. [2] "It didn't reflect the fact that we're the boss. The whole idea of the agreement was repugnant to the Bush administration."

"We have no illusions about this regime," said Secretary of State Colin L. Powell. "We have no illusions about the nature of the gentleman who runs North Korea. He is a despot, but he is also sitting on a failed society that has to somehow begin opening if it is not to collapse." [3] Powell added that the administration was extremely concerned about North Korea's "efforts toward development of weapons of mass destruction and the proliferation of such weapons and missiles and other materials to other nations, not only in the region but around the world."

Because of North Korea's apparent violation of the '94 agreement, both the Clinton and Bush administrations delayed construction of the two promised power plants to pressure the government to allow inspections of its nuclear facilities. As of early 2003, the plants were far from completion. [4]

Bush's condemnation of North Korea — officially known as the Democratic People's Republic of Korea (DPRK) — intensified after the Sept. 11, 2001, terrorist attacks in the United States. In his January 2002 State of the Union address, the president branded North Korea, Iraq and Iran as an "axis of evil" bent on obtaining weapons of mass destruction to use against the United States and its allies.

Moreover, two key Pentagon documents issued last year specifically linked North Korea to contingencies that might call for pre-emptive military action, possibly including the use of nuclear weapons. [5]

Then last summer, when *The Washington Post's* Bob Woodward interviewed Bush, he reported that the president nearly jumped out of his chair when asked about Kim. "I loathe Kim Jong Il!" Bush shouted. "I've got a visceral reaction to this guy because he is starving his people. And I have seen intelligence on these prison camps — they're huge — that he uses to break up families and to torture people. . . . Maybe it's my religion," said Bush, who often invokes his Christian faith, "but I feel passionate about this." [6]

In response to Bush's policy changes, North Korea accused the United States of reneging on its 1994 commitment to build the two nuclear plants — desperately needed to power the country's collapsing industries and farms — and declared that Bush's policies and statements amounted to a threat of aggression.

"A dangerous situation where our nation's sovereignty and our state's security are being seriously violated is prevailing on the Korean Peninsula due to the U.S. vicious, hostile policy towards the DPRK," the government said on Jan. 10. "After the appearance of the Bush administration, the United States listed the DPRK as part of an 'axis of evil,' adopting it as a national policy to oppose its system, and singled it out as a target of pre-emptive nuclear attack, openly declaring a nuclear war." [7]

Many analysts say North Korea's fear of U.S. aggression is genuine. "From the North Korean point of view, the United States would like to bring about the downfall of their government as a totalitarian regime that we don't like," Harrison says. "They also

The North's Focus on Nuclear Weapons

Facilities to research, develop and produce nuclear fuels and weapons are thought to be scattered throughout North Korea, including several in Pyongyang, the capital. After decades of mismanagement, North Korea relies heavily on international food aid while spending needed capital maintaining its large army and developing long-range missiles and nuclear, chemical and biological weapons. Last December, North Korea expelled U.N. monitors and repudiated a 1994 agreement that shut down its nuclear reactors, intensifying fears it would produce nuclear weapons.

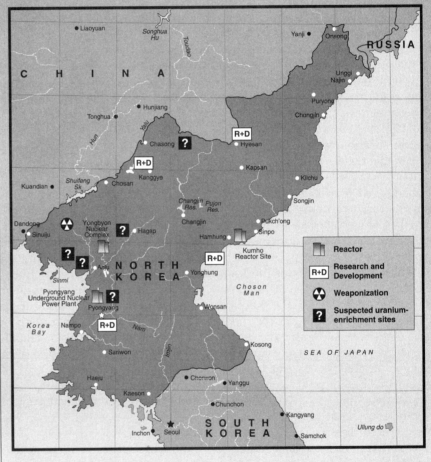

Sources: CIA, The World Factbook 2002; *Center for Non-Proliferation Studies*

think the [new] national security doctrine legitimizing the idea of a pre-emptive military strike against any country we think might be a threat was definitely targeted toward them."

Tensions had escalated even more last October, when State Department

officials traveled to Pyongyang, the capital, to present evidence that North Korea had a secret program to enrich uranium that could be used for nuclear weapons. North Korea acknowledged the U.S. claim that it had a uranium-enrichment program, though it

North Korea at a Glance

North Korea, one of the world's most highly controlled and isolated economies, faces desperate conditions. Industrial capital stock is nearly beyond repair, and industrial and power output have declined. Despite a good harvest in 2001, the nation faces its ninth year of food shortages. Massive international food aid since 1995-96 staved off mass starvation, but the population remains vulnerable to prolonged malnutrition. The regime recently has emphasized earning hard currency, developing information technology, addressing power shortages and attracting foreign aid, but without undergoing widespread market-oriented reforms. Last year, heightened political tensions with key donor countries and general donor fatigue reduced desperately needed food aid.

Area: *47,386 sq. mi., slightly smaller than Mississippi.*

Geography: *Strategic location bordering China, South Korea and Russia; the mountainous interior is isolated, sparsely populated.*

Natural resources: *coal, lead, tungsten, zinc, graphite, magnesite, iron ore, copper, gold, pyrites, salt, fluorspar, hydropower.*

Population: *22.2 million (July 2002 est.)*

Life expectancy: *71.3 years*

Religion: *traditionally Buddhist and Confucianist, some Christian and Chondogyo (Religion of the Heavenly Way)*

Government: *authoritarian socialist; Kim Jong Il has ruled since his father and the country's founder, Kim Il Sung, died in 1994.*

Capital: *Pyongyang; population, 2.5 million (2002 est.)*

GDP: *$22 billion; growth rate, 1%; per capita, $1,000 (2002 estimates).*

Labor force: *9.6 million; agricultural 36%, non-agricultural 64%*

Industries: *military products, machine building, electric power, chemicals, mining, metallurgy, textiles, food processing, tourism.*

Agriculture: *rice, corn, potatoes, soybeans, pulse, cattle, pigs, eggs.*

Exports: *$826 million (2001 est.); minerals, metallurgical products, manufactures (including armaments), textiles, fishery products; main partners: Japan 36.3%, South Korea 21.5%, China 5.2% (2000)*

Imports: *$1.8 billion (2001 est.); petroleum, coking coal, machinery and equipment, textiles, grain; main partners: China 26.7%, South Korea 16.2%, Japan 12.3% (2000).*

Source: CIA, The World Factbook 2002

denied it was for making nuclear weapons. However, it subsequently announced it was pulling out of the NPT and expelled International Atomic Energy Agency (IAEA) monitors from its plutonium-reprocessing facility at Yongbyon. The U.S. and its allies promptly stopped fuel oil shipments to North Korea.

Relations quickly deteriorated further. In December a U.S. Navy ship temporarily seized 15 North Korean-made Scud missiles on a Yemen-bound North Korean freighter. In February, North Korea reactivated its 5-megawat reactor at Yongbyon, which can produce enough plutonium to produce up to six nuclear weapons. (*See story, p. 289.*) On March 1, four North Korean fighter jets shadowed a U.S. spy plane in international airspace off North Korea's coast, the first such incident since 1969. Later that month, North Korea launched two cruise missiles into the Sea of Japan — an act that Pyongyang has frequently employed to express its displeasure with policies of the U.S. or its allies in the region.

Today, Washington and Pyongyang are at an apparent stalemate. North Korea wants the United States to resume food and energy assistance, promise not to invade and participate in bilateral negotiations, which the Bush administration rejects as caving in to "nuclear blackmail" and "rewarding bad behavior." Washington says North Korea must first shut down its nuclear-weapons program and insists on including South Korea and the other regional powers — China, Japan and Russia — in any talks.

The war with Iraq has further complicated the policy dilemma. North Korea declared on March 21 that the U.S.-led operation to topple Saddam Hussein would have "disastrous" consequences and accused the United States of pushing the Korean crisis toward an "explosive phase." Moreover, many analysts believe that while the world is watching Iraq, North Korea will restart its Yongbyon plutonium-reprocessing plant. [8]

"We should be prepared for North Korea to try to take advantage of our distraction in Iraq," says Michael Levi, director of the Federation of American Scientists' Strategy Security Project. "I don't know exactly what they would do, perhaps restart their reprocessing plant. But certainly they'd like to be getting more attention."

For the moment, the U.S. is standing firm. "The administration has decided that we shouldn't be cowed into submission or forced into dialogue, and that we should actually stand them down," says Victor D. Cha, an associate professor at Georgetown University's School of Foreign Service and an administration adviser on Korea. "If that fails, then we're looking at isolation and containment. And if that fails, or if the North is found to be exporting weapons of mass destruction, then I think a military option will get talked about a lot more."

Indeed, says Michael A. McDevitt, director of the Center for Strategic Studies at the Center for Naval Analyses, "The beginning of wisdom in dealing with North Korea is the realization that there are no good choices — only bad and less-bad choices. You don't want to reward bad behavior, and clearly North Korea has been doing really dumb, bad things.

"So the options you face are either rewarding bad behavior by going into negotiations or refusing to negotiate, which allows North Korea to control

the process, continue doing bad things and escalate tensions."

As the political stalemate drags on, these are some of the questions being asked:

Does North Korea's nuclear program pose an immediate threat to the United States?

The North Korean government admitted last fall that it has conducted a clandestine program to develop nuclear weapons, in violation of both

North Korean soldiers march in Pyongyang on March 26, 2002. After World War II, North Korea poured its resources into creating a million-man army equipped with some 11,000 artillery pieces. Now leader Kim Jong Il is thought to be developing nuclear weapons.

its 1994 Agreed Framework with the United States and the NPT, which it signed in 1985. Analysts now suggest it may be on the verge of producing nuclear weapons from either enriched uranium or reprocessed plutonium, or both.

Even if the regime halted its weapons programs tomorrow, U.S. intelligence suggests it already has enough fissile material for at least one nuclear bomb. "North Korea probably has one or two nuclear weapons," says Levi of the

Federation of American Scientists. "That's the most obvious danger."

South Korea and Japan also think North Korea has nuclear weapons. And recent reports suggest the Bush administration has quietly acknowledged that reality and shifted its efforts from blocking North Korea's development of nuclear weapons to stopping it from exporting them. [9]

It is uncertain how soon Pyongyang could add to its nuclear arsenal. The Yongbyon reactor, deactivated under the 1994 agreement, could be restarted quickly and used to reprocess the plutonium contained in some 8,000 spent fuel rods stored at the site. "The plutonium reprocessing is probably much closer to realization than the uranium-enrichment program," Levi says. "They would simply take material that had been generated by operating the nuclear reactor over a decade ago and in six months convert it into as many as six nuclear bombs."

Uranium enrichment is a more complex process, but easier to hide from spy-satellite cameras. Analysts believe several enrichment labs may be hidden around the country, including underground facilities. But North Korea would be unable to produce uranium-based weapons for at least another year, most experts say.

But James A. Kelly, assistant secretary of State for East Asian and Pacific affairs, recently told the Senate Foreign Relations Committee the enriched-uranium issue is not "somewhere off in the fog of the distant future." Rather, he said, "it is only probably a matter of months, and not years, behind the plutonium." [10]

AFP Photo/Goh Chai Hin

Further fueling America's anxiety, CIA Director George J. Tenet told a congressional panel last month that North Korea's Taepodong-2 ballistic missile — which could carry a nuclear warhead — is capable of reaching the Western United States. [11] However, the missile has never been tested — casting doubt on its ability to actually reach such a distant target.

Some experts downplay Pyongyang's nuclear threat. Using nukes to drive the Americans out of South Korea would be suicidal, they point out, because a large portion of the peninsula would be destroyed or contaminated with deadly radioactive fallout. It also would invite U.S. retaliation in kind.

"If they wanted to damage the South, they could do it with artillery," says Georgetown's Cha, noting North Korea has about 11,000 missiles.

Alternatively, North Korea could attack the United States and its allies indirectly by providing the weapons to terrorist organizations like al Qaeda. "With the six or seven nuclear weapons it could have in a year or so, North Korea could carry out a test explosion, target South Korea and Japan, hold a few bombs in reserve and even sell plutonium to eager buyers," wrote Robert J. Einhorn, a senior CSIS adviser who served as assistant secretary of State for non-proliferation in the Clinton administration. "Within several more years, it could be producing large quantities of fissile material from its uranium-enrichment plant and three plutonium reactors." [12]

But other experts discount the threat. "In the short run, you don't have to worry about North Korea selling off its nuclear material," says David Albright, president of the Institute for Science and International Security, a Washington think tank. "Because it is extremely worried about being attacked by the United States, I find it very difficult to believe North Korea would sell any of its precious plutonium to a terrorist group." Albright estimates that Pyongyang could devel-

op no more than five to eight nuclear weapons by the end of this summer. "That's not very many if you're facing an invasion by the United States."

Nonetheless, many experts say it would be foolhardy to dismiss the hostile statements coming out of Pyongyang today as groundless bluster. "North Korea has been systematically shedding any inhibitions about building nuclear weapons," says McDevitt of the Center for Strategic Studies. "They've walked away from the Agreed Framework, they've told the IAEA inspectors to get out of Yongbyon and they've said they were leaving the NPT. Now there's a big question as to whether we can get them out of the [nuclear] game."

Indeed, some longtime observers say it may already be too late. "This is not just a bluff," says Donald P. Gregg, president of the Korea Society and a former U.S. ambassador to South Korea. "The Bush administration says it will not allow North Korea to become a nuclear power. Now that they've announced that they're going to become one, the question [for Washington] becomes: 'What are you going to do about it?'"

Should the United States hold bilateral talks with North Korea?

Since Pyongyang acknowledged its uranium-enrichment program last October, it has called on the United States to sign a non-aggression treaty promising not to attack North Korea and to enter into direct, bilateral negotiations to resolve tensions between the two nations. The Bush administration has emphatically rejected the proposal, especially in light of steps taken by North Korea to accelerate its weapons program.

"Each of these North Korean provocations is designed to blackmail the United States and to intimidate our friends and allies into pushing the United States into a dialogue with the North — giving the North what it wants, and on its terms," said Assistant Secretary of State Kelly. "We tried the bilateral

approach 10 years ago, by negotiating the Agreed Framework. . . . And we found the North could not be trusted. This time, a new and more comprehensive approach is required." [13]

The Bush approach to negotiations with North Korea would include South Korea and Japan — the United States' principal allies in Northeast Asia — as well as China and Russia, both of which have historic ties to North Korea and are eager to remain the region's only two nuclear powers. (*See sidebar, p. 285.*)

Many experts outside the administration fault Bush for ignoring North Korea's call to the negotiating table. "The administration has made a mistake by equating diplomacy with appeasement," says Campbell of CSIS. "Diplomacy was invented to deal with unpleasant people and circumstances, the very situation we're facing in North Korea. Among all the bad options on the Korean Peninsula — including war, serious proliferation problems and the prospect of triggering regionwide insecurity — diplomacy is really the only way to go."

Campbell does not dismiss the administration's goal of multilateral dialogue, but he says bilateral talks are a necessary first step. "Direct, bilateral negotiation is the way forward toward progress on multilateral talks," he says. "Direct talks are essential to bringing our allies together for potentially more serious options if things go poorly in those negotiations."

Some experts say bilateral talks could not only resolve the nuclear crisis but also pave the way for more sweeping changes on the peninsula. "If we can get this nuclear issue behind us and normalize relations with North Korea, maybe they'll begin to open up," says McDevitt. "Maybe they'll begin to change their economy, as the Chinese did. Maybe things will turn out so well we can get to a state of peaceful coexistence between the two Koreas."

Continuing to reject Pyongyang's call for bilateral talks and a non-aggression treaty could backfire on the

The State of Nuclear Proliferation, 2001

The 1968 Non-Proliferation Treaty restricts Nuclear-Weapon States status to nations that "manufactured and exploded a nuclear weapon or other nuclear explosive device prior 1 January 1967." The CIA estimates that North Korea has diverted enough plutonium to develop one or two nuclear weapons.

Recognized Nuclear-Weapon States (NWS)	No. of strategic warheads	Unrecognized Nuclear-Weapon States	Estimated no. of warheads	States of Immediate Proliferation Concern	Recent Adherents to the Non-Proliferation Treaty
China	300	India	45-95	Iran	Algeria, Argentina,
France	Less than 500	Israel	75-125	Iraq	Belarus, Brazil,
Russia	6,094 deployed	Pakistan	30-50	Libya	Kazakhstan, South
United Kingdom	Less than 200			North Korea	Africa, Ukraine
United States	7,295 deployed				

Source: Arms Control Association, March 12, 2003, www.armscontrol.org

administration, some experts say. "It's quite clear to me that if we do not talk directly to them and answer their security concerns, North Korea will at some time this year announce that it is going to build nuclear weapons," says former Ambassador Gregg. "I am told that there is still a window of time, but that that window is not going to stay open too much longer."

With its hands full in Iraq, however, the Bush administration is showing little inclination to shift its hard-line stance. "There is zero support for a proactive engagement of North Korea," says L. Gordon Flake, executive director of the Mansfield Center for Pacific Affairs, which promotes cooperation between the United States and Asia. "There are some who are willing to deal with the North Koreans if they unilaterally capitulate on their nuclear program. But no one in the administration thinks that we should approach the North Koreans with a plan, that we should try to engage them — no one in this administration, period."

Supporters of the administration's position say acceding to Pyongyang's demands for both a non-aggression treaty and bilateral talks would severely limit Washington's hand. "People who say we

must negotiate with the North Koreans also say we have to renounce the use of force and the threat of sanctions," says administration adviser Cha. "That's a very difficult position to negotiate from."

The supporters also contend that accepting bilateral talks would relieve South Korea, Japan, China and Russia — who don't want North Korea to become a nuclear power — from taking responsibility for the outcome. "If this were something that didn't directly affect the security interests of all the countries in the region, then you might be able to say that it's alright to leave the United States to deal with it alone," Cha says. "There are some countries that would like the problem to just go away and free-ride off the United States. But these are all grown-up countries now, and the administration is on the right track by pushing the multilateral effort and trying to get other countries on board."

Should the United States consider military action to halt North Korea's nuclear program?

For many months after citing the Pyongyang regime as part of an "axis of evil" bent on destroying the United States, President Bush took pains to reassure North Korea the United

States had no plans to attack. But the president recently has hardened his stance toward North Korea.

"I still believe this [crisis] will be solved diplomatically," Bush said in February. But for the first time, he also hinted at the possibility of further action if diplomacy fails. "All options are on the table, of course," he added. Underlining the president's statement, White House spokesman Ari Fleischer said the United States has "robust plans for any contingencies" involving North Korea, including the use of force. [14]

Concerned that Kim might try to take advantage of the diversion of U.S. forces to the Middle East, the Pentagon in early March deployed 24 long-range bombers to Guam, within striking distance of North Korea. While still hoping to halt North Korea's nuclear program through diplomatic efforts, the president said, "If they don't work diplomatically, they'll have to work militarily." [15]

Likely military scenarios include a "surgical" strike at the Yongbyon reactor. But even if it destroyed the facility, critics say it probably would not end Pyongyang's nuclear capability. "Even if there were only one plutonium-reprocessing program, North Korea could reconstitute the program in a matter of

Global Nuclear-Weapons Stockpiles

The 1968 Nuclear Non-Proliferation Treaty (NPT) recognizes the five permanent members of the U.N. Security Council — the U.S., Russia, France, United Kingdom and China — as Nuclear-Weapon States, or countries that had "exploded a nuclear weapon" before Jan. 1, 1967.

The treaty designated the International Atomic Energy Agency (IAEA) as the monitoring agency. Countries that signed the NPT agreed to refrain from producing or stockpiling nuclear weapons. [1]

The NPT, which now has 187 signatories, has the broadest support of any arms-control treaty. Only four countries — Cuba, India, Israel and Pakistan — have not signed the pact. Of these, only Cuba has not actively developed a nuclear capability.

But the near-unanimous global support for the NPT in principle has not removed the threat of nuclear proliferation. According to the Nuclear Threat Initiative, a nonprofit organization founded by media mogul Ted Turner and former Sen. Sam Nunn, D-Ga., "More than a decade after the end of the Cold War, there are still some 30,000 strategic and tactical nuclear weapons in the world (mainly in U.S. and Russian arsenals). "The world's stockpiles of separated plutonium and highly enriched uranium (HEU) are estimated to total some 450 metric tons of military and civilian separated plutonium, and some 1,600 tons of HEU — enough to make nearly a quarter-million nuclear weapons." [2]

India, Israel and Pakistan are believed to possess finished nuclear weapons or components that could be rapidly assembled. In 1998, India and Pakistan — engaged in a longstanding border dispute — acknowledged their nuclear status. Israel, the only other unrecognized nuclear state, began developing its nuclear capability in the 1950s with French assistance. The United States has refrained from pressing its chief Middle Eastern ally to end its nuclear program, and Israel has never acknowledged its arsenal, estimated at 75 to 125 warheads.

North Korea, along with Iraq, Iran and Libya, are "states of immediate proliferation concern" — believed to be seeking a nuclear capability in violation of the NPT. In 1993, North Korea announced that it would withdraw from the treaty, but rescinded that decision after signing the 1994 Agreed Framework with the United States, promising to freeze its nuclear program in exchange for food and fuel assistance.

However, citing its right to self-defense after the Bush administration's condemnation of North Korea as part of an "axis of evil," North Korea in 2002 again announced it was withdrawing from the NPT. The United States estimates that North Korea has enough fissile material to make one or two nuclear bombs.

Iraq was trying to develop nuclear weapons when Israeli air strikes destroyed its French-supplied reactor in 1981. Iraq was ordered to disarm after the 1991 Gulf War, but shortly after the war IAEA inspectors discovered a large, secret nuclear-weapons program in violation of the NPT. By 1998, when Iraqi leader Saddam Hussein expelled the inspectors, the IAEA had concluded that Iraq was no longer able to produce nuclear weapons. During their recent return to Iraq, halted before the March 19 U.S.-led invasion, weapons inspectors failed to turn up fresh evidence of Iraqi non-compliance with the NPT, despite U.S. and British allegations that Iraq was seeking nuclear weapons.

The United States believes that Iran, which shares a border and longstanding animosity with Iraq, is also secretly pursuing a nuclear-weapons program, although the IAEA still considers it in compliance with the NPT. Since the mid-1990s, Russia has assisted Iran in building nuclear-power plants, but acceded to U.S. demands not to sell the Iranians uranium-enrichment technology that could be used to build weapons.

Russia also has begun discussions to help Libya modernize its nuclear reactor. The United States suspects that Libya is trying to build nuclear weapons. On a positive note, seven countries have forsaken nuclear weapons over the past decade. Belarus, Kazakhstan and Ukraine, which inherited weapons stockpiles from the Soviet Union when it collapsed in 1991, have returned the nuclear weapons to Russia and joined the NPT as independent countries. South Africa, which developed six nuclear bombs in the 1980s, dismantled its arsenal and declared itself nuclear-free in 1994. After the discovery of its nascent program in 1991, Algeria renounced nuclear weapons and acceded to the NPT in 1995. Argentina and Brazil ended their programs and signed the NPT in the late 1990s.

But there is lingering concern about the potential theft of poorly guarded nuclear weapons and fissile material in the former Soviet Union. Since 1992, the United States has spent some $4.1 billion to secure nuclear weapons and material stored there. Much of the money has gone to the Defense Department's Cooperative Threat Reduction program, created by legislation sponsored by Nunn and Senate Foreign Relations Chairman Richard G. Lugar, R-Ind.

But House Republicans, claiming the program has failed to gain sufficient Russian support, have blocked a Bush administration request to expand the program and spend up to $50 million in fiscal 2003 and 2004 to secure weapons of mass destruction materials outside the former Soviet Union, including in Iraq. [3]

Concern about nuclear proliferation has mounted since the Sept. 11, 2001, terrorist attacks. "We are in a new arms race between terrorist efforts to acquire nuclear, biological and chemical weapons and our efforts to stop them," said Nunn. [4]

---

[1] Unless otherwise noted, information in this section is based on Arms Control Association, "The State of Nuclear Proliferation, 2001," www.armscontrol.org. For background, see Mary H. Cooper, "Non-Proliferation Treaty at 25," *The CQ Researcher*, Jan. 27, 1995, pp. 73-96.

[2] Nuclear Threat Initiative, "Controlling Nuclear Warheads and Materials: The Global Threat and Urgent Steps to Address It," www.nti.org.

[3] See David Ruppe, "U.S. Response: House Rejects Bush Cooperative Threat Reduction Request," *Global Security Newswire*, April 2, 2003.

[4] Nunn addressed the World Affairs Council in Washington, D.C., Oct. 22, 2002.

years," says Levi of the Federation of American Scientists. "There isn't a military option that provides the same comprehensive solution that diplomacy might."

Moreover, Levi adds, taking out Yongbyon would not affect what experts say is North Korea's highly secret uranium-enrichment program, which may include numerous underground locations. "It's very hard for us to verify how far along they are because we don't know where the uranium facilities are," Levi says. "That means there is no military option short of regime change that will completely remove the North Korean nuclear threat."

Critics of the military option say that despite its much-vaunted ability to fight two wars simultaneously, the United States may not be up to the task as long as the fighting continues in Iraq. "In foreign affairs, Washington is chronically unable to deal with more than one crisis at a time," wrote former Secretary of State Warren Christopher nearly three months before the invasion of Iraq. "While Defense Secretary Donald H. Rumsfeld may be right in saying that our military can fight two wars at the same time, my experience tells me that we cannot mount a war against Iraq and still maintain the necessary policy focus on North Korea and international terrorism." [16]

In any event, North Korea repeatedly has warned that an attack on its nuclear facilities would trigger all-out war, the consequences of which would be catastrophic, even if Pyongyang did not use a nuclear bomb, military experts warn.

North Korea has more than 8,000 artillery pieces deployed along the DMZ as well as 70 percent of its 1.2 million troops. "Military pre-emption has an incredibly high risk of starting another Korean war," says McDevitt, of the Center for Strategic Studies. "Unlike other areas of the world, the geography of the Korean Peninsula is such that North Korea could lash out immediately and

cause a lot of death and damage in the South. It would not be hard to destroy that reprocessing plant militarily. It's the consequences that you have to be able to deal with." ∎

BACKGROUND

Korea's Roots

North Korea emerged from the ashes of World War II in 1945 to become one of the most enduring vestiges of the Cold War. But the culture and political ideology of the communist state are unique, owing as much to the Korean Peninsula's troubled history as to Cold War rivalry. Indeed, the authoritarian, paternalistic, isolationist and highly militaristic regime that rules North Korea today has its roots in Korea's troubled dealings over the millennia with its powerful neighbors — China, Russia and Japan. [17]

For many years, Korea managed to ward off Western encroachment, which began in earnest with U.S. Navy Commodore Matthew C. Perry's opening of Japan to foreign trade in the mid-19th century. Indeed, Americans' first attempt to penetrate Korea's isolation ended badly. In 1866, when the U.S.S. *General Sherman* steamed up the Taedong River to the outskirts of Pyongyang, local inhabitants burned the ship and killed all its crew. North Korea's late leader, Kim Il Sung, claimed that his great-grandfather participated in that attack, now celebrated as a heroic victory against foreign invaders.

Korea's isolation was short-lived. Japan annexed the peninsula in 1910 and turned it into a colony whose natural resources would help build the Japanese war machine. Korea's occupiers industrialized the peninsula, building factories, roads and hydroelectric dams and

laying the foundations of later private industrial development in the south and state-controlled industry in the north.

The colonial experience, which ended with Japan's defeat in World War II, left a lasting impression of national humiliation that would feed Korean aspirations for independence.

Korean resentment of its colonial status fueled intermittent protests and insurrections that were brutally suppressed by Japanese administrators. Exiled to China and the Soviet Union, some of the dissidents, including Kim Il Sung, gained military training. After Japan annexed Manchuria in 1931, the rebel leaders returned to the region and led guerrilla actions against the Japanese occupation forces, which had a profound influence on North Korea's military and ideological development. Indeed, Kim and his resistance compatriots would occupy most leadership positions in North Korea for the next 50 years.

Korean War

Even before World War II ended, the United States and its allies began deliberating the future of Korea. At a meeting in Cairo, Egypt, in December 1943, they endorsed President Franklin D. Roosevelt's vague proposition that upon Japan's defeat Korea would become independent "in due course." The Roosevelt administration also reversed traditional American non-involvement in Korean affairs by defining security on the peninsula as important to postwar Pacific — and therefore U.S. — security.

On Aug. 11, 1945, War Department officials, without consulting Korean or Soviet officials, made the fateful decision to divide Korea into Soviet and U.S. zones separated along the 38th parallel. In early September, 25,000 American soldiers occupied southern Korea, ending the hated Japanese occupation of the peninsula. But they

Chronology

1940s-1980s
Korean War ends in a stalemate, and a tense standoff on the Korean Peninsula ensues.

Aug. 11, 1945
As World War II draws to a close, U.S. officials decide to divide Korea into Soviet and U.S. zones, separated along the 38th parallel. In September, 25,000 American soldiers occupy southern Korea.

May 1948
U.N.-supervised elections result in the creation of the Republic of Korea (South Korea).

Sept. 9, 1949
The People's Democratic Republic of Korea — North Korea — is established with guerrilla leader and Korean Workers' Party head Kim Il Sung as its leader.

June 1950
North Korean forces invade South Korea. Although U.S.-led United Nations forces repel the invasion, hostilities continue until July 27, 1953, when the two sides sign an armistice.

1965
Soviet engineers help build North Korea's nuclear reactor at Yongbyon.

1984
North Korea tests missiles based on Soviet Scud technology.

1985
North Korea signs the 1968 Nuclear Non-Proliferation Treaty (NPT).

1990s
The United States and South Korea try to ease tensions on the Korean Peninsula through a policy of engagement with North Korea.

March 12, 1993
As one of his last major acts before handing over the country to his son, Kim Jong Il, Kim Il Sung announces his intention to withdraw from the NPT.

Oct. 21, 1994
The United States and North Korea sign an Agreed Framework in which Pyongyang promises to adhere to the NPT and freeze its nuclear-weapons program in exchange for food and energy assistance.

1998
North Korea test-fires a longer-range Taepodong-1 missile over Japan.

2000s
The Bush administration shifts U.S. policy toward North Korea.

October 2000
During the Clinton administration's waning days, Secretary of State Madeleine K. Albright makes a historic visit to North Korea but fails to reach an agreement that would halt North Korea's exports of missile technology to Pakistan and other countries. North Korea's second in command, Vice-Marshal Jo Myong Rok, visits Washington and signs a joint non-aggression pact. North Korea agrees to a moratorium on long-range missile tests and continues the freeze at Yongbyon.

March 2001
President Bush repudiates the Agreed Framework and Clinton's engagement policy toward Pyongyang.

Sept. 11, 2001
Members of the al Qaeda terrorist organization kill some 3,000 Americans in New York City, the Pentagon and rural Pennsylvania.

January 2002
In his State of the Union address, Bush lumps North Korea with Iraq and Iran as an "axis of evil" bent on obtaining weapons of mass destruction to use against the United States and its allies or provide to anti-American terrorists.

October 2002
A U.S. State Department delegation to Pyongyang confronts North Korea with evidence that the regime has started a uranium-enrichment program in violation of the 1994 agreement. North Korea acknowledges the program and says it will withdraw from the NPT.

Feb. 7, 2003
Bush for the first time suggests that the United States may consider the use of military force to halt North Korea's nuclear program.

March 1, 2003
Four North Korean fighter jets shadow a U.S. spy plane in international airspace off the North Korean coast. North Korea launches two cruise missiles into the Sea of Japan.

March 12, 2003
Central Intelligence Agency Director George J. Tenet tells a congressional committee that North Korea possesses the missile technology to reach the Western United States.

March 19, 2003
The United States leads an invasion of Iraq to topple its leader, Saddam Hussein. North Korea declares that the U.S.-British operation will have "disastrous" consequences and accuses the United States of pushing the Korean crisis toward an "explosive phase."

immediately faced opposition among Koreans who saw the U.S. presence as a continuation of colonialism and resented the notion that they were not ready for independence. Meanwhile, Soviet forces occupied Korea north of the 38th parallel and brought with them Kim Il Sung and other communist leaders who had left the country during the Japanese occupation.

Soviet leader Josef Stalin had quietly accepted the partition of Korea, but U.S.-Soviet relations quickly chilled. Although Korea was home to one of the oldest communist movements in Asia, the United States saw the emergence of communist leanings in the South in late 1945 as evidence of a Soviet plan to dominate the entire peninsula.

In 1947, President Harry S Truman called for the containment of communism within existing boundaries — the so-called Truman Doctrine. The U.S. won United Nations support for U.N.-supervised elections for all of Korea if the Soviet Union approved the plan. When it didn't, elections were held in the South in May 1948, resulting in the establishment of the Republic of Korea and the ascendance to power of Syngman Rhee, the first of several authoritarian leaders who would rule South Korea for the next three decades. [18]

Kim, meanwhile, had emerged as the leader of the communist movement that consolidated power in the North and established a central government in February 1946. Over the next year, land and industries were nationalized and brought under a system of central planning along the Soviet model. Bolstered by his earlier activities as a nationalist guerrilla, Kim became highly popular, far more than the new leaders in the South, who were regarded by many Koreans as puppets of the American colonial occupiers.

Kim strengthened his hold with the merger of communist parties in 1949

into the Korean Workers' Party, which dominated the new Democratic People's Republic of Korea (DPRK) from its founding on Sept. 9, 1948, three weeks after the Republic of Korea's formation.

In contrast to Soviet-supported regimes in Eastern Europe, Kim's brand of communism was no mere copy of the Soviet model — partly because of Stalin's withdrawal of Soviet forces from Korea in 1948. Kim infused a singularly Korean theme into his communist system through the adoption of *chuch'e* ideology. Defined roughly as keeping foreigners at arm's length, *chuch'e* appealed to the traditional Korean ideals of self-reliance and independence. Kim put his doctrine into action in 1955, when he distanced his regime from the Soviet Union, and throughout his rule by subjecting North Koreans to continual political indoctrination.

In 1949, Kim had himself named *suryng*, an old Korean word for "leader" that was modified to mean "great leader." That year he began condemning South Korea as a puppet state.

Although neither Seoul nor Pyongyang recognized the 38th parallel as a legitimate boundary, historians generally blame the North — and not the South — for the outbreak of the Korean War. Bolstered by some 100,000 war-trained forces and support from China and, to a lesser degree, the Soviet Union, North Korean forces invaded South Korea on June 25, 1950, and took control of all but a small corner of southeastern Korea around the port city of Pusan.

In September, U.N. and South Korean forces led by U.S. Gen. Douglas MacArthur drove out the invaders. The war dragged on for another three years, costing the lives of some 800,000 Koreans on both sides of the parallel, 115,000 Chinese and 37,000 Americans and laying waste to much of the peninsula. An armistice was signed in the summer of 1953 recognizing the de facto division of Korea.

Military Ambitions

The war's conclusion 50 years ago this July 27 came not with a peace treaty but with an armistice that merely suspended the hostilities and separated the two sides at the 38th parallel. To bolster South Korea's military forces, the United States retained a sizable military presence in South Korea, backed by naval forces in the Pacific and, ultimately, its superpower nuclear deterrent. Faced with such a formidable adversary, North Korea poured its resources into creating one of the most militarized societies on Earth — eventually building a million-man army equipped with some 11,000 artillery pieces.

It was not long before the North sought to move beyond its conventional arsenal. As early as 1964, Pyongyang set up a nuclear-energy research complex at Yongbyon, where the Soviets built Korea's first nuclear reactor a year later. A plutonium-reprocessing plant and other support facilities appeared over the next two decades.

Despite signing the NPT in 1985 — which barred signatories without nuclear weapons from developing them — barely two years later Pyongyang began hindering U.N. inspections of its nuclear facilities to ensure compliance with the treaty. The IAEA inspectors did not gain access to North Korean nuclear facilities until May 1992. Amid intelligence reports that North Korea was secretly continuing its nuclear program at clandestine sites, their findings were inconclusive.

Besides pursuing a nuclear capability, North Korea also is believed to have developed biological and chemical weapons beginning in the early 1980s, even though in 1987 it acceded to the 1972 Biological and Toxin Weapons Convention banning pathogens for military uses. But, according to the Washington-based Nuclear Threat Initiative, North Korea produced weapons containing anthrax, botulinum toxin and plague. [19]

Does North Korea Have the Bomb?

The Bush administration and many non-governmental experts say North Korea already has enough fissile material to make two nuclear weapons and may be on the threshold of making many more. But the self-imposed isolation and secretiveness of the regime in Pyongyang make estimates sketchy at best. [1]

North Korea appears to possess the technology to produce nuclear weapons using two different materials — reprocessed plutonium and enriched uranium. Both techniques require the ability to mine and mill uranium.

To make a plutonium-based bomb, milled uranium is processed into reactor fuel and "burned" in a reactor. Plutonium is then extracted from the spent fuel and formed into the core of a fission-implosion weapon. High explosives are used to initiate the fission process that ends with the nuclear explosion.

A uranium-based bomb contains milled uranium that has been enriched to produce a Hiroshima-sized blast or an even more destructive weapon. An advanced uranium-based weapon would include tritium, a radioactive gas that can enhance the bomb's power.

Korea-watchers are most immediately concerned about North Korea's ability to reprocess plutonium from some 8,000 spent nuclear fuel rods stored near the 5-megawatt Yongbyon nuclear reactor. Under the 1994 Agreed Framework with the United States, Pyongyang shut down that reactor in exchange for U.S. food and fuel assistance.

Both sides abandoned the agreement last October, however, after Pyongyang admitted to U.S. State Department officials that it had launched a uranium-enrichment program. The Yongbyon facility, together with a smaller research reactor, could reprocess enough plutonium to build up to 50 bombs a year if North Korea can overcome technical problems at its antiquated plants and bring them both up to full operation. [2]

The status and location of North Korea's uranium-enrichment program are unknown, but experts believe it may be able to produce about 100 kilograms of weapons-grade uranium a year by 2005, at the earliest.

---

[1] Information based on "North Korean Nuclear Capabilities," Nuclear Threat Initiative and Center for Non-Proliferation Studies, www.nti.org.

[2] See Glenn Kessler and Walter Pincus, "N. Korea Stymied on Plutonium Work; Reprocessing Lab Called Antiquated," *Washington Post*, March 20, 2003, p. A24.

The group also estimates that North Korea has 12 chemical-weapons plants producing some 4,500 tons of mustard, phosgene, sarin and other chemicals — and that annual production could reach 12,000 tons in case of war. Unlike the United States, North Korea never signed the 1993 Chemical Weapons Convention, which bans chemical weapons and provides for monitoring compliance, including intrusive inspections and allowances for sanctions and the use of force against violators. In addition, North Korea's thousands of artillery systems can deliver chemical weapons into the DMZ and Seoul. [20]

Since the 1970s, military experts say North Korea has been developing missiles capable of reaching targets beyond the range of conventional artillery. By 1984, it had tested a ballistic missile based on the Soviet Scud technology, and it has since produced several types of missiles, including 100 of the advanced, 800-mile-range Nodong. The even longer-range Taepodong-1 failed during a 1998 test launch, while the newer Taepodong-2, which po-tentially could reach the U.S. West Coast, is reportedly almost ready for testing.

Although there is no evidence that North Korea has exported its weapons of mass destruction, it has sold its missile technology to several countries, including Egypt, Iran, Libya, Pakistan, Syria and Yemen.

Hardship and Repression

Missile sales are among North Korea's few sources of hard currency. The government maintains a strict policy of self-sufficiency, even in the face of economic collapse since the early 1990s. The Soviet Union's demise and the rejection of the communist model throughout Eastern Europe at the beginning of the decade abruptly halted North Korea's main source of fuel oil and coal to generate electricity, power industrial plants and make fertilizers.

Moreover, a series of droughts and floods destroyed much of its agricul-tural output. Food shortages began in the early 1990s with the loss of electricity-driven irrigation systems and fertilizers. As the government continued to allocate most food and consumer goods to the military, the shortages produced a nationwide famine that prompted many foreign governments, including the United States, to ship food to North Korea. Up to 3.5 million North Koreans, out of a pre-famine population of some 22 million, are believed to have succumbed to malnutrition and starvation. [21]

North Koreans who try to flee their plight have little hope of success. Most try to wade across the icy Tumen River into China, where an estimated 300,000 North Koreans have quietly settled among the region's ethnic Koreans. Many are abused and exploited. Others are aided by foreign Evangelical Christian missionaries, who help them escape to South Korea via an "underground railroad." [22]

But China, eager to prevent a destabilizing influx of millions of North Koreans, refuses to grant them refugee status. Appeals for asylum in the Japanese consulate in China also go unheeded, with North Korean refugees often dragged from the gates of the consulate. [23]

The vast majority of would-be refugees are arrested and forcibly repatriated to North Korea, where they face imprisonment and sometimes execution. [24]

According to the U.S. State Department's 2002 human rights report, the North Korean government has detained 150,000 to 200,000 political prisoners in prisons and forced-labor or "re-education camps." North Koreans can be detained indefinitely without a trial for "crimes against the revolution," such as speaking with South Koreans, reading foreign literature or practicing Christianity. Defectors and refugees, the report says, tell of extrajudicial killings and "disappearances" and prisoners — including newborn babies — being routinely executed. Others are beaten, sexually assaulted, tortured and used as guinea pigs in experiments using chemical and biological warfare agents, the report says. [25]

Evangelical Christians and missionaries from the United States, South Korea and around the world are particularly upset about the alleged persecution of Christians in North Korea, which with the South was once a Christian stronghold in Asia. South Koreans claim an estimated 6,000 Christians are imprisoned in the North, although a State Department report on religious freedom says there is "no reliable information" on how many religious prisoners are in North Korea. However, defectors say Christian prisoners are

considered insane, and their families are "identified for extermination for three successive generations," according to the report. [26]

Agreed Framework

On March 12, 1993, as one of his last major acts before handing the country over to his son, Kim Il Sung withdrew from the NPT, thus ending North Korea's commitment not to develop nuclear weapons. The announcement sparked concern throughout the region that Pyongyang would

North Korean leader Kim Jong Il toasts Secretary of State Madeleine K. Albright during her historic visit to Pyongyang, on Oct. 24, 2000. She failed, however, to convince Kim to stop exporting missile technology to Pakistan and other countries.

join China and Russia to become Northeast Asia's third nuclear power and fuel a regional arms race that might include South Korea and Japan.

After 18 months of bilateral negotiations aimed at ending the crisis, led by former President Jimmy Carter, the United States and North Korea signed the Agreed Framework on Oct. 21, 1994. [27] "This agreement will help achieve a longstanding and vital American objective — an end to the threat

of nuclear proliferation on the Korean Peninsula," then-President Clinton said on Oct. 22.

Pyongyang agreed to remain a party to the NPT and freeze the construction and operation of nuclear reactors capable of producing weapons-grade material in exchange for a U.S. promise to provide two nuclear-power reactors to generate electricity. Pending completion of the reactors, considered to be proliferation-resistant, the United States would supply North Korea with heavy fuel oil to meet its energy needs. A new international consortium — the Korean Peninsula Energy Development Organization (KEDO) — was created to implement the agreement.

The agreement committed both sides to remove barriers to full economic and diplomatic relations. To that end, the Clinton administration relaxed longstanding U.S. economic sanctions against North Korea, including the Trading with the Enemy Act and the Defense Production Act — both in place since 1950 — and the 1979 Export Administration Act. The agreement left in place bans on government military assistance and U.S. exports to North Korea of military and "dual-use" items — goods produced for civilian purposes but potentially adaptable to military use. The agreement also committed both countries to keep the Korean Peninsula free of nuclear weapons, including a U.S. promise to "provide formal assurances" not to threaten or attack North Korea with nuclear weapons.

The Agreed Framework identified several specific obligations for both parties. North Korea agreed to freeze operation of its 5-megawatt reactor and

AFP Pool Photo/Chien-min Chung

plutonium-reprocessing plant at Yong-byon and halt construction of a 50-megawatt reactor at Yongbyon and a 200-megawatt plant at Taechon. Both of the larger reactors would have to be dismantled entirely before the United States would complete the second reactor. North Korea also agreed to "can" all spent fuel from its reactor at Yongbyon, pending its eventual removal from the country, and allow IAEA inspectors complete access to all nuclear facilities.

For its part, the United States agreed to set up KEDO, which it did on March 9, 1995, to provide fuel oil and assistance in implementing the agreement. KEDO, which includes the 15-member European Union and 12 other countries, delegated to Japan and South Korea responsibility for financing and building the two 1,000-megawatt, nuclear-powered reactors at a cost of $4 billion.

After numerous delays, ground was broken at the site in the North Korean coastal city of Kumho in August 2001, and initial construction began a year later. To compensate for the loss of electricity generation caused by the shut-down of North Korea's existing nuclear plants, the agreement committed the United States and its KEDO partners to provide 500,000 metric tons of heavy fuel oil until the new power reactors came on line.

But another crisis had erupted in August 1998, when North Korea test-fired its Taepodong-1 medium-range ballistic missile over Japan. That test, paired with evidence that North Korea was developing a long-range missile that could reach the United States, prompted calls to abandon the Agreed Framework. Clinton established an outside policy review committee, chaired by former Defense Secretary William J. Perry. The committee issued a joint U.S.-South Korean-Japanese statement in May 1999, calling on North Korea to verifiably eliminate its nuclear-weapons and missile programs in return for a U.S. af-

firmation that it had no "hostile intent" toward North Korea.

The Clinton administration's policy of engagement with North Korea provided the security guarantee that enabled South Korean President Kim Dae Jung to advance his "sunshine policy" of phased reconciliation with North Korea. The first North-South summit meeting, held in Pyongyang on June 13-15, 2000, paved the way for numerous follow-up official contacts, exchanges of letters between family members separated since the Korean War and the return, in 2002, of several Japanese citizens kidnapped decades earlier by North Korea. The two governments agreed to reopen rail and road links across the border and once again allow South Korean tourists to visit scenic Kumgang Mountain, just inside North Korea. North Korea announced plans to establish two special economic zones, similar to those that launched China's trade boom in the late 1970s, at Kaesong and Sinuiju. [28]

In October 2000, as the Clinton administration drew to a close, Secretary of State Madeleine K. Albright made a historic visit to North Korea. She failed, however, to reach an agreement that would halt North Korea's exports of missile technology to Pakistan and other countries.

The same month, North Korea's second in command, Vice-Marshal Jo Myong Rok, visited Washington and signed a joint communiqué in which both countries promised: "Neither government would have hostile intent toward the other." North Korea also agreed to a moratorium on tests of long-range missiles and continued the freeze at Yongbyon. Improving relations between North and South Korea culminated in a now-controversial summit meeting between the leaders of the two countries. [29] Finally, in an effort to ease relations with Japan, North Korea returned several Japanese citizens who had been kidnapped several decades earlier. ■

CURRENT SITUATION

Bush's About-Face

The easing of tensions on the Korean Peninsula was short-lived. In March 2001, two months after his inauguration, Bush stunned South Korean President Kim during a visit to Washington by repudiating his "sunshine policy." Bush's reversal essentially halted further improvements in North-South relations. Bush then repudiated the seven-month-old U.S.-North Korea joint communiqué abjuring hostile intent.

Bush's antipathy toward both the North Korean regime and the Clinton administration's engagement with it mounted after a December 2001 report by the National Intelligence Council. It revealed that U.S. intelligence agencies had concluded in the mid-1990s that North Korea had produced enough fissile material to assemble one, possibly two, nuclear weapons in violation of its NPT commitments. [30]

Several months later, U.S. intelligence agencies discovered that Pakistan, which had joined the nuclear club in the late 1980s, had provided Pyongyang with materials for a highly enriched uranium production facility. In exchange, North Korea helped Pakistan build a version of its Nodong medium-range ballistic missile, which Pakistan test-fired in 1998. The missile could be armed with a nuclear warhead and could reach deep into India, Pakistan's longstanding, nuclear-armed adversary.

In the year following the Sept. 11 terrorist attacks in the United States, the Bush administration issued three major policy statements identifying North

Korea as a significant threat to U.S. security that the United States was prepared to address, militarily if necessary.

First, the "Nuclear Posture Review," a long-range planning document submitted to Congress on Dec. 31, 2001, cited North Korea as a potential target of a U.S. nuclear strike. "In setting requirements for nuclear-strike capabilities, distinctions can be made among the contingencies for which the United States must be prepared," the document states. "Current examples of immediate contingencies include an Iraqi attack on Israel or its neighbors, a North Korean attack on South Korea or a military confrontation over the status of Taiwan. . . . North Korea, Iraq, Iran, Syria and Libya are among the countries that could be involved in immediate, potential or unexpected contingencies. All have longstanding hostility toward the United States and its security partners; North Korea and Iraq in particular have been chronic military concerns. All sponsor or harbor terrorists, and all have active weapons of mass destruction and missile programs." [31]

Second, in his 2002 State of the Union address, Bush identified North Korea, Iraq and Iran as enemies. "States like these, and their terrorist allies, constitute an axis of evil, arming to threaten the peace of the world," Bush said. "By seeking weapons of mass destruction, these regimes pose a grave

and growing danger. They could provide these arms to terrorists, giving them the means to match their hatred. They could attack our allies or attempt to blackmail the United States. In any of these cases, the price of indifference would be catastrophic. . . . I will not stand by, as peril draws closer and closer. The United States of America will not permit the world's most dangerous regimes to threaten us with the world's most destructive weapons." [32]

Finally, in September, Bush's message assumed more concrete form in an updated version of the country's "National Security Strategy," the first to incorporate the policy implications of the Sept. 11 terrorist attacks. For the

first time, the doctrine envisioned a first-strike strategy against terrorist organizations and "rogue states," including Iraq and North Korea.

"We must be prepared to stop rogue states and their terrorist clients before they are able to threaten or use weapons of mass destruction against the United States and our allies and friends," the document stated. [33]

Secretary of State Colin Powell meets with South Korean President Roh Moo Hyun at the presidential Blue House in Seoul, on Feb. 25, 2003, during Powell's efforts to build international support for U.S. efforts to disarm Iraq and North Korea.

AFP Pool Photo/Kim Jae-Hwan

Pyongyang's Response

The Bush administration's shift from a policy of engagement to what Cha of Georgetown calls "hawk engagement" has prompted North Korea to respond with a series of belligerent statements and actions. [34] When Assistant Secretary of State Kelly led a delegation to Pyongyang last October to confront the regime with evidence that it had started up a uranium-enrichment program, North Korea readily acknowledged it, abandoned the NPT and expelled the IAEA inspectors monitoring Yongbyon for treaty compliance.

North Korea has cited the Bush administration's policy statements to explain its insistence on a new non-aggression pact and its call for immediate bilateral negotiations to defuse tensions on the peninsula. As Washington demurred, Pyongyang turned up the heat, sending four MIGs to shadow a U.S. spy plane off the North Korean coast and launching two cruise missiles into the Sea of Japan.

At Issue:

Should the Bush administration hold bilateral talks with North Korea?

SEN. RICHARD G. LUGAR, R-IND.
CHAIRMAN, SENATE FOREIGN RELATIONS COMMITTEE

FROM A STATEMENT BEFORE THE COMMITTEE, MARCH 6, 2003

*t*he events of the last several weeks have confirmed and re-confirmed how volatile . . . the situation on the Korean Peninsula has become. The North Korean regime has taken highly provocative actions toward the United States and its neighbors. All of us remain concerned about the potential for miscalculation that could lead to a deadly incident or broader conflict.

North Korea . . . requires immediate attention by the United States, thoughtful analysis about our options and vigorous diplomacy to secure the cooperation and participation of nations in the region. Compared to most nations, our information on North Korean decision-making is scant. The actions of the North Korean regime and the military often stray from a course that we perceive as consistent with rational self-preservation. But we must . . . avoid simplistic explanations of North Korean behavior. . . .

In 1994, the United States and North Korea signed the Agreed Framework — the agreement under which North Korea was to shut down its nuclear facilities in return for shipments of heavy oil and the construction of two light-water nuclear reactors. . . . The Clinton administration had hoped to secure a freeze of North Korea's nuclear program and to prevent it from producing weapons-grade plutonium. It also intended that the Agreed Framework would be the basis for ongoing contacts with Pyongyang. But these goals have not been realized, and circumstances require the United States to develop a new approach.

The Bush administration has been reluctant to agree to a bilateral dialogue with North Korea until the regime satisfies U.S. concerns over its nuclear program. The administration has instead focused on proposals for multilateral talks involving North Korea and other countries. Multilateral diplomacy is a key element to any long-term reduction of tensions on the Korean Peninsula. But it is vital that the United States not dismiss bilateral diplomatic opportunities that could be useful in reversing North Korea's nuclear-weapons program and promoting stability. We must be creative and persistent in addressing an extraordinarily grave threat to national security.

While some American analysts oppose any dialogue with North Korea . . . I do not believe we have the luxury to be this absolute. The risks are too immediate, and the stakes too high. The United States must maintain military preparedness and should not tolerate North Korea's nuclear-weapons programs.

But the mere initiation of a bilateral dialogue, with American authorities concurrently consulting with the South Korean government, does not compromise our national-security interests.

JAMES A. KELLEY
ASSISTANT SECRETARY OF STATE, EAST ASIAN AND PACIFIC AFFAIRS

FROM TESTIMONY BEFORE THE SENATE FOREIGN RELATIONS COMMITTEE, MARCH 12, 2003

*w*e tried the bilateral approach 10 years ago, by negotiating the U.S.-[North Korea] Agreed Framework. . . . In 1993 and 1994, and over the past decade . . . we found the North could not be trusted. This time, a new and more comprehensive approach is required. The stakes are simply too high. . . .

To achieve a lasting resolution, this time the international community, particularly North Korea's neighbors, must be involved. While the Agreed Framework succeeded in freezing the North's declared nuclear-weapons program for eight years, it was only a partial solution of limited duration. That is no longer an option.

That is why we are insisting on a multilateral approach, to ensure that the consequences to North Korea of violating its commitments will deny them any benefits. . . . It was easier for North Korea to abrogate its commitments to the United States under the Agreed Framework, thinking it would risk the condemnation of a single country. In fact, the past six months have shown that the international community is united in its desire to see a nuclear weapons-free Korean Peninsula. . . .

If our starting point for a resolution is a multilateral framework, we believe that this time it will not be so easy for North Korea — which seeks not only economic aid but also international recognition — to turn its back on all its neighbors and still expect to receive their much-needed munificence. This would further North Korea's own isolation, with an even more terrible price to be paid by its people, who are already living in abject poverty and face inhumane political and economic conditions.

States cannot undertake this task alone. International institutions, particularly the International Atomic Energy Agency and the U.N. Security Council, will have an equally crucial role to play. Thus . . . we are moving forward with plans for multilateral, rather than bilateral, talks to resolve this issue. But the rubber hits the road when we are faced with violations of those agreements and commitments. Moreover, it is important to underscore that multilateral support for such regimes, as reflected in the [Nuclear Non-Proliferation Treaty], is critical.

We must, in dealing with North Korea, be mindful that other would-be nuclear aspirants are watching. If North Korea gains from its violations, others may conclude that the violation route is cost-free. Deterrence would be undermined, and our non-proliferation efforts — more critical now than ever — would be grossly jeopardized.

The regime's rhetoric has been as provocative as its actions. "The U.S. loudmouthed 'development of nuclear weapons' by the DPRK is nothing but a subterfuge to internationalize its moves to pressure and isolate the DPRK and ignite a new war of aggression against it," the official news agency stated recently. "It is quite senseless and unreasonable for the U.S. to insist that the DPRK poses a 'nuclear threat' to the U.S. . . . The U.S. is well advised to give up its stand to stifle the DPRK and properly approach dialogue and thus fulfill its responsibility as the direct party concerned with the settlement of the nuclear issue on the peninsula." [35]

Even before the spy plane incident — but after Bush began suggesting that he would consider using military force to halt North Korea's nuclear-weapons program if diplomacy failed — the Pentagon sent two-dozen B-52 and B-1 long-range bombers to the Western Pacific island of Guam. White House officials said the deployment was to discourage North Korea from invading South Korea while the bulk of U.S. forces were fighting in the Iraq war, which began March 19.

"These moves are not aggressive in nature," Pentagon spokesman Lt. Cmdr. Jeff Davis insisted. "Deploying these additional forces is a prudent measure to bolster our defensive posture and as a deterrent." [36]

Policy Debate

As media attention focuses on Iraq, the crisis on the Korean Peninsula has escalated largely out of the public eye. But Korea experts and lawmakers are debating what the United States should do to resolve the crisis before it erupts into hostilities. A year ago, a task force of academics, former ambassadors and government officials began work on policy options.

In February they recommended direct negotiations with North Korea aimed at ending Pyongyang's nuclear ambitions and providing more food and fuel for its starving population.

According to Harrison, chairman of the task force, the Bush administration must first drop its insistence on multilateral talks with North Korea and accede to their demand for direct, bilateral negotiations. "We're the ones that North Korea is afraid of," Harrison says. "Their whole policy of pursuing a nuclear-weapons option reflects the fact that they feel they have to deter us from both a possible preemptive military strike and pressure to bring down the regime."

The task force also endorsed a joint U.S.-North Korean declaration of nonaggression, which would become permanent upon the dismantlement of North Korea's nuclear-weapons program. "The declaration would also include a pledge to respect North Korea's sovereignty, meaning we won't try to bring about their collapse," Harrison says. "That way we would address their security concerns in the broadest sense."

Only then, he says, would the administration's multilateral approach come into play. "There could be regional security guarantees and economic cooperation that would help North Korea," Harrison continues. "The problem is the Bush administration's attitude. What they have in mind is the use of multilateral action to pressure North Korea with no incentives — just all sticks and no carrots. So North Korea has no intention of going into such a multilateral gathering unless it has inducements attached to it."

Harrison says Bush's call for multilateralism in dealing with North Korea may fall on deaf allied ears, after the administration eschewed multilateral actions and opinions regarding the U.S. invasion of Iraq, which was widely criticized in the U.N. Security Council. "The Bush administration is not really embracing multilateral cooperation; they're embracing multilateral action under U.S. leadership to confront, isolate and pressure North Korea," Harrison says. "Just as they're trying to enlist the United Nations to do what [the U.S.] wants [in Iraq], they're trying to enlist the countries of the region to do what [America] wants — not as a way of accommodating other countries or taking action that reflects a common position on policy."

Indeed, when Secretary of State Powell visited East Asia to win support for U.S. policy toward North Korea, he failed to gain any pledges from China, Japan or South Korea, which would play key roles in Bush's multilateral approach to the North Korea problem. In South Korea, Powell attended the swearing-in ceremony for newly elected President Roh Moo Hyun. Roh, who had run on a platform stressing rapprochement with North Korea, won handily amid growing anti-American sentiment in South Korea. Although Powell announced the United States would resume shipments of food aid to North Korea, which it had suspended two months earlier in retaliation for Pyongyang's resumption of its nuclear program, Roh said the issue "must be dealt with through dialogue." [37]

Some Korea experts say the key to resolving the Korean crisis is to find a middle road between acceding to North Korea's demands for bilateral talks and Bush's hard-line alternatives. "Don't bomb and don't grovel," says Henry D. Sokolski, executive director of the Nonproliferation Policy Education Center, who was deputy Defense secretary for non-proliferation policy during the administration of President George Bush. "This would be a lot easier if the administration had a unified view on North Korea, but they're still divided pretty seriously between those who want to patch things over and please most of the governments in the region over the short run, and those who essentially are less concerned about them and want to put the North Korean regime out of commission."

In Sokolski's view, the United States could gain regional support for ending Pyongyang's nuclear-weapons program by taking smaller steps, such as helping Japan end North Korea's shipments of illegal methamphetamine to Japan, a trade that reportedly nets the North Korean military some $8 billion a year in hard currency. [38]

"Modest steps such as these could provide U.S. leadership in the region," he says. "We need to start with what the market will bear, which is not bombing. But it also is not accepting a nonaggression pact with North Korea." ∎

OUTLOOK

Iraq War's Impact

Predictions of a North Korean military attack on South Korea to coincide with the U.S.-led invasion of Iraq thus far have proved wrong. Indeed, Pyongyang has been uncharacteristically silent in recent weeks, despite warnings that it would consider U.S.-South Korean military exercises as evidence of plans to invade North Korea. In addition to the 37,000 U.S. troops stationed in South Korea, some 5,000 American soldiers joined South Korean troops in the country's annual war games, which took place without incident from March 4 to April 2.

Pyongyang also stopped short of retaliating against Japan for its planned launch of a spy satellite. Instead of testing another long-range ballistic missile as it did in 1998, North Korea in late March fired a short-range, surface-to-ship missile that landed harmlessly off the North Korean coast.

But experts warn that the lull in hostile actions emanating from Py-

ongyang may be short-lived. "North Korea has some hard-liners that would make Americans turn white," says Albright, of the Institute for Science and International Security. "It's clear that they're hostile to the United States, and some of them probably would like to start a war right now. This is a very serious situation."

Barring an immediate escalation of tensions by Pyongyang, the war against Iraq makes it likely the Bush administration will continue to ignore North Korea's demands for the time being. But there is little hope that the nuclear crisis on the Korean Peninsula will subside on its own.

"Deferring the problem will not remove the risk of war in Korea," says McDevitt of the Center for Strategic Studies. "Long after the situation in Iraq is settled, the same dilemmas that we face today in thinking about military coercion in Korea will remain. Those dilemmas are not going to change."

Administration critics fear that the war in Iraq will only embolden would-be nuclear powers to hasten their nuclear programs. "Our attention is going to be occupied in Iraq for quite awhile, beyond the military confrontation," says Levi of the Federation of American Scientists.

Levi fears that the Iraq war by itself is sending the wrong message, not only to North Korea but also to other countries that either have or are considering obtaining nuclear weapons. "The administration also now has to worry about Iran, which is on the brink, and it may have to expand the 'axis' [of evil] if Libya makes significant strides in the next couple of years. The lesson of all this to other countries is to get nuclear weapons faster."

The most pessimistic observers fear that the United States may well be facing a war with North Korea. "We have backed ourselves into a polemical position where we cannot and will not back down," says Flake of the Mansfield Center. "We're not going to re-

ward their bad behavior, we're not going to give into blackmail and we're going to continue to increase pressure.

"For their part," he continues, "the North Koreans are hard-wired for paranoia, and there's almost nothing we could do at this point that would cause them to give up their nukes. So, I expect that we're going to see a gradual ratcheting up of the pressure, and eventually someone is going to cross the line. The most likely scenario at this point is a war."

The Bush administration continues to express optimism that the crisis can be resolved diplomatically. "I think we're chipping away at this one, despite some of the criticism that is leveled at us that we won't simply . . . get in the room with the North Koreans," Secretary of State Powell said recently.

"We have a position, they have a position, and we are trying to find a way forward. I think the overall situation has improved . . . in that the tension has been lowered." [39] ∎

Notes

[1] For background, see Kenneth Jost, "Future of Korea," *The CQ Researcher*, May 19, 2000, pp. 425-448.

[2] "Turning Point in Korea: New Dangers and New Opportunities for the United States," Task Force on U.S. Korea Policy, February 2003.

[3] Powell testified March 8, 2001, before the Senate Foreign Relations Committee.

[4] See Phillip C. Saunders, "Confronting Ambiguity: How to Handle North Korea's Nuclear Program," *Arms Control Today*, March 2003, p. 11.

[5] For background, see Mary H. Cooper, "New Defense Priorities," *The CQ Researcher*, Sept. 13, 2002, pp. 721-744.

[6] Quoted in Richard Wolffe, "Who is the Bigger Threat?" *Newsweek*, Jan. 13, 2002, p. 20. See also Bob Woodward, *Bush At War* (2002), p. 340.

[7] North Korea's statement was published Jan. 10, 2003, by KCNA, the state news agency.

[8] Published by KCNA, March 21, 2003. See also "North Korea Delays Inter-Korean Talks,

Citing Military Tensions," *The New York Times*, March 23, 2003, p. A47.

[9] See Doug Struck and Glenn Kessler, "Foes Giving In to N. Korea's Nuclear Aims," *The Washington Post*, March 5, 2003, p. A1.

[10] Kelly testified March 12, 2003, before the Senate Foreign Relations Committee.

[11] Tenet testified March 12, 2003, before the Senate Armed Services Committee.

[12] Robert J. Einhorn, "Talk Therapy," *The New York Times*, Feb. 12, 2003, p. A37.

[13] Kelly testified March 12, 2003, before the Senate Foreign Relations Committee.

[14] Bush made his comments Feb. 7, 2003, in response to reporters' questions at the Treasury Department. Fleischer spoke Feb. 6. See "Bush: 'All Options on Table' on N. Korea," The Associated Press, Feb. 8, 2003.

[15] Bush spoke with reporters on March 3, 2003. See "N. Korean Jets Stalk U.S. Plane," *Los Angeles Times*, March 4, 2003, p. A1.

[16] Warren Christopher, "Iraq Belongs on the Back Burner," *The New York Times*, Dec. 31, 2002, p. A19.

[17] Unless otherwise noted, material in this section is based on "North Korea — A Country Study," Library of Congress, June 1993.

[18] For more information on Korea's postwar history, see Selig S. Harrison, *Korean Endgame* (2002).

[19] "North Korea Overview," *Nuclear Threat Initiative*, January 2003.

[20] For background, see Mary H. Cooper, "Chemical and Biological Weapons," *The CQ Researcher*, Jan. 31, 1997, pp. 73-96.

[21] Marcus Noland, Sherman Robinson and Tao Wang, "Famine in North Korea: Causes and Cures," Institute for International Economics, 1999.

[22] See Valerie Reitman, "Leading His Flock of Refugees to Asylum," *Los Angeles Times*, Oct. 27, 2002, p. A1.

[23] James Brooke, "A Human Face on North Koreans' Plight," *The New York Times*, Aug. 15, 2001, p. A6.

[24] See Human Rights Watch, "The Invisible Exodus: North Koreans in the People's Republic of China," November 2002.

[25] The report can be found at www.state.gov/g/drl/rls/hrrpt/2001/eap/8330.htm.

[26] Quoted in Doug Struck, "Keeping the Faith, Underground; N. Korea's Secret Christians Get Support From South," *The Washington Post*,

---

FOR MORE INFORMATION

Arms Control Association, 1726 M St., N.W., Washington, DC 20036; (202) 463-8270; www.armscontrol.org. A nonpartisan organization dedicated to promoting effective arms control policies.

Center for Strategic and International Studies, 1800 K St., N.W., Suite 400, Washington, DC 20006; (202) 887-0200; www.csis.org. A research organization dedicated to providing insights and policy options on strategic global issues.

Federation of American Scientists, 1717 K St., N.W., Suite 209, Washington, DC 20036; (202) 546-3300; www.fas.org. A research and educational organization that supports global nuclear disarmament.

Institute for Science and International Security, 236 Massachusetts Ave., N.E., Suite 500, Washington, DC 20002; (202) 547-3633; www.isis-online.org. Dedicated to stopping the spread of nuclear weapons.

Korea Society, 950 Third Ave., Eighth Floor, New York, NY 10022; (212) 759-7525; www.koreasociety.org. Promotes better U.S.-Korea relations.

Korean Central News Agency, Democratic People's Republic of Korea; www.kcna.co.jp. North Korea's state-run news agency.

Mansfield Center for Pacific Affairs, 1401 New York Ave., N.W., Suite 740, Washington, DC 20005; (202) 347-1994; www.mcpa.org. Promotes understanding and cooperation between the United States and Asia.

Nonproliferation Policy Education Center, 1718 M St., N.W., Suite 244, Washington, DC 20036; (202) 466-4406; www.npec-web.org. Supports a more robust non-proliferation policy.

April 10, 2001, p. A1.

[27] Information in this section is based on "The U.S.-North Korean Agreed Framework at a Glance," Arms Control Association, January 2003.

[28] See Jost, *op. cit.*

[29] Howard W. French, "Former Leader Is Caught Up In South Korean Maelstrom," *The New York Times*, April 6, 2003, p. A12.

[30] National Intelligence Council, "Foreign Missile Developments and Ballistic Missile Threat Through 2015," December 2001, p. 11. The council provides strategic analyses for the Central Intelligence Agency and other U.S. intelligence agencies.

[31] U.S. Defense Department, "Nuclear Posture Review Report," Jan. 8, 2002, p. 16.

[32] Bush delivered his State of the Union address on Jan. 29, 2002.

[33] The White House, "National Security Strategy of the United States," September 2002, p. 18.

[34] Victor D. Cha, "Korea's Place in the Axis," *Foreign Affairs*, May/June 2002, p. 81.

[35] Korea News Service (KCNA), March 17, 2003.

[36] See David E. Sanger and Thom Shanker, "U.S. Sending 2 Dozen Bombers in Easy Range of North Koreans," *The New York Times*, March 5, 2003, p. A1.

[37] See Doug Struck, "Powell Makes Few Gains on Asia Tour," *The Washington Post*, Feb. 26, 2003, p. A16.

[38] See Henry Sokolski, "Curbing the North Korean Threat: The U.S. Must Stop Aiding Its Military," *National Review Online*, March 10, 2003.

[39] Powell spoke March 29, 2003, during an interview by *The New York Times*, posted on the State Department's Web site, www.state.gov.

Bibliography

Selected Sources

Books

Harrison, Selig S., *Korean Endgame: A Strategy for Reunification and U.S. Disengagement*, Princeton University Press, 2002.

A longtime Korea-watcher, who played a key role in talks leading to the 1994 nuclear freeze accord with North Korea, presents a detailed history of the peninsula and recommends how to forestall the North's nuclear-weapons program.

Noland, Marcus, *Avoiding the Apocalypse: The Future of the Two Koreas*, Institute for International Economics, 2000.

Noland examines three concurrent crises on the Korean Peninsula — the U.S.-North Korean nuclear confrontation, famine in North Korea and the financial crisis in South Korea.

Sokolski, Henry D., *Best of Intentions: America's Campaign Against Strategic Weapons Proliferation*, Praeger Publishers, 2001.

The executive director of the Nonproliferation Policy Education Center presents an exhaustive history of U.S. efforts to halt the spread of strategic weapons since World War II.

Woodward, Bob, *Bush At War*, Simon & Schuster, 2002.

The legendary Washington reporter describes the evolution of President George W. Bush's foreign policy after the Sept. 11, 2001, terrorist attacks in the United States, including his attitudes about North Korea.

Articles

Brooke, James, "A Human Face on North Koreans' Plight," *The New York Times*, Aug. 15, 2001, p. A6.

Brooke documents the hardships and repression suffered by North Koreans who try to flee the country.

Cha, Victor D., "Korea's Place in the Axis," *Foreign Affairs*, May/June 2003, pp. 79-92.

A Georgetown University professor and Bush administration adviser on Korea endorses the current U.S. stance toward North Korea, which he describes as "hawk engagement" to distinguish it from the Clinton administration's more accommodating "engagement" policy.

Garfinkle, Adam, "How to Overthrow Pyongyang — Peacefully," *The New Republic*, Nov. 4, 2002.

The editor of *The National Interest* writes that concern over North Korea's nuclear-weapons program underscores the justification for invading Iraq to prevent Saddam Hussein from developing a nuclear capability.

Hersh, Seymour M., "The Cold Test," *The New Yorker*, Jan. 27, 2003, pp. 42-47.

The Bush administration's intense focus on overturning the Iraqi regime has undermined U.S. policy toward North Korea, described as "a mixture of anger and seeming complacency."

Hertzberg, Hendrik, "Axis Praxis," *The New Yorker*, Jan. 13, 2003.

President Bush's lumping together of North Korea, Iraq and Iran — three disparate countries — as a homogeneous "axis of evil" has led to what the author calls "a fairly comprehensive botch" of U.S. policy toward these countries, especially North Korea.

Kim, Suki, "A Visit to North Korea," *The New York Review of Books*, Feb. 13, 2003, pp. 14-18.

A Korean-American visits North Korea and finds what she describes as an alien culture based primarily on obeisance to the reclusive country's leader, Kim Jong Il.

Saunders, Phillip C., "Confronting Ambiguity: How to Handle North Korea's Nuclear Program," *Arms Control Today*, March 2003, p. 11.

Accepting bilateral negotiations with North Korea, rejected by the Bush administration as caving in to nuclear blackmail, would offer political benefits that probably would not result from engaging other regional powers in multilateral talks.

Reports & Studies

Human Rights Watch, "The Invisible Exodus: North Koreans in the People's Republic of China," November 2002.

The independent human rights monitoring group documents extensive mistreatment of North Korean refugees attempting to flee famine in their country, only to be forcibly repatriated by the Chinese government.

Niksch, Larry A., "North Korea's Nuclear Weapons Program," Congressional Research Service, Sept. 21, 2001.

The Library of Congress' research branch reviews North Korea's efforts to develop nuclear weapons and U.S. responses.

Task Force on U.S. Korea Policy, "Turning Point in Korea: New Dangers and New Opportunities for the United States," February 2003.

A group of Korea experts call on the United States to take up North Korea's invitation to start bilateral talks with the aim of formally ending the Korean War, reducing the U.S. military presence in South Korea and dissuading North Korea from pursuing nuclear weapons.

16 New Defense Priorities

MARY H. COOPER

During the Cold War, the U.S. military amassed an arsenal of unprecedented power, including thousands of nuclear weapons, bombers, aircraft carriers, tanks and submarines.

But nothing about the Sept. 11 terrorist attacks on New York City and the Pentagon corresponded to the conventional, doomsday war scenarios anticipated by the Pentagon — a Soviet land invasion of Europe or nuclear missile attack against the United States.

Nevertheless, President George W. Bush responded to the attacks in a conventional manner. He declared a "war on terrorism" and sought international support for military action. Then he mounted a U.S.-British offensive against the alleged mastermind of the attacks, Saudi exile Osama bin Laden, his Islamic terrorist organization Al Qaeda and its Taliban supporters in Afghanistan. [1]

Although Operation Enduring Freedom used some of the Pentagon's most sophisticated new communications systems and "smart" weapons, many Al Qaeda leaders escaped capture. The operation succeeded in toppling the Taliban, but Bush's larger war on terrorism continues amid questions about U.S. preparedness for such unconventional combat.

"As the cliché goes, the generals are always preparing for the last war," said Ranan R. Lurie, a senior associate at the Center for Strategic and International Studies (CSIS). "But there

From *The CQ Researcher,*
September 13, 2002
(Revised June 2003).

Secretary of Defense Donald H. Rumsfeld calls for transforming the military to enable it to counter "asymmetric" threats from unconventional forces like the Al Qaeda Islamic terrorist organization. The administration applied some of its new military priorities in the war to oust Iraq's Saddam Hussein, who President Bush said was developing weapons of mass destruction.

AFP Photo/Tim Sloan

will never be a war that is so different from previous wars as this one is, and we would be extremely irresponsible not to recognize that fact."

But almost two years after Sept. 11, it is still unclear how the attacks will affect U.S. defense policy. In his first effort to adapt strategy and weaponry to a rapidly changing international security environment, Defense Secretary Donald H. Rumsfeld emphasized the need to "deter and defeat" unconventional adversaries like bin Laden. He called for a stronger homeland defense and preparations for countering "asymmetric" warfare — unconven-

tional attacks by forces, like Al Qaeda, which cannot match the United States' military strength on the battlefield. [2] Indeed, the Sept. 11 hijackers were not regular soldiers, and their commanders acted on behalf of no recognized government.

Since the attacks, Bush has requested, and obtained from Congress, an immediate infusion of money to conduct the war on terrorism. Lawmakers approved a record $382.2 billion military-spending measure for fiscal 2003 — a 10 percent, or $34.4 billion, increase over 2002. The Pentagon has requested $399.1 billion for fiscal 2004, a 4.4 percent increase over last year. [3]

Rumsfeld's Pentagon is forging ahead with efforts to build what Rumsfeld says will be a more flexible, mobile military capable of using the latest technology to quash the kinds of asymmetric warfare likely to threaten national security in the future.

"Big institutions aren't swift on their feet," Rumsfeld said on Sept. 3, 2002. "They're ponderous and clumsy and slow." A terrorist organization, meanwhile, "watches how you're behaving and then alters and adjusts at relatively little cost, [in] relatively little time, [with] relatively little training to those incremental changes we make in how we do things." [4]

The solution, Rumsfeld said, is to change the way the U.S. military does things. "Business as usual won't do it," he said.

In the process, Rumsfeld is planning to scuttle some traditional weapons, such as the Crusader, a heavy cannon designed for old-style battlefield combat.

U.S. Strength vs. Potential Enemies

The United States far surpasses in manpower and materiel the countries historically identified by the Department of Defense as potential enemies. Moreover, the comparison understates the full military strength of the U.S. because of the higher capability of U.S. weaponry, training and communications, according to the independent Center for Defense Information.

	Active Troops	Reserves	Heavy Tanks	Armored Vehicles	Planes	Helicopters	Warships
U.S.	1,400,000	1,200,000	8,303	24,075	9,030	6,779	200
Iran*	513,000	350,000	1,135	1,145	269	718	8
Iraq	429,000	650,000	2,200	4,400	350	500	--
Libya	76,000	40,000	2,210	2,620	594	202	4
North Korea	1,100,000	4,700,000	3,500	3,060	1,167	320	29
Sudan	104,500	--	170	488	46	28	--
Syria	316,000	396,000	4,850	4,785	640	221	2

*Iran has been historically defined as a potential U.S. enemy, but the Department of Defense removed Iran from the list in March 1999.

Sources: Center for Defense Information, Military Almanac 2001-2002, based on data from U.S. Department of Defense and the International Institute for Strategic Studies

Eliminating the $11 billion program — which is already under way — may be the first of several major changes in ongoing weapons systems. The latest "defense planning guidance," which lays out the administration's defense investment priorities for fiscal 2004-2009, calls for the review — and possible elimination — of several other major systems now considered outmoded for future combat scenarios (*see p. 309*).

Aside from the expanded spending bill, however, there are few signs that the attacks have prompted major defense-policy changes. "Although Sept. 11 has created a greater sense of threat and a greater willingness to spend money on national security, the long-term plans of the military establishment's senior policymakers have changed relatively little in response to Sept. 11," said Loren B. Thompson, a defense analyst at the Lexington Institute, a think tank in Arlington, Va. "Judging from the defense planning guidance, what they're

trying to achieve and what priorities they plan to pursue are remarkably similar to the goals and terminology used prior to Sept. 11."

Bush's most visible defense-related initiative is the new Department of Homeland Security — a massive, $34.7 billion undertaking to merge some 170,000 federal workers from 22 agencies into a new, Cabinet-level agency dedicated to protecting the United States from terrorist attack. [5]

"But that is almost entirely separate from the military establishment," Thompson said. "Defense spending has increased, but for the most part not because of Sept. 11. So it is somewhat misleading to think that the surge in money for homeland security is synonymous with increased defense spending."

But others warn against radical changes in the Pentagon's ongoing effort to transform the military. "There is danger in taking an overly milita-

rized view of the war on terrorism," said Joseph Nye, dean of Harvard University's John F. Kennedy School of Government. "It's important to realize that the military is only a part of what is needed to protect against terrorism, and maybe not even the dominant part."

Nye, who served as assistant Defense secretary for international security affairs under former President Bill Clinton, says the attacks did not significantly change the nature of emerging post-Cold War threats to U.S. security — such as the possibility that Iraq and other so-called rogue states may be developing nuclear weapons. "We have to have an intelligent defense strategy" to deal with such threats, he said.

In fact, Bush's recent war to effect "regime change" in Iraq represents one of the major shifts in the administration's military policy. Bush has often warned that he would consider preemptive strikes against any states or terrorist groups trying to develop nuclear, biological or chemical weapons — so-called weapons of mass destruction — that could be used against the United States.

"We must . . . confront the worst threats before they emerge," Bush told the graduating class of West Point on June 1, 2002. "In the world we have entered, the only path to safety is the path of action. And this nation will act."

Preemptive-strike proposals stem from frustration over the U.S. military's inability to prevent the Sept. 11 attacks as well as from fear that in the era of the suicide bomber, America's longstanding strategy of deterrence may not be enough.

"Most countries are deterred from attacking us, even if they have nuclear weapons, by the fact that we also have nuclear weapons and could do considerable damage to them," said Peter W. Galbraith, a professor at the National War College, which trains senior Pentagon officers. But Al Qaeda has "no return address," he pointed out. "If they smuggle [a nuclear weapon] in and blow it up in Washington or New York, we can do nothing to hit back except what we've been trying to do, apparently unsuccessfully, for the last year, which is to get Mr. bin Laden, dead or alive."

Bush enjoyed widespread bipartisan support for his military actions in Afghanistan following the Sept. 11 attacks. But the war to oust President Saddam Hussein of Iraq, absent overt aggression against the United States, raised concerns at home and abroad. Senate Foreign Relations Committee Chairman Joseph R. Biden Jr., D-Del., held a hearing on the issue several months before the U.S. invasion began in March. "I want [administration officials] to define their objectives in Iraq," Biden said. "I want to know what scenarios there are for eliminating the chemical and biological weapons that Iraq may use if we attack. I'd like to know how important

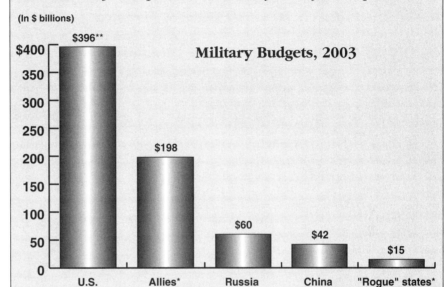

U.S. Military Spending Dwarfs Other Nations'

The proposed U.S. military budget for 2003 exceeds the combined military budgets of the world's other major powers and the "rogue" nations identified as potential enemies by the Defense Department.

(In $ billions)

Military Budgets, 2003

U.S. $396**
Allies* $198
Russia $60
China $42
"Rogue" states* $15

Allies include the NATO countries, Australia, Japan and South Korea. Rogue states are Cuba, Iraq, Iran, Libya, North Korea, Sudan and Syria.

**Includes requests for Energy Department nuclear-weapons programs and military construction in addition to the core Defense Department budget request.*

Source: Center for Defense Information, Military Almanac, 2001-2002, *based on data from the International Institute for Strategic Studies and the Department of Defense*

our allies are in this." [6]

In response to such concerns, Bush announced on Sept. 3 he would not take action before seeking the approval of Congress. Later, he discussed his concerns about Iraq with leaders from Britain, France, Russia, China and other nations. Only Britain agreed to join the United States in the war.

As lawmakers debate the nation's post-9/11 defense policy, these are some of the issues being considered:

Should the United States embrace the preemptive-strike doctrine?

President Bush has described Iraq, Iran and North Korea as part of an "axis of evil" bent on destroying the United States and its allies. Iraqi Pres-

ident Hussein rose to the top of that list, the administration said, because he had biological and chemical weapons, was developing nuclear weapons and allegedly supported anti-U.S. terrorist groups.

The president's father, former President George Bush, ousted Iraq from Kuwait in 1991 but stopped short of invading Baghdad and going after Hussein. [7]

Hussein defied a United Nations resolution mandating inspections of suspected Iraqi nuclear, biological and chemical weapons production sites — a provision of the peace agreement Iraq signed when it surrendered. The second Bush administration charged that Iraq continued to develop weapons

Bush's Go-It-Alone Nuclear Policy

The Bush administration's call to overthrow Iraqi President Saddam Hussein — suspected of developing nuclear weapons for possible use against the United States or its allies — represents a radical departure in U.S. arms-control policy. That policy, in essence, called for negotiation rather than unilateral action.

During the Cold War, the United States and the Soviet Union developed a series of negotiated agreements to avert a potentially catastrophic nuclear exchange. Those treaties included the 1972 Anti-Ballistic Missile Treaty (ABM) and the SALT I and II treaties, negotiated in the 1970s and 1980s.

When the Soviet Union dissolved in 1991, the SALT treaties became obsolete, and the United States and leaders of the new Russia negotiated new treaties, starting with the 1991 Strategic Arms Reduction Treaty (START I). It limited each side to 6,000 warheads and 1,600 long-range bombers and missiles. The treaty also applied to the Soviet successor states of Russia, Ukraine, Belarus and Kazakhstan, then the repositories for the former Soviet arsenal. [1]

As bilateral relations steadily improved, the United States and Russia agreed to further nuclear-arms reductions. In January 1993, even before START I took effect (December 1994), they signed START II, which called for nearly halving each country's strategic nuclear warheads, to 3,500. The U.S. Senate ratified the treaty in January 1996, the Russian legislature in 2000.

In March 1997, President Bill Clinton and Russian President Boris Yeltsin agreed to begin negotiations on START III, once START II entered into force. The new treaty would have re-

duced each side's nuclear arsenals to 2,000-2,500 warheads and set limits on shorter-range, or tactical, nuclear weapons.

By 2001, when President Bush took office, START II had yet to enter into force. As a critic of traditional arms-control policy, Bush strongly supported the accelerated construction of a national missile-defense system. But the ABM Treaty prohibited such a nationwide defensive system, on the theory that it would spark the building of more nuclear arms to overcome it.

The ABM Treaty allowed each country to install a single missile-defense site, with no more than 100 interceptors, provided they did not provide nationwide coverage. The treaty was part of a broad agreement limiting both sides' ballistic-missile arsenals. (The 1979 SALT II Treaty contained a second set of limits, but the Senate refused to ratify it after the Soviets invaded Afghanistan in 1980.)

On Dec. 13, 2001, Bush announced his intention to unilaterally withdraw from the ABM Treaty, calling it out of date. Over Russian objections, the United States officially withdrew from the treaty on June 13, 2002.

At the same time, Bush announced — again unilaterally — plans to continue reducing the U.S. nuclear arsenal. Instead of pursuing his predecessor's efforts to conclude START III, Bush bypassed the negotiation process and declared that the United States would cut its nuclear arsenal to below the levels agreed to under START II. Russia, however, called for a formal, bilateral agreement binding the two sides to any further nuclear arms reductions.

On May 24, 2002, Bush and Russian President Vladimir

of mass destruction despite U.N. economic sanctions intended to force Hussein to readmit weapons inspectors.

After the 1991 Persian Gulf War, the U.S. sought to prevent further Iraqi aggression. Britain and the United States enforced "no-fly" zones designed to keep Iraqi forces out of northern and southern regions of the country, home to persecuted Kurdish and Shiite Muslim populations.

But after the Sept. 11 attacks, the administration turned up the rhetorical heat against Iraq. "It's the stated policy of this government to have a regime change," Bush said on July 8, 2002. "And we'll use all the tools at our disposal to do so." Earlier that year, the president reportedly signed an order directing the Central Intelli-

gence Agency (CIA) to initiate a covert program to overthrow Hussein. [8]

To justify such an offensive, the administration articulated a new preemptive doctrine allowing the president to initiate military action — without congressional approval — against rogue states with weapons of mass destruction.

"Deterrence — the promise of massive retaliation against nations — means nothing against shadowy terrorist networks with no nation or citizens to defend," the president said at West Point. "If we wait for threats to fully materialize, we will have waited too long. [O]ur security will require all Americans to . . . be ready for preemptive action when necessary to defend our liberty and to defend our lives."

In fact, preemption isn't a new doctrine, said the war college's Galbraith. "It's long been the case that if we thought that someone was about to attack the United States we would take action against them," he said. "This is an evil regime that has practiced genocide against its own people, would do it again if unrestrained and certainly is going to cheat on every agreement it has made with regard to weapons of mass destruction. The Iraqi people will be very supportive of our taking action to liberate them."

Galbraith wonders, however, about the administration's logic of announcing — and then debating — preemptive action. "It doesn't make sense to announce it, particularly if you're dealing with someone like

Putin signed a new Strategic Offensive Reductions Treaty. Known as the Treaty of Moscow, it calls for cuts in each country's deployed nuclear warheads to between 1,700 and 2,200 by the end of 2012. As the Senate prepares to consider the treaty, Senate Foreign Relations Committee Chairman Joseph Biden Jr., D-Del., and some other lawmakers are pressing for controls on short-range nuclear warheads as well. Russia's stockpile of thousands of tactical weapons is poorly guarded, and lawmakers worry that terrorists could obtain some warheads and make easily concealed "suitcase bombs" that could be detonated in a U.S. city. [2]

Meanwhile, the administration has stated it will not seek ratification of the 1996 Comprehensive Nuclear Test Ban Treaty (CTBT). By prohibiting all nuclear tests, the treaty aims to halt the improvement of existing nuclear arsenals and the development of new nuclear weapons. Signed by President Clinton and 164 other countries, it would enter into force after ratification by the 44 countries that already have nuclear weapons or nuclear reactors. To date, 31 have done so, including Russia, the United Kingdom, and France.

Iraq's Saddam Hussein meets in August with Foreign Minister Sheikh Hamad of Qatar, the first Gulf state to re-establish ties with Iraq after the 1991 gulf war.

AFP Photo/Ramzi Haidar

In the United States, critics have argued that some signatories might secretly test weapons or improve their nuclear stockpiles while the treaty-abiding United States would be left with a deteriorating arsenal. On the basis of these objections, the Senate rejected the treaty in 1999.

But a panel of experts convened by the National Academy of Sciences recently found that fear unfounded. "We judge that the United States has the technical capabilities to maintain confidence in the safety and reliability of its existing nuclear weapon stockpile under the CTBT," the panel concluded, "provided that adequate resources are made available." [3]

Although the administration will not seek ratification of the CTBT, it says it intends to observe a nuclear-testing moratorium in place since October 1992.

---

[1] Information in this section is based in part on Amy F. Woolf, "Nuclear Arms Control: The U.S.-Russian Agenda," *Congressional Research Service,* June 13, 2002.

[2] See Miles A. Pomper, "U.S.-Russia Nuclear Arms Treaty Debated," *CQ Weekly,* July 13, 2002, p. 1897.

[3] National Academy of Sciences, "Technical Issues Related to the Comprehensive Nuclear Test Ban Treaty," July 31, 2002.

Saddam Hussein," he said. In fact, he added, announcing it in advance removes any reason for Hussein "not to use whatever weapons he has."

Supporters of Bush's emerging preemptive-strike policy argue that terrorist organizations and hostile governments that threaten the United States are unlikely to respond to traditional methods of deterrence.

"There is no give and take between such regimes and our country," said Lurie of the CSIS. The fact that North Korea, Iran and Iraq either have or are developing nuclear weapons and are hostile to the United States fully justifies a preemptive doctrine, he added. "The danger is immense. I would hate to see a situation where people are standing around scratch-

ing their heads, if they still have heads, and wondering, 'Why didn't we see it coming?'"

But preemptive action may have unintended consequences, critics say. Because it would permit the United States to launch a military operation unilaterally, the doctrine would alienate longstanding U.S. allies and may undermine the credibility of the United Nations and other international institutions, which the United States helped build. Indeed, widespread opposition from France, Germany and other allies to the U.S.-led war has produced the biggest strains in transatlantic relations since the end of World War II.

"It is not only politically unsustainable but diplomatically harmful," wrote

G. John Inkenberry, a political science professor at Georgetown University. "And if history is a guide, it will trigger antagonism and resistance that will leave America in a more hostile and divided world." [9]

Others are more concerned about the administration's suggestion that a preemptive strike against Iraq might involve the use of nuclear weapons. After the gulf war, the Iraqi military moved some of its essential communications — and weapons — into deep underground bunkers. To destroy those installations, the Pentagon called for developing small, "bunker-busting" tactical nuclear warheads. [10]

"Tac-nukes," as they are called, were first developed as a last-resort defense

Defense Dominates Discretionary Spending

Defense spending is expected to comprise 18 percent of the nation's $2.1 trillion budget this fiscal year. However, military spending comprises almost half of the $792 billion the nation spends annually on discretionary items, such as foreign aid.

Projected U.S. Spending, Fiscal 2003
(in $ billions)

Non-defense **$415**

Social Security/ Medicare **$743**

Defense **$377**

Means-tested programs **$302**

Interest payments **$157**

Other expenses **$155**

Mandatory Spending
($1.2 trillion)

Discretionary Spending
($792 billion)

Interest Payments
($157 billion)

Total: $2.1 Trillion

Source: Congressional Budget Office, January 2003

against a massive Soviet invasion of Europe. They have never been used, and critics warn that deploying such nuclear weapons would lower the threshold for the future use of similar or even more lethal weapons. Although none were used in the war against Iraq, Congress has approved funds to develop nuclear bunker busters in the 2004 budget.

"It is politically inconceivable that the United States could ever be the first to use nuclear weapons," Galbraith said, adding that it would also be "militarily disastrous" for the United States. "If you have, as we do, the most powerful conventional forces in the world, the last thing you want is

for it to become acceptable for people to ever think about using nuclear weapons against our forces."

Moreover, said Michael E. O'Hanlon, a senior fellow at the Brookings Institution, it is doubtful that conditions favorable to implementing a nuclear first-strike would ever arise. "You'd have to have Saddam deep in some underground bunker out in the middle of nowhere, where prevailing winds would not carry the fallout toward major cities," he says. "He's more likely to be where there are a lot of civilians, because that's his best defense against attack.

Supporters of preemption say the changing security environment warrants an equally radical shift in think-

ing. "During the Cold War, we had one enemy that mattered, and we relied on deterrence because we couldn't defend ourselves against a large Soviet attack," said the Lexington Institute's Thompson. "Today, we not only have other options, but we've also got lots of other enemies, and we don't understand some of them. So the administration's basic logic is valid: Not only are new enemies less predictable, but they may be less deterrable. So just trying to discourage aggression isn't enough any more."

Should the Pentagon play a bigger role in homeland security?

Traditionally, the Defense Department was charged with defending the United States abroad while a broad array of agencies protected Americans on U.S. soil. Tragically, the Sept. 11 attacks revealed a gaping hole in that division of labor.

The Bush administration responded immediately by creating the White House Office of Homeland Security, headed by former Gov. Tom Ridge of Pennsylvania. On June 6, 2002, Bush proposed transforming the office into a new, Cabinet-level Department of Homeland Security, merging all or parts of the 22 agencies that protect the United States from terrorist attacks. Congres approved the new department, and Ridge was sworn in as its secretary on Jan. 24, 2003.

The Pentagon has a limited role in the new department, due in large part to the longstanding legal separation of military and police functions. The 1878 Posse Comitatus Act prohibited using military forces for domestic law enforcement. Adopted in response to excesses by federal troops deployed in the South during Reconstruction, the law has been amended to allow for limited military involvement in drug interdiction and a few other exceptions.

Pentagon officials traditionally have opposed exceptions to the law, fearing domestic assignments could weaken the military's readiness overseas. However, the terrorist attacks blurred that distinction. While the attacks took place on U.S. soil, they were conducted by foreign nationals and supported by overseas leadership and funding. As a result, the military was immediately pressed into service after the attacks: Air Force jets patrolled over American cities while National Guard troops guarded airports and assisted at border checkpoints.

The administration, eager to strengthen local defenses against terrorist attack, has asked for a review of the law's ban on domestic military involvement.

The Pentagon's new domestic role is managed through the recently created office of the assistant secretary of Defense for homeland security. But Air Force Gen. Ralph E. Eberhart, who heads the Northern Command, created after Sept. 11 to boost domestic security, is among a handful of military brass who advocate amending the law to enhance the military's contribution to homeland defense. "My view has been that Posse Comitatus will constantly be under review as we mature this command," he said.

The command, which began operations Oct. 1, 2002, at its headquarters in Colorado Springs, is authorized to deploy military personnel to back up domestic agencies such as the FBI and the Federal Emergency Management Agency (FEMA), as needed in emergencies. [11]

Some experts say the ban on military involvement in domestic law enforcement is a waste of vital military know-how and manpower. "Our Department of Defense has more tools, training, technology and talent to help combat the terrorist threat at home than any other federal agency," said Sen. Joseph I. Lieberman, D-Conn., chairman of the Senate Armed Services Airland Subcommittee. He would give the 460,000-member National Guard —

essentially a 50-state militia that can be mobilized in state and national emergencies — an especially prominent role in homeland security.

"Our military has proven capable of brilliance beyond our borders," Lieberman said. "Now we must tap its expertise and its resources within our country by better integrating the Defense Department into our homeland security plans." [12]

But some experts agree with Pentagon officials who say the line between the military and law enforcement should remain strong. "The job of the Pentagon is to deter and defeat adversaries," said Thompson of the Lexington Institute. "Dragging them into an already overcrowded homeland defense arena would be a big mistake. We really don't need aircraft carriers defending our coastlines."

Other experts want the National Guard and the reserves to focus primarily on external threats, because that's where the risk is most serious. "If there is a catastrophe here at home, the National Guard is not going to be on hand quickly enough to be the most important player in the first few hours after an attack," said O'Hanlon of the Brookings Institution. "It's going to be local fire, police and rescue personnel. These first responders should get most of the resources, and the Guard should remain focused primarily on overseas combat."

Would a national missile-defense system protect the United States?

In one of the first major arms-control agreements of the Cold War era, the United States and the Soviet Union agreed to refrain from building defenses against the biggest perceived threat of the time — a massive nuclear attack by one superpower against the other. By prohibiting defenses against such a nuclear holocaust, the 1972 Anti-Ballistic Missile (ABM) Treaty assured each Cold War

adversary that the other side was essentially defenseless. Moreover, the strategy — known as Mutual Assured Destruction (MAD) — theoretically reduced the incentive to build more nuclear weapons. [13]

Toward the end of the Cold War, however, President Ronald Reagan rejected the ABM Treaty's logic and called for the development of a space-based system capable of intercepting incoming missiles. Although critics ridiculed the plan as technically unfeasible — dubbing it "Star Wars" after the popular movie of the time — the Strategic Defense Initiative received funding that continued even after the Soviet Union's collapse in 1991. President Clinton later endorsed a more limited approach aimed at deflecting attacks from hostile states like Iraq, Iran and North Korea that had or were developing nuclear weapons.

George W. Bush entered the White House promising to remove the main legal obstacle to missile defenses by jettisoning the ABM Treaty altogether, which he did, effective June 14, 2002. The next day, on June 15, construction began on a missile-defense facility at Fort Greely, Alaska, the first component of a larger system that could total $238 billion by 2025. [14]

The attacks of Sept. 11 merely confirmed the views of missile-defense critics who had warned all along that long-range missiles no longer posed the biggest threat to U.S. security and that defending against them entailed huge technical obstacles.

"President Bush will not and cannot deploy any meaningful missile defense anytime this decade," wrote Joseph Cirincione, an analyst at the Carnegie Endowment for International Peace, who argues that the program has greater political than practical value. "Missile defense plays well for the Republicans. It shows that President Bush is keeping the faith with the Reagan revolution, and it remains an applause line for his core, conservative constituency." [15]

Harvard's Nye argues that the missile-defense program would be useless against today's immediate threats. "The idea of being able to defend ourselves against missiles from second-tier states at some point in the future is a worthy objective," he said. "The key questions are how much you spend, how fast you develop the program and how effective it will be."

Nye worries that emphasizing missile defenses may divert resources away from other weapons of mass destruction, such as nuclear "suitcase" bombs that could be smuggled across inadequately policed borders. "The danger is that we spend a lot of money nailing the door shut while leaving the windows open," he said.

Moreover, he said, "Getting rid of the ABM Treaty may make people think that other threats have gone away, and they haven't."

Some missile-defense advocates say that the terrorist attacks strongly suggest the program's design should be altered. O'Hanlon of Brookings supports a "relatively small" system, partly to avoid fueling a nuclear arms race with China, which has a limited nuclear arsenal.

But, he concedes, the threat from China is "not so dire as to constitute [an] urgent reason for investing huge numbers of national security dollars."

In addition, huge technical obstacles to developing an effective missile-defense system remain. "The administration is probably right that countries that don't now have missiles will be more inclined to acquire them if we are defenseless," said Thompson of the Lexington Institute. "But that doesn't address the main question, which is whether the defenses will work, and on that the jury is still out."

Like O'Hanlon, Thompson worries that a major missile-defense system would spur China to expand its nuclear arsenal. "But the missile defense system we are planning to deploy, at least during the Bush years, will be

very modest," Thompson said. "It could cope with a North Korean missile attack or a handful of missiles accidentally launched by China or Russia, but not much else."

Meanwhile, Thompson echoed the skeptical views of many defense experts on both sides of the debate. "Although missile defense is still a worthwhile undertaking, Sept. 11 essentially confirmed the critics' complaints that there are many other ways that we could be attacked." ■

BACKGROUND

Post-Cold War Shift

The ongoing evolution in U.S. military strategy dates from the Soviet Union's collapse in December 1991. [16] Besides ending the Cold War, it abruptly eliminated the rationale for America's military strategy since the end of World War II.

The United States and the communist-led Soviet Union spent the early years of the Cold War in a race to build nuclear arsenals. As it became clear that neither country could defeat the other without destroying itself in the process — the MAD notion — they negotiated a series of bilateral arms-control agreements to slow the arms race. (*See sidebar, p. 302.*)

The Cold War also shaped the superpowers' arsenals of non-nuclear weapons. Assuming that the biggest threat was a massive land invasion of Warsaw Pact forces across West Germany's Fulda Gap, the United States arrayed heavy tanks, artillery and ground troops along the so-called Iron Curtain — the border between Soviet-dominated communist Eastern Europe and democratic Western Europe.

As the superpowers refrained from direct hostilities in Europe, the Cold War devolved into a series of U.S.-Soviet proxy wars in Africa, Asia and Latin America — wherever socialist- or communist-leaning rebels were active in a country run by a pro-U.S. government. These far-flung conflicts and face-offs required the deployment of troops and equipment at military bases around the world.

The prevailing military doctrines were containment and deterrence. Containment — a term coined in 1947 by U.S. diplomat George F. Kennan — called for preventing the Soviet Union from expanding beyond a handful of bordering countries, which together became known as the Communist Bloc. Deterrence, reflecting President Theodore Roosevelt's admonition to "speak softly and carry a big stick," called for building a military strong enough to dissuade the enemy from attacking.

But both doctrines became less relevant after democratically elected governments replaced the communist regimes in the former Soviet states and Eastern Europe. U.S. policymakers anticipated a hefty "peace dividend" — more funds for domestic needs — as overseas military commitments, military bases and defense spending were cut. The transformation left Pentagon planners scrambling to define new strategies for dealing with a radically different set of security concerns.

Some of these threats had been emerging even before the Soviet collapse, as Iraq, North Korea and a few other regional powers began building arsenals of advanced conventional weapons and, in some cases, weapons of mass destruction. [17] To cope with the threat of what the State Department called rogue states, Pentagon planners began assembling the forces necessary to prevail against two regional powers simultaneously. They also began shifting procurement priorities from massive tanks and artillery

Chronology

1950s-1970s
Cold War shapes U.S. defense policy; superpowers sign nuclear arms control treaties.

1972
The U.S.-Soviet Anti-Ballistic Missile (ABM) Treaty is signed, prohibiting the superpowers from erecting a ballistic missile-defense system.

1973
War Powers Resolution calls for Congress and the president to share in decision-making over going to war.

1980s-1990s
As the Cold War winds down, hostile "rogue" states and Islamic terrorists replace the Soviet Union as the United States' main security concern.

1991
The U.S. leads an international coalition to drive Iraq from Kuwait. The Soviet Union collapses in December, ending the Cold War. U.S. and Russia sign START I treaty limiting nuclear weapons.

1993
The first major study on transforming the military after the Cold War reaffirms the "two-war strategy" — calling for military preparedness to fight two regional wars at once. In January, Russia and the U.S. sign START II, calling for halving each country's nuclear warheads. On Feb. 23 Arab terrorists bomb the World Trade Center, killing six and injuring 1,000.

1994
The National Defense Authorization Act orders a Pentagon review of broad strategic goals every four years. U.S. forces withdraw from Somalia on March 25 after 18 American soldiers are killed during a failed U.N. peacekeeping mission. U.S. troops oust a Haitian military regime that had seized power from the elected president.

June 25, 1996
Terrorists bomb U.S. military barracks in Saudi Arabia, killing 19.

1997
The first Quadrennial Defense Review (QDR) directs the military to prepare for a broad range of conflicts and threats. Critics say retaining the two-war strategy fails to consider new security threats, such as terrorism, requiring more mobile forces.

August 1998
On Aug. 7, terrorists bomb U.S. embassies in Tanzania and Kenya, killing 224; U.S. retaliates on Aug. 20 by attacking Al Qaeda camps in Afghanistan.

1999
The United States leads a NATO campaign to halt Serb repression of ethnic Albanians in Kosovo. Critics blame civilian casualties on the U.S. military's reluctance to place troops on the ground.

2000s
Continued terrorist attacks prompt changes in defense policy.

Oct. 12, 2000
USS Cole is bombed in Yemen by militant Muslims, killing 17.

January 2001
President George W. Bush asks for the largest defense budget increase since the 1980s and orders review of the nation's military capability.

Sept. 11, 2001
Al Qaeda terrorists attack World Trade Center and the Pentagon, killing 3,000.

May 8, 2002
Defense Secretary Donald H. Rumsfeld says he wants to cancel the $11 billion Crusader cannon, one of several weapons systems that critics say are ill-suited to current threats.

May 24, 2002
U.S. and Russia sign Treaty of Moscow, calling for more cuts in nuclear arms.

June 1, 2002
Bush announces plans to use preemptive strikes against states or terrorist groups trying to develop weapons of mass destruction.

June 13, 2002
Bush withdraws U.S. from ABM treaty.

July 8, 2002
Bush says his government wants "a regime change" in Iraq.

Sept. 4, 2002
Bush promises to ask Congress and the U.N. Security Council for approval to attack Iraq.

Sept. 12, 2002
Bush is scheduled to address the U.N. General Assembly to present his case for attacking Iraq.

March 20, 2003
The United States and Britain invade Iraq and topple the government of President Saddam Hussein.

May 1, 2003
Bush declares victory in Iraq.

with the latest in high-technology hardware, from night-vision equipment to precision-guided "smart" bombs, the 500,000 U.S. and allied forces of Operation Desert Storm drove Iraq out of Kuwait in just seven weeks in 1991.

The United States' first major post-Cold War conflict also revealed some weaknesses in the new U.S. strategy. Lightly armed 82nd Airborne Division soldiers — who were deployed early — were vulnerable to Iraqi attack for weeks before more heavily armed reinforcements could arrive by ship. In addition, several "smart" bombs missed their targets and killed civilians, and Iraqi Scud missile launchers evaded detection long enough to cause significant damage in Israel and Saudi Arabia.

There was another problem with the smart bombs and other precision weapons that could be employed far from the battlefield. While they kept U.S. combat casualties to a minimum, they also fostered a reluctance to place U.S. troops in harm's way. It was this caution, critics say, along with fears that Iraq might disintegrate, that led then-President George Bush not to pursue Iraqi troops to Baghdad.

Clinton's Changes

President Clinton (1993-2001) continued the process of "transforming" the military. During his administration, calls mounted for more than just modernization but for a true revolution in military affairs that would incorporate rapidly developing technology into weapons systems and adjust strategy to accommodate them.

Such a technological transformation would be as revolutionary as the introduction of gunpowder or the development of aircraft carriers before World War II. Military planning, advocates said, should acknowledge that future adversaries, unable to match the United States'

AFP Photo

AFP Photo/Chris Bouroncle

Weapons of Choice

In an effort to save money, the Pentagon is retaining the less-expensive F-35 Joint Strike Fighter (top), while some older warplanes may be dropped or phased out. Pentagon planners also may shelve plans to replace the Navy's nine Nimitz-class aircraft carriers (bottom) with a new generation of nuclear-powered carriers.

to lighter, more mobile weapons that could be quickly transported from bases in the United States.

Iraq's Hussein put the new plans to the test in 1990, when he invaded Kuwait, launching the Persian Gulf War. Equipped

overwhelming force superiority, would try to use surprise and unconventional uses of the weapons at hand to engage the world's sole superpower in "asymmetrical" warfare.

However, the most visible changes during this period were in so-called force downsizing. The Clinton administration closed 97 major bases — including 24 in California and seven in Texas — and downsized 55 others. Gen. Colin L. Powell, then-chairman of the Joint Chiefs, supported the development of a "base force" — the minimum number of troops and weapons needed to protect U.S. national interests while maintaining enough capacity to win two major regional wars simultaneously.

In 1993, the first major study on transforming the military after the Cold War — the so-called Bottom Up Review — reaffirmed the two-war strategy, despite criticism that it was unrealistic and expensive to fund, and supported a controversial new role for the military as peacekeepers. [18]

Meanwhile, the Clinton administration faced several military challenges that tested the president's goal of broadening the role of U.S. forces to include peacekeeping and other non-traditional missions. These would take U.S. troops to parts of the world where the United States had little or no prior military presence. On March 25, 1994, one such operation ended

Despite calling for a sweeping transformation of the U.S. military, the Bush administration has canceled only one major weapon system to date — the Crusader, a heavy cannon designed for old-style battlefield combat. Defense Secretary Donald H. Rumsfeld asked that the $475 million initially requested for the $11 billion Crusader program in 2003 be used instead to speed development of lighter, more mobile artillery.

in disaster, when U.S. forces withdrew from Somalia after 18 American soldiers were killed during a failed U.N. peacekeeping mission in Mogadishu. A more successful operation came on Sept. 19, 1994, when Clinton sent troops to Haiti to oust a military regime that had seized power from the elected president.

A congressionally mandated commission reassessed the international-security environment as part of the

1994 National Defense Authorization Act and recommended retaining the two-war standard. But in view of the rapidly changing global situation — including regional conflict in the Balkans and threats from Iraq and North Korea — the commission suggested that the Pentagon review its broad strategic goals every four years. In 1996, Congress agreed with the panel and required the Defense Department to conduct a comprehensive examination of America's defense needs at four-year intervals.

The first Quadrennial Defense Review (QDR), issued in 1997, directed the military to prepare for a variety of conflicts and threats, ranging from illegal drug trafficking to terrorism to major wars. But because it kept the two-war standard for determining force strength, critics continued to accuse the Pentagon of exaggerating defense needs to meet budget targets.

Congress had stepped into the debate in 1996 when it passed the Military Force Structure Review Act, which created another panel to assess ongoing defense policy changes. The following year, the National Defense Panel challenged the two-war scenario as a Cold War holdover and faulted the 1997 QDR for failing to adequately plan for the kind of military transformation required to deal with future challenges, such as asymmetric threats.

To pay for new weapons better suited for dealing with the emerging threats, the panel also asked the Pentagon to

U.S. Military Manpower Has Declined

The number of active-duty military personnel declined and then leveled off in the post-Cold War period. High levels in previous years reflect the world wars and the Korean and Vietnam wars.

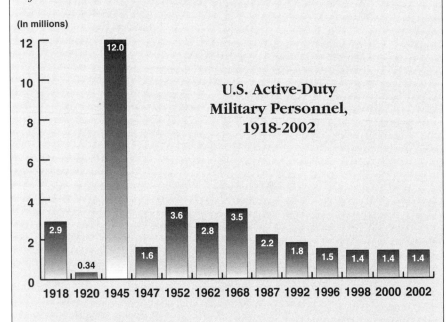

(In millions)

U.S. Active-Duty Military Personnel, 1918-2002

1918: 2.9
1920: 0.34
1945: 12.0
1947: 1.6
1952: 3.6
1962: 2.8
1968: 3.5
1987: 2.2
1992: 1.8
1996: 1.5
1998: 1.4
2000: 1.4
2002: 1.4

Source: Center for Defense Information, Military Almanac, 2001-2002

consider scaling back or eliminating several programs that critics said were either too expensive or antiquated "legacy systems," such as the Army's Crusader artillery vehicle, the Comanche helicopter, the Navy's last *Nimitz*-class aircraft carrier and several tactical, or short-range, aircraft.

By the end of the Clinton administration, some of the Pentagon's efforts to transform the military had begun to bear fruit. In early 1999, Clinton ordered U.S. forces to lead NATO's Operation Allied Force to halt Serb repression of ethnic Albanians in Kosovo. The almost exclusive use of air power and precise munitions enabled the allies to prevail in 11 weeks with few U.S. casualties. However, the deaths of some 500 civilians from stray bombs once again demonstrated the shortcomings of such heavy reliance on long-distance warfare.

Operation Allied Force also demonstrated the limited usefulness of some Cold War systems, such as the Army's big tanks, which were too wide and heavy for Kosovo's narrow roads and rickety bridges.

Bush's Priorities

During the 2000 presidential campaign, candidate George W. Bush criticized then-President Clinton for underfunding U.S. defenses and failing to prepare both military strategy and weaponry for 21st-century contingencies. He repeatedly promised the military, "hope is on the way."

Upon taking office in January 2001, Bush ordered Rumsfeld to conduct a comprehensive review of the nation's military capability. "To meet any dan-

gers, our administration will begin building the military of the future," Bush said after asking for the biggest increase in military spending since President Ronald Reagan's massive Cold War buildup in the 1980s. "We must and we will make major investments in research and development." [19]

High on Bush's priority list was the national missile-defense system. Although Clinton had supported research into a similar system, he had opposed its actual development because the ABM Treaty banned such systems. Declaring the treaty obsolete, Bush abandoned the agreement and pushed ahead.

When the Pentagon released its second Quadrennial Defense Review on Sept. 30, 2001 — barely two weeks after the terrorist attacks — its central objective was to "deter and defeat adversaries who will rely on surprise, deception and asymmetric warfare to achieve their objectives," said Rumsfeld. "The attack on the United States on Sept. 11, 2001, will require us to move forward more rapidly in these directions, even while we are engaged in the war against terrorism." [20]

But many defense analysts were disappointed that the QDR lacked clear recommendations on how to achieve such a radical shift in focus.

"There is nothing in the QDR that envisions a significant increase in the new war-fighting technologies everyone agrees are critical," wrote Steven J. Nider, director of foreign and security studies at the Progressive Policy Institute, a liberal think tank. Calling the review "maddeningly vague," he charged the Rumsfeld Pentagon with the same inertia that had stymied change since the end of the Cold War. [21]

"More than just a broken campaign promise," he concluded, "it represents a missed opportunity to reshape our military to wage a new kind of war against new threats and enemies." ∎

European Allies Oppose Attack on Iraq

Almost from the moment President Bush took office last year, America's European allies have accused him of adopting unilateral defense and foreign policies. One of the sole exceptions to such complaints was the outpouring of sympathy and solidarity after the Sept. 11 terrorist attacks.

Bush has strained transatlantic relations by rejecting several international agreements that enjoy broad support in Europe — including the Kyoto treaty to slow global warming, the U.S.-Soviet Anti-Ballistic Missile (ABM) Treaty and the treaty creating the new International Criminal Court.

Now, his insistence on preemptive U.S. military action to overthrow Iraqi leader Saddam Hussein has injected a new source of tension between the United States and its military allies in the North Atlantic Treaty Organizaton (NATO).

Ever since the president's father — President George Bush senior — led a broad, U.N.-sanctioned coalition to expel an Iraqi invasion of Kuwait in 1991, America's staunchest ally in the quest to contain Iraq has been Britain. Since the Persian Gulf War, British and U.S. air forces have jointly enforced "no-fly" zones over northern and southern Iraq to prevent Iraq from threatening its neighbors and persecuting Kurdish and Shiite Muslim minorities. Since 1998, U.S. and British aircraft have stepped up their attacks on Iraqi ground installations, completing more than 40 so far this year alone.

British Prime Minister Tony Blair, left, meets with President Bush at Camp David in early September. Blair supports military action against Iraq only if the U.N. fails to resolve the conflict.

On Sept. 10, in one of his strongest statements yet, British Prime Minister Tony Blair called Hussein "an international outlaw" and said he believed it was right to deal with the Iraqi leader through the United Nations. "Let it be clear," Blair said, "that he must be disarmed. Let it be clear that there can be no more conditions, no more games, no more prevaricating, no more undermining of the U.N.'s authority. And let it also be clear that should the will of the U.N. be ignored, action will follow." [1]

America's other NATO allies have been adamantly opposed to military action against Iraq from the start. It's not that the Europeans are unconcerned about threats posed by Iraq, but they insist on obtaining a clear mandate from the international community before undertaking any military action. French President Jacques Chirac, who on Aug. 29 criticized "attempts to legitimize the use of unilateral and preemptive use of force" in Iraq, argues that the U.N. Security Council must approve any military operation. German Chancellor Gerhard Schroeder opposes an attack even with U.N. blessings, and indeed has made his opposition to invading Iraq a part of his current campaign for re-election. The goal, he said, should be to pressure Hussein to allow weapons inspectors — whom he expelled in 1998 — back into Iraq, not to go to war regardless, as Vice President Dick Cheney has suggested. "The problem is that [Cheney] has or seems to have committed himself so strongly that it is hard to imagine how he can climb down. And that is the real problem, that not only I have but that all of us in Europe have."

Non-European voices have been equally forceful. "We are really appalled by any country, whether it is a superpower or a poor country, that goes outside the United Nations and attacks independent countries," said former South African President Nelson Mandela. Russian Foreign Minister Igor Ivanov warned, "Any decision to use force against Iraq would not only complicate an Iraqi settlement but also undermine the situation in the gulf and the Middle East." The Arab League warned that an attack on Iraq would "open the gates of Hell" in the Middle East. Foreign ministers from 20 Arab states called for a "complete rejection of threats of aggression against some Arab countries, in particular Iraq." [2]

Joseph Nye, dean of Harvard University's John F. Kennedy School of Government, says European allies might support U.S. action if the emphasis were not just on changing the regime but rather on stopping Hussein from obtaining weapons of mass destruction. "That means going through the U.N. inspection system and proving that he's not living up to his multilateral commitments, that he's developing nuclear weapons and that those pose an imminent threat," says Nye, who was former President Bill Clinton's assistant secretary of Defense for international security affairs. "Those are the key steps for gaining international support."

---

[1] Quoted in Terrance Neilan, "Blair Says 'Action Will Follow' if Iraq Spurns U.N. Resolutions," *The New York Times online*, Sept. 10, 2002.

[2] Quoted in Nicholas Blanford, "Syria worries US won't stop at Iraq," *The Christian Science Monitor*, Sept. 9, 2002.

CURRENT SITUATION

Afghanistan Victory

T he most salient lesson learned from Operation Enduring Freedom is that it was an astounding success, said Lurie of the CSIS. "What happened in Afghanistan was definitely an American victory," he said. "Someone may still be shooting a mortar here and there, but the fact of the matter is, we took over Afghanistan in a few weeks, something that the Soviets couldn't do in 10 years."

Thanks to the Bush administration's coherent reaction to the Sept. 11 attacks, "Every country now knows what to expect if it allows its own forces or terrorists acting from its territory to attack the United States," Lurie said. "As the old saying goes, 'If you can't kill the lion, don't sting it.'"

Enduring Freedom also introduced several innovations in hardware and tactics. Special-operations forces used laser range-finders and global-positioning systems to help pilots home in on and destroy targets with much greater precision even than during the Gulf War. [22] Unmanned aerial vehicles (UAVs), together with older imaging satellites and the Joint Surveillance Target Attack Radar System, enabled U.S. commanders to obtain vital information about remote battlefield conditions without placing American pilots in danger. And improvements in communication networks relayed the information faster than ever.

Moreover, for the first time unmanned planes, like the CIA's Predator UAVs, were used offensively to fire Hellfire air-to-surface missiles at enemy targets. And precision weapons — such as laser-guided missiles and JDAMS (guided bombs better suited to poor weather) — were first used as the predominant form of ordnance fired on enemy targets.

With the hostilities winding down, Pentagon planners said they had

U.S. soldiers search for enemy forces in eastern Afghanistan in March, 2002. Despite its success in routing the Taliban, Operation Enduring Freedom fell short of its primary objective, capturing Osama bin Laden and destroying his terrorist organization. Critics say the United States' unwillingness to commit adequate manpower to the Tora Bora campaign allowed Taliban and Al Qaeda forces to slip away.

learned several lessons that would guide them in further transforming the military. Brookings' O'Hanlon argues that the mission's success depended not so much on the latest aircraft, ships and ground vehicles, as on improved communications, better-prepared troops and more coordination between special-operations forces on the ground and Air Force and Navy aircraft.

"It's dangerous to infer too much from one conflict, especially in this situation, where the Taliban really didn't have good air defenses," O'Hanlon said. "But I would still argue that Operation Enduring Freedom makes the case for smart munitions being very effective, and sometimes being good enough that you don't need to have the fanciest airplane from which to drop them."

But others warn about the unwillingness to commit adequate manpower to complete the job. "Instead of putting American troops on the ground in the Tora Bora campaign, which would have been costly and might have involved more casualties, we relied on Afghan allies who were hardly tested," said Galbraith of the National War College. "These guys weren't trained, and they operated in the Afghan manner, which is to serve whomever pays the highest price. They simply let the Al Qaeda people slip away. There should have been more U.S. forces up there to seal up the escape routes."

Galbraith also questions the growing reliance on high-technology munitions. "There's a belief that high-tech is a magic wand, and that's not true because it depends on intelligence, which is never going to be that good," he said.

Galbraith cites the tragic U.S. bombing of a July 1 wedding party in Oruzgan Province, killing at least 54 civilians. American forces reportedly mistook the traditional firing of rifles into the air by wedding guests for an Al Qaeda attack.

"You're just not going to ever get 100 percent intelligence as to whether something is a wedding or a gathering of [Taliban leader] Mullah Omar and his buddies," Galbraith said. "[So,] troops on the ground are probably essential."

Indeed, despite its success in routing the Taliban, the Afghanistan campaign

At Issue:

Are the Pentagon's efforts to transform the military on track?

PAUL WOLFOWITZ
DEPUTY SECRETARY OF DEFENSE

FROM TESTIMONY BEFORE THE SENATE ARMED SERVICES
COMMITTEE, APRIL 9, 2002

Our overall goal is to encourage a series of transformations that, in combination, can produce a revolutionary increase in our military capability and redefine how war is fought. . . .

Long before Sept. 11, the department's senior leaders — civilian and military — began an unprecedented degree of debate and discussion about where America's military should go in the years ahead. Out of those intense debates, we agreed on the urgent need for real changes in our defense strategy. The outline of those changes is reflected in the Quadrennial Defense Review (QDR) and the 2003 budget request. . . .

Setting specific transformation goals has helped to focus our transformation efforts, from investments to experimentation and concept development. The six goals identified in the QDR are:

- To defend the U.S. homeland and other bases of operations, and defeat nuclear, biological and chemical weapons and their means of delivery;
- To deny enemies sanctuary — depriving them of the ability to run or hide — anytime, anywhere;
- To project and sustain forces in distant theaters in the face of access-denial threats;
- To conduct effective operations in space;
- To conduct effective information operations; and,
- To leverage information technology to give our joint forces a common operational picture. . . .

Taken together, these six goals will guide the U.S. military's transformation efforts and improvements in our joint forces. Over time, they will help to shift the balance of U.S. forces and capabilities. U.S. ground forces will be lighter, more lethal and highly mobile. . . . Naval and amphibious forces will be able to assure U.S. access even in area-denial environments, operate close to enemy shores and project power deep inland. Air and space forces will be able to locate and track mobile targets over vast areas and strike them rapidly at long ranges without warning. . . .

Even as we fight this war on terror, potential adversaries scrutinize our methods, they study our capabilities, they seek our weaknesses. . . . So, as we take care of today, we are investing in tomorrow. We are emphasizing multiple transformations that, combined, will fundamentally change warfare in ways that could give us important advantages that can help us secure the peace.

We realize that achieving this goal requires transforming our culture and the way we think. We must do this even as we fight this difficult war on terrorism. We cannot afford to wait.

ANDREW F. KREPINEVICH
*EXECUTIVE DIRECTOR, CENTER FOR STRATEGIC
AND BUDGETARY ASSESSMENTS*

FROM TESTIMONY BEFORE THE SENATE ARMED SERVICES
COMMITTEE, APRIL 9, 2002

While the Defense Department's rationale for transformation is persuasive, its process for effecting transformation is more difficult to discern and, hence, to evaluate. A transformation process is needed to validate vision, to identify the best means for addressing critical challenges and to determine if opportunities can be realized. . . .

The process should enable feedback on transformation initiatives (for example, new operational concepts, doctrines, systems, networks, force structures). This will enable senior Defense leaders to gauge whether the transformation path being pursued is, in fact, the correct path, or to make the appropriate adjustments if it is not. Such a process can help inform choices about investments in future capabilities — R&D, procurement, personnel and force structure — so as to reduce uncertainty in a resource-constrained environment.

Unfortunately, the Defense Department's modernization strategy today remains much the same as it was during the Cold War era, with its emphasis on large-scale, serial production of relatively few types of military systems and capabilities. To the extent possible, we should avoid premature large-scale production of new systems . . . until they have clearly proven themselves helpful in meeting critical operational goals. . . .

The United States military must transform itself, and it must begin now. As [Defense] Secretary [Donald] Rumsfeld has said, "Transformation is not a goal for tomorrow, but an endeavor that must be embraced in earnest today. The challenges the nation faces do not loom in the distant future, but are here now."

To its credit, the Bush administration has both clearly defined what transformation is, and provided a persuasive case as to why the world's best military needs to transform. Unfortunately, it has not yet developed either a transformation strategy or a process to ensure that transformation will come about. This is most clearly demonstrated in the absence of plausible service and joint war-fighting concepts for addressing the new, emerging critical operational goals, and finds its ultimate expression in the administration's program and budget priorities, which for the most part sustain the course set by the Clinton administration. . . .

If the Defense Department fails to seize the opportunity to transform our military — we run a very real risk of investing a substantial sum of our national treasure in preparing our military to meet the challenges of today, and yesterday, rather than those of tomorrow. Should that occur, payment could be exacted not only in lost treasure but also in lives lost.

fell short of its primary objective, capturing bin Laden and destroying his organization.

Some critics contend that no matter how well equipped, the U.S. military cannot win this kind of war on its own. "The military solution was very good in toppling the Taliban, but not at getting rid of Al Qaeda, which still has cells in some 50 countries," says Harvard's Nye. "The only way you're going to get rid of them is through very careful intelligence-sharing with many other countries."

But other countries may not be so willing to share intelligence if another potentially sweeping change in Pentagon planning and missions is adopted. Rumsfeld reportedly is considering expanding the role of special-operations forces to capture or kill Al Qaeda leaders.

Such clandestine missions — usually limited to the CIA under legally defined conditions — could potentially involve U.S. combat forces in covert actions inside countries with whom the United States is not at war, without the knowledge or consent of the local governments. Pentagon officials reportedly said the expansion of the military's role into covert missions could be justified as "preparation of the battlefield" in the war against terrorists who do not recognize national boundaries. [23]

Defense Budget

The Bush administration has called for speeding plans to transform the military. In 2002, for example, it canceled the $11 billion Crusader cannon. Rumsfeld asked that the $475 million initially requested for the Crusader in 2003 be used instead to speed development of lighter artillery weapons for the Army. [24]

"So little is certain when it comes to the future of warfare, but on one point we must be clear," Rumsfeld wrote in defending his decision to drop the program. "We risk deceiving ourselves and emboldening future adversaries by assuming [the future] will look like the past. Sept. 11 proved one thing above all others: Our enemies are transforming. Will we?" [25]

Besides the Crusader, four other major programs may be sacrificed in the interest of transformation, though the Pentagon has deferred a final decision on their fate. The list includes key weapons currently under development by all four branches of the armed services.

For instance, the F-22 fighter — designed to replace the Air Force's F-15 — may be dropped in favor of the cheaper F-35 Joint Strike Fighter, which is already under development. The Marine Corps' V-22 Osprey, which has a tilt rotor that enables it to land and take off like a helicopter and fly like a plane, also is under review. Development of the Osprey has been plagued by accidents that have cost the lives of 23 servicemen. The Army is also scrutinizing its Comanche helicopter, another troubled program under development for nearly two decades and still at least 10 years from becoming operational. Finally, Pentagon planners are eyeing the Navy's proposed CVNX nuclear-powered aircraft carriers, designed to replace the nine *Nimitz*-class carriers deployed beginning in 1975.

"The administration [believes] the world is changing very rapidly and that something more than evolution [in strategy and weapons design] is required to prepare for future threats," said Thompson of the Lexington Institute. He sees two problems with the administration's approach.

"First, they don't have a clear idea of what the future threat is," he said, "so there's a danger that much of what they do may be inappropriate. Secondly, it's much easier to kill programs . . . than to build a legacy of replacement programs, which takes more time than a single administration has to complete. So the danger is that the Bush administration will be all too ef-

fective at eliminating key programs and not effective at all at building a foundation for modernization that is sustained by its successors."

Some experts applaud Rumsfeld's decision to terminate the Crusader as a step in the right direction. "Up to now, every service has been getting their dream piece of equipment, and killing the Crusader dealt a blow at that trend," Harvard's Galbraith said. "It certainly hasn't completely transformed the military, but looking for lighter, more mobile forces is the right idea."

Galbraith is less supportive of the administration's $7.8 billion request for the national missile-defense program, which Congress is expected to approve in full. [26] "The threat isn't a rogue country firing off a missile, because wherever that missile comes from it's going to have a return address," he said. "The real threat is that somebody will acquire or build a nuclear weapon, smuggle it into the country and set if off in Manhattan or Washington, and we won't know where it came from."

In his view, a far better use of those funds would be to develop technologies to detect nuclear weapons and inspect everything that enters the country. "I'm no techno-wizard," he said, "but I sense that money spent that way would be much better than on a missile defense that deals with a very unlikely threat."

Other experts say the Pentagon has not fully applied the lessons of either Desert Storm or Enduring Freedom to the military budget. "I would put more money into munitions, command-and-control networks, information processing and unmanned aerial vehicles and less into the major combat platforms that are carrying those smaller capabilities," O'Hanlon of Brookings said.

Lurie of the CSIS agrees that large weapons systems continue to receive an inordinate share of the defense budget.

"I would like to see a much bigger chunk dedicated to intelligence," he said. "That is probably our most crucial weapon to counter terrorism." ∎

OUTLOOK

Lessons from Iraq

The past year has put the Bush administration's defense priorities under the spotlight. Faced with growing concern in Congress about the potential risks involved in preemptively attacking Iraq, administration officials insisted that Hussein possessed chemical, biological and nuclear weapons and that the risks of inaction were far greater.

Left to deploy nuclear weapons, Vice President Dick Cheney warned, the Iraqi leader would "seek domination of the entire Middle East, take control of a great portion of the world's energy supplies, directly threaten America's friends throughout the region and subject the United States or any other nation to nuclear blackmail." [27]

Bush assured legislators he would seek congressional approval before taking action against Iraq and consulted with the other members of the United Nations Security Council — the leaders of Russia, China, Britain and France — to explain his position. [28] Finally, the president presented his case to the United Nations in New York on Sept. 12 — the day after the one-year anniversary of the terrorist attacks.

In effect, Bush was seeking approval from Congress, the country and America's allies for his preemptive-strike policy. "We're in a new era," Bush said. "This is a debate the American people must hear, must understand. And the world must understand, as well, that its credibility is at stake." [29]

As the months wore on, Bush's argument swayed many in the United States, but hardly anyone else. He won overwhelming approval in Congress

for a war resolution, and he convinced the Security Council to unanimously adopt Resolution 1441, ordering Iraq to fully and voluntarily disclose the status of its weapons programs. Even after the war began, he kept the unwavering support of the American people, who backed the conflict by a ratio of three-to-one.

But Bush's determination to proceed with the invasion even after weapons inspectors failed to disclose evidence that Iraq possessed weapons of mass destruction alienated many of America's traditional allies. After France and Germany condemned the administration's preemptive war plan, the United States was left with just Britain as a major partner in what Bush called the "coalition of the willing" to invade Iraq. Fellow NATO member Turkey refused to let U.S. forces use its territory across the border from Iraq as a staging area for the impending invasion.

On March 20, Operation Iraqi Freedom began with heavy air strikes, dubbed "shock and awe," against military targets in Iraq, followed by a ground invasion of coalition tanks from Kuwait northward toward Baghdad, the Iraqi capital. From the beginning, critics charged that Rumsfeld had placed too great an emphasis on high-tech weaponry and left ground forces with too few troops. But Iraq's armed forces failed to mount a strong counterattack, and Baghdad fell to coalition forces within weeks. On May 1, Bush formally claimed victory.

In the end, the United States lost just 110 in Operation Iraqi Freedom, fully a quarter of whom died in non-combat accidents. Supporters of Rumsfeld's military transformation attribute the rapid victory and lack of massive casualties to the United States' advanced, satellite-assisted communications equipment, advanced aircraft and smart munitions.

But the military victory left the administration with the much more ar-

duous task of rebuilding Iraq, devastated not only by the war but also by decades of authoritarian rule. Indeed, the post-war mission may prove to be a far greater challenge than the war itself.

Bush has long criticized the use of American troops in peacekeeping operations in the Balkans and elsewhere. But U.S. allies contribute the bulk of peacekeepers now deployed in Afghanistan.

"You would have to assume that we'd be looking at a multiyear stability operation that would make the efforts in the Balkans look relatively modest by comparison," Brookings' O'Hanlon said.

The United States provides about 15 percent of peacekeeping forces in the Balkans. "We'd have to be closer to 25 percent of the total force in Iraq because it would be seen as very much our war," O'Hanlon predicted. "We couldn't do what we've done in Afghanistan and essentially ask our allies to do the whole thing for us."

Indeed, while transatlantic relations have improved somewhat since the war's end, the job of peacekeeping and nation-building in Iraq has fallen squarely on the shoulders of the United States and Britain. Some 150,000 U.S. soldiers — and only 12,000 allied troops — remain in Iraq, helping restore basic services, hunting for weapons of mass destruction and acting as policemen in anticipation of a new civilian government that can take over these missions. That could take months or even years, analysts predict. Meanwhile, persistent attacks on U.S. troops have prompted the military to launch a new mission, dubbed Operation Desert Scorpion, to aggressively hunt down Hussein supporters and beef up humanitarian aid to win over Iraqi public opinion.

Although a majority of Americans still support the military action in Iraq, the administration is coming under scrutiny by critics who charge that Bush misled Americans about the dangers posed by Hussein's regime. Nine weeks after the war's end, the United States had failed to produce clear evidence that Iraq possessed weapons of mass destruction. ■

Notes

[1] For background, see David Masci and Kenneth Jost, "War on Terrorism," *The CQ Researcher*, Oct. 12, 2001, pp. 817-848.

[2] Donald H. Rumsfeld, Foreword, *Quadrennial Defense Review Report*, Department of Defense, Sept. 30, 2001, p. iv.

[3] See Carl Hulse, "Senate Easily Passes $355 Billion Bill for Military Spending," *The New York Times*, Aug. 2, 2002.

[4] " 'The American People Have Got the Staying Power for This,'" *The New York Times*, Sept. 3, 2002.

[5] Adriel Bettelheim, "Congress Changing Tone Of Homeland Security Debate," *CQ Weekly*, Aug. 31, 2002, pp. 2222-2225.

[6] See James Dao, "Senate Panel to Ask Bush Aides to Give Details on His Iraq Policy," *The New York Times*, July 10, 2002.

[7] Mary H. Cooper, "Energy Security," *The CQ Researcher*, Feb. 1, 2002, pp. 73-96.

[8] See Bob Woodward, "President Broadens Anti-Hussein Order," *The Washington Post*, June 16, 2002.

[9] John G. Inkenberry, "America's Imperial Ambition," *Foreign Affairs*, September/October 2002, p. 45.

[10] See William J. Broad, "Call for New Breed of Nuclear Arms Faces Hurdles," *The New York Times*, March 11, 2002.

[11] Quoted by Eric Schmitt, "Wider Military Role in U.S. Is Urged," *The New York Times*, July 21, 2002.

[12] Lieberman addressed a June 26, 2002, forum on homeland security sponsored by the Progressive Policy Institute.

[13] For background, see Mary H. Cooper, "Missile Defense," *The CQ Researcher*, Sept. 8, 2000, pp. 689-712.

[14] See Pat Towell, "Bush Wins on Missile Defense, But With Democratic Stipulation," *CQ Weekly*, June 29, 2002, pp. 1754-1757.

[15] John Cirincione, "No ABM Treaty, No Missile Defense," *Carnegie Analysis*, June 17, 2002, www.ceip.org.

[16] This section is based in part on Mary H. Cooper, "Bush's Defense Strategy," *The CQ Researcher*, Sept. 7, 2001, pp. 689-712.

[17] For background, see Mary H. Cooper, "Weapons of Mass Destruction," *The CQ Researcher*, March 8, 2002, pp. 193-216.

[18] Unless otherwise noted, information in this section is based on Jeffrey D. Brake, "Quadrennial Defense Review (QDR): Background, Process, and Issues," *CRS Report for Congress*, Congressional Research Service, June 21, 2001.

[19] Speech at the American Legion convention, San Antonio, Texas, Aug. 29, 2001.

[20] Rumsfeld, *op. cit.*, p. iv.

[21] Steven J. Nider, "New Military Strategy Falls Short," *Blueprint Magazine*, Nov. 15, 2001.

[22] Unless otherwise noted, information in this section is based on Michael E. O'Hanlon, *Defense Policy Choices for the Bush Administration*, Second Edition (2002), pp.

99-102.

[23] See Thom Shanker and James Risen, "Rumsfeld Weighs New Covert Acts by Military Units," *The New York Times*, Aug. 12, 2002.

[24] See Pat Towell, "Crusader May Be Precursor to More Defense Cuts," *CQ Weekly*, July 20, 2002, pp. 1963-1967.

[25] Donald Rumsfeld, "A Choice to Transform the Military," *The Washington Post*, May 16, 2002.

[26] See Pat Towell, "Missile Defense Money Pivotal for House and Senate Conferees," *CQ Weekly*, Sept. 7, 2002, pp. 2321-2322.

[27] Cheney addressed a convention of veterans in Nashville, Tenn., on Aug. 26, 2002. See Elisabeth Bumiller and James Dao, "Cheney: Nuclear Peril Justifies Iraq Attack," *The New York Times*, Aug. 27, 2002.

[28] Elisabeth Bumiller, "President to Seek Congress's Assent Over Iraq Action," *The New York Times*, Sept. 5, 2002.

[29] Bush's remarks are found at www.whitehouse.gov/news/releases/2002/09/20020904-1.html.

FOR MORE INFORMATION

Brookings Institution, 1775 Massachusetts Ave., N.W., Washington, DC 20036; (202) 797-6000; www.brook.edu. An independent research organization devoted to public policy issues.

Center for Defense Information, 1779 Massachusetts Ave., N.W., Washington, DC 20036; (202) 332-0600; www.cdi.org. A nonpartisan, nonprofit educational organization that focuses on security policy and defense budgeting.

Center for Strategic and International Studies, 1800 K St., N.W., Washington, DC 20006; (202) 887-0200; www.csis.org. A bipartisan organization that analyzes challenges to U.S. national and international security.

Council on Foreign Relations, 58 E. 68th St., New York, NY 10021; (212) 434-9400; www.cfr.org. A nonpartisan research organization dedicated to increasing America's understanding of the world and contributing ideas to U.S. foreign policy.

Lexington Institute, 1600 Wilson Blvd., Suite 900, Arlington, VA 22209; (703) 522-5828; www.lexingtoninstitute.org. A nonprofit, nonpartisan organization that supports a limited role for government and a strong military.

Nuclear Threat Initiative, 1747 Pennsylvania Ave., N.W., 7th floor, Washington, DC 20006; (202) 296-4810; www.nti.org. Co-chaired by Ted Turner and Sam Nunn, this nonprofit organization works to reduce the global threats from nuclear, biological and chemical weapons.

U.S. Department of Defense, Washington, DC 20301-7100; www.defenselink.mil. The Pentagon's Web site is the most complete source of DOD information.

Bibliography

Selected Sources

Books

Butler, Richard, *Fatal Choice: Nuclear Weapons and the Illusion of Missile Defense*, Westview, 2002.

The former head of the U.N. Special Commission on Iraqi weapons programs argues that the Bush administration's plan to build a missile-defense system will only prompt China and other countries to build more nuclear weapons.

Cohen, Eliot A., *Supreme Command: Soldiers, Statesmen, and Leadership in Wartime*, The Free Press, 2002.

A defense analyst argues that the Powell doctrine has severely limited the military's ability to defend U.S. national interests. Attributed to Secretary of State Colin Powell, the doctrine directs the U.S. to abstain from foreign military incursions unless vital national interests are at stake and to use overwhelming force once it decides to act.

O'Hanlon, Michael E., *Defense Policy Choices for the Bush Administration (2nd ed.)*, Brookings Institution, 2002.

A Brookings analyst argues that the Bush administration, despite promises of a radical overhaul, has essentially continued the "transformation" begun by its predecessors.

Articles

Boyer, Peter J., "A Different War," *The New Yorker*, July 1, 2002, pp. 54-67.

The Army, with its legacy of heavy, slow-moving weapons, is the target of much of Defense Secretary Donald Rumsfeld's campaign to revolutionize the military, including increased reliance on long-distance precision strikes using Navy and Air Force aircraft and weapons.

Carr, David, "The Futility of 'Homeland Defense,' " *The Atlantic Monthly*, January 2002, pp. 53-55.

Carr argues the U.S. cannot defend itself completely against attacks involving nuclear, biological or chemical weapons, which could be smuggled in shipping containers, without destroying its free-trade policy.

Homer-Dixon, Thomas, "The Rise of Complex Terrorism," *Foreign Policy*, January/February 2002, pp. 52-62.

The Sept. 11 attacks offer a glimpse of future terrorist actions, a University of Toronto political scientist writes. Wealthy countries, with their widespread energy and industrial facilities, provide myriad targets for far more devastating attacks.

Kagan, Fred, "Needed: A Wartime Defense Budget," *The Wall Street Journal*, April 3, 2002.

A military historian argues that the U.S. armed forces have been so profoundly weakened over the past decade that they will be unable to conduct future operations, including an incursion against Iraq, unless defense spending grows by at least triple the $150 billion increase requested this year by President Bush.

Nather, David, "For Congress, a New World — And Business as Usual," *CQ Weekly*, Sept. 7, 2002, pp. 2274-2288; 2313-2322.

Nather's comprehensive report leads off the magazine's Special Report on congressional and defense issues on the one-year anniversary of the Sept. 11 terrorist attacks. Topics covered include President Bush's efforts to sell lawmakers on preemptive strikes against Iraq, missile defense and Attorney General John Ashcroft and national security.

Perry, William J., "Preparing for the Next Attack," *Foreign Affairs*, November/December 2001, pp. 31-45.

Former President Clinton's Defense secretary says the most immediate threat to the U.S. is a small nuclear or biological weapon unleashed in a major city, and that the best defense is vigorous efforts to halt weapons proliferation.

Wallerstein, Immanuel, "The Eagle Has Crash Landed," *Foreign Policy*, July/August, 2002, pp. 60-68.

A Yale University historian argues that the U.S., like all other great powers before it, is destined to decline in power, and indeed has been losing ground since the 1970s.

Weinberg, Steven, "Can Missile Defense Work?" *The New York Review of Books*, Feb. 14, 2002, pp. 41-47.

A Nobel laureate in physics argues that the national missile-defense system being pursued by the Bush administration will not work against the most dangerous threat — an accidental launch of one of Russia's 3,900 nuclear warheads — and may prompt other countries to develop or expand their own nuclear arsenals.

Reports and Studies

Grimmett, Richard F., "War Powers Resolution: Presidential Compliance," *Issue Brief for Congress*, Congressional Research Service, updated June 12, 2002.

The 1973 War Powers Resolution, meant to ensure that the president and Congress share in war-making decisions, is coming under scrutiny once again as President Bush contemplates action against Iraqi leader Saddam Hussein.

U.S. Department of Defense, "Quadrennial Defense Review," Sept. 30, 2001.

The Bush administration's first QDR provides few major changes from earlier calls for "transforming" the military by developing more flexible, high-tech weapons to deal with new threats to U.S. security.